COUNTER-ARCHIVE

FILM & CULTURE SERIES

JOHN BELTON, GENERAL EDITOR

Côte d'Or
Dordogne
Ille et Vilaine
Côtes du Nord
Finistère
Gironde
Jardin de Boulogne
Haut Rhin ruines
Seine
Haut Rhin
Haute Savoie
Seine

COUNTER-ARCHIVE

FILM, THE EVERYDAY, AND
ALBERT KAHN'S ARCHIVES DE LA PLANÈTE

PAULA AMAD

COLUMBIA UNIVERSITY PRESS | NEW YORK

COLUMBIA UNIVERSITY PRESS

Publishers Since 1893

New York   Chichester, West Sussex

Copyright © 2010 Columbia University Press

All rights reserved

The author and Columbia University Press gratefully acknowledge
the support of the University of Iowa Office of the Vice President
for Research in the publication of this book.

Frontispiece: Photography of original autochrome boxes at
Museé Albert-Kahn by Nick Yablon.

Library of Congress Cataloging-in-Publication Data

Amad, Paula.
Film, the everyday, and Albert Kahn's Archives de la Planète / Paula Amad.
p. cm. — (Film and culture)
Includes bibliographical references and index.
ISBN 978-0-231-13500-9 (cloth : alk. paper) —
ISBN 978-0-231-13501-6 (pbk. : alk. paper) —
ISBN 978-0-231-50907-7 (e-book)
1. Actualities (Motion pictures)—History and criticism.
2. Archives de la Planète. 3. Kahn, Albert, 1860-1940. I. Title. II. Series.

PN1995.9.D6A43 2010
791.43'3—DC22

2010018855

TO NICK

CONTENTS

i

ILLUSTRATIONS

ACKNOWLEDGMENTS

THIS BOOK IS INDEBTED to the scholarship and teaching of Tom Gunning and Miriam Hansen. From the moment he kindly offered me a tape of the Kahn films to investigate, Tom's intellectual generosity, curiosity, and guidance enabled me to pursue and finish the first version of this project. I am equally grateful for his patient and helpful advice over the years. Miriam first introduced me to the pleasures and peculiarities of silent cinema. She has been a constant source of intellectual and personal inspiration as well as a warm and caring friend and mentor. Thanks also to the helpful suggestions I received early on from Leora Auslander, Homi Bhabha, and James K. Chandler at the University of Chicago.

The project has developed significantly beyond its first version. For generously reading and providing feedback on sections of the current book, I am grateful to my colleagues at the University of Iowa, Steve Choe, Lauren Rabinovitz, and Steve Ungar. Thanks also to Rick Altman, Corey Creekmur, Kathleen Newman, Russell Valentino, and especially Kathy Lavezzo, for their support during the book's completion, and to Erica Stein for her help with the proofreading.

The decade-long research for this book would not have been possible without the generous help and expert knowledge of the present and former directors of the Musée Albert Kahn in Boulogne, Gilles Baud-Berthier and Jeanne Beausoleil. Special thanks go to their team, including Flore Hervé and Jocelyne Leclerq, and especially Frédérique Le Bris, for welcoming me on numerous occasions to the museum and for dealing with my endless requests. Beyond the Kahn museum, the majority of primary research was conducted at various sites of the Bibliothèque Nationale Française, the Bibliothèque du Film at the Cinémathèque Française, the Bois d'Arcy Film Archives, and the Fort d'Ivry Établissement de Communication et de Production Audiovisuelle de la Défense. For helpful conversations and suggestions during my Paris research trips, I would like to thank Yannick Bellon, Christa Blümlinger, François de la Bretèque, Béatrice de Pastre, Philippe Dubois, Christophe Gauthier, Noëlle Giret, Christophe Karabache, Michèle Lagny, Magdalena Mazaraki, Eric LeRoy, and Dimitri Verzyroglou.

Diverse funding sources have been central to the research for this book. I am grateful to the American National Can Dissertation Fellowship for 2000, and most importantly, the Getty Postdoctoral Fellowship for 2006–2007, which gave me the much-needed time to develop key areas of research. Thanks also to the University of Iowa Office of the Vice President for Research for a book subvention grant.

The project has benefited greatly from the responses, advice, and criticism of many people at various workshops, conferences, and presentations in America and Europe. I would like to thank in particular Richard Abel, Jennifer Bean, Angela dalle Vacche, Lorraine Daston, Jane Gaines, Oliver Gaycken, Alison Griffiths, Richard Grusin, Sabine Haenni, Gregg Mitman, Bill Nichols, Jennifer Peterson, Michael Renov, Catherine Russell, Dan Streible, Yuri Tsivian, Haidee Wasson, and Kelley Wilder. For being wonderful colleagues to me during my year at Indiana University, Bloomington, a warm thanks to Barb Klinger and Jim Naremore. And for their early and ongoing encouragement, thanks to Terry Collits and John Hartley. I would also like to thank the committee who awarded me the Honorable Mention in the 2003 Society for Cinema and Media Studies Dissertation Award and the suggestions in their report that encouraged me to develop specific areas of the project.

At Columbia University Press, I am grateful for the support of John Belton, Jennifer Crewe, and Afua Adusei-Gontarz and deeply appreciative of the feedback provided by the anonymous press readers. I am especially indebted to Roy Thomas for his expert and cheerful copyediting. I would also like to thank John Libbey and Duke University Press for allowing me to include revised material from my previously published articles: "Cinema's 'sanctuary': From Pre-documentary to Documentary Film in Albert Kahn's *Archives de la Planète*, 1908–1931," *Film History* 13.2 (2001): 138–59; "'These spectacles are never forgotten': Memory and Reception in Colette's Film Criticism," *Camera Obscura: Feminism, Culture and Media Studies* 59 (2005): 119–64; and "Between the 'familiar text' and the 'book of the world': Touring the Ambivalent Contexts of Travel Films," in Jeffrey Ruoff, ed., *Virtual Voyages: Cinema and Travel* (Duke University Press, 2006), 99–116.

This book may have been written far away from my first home in Melbourne, Australia, but my family and friends were never far from my mind and heart. Thanks especially to my parents, Marie and Peter, for their unconditional love and support; to my siblings, Martin, Lisa, Nicole, and Danielle, and cousins Margaret-Anne and Lisa, for always reminding me there is life beyond academia; to my girlfriends both in Australia and everywhere else, Natalie Elliott, Eliza Hope, Michele

Pierson (who also provided helpful feedback on parts of the manuscript), Kim Reid, Emily Shelton, Susannah Stoney, and Neradine Tisaj, for their friendship; and to Doris Steel, Rosemary and Tony Yablon, and Emma Parlons for welcoming me on trips to London. Closer to my second home in Iowa City, I would also like to thank my neighbors Chris and Nora Roy for their always jovial chats over the back-yard fence. And finally, none of this would have been possible, worthwhile, or half as much fun without Nick Yablon, who, in addition to fully sharing this intellectual journey, patiently provided me with invaluable, detailed, and insightful feedback on the entire manuscript—sentence by sentence. His love sustains me every moment of every day.

ABBREVIATIONS

THE FOLLOWING ABBREVIATIONS are used in the book for frequently referenced works or institutions:

ADLP	Archives de la Planète
AK	*Albert Kahn: Réalités d'une utopie, 1860–1940*
BiFi	Bibliothèque du Film/Cinémathèque de France, Paris
BNF	Bibliothèque Nationale de France, Paris
BNF-AS: Rk	Bibliothèque Nationale Française: Département des Arts et Spectacles, Rondel Collection, Paris.
CE	Henri Bergson, *Creative Evolution*
FVP	Fonds Victor Perrot
GH	Jean Brunhes, *La Géographie humaine*
HC	Marc Bloch, *The Historian's Craft*
HG	Jean Brunhes, *Human Geography* (Abridged Edition, 1910)
JB	*Jean Brunhes: Autour du Monde, regards d'un géographe/regards de la géographie*
L	Henri Bergson, *Laughter*
MAK	Musée Albert-Kahn—Département des Hauts-de-Seine, France.
MM	Henri Bergson, *Matter and Memory*
WD	Henri Bergson, *The World of Dreams*

COUNTER-ARCHIVE

INTRODUCTION

The photographic archive assembles in effigy the last elements of a nature alienated from meaning.... The capacity to stir up the elements of nature is one of the possibilities of film.

SIEGFRIED KRACAUER (1927)[1]

The cinema is a machine for regaining time all the better to lose it.

ANDRÉ BAZIN (1947)[2]

MOST ARCHIVES INCITE a fascination with a return to origins, beginnings, and sources. Yet they may also direct our attention in the opposite direction, toward an uncertain future. At the conception of every archive—traditionally understood as a repository for state, unpublished records no longer in use—there resides a gamble with time in general. The archive bets on its indispensability not only to the present (soon-to-be-past), but, more importantly, to the future, in the hope that its salvaged documents will be remembered, consulted, and studied. The researcher in the present, who is always removed from the archive's own original temporal vortex, should thus be careful not to overlook the fantasies of the future nestled amidst the documents in which she pursues the facts of the past. Mindful of this warning, the study I have produced of Albert Kahn's Archives de la Planète is as interested in its unfinished, utopian projections as in its actual documents and accomplishments.

Unlike the documents in a conventional paper-based archive, stored and organized according to the systematic rules of a classificatory logic, those belonging to the Archives de la Planète are not filed away methodically in dusty cabinets or publicly accessible centers of research. They cannot be touched, not even with white gloves. Tactility is not one of the customary pleasures of research in a film archive. Given their original basis in nitrate film and autochrome glass plates, the proverbial experience of dust in the archives—an experience that is at the center of conflicting accounts that have coveted, decoded, revalorized, and even mocked the practices and passions of archive users, and that has a fatal dimension in the case of nitrate film—will not be mine.

The inaccessible state of the original Kahn documents is a reminder that distance and absence have always been a part of the identity of film since 1895. As a medium intended for the projection of moving images whose discrete photographs could never be held, whose frames could never be turned like the pages of a book, whose illusion of movement depended upon what the eye could not see, and whose lifelike resurrection of ghosts so frequently recalled death, film's presence has always been accompanied by absence. Likewise, its ability to find and uncover the past has always been supplemented by its confirmation of the past as lost and unrecoverable. Nearly a half century after its birth, André Bazin, reviewing a compilation film that happened to include a scrap from the Kahn film archive, summarized the medium's paradox as "the specifically cinematographic Tragedy, that of Time."[3] In other words, like the archive, film too poses a dangerous gamble with time.

A more prosaic avenue into the Kahn films' hide-and-seek relation to the past opens up before us just a few steps from the Boulogne terminus of Paris's No. 10 Metro line at the Musée Albert-Kahn. There one can view a selection of Kahn's documents, albeit at least twice removed from their original but inaccessible dust-to-dust state of nitrate fragility, in the form of video and digital reproductions. In a darkened corner of the museum I sit on an uncomfortable metal chair in front of a computer monitor attached to a keyboard with a television screen above. Behind me are window shutters that protect the viewing area from the rich foliage and sunlight just beyond the walls. Between me and the visual treasure trove to which Kahn devoted his fortune and the better part of his life, the classificatory interface of the computer search program stands guard. Drawing upon the elision of taxonomic labor that my own life's acquaintance with the keyboard and "search" function allows, it takes only a few minutes to learn how to navigate the Archive's public contents according to country, city, date, or person.[4] Alternatively, I can enter a variety of themes and topics, ranging from daily life, women, sports, and agriculture to brothels, exhibitions, and deaths. While I wait for the document, I watch a television screen above that shows the electronic arms of a once state-of-the-art robot (that matches the equally outdated Minitel-style keyboard in front of me) scanning rows of video cassettes before choosing the one containing the footage I have requested. The collection of videos that can be accessed at the museum, as well as the robot who dutifully retrieves them, are thus always being watched, either at the viewing stations where I am seated or toward the other end of the museum on display behind a glass wall for an implied (though to my eyes, never present) rapt audience: a veritable archive (of technology) on show *within* the archive. (As expected, since my original research began around 1998, the analogue monolith has vanished into the renovation of the museum's new digital *dispositif*.) Before I view my films I am thus obliged to observe the automated retrieval of the video in a sort of techno-archivophilic peepshow, the velvet curtains of the Archive's stage parting just in time for the main feature to begin.

From other research visits, I know that there is an older, informal "museum to the archive" on the other side of the property, off limits to the public, in one of the original villas, which in conjunction with his world-themed gardens, provided the cornerstones of Kahn's unique Boulogne heterotopia. In that turn-of-the-century building one will find a room outfitted to store the planet, with wall-to-wall shelves filled with the original boxes containing the fragile autochrome glass plates (although they too have recently been removed to a safer storage area).[5] Back in the newer public spaces of the museum, within a few moments after the camera on the Archive has shut its eye, the screen flickers open onto a journey through what might best be described as an intimate visual stocktaking of the planet in the early twentieth century. The only thing that distracts me from the journey and its alternative Borgesian universes hinted at in other possible search options are the occasional footsteps of other museum visitors and the slivers of light from the windows behind reflecting the shimmering verdant exterior onto the screen. During a long series of first viewings of these fragments of film, I thus watch Albert Kahn's planet as he might have wished, through a filter of foliage: a cinematic world packaged in layers of leaves. Being caught between the organic and the inorganic, darkness and light, silence and noise, stillness and mobility, text and image, the public and the private, is perhaps the optimum condition for experiencing the vertiginous balancing act of the archive's and film's gamble, that condition one meets halfway between the past and the future in a split (call it the crisis of the present and presence) that accompanied the conceptual birth of the film archive.

IN HIS PAMPHLET "A New Source of History" (1898), the Polish cameraman Boleslas Matuszewski campaigned vigorously for the creation in Paris of what would have been the first official French film archive, what he called a "depository of historical cinematography."[6] In that text, he argued that film was fated to fulfill an archival mission due to its affinity for storing "actions and spectacles of a documentary interest" marked by "an authenticity, exactitude, and precision that belongs to it alone" (12). As confident as Matuszewski seemed in the film camera's ability to record objectively the march of time—such as "the meeting of Heads of State" (7)—that would be of interest to future historians interested in the chronology of political and diplomatic history, his pamphlet also revealed a degree of concern regarding the cameraman's potential to "slip into" the less official terrain of what he calls "anecdotal History."[7] Thus, if on the surface Matuszewski's manifesto trumpeted the idea that the traditional "historical fact" had found its most accurate reproduction in film, at its margins it also recognized the new medium's challenge to the traditional definition of the historical event by invoking this different type of unreliable, anonymous, unofficial, and uneventful history to which the film camera seemed fatally drawn.

In contrast to Matuszewski's guarded appreciation of the camera's power to expose history's minor themes, earlier commentators seized upon and celebrated the medium's attraction to incidental, undramatic events. Reviewing an early public projection of the Lumiere brothers' *cinématographe* at Paris's Salon Indien in 1895, one critic claimed that what was so astonishing about the recent invention was its capacity to capture ordinary people "surprised in their everyday activities . . . with a perfect illusion of real life."[8] This critic went on to suggest that if "[s]peech has already been collected and represented" with the phonograph, then the arrival of the cinematograph—with its unique ability to record movement—meant that "now life [could be] collected and reproduced," making it "possible to see one's loved ones active long after they have passed away." Once again, in this vision of an intimate archive of life, we see the desire to actualize film's potential to capture, organize, and store for future referral and resuscitation the unclassifiable, but nonetheless highly valued, fragments of private rather than public life, ordinary rather than extraordinary events, and unceremonious rather than epic history.[9]

In our more recent fin-de-siècle, as a symbol for the possibilities and limitations of memory, the archive has become a touchstone in contemporary debates and practices across history, philosophy, art, and especially new media. *Counter-Archive* returns us to the origins of these debates in the archival mediascape of the early twentieth century, when film's unique documentary qualities appeared to revolutionize the traditionally text-based concept of the archive. Promising the historicist dream of total recall while also threatening the nightmare of infinite memory, film presented what I call a "counter-archival" challenge to the positivist archive's sacred myths of order, exhaustiveness, and objective neutrality. This challenge inspired both utopian and dystopian discourses and projects that sought to discipline or unleash film's excessive evidentiary capacities. At the core of film's counter-archival record of reality was its attraction to the everyday fragment as the history of the present, in direct contrast to nineteenth-century archives' dedication to the political document as the history of the past.

I explore film's counter-archival origins through the unique lens of the Archives de la Planète (1908–1931), a first-of-its-kind multimedia archive comprised of color photographs and unedited nonfiction films founded by the Alsatian-born Jewish-French banker Albert Kahn with the express purpose of capturing and storing the transformation of everyday life in the modern world. Inspired by his lifelong mentor and the most prominent philosopher of the day, Henri Bergson, yet largely overlooked by contemporary film cognoscenti, the Archives de la Planète remains one of the twentieth century's most utopian experiments in world memory and modern media. My book presents an alternative history of French modernity viewed from the specific example of Kahn's Archive and the general perspective of film's formative engagement with the institutionality of the archive and the informality of the everyday.

Six overlapping inquiries underpin *Counter-Archive*: a theorization of the relevance of the archive, as site and concept, for understanding film's challenge to positivist conceptions of time, memory, and history; a study of the status of the everyday in early-twentieth-century philosophy, geography, historiography, and film criticism; a recovery of the overlooked dialogue between diverse pre-documentary nonfiction films and the 1920s avant-garde; a rereading of the cinematic imaginary in Bergson's philosophy in light of his connection to the Kahn Archive; a reconsideration of the material and philosophical interrelationship between photography and film; and a reassessment of the lost origins of Kracauer and Bazin's "realist" film theory in the counter-positivist approach to the everyday that characterized French film criticism of the late teens and twenties. These concerns are related to an overarching investigation into early cinema's classificatory drive to capture and store the mundane moments of contemporary everyday life, and the mnemonic challenge film posed to those wanting to take stock of its endless chronicle of evidence. Methodologically, the book works simultaneously on two fronts as a theorization of film history and a historicization of film theory. *Counter-Archive* is therefore a study of how the cinema developed out of both narrative and non-narrative impulses having to do with the realist legacy of basing art in the ordinary, the naturalist tradition of scientific observation, as well as textual- and photographic-based archival practices central to the intended, although never complete, management of modernity's memory.

Film's ability to record and store the raw data of routine experience, transient details, uneventful moments, ordinary gestures, and casual occurrences—that side of life that Bergson summed up with the word *habitude*—produced one of the central topoi, or network of ideas and associations, of interwar French film culture. To be sure, the topos of film's archival fascination with the everyday might at first seem extraneous to mainstream film history. After all, the category of the "everyday" was already a literary cliché (after the height of realism and naturalism) at the beginning of cinema, and the discovery (or rediscovery) of the everyday in and through film had also become a cinematic cliché by the late thirties with French poetic realism's stylization of the "ordinary tragedies of daily life."[10] Indeed, the backlash against film's special relationship to the everyday had begun even earlier. Dziga Vertov's 1927 slogan "down with the staging of everyday life. Film us as we are" declared an outright attack upon Hollywood's cooptation of the cinematic everyday via the conventions of realism, while in one of the first manifestos of surrealism André Breton was already complaining in 1924 that "our brains are dulled by the incurable mania of wanting to make the unknown known, [and] classifiable."[11]

Regardless of their eventual taming by institutional and stylistic conventions, the archive and the everyday were key categories of film criticism, practice, and history of the first three decades of cinema in general and nonfiction film in particular. In order to trace the early cinematic evolution of these categories, *Counter-Archive* offers a history of French film culture in the period 1895 to 1930 prior to the ascendancy of mass culture in France, the Hollywood classical style of narrative filmmaking, the Griersonian ideal of documentary, poetic realism's hyperstylization, and the Cinémathèque Française's model of film archiving. This was a period in which film's multifaceted relationship with the everyday had not yet succumbed to the stylistic stasis of convention and its archival applications were not yet reduced to the preservation of fiction art films in national archives. During this era, film's capacity to record and store the historically marginalized or overlooked dimensions of daily life as the history of the present evoked a wide spectrum of responses, both negative and positive, and gave rise to an array of alternative visions for cinema.

Albert Kahn's Archives de la Planète constitutes one of the most ambitious of the great expectations that the new medium of film aroused. Whereas others dreamed about and debated film's archival and everyday affinities, Kahn constructed a literal film archive devoted to recording the diversity of global daily life. His Archive was primarily made up of nonfiction films and color autochrome photographs shot across the planet with the intention of capturing and containing a world that stood on the threshold between the traditional and the modern, the local and the global, all with a view to facilitating international peace and cooperation. Entirely financed by Kahn, the Archives de la Planète (its official name) was in operation from 1908 to 1931, by which time the after-effects of the stock market crash had eroded the fortune that had fueled its global ambitions.[12] During the Archive's two decades, Kahn employed eleven independent cameramen and photographers, as well as the pioneering biologist Dr. Jean Comandon, to record and collect life—understood in the social, philosophical, and biological sense of the term—in over forty countries.[13] Kahn's cameramen amassed a vast, multimedia, ethno-geographic visual inventory of the globe made up of 72,000 color autochrome photographs (the largest collection of its kind in the world), 4,000 stereographic images, and approximately 183,000 meters (or about 100 hours) of 35mm black-and-white silent film in addition to a small amount of color film (using the Keller-Dorian process).[14] The majority of the *film* Archive, the primary focus of this study, consists of unedited footage, making it one of the most unique extant collections of early nonfiction film in the world. Although the Kahn Archive and the gardens attached to them command a certain renown in France, its documents, *especially* its films, have until very recently remained in limbo, confined to the a-cinematic slumber of the unprojected film reel.[15] It follows that Kahn's films have also eluded detailed academic attention. *Counter-Archive* is the first book-length study of Kahn's films based on extensive primary research and theoretical inquiry into their aesthetic, intellectual, and historical context.[16]

Rather than providing the triumphant inevitability of what Siegfried Kracauer called "[h]istory as a success story," my study of the Kahn Archive composes a chapter in the film history of "lost causes" and "unrealized possibilities."[17] Far from being forgotten, however, the content of these failures and gaps in the historical record have in recent decades inspired diverse rewritings of film history. No longer abandoned by history, and benefiting from the unusual synchrony in the academic and commercial appeal of "treasures from the archives," film history's former outcasts are increasingly finding homes beneath the conceptual and institutional shelter of terms like "orphan" or "unseen cinema."[18] *Counter-Archive* joins attempts to revise our knowledge of silent cinema from the perspective of previously marginalized genres and sites of exhibition: nonfiction, non-narrative, noncommercial, and nontheatrical, private cinema.[19] Unlike the orphaned majority of early nonfiction films, which are notoriously difficult to contextualize with regard to date, place, and cameraman, the Kahn Archive offers a rare, intact, information-laden collection of purpose-made nonfiction films. Nonetheless, even a brief viewing of some of Kahn's films makes it apparent that conventional institutional categories of film history such as production, distribution, exhibition, and reception fall short regarding the Kahn Archive. The same holds for models of representational and stylistic evolution. Even though I will trace the Kahn films' affinities with older or recently emerging nonfiction styles, from the Lumière shorts of the turn of the century to the newer documentary traditions of the late twenties, their largely non-edited form makes them recalcitrant objects of comparison.

In other respects, their radical difference from mainstream film culture highlights other unlikely affinities—for example, between Kahn's films and the avant-garde's preoccupation with the archival and everyday dimensions of nonfiction film. The avant-garde's fascination with nonfiction film in general and scientific film in particular was inseparable from their attraction to the non-narrative excesses of fiction film. By focusing on the vital exchange that existed between nonfiction *and* fiction film in the late teens and early twenties, one that impacted film theorists with a particular interest in non-narrative dimensions of cinema, like

Kracauer and Bazin, we are better able to understand film's relation to the every-day without reducing it to the imputed "realist" status of filmic representation. We are also better positioned to uncover alternative dimensions of spectatorial experi-ence and pleasure that prevailed before and continued into (if only marginally) the era of the star- and genre-driven Hollywood classical cinema and the anti-mod-ernist, no-nonsense sobriety of Griersonian documentary.

In bringing together the categories of the everyday and the archive, I am also consciously engaged in a methodological endeavor to work at the intersections of history and theory. Each of these categories refers at once to the irreducible ma-teriality of history and to the conceptual domain of theory, while also challenging the supposed monopoly on the particular held by the former and the general or abstract held by the latter. Both historical and theoretical dimensions of the cat-egory of the everyday crossed paths in the Kahn Archive. It was dominated by an empirical focus on daily life deemed archivable because of film's affinity with unre-hearsed actuality, and it was directly associated with intellectuals (Henri Bergson and Jean Brunhes, the official scientific director of the Archive) for whom "habit" and "the familiar" were crucial topics of academic analysis. Reflective of this mix, I use the term *everyday* within multiple registers: film's connection to minor or non-eventful history; the actual social domain of daily unofficial life often repre-sented on and in front of the screen in the embodied moviegoing experience; early twentieth-century theories of habit and type; and early film theory's negotiation of the medium's uniquely temporal purchase upon the contingent details and flux of the natural and urban world. The intermingling of the historical and the theoreti-cal is also apparent in my use of the term *archive*. My study of the Archives de la Planète combines at least four instantiations of the archive: as a storehouse for records of historical importance; as a metaphor to describe memory, and by exten-sion film's unprecedented mnemonic capacities; as a category crucial to determin-ing the production and parameters of history (in this case, both the history of film in general and film's claim to an alternative historicity); and as an institution and concept theorized by diverse poststructuralist thinkers as a central epistemological technology for the regulation *and* undoing of modern discourse and memory.

As a topos rather than a movement, the attraction between the archive and the everyday in early cinema was not represented in any programmatic manifesto, even though it found its most extreme experiment in Kahn's Archives de la Pla-nète. And yet the latter too is lacking any mission statement, let alone a central-ized inventory. Moreover, if we tried to give an exhaustive description of the films in the Archive, we would run the risk taken by those fantasists who conjure the imaginary worlds of Jorge Luis Borges's short stories: the danger, that is, "of exac-titude in science," of being faithful to scale in the fantasy of representing a vastness via another vastness.[20] If the Archive's own desire to map the world visually was helped along by deformations of scale such as micro- and aerial cinematography (as I show in chapter 8), my own desire to map the Archive recognizes that a collection of still and moving images that is as fragmented, extensive, and inaccessible as Kahn's cannot be described exhaustively without producing another archive.[21] Put simply, forgetting is literally essential to the pragmatics of remembering the Archives de la Planète. Furthermore, while my book offers a detailed history of the Kahn Archive, it is neither a catalogue nor a user's manual. Rather, it is a cultural ethnography of the Kahn Archive's evolution, use, and habitat that also opens out onto a general hermeneutics of the transformed nature of the archive in the age of cinema. As with all ethnography, I present a selective narrative from the field notes taken amidst the foreign world of Kahn's Boulogne compound. Regardless of the selection involved, my analysis claims that the original coordinates of the films' temporal and spatial fragments were plotted by the Archive's central itinerary: a journey through modernity via the path of the everyday.

This is not to say that daily life is the only topic of the films. Kahn's Archive contains many films that register the events that Matuszewski believed film should archive, for the kind of history French historians would later call *histoire événementielle*—the terrain of local, national, and international politics.[22] These would include those films in the Archive that harbor the emergence of important political events, many pertaining to the violent history of postimperial nation-state formation (the fall of the Mandchou Empire in China in 1912; the "ethnic cleansing" of Macedonia following the Balkan Wars (1912–13 and 1913); the victory of the social-democrats in Vienna in 1919; the rise of Czech nationalism in Prague in 1920; the revolution in Turkey in 1922; and Lord Balfour's visit to Palestine in 1925).

As drawn as the Archive was to the surface disruptions of *histoire événementielle*, the uniqueness of its films resides in their capturing of the spatial and temporal webs of daily life—eating, working, playing, walking, reading—that weave their way around these nodal points of chronological history. The everyday life captured in the Kahn films is not, however, separate from or neatly opposed to political or economic history. As suggested in the most succinct of Kracauer's many cinematically inflected definitions of the everyday, far from being an isolated, private domain, everyday life forms a "matrix of all other modes of reality."[23] The everyday thus appears in Kahn's films as this connective matrix, subtly supporting and surrounding in a usually taken-for-granted manner the more visible edifices and evolutions that make up official history.

Certainly, the fascination with recording and preserving fragments or documents pertaining to everyday life did not emerge with the advent of publicly projected film in 1895 or the establishment of Kahn's Archive in 1912. Turn-of-the-century France witnessed an unprecedented interest in the material and mental transformation of everyday life across a variety of aesthetic, intellectual, and technological fields, only some of which—in particular photography—were archivally inflected. The vast topic of daily life had of course been addressed aesthetically by painters and novelists since early periods of industrialization across Europe and was anticipated even before that.[24] Nonetheless, this renewed attention to an age-old object of representation and inquiry was distinguished in the late nineteenth century by a sense of the urgent need to account for a radically new configuration of lived experience brought about by the increasingly palpable effects of an expansive period of industrialist, imperialist, and consumer capitalism. To rehearse a by now well-known description, modern daily life in European cities metamorphosized during this period at unprecedented speeds due to a series of interconnected developments that included the increased mechanization and electrification of urban life, the availability of faster transport, the expansion of standardized consumer items on display and for sale, the increasing circulation of cheaper mechanically reproduced images capable of bringing the world home in ever more intimate ways, and the widespread occurrence of mass migrations resulting in rural depopulation and urban growth. This rural exodus was accompanied by a transformation in gender roles and a transition from traditional forms of social existence and memory rooted in the family or village to increasingly abstracted social relations rooted in the anonymous market place. In short, to use Henri Lefebvre's summary of the outcome of market uniformity in the late nineteenth century—"everything (objects, people, relations) changed under the influence of this predominant feature that turned the world to prose."[25] Conceived with the express purpose of capturing diverse ways of life that were in danger of disappearing or being homogenized, Kahn's Archive must first be read as a reaction to this state of flux. Although Kahn and his contemporaries were not the first to experience the unpoetic "prose" of modern alienation, repetition, and standardization, the collective perception of a decisive and irreversible change in the nature of daily life (as numerous theorists of modernization, from Georg Simmel and Georg Lukács to Lefebvre, have argued) contributed to a *new* conceptualization, awareness, and validation of the everyday as a topic of critical concern.[26]

This intensified scrutiny of daily life, especially from "above" but also from "below," was associated with multiple mid- to late-nineteenth-century developments, from the aesthetic legitimacy of ordinary people within the realist and naturalist movements in art and literature, and the Marxist demystification of the mysterious obviousness of the commodity to the Freudian reclamation of trivial slips of the tongue as the language of the unconscious, the anthropological retrieval of once undervalued regional, rural, or "primitive" cultures, and the scientific visualization of life's unseen complexity. Beneath high culture, a broad interest in the representation and reproduction of slice-of-life reality also manifested itself as a commodified attraction in the emerging forms and venues of mass culture entertainments. For example, in the proliferation of folk and wax museums and the increasingly sensationalized nature of newspaper reportage, the reframing of the everyday as spectacle came to define new modes of visual fascination and consumption.[27] Meanwhile, in the juridico-medical domain, we see the proliferation of vast textual and photographic archives intended for the social disciplining of ordinary individuality.[28] Regardless of the extent to which this everyday was radically new, one thing is certain: by the end of the nineteenth century the seemingly insignificant moments of day-to-day existence (culled from the margins of both material and mental life) had lost their innocence, inconsequentiality, and invisibility forever.

With their capacity to record and disseminate the minute details and rhythms of ordinary perception and daily experience with unparalleled accuracy, economy, and speed, photography and film played a special role in this multifaceted rediscovery and appropriation of everyday life. In addition to enabling diverse demystifications of daily life, photography and film also acted as catalysts for the reenchantment of the everyday. From the epic anonymity of the pedestrian frozen in time as he waits to have his shoes shined in a boulevard daguerreotype and the joyous indecency of the casual, nonaestheticized body jumping and running in later instantaneous photographs to the secular miracle of perfectly rendered movement found in the natural stars—the crowds, waves, and leaves—of early cinema, new technologies of reproduction were central to the modern revelation of the ordinary as extraordinary.[29]

By the late 1910s and early 1920s, it seemed that the cinema in particular promised to disrupt the cycle of aesthetic obsolescence that had condemned earlier efforts to defend the contemporary everyday in all its ordinary heroism (central to the political and aesthetic disruptions of Gustave Courbet's realism, Edgar Degas' impressionism, and Charles Baudelaire's modernity). If the everyday had become entrapped in an outmoded aesthetic tradition, succumbing to its opposite, stylization, the moment it became a respectable subject of art, the first wave of independent film critics in France argued that film offered a different relationship to daily life. Louis Delluc summarized this difference when he argued that film subtracted traditional aesthetics from representation's habitual equation with everyday life, leaving behind the remainder of not simply "life itself" but life as revealed by the camera—in other words, a profoundly modern everyday life.[30] Delluc and other critics believed the cinema would be able to escape the cycle of inevitable decline into conventionality because of its technologically mediated character, its potential mass audience, its photographic base as an arbitrary and indexical (which is to say indeterminate yet objective) record of reality, and its temporal plasticity. They also recognized that if the fate of the everyday had been inextricably bound to a quest to make the invisible visible, then the camera, modernity's new vision machine, reinvented this quest. These critics understood, from often opposing positions regarding film's status as an art, that the camera could satisfy the late-nineteenth-century's thirst for evidence of an "incorruptible objectivity" while also mounting a challenge to the rationalist dimensions of positivism.[31] In other words, film was just as likely to be appreciated for catching the surprise in the corner of the eye of ordinary human perception (often via film's manipulation of time and space) as for being able to revive in real time, with a mathematical precision, simple, humble, and familiar events that had actually occurred in front of the camera. French film criticism of the period thus offered a dialectical appreciation of film as a faithful witness to the passage of events understood in their uniqueness and unpredictability, as well as their repeatability and familiarity. Most importantly, unlike post–Second World War traditions of theorizing the everyday, these earlier film critics did not perceive the uniqueness of the everyday as liberatory and progressive nor its repeatability as reactionary and repressive. For them, the ideological correspondences of film's two-sided affinity for the everyday were still up for grabs.

Far from exhausting the relevance of the topic of everyday life, these late-nineteenth and early-twentieth-century discourses have bequeathed to our more recent fin-de-siècle an even livelier fascination with the topic of the everyday and its relationship to modernity and cinema. Few categories in the humanities and social sciences have received such debated attention in the last two decades as that of "the everyday." The uncomfortable fit between the notoriously vague concept of "the everyday" and academic principles of transparency (which arise as a result of the term's propensity to connote the specific and irreducible particulars of day-to-day existence as well as the general and abstract condition of modern experience) often finds relief when "the everyday" attaches itself to the more concrete, socially denotative terrain of "everyday life." The continuing challenge posed by this deceptively straightforward category can be seen from the frequency with which works dealing explicitly with the topic of "the everyday" rather than "everyday life" begin in a mood of uncertainty, cautiously approaching the worrisome word using a variation of the phrase "something that we can call the everyday."[32]

There are significant reasons for such persistent trepidation in the presence of this seemingly simple yet frustratingly vague term. They recall not only the once marginalized status within academia of the banal and trivial particulars of daily life, and thus the need to continually define and justify reference to the everyday, but also the perpetual problem with representation and narration that the category poses. Our recent dealings with the topic point to a default assumption that whatever the everyday signifies—be it Baudelaire's "transient, fleeting, and contingent," Bergson's "duration"-negating realm of "habit," or Bronislaw Malinowski's "all that is permanent and fixed," to take just three significant aesthetic, philosophical, and anthropological versions of the modern everyday from the period under investigation here—by nature it inevitably eludes, or should elude (depending on the extent to which you view it as a site of oppression or resistance), representational codification.[33] As several critics have noted, the everyday incites a perpetual game of deferment, exceeding as much as stimulating the temptation to register or narrate it.[34] For a Marxist like Henri Lefebvre, the problem of the everyday understood as a problem of definition was ideological *tout court*. We cannot define the everyday because it points to the distortions of ideology: that which we experience but do not know; that which we live through as "the residuum" of social experience but are not accustomed to thinking about as the core of social meaning; that which we practice but do not normally theorize, let alone successfully capture on film.[35] According to the logic of this critique, once the everyday is visible it is no longer valuable as a space for the enforcement or critique of ideology, in the same sense that once ideology is unmasked, it no longer functions.

One need take only a cursory glance across work in the humanities and social sciences of the past few decades to realize that the invisibility of the everyday in academic discourse is a thing of the past.[36] Defining it, reclaiming it, critiquing it, decolonizing it, and reappropriating it have all in different ways been central to the politicization of the personal in feminist studies, the emphasis upon history "from the bottom up" by social historians in the 1970s, the renewed attention to the local and the particular by cultural historians in the 1980s, the elevation of the anecdotal in New Historicism, and the debates about resistance and popular culture by cultural studies scholars in the 1990s.

Within film studies, however, the everyday as a critical concept has more often been addressed in an indirect manner. Certainly, the claim about the "medium's primordial concern for actuality" and "the familiar" (as Kracauer put it in *Theory of Film*) has been a common trope within so-called realist film theory from Kracauer to André Bazin.[37] Yet the more radical potential of this tradition—whose origins I partly trace to the Bergsonian influenced, post-positivist climate of film criticism of the late teens and twenties—has been generally overlooked and is only beginning to be redressed.[38] We might trace this oversight to the negative reading of realist film theory that characterized 1970s *Screen*-related apparatus theory. Developed across numerous exposés of the ideological determinations of narrative film and the cinematic apparatus, this reading uncovered an implicitly conservative conspiracy of sorts between the everyday and realism. This paradigm of studying film tarred realism (or the classical style of Hollywood narrative cinema) and realist film theory (from Kracauer to Bazin) with the same brush. Everyday life was made to resemble the hangover of collective false consciousness—a state we should all want to get over quietly, rather than explore for its own ideological complexities and political possibilities.

Emerging partially as a response to the perceived limitations of 1970s ideology critique, historical analyses of the multifaceted dimensions of the moviegoing experience now form one of the strongest traditions for thinking about the everyday and cinema.[39] Without explicitly addressing the theoretical discourse that now accompanies the everyday, many of these works charted the evolution of film exhibition and reception as a function of changing social and cultural patterns, and they have done much to expand our understanding of the specific social experience of film viewing (differentiated according to class, racial, national, generational, and gender dynamics).[40]

As for the period that concerns me most, 1895 to 1931, we have seen a particularly productive exploration of the issue of early cinema's connections to everyday life in the past two decades. This work has focused on film's relation to the broader forms and experiences of modern urban culture. In the words of Anne Friedberg, it has "argued for widening the focus of social and psychic accounts of cinematic spectatorship to include [for example] advertising, illustrated print journalism, fashion, and other modes of 'screen practice': in short, the everyday."[41] Furthermore, insofar as they are concerned with vernacular culture as a significant factor of modernity while accounting for the cinema as a key institution within that historic shift, many of these studies belong to a wider reinvestigation of modernity from the perspective of everyday life.[42] Across many fields, modernity has come to be analyzed as a period whose defining features—whether figured in the individual experience of speed, fragmentation, memory strain, or the collective processes of rationalization, alienation, and commoditization—were often experienced at the level of banal, daily events as opposed to the domain of official and formal culture. Such a perspective occurs in a number of projects that now employ the networks of everyday culture—mass media, material culture, domestic space, micro-politics— to analyze the key institutions (from museums and archives to nation-state formations) and practices (from consumerism and colonialism to state-sponsored terror and torture) of both Western and alternative "modernities."[43]

Counter-Archive builds on and departs from the above models in several ways. I not only share the assumption of the centrality of everyday life to early cinema, but I focus more explicitly on the first generation of scholars and film critics who articulated, debated, and experimented with these assumptions. For example, the Kahn films evolved in direct contact with two intellectuals who reshaped their disciplines through their conceptualizations of the everyday: the philosopher Henri Bergson and the geographer Jean Brunhes. Although it is more common to study the conceptual status of the everyday in this period through the discipline of anthropology or the writings of Sigmund Freud, I argue that the tradition of thinking about the "habitual" and the "typical" in Bergsonian philosophy and human geography provide two missing cinematically mediated supplements to France's early-twentieth-century discourse on everyday life. Most importantly, I argue that Bergson's philosophy permits a progressive encounter with (rather than, as has usually been argued, an outright opposition to) the mechanistic and habitual tendencies of everyday life and cinematographic methods to which the Kahn Archive is a monument. This new reading of Bergson leads to the book's major theoretical intervention: to interpret the Kahn Archive and films in proximity to the latent, counter-archival ambivalences of Bergson's attack upon the notion of memory as an archive-like site of storage. The counter- rather than anti-archival tendency in

Bergson's thinking provides the framework for understanding Kahn's films in their simultaneous dependence upon and challenge to a positivist, inventorial, ocular-centric, and voluntary notion of memory. This retrieval of Bergson's philosophy is also central to my historicization of the previously unexamined Bergsonian debates of early French film theory.

Whether felt by philosophers, geographers, or film critics, an articulated concern with the new experiences of modern life constituted one of the dominant aesthetic, social, and discursive horizons against which diverse communities engaged with and reflected upon the medium in the first three decades of cinema. The richness of this discourse in France explains why Kracauer flashes back so often to the French film critics of the 1920s (especially Louis Delluc, Germaine Dulac, Jean Epstein, and Fernand Léger) in *Theory of Film* (1960)—arguably the most probing theoretical examination of film's relationship with "the common everyday world" (200).[44] Sharing the French critics' conception of the everyday as a condition we cannot step outside of to actually see, Kracauer diagnosed the problem of the everyday *in its cinematic guise* as that which is "part of us like our skin," that which we know "by heart" (local faces, streets, houses) but "do not know . . . with the eye."[45] Yet the Kracauer who is just as important to this period is the Kracauer who was contemporary to its culture and who set out in essays like "The Mass Ornament" (1927) and "Photography" (1927) to illuminate human perception's and historical understanding's habitual blindness to the visible but unseen significance of everyday culture. Of particular relevance here is his essay on photography, which peels away the surface of the modern mediascape, in the process producing the era's most illuminating discussion of the negative and positive aspects of modern media's archival qualities. In that essay Kracauer argued that thanks to its photographic-based, archival qualities of accumulation, film had the capacity to stir up and rearrange its positivist warehousing of daily life, in the process archiving the world anew and revealing the provisional, denaturalized, and open nature of history. And finally, just as important to my interest in the Kahn Archive's challenge to positivist history, is another of Kracauer's books that has its roots in the 1920s, his last work, *History: The Last Things Before the Last* (1969), which explored the connections between photographic media and the discipline of history read along the lines of their shared responsibility to the indeterminacy and randomness of daily life. For all these reasons and others, including his vague attraction to *lebensphilosophie*, Kracauer is central to this book's genealogy of the cinematic conceptualization of the everyday.

The historical focus of this genealogy is the discussions of film's affinity for the everyday in France during the 1910s and 1920s. During this period the stakes of film's ability to make the everyday known to the eye through the camera-eye were still being negotiated in practical and theoretical projects as diverse as the Kahn Archive and the first wave of French film criticism—in a period, that is, prior to the tendency to position the everyday according to the either-or logic of a reviled or hyper-valorized object of study. Contrary to Lefebvre's deeply pessimistic understanding of cinema after the Second World War as an "illusory reverse image" of the real, interwar film criticism presented less negative precursors to his conception of the everyday as the "residuum" of official life.[46] For instance, Kracauer himself rooted his 1920s' essayistic histories of the present in what he also referred to, albeit in a more positive light, as the era's cultural "residuum" (chiefly photography and film).[47] Less than a decade later a similar sentiment underpinned Germaine Dulac's promotion of the overlooked detritus of cinema culture, namely newsreels, as the unconscious history of the present, "the importance of which has not immediately been grasped."[48] And in the immediate years after the Second World War, Bazin too analyzed the radical temporality and unintentional beauty of reedited, salvaged newsreels and fiction films.[49] Although this book's central film critics are Dulac and her peers, it reconnects their writings on film's history of the everyday with the non-representationalist potential of Kracauer and Bazin's later realist theories of film.

Counter-Archive also uncovers the strange legacy of positivism's progressive and conservative impulses within the cinematic sphere of French modernism. Understood as a diffuse set of tendencies related to a belief in rational progress, empirical realism, causal determinism, objective truth, and an overarching faith in applying the model of the natural sciences to understanding human behavior, positivism had been on the defensive since the late 1890s. Within early film theory, itself a major if mostly unrecognized contributor to French modernism, positivism's residual traces appeared under the influence of a broader Bergsonian anti-mechanistic climate reflective of a widespread distrust of, yet lingering attraction to, science and rationalism. For example, the avant-garde film criticism and practice of Delluc, Dulac, and Epstein in the interwar years displayed a fascination with the medium's ability (in fiction film) to reveal the secret life of things as well as offer (in nonfiction actualities) the secret life of history. This fascination cannot be understood outside an appreciation of the quasi-scientific and quasi-magical aura in which their love of film blossomed. Their critical discourses also need to be reinserted into the context of a residual if newly radicalized naturalism. For if both avant-garde and documentary movements of the 1920s coalesced around a modernist vision of an "everyday shared secular reality" that was interested in—to use Vertov's words—the "decoding of life as it is," such defamiliarizing strategies also appeared in the alienating encodings of hyper-naturalist representation.[50] Seeking to uncover modernism and naturalism's overlapping terrain, I am interested in exposing the connections between the documentary-aligned modernist cinema and those nonfiction projects of the period, like Kahn's, that did not self-consciously defamiliarize everyday reality (through montage) so much as refamiliarize the camera to the quotidian by incessantly and excessively observing, recording, and storing daily life as the self-conscious history of the present. My uncovering of Bergson's counter-positivist influence on both early French film theory and the Kahn films will help us make these connections by opening a new perspective upon the radical revision of naturalism and historicism within French film history in general, and nonfiction film and realist film theory in particular.

In addition to rethinking the status of the everyday in their disciplines, Bergson and Brunhes were preoccupied with rethinking the categories of time and space (and memory and place). They therefore have much to tell us about early cinema's archival context: the connection, that is, between the early-twentieth-century perception of film as the most radical technological intervention into the human experience of space and time, and the notion of an archive as a *space in which time is stored and retrieved*. Contrary to Michel Foucault's too convenient distinction between a temporally dominated nineteenth century and a spatially fixated twentieth century, the possibility of a film archive (as a space where time is stored) at the threshold between these centuries announces the indivisibility of the temporal-spatial continuum, personified in the Kahn Archive via the figures of Bergson (a philosopher of time) and Brunhes (a geographer of space).[51]

This shift to the spatio-temporal inventiveness posed by film brings me to the distinguishing feature of my investigation into film's affinity for the everyday, namely, its archival contexts. A nonaesthetic, and non-narrative, archival tradition of thinking and organizing information about the everyday underpinned early cinema's scientific and classificatory drives and contributed to French cinema's indebtedness to the naturalist and positivist tradition. Stated succinctly, the twentieth-century emergence of a possible film archive disrupted the traditional print-based archive and its associated models of history, temporality, and memory. Film's paradoxical archival nature, suggested in Bazin's diagnosis of the cinema as "a machine for regaining time all the better to lose it," unfolded under the affliction of (as Bazin also went on to note) the medium's tragic relation to time: its fate, that is, to record events not only as they had been at one time but as they existed (and continued to exist) in and through the preservational *and* destructive aspects of time. Inserting the everyday into the archive, I show how film's particular temporal purchase on ordinary reality—its ability to revive small-scale events, casual gestures, and accidental details—was understood (well before Bazin) not simply in terms of the technology's representational superiority (that is, its supposed affinity for verisimilitude of a historicist order), but in reference to the revelatory capacities of the medium as it captured, distorted, and itself survived the passage of time.

The archive is not simply the neutral space in which the Kahn films of daily life were stored; it is the logic acting upon each frame of film. Keeping this archival logic in mind, I have chosen to work my way out from one nodal point within the highly diffuse topos of film's archival longing for the everyday—the Kahn Archive and its surrounding culture—while attending to the more general historical and conceptual underpinnings of this new archival imaginary. As a private, noncommercial Archive that was never intended for public consumption, the Archives de la Planète is a particularly instructive example within the multifaceted articulation of film's archival relation to the everyday. From the outset, for instance, the Archive upturns the popular culture bias of late-twentieth-century theories of the everyday. The Kahn Archive was a bastion of elitism. Furthermore, the nonfiction bias and implied *savant* constituency of Kahn's project intersected with a revitalized concern with the quotidian in nonpopular realms, from the fields of philosophy, geography, and history to avant-garde and documentary film practice and theory, all of which form a crucial, if previously underexamined, elitist supplement to our current understanding of the broader stakes of cinema's vernacular affinities.

Like the category of the everyday, the archive also has an important conceptual history that peaked in the years of the Third Republic but that dates back at least to the eighteenth century and Denis Diderot's dream for a totalizing compendium of knowledge. The fate of the Encyclopedists' aspiration to know all, materialized in the medium of print, was taken up in the Kahn Archive's aspiration to see and save all, materialized in the medium of film. In its ambition to stockpile (if not publicly display) the planet in visual form, the Kahn Archive combined the Encyclopedic culture of the eighteenth century with the colonial "scramble" mentality of the late nineteenth century, while also sharing affinities with the exhibitionary sites and pleasures of its time, figured in institutions like the museum, the botanical garden, the universal exposition, the department store, and other visual compendia such as postcards and stereographic tours of the world. But more importantly, Kahn's pocketing of the world as visual inventory also inherited the instability common to the encyclopedic, exhibitionary, and especially archival enterprises—that is, their tendency, especially in their most ambitious instances, to expose the arbitrariness of classificatory arrangements of knowledge. As Foucault argued in *The Order of Things* (1966), "there is nothing more tentative . . . than the process of establishing an order among things."[52]

In accordance with the emphasis upon the arbitrary in the Foucauldian-inaugurated poststructuralist turn to the archive, it has become almost a cliché to note that meaning in the archive, accessible in the form of the document and conventionally associated with the writing of history, may appear to be found, innocent, and neutral but is always produced, ideological, and often deeply personal.[53] Interpreted by Michel de Certeau as a sort of factory for manufacturing the product we commonly call history, the archive has become a figure for the obfuscation of history writing. Afflicted by what de Certeau calls (uncannily echoing Bazin on film) the "perversion of time," history in general, and the archive in particular, make us forget that which they are supposed to represent, the past.[54] Moving more in the direction of de Certeau's than Foucault's formulations, Jacques Derrida contributed to the analysis of this temporal paradox by emphasizing the contradiction inherent in the archive ("The archive always works, and *a priori*, against itself") as an institution that claims to impose a coherent monolithic meaning while always gesturing to the remainder, or shadow, that lies outside, permanently threatening the order of its available stock.[55]

Of these three philosophers, Foucault had the largest impact on the field of visual studies. In the 1980s his work inspired interpretations of the archive as an epistemological device bent on maintaining an illusory segregation of knowledge and power. Subsequent readings emphasized the archive's function for the hegemony of institutional and state discourses, ranging from those related to penal, juridical, medical, and colonial practices, as well as others related to visual entertainment technologies.[56] Not surprisingly, given their concrete use in the disciplining of socially marginalized bodies, photographic archives (such as Jean-Martin Charcot's La Salpêtrière experiments or Alphonse Bertillon's police photography) provided the most undisguised evidence of the archive's connection to power. It was precisely this power-knowledge connection that traditional art history had obfuscated for too long (according to Rosalind Krauss), as seen in the discipline's tendency to liberate photographs from their original archival context into the ideological weightlessness of connoisseur readings.[57]

In response to the now dominant poststructuralist framing of the archive that emerged from the above debates, the feminist social and cultural historian Carolyn Steedman has objected to two of its outcomes: first, the mechanical collapsing of the archive onto state apparatuses which had led to its reputation as the default bad object of modernity, inflated beyond all material specificity to unquestionably denote coercion and state power; and second, the increasingly abstract application of the term as a stand-in for memory.[58] Not unlike Allan Sekula (although without his focus on photography), Steedman has argued for a more materialist (although no less poetic and personal) approach to the archive's diverse histories of use while also critiquing its sacred status for working-class social history.

In light of these archival quarrels, film studies' own belated rush to the archives in recent years offers a critical opportunity for reflection upon the future of film history. Given the infamously incomplete state of early cinema's archive, working in and writing from film-related archives from this period require new theoretical models of creative and critical empiricism. The stakes of such research become even higher when confronted with the "aggressive empiricism" (to use Sekula's words) that underlines those rare, actually self-identified archives like the Archives de la Planète.[59] The glaring gaps in cinema's historical record do not constitute a handicap for history but a challenge to produce a more sensitive historiography that moves beyond the historicist myth of the all-knowing sovereign archive.

Acknowledging Steedman's reservations regarding the archive-as-metaphor, while supporting a reinvigoration of theory in literal archives, this book also aims to retrieve both the archive and Foucault from the monolithic appropriation of

Discipline and Punish. The phenomenal impact of that work has led to a re-
grettably orthodox situation in which representations anywhere in the vicinity of
modernity, and especially within the confines of archives, are assumed to function like two-dimensional Benthamite panopticons, ready to reveal the straightforward evidence of surveillance and constraint necessary to the production of
modern, docile subjects. Ironically, where the everyday has assumed in critical
discourse an elusive identity, the archive has been stamped with an unquestionable, definite profile. *Counter-Archive* questions the obviousness of the archive
by returning us to the elusiveness of its early cinematic incarnation. Central to
my retrieval must be the recognition that unlike photography, film was not dominated by—although it certainly took influential detours through—archival applications in its first decades. And even when it was, as with the Archives de la
Planète, the film archive did not successfully submit to the filing cabinet or card
catalogue as previous photographic archives did.[60] Certainly, as one of the first
"media fantasies" that accompanied cinema's emergence, the archival imaginary
had a hold upon film discourse (the topic of chapter 4), but cinema soon became
dominated by a narrative-based entertainment context.[61] If this should give us
reason to question the applicability of what I call the "panoptic-archive" model,
it should not deter us, however, from returning to Foucault's earlier anti-positivist method of archaeology in trying to deal with the specific rupture posed by
the paradox of a film archive that appears before the emergence of film archives
proper. There remains much in Foucault's work (particularly in his model of history in *The Order of Things* and *The Archaeology of Knowledge*, but also in his
attention to the utopian-heterotopian dialectic that animates his writings on the
new spatio-temporal forms of modernity) that is crucial for a nondeterministic
study of the film archive in its literal and conceptual manifestations and a counter-positivist understanding of film's access to a history of the everyday. Applying
Foucault's focus on regularities *and* incongruities to the Kahn Archive reveals
the instabilities within the positivist project that underpinned it from the outset
while also recognizing the position of privilege and power that enabled its execution given the historical connection between French archives and nation-state
and colonial power.

     If Kahn's filmic circumference of the globe should not be reduced to the French
state's disciplining functions—which would make it a sort of *Policeman's Tour of
the World* (to appropriate the title of a 1906 Pathé film)—it should also not be
abstracted into an aestheticized, apolitical experiment in *visual Esperanto*. The
hermeneutics of the archive that I propose begins, therefore, from the assumption
that when studying archives one should not have to make a choice between an analytic framework devoted to original context and documentary evidence versus one
attracted to aesthetic formalism and theoretical abstraction.

   This book is committed to tracing at both theoretical and historical levels the unevenness and distinctiveness of the emergence of film as an archive-inflected medium. Unlike the mostly abstract and generalist discussions to date of film's ties to an archival logic, this book grounds a conceptual interrogation of the archive within a specific material history of its early cinematic application.[62] At the same time, I am not interested in opening up the Kahn Archive just for the sake of expanding our stock of silent cinema. Rather, my interest lies in opening up the concept of the archive itself—a concept hitherto dominated by discussions in photographic history and historical methodology—to the challenge posed by film. As much as Foucault and Derrida deconstructed the concept of the archive, for the most part their work neglected the material example responsible for unwittingly reinventing that concept in the early twentieth century, the *film archive*.[63] *Counter-Archive* illuminates this blind spot by attending to the diverse ways in which film was imagined and mobilized under the sign of the archive. Not surprisingly, film's transformation of the concept of the archive embodied a nascent challenge to the practice most often associated with archives: the writing of history. Accompanying the perception of film as the most advanced medium for archiving everyday life was the more troubling recognition of film's potential to destabilize its archival properties and historicist applications. Film's mechanical-based nature as an automatic, arbitrary, and anonymous record of contingent information on everyday life meant that, in addition to having the potential to be an exhaustive, visual storehouse, it also displayed a tendency, as Kracauer understood, for a level of "endlessness" and "indeterminacy" that unsettled the finite needs of historicist evidence.[64]

   It is film's multifaceted challenge to historicism that I understand to be counter-archival. A central concern of this book is to show how the film medium brought to the surface the internal contradiction within the modern desire to archive everyday life, at once understood as a dream of complete knowledge and a nightmare of totalizing inscription. If, as Sekula has argued, the index card, filing cabinet, and archive were in fact the external guarantors of photography's questionable optical realism, then film, with its even more arbitrary and undisciplined style of evidence inevitably undermined even further the archival support it inherited from photography, thus establishing a relation to the archive that I call counter-archival. Once translated into the age of cinema, the archive thus mutated into the counter-archive, a supplementary realm where the modern conditions of disorder, fragmentation, and contingency came to haunt the already unstable positivist utopia of order, synthesis, and totality.

   I mobilize the term *counter-archive* in four related ways in this book, all of them breaching the supposed impasse between historical and theoretical approaches to silent cinema. First, at the broadest level, counter-archive denotes the unconventional way in which I read the relationship between film, the everyday, and French modernity from the perspective of noncanonical films that challenge the commercial, theatrical, and narrative bias of traditional film history. In its second hyphenated sense, counter-archive purposely collapses two terms, the archive and its contradictions, in order to connote two directions in the archival conceptualization of film that form an underlying struggle in the Kahn Archive and film in general.

This conjoining leads to the third and more explicitly theorized adjectival sense of the term, in which counter-archival refers to all those qualities within film that tempted but ultimately subverted positivist history. I find these qualities theorized in Bergsonian philosophy, exemplified in the Kahn Archive, impressed upon the early Annales theory of history, and experimented with in avant-garde film theory and practice. The uniqueness of the Kahn Archive as an extreme test case for the archive is central in this regard. In contrast to conventional archives established in a *post hoc* (after the fact) fashion intended to preserve documents removed from their original function, the Archives de la Planète existed in a *pre hoc* state; its documents were born in, rather than retired to, an archive.

The fourth sense in which I am using the term *counter-archival* refers to my revisionary reading of the French intellectual tradition of critiquing the archive (from Baudelaire to Bergson, Marc Bloch to Pierre Nora, Foucault to de Certeau, and Derrida to Deleuze). Instead of foregrounding the anti-archival bias in the French suspicion of the archive, I uncover with reference to film a counter-archival dimension in this tradition. Rather than emphasizing the deficiencies of the film-as-archive equation, I have thus chosen to explore the unique capacities—which I term counter-archival—of film's relation to memory, the past, and history.

If the archival paradigm has provided a dominant framework for the history of modern photography throughout the twentieth century, it has only recently made an impact upon analyses of film. It has mainly served to highlight the postmodern archival interface that mediates our contemporary access to early cinema, as displayed in the exponential expansion of the meaning and reception of early film due to new digital technology or the diverse range of filmmakers currently recycling the past by raiding archives for their aesthetic and historical secrets. In contrast to the largely postmodern framing of our present approach to film's archival qualities, this book argues that early cinema was already located in a complicated modern *counter*-archival culture and logic of its own, which contested the positivist conception of the archive as a source for history based in linear time.

To approach the Kahn Archive as a counter-archive is to show how it continued as well as contested the positivist heritage that informed the evolution of France's first archives, a positivist heritage that also influenced history, naturalism, geography, and, of course, the early applications of film itself. Such challenges may have been already implicit within diverse nineteenth-century positivist monuments, any number of which (museums, world expositions, state archives) harbored their own auto-critique or counter logic. But in the early twentieth century, under the pressure from new technologies like film, this instability in the archive became more widespread and explicit. The Kahn Archive thus embodied film's anarchic, potentially liberating ability to disrupt the overarching ideal of an exhaustive classification of daily life. And although it was conceived as a literal archive, to be consulted by a national elite, it was also from its inception a virtual archive—unfinished, impossible, and until very recently, unseen. But the Archive's voyage into the realm of the counter-archival was never simply a function of its forced closure with the financial ruin of Kahn after 1929. It was reflective of the project's inherent impossibility due to its dependence on a medium and an aspect of life resistant to classification. By integrating the archive, a quintessential nineteenth-century institution of the state, with film, an equally representative twentieth-century medium of entertainment, Kahn created a project that was both backward- and forward-looking in its aspirations, both disciplining and distracting in its attention to the everyday, and both reassuringly meticulous and curiously casual in its archival procedures.

If the Archives de la Planète did not follow the definition of the archive as the guardian of the afterlife of documents no longer in use, it was, however, based in a profound sense of the afterlife of the planet, or more precisely, the apocalyptic feeling about the world that existed as it entered and exited the First World War. Where older planetary pictorial traditions like the atlas proposed a God's-eye unity, Kahn's global visual compendium offered a world gathered, described, and left in fragments. Confronted by the vast and discontinuous nature of the Kahn Archive's holdings, I have found it useful to shape the book via a kaleidoscopic mode in which each chapter shifts our perspective onto the puzzling shards of Kahn's multifaceted world. True to the workings of a kaleidoscopic vision, each chapter shift produces an image that allows the reader to keep the macroscopic and microscopic in view via a methodology inspired by Kracauer's cinematically inflected notion that the "the big can be adequately rendered only by a permanent movement from the whole to some detail, then back to the whole."[65] Just as a kaleidoscope's views are not infinite but limited in their capacity to reorganize the glass splinters into new perspectives, so too are these chapters prearranged according to my own fixed interest in the central topos of the archive, the everyday, and film. I do not claim that this topos authorizes me to uncover the single truth lying somewhere hidden in Kahn's Archive. It will also not be my job to disclose a single authoritative meaning behind Kahn's films, or to fall prey to the fantasy of awakening the sleeping documents with the (death) kiss of finite interpretation. Rather, following Foucault's critique of archival-based history in *The Archaeology of Knowledge*, I try "to follow them through their sleep," attending to the "forgotten, and possibly even destroyed" context of the films' emergence, without giving up entirely on interpretation, the ethical subject behind and/or in front of the camera, or the unpredictable challenges to which the rules and regulations of discursive formations are historically subject.[66]

Chapter 1 outlines the evolution of the Kahn Archive in reference to Kahn's biography, the cultural shift from travel to tourism, the heterotopian nature of Kahn's world, and the interrelationship between photography and film. Chapter 2 provides an overview of the Kahn Archive's films emphasizing their transitional status between pre-documentary and documentary genres. Deploying Bergson's hitherto unexamined connection to the Kahn Archive as a way to revisit the Bergsonian cinema debate, chapter 3 argues for the interaction, rather than opposition, in Bergsonian philosophy, between, on the one hand, *la durée*, and on the other hand, the everyday, film, memory, and the archive. Chapter 4 discusses the first discourses and practices related to the concept of the French film archive, and chapter 5 investigates the rupture to traditional *histoire événementielle* posed by film as reflected in the shift from the *école méthodique* to the Annales school of history. Chapter 6 analyzes the rediscovery of the everyday as a central topic in early French film theory and chapter 7 brings this theory to bear upon an analysis of the reception context of the Kahn films. Returning to the ideological dimensions of world travel through the optic of the aerial view, chapter 8 situates the Archive in relation to the connections between geography, film, and colonialism.

Finally, *Counter-Archive* is also unabashedly a product of, if not an extended reflection upon, the experience of working day after day in archives: equal parts boredom and exhilaration, alienation and enchantment, loneliness and sociality, patience and frustration. The experience often resembles a balancing act of feeling overwhelmed and in control, feeling relief at having finally gotten in mixed with concern over when I will ever get out—all dominated by a sense of the preciousness of time mixed with the need to approach each day's work as if one had all the time in the world. Not coincidentally, the vertiginous relation to time and space that archival research provides—a feeling of being lost and found, at once—is as good as any definition I can ultimately offer of the everyday.

WORLD SOUVENIR

"MR. K" AND THE ARCHIVES DE LA PLANÈTE

A Cinema Museum: Though little spoken of this museum exists and already stores within its cabinets an impressive number of kilometers of film, especially documentary films on social life. The creation of this museum is the work of the generous patron M[onsieur] K. . . . It is installed in a magnificent park in Boulogne-sur-Seine. Up until now the museum has been private property but it will return to the State after the death of the founder.

LE JOURNAL DU CINÉ-CLUB (OCTOBER 1, 1920)[1]

I have traveled a lot—I have read a lot and I knew all the famous men of my time, trust me, I don't say this out of vanity, and yet I only considered all this knowledge as a partial goal, what I was searching for was life's path and the universe's functioning principles, which is why I assembled a documentation in which all the world's events have been studied.

ALBERT KAHN (1938)[2]

"[Films] virtually make the world our home."

SIEGFRIED KRACAUER (1960)[3]

THE ABOVE NOTICE from the *Journal du Ciné-Club* is one of the very few contemporary references in the French film press to the kilometers of nonfiction footage that make up the film component of Albert Kahn's Archives de la Planète. The publication in which it appeared, the *Journal du Ciné-Club* (1920–21), was founded and edited by the most influential film critic of his generation, Louis Delluc, and it played a central role in the intellectual and creative blossoming of French film discourse and practice in the late teens and early twenties. Given the magazine's position at the epicenter of French film culture, we might consider it strange that the *Journal du Ciné-Club* appears to have only registered Kahn's monumental cinematic project in the margins of its pages. This chapter begins the process of explaining the apparent estrangement between the Archives de la Planète and film culture of the period by addressing four interrelated issues: Kahn's biography and his status as the absent center of the Archive; the heterotopian features of his *oeu-vre's* major sites; the origins and motivations for the establishment of the Archive as expressed, on the one hand, in its unofficial beginnings in the images taken by Kahn's chauffeur Albert Dutertre and, on the other hand, in its official inaugura-tion by the human geographer and scientific director of the Archive, Jean Brunhes; and the unique multimedia makeup (stereographs, films, and color autochrome photography) of the Archive.[4] The overarching context for all of these issues is the transitional culture and experience of modern travel—a condition bookended by Kahn's own founding "exile" from his birthplace, Alsace, and his later expression of world-weariness: "I have traveled a lot." Far from serving his loftier goals in a pure-ly ancillary way, as Kahn claimed retrospectively in the above epigraph, travel—and the crisis it faced due to its new "other," tourism—shaped Kahn's multifaceted projects through and through.[5]

The easily overlooked notice in the *Journal du Ciné-Club* reminds us that one possible explanation for the Archive's absence from the pages of the contemporary film press appears in the strict anonymity and low profile maintained by Kahn throughout his life, evident in the way he hides in the journal's text behind the mysterious screen of "Mr. K." A more extreme symptom of Kahn's obsessive privacy (not so unusual for a Jewish millionaire living in the anti-Semitic, post–Dreyfus Affair climate of early-twentieth-century France) appears in his curious camera-phobia. Kahn posed willingly for only a single formal photograph during his adult life (fig. 1.1).[6] Not coincidentally, he agreed to that singular portrait only because it was to be used for his passport. In other words, it bore an instrumental relation to fulfilling Kahn's understanding of travel as the search for "life's path and the universe's functioning principles." Thus, while Kahn spent his fortune developing an exhaustive photo-cinematographic surveillance of the daily lives of others, he spent a good part of his own daily life evading (sometimes unsuccessfully) those very same cameras. Behind the scenes of "Mr. K's" grandiose and public contribu-tion to modernity's exhibitionist complex there existed a deeply personal, albeit socially determined, need for invisibility apparent in the disappearing act Kahn performed before his cameras day after day.

The enigmatic reputation of camera-shy "Mr. K" has also spread due to his sim-ilarly paradoxical semidisappearance from paper archives. There is only a small amount of extant information on Kahn. This situation could be partly attributed to the fact that he died in 1940 shortly after the Germans invaded Paris and just before, to use the words of Philip Nord, "Vichy and the right dismissed the [Third] republic as a cabal of Protestants, Freemasons, and Jews."[7] Given Kahn's affinities with that imaginary Third Republican "cabal" (whose invention dates back to the polarizing effects of the Dreyfus Affair of the 1890s), one can surmise why the remains of a

FIGURE 1.1   The only known posed photographic portrait of Albert Kahn on the balcony of his office, 102 rue de Richelieu, Paris. (*Photo*: Paul Ducellier, c. 1928 [MAK])

wealthy Alsatian Jewish financier, whose only signed publication (from 1918) was filled with postwar anti-German rhetoric, mysteriously disappeared.[8] The possibility that Kahn did leave behind documents that were confiscated by the Germans is likely, especially given that in 2002 paper documents relating to one of his projects, the Société Autour du Monde, were returned to the Musée Albert-Kahn from Russian state archives.[9] Although we can never be sure whether extensive records existed, were confiscated, or simply lost over time, it is undeniable that Kahn left behind a surprisingly small amount of documentation (no personal diary or business records). When it comes to his own personal archives, it seems that Kahn—the preserver of an Archive for the planet—either willfully removed himself from history by refusing to leave behind traces, or else fell victim to the politicized fate of archives as the potential spoils of war. Either way, his end was overshadowed by the messy (and, as I will explain in chapter 8, murderous) *realpolitik* of archives that in many ways he had devoted his life to transcending in the form of a humanist global Archive. Nonetheless, just as the figure of Kahn was in fact captured surreptitiously by at least some of his film cameras, so, too, are the facts about Kahn not entirely lost to history.[10]

THE MYSTERIOUS "MR. K"

Abraham Kahn was born on March 3, 1860, to a Jewish merchant family in the small Alsatian town of Marmoutier in northeastern France, a regional home to a large Jewish community.[11] In the century after emancipation (1791), when civil rights for Jews came slowly and at the price of assimilation, the community to which Kahn belonged found itself to be the target of distrust due to its proximity to Germany.[12] This suspicion increased dramatically following the 1871 annexation of Alsace-Lorraine to Germany as a result of the Franco-Prussian War. Jewish families, including Kahn's, became exiles in their own land. They had to decide between staying and becoming German or leaving and opting for French national identity. The patriotism of Alsatian Jews was thus often met with "suspicions of 'dual loyalties'" that eventually deepened the division of the nation during the Dreyfus Affair when Captain Dreyfus, a Jew from Alsace, was falsely accused of being a German spy.[13]

As one of the "Jews of the Alsatian exodus" (to borrow the self-description of another Alsatian Jew, the Annales historian Marc Bloch), Kahn arrived in Paris with the christianized first name Albert around 1875–76.[14] He soon became an employee of the Goudchaux bank and in 1879 began to study for his *baccalauréat* with a teacher one year his senior, the then unknown Henri Bergson. This tutorship initiated the bond that would lead to the defining friendship of his life. Installed in the capital, Kahn quickly proved himself to be gifted in taking advantage of the financial opportunities opened up by colonial expansion. After a trip to South

Africa in 1888, he reputedly speculated with great success on options in the De Beers diamond and Rand gold mines.[15] Kahn's business trips also took him to Tonkin (present day Vietnam)—perhaps spurred on by recent French colonial incursions into that region—as well as Venezuela, Egypt, Russia, and Ireland before 1900.[16] As a result of his early financial coups, by 1892 at the age of thirty-two, Kahn had become a joint owner of the Goudchaux bank.

The young banker was thus positioned at the turn of the century to experience both the rise to social legitimacy for Jewish financiers in France's Third Republic (1870–1940) as well as the accompanying reactionary growth in popular anti-Semitism that planted its deepest roots during the Dreyfus Affair. While not religiously observant himself, Kahn clearly embodied what Philip Nord and others have called "Jewish Republicanism." He was shaped by a shift in Jewish relations to French citizenship distinguished by a "conception of Jewish selfhood that embraced the republic as a secular incarnation of values embedded in Jewish tradition" and that identified strongly with a "commitment to an enlightened and fraternalist universalism."[17] Above all, Kahn's republican, liberal, pacifist, and secular patriotism was indelibly marked by the experience of a lost homeland. Like many Alsatian Jews who emigrated and opted for French national identity over native soil when given the choice after 1870, it might be said of Kahn (as it has been said of Bloch) that he "claimed the capital as [his] home, the Revolution as [his] liberator, and the Third Republic as [his] benefactor."[18]

In 1895, the same year Auguste and Louis Lumière held the first public screening of their *cinématographe*, Kahn purchased a vast property in Boulogne just to the southwest of Paris. There he embarked on building the first of two virtual attempts to make the world his home (to invoke Kracauer) in the form of his world-themed gardens. (The second of these attempts, the Archives de la Planète, would rival the global cinematic reach of the Lumières.) If the Boulogne gardens announced, at least in a superficial way, his membership in an elite group of mostly urban, assimilated Jews who were allowed entry into the upper echelons of fin-de-siècle French society, they also commemorated his rural past, particularly in the garden's miniature Vosgean forest devoted to the landscape of his birthplace.[19]

By 1898 Kahn had opened his own merchant bank and established himself as one of the first Western financiers to enter the Japanese market, where his fortune grew thanks to the international loans he organized. Yet Kahn never seems to have been at ease with his financial success. Embodying the cliché of the restless millionaire, Kahn grew dissatisfied with the mere accumulation of capital and began searching for worthy applications and legitimations for his vast wealth. Stimulated by his Japanese dealings, he began to nurture, following the already prominent tradition of French *japonisme*, what he himself called a deep "affinity" for Japanese "sensibility" and culture.[20] In addition to memorializing his past in the Vosgean forest, his gardens also contained a living homage to his acquired,

FIGURE 1.2   The Japanese "corner" of Kahn's world-themed gardens. (*Photo*: Auguste Léon, April 1911 [MAK: from original color autochrome B 62])

Far Eastern "sensibility" in the form of a Japanese garden that Kahn referred to as his transplanted "corner of Japanese soil" (fig. 1.2).[21] Not surprisingly, this cultural turn to Asia was double-sided: the financial roots of Kahn's Japanese garden found their source in the investments he was making in colonial interests in Taiwan and China.

If the enigma surrounding "Mr. K" is somewhat dispelled by the above account, surviving testimonies only reestablish the mystery. Several splintered portraits emerge of Kahn from those who knew him personally.[22] Mariel Jean-Brunhes Delamarre, the daughter and collaborator of the geographer Jean Brunhes (official director of the Archive), who lived on Kahn's estate while her father worked for him, remembered Kahn as a "man of mystery and concentration" who was gifted with the capacity for "seduction," exemplified in the magnetism of his eyes: "There was an extraordinary radiance which came from his gaze. He had a sparkle to his eye and seemed entirely preoccupied by his grand projects."[23] Also struck by Kahn's powers of seduction was Brunhes' teacher, Paul Vidal de la Blache, founder of the French school of human geography. He wrote to Brunhes with these words of advice: "You will be taken aback by the largeness of mind, mixed somewhat with a utopian streak and a considerable personal seduction that is wielded by this man whose daily practice of business renders him only bolder in the area of ideas."[24]

The banker Georges Wormser was more attached to the memory of Kahn as a vegetarian who always wore the same simple suit and who considered Bergson a god. Alain Petit, a recipient of Kahn's travel fund, also emphasized the paradoxical qualities of the Alsatian banker. He noted with irony that Kahn, who spent a fortune on importing rare trees, plants, and even Japanese gardeners to build his Kyoto-inspired "corner," could himself easily be mistaken for an employee of his gardens, given his unassuming clothes and small stature.[25] Other portrayals of the lifelong bachelor allude to his partiality to wearing a large slightly tilted hat and cape, in winter or summer; his unassimilated Alsatian accent; his nightly habit of reading Jean-Henri Fabre's *Souvenirs entomologiques* (a popular entomological study); or his fondness for ending a busy week by having his chauffeur drive him out of town where he would sleep in his convertible under the stars.[26] Kahn's correspondence with Bergson reveals a man fond of excursions and hiking while other sources point to his love of Richard Wagner and the sculptures (which he collected) of Auguste Rodin, with whom he attended the Wagner festival in Bayreuth.[27] And in another appraisal by the poet and literature professor Fernand Baldensperger, most likely tinged with an anti-Semitism that cast all Jews as outsiders and foreigners, Kahn appears under the disparaging guise of a "bizarre man of money."[28]

What remains constant across these composite portraits—Kahn as a philosopher-banker, ascetic-millionaire, humanist-misanthrope, wanderer-recluse, provincial-nipponophile—is his abiding passion for the "patriotic and humanitarian mission" he embarked upon around the same year as the Lumières launched their "invention without a future."[29] Far from constituting a passing fad, as the *cinématographe* seemed to be for the Lumières, Kahn's mission, described by Émile Borel as furthering "the *oeuvre* of mutual comprehension of peoples and international rapprochement," obsessed him until his dying days.[30] One of his secretaries, Paul Ducellier, recalled how after all his properties and belongings had been sold when he lost his fortune in the 1929 stock market crash, Kahn continued to act as though nothing had changed and never stopped believing that he would one day rebuild his fortune and continue the unfinished Archive.[31] This would not happen. Kahn died on November 14, 1940, just a few months after the German invasion of Paris and two months before Bergson's death—two events that marked the passing of the political ideal and philosophical inspiration that had guided his life's work.

KAHN'S *OEUVRE*

Far from being the sole object of Kahn's attentions, the Archives de la Planète constitutes just one element of the banker's multifaceted *oeuvre*. Although no master document remains that fully explains the relations among Kahn's various projects, the autochromes and films existed in an organic relationship with his wider network of botanical, publishing, and philanthropic-related projects. The public face

of Kahn's mission predated the Archive itself with the creation in 1898 of the Autour du Monde (Around the World) travel scholarships. As described in the instructions for the foundation that oversaw the travel fund, which was administered by
the Sorbonne with instructions not to divulge the donor's identity, the grants were
intended to enable young teachers chosen from the "intellectual and moral elite of
the nation" to "enter into sympathetic communication with the ideas, feelings and
lives of other peoples."[32]

In contrast to the emphasis upon the acquisition of impartial data in seventeenth-century travel, summarized by Judith Adler as a practice "capable of yield-
ing a corpus of 'objective' knowledge, based on the observations of gentlemen
scholars," Kahn's instructions stressed repeatedly the value of personal experience.[33] Supporting this commitment to subjective rather than objective knowledge, Kahn elsewhere stated that he hoped the travel funds discouraged future
teachers from being "content with a purely abstract knowledge."[34] Most importantly, the fund was devoted to Kahn's belief that travel enabled one to "come into
real contact with life."[35] The travel fund harnessed the vision-observation-knowl-
edge continuum of a somewhat outdated, elitist rationale for travel to the Third
Republic's cult of education. It also fashioned its end product, that is, the returned
travel grant recipients (*boursiers*), as emissaries of a reinvigorated cosmopolitanism bound by a duty to "explain to their peoples that attachment to a State and a
national civilization didn't prevent one from feeling oneself to be a citizen of the
world."[36] The travel grants thus combined many of the key ideological currents in
the Kahn project, from republican secular pedagogy and French cosmopolitanism
to the renovation of scientific positivism from the angle of subjective insight.

The Autour du Monde scholarships directly fed into the creation of the Société Autour du Monde (1906–1949), a convivial international intellectual circle
established to continue the pursuit of intercultural cooperation and knowledge
begun by the grant recipients during their world voyages.[37] At its height in 1931,
the Société (whose archives would be of great interest to the German occupiers
during the Second World War) counted 186 members and, in the same year, the
club was fêted at its twenty-fifth anniversary as "an *oeuvre* in which one recognized
the true face of our country, of a pacifist, hardworking, and humane France."[38] The
Société convened every Sunday for informal luncheons in one of the buildings on
Kahn's Boulogne property and opened its doors to an array of international guests
from the world of politics, religion, industry, military, science, literature, and the
arts, including Rabindranath Tagore, Lord Robert Cecil, Thomas Mann, Albert
Einstein, H. G. Wells, Edmund Husserl, Rudyard Kipling, Auguste Rodin, Léon
Bourgeois, Paul Rivet, Lucien Lévy-Bruhl, Marie Curie, Anatole France, André Mi-
chelin, Louis Lumière, Paul Valéry, and Colette.

In addition to these luncheons, the Société also organized private (by invitation
only) autochrome projections and film screenings on the Kahn property.[39] In other

words, unlike films in a commercial context or documents in a state archive, Kahn's filmed documents were never intended for commercial or public exhibition, circulation, or consultation. During Kahn's lifetime, he reserved his visual documents for viewing by a cultural and intellectual elite. Their distribution was thus limited to two noncommercial audiences. The first, internal audience included Kahn and members and guests of the Société Autour du Monde. The second, external audience mainly derived from Brunhes' functions as a teacher at the Sorbonne, the Collège de France, and occasionally overseas.[40]

Set up with a similar devotion to intellectual elites, although assembling beyond the cloistered environs of Kahn's "Boulogne community" (as Bergson called it), Kahn also funded the Comité National d'Études Sociales et Politiques (National Committee of Social and Political Studies) (1916–1931)—a multidisciplinary forum for a host of national leaders (from the state, church, army, unions, universities, industry) of diverse ideological and political persuasions. Its participants ranged from Bergson, Albert Thomas, André Michelin, and Marcel Mauss to Le Corbusier, General Hubert Lyautey, and General Ferdinand Foch.[41] The Comité met on average once a fortnight for sixteen years in the Court of Appeal in Paris and debated the major social and political issues of the day, from war reparations and the fight against venereal disease, to the status of France's colonies and the rise of communism and fascism.

The printed summaries of these meetings made up one of the fourteen titles in Kahn's encyclopedic publication series. Together, these publications provide the written component of what Kahn referred to collectively in this chapter's epigraph as the "documentation" he funded in which "all the world's events have been studied."[42] Between 1917 and 1931, fourteen separate bulletins were thus printed and distributed for free to an elite international constituency including university professors, ministers, and various heads of state. The publications, which mostly took the form of commentaries, extracts, and summaries collected on a daily basis from world newspapers, constitute a vital textual and analytical accompaniment to the discussion-based Comité National d'Études Sociales et Politiques and the visual-based Archive. Though Kahn envisioned the bulletins as an organic encyclopedia of the times, they more closely resembled a world scrapbook. Apparently never arriving in time to be of immediate impact (thus in a certain way echoing the fate of the films, which were in fact rarely screened compared to commercial standards), the bulletins were sent off into the world from Boulogne, like the eager *boursiers*, as so many hopeful messages in a bottle.

Kahn's devotion to institutes of higher education, typical of his loyalty to the Third Republic's investment in secular education, culminated in the founding of the Centre de Documentation Sociale in 1920. Housed at the École Normale Supérieure on the rue d'Ulm (where Bergson, Brunhes, Dr. Jean Comandon, and many other members of Kahn's circle had studied), the Centre de Documentation Sociale was a pioneering intellectual endeavor run by the sociologist Celestin Bouglé (a former student of Émile Durkheim) that focused on developing social science research with an emphasis upon contemporary society.[43] Although Kahn himself was more an autodidact and had not attended elite institutions of higher learning, he retained his faith in their role as the ultimate arbiter of his *oeuvre*. In April 1929 he signed an agreement known as the *Centrale de recoordination* that would have transferred the entirety of his projects to the Sorbonne in return for 500, 000 francs and an additional 9.5 million francs on his death. Although the loss of his fortune voided this agreement and left many of his projects without further funding, several continued to operate after 1932. For instance, the Centre de Documentation Sociale continued under Kahn's watchful eye until 1940, with help from the Rockefeller Foundation. And in a move that speaks of its courageous commitment not merely to social science research, the Centre offered a home in July 1933 to members of the Frankfurt School recently exiled from Germany.[44]

Besides the Archives de la Planète, Kahn's involvement in film projects extended to funding a biological laboratory on the Boulogne property in 1926 for Dr. Jean Comandon, the celebrated pioneer in microcinematography. After his initially fruitful collaboration with Pathé turned sour in 1926, Comandon seems to have been approached by Kahn with an offer he could not refuse. The nineteen or so scientific films that Comandon made in Boulogne with his collaborator Pierre de Fonbrune, using a specially made ultramicroscopic camera funded by Kahn, constitute one of several cinematic satellites to the Archive proper.[45]

THE GARDEN IN THE ARCHIVE

As distinct as each of the above projects is, no single element of Kahn's *oeuvre* existed in isolation. The organic relation between the parts of his *oeuvre* is nowhere more evident than in the most famous trace of Kahn's legacy, his magnificent "world" gardens. Given Kahn's desire for anonymity, it is ironic but fitting that his name should be most commonly associated today with his gardens—the one piece of the puzzle he kept most to himself before they became open to the public in 1937.[46] In Kahn's lifetime, use of the gardens was strictly limited to himself and his invited guests. Even the members of the Société Autour du Monde were forbidden from using them apart from Sundays between two and five in the afternoon. Yet far from constituting a space apart from his global laboratory of universalist experiments, the gardens, like several other seemingly ancillary aspects of the Archives de la Planète (such as Comandon's films or Kahn's relationship with Bergson), are best understood as integral components of the comprehensive if eccentric methodology and vision linking Kahn's diverse projects. The gardens are especially important because they materialize the heterotopian relation to travel that underpins Kahn's enterprises.

As theorized by Michel Foucault in his 1967 lecture "Of Other Spaces," het-erotopias differ from the "fundamentally unreal" condition of utopias in that they are actually existing "counter-sites" in which society's real sites are "simultaneously represented, contested, and inverted."[47] Conspicuous among the heterotopias out-lined by Foucault are three sites that define the topography of Kahn's *oeuvre*: the cinema, the garden, and the archive. Foucault offers the cinema, with its multiva-lent spaces enfolded into the conventional screening room, as a modern example of the heterotopian principle of "juxtaposing in a single real space several spaces" (25). Then, as though he had Kahn's Boulogne heterotopia in mind, in the same sentence he contrasts the cinema with the "oldest example" of these forms of "con-tradictory sites," the garden. Even more relevant to Kahn's world-themed gardens is Foucault's contention that a "garden is the smallest parcel of the world and then it is the totality of the world" (26). After his reference to cinemas and gardens, Foucault makes a crucial shift to the temporal register in his essay (presaged, not coincidentally, by the preceding treatment of the cinema) in highlighting a further principle of heterotopian counter-sites, namely, their link "to slices in time" (26) as exemplified by those key archival sites of nineteenth-century modernity—mu-seums and libraries. If, for Foucault, these spaces brought modernity into general being through a devotion to "the idea of accumulating everything, of establishing a sort of *general archive* [my emphasis]," they did so because they represented that century's overarching obsessions with time and history.

As resonant as Foucault's idea of heterotopia is for the Kahn Archive, it fails, of course, to describe it fully because Foucault stops short of the twentieth century and the rupture (for history and heterotopias) posed by the possibility of a film archive. For instance, his theorization of discourse and the archive in *The Archae-ology of Knowledge*, published a year after "Of Other Spaces" and dominated by a print-based, nineteenth-century conception of communication, does not broach the challenge of modern photographic media. Nonetheless, as we will see with the Archives de la Planète, it is the film archive, this new twentieth-century site for spatio-temporal storage obsessions, that fulfills *and* challenges exactly what Fou-cault claimed was at the heart of the nineteenth-century obsession with history, namely, the "will to enclose in one place all times, all epochs, all forms, all tastes, [and] the idea of constituting a place of all times that is itself outside of time and inaccessible to its ravages" (26).

As the elements of Kahn's *oeuvre* that have most successfully survived, against all odds, the ravages of time, the films, gardens, and Archive (which still exist as they were intended together on the Boulogne estate) form a concentration of inter-penetrating heterotopian sites and impulses as described by Foucault. But if there is one force around which they all gravitate, it is, without doubt, the gardens. In them, Kahn sought to bring together the views and spaces of Oriental, Mediter-ranean, and European landscapes into a model voyage through cultural difference, harmonizing if only through the imaginary ideal of international cooperation what in many ways the unedited films allude to but leave suspended in the unfinished Archive.[48] The gardens and films also coincide on a formal level in their fragmented nature. Any walk through the different sections of Kahn's gardens reveals that they are actually discontinuous slices of landscapes—topographical equivalents of the mostly unedited footage that make up the film component of the Archives de la Planète. In fact, the characteristic feature of his botanical world in miniature is that no effort has been made to suture over the discontinuities between the geographically incongruous corners of the globe. The result is that the mini-landscapes do not so much flow into each other as contrast discordantly with one another. Rather than a utopian harmonious amalgam of the world, Kahn's gardens choreograph an acute experience of topographical difference whose temporal-spatial collisions evoke the disruptions and violent artifice that (according to Foucault) characterize heterotopias and that lie just beneath the surface of this once secret garden.[49]

But the heterotopian qualities of Kahn's world are not limited to the gardens or the films' materialization of a "perpetual and indefinite accumulation of time in an immobile place" (26). In his ultimate example of a heterotopian space, the boat (27), Foucault suggests the link that holds together Kahn's heterotopian universe, that is, the connection between Kahn's three counter-sites (the cinema, the gardens, the archive) and travel, understood either literally, as with the travel funds, or in a virtual or metonymical form, as with the films, gardens, and planetary archive.[50] This connection speaks to Foucault's insistence that heterotopias begin to function at full capacity on the threshold of one of the central experiences of modernity in general and travel in particular, that moment of crisis (to which the Kahn Archive is a reaction) when "men arrive at a sort of absolute break with their traditional time" (26). It is to the relationship between Kahn's heterotopian universe and travel's basic structure as a confrontational movement through space *and* time that I now want to turn.

HETEROTOPIA AND TRAVEL

The earliest components of Kahn's *oeuvre*, the gardens and the travel scholarships (begun respectively in 1895 and 1898), are monuments to a centuries' long tradition of world voyages undertaken by privileged Western subjects. In the case of the gardens, the monument is turned inward, the world condensed and contained in the off-limits metonymy (as Foucault said, "the heterotopic site is not freely accessible like a public space" [26]) of a Parisian-bound global landscape. By contrast, in the travel scholarships the monument gestures outward in the gift given to middle-class educators to help open their eyes to the benefits of knowledge beyond book learning. Both projects held sacred the possibility of knowing (and control-

ling) the world in all its plurality. They also reflected the ideological histories embedded in diverse European "atlas" traditions of observing, describing, collecting,
ordering, and displaying the world.[51]

There never seemed a better time to know the world through firsthand observation than in the early twentieth century, due to developments in technologies of transportation and of visual recording. Yet this period of ascendant tourism
contributed to a crisis in the epistemological heritage of travel resulting from the
democratizing effects of those very same technologies. Reflecting this crisis, Kahn's
diverse enterprises were split by the increasingly untenable oppositions between
travel and tourism, the former understood as the practice of a privileged, usually
male subject undertaking a demanding voyage in search of active experiences, useful knowledge, and visionary insight, the latter associated with the practice of de-
mocratized and feminized masses signing up for recreational tours in search of
distracting experiences, recognizable attractions, and sightseeing. Both forms of
journeying were also subject to a common set of tensions—home and away, stasis
and movement, memory and forgetting, the familiar and the new, self and other.[52]
In short, travel functioned within Kahn's Archive not merely as a means to collect
"views" from around the world; travel also infused the project in its pedagogical,
epistemological, philosophical, colonial, and not least, cinematographic turns. In
regard to the latter, as a technology of reproduction wedded to a *mobile* representation of a past event from another place (from the time and space of the viewing
experience), early cinema's elsewhere- and elsewhen-ness embraced time travel
and spatial displacement as a standard condition of its reception.[53]

As for Kahn himself, his experience of forced displacement from Alsace can
now be understood as a personal connection (reflecting the doubly exilic identity
of the post-1870 Alsatian Jew) to a national trauma (the defeat of 1870 and the annexation of Alsace and Lorraine) that haunted his Archive and the entire French
imaginary until and even beyond the return of the so-called "lost provinces" at the
end of the First World War. Indeed, Kahn's biography is enmeshed in some of the
central narratives surrounding turn-of-the-century travel. These include travel as
the burden of forced migration or expulsion, resulting in the condition of permanent exile; travel as the mobilization of expansionist and exploitative economic
impulses; and travel as the conduit to a humanist, world-citizen outlook. As a
citizen for whom spatial displacement—voluntary and involuntary, willing and unwilling—provided a lifelong condition, Kahn found that his life intersected with
the oppressive and liberatory histories behind modern travel. As a result, journeys
away from and back to home, within that fraught modern passage that Rabindranath Tagore (a frequent visitor to the Kahn property) called "the home and the
world," reveal a crisscrossing restlessness beneath the calm surface of Kahn's photo-cinematographic *mappa mundi*.

GRAND LIVRE DU MONDE

It was on one such journey to America and Asia, undertaken partly for business, partly for pleasure, between November 1908 and May 1909, that initial plans for the Archives de la Planète evolved. The hybrid nature of this trip epitomizes Kahn's efforts to reconcile his search for new capital markets with the desire for, as one of his Japanese co-utopianists put it, "the unification of the world" based on the destruction of "racial and religious intolerance."[54] Insofar as it combined financial interests with cultural pursuits, blurring the distinction between capitalist ventures and touristic adventures so typical of travel during this period, this trip was probably much like any other Kahn had taken over the past twenty years.

There was, however, one notable difference—Kahn enlisted his chauffeur Albert Dutertre to document their voyage with a Vérascope Richard color stereograph camera and a Pathé film camera.[55] Dutertre also produced a diary, thus adding to the significant number of travel *récits* that make up the textual documents surrounding the Kahn Archive (the other major example being the accounts written by the Autour du Monde grant recipients on their return).[56] Although Dutertre's mostly factual diary sheds little light on the wider rationale behind his photographic and cinematographic documentation, it does indicate how he and Kahn participated in the masculinist, elitist adventurer-explorer mode and myth of travel undertaken by scores of missionaries, colonists, orientalists, and geographers before them.

Typical of this travel myth, the diary reveals how they consciously opposed the practices of tourists by traveling during the off-season and visiting out-of-the-way places (like the Great Wall of China) in search of new knowledge. Their travel was not intended, as it supposedly was for the tourist, as a pleasure or end unto itself. Tellingly, Kahn himself was careful to distinguish his life's travels from purposeless "roaming."[57] And one of Kahn's travel grant recipients, Madame Antoine, echoed this aversion to superficial sightseeing when she justified her visit to Yellowstone Park in America "not for the pleasure of tourism but in order to understand volcanic phenomena."[58] It is clear that Kahn and the "Boulogne community" who participated in his network of projects self-consciously aligned themselves with the elite, knowledge-seeking, and altruistic labor of travel rather than the mass-marketed, commodified, and sensation-seeking pleasures of tourism that began to transform (in large part due to photography and film) the culture of world tours in the late nineteenth and early twentieth centuries.

Supporting this utilitarian justification for travel, Kahn's own wanderlust directly fed into his plans for the Archives de la Planète as a corrective to the out-of-date travel guides and dusty academic studies that had so frustrated him on his journey with Dutertre to Japan and China in 1909. Resisting the rising discourses and practices of Thomas Cook–style middle-class tourism, while also reflecting a distrust of scholarly academicism, Kahn would eventually fashion the Archive as an updated version (due to the superior eye-witness claims of photography and cinematography) of the centuries-old traveler's quest for "on-the-spot" observations. In line with this mission to modernize the ocularcentric and experiential bent of the Enlightenment travel-as-knowledge equation, Kahn and Henri Bergson compared the Archive separately (invoking Descartes' vocabulary) to the *"Grand Livre de l'Homme"* ("Great Book of Man") and the *"Grand Livre du Monde"* ("Great Book of the World").[59] Such allusions to the Archive's association with the world-as-book idea were intended clearly to distinguish the project from anything resembling a tourist's guidebook or an abstract academic study.

A CHAUFFEUR'S TOUR OF THE WORLD

Even though Kahn replaced his chauffeur with a professional when he returned from the 1908–1909 tour, Dutertre's documentation forms an indispensable amateur prologue to the Archive proper. To be sure, the chauffeur's stereographs and films may not be as technically expert as those of the professionally trained cameramen working for Kahn (like Auguste Léon, Stéphane Passet, Camille Sauvageot, or Lucien Le Saint).[60] Nonetheless, they were probably shot in the presence or at least the proximity of Kahn's orders. For this reason alone, they offer a possible clue to the style of documentation Kahn was hoping his future Archive might pursue. In this regard, it is interesting that Dutertre's documentation—particularly in the format with which he was most successful, stereography—was oriented more toward tourist photography than professional expeditionary photography.[61]

Dutertre's touristy orientation was partly determined by the fact that stereomania's hold in the second half of the nineteenth century (when it was used mainly as a parlor entertainment) also overlapped significantly with the beginnings of middle-class tourism. Indeed, stereography had evolved commercially in the nineteenth century as the format *par excellence* for materializing the traveler's dream of imaging and organizing the world in all its diversity. Inverting the gigantism implicit in formats like the panoramas and dioramas, stereographic collections allowed their owners to contain the world in a box. The phenomenal popularity of the format thus stimulated the Western subject's insatiable appetite for cataloguing, collecting, and consuming world *views* (as the stereographic cards were called) of landscapes, monuments, voyages, and peoples according to enumerative and archival systems of knowledge provided by the series, sequences, and inventories that one could purchase in a container not much bigger than a shoebox.[62] Stereograph customers were even able to pick and choose from a catalogue the sites to which they would eventually travel—with the added immersive sensation of being there provided by the three-dimensional effect—from the comfort of their armchairs. When not engaging in armchair travel, consumers of stereographs stored them in archival-like cabinet and multiple-viewing units that transformed the domestic viewer into a pictorial taxonomer of sorts. Stereographic tours thus marked an important step in the evolution of one of the central visual obsessions of European modernity in general and the Kahn Archive in particular: the drive to bring the previously ungraspable proportions of the world into intimate focus and manageable order.

Although the popularity of the stereoscope declined after its heyday in the 1860s with the rise of the *carte de visite* and the postcard, it experienced a revival in the early twentieth century thanks to the exact type of camera Dutertre used. Invented in 1894, the Vérascope Richard was the first mass-produced, amateur-marketed camera of its type.[63] The presence of stereography in the preparatory stages of the Archive suggests a number of things. As a visual format that typified early tourist industries and mass culture entertainments, bringing a new intimacy and popularization to the previously elite aura of world collections and visual taxonomies, stereographs personified the Kahn Archive's hybrid approach to mapping the world visually. This approach reflected an inclusive visual methodology that was simultaneously scientific and amateur, organized and roaming, rigorous and casual, systematic and idiosyncratic, global and local. Above all, the gaze that typified this methodology was one that wandered across the borders between travel and tourism.

Central to this convergence of the putatively separate realms of travel and tourism was a common emphasis on the redemptive potential of the daily life of "other" cultures, experienced as the authentic, often premodern, antidote to the Western traveler's own increasingly alienated quotidian life.[64] Walter Williams, an American journalist and Autour du Monde grant recipient, expressed this valorization of the everyday life of "other" cultures from the anti-touristic stance of the traveler:

> Famous views have not the slightest charm for me. It is infinitely more interesting to learn how the Egyptians live than to see the Sphinx by the light of the moon, to observe the customs of the French and Germans in the interior of their homes than to contemplate Napoleon's tomb in Paris.[65]

Williams clearly supported the idea that knowledge about the "other" depended on penetrating the "interior" domestic realm rather than remaining satisfied with the superficial surface of a culture's "famous views." In line with this rejection of postcard culture and support for a more anthropological observation of local customs, one theme comes across clearly in Dutertre's stereographs: that of everyday life framed within and against the visual conventions of a "famous views"-style tourist iconography.

Captured *sur le vif* and *en plein air*, Dutertre's images offer a vision of reality focused unabashedly on the informal, uneventful, and ordinary scenarios of daily life, whether depicting a woman and child playing a ball game on a Japanese street,

FIGURE 1.3   Migrants aboard the *Amerika* during Kahn and Dutertre's crossing from Cherbourg to New York. (*Photo*: Albert Dutertre, November 13–21, 1908 [MAK: one half of black-and-white stereograph D122–3538])

water carriers filling up at a well in Beijing, or a New York woman adjusting her hat as she walks down an expansive boulevard. Interestingly, Dutertre himself distinguished these images from those he shot (of Japanese temples, ceremonies, and especially gardens) in what he called the "picturesque" style, thus mirroring the aversion to a merely "picturesque interest in exotic things" expressed by many Kahn travel grant recipients.[66] In contrast to the highly staged topographical and pornographic views that dominated more conventional commercial applications of the stereographic process in France, Dutertre's work exemplifies the passion for instantaneity and on-the-fly depictions fueled in part by tourism's ever-renewable quest for the authentic, behind-the-scenes experience that enthused so many turn-of-the-century amateur users of faster, lighter photographic and stereographic cameras.[67]

Although Dutertre also recorded the sensational, the picturesque, and the exotic (for example, the 1906 San Francisco earthquake ruins, Japanese gardens, and musical ceremonies), it is the more trivial and uneventful aspects of, to invoke Walter Williams, ordinary life that define the uniqueness of his images.[68] Even when documenting often once-in-a-lifetime events such as migration, Dutertre still focused on everyday activities, as in his images of Asian migrants cooking, doing laundry, or gambling during the Pacific crossing of his journey.[69] On the earlier Atlantic passage, his image of huddled migrants (fig. 1.3) offers another example

FIGURE 1.4 *(ABOVE AND OPPOSITE)*   Stereographic pair of images of anonymous woman on a New York City street, taken during Kahn and Dutertre's 1908–1909 tour. (*Photo*: Albert Dutertre [MAK: N170])

of his interest in the socially inflected passage of time. To be sure, if viewed from the perspective of art photography, Dutertre's image resonates uncannily with the most iconic portrait of transatlantic passage (and perhaps of modern photography), Alfred Stieglitz's *The Steerage* (1907, published 1911). In stark contrast to *The Steerage*, whose acquired social documentary fame exceeds Stieglitz's original, exclusively formalist interest in the subject matter, the primary interest in Dutertre's image is an intimate encounter with the temporal experience of waiting and passing time that weighs upon this heterotopian passage between ports when "traditional time" is held in suspense.[70]

But it is the stereographic format itself that particularizes Dutertre's focus on everyday life. His rendition of the everyday depends on his successful exploitation of the stereographic illusion of depth, which traditionally becomes legible where the demarcation between foreground, middle ground, and background is exaggerated because objects or people mark these spatial distances. Dutertre's stereographs, however, were not always composed to maximize the effect of depth. Many contain people walking into or out of the frame, in some cases blurred. Though probably unintended, such random inclusions of parts of people poking in from

the edges of the frame accentuate the dominant theme of a spontaneously unfolding reality that characterized Dutertre's images. These imperfections implicate
a sense of space and movement continuing beyond the frame. Indeed, Dutertre
seems to use the Vérascope Richard as an extension of his Pathé camera. We can
see this intermedia practice in his unstaged stereograph of an upper-class lady on
a foggy New York City boulevard, caught in an off-guard intimate instant as she
smiles in response to the mischievous male intruder into her pedestrian path (fig.
1.4). Switching between different technologies of reproduction, the novice cameraman nonchalantly activates diametrically opposed media as though they were
interchangeable in their service to capturing the unmanageable unpredictability of
daily, and especially street, life. As a result, Dutertre's stereographic portraits of the
everyday are left quivering, oscillating between the stasis of still photography and
the motion of moving pictures.

Dutertre's interest in recording the spontaneous continuum of daily life even
appears when his photographs invoke a more familiar ethnographic fascination
with foreign "types." The modern French representational fascination with the
classification of urban types, to which Dutertre would no doubt have been exposed,

dates back to the second half of the nineteenth century.[71] Another example of the nineteenth century's heterotopian mania for what Foucault called "indefinite accumulation," the national appetite for classificatory-based types, both old and new, folkloric and modern, normal and aberrant, fed off numerous forms beyond the stereograph, including the highly developed literary genre of the "physiologies" (or examinations of types in the street) and the mass-produced illustrations of *types parisiens*.[72]

One of the most well-known photographic contributions to the *types parisiens* tradition was produced by the photographer—or as he referred to himself, maker of *documents*—Eugène Atget, in the series he photographed from the turn of the century devoted to Paris's *petits métiers*, or traveling tradespeople and vendors.[73] Atget's *petits métiers* images typically depict the tradesperson positioned like a cutout, depthless figure placed incongruously on a vague urban stage. In contrast to Atget's decontextualizing approach, Dutertre's stereographic "types" (which also include images of pushcart drivers, firemen, waiters) are deeply contextualized. He rendered his subjects as integral components of their environment. Dutertre's focus on the interpenetration of humans and milieux—reinforced, no doubt, as a result of their representation in a three-dimensional format—reflected the shift occurring at the time in anthropological *and* popular displays and representations of human types. This shift signaled a move away from an abstracted focus on bodies as racial signifiers in anthropometric-related portraits (rooted in a typological hierarchy of the races) to a more immersive contextualization of humans in their local and *especially everyday* environments.[74]

An example of Dutertre's interest in the human-milieu continuum appears in the stereograph he shot from the middle of a quiet Japanese street that curves in the background to the right and is lined on either side by wooden stores.[75] Viewing the scene before him through the universalized lens of *petits métiers* conventions, Dutertre captures two "types" reminiscent of Atget's taxonomy and still visible on the streets of Paris through which he chauffeured Kahn on a daily basis—the water carrier and the cart-puller.[76] The Japanese water carrier happens to be exactly center frame as he walks away from the camera and up the road while the cart-puller is facing the camera and is positioned on the right side of the road. Recalling Atget's *Chiffonnier, Avenue des Gobelins* (June 1901), which focuses on a ragpicker posed with his overloaded cart, Dutertre's cart-puller also appears semiposed with his hands folded and his face staring straight toward the camera.

Where Atget's portrait is entirely focused on the almost indivisible assemblage of tradesperson and trade (that characterizes the entire series) against a blurred background, in contrast Dutertre's image maps out a clearly intelligible space around the cart-puller. The Japanese cart-puller is surrounded by a wealth of contextual information: surrounding stores, shop-wares, signs, and telegraph poles. The human and the inanimate, the significant and the insignificant thus compete for our attention in the refocusing game that all stereographic perception requires and that was also a feature of early cinema's even less hierarchical, chaotic survey of everyday life. Ultimately, the object of Dutertre's fluid intermedia interest is the immersive and unpredictable drama of the *street* in collaboration with the predictable "types" who inhabit, rather than pose, on its stagelike surface.

PROLOGUE TO AN ARCHIVE

I have begun my analysis of the Kahn Archive from its margins for several reasons. Even in its unofficial prologue, one can detect a set of ideas for representing and organizing the everyday, shaped between the cultural impact and practices of travel and tourism, which continued to guide the Archive in the years to come. Motivated by an interest in the dynamic interaction between humans and their milieux that was indebted to the cultural and scientific roots of naturalism, and reflective of a geographically inflected turn to cultural context in anthropological and popular representations, the Archive sought to map the everyday in the context of pivotal transitions between tradition and modernity that privileged the banal, routine, and typical aspects of daily life over and above the more picturesque, exotic, and sensational dimensions of culture.

Underpinning this mode of observing humans in their environment would be the acknowledged position of the photographer or cameraman himself. In the Kahn Archive, the everyday was not simply to be found elsewhere, comfortably discovered beyond the familiar, the near, or the self, in some ideal objective terrain of the world-turned-laboratory; it was also to be examined closer to home (whether understood as France, Europe, or some cosmopolitan vision of the world), and closer to the self, no matter how bent on self-effacement Kahn himself might have been. The Archive's focus on a proximate, familiar everyday thus implies the geographical dominance of France and its colonies, while also reflecting the unswerving orientation of its own cultural origins even when operating far from home. Put simply, Dutertre's stereographs tell us just as much about Dutertre the Parisian chauffeur as they do about the local customs of people he came across on his journey with Kahn. Furthermore, the acknowledged position of the observer—a dominant feature in Dutertre's images and Kahn's films—also poses a threat to the Archive's positivist alliance with scientific naturalism's traditional aspiration to record, name, and classify the planet through impersonal, *unseen* observation.[77] The camera is always seen in Kahn's films. As a result, the Kahn films' gaze upon the familiar appearances of a culture often manifests the radical excesses of naturalist observation, figured in the desire to go beyond subjective effacement, surface reality, and the limits of conventional human perception. The indiscrete quality of the Archive's naturalist bent—hinted at in Walter Williams' goal of reaching the "interior" of the cultures to which he traveled—would be most blatantly displayed in the previously invisible dimensions of space and time disclosed in Dr. Comandon's scientific films of the inside of the human body and the inner life of plants.

Dutertre's stereographs are additionally instructive as they highlight the difficulty of interpretation vis-à-vis the Kahn Archive. Besides the obvious problems relating to the ungraspable vastness and multimedia plurality of the Archive's documents, interpretative fault lines arise due to the inconsistency between the Archive's status as one element of Kahn's wider *oeuvre* (with all the authorial implications of that term) and its day-to-day functioning as a sort of anonymously generated "factory of facts" (to use Dziga Vertov's phrase for his own idea for a nonfiction archive).[78] As inconvenient as this inconsistency is for Foucault's reconceptualization of the archive (dominated by the notion of the anonymous production of discourse), the Kahn Archive is both ego-driven and authorless, centered and dispersed, individual and collective, expressive and artless, deeply personal and clinically impersonal.[79] These irreconcilable divisions also play out across the gap between the Archive's scientific purposefulness and the casual aimlessness of so much of its recordings.

By placing Dutertre's amateur images alongside those of a founder of modern photographic art (Stieglitz) and perhaps the most celebrated "found" artist of the photographic medium (Atget), I have sought to highlight from the outset the problematic issue of authorship, ownership, and semantic fluidity in the interpretation of photographs whose origins are shaped less by the institutions of art than by that of the archive. Beyond general affinities between his and Dutertre's interest in "types," Atget's work is especially important for a consideration of the larger Kahn Archive because his visual inventory of Paris, indebted to classificatory and commercial practices of archiving, presents the canonical counterpoint to the less known archiving of Paris done by Kahn's photographers and cameramen. Historians and theorists of photography such as Allan Sekula, Rosalind Krauss, and John Tagg have all cautioned against the historically irresponsible liquidation of meaning that occurs when photographic documents (Atget's being a major case in point) are divorced from their original archival function.[80] This warning regarding photography's unstable signification as it moves across institutions of the archive and the museum has correctly sought to highlight distinctions between commercial versus art photography; documentary objectivity versus authorial intent; use value versus exchange value; utilitarian origins versus aesthetic appropriation. While the Archives de la Planète does not conform to some of the best-known photographic archives, as it was neither the product of a commercial exchange between photographer and client or patron (as was Atget's archive), nor a disciplinary encounter between state and citizens (as was Alphonse Bertillon's police archive), it cannot be understood outside the archival context that frames so much of photographic history.[81] The documents that would be produced for this Archive thus testify as much to the production of and desire for a taxonomic relation to the data of daily life on the part of Kahn and his cameramen themselves as they do to any authentic disclosure of "life as it is" that they managed to document.

Still, as important as it is to resist museums' disavowal of photography's archival affiliations (in this regard, it is interesting to recall that it is the Albert Kahn Museum that today houses the Archives de la Planète), we should be just as careful not to reduce all photographic-based archives to a preconceived juridico-medical model. The question, perhaps reflective of a false choice, of whether to interpret the Kahn images as documents or art becomes all the more complicated when the images in question are *archival films*. Not to be mistaken with the phenomenon of what I call post-archival films (that is, films that reuse and recontextualize footage appropriated from the general world "archive" of film), archival films refer to footage purposefully shot for inclusion in a self-identified archive, the Archives de la Planète probably constituting the first full-scale mobilization of this definition.[82] Archival films like Kahn's exist in a pre-hoc state, arriving before the event of history that they seek to court, whereas the more common post-archival films exist in a post-hoc state, coming after the global cinematic deluge that they seek to dam or reroute semiotically through recontextualization.

The Kahn Archive is also unconventional in that it did not follow the usual effacement of the individual document-maker in archival contexts. The Archive's director, Jean Brunhes, actually encouraged his cameramen and photographers to imprint if not sign their documents. Brunhes' promotion of the cameramen's personal input reveals just one of several ways in which Kahn's Archive opposed a model of the photographic archive based on anonymous, objective, artless documents. This openness to the subjective does not mean we need to recover the undiscovered artistry or the signature style in Dutertre, Le Saint, or Sauvageot's work, thereby losing sight of the original collective context in which they were all employed. Reading the archive "from below" can go hand in hand with a reading "from above." Visual archives can claim both a style and a system. The particular emphasis given to the individual initiative of the Kahn cameramen does suggest, however, the need to rethink the issue of anonymity (beyond a simplistic restoration of the unified biographical subject) vis-à-vis archival documents. Only then can we attend to the multiplicity—cinematographic as well as photographic, private as well as state, amateur as well as scientific, utopian as well as propagandistic—that exists within the uneven history of actual visual archives.

Dutertre's stereographs also foreground the tension between the Archive's elitist purviews and the democratic effects of the Kahn travel grants, a contradiction that in many respects ultimately reflects the Archive and French modern elites' ambiguous relationship to emerging mass culture. For all the appearances of anti–mass-culture sentiment that surround the "Boulogne community," by extending travel to the largely middle-class teaching population, Kahn's Autour du Monde travel fund directly participated in tourism's democratizing effects. Furthermore, Kahn's funds moved the feminized associations of tourism (often derided in gendered terms as the passive consumption of prepackaged sites) in a progressive direction. At a time when women had just been given permission in France to take the *aggrégation* exam that led to a career in administration or teaching, Kahn boldly opened his travel funds in 1905 to both sexes.[83] Challenging barriers of culture, class, and gender, the Kahn Archive undermines itself from within, its ambitious overreaching in one area leading to a compromise in another.

Finally, in appraising Dutertre's collection, we are confronted by the specific nature of stereoscopy. On the one hand, stereographs popularized the classificatory traditions of encompassing the world visually. On the other hand, in Dutertre's intermedia use of the Vérascope Richard we are given a hint of the open-ended, intentionally unfinished nature of the individual documents that would eventually become part of a multimedia Archive *avant la lettre*. The latter features introduce us to the ontological instability of Kahn's documents. Neither just photographs nor just films but documents always in dialogue with each other, Kahn's autochromes and films resist medium-specific expectations of stasis and mobility.

But the most curious feature of the stereographs—at least from the perspective of their connection to the future Archive—resides in the *virtuality* of their documentation.[84] The full impact of the stereographic image is in practice impossible to box because its illusion of depth can only be actualized with the aid of supplementary optical devices. Even then the effect is an apparition in the head of the individual viewer. In other words, the format makes for a suspect form of objective, transportable, comparable, evidence. Although from 1891 it was possible to produce the illusion of depth via projection, in its most typical use the stereographic image, actualized with the illusion of depth, could not be held or examined very easily in a comparative, collective context. The fact that its representation remained in the head of the (more commonly) isolated viewer explains why the process, at least in France, was rarely exploited for formal educational purposes.[85] The informational potential of the stereograph resides not just in the eye but in the body of the beholder, operating more at an experiential rather than factual level. Consequently, even more than the autochrome photographic plates and motion pictures, which one could also not hold or examine as they both generally relied on projection, whatever evidence the stereographs contained remained stubbornly virtual and fleeting.

The stereograph's evidence was also vulnerable because subject to the refocusing game that stereographic reception requires. When this refocusing game literally fails, as it frequently does in Dutertre's images that include spontaneous intruders whose position in the extreme foreground unbalances the view's three-dimensional legibility, the randomness of the street's flow of life warps the classically perspectival conventions necessary for the stereographic illusion. These everyday intrusions bring to the surface the "immanent disorder" that Jonathan Crary has argued is central to the stereograph's optical address ("producing a patchwork of different intensities of relief within a single image") and that would, in part, lead to its disappearance.[86] Not surprisingly, Dutertre's stereographs constitute the last time this process would be used in the Archive. Nonetheless, virtuality, as well as the attendant experiential and sensual effects of stereoscopy's inexact and indeterminate documentation, remained at the core of Kahn's films and their ultimately troubled relation to a straightforward positivist application of visual evidence.

WHILE THERE WAS STILL TIME

Although we cannot be certain that Kahn undertook his world tour with Dutertre as an experiment for the scope of his larger project, there is little doubt that the 1908–1909 trip fundamentally shaped his vision for the Archive. In November 1911 Kahn unveiled the plans for his Archive, whose details he had only so far shared with Bergson, to the geologist Emmanuel Jacquin de Margerie. Not long after, in a letter dated January 12, 1912, de Margerie informed Jean Brunhes (a professor of Human Geography at the University of Fribourg whom he would recommend as head of the Archive) about the project in terms that stressed the urgency of its execution:

> This morning I received a visit from Mr. Albert Kahn, the founder of the Autour du Monde scholarships, who came to ask me if I could not help him in the realization of his vast plans, which he had already been working on for some time, and about which he had spoken briefly in November at one of the Boulogne lunches. While there was still time, Mr. Kahn was wanting to create what he called the Archives de la Planète, that is, to put into effect a sort of photographic inventory of the surface of the globe as inhabited and developed by Man at the beginning of the twentieth century.[87]

In addition to outlining the skills he was looking for in the future Archive director, Kahn himself highlighted to de Margerie (as retold in the letter above) the role that film would play in this global inventory, specifying it would be based on "stereographic photography, projections, and *especially* cinematography."[88] So although the original plans for the Archive did include stereographic photography (which would be replaced by autochromes once Brunhes joined), it was clearly film that was most technologically suited to Kahn's primary goal—to "fix once and for all, the look, practices, and modes of human activity whose fatal disappearance is just a question of time."[89] Defined by its ability to capture movement, or what Brunhes would call (once he had signed onto the project) in unmistakably Bergsonian terms, "the rhythm of life," film seemed especially equipped to record the dynamic evolution of human activity that Kahn hoped to capture in his entropic narrative (this time global, rather than biographical) of "fatal disappearance."[90]

On the advice of de Margerie, who gave much thought to the banker's need for "an active and sufficiently youthful man, who was both used to traveling and teaching and who was well recognized as a geographer," Kahn approached the up-and-coming professor Brunhes as a possible candidate.[91] Although no records remain of the first meeting between Kahn and Brunhes (with Bergson presiding) over lunch at the banker's Boulogne villa in February 1912, it is clear that Brunhes fit the job description perfectly, particularly in its privileging, much like the Autour du Monde scholarships, of the figure of the traveler-teacher.[92] Brunhes was a highly experienced and well-connected professional traveler and photographer who had published several articles, one in a travel magazine conspicuously titled *Tourista: Revue pratique de voyages*, on the application of stereographic photography to geographic study.[93] Also in Brunhes' favor was the fact that he had already embarked on a similar collaborative and global stereo-photographic inventory, the *Atlas photographique des formes du relief terrestre* (1908–1914), which, had the war not intervened, would have resulted in the world's most advanced carto-photographical survey.[94]

In addition to his multiple photo-geographic skills, there was Brunhes' well-known participation in the Social Catholic movement. To be sure, Brunhes' work for the Social Catholics took a backseat once he began directing the Archive. Nonetheless, his formative connection to a movement that defined itself as an alternative avenue of social critique, that "insisted upon the role of educated elites as leaders who were responsible for the moral welfare of society at large," and that sought to reconcile morality with science in the drive "to collect and coordinate the social facts of our times and to interpret them," obviously impacted the Archive.[95] In short, Brunhes' Social Catholic allegiances aligned him with that French group of reluctant modernizers whose ambivalence toward the effects of industrial modernity appeared in all Kahn's projects.

Yet perhaps the strongest aspect of Brunhes' candidacy was the specific type of geography that he practiced. The school of geography known as human geography that Brunhes helped pioneer applied an interest in the dynamically evolving interaction between humans and their environment that we saw in Dutertre's amateur photographs to the redefinition of a discipline. Indeed, Kahn's own definition of the Archive as a study of "the surface of the globe as inhabited and developed by Man" could also serve as a layman's definition of human geography, elsewhere abbreviated by Brunhes as "the 'interaction' or the result of reciprocal actions between the natural milieu and man."[96] Of particular note is the inclusion of humans and a related anthropological introduction of culture, customs, and costume into the conception of the geographical landscape. Human geography's links to anthropology thus appears in its emphasis on the human-milieu dynamic, which developed in opposition to the formalist and static concerns of physical geography, just as the newer cultural anthropology's shift to representations based in detailed cultural context emerged in reaction to the former abstractions of anthropometric representation associated with physical anthropology.[97] The Kahn Archive reflected these shifts by applying the immersive, detailed, sociological data of the naturalist worldview into a new network of geography, anthropology, and cinema.

Kahn's need to secure cultural and scientific legitimation for the Archive dovetailed with Brunhes' own professional interest in consolidating academic credentials for his recently founded discipline. Those credentials were secured in May 1912 when Kahn funded the first French Chair of Human Geography at the Collège de France. By July of the same year, Brunhes occupied that Chair (helped along in the elections by a vote from Bergson, who was an esteemed member of the Collège). On December 9, Brunhes delivered his inaugural class and in the same month the first official Archives de la Planète mission (as the image-gathering trips were called) to China and Mongolia began with the recruitment of Stéphane Passet as cameraman. Thus, by the end of 1912 Kahn was on his way to transforming his vision of what he would later refer to as an "inexhaustible haven" of information into a functioning, if nonetheless one-of-a-kind, multimedia Archive.[98]

A SPECK IN THE EYE

Although it is relatively easy to understand what brought Kahn and Brunhes together, it is more difficult to determine how these two men actually shaped the Archive itself. A fitting place to investigate their impact is in the actual images of Kahn and Brunhes that remain in the Archive's cabinets. In spite of Kahn's obsessive pact with anonymity, one of the most persistent chance occurrences recorded by his cameramen (also indicative of their willingness to test the boss's orders) is the unexpected, fleeting appearance of Kahn himself. Often obliged to enter the field of vision of his Archive's planetary gaze as he guided important guests (like Rabindranath Tagore, Lord Arthur James Balfour, General Henri Gouraud) around his gardens, these candid "home movies" of Kahn usually find him head down wearing a large black hat, pointing to this or that botanical treasure or occasionally raising a disciplinary finger at the cameraman for having filmed him (fig. 1.5).

The footage of Kahn filmed by Camille Sauvageot on August 10, 1920, is particularly evocative (fig. 1.6).[99] Barely visible at the upper right of the frame, nearly lost amidst a blur of vegetation, Kahn cannot entirely escape Sauvageot's camera-eye and is finally captured standing as if turned to stone in rapt adoration of his gardens, his arms wide open (not captured in fig. 1.6) in a gesture of pride and wonder. Caught in the cross-fire of his cameras' range, Kahn's presence (whether accidental or not) subverts the ideal of panopticism (defined by Foucault as the experience of seeing without being seen) that his Archive seems to promise, though rarely fulfills.[100] The invisible "Mr. K's" presence on film irritates the ideal of hidden surveillance, like a speck in the eye of the panoptic archival gaze. Put differently,

FIGURE 1.5   Albert Kahn receives General Henri Gouraud in Boulogne. (Camille Sauvageot, November 3, 1919 [MAK: frame enlargement 87718])

Kahn's unsuccessful refusal to be the docile object of an invisible eye leaves behind traces of the supposedly inviolable archival gaze itself being disciplined, returned, managed, and pulled up. And in that finger raised toward the cameramen—an at once threatening and futile gesture—power (for Foucault, the real meaning of the archive) loses its unidirectionality and unequivocal meaning.

Just as Kahn appears and disappears from the films, so, too, is he a fleeting but significant presence in the production of the Archive. His hand can arguably be detected in at least two crucial decisions. First, Kahn risked aligning his Archive with the newly evolving discipline of human geography rather than with more established fields of knowledge—like history, anthropology, or sociology—with their own significant claims on the study of daily life.[101] A second crucial factor shaping the Archive can be traced back to Kahn's decision to recruit a team of independent cameramen instead of contracting out the technical and filming side of the Archive to Gaumont.[102] It was also during the early teens that Kahn rejected Brunhes' proposal to hire scientific specialists to be in charge of each mission, leaving the organization of the trips and classification of documents (especially the autochromes) to Brunhes. By maintaining his own team of paid cameramen under the guidance of one scientific director, Kahn was probably attempting to ensure the financial efficiency of the daily operation of the Archive while strengthening the integrated vision underpinning the films in light of their relevance to his wider utopian

FIGURE 1.6   Rabindranath Tagore and party visiting Kahn's Boulogne gardens. Kahn can be seen in the background upper right. (Camille Sauvageot, August 10, 1920 [MAK: frame enlargement 87724])

projects. We can thus presume that uniformity of visual methodology provided the (not always realized) ideal standard against which the cameramen were supposed to produce their photographic and film documents.

Kahn may not have had a hands-on role in every aspect of the Archive, but he still appears to have been more responsible than Brunhes for what was filmed, especially in Paris. Given the direct connection between key topics in the bulletins he published and the subjects filmed, it is highly likely that Kahn directed the cameramen's gaze to certain events.[103] Evidence for this assertion can be drawn from what we know about Kahn's overseeing of the fourteen bulletins published at the Boulogne property. He apparently began each day reading a sample of the world's newspapers between 5.30 and 7.30, followed by a meeting with his publication collaborators to discuss the day's events and to set the agenda for the bulletins. Kahn may have used these daily briefings and his own intuitive "antennae" (as he called them) to suggest newsworthy and other events that the cameramen should film.[104]

Providing more than literal evidence for film's resemblance to a "living news-paper" (a common metaphor of the period), the contribution of the mass dailies to Kahn's films of daily life—made literal in certain films that actually feature head-line-wielding newspaper boys (fig. 1.7)—suggests two things.[105] First, the presence of newspapers indicates another significant example of the Archive's competitive

FIGURE 1.7   Newsboys displaying newspaper headlines to the camera. (Camille Sauvageot, May 1, 1926 [MAK: frame enlargement 73 603])

engagement with (rather than outright rejection of) mass culture in general and
global journalism in particular. Second, the newspapers' contribution to a collection of films predominantly focused on daily life challenges the way in which
newspapers have often been maligned in French critical thought as the enemy of
the everyday. For example, both Henri Lefebvre and Fernand Braudel reduce the
newspaper to the superficial realm of *histoire événementielle*, that is, a type of history that distracts us from "the manner in which ordinary men and women spent
[their] day" (Lefebvre).[106] To the extent that newspapers enabled Kahn's cameramen to be present at unforeseen events (such as the fragmentation of the French
Socialist Party at the Congrès de Tours in 1920, which they alone filmed), and to
capture the seemingly uneventful *histoire non-événementielle* that is the bread and
butter of their filming, they contained more of the unofficial history of daily life
than Lefebvre and Braudel would have been willing to recognize.[107]

Nonetheless, no matter how Kahn might have read the daily newspapers' history of the present (whether with or against the grain), it would be a disservice to
the collaborative nature of the Archives de la Planète to overestimate his personal
influence. Even though Kahn may have decided *where* the cameramen were sent,
Brunhes probably had more of an influence on *how* the films were shot, even if it
seems, as I will explain further in the next chapter, that the cameramen adhered to
the already supple scientific aspect of his instructions in a loose manner.

DREAMING IN COLOR

While they may have disagreed over other elements of the Archive, Kahn and Brunhes seemed to have agreed on the defining decision to base the still photography component on autochromes. By the time of the first missions to Bosnia, China, Mongolia, and Morocco, Kahn had abandoned his original plans to include stereographic photography (perhaps because of that medium's association with amateurs, entertainment, and other more licentious experiences). Instead, the autochrome—one of the first color photographic processes perfected and put on the market by the Lumière brothers in 1907—was chosen to distinguish the Archive.

The popular reception of autochromes was most associated in Paris with figures like Jules Gervais-Courtellemont, a celebrated orientalist explorer-photographer-lecturer whose famous "Visions of the Orient" (1908–1909) projections at the Salle Charras "all of Paris was wanting to see."[108] Kahn and maybe Brunhes also seem to have been among his admirers as the first eighty-four autochromes in the photographic inventory of the Archives de la Planète (probably purchased rather than commissioned) were shot by Gervais-Courtellemont.[109] Beyond the wonders of the new color medium—a uniquely diffuse color described by John Wood as "an idyllic light, a lying light, because it gives the world a softness . . . it has never known"— Kahn and Brunhes would have been well aware of the autochrome's drawbacks.[110] Not only extremely expensive compared with black and black-and-white photographic processes, the autochrome glass plates, coated with dyed potato starch grains, were heavy and fragile with a life span of only a few months. This led to endless problems of transportation and handling, not to mention eventual storage and preservation. Further limitations arose from the fact that the autochrome was a "unique positive," a developed glass slide from which further slides could not be produced. Autochromes were therefore even more *virtual* than the stereographs in that they largely remained trapped on glass rather than liberated through reproduction on card or paper. And although they could be viewed, like stereographs, through hand-held and table-top viewing devices, for full effect (as Kahn realized) they required projection.[111]

The most striking disadvantage of the process, however, was that it required an uncommonly long exposure time of a few seconds—roughly twenty times as long as the exposure required for a fast plate—when used in natural light. For studio portraits dependent on artificial light, the exposure time expanded to a couple of minutes.[112] In order to avoid blurred images, this latter feature mandated that for the sake of color, the photographic component of the Archive be content with immobile and posed human subjects or environments cast in an impressionistic rather than documentary light. Against the background of an era defined by speed, transformation, and flux, matched by increasingly fast instantaneous photography and light cameras put to the use of ever more graphic documentary functions, the

Kahn Archive's tripod-restricted still photography section opted for the antithesis: representations cloaked in a counter-modern aura of tradition, nostalgia, slow time, and aesthetic contemplation.

It is no surprise then, that the autochromes have been the privileged, indeed fetishized, object of study, publication, and especially exhibition for the Kahn Museum since it opened in the 1980s.[113] The nostalgic and painterly "look" of the autochromes has been enhanced over time due to the rarity of the process, while their exhibition limitations have been overcome through new forms of projection and printing. Sidelined due to the halo of visual wonder that increasingly surrounds Kahn's autochromes, his films have become the ugly duckling of the Archive, these seemingly meaningless, nonsequential scraps of black-and-white footage that refuse any easy aesthetic or documentary appeal.

BETWEEN PHOTOGRAPHY AND CINEMATOGRAPHY

One cannot, however, appraise the autochromes in isolation from the films, nor vice versa. Although this book redresses the historical neglect of Kahn's films by privileging them rather than the autochromes, I also account for the unique impact of the autochromes on the Archives de la Planète. The coexistence of autochromes, films, and to a lesser degree stereographs constitutes one of the defining features of Kahn's Archive. In this regard it is crucial to note that these were not the only recording media Kahn considered, as sound recording equipment was also at Dutertre's disposal during the 1908–1909 trip with Kahn. His inability to use sound technology may have put an end to the possibility of the Archive adding a sonic dimension to its multimedia goal of total reality (apparent in its eventual reproduction of the world, in black and white as well as color, still as well as moving images, and two- as well as three-dimensional views). Given Kahn's multimedia interests, it is tempting to position him as one of those dreamers obsessed with the "Myth of Total Cinema" as described by André Bazin (the dream, that is, to create "a perfect illusion of the outside world in sound, color, and relief").[114] It is more correct, however, to emphasize that Kahn was primarily wedded to a less cinema-centric notion of total reality, in which film was just one part of a larger multimedia, multisite mosaic of documentation.

The intermedia duality of the Archive's two major forms of mechanical reproduction—autochromes and films—takes us back to the first projection of the Lumière *cinématographe* in March 1895. The Lumière films premiered that day, we should recall, not as the top-billed act, but as an additional attraction to the showcasing of color photographs (based on the Lippman process).[115] Color photography, not film, was the true passion of the Lumière brothers. Though their film production had ceased before the Kahn Archive began, ironically it was the new color photography to which the Lumières devoted themselves—the autochrome process

FIGURE 1.8   Louis Lumière during his visit to Kahn's Boulogne property. (*Photo*: Georges Chevalier, June 17, 1930 [MAK: From original color autochrome A 63083])

that they perfected in 1907—that would be fundamental to the establishment and identity of the Kahn Archive. In a sense then, the Kahn Archive was indeed not only the ideal customer for the Lumière product but also the ideal monument to the Lumière legacy, combining what the Lyonnais brothers had left behind, film, with what they had turned or rather returned to, color photography. No wonder, then, that Louis Lumière looks into the lens with such a twinkle of pride and a posture of knowing patience as his autochrome portrait was taken during his visit to Kahn's property on June 17, 1930 (fig. 1.8).

The Kahn films also inherited the important role that amateur still photography played in the Lumière films.[116] A fascination with adding movement to the humble portraits, awkward gestures, and unclassical poses of amateur photography appears across many of Kahn's films, from the one of Dutertre's son jumping for joy in the arms of his mother (fig. 1.9), to that of a sailor having his tooth pulled in the bowels of a ship, to that of a bride toasting her guests at a wedding luncheon. These films display an interpenetrating, intimate social field of everyday human gesture and motion made possible by the camera's capacity to capture movement. As he made clear in his promotion of the Archives de la Planète as an improvement

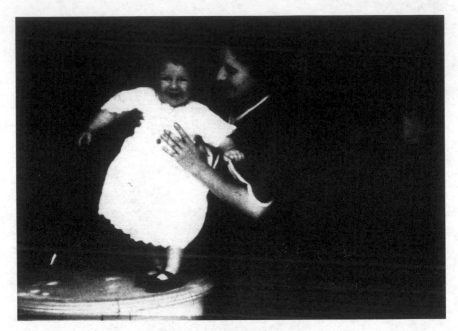

FIGURE 1.9   The son of Albert Dutertre, Albert Kahn's chauffeur, filmed at Boulogne. (Camille Sauvageot, 1921 [MAK: frame enlargement 103153])

upon the collections of "dead plants," "wax dummies," and "posed photographs" that typified the botanical or ethnographic museums of the nineteenth century, Brunhes believed its film-based component was most suitable to "captur[ing] man in the very truth of his present bearing."[117] He also emphasized the suitability of film for Kahn's mission to archive the non-archivable—life itself: "Amongst all the graphic and photographic processes of reproduction, it is the cinematograph . . . which guarantees an exact and perfect recording of all which is of the domain of life; it must become more and more a tool for scientific research."[118] Nonetheless, Kahn's films never escape their proximity to the autochrome stills and their material base in a series of individual frames on a filmstrip. In the Kahn Archive's split between still and moving images, and between time frozen and time relived, we have the ambiguity of film writ large. The films thus exist in a rocking-chair state of vacillation between stasis and mobility, death and life, that is at the heart of the Lumièrean (and the Bergsonian) cinematic equation.

Given the exaggerated stillness of the autochromes and the often frenetic movement in the films, we could read the Archives de la Planète as an experiment in the dialectic of stasis and mobility that is at the center of cinema's theatrical and philosophical attraction in these years. Indeed many of the antinomies of Kahn's project are brought to the fore in the dialectical relation between the autochromes and the films. Even though the autochromes' pioneering ability to capture color made them revolutionary, their unreproducibility and impressionistic, dreamlike quality harked back to what Walter Benjamin would call the auratic culture of unique, authentic, and indeed painterly artifacts.[119] In fact, if the autochrome process was described at the time of its appearance as the greatest discovery since the daguerreotype, it also seemed to be the color reinvention of the daguerreotype process.[120] The autochromes may have quickly become a commercial success for the Lumières (by 1913 they were producing 6,000 plates a day), but they carried within them a reminder of the preindustrial phase of photography, especially in their similarities to the non-reproducibility and long exposure time of the daguerreotype.[121] Film, by contrast, heralded a future-oriented culture of movement, rapid recording, mass reproducibility, and borderless dissemination. And yet if there was an air of anachronism about the autochromes, we should be careful not to position them as anti-modernist but instead as suggestive of other slower countercurrents within the more commonly perceived rapids of French modernism.[122] Confounding further our conventional opposition between still and moving images, the Kahn autochromes were, in fact, also used by Brunhes to form dynamic, temporally motivated series of images, while the films (in rejection of the commercial context of most film production) were never instantaneously allowed to reach a mass audience, remaining for the most part sleeping documents betrothed to some future reawakening.

We can conclude this exploration of the paradoxical appeal of the autochrome by returning to the slippery question of Kahn and Brunhes' influence upon the Archive. While Kahn maintained a certain distance from the practical operations of the Archive, Brunhes was decidedly hands-on. This distinction is demonstrated quite literally in a candid autochrome of Brunhes from October 23, 1913, taken by Auguste Léon in Montenegro, Yugoslavia (fig. 1.10). Dressed in a three-piece suit, tie, and hat, Brunhes barely makes it into the right edge of the frame, standing diagonally to a man in traditional costume who is sitting on a rock, just left of center, with his body turned three quarters to the right and his face in profile, in the process of carefully posing. Doing everything he can to mitigate the autochrome process's infamous intolerance of human intervention, especially at the developing stage, Brunhes holds up his hands squarely in front of his chest as he frames and directs the soon-to-be-captured pose of the "typical" villager.[123] As with Sauvageot's film of Kahn in the garden, Brunhes has also entered the Archive's gaze accidentally. But Brunhes did so with the express intention of guaranteeing that significant "facts" would be captured by the highly selective slow exposure of the autochrome camera, whereas Kahn accidentally entered the frame as he could not avoid the more inclusive, and in a sense uncontrollable, survey of reality unleashed by the motion picture camera. In both candid portraits, we see the two "leaders" of the Archive wrestling with the excesses of each technology. Brunhes tackles the autochrome process's tendency for obsessive order (connected to the recent history of

FIGURE 1.10   Jean Brunhes preparing a subject to be autochromed on a mission in Montenegro. (*Photo*: Auguste Léon, October 23, 1913 [MAK: from original color autochrome])

anthropometric photography with its fixation upon a highly regulated, abstracted survey of the human body as a racially signifying landscape intended for collection, classification, and comparison). On the other hand, Kahn finds himself subject to film's tendency to err on the side of disorder (capturing new levels of excessive detail, chance occurrences, and indeterminate meaning).

If Kahn and Brunhes shared a broadly conservationist attitude to the unprotected museum of global daily life, there were considerable differences in how they understood this quest. Kahn's vision for the Archive, which was at its foundation a quest for the immaterial, figured in his vaguely Bergsonian yearning "to decipher the meaning of life," ultimately could not have survived without Brunhes' more pragmatic approach that harnessed the Archive to a legitimate scientific rationale grounded in more measured ambitions. Brunhes' pragmatism is visible in an article published in 1913 in the *Bulletin de la Société d'Ethnographie de Paris*, in which he brought Kahn's utopian rhetoric down to earth by promoting the "essential task" of the Archive in the following straightforward manner: "to employ those instruments which have just been born in order to capture and conserve the facts of the planet which are going to die."[124] Directly echoing the sense of urgency in Kahn's earlier description of the project ("to fix once and for all," "while there is still time"), Brunhes also outlined the methodological logic of the multimedia

Archive, when he defined it as "a sort of true picture of life in our age, constituting the monument *par excellence* of consultation and comparison for those who will come after us."[125]

Brunhes' goal of a comprehensive storehouse of visual knowledge conducive to a future-oriented comparative study of humanity positions the Archive as the direct inheritor of Foucault's nineteenth-century monuments to infinite storage: the museum, the library, and the archive. In their desire to fix, collect, and preserve the fleeting moments and practices of everyday life, both Kahn and Brunhes thus expressed a common response to the break with traditional time and the threat of accelerated history in modernity. This response was perhaps nowhere better exemplified than in their use of a process, the autochrome, that seems to deny time. Thus in addition to being fashioned as a place in which space, the key category of geography, could be collected and classified, the vastness of the globe sliced up into views, organized in boxes, and stored on floor-to-ceiling shelves, the Archives de la Planète aspired to being a place in which time might be brought to a standstill.

CONCLUSION

Kahn and Dutertre's 1908–1909 world tour provides us with the springboard for understanding the significance of diverse cultures of travel to the production and ideology of the Archive in its most humble and ambitious dimensions. In conjunction with Kahn's Autour du Monde fund, his own "around the world" voyage confirms how the multifaceted logic of travel—embedded in the modern capitalist networks of transportation, reproduction, and colonialism, the heterotopian dimensions of those networks, and the private experiences of movement away from home through space and time—was central to the evolution of the Archive. But it is Kahn's travel companion and visual chronicler, Dutertre, who allows us to glimpse the contradictions that would beset this tribute to world travel. To remind us of these contradictions, it is useful to recall that Dutertre returned from the trip in possession of a small souvenir from the Chinese New Year's celebrations (that he mentions purchasing in his diary), whereas his *patron*, Kahn, returned trying to grasp a much larger travel token—the Archives de la Planète.

There is no doubt that the Kahn Archive aspired to an anti-touristic mode, elevating the idle curiosity of sightseeing into the useful knowledge of travel, and substituting the inauthentic everyday with a truer representation of daily life. As tourism expanded within and between France and her colonies, however, the early twentieth century saw an intensified exchange rather than separation between tourism and travel. As seen in Dutertre's images, this crossover was particularly evident in both the touristic *and* anthropological shift away from depicting the "other" as a morphological specimen beneath a microscope to a multidimensional agent within a detailed contextualized environment of daily life. The contradiction in maintaining distinctions between the traveler and the tourist's gaze in the Archive would become even more pronounced as a result of the decision to privilege film, a medium haunted by associations with unhealthy curiosity, as the recording device most suited to capturing the daily "rhythm of life." Dutertre no longer contributed to the Archive by the time it became professionalized in 1912, but the chauffeur's preference for aimless and idiosyncratic recording would continue into the official instructions given to Kahn's cameramen, which as we will see in the next chapter combined *laissez-faire* gawking with geographical surveying.

As different as Dutertre and Kahn's travel trinkets were, they reinforce the Archive's affinities (also found in its stereographs) with two of the key by-products of the material culture of travel—the souvenir and the collection. If the Kahn Archive and gardens resemble the souvenir in its nostalgic concern with the past and what Susan Stewart describes as a longing for a "place of origin" made palpable through a tendency to miniaturize the planet so that it can be held in the hand, it also approaches the collection in its anticipatory and future-oriented open-endedness (collect everything while there is still time), appended to a belief that the unfathomable endlessness of the world might be grasped through modes of ordering and classifying.[126] On the other hand, the scale and ambition of the Archive render it oversized for the intimacy of the conventional souvenir, while the manufactured rather than found or purchased nature of what it gathered—films and autochromes—not to mention their immaterial rather than tactile quality, removes it from the exchange economy and display-case fixations of the traditional collector. Ultimately, therefore, the Kahn Archive conforms to neither the souvenir nor the collection, except perhaps if we were to imagine a new category that merges miniaturization with magnification—namely, the world souvenir. Recombined, however, in the impossible hybrid of the world souvenir, the souvenir and the collection still disclose much about Kahn's Archive. As modern "devices for the objectification of desire" (Stewart) as it negotiates the passage between the home and the world, the souvenir and the collection (like film) also remind us that the Archive is not just a space of regulation and control. It is also, to quote Carolyn Steedman's anti-Foucauldian reconsideration of the archive, a potential place for "the counting house of dreams"—a site, that is, particularly suited to a banker with a utopian streak and ironically well-matched to Foucault's "other" heterotopian archive.[127] Far from staging a relation between the self and the world structured by mastery and distantiation, the Kahn Archive reveals an anxious uncertainty over the self's (that is, Kahn's, the *boursiers'*, the cameramen's, and ultimately France's) place in the world and the self's ability to make a home in that world. It was from this position of modern exile that Kahn (like Kracauer in the epigraph to this chapter) looked to film as the bridge between the home and the world.

The conservative connotations of the Archive's preservationist ethos cannot be denied, especially when applied to the collection of human types, and particularly when viewed only from the perspective of the exaggeratedly frozen-in-time auto-chromes. Yet the Kahn Archive's relation to time is not simply nostalgic, and its relation to space is not only acquisitive. Much like the uneasy balance between past and present, mobility and stasis, that we find within and between the autochromes and films, their relationship with categories of space and time is equally unsettling and speaks to how the project is embedded in some of the central contradictions by which Bergson understood modernity. Although the Kahn Archive resembled a "sort of perpetual and indefinite accumulation of time in an immobile place" (to return to Foucault's definition of the museum), to understand its unique spatio-temporal identity we will need to explore further the role of film in the unique archival context of the Archives de la Planète. Likewise, if the question of autho-rial intent vis-à-vis anonymous documents (and discourse) problematizes the Ar-chive's association with established visual and print-based archival practices (espe-cially in the domain of photographic archives and the profession of history in the late nineteenth century), this problem only increases once we factor in—as I will do in the next chapter—the filmic specificity of a vast portion of the Kahn docu-ments. Then we will also need to address the Archive's relationship with the era's key philosopher of life and time, Henri Bergson, a profoundly anti-spatial thinker, who among other things, criticized the logic—to see is to know the world—and the related medium—film—that together underpinned the Archive's foundations in actual and virtual travel.

"KEEP YOUR EYES OPEN"

FROM PRE-DOCUMENTARY TO
DOCUMENTARY FILM IN THE KAHN ARCHIVES

> Just when he was about to abandon hope, the lecture-room would fill up to half
> capacity with children accompanied by their mothers or nursemaids. . . . To this
> mixture of moth-eaten ghosts and restless infants the lecturer was privileged—
> as the supreme reward for so much effort, care and hard work—to reveal his
> precious store of memories. . . . Such, then, was the anthropologist's return.
>
> CLAUDE LÉVI-STRAUSS (1955)[1]

IN THE OPENING PAGES of *Tristes Tropiques*, Claude Lévi-Strauss recalls with
a mixture of embarrassment and nostalgia the poorly attended anthropological
lectures held weekly at Paris's zoological museum in the 1920s. He drags out this
half-forgotten scene of amateurishly illustrated lectures in the "dilapidated amphitheatre" of Paris's Jardin des Plantes with a view to criticizing the more professionalized and mediated travel lectures that filled the Salle Pleyel in the 1950s.
Lévi-Strauss's distaste for the latter venue—whose commercial travel lectures were
similarly targeted for criticism around the same time by André Bazin in an essay
("Cinema and Exploration") that praised the aesthetic of amateur travel films over
professional ones ("characterized by a shameless search after the spectacular")—
embodies the antinomy between authentic travel and inauthentic tourism that
formed the background to the introduction of the Kahn Archive in the preceding
chapter.[2]

The anthropologist's recollections of a key exhibition site for early visual anthropology also directs us to a series of relationships that are at the core of this chapter's contextualization of the production and stylistic history of the Kahn films: the connection between still and moving-image projections of a nonfiction nature; the relation between the preoccupation with daily life in anthropology and human geography; and the impact of both relationships upon the shift from pre-documentary to documentary film proper. Beginning with an exploration of Lévi-Strauss's undoing of the antinomy between travel and tourism (which provided the base from which he launched his career), this chapter also explores how a related series of breakdowns—emerging from the collapse of distinctions between science and art, professionalism and amateurism, objectivity and subjectivity, the other and the self—influenced the instructions given to Kahn's cameramen and ultimately helped shape their films as examples of a hyper-naturalist tendency in French documentary filmmaking. If my primary intention in this chapter is to show how Kahn's films occupy a transitional, anthropo-geographical space between pre-documentary and documentary nonfiction film, a secondary related concern aims to highlight the specifically French contribution to that transition. Over the template of what Bill Nichols has identified as the "passage from document to documentary"—the path, that is, from a fragmented accumulation of filmed views to a deliberate arrangement of filmed facts within a larger poetic or persuasive narrative form—I will thus situate Kahn's films between what film historian Tom Gunning describes as the "aesthetic of the view" and what the filmmaker Jean Vigo called in 1930 the "documented point of view."[3]

Distancing himself from the 1950s explorer-as-showman who was motivated by the "desire to impress" and the goal of "covering a great many miles and assembling lantern-slides or motion pictures, *preferably in color*, so as to fill a hall with an audience for several days" (18; my emphasis), Lévi-Strauss begins his autobiographical travelogue by claiming that his predecessor, the Jardin des Plantes lecturer, had traveled with a purer goal, that of "discovering hitherto unknown facts after years of study" and communicating them to an audience who themselves "traveled very little." However, this neat divide between inauthentic and authentic collectors of daily life (the former merely assembles "pictures," whereas the latter discovers "facts") does not hold up for long. As a professional traveler himself, Lévi-Strauss then needed to distinguish his own travel narrative from the more popular "accounts of expeditions." More to the point, his opening reflections display an acute anxiety regarding the narrative value of the uneventful. Lévi-Strauss frames this apprehension toward the everyday with a question: in the face of the "platitudes," "commonplaces," and "scraps of hackneyed information" that constitute the bulk of popular accounts of journeys to faraway lands, how can he possibly overcome the sense of "shame and repugnance" that prevented him for so many years from publishing his own "trivial circumstances and insignificant happenings" that occurred during his research trip to Brazil between 1935 and 1939?

At the heart of Lévi-Strauss's travel malaise, in which the weary optimism of Kahn's "I have traveled a lot" has dwindled into the outright pessimism of Lévi-Strauss's opening disclaimer "I hate traveling and explorers" (17), is a struggle over the significance of representations of daily life within the specific domain of anthropology due in part to the broader epistemological crisis of modern travel. As a conceptually divided category, the everyday operates across several registers in the opening to *Tristes Tropiques*. Its meaning changes according to the narrative in which it appears (there are exactly three "tellers of tales"), the technology by which it is recorded and exhibited (writing, photography, film), and the audience to whom it is addressed (popular audiences; professional scientists; mothers, children, and nurses). Yet if Lévi-Strauss's reference to the "anecdotes" and "platitudes" of the commercial travel lecturers of the 1950s positions the everyday as the inauthentic, it is somewhat more difficult to unravel the anthropologist's own attitude to the inventory of daily activity he had been carrying inside himself for so many years. Aligning himself with the Jardin des Plantes lecturer, Lévi-Strauss suggests that it is the anthropologist's job to endure the "dross" of everyday routine, "the thousand and one dreary tasks which eat away the days to no purpose" only to the extent that they deliver some "unknown" or "new" information about the peoples one has traveled so far to study. In this formulation, the everyday is that which one survives, the labor one puts up with in order to attain a knowledge (that is ironically about the everyday life of "others"), which then allows one to claim the rights to an "anthropologist's return."

Before Lévi-Strauss, the dominant schools of anthropology had depended upon a formulation whereby the everyday (of habits, daily rituals, household tools) existed in relation to nonliterate societies much as history (of written texts, books, and archives) did to literate societies. Lévi-Strauss's approach opened the way to recognizing similarities between the two societies at the transhistorical and universal level of everyday life. His valorization of "their" everyday (over and above the "dross" of anthropological work) thus entails an implicit understanding that the seemingly insignificant doings of daily life hold the key to unlocking the deep structure and mythic categories of not only so-called primitive societies but also civilized ones. This recognition occurs at the climactic point in his narrative, where the home and the world truly collide and where travel account, scientific ethnographic description, and autobiography clash in the epiphany of self-critique experienced at the plateau of the western Matto Grosso in Brazil.

Just when he should be celebrating his proximity to the holy grail of ethnography, described by Bronislaw Malinowski in 1922 as the ability to "grasp the native's point of view, his relation to life, to realize *his* vision of *his* world," Lévi-Strauss becomes waylaid by his own point of view.[4] Offered the discovery of a lifetime, he recalls shamefully how he was haunted "not by the things that lay all around me and that I would never see again, but by a hackneyed melody"—Chopin's Étude no.

3, opus 10—that "now seemed to epitomize all I had left behind" (377). Perched precariously on the threshold of new knowledge of the other, sitting opposite a treasure chest of untouched "facts" just waiting to be collected for the West's ever-expanding archive of soon-to-disappear primitive data, he is drawn back home, to the old, seemingly banal memories of his former self: "fleeting visions of the French countryside I had cut myself off from, or snatches of music and poetry which were the most conventional expressions of a culture which I must convince myself I had renounced" (376). In this rush of the repressed trivial "self," where the young anthropologist finds himself distracted by the more personal items in his "precious store of memories," private rather than public memory unleashes another competing version of the everyday. Gripped by a fear of the disorderly detail and the need to secure signification for even the most insignificant element of daily life (at the level of structure if not content), Lévi-Strauss's professional devotion to underlying structure meets a formidable challenge in this loose thread from the past. In addition to the commercialized "platitudes" and "commonplaces" of tourist discourses, Lévi-Strauss's narrative is thus equally troubled by a potentially swarming array of historical contingency, those fragments of experience ("a useless shred of memory," a "pitiable recollection," "fleeting visions," "snatches of music and poetry") that refuse to remain in the past, no matter how consciously "renounced" by his present self.

Although Lévi-Strauss's structural anthropology is most associated with the era after the Second World War, his quest to record and order a mass of data about vanishing quotidian life tied him to earlier efforts to collect the everyday. It was some three decades before Lévi-Strauss journeyed to Brazil, during a period when (as Lévi-Strauss noted) "people traveled very little" (18), that Albert Kahn embarked on his own globe-trotting mission to capture and store, primarily in visual rather than literary form, diverse, threatened ways of life. Interestingly, Kahn's Archive has in fact been described as the halfway point between Bergson and the League of Nations on the one hand, and Lévi-Strauss and the Musée de l'Homme on the other.[5] Leaving his relationship with Bergson for the next chapter, we might assess Kahn's more distant affiliation with Lévi-Strauss by noting that no matter how much both men wished to disappear into the sea of data they collected, the works they left behind testify to the impossibility of that self-effacement. As for their preoccupations with daily life, Lévi-Strauss's struggle to maintain a bifocal view—that would allow him to focus as much on the new and formerly unseen as on the old and already known—echoes the dual vision of the everyday in the Kahn Archive. As we shall see, the focus upon the familiar manifestations of a culture played a defining role in the evolution of human geography, a rival discipline to anthropology that Kahn chose to legitimate his Archive. In turn, human geography's privileging of the surface appearance of quotidian reality (what Lévi-Strauss refers to as the "conventional expressions of a culture" [377]) directly influenced the documentary practices of Kahn's photographers and cameramen.

Guaranteeing the Archive's scientific credentials, Jean Brunhes formulated a new anthropo-geographical methodology based ironically on a professed *anti*-systematicity that aimed to capture the everyday interactions between humans and their environment within the net of a supple classificatory system of knowledge. In striking contrast to Lévi-Strauss's portrait of the technologically awkward lecturer at the Jardin des Plantes with his "faint images" and "over-large screen" (18), Brunhes championed the professionalized use of photography (in particular stereography and color photography), and to a lesser extent film, in providing geographical evidence, a predilection he put to the test in his Collège de France lectures between 1912 and 1917, which were illustrated by autochromes from Kahn's Archives de la Planète. Moreover, in direct contrast to Lévi-Strauss's suspicion of *color* images, traditionally deemed less scientific (because sensuous) than black-and-white photography, Brunhes embraced the latest in color reproduction and with it the impressionistic anti-systematicity of the new autochrome technology.

Resembling more Lévi-Strauss's 1950s showman than his 1920s underappreciated scientist, Brunhes confidently described in 1912 the ambition of the Archive: "to employ those instruments which have just been born [color photography and cinematography] in order to capture and conserve the facts of the planet which are about to die."[6] He then stressed the importance of the Archive as "a sort of dossier of humanity captured in the fullness of life, at the beginning of the twentieth century and at the critical moment of one of the most complete economic, geographic and historic 'shifts' that we have ever been able to observe." In these inaugural definitions of the Archive, Brunhes condenses three motivations articulated between the twin-poles (as the first description indicates) of life and death: (1) an urgent awareness of the early twentieth century as a pivotal moment of change, when the forces of modernity were transforming daily life around the world with unprecedented speed; (2) an implicit if paradoxical faith that the tools of modernity and progress—"these new processes of technology and science"—would act as "fact"-gathering, document-storage machines capable of observing and recording (if not stilling) the contemporary phenomenon of movement and change for the purpose of a comparative global source of documentation; and finally, (3) an understanding of the interlocking aesthetic and evidentiary context of those photographic and cinematographic "instruments."

If the new discipline of human geography provided one context for the Archive's approach to the everyday, the similarly nascent tradition of documentary film provided a second.[7] Ascertaining the relation between Kahn's films and the documentary film tradition requires us to go back in time (which I do for the first part of this chapter) as well as forward in time (the second part of the chapter) from the Archive's 1912 official inception. The pre-cinematic heritage of the illustrated lecture (recalled by Lévi-Strauss's Jardin des Plantes lecturer) provides a crucial context for understanding the informational and aesthetic mix of Kahn's documents and their relation to the "aesthetic of the view," a mode of representation that Gunning argues characterized pre-documentary nonfiction film (dominated by representational techniques of showing and displaying rather than telling or narrating) before the First World War.[8] But we will also need to move beyond the war in order to read Kahn's films in the context of the emerging international conventions and rationales for documentary film in the twenties and thirties. Even though Kahn's films cannot satisfactorily be categorized as documentaries in the sense provided by John Grierson (undoubtedly the most energetic promoter and codifier of documentary practice and discourse in the interwar period), it is undeniable that they intersect at points with that evolving tradition.[9]

PRE-DOCUMENTARY FILM AND HUMAN GEOGRAPHY

The standard history of documentary film has been transformed in recent years by new research into the diverse nonfiction genres that existed before the emergence of documentary film in the 1920s. New scholarship has put to rest the tired notion that documentary film was brought to life in three stages: conception with the Lumière brothers at the turn of the century; gestation around 1921–22 with Robert Flaherty and Dziga Vertov; and delivery in 1926 by John Grierson under the name of "the creative treatment of actuality."[10] A central concern of this recent turn to early nonfiction films has been to excavate documentary film's disavowed past within the complex field of nonfiction film before Flaherty. The canonical proclamation of this disavowal is Grierson's first full description of documentary film in 1932 in which he positioned it explicitly (and perhaps nationalistically) in opposition to the heterogeneous mixture of nonfiction forms denoted by the French origin of the term, *film documentaire* (which we have already seen used by the *Journal du Ciné-Club* in 1920 to describe Kahn's films).[11] Rethinking this opposition, recent scholarship on pre-documentary film has questioned the division between fiction and nonfiction (in fiction and war propaganda films), and between actuality and spectacle (in the travelogue genre), while in other instances revealing the need to emphasize the difference between pre-documentary and documentary film and between scientific research films and popular science films.[12]

One element of the complex mix of nonfiction film that has not yet been explored, and that sheds light on the curious impact of the natural sciences and naturalism on the evolution of French documentary traditions, as well as an obsession with the human-milieu continuum in Kracauer and Bazin's realist film theory, is that of human geography. Even though Grierson defined "the fuller art of documentary" in opposition to the earlier nonaesthetic genres of nonfiction film (travelogues, educationals, scientific film, newsreels, lecture films) as well as the simultaneously developing overaestheticized work of the avant-garde (especially the "city symphony" films), all three modes of filmmaking in France (pre-documentary,

documentary, avant-garde) operated upon a common ground, the human geography of everyday life.[13] Whatever form they gave to their observational impulse (as Grierson himself wryly noted, observation could be plain, fancy, or creative), they all operated between two positions: a commitment to "observing and selecting from life itself" (Grierson) and an understanding that this process necessarily involved subjective selection if their primary intention was to move representation beyond empiricist evidence and "cast the familiar in a new light" (Nichols).[14]

The Archive's indebtedness to human geography appears in its commitment to both objective *and* subjective observational modes. In addition to being an articulated goal of the Archive ("to establish a sort of dossier on humanity captured in the fullness of life"), direct observation "from life itself" formed a central tenet of the new form of geography practiced by Brunhes.[15] It also pointed to a strong connection between human geography and the major aim of literary and scientific naturalism: to study both natural and social phenomena in their organic settings. Sometimes referred to as anthropo-geography, human geography developed in the late nineteenth century in opposition to physical geography, until then the discipline's hegemonic paradigm. A more positivist development of early geography (which had been dominated by the encyclopedic collection of inventories, lists, and maps), physical geography set out to describe how the major geographical features of the earth determined the evolution of humanity. In contrast, the human geography of Brunhes' teacher, Paul Vidal de la Blache, renovated the discipline according to a more flexible approach, offering a new definition of geography as the "scientific study of places."[16] Defining "place" as the reciprocal and constantly evolving relations between humans and their *milieu* or environment, Vidal de la Blache inherited this social conglomerate from Tainean determinism but also remade it under the more fluid concept of *genre de vie* (literally "lifestyle" but often translated as "culture")—a comprehensive category which opposed the rigid determinism of physical geography.

Brunhes described the distinction between physical and human geography in the following terms: "Between the facts of physical order, there is sometimes a relationship of causality; between the facts of human geography, there are scarcely any causal connections."[17] Where physical geographers saw the relationship between humans and the earth in fixed and eternal terms, human geographers like Brunhes offered a decidedly more complex, noncausal network: a "space of collaboration, cooperation, adaptation and incessant readaptation."[18] In order to develop a more "supple" and "less certain" method for explaining this continually morphing geographical reality subject to time and history, human geography embraced fieldwork and direct observation as cornerstones of geographical practice, leaving behind the armchair and text-bound mode of learning that had characterized physical geography and that Kahn specifically rejected in his ideas for the Archive.[19] Practical rather than abstract study and location-based rather than laboratory-based research were to be the hallmarks of human geography.

Brunhes embraced his teacher's privileging of practical, visual experience, maintaining that geography (like the natural sciences) was "above all else a science of observation."[20] But just as Lévi-Strauss was not content with the mere accumulation of facts, so too did Brunhes push beyond the empiricism of positivism and naturalism, whose limits he derisively referred to as "the mere observation of phenomena."[21] Rather, he intended to "study [phenomena] in series and to seek for the principle that connects them"; in other words, Brunhes expected an order to arise out of the disorder of multiple facts in constant evolution that characterized the true geographical landscape.

If in his later career he hoped that the Archive would provide the overarching system for this quest for order, in his early years Brunhes turned to photography as a key tool for extracting geographical knowledge from the disorder of reality. In stark contrast to the discipline of anthropology, which appears not to have officially welcomed photography and film until much later, human geography embraced the photographic camera early on as an essential (if always subordinate) aid for geographical research.[22] It is not surprising then that Brunhes mobilized photography, and especially stereography, the most objective record at the time of observation in space, to aid him in his early research trips between 1895 and 1900. Brunhes even went as far as referring to the photographic image as the master metaphor for the geographic method.[23]

By the 1910s, geographers had also enlisted cinematography as an educational tool within geography. The nascent film educational movement of the period considered geography to be the subject most suitable for cinematic mediation.[24] Although Brunhes was not affiliated with any film industry interests, he too contributed to that small group of scientists in France hoping to convert the cinema to scientific and educational purposes. He thus echoed the aspirations of diverse men of science, from Félix-Louis Regnault to Dr. Jean Comandon, when in promoting the Archives de la Planète he argued that "amongst all the processes of graphic and photographic reproduction, the cinematograph . . . authorizes an exact and perfect recording of all that comes from the domain of life" and that "more and more it will become an apparatus of scientific research."[25]

Even before he met Brunhes, Kahn's philosophy shared three central tenets of human geography: a nondeterminist, noncausal approach to the constantly evolving relationship between humans and environment; a dedication to practical rather than theoretical accumulation of knowledge; and a privileging of direct, *en plein air* observation (albeit mediated by photography and film). Brunhes' Bergsonian interest in "the domain of life" spoke directly to Kahn's preferences for life over matter. These were exemplified in the latter's rejection of the geologist Emmanuel Jacquin de Margerie as a possible scientific director for the Archive because what interested Kahn most (according to de Margerie) was not the dead matter of rocks and stones, but "the living and human element."[26] In addition to these shared interests, it was most likely Brunhes' vast experience with various types of photography and human geography's emerging affinity with film that would have consolidated Kahn's interest in having this new branch of knowledge legitimate his unconventional Archive.

Of course, as mentioned in chapter 1, Brunhes favored a type of photography, the autochrome process, that entailed distinct advantages and disadvantages. On the positive side, if used correctly the autochrome process allowed previously unrecordable detail, such as the colors of the traditional costume worn by the Montenegrin villager (fig. 1.10), to be saved for posterity within the format of what Brunhes described as a "rigorously exact" document ready for "ethnographic research."[27] Due to its long exposure time, autochrome photography required Brunhes to manipulate and shape the surface features of culture (clothes, people, houses) in front of the camera—to wrest them, in effect, from the unsettling traces of time and the monochrome blandness of conventional photographic space—in a way that would have been impossible with the movement-oriented and black-and-white dominated medium of film.

On the negative side, Brunhes' decision to use autochrome photography thus meant that "the living and human element" so cherished by Kahn was sacrificed to some degree for the additional evidence of color. In contrast to the split-second arbitrary moment or series of moments of instantaneous photography or cinematography respectively, the autochrome offered an anachronistically drawn-out passage of time. Not finding this a drawback, Brunhes actually believed that the autochrome's distillation of time (figured in the literal duration of the exposure) allowed for a "translation" of the most distinctive characteristics of a race to be read from the gestures, movements, and looks condensed in the still photograph.[28] Although Brunhes was always careful to claim that he and his photographers shot only what they observed and never tampered with the "details" that might appear naturally in an image, the technology he was using (as mentioned above) required more than a minimum amount of arrangement and selection of the scene before the camera to ensure the success of that process of translation.[29] Put simply, the autochrome process forced Brunhes to still (and stage) life in front of the camera so that previously unrecordable and invisible aspects would supposedly come to the surface.

But if the autochrome process sanctioned human intervention at the pre-shot stage, it did not tolerate even a hint of manipulation during the highly complex development stage. As with the much earlier daguerreotype, it was not possible "to remedy any faults by means of retouching" and "all hand work [was] out of the question" while the autochrome plate was being developed.[30] This meant that each autochrome was not only unique and non-reproducible but could not be subject to accusations of manipulation, as so often happened with black-and-white photography, and was increasingly the case with cinematography in the 1910s.[31] In step with his supple approach to science, Brunhes thus wielded a flexible rather than totally inviolable scientific document with the autochrome process: admitting subjective intervention and prearrangement of reality at one end, while assuring impersonal objectivity and "truth" at the other.

THE "AESTHETIC OF THE VIEW" ACROSS PHOTOGRAPHY AND FILM

This split in Brunhes' scientific approach returns us to the complimentary and contradictory relationship between the Kahn Archive's autochromes and films. Beyond their specific combination in the Archive, their connection speaks to the fluid aesthetic, semiotic, and exhibitionary relationship between still and moving images in the early cinema period. Central to Gunning's analysis of nonfiction film from this period according to an "aesthetic of the *view*" is the overlapping territory of photographic and cinematographic views, a word whose French translation, *vues*, referred to both photographic (including magic lantern slides and stereographs) and cinematographic images during this period.[32]

Gunning offers the "aesthetic of the view" as the implicit other to what Grierson called "documentary proper"; which is to say, it typified the raw, unarranged, "natural material" of on-the-spot cinematic recording as opposed to the interpretive rearrangement of recordings required by Grierson's definitions.[33] Clearly in line with the "view" aesthetic, the majority of Kahn's films were patterned more by the single-shot, non-narrative logic of the "cinema of attractions" context of early nonfiction film than by the multishot narrative dictates of the post-1920s documentary tradition based on the realistic elaboration of a story grounded in historical truth. Gunning, however, goes even further than this initial opposition in arguing that early nonfiction films were not simply concerned with presenting a place, event, or process (what Grierson derisively referred to as representations of "doing or process").[34] Most importantly, pre-documentary nonfiction films were distinguished by the frequency with which subjects or events in them offered a "mimesis of the act of looking and observing." True to the view-hungry tourist who is often their implied spectator, these films highlight "the act of seeing as much as the sight to be seen."[35] Thus, in contrast to what we might term Grierson's aesthetic of "virtue," which proclaimed that poetic truth and civic uplift were to be at the center of the argument-driven documentary narrative, early nonfiction films' "aesthetic of the view" refers to their unadulterated focus on displaying, seeing, and observing.[36]

One of the most recognizable ways in which pre-documentary film emphasized the simple, if never innocent, process of "just looking" is through the omnipresent acknowledgment of the camera by those being filmed—one of the dominant characteristics of the Kahn films. In reaction to the overwhelmingly visible (or acknowledged) camera in early nonfiction films, by the 1920s support had developed for the idea that a hidden (or unacknowledged) camera resulted in a more candid and truthful depiction (and eventual decoding) of everyday life. This position actually became a point of principle in emerging and more socially radical forms of "fly on the wall" observational filmmaking (to be seen in Dziga Vertov's championing of "life caught unawares" and Jean Vigo's intolerance for "conscious behavior" in those being filmed).[37] Kahn's films, however, encapsulate a prior model of filming in which the disclosed witnessing of social reality—implicitly (if not explicitly) understood as a reality necessarily (and even more so in the case of the autochromes) shaped by the presence of the camera—provided the norm. Manifestations of this norm in the Kahn films range from the ubiquitous gaze at the camera by children, attracted like metal filings to the bottom edges of the film frame, to the woman eating in a soup kitchen who tries to shield her identity from the camera's gaze, to those adults who appear in countless other films doffing their hats to the cameraman or imitating the cranking of the camera.[38] Yet in addition to these embodied examples of "looking," further evidence of the Kahn Archive's affinity with an aesthetic of the view appears in the exhibition of Kahn's still images during Brunhes' weekly public lectures at the Collège de France and in the influence that human geography had upon Kahn's cameramen.

The focus upon non-narrative and descriptive modes of showing and seeing is a feature of Brunhes' geographical work. Even his written texts have been described as employing a "monstrative" rather than "demonstrative" methodology; that is, they emphasize displaying and describing rather than narrating and arguing.[39] In contrast to the enumerative inventories of early geography, the theoretical formulations of physical geography, or the poetic descriptions of Vidal de la Blache's writings, Brunhes' texts and lectures were dominated by a rhetoric of exhibitionism, a fascination with observation, and a tendency to overdescribe (all key features of naturalist description as defined by Georg Lukács).[40] Brunhes' lectures at the Collège de France were replete with the vocabulary of seeing and showing that recalls the pre-cinematic precedents for early nonfiction film's aesthetic of the view.[41] Although Brunhes spoke to a larger crowd than the one that customarily appeared before Lévi-Strauss's lecturer at the Jardin des Plantes amphitheatre, both audiences were no doubt treated to a show that appealed through the popular *and* elite pleasures of the magic lantern tradition with its mix of spectacular delights and didactic lessons.

Often central to the arousal of these hybrid pleasures was the lecturer (in French, the *bonimenteur*), whose presence in screen venues of the period, as Rick Altman has demonstrated, reminds us that "early cinema was a world not of films but of performers."[42] Well trained in the art and craft of the illustrated lecture that was such an important cultural reference for the exhibition landscape of cinema even into the 1910s, Brunhes was both performer and showman. His insistence upon the act of seeing within his lecture performances appears in the references he employed to summon, introduce, or summarize an autochrome ("you are going to see," "here is the figure of the man himself," "a small scene just as it was observed," "I would like to now place before your eyes photographic documents"). His attention to spatial and temporal qualifiers, of here and there, and now and then, are evident in the references that serve to transport the audience into the world of the image itself ("here we are in the town of Tirrana," "We are now going to leave the limits of Albania, but we will see the Albanians again," "We are going still further").[43] Interpreted according to Lukács' hierarchical distinction between literary naturalism and realism, what Brunhes reaches for in these performances is the interpellation of the audience member as both naturalist observer (of detail, description, and space) *and* realist participant (of action, events, and time).[44] The contrasting (two-dimensional) aspects of this representational style—passive and active, distant and immersed, spatial and temporal—are fully displayed in his narration for a series of autochromes depicting the journey to and entrance into an old fortress: "We climb up to the fortress; we see the door of this old fortress; we are going to enter and, and once inside, we will take a look behind us and notice all the details." Conjuring a fluid, indeed cinematic space between the discrete two-dimensional views, Brunhes also skillfully guides his audience as though they were participants in a tour ("we climb up") and acutely trained and engaged observers of his photographic (not verbal) descriptions ("notice all the details").

While Brunhes' book *La Géographie humaine* may have "subordinate[d]" its black-and-white photographs "to [the] exposition of facts and theories," his public lectures could not have tamed the visual so easily.[45] In the learned hall, the autochromes more frequently structure his presentation as a spectacle whose major attraction is not geographical knowledge but the wondrous experience of over fifty years of technological endeavor: the reproduction of natural color. Carefully mobilizing the images as the visual punctuations within the drama of his larger talk, Brunhes seems aware of the excessive sensual appeal within the autochrome projection (the exact problem with color that Lévi-Strauss will express in his disdain for the illustrated lectures of the 1950s). But there are also moments where Brunhes is prepared to use this visual curiosity to his advantage, giving in to color's potential to take over the presentation and undermine its didactic function. For example, in a lecture on Syria and Lebanon on April 25, 1929, one of only a few that he presented as public exhibitions of the Archives de la Planète in the Grand Auditorium of the Sorbonne, Brunhes concludes by projecting, almost as an applause-seeking climax, a spectacular autochrome of a sunset (already a classic theme in the autochrome genre) over the ruins of Palmyra.[46] Again drawing on the hybrid conventions of the popular and scientific illustrated lecture format, Brunhes' slide-shows were part promotion (for the new discipline of human geography), part visual entertainment, and part geographical lesson.

It is obviously not enough, however, to analyze the Archive from the perspective of its director. What sort of training did Kahn's photographers and cameramen undergo once Brunhes employed them? Before they departed on their "missions" they were given rudimentary lessons in how the principal classifications of human geography should shape the way they saw, recorded, and visually mapped the world. It seems they were supposed to organize their "views" according to the three central categories by which Brunhes classified the "facts" of human geography: "First group: Evidence of nonproductive use of land: a) houses b) roads; Second group: Evidence of plant and animal conquest: c) domestic animals d) fields and gardens; Third Group: Evidence of economic destruction: e) plant and animal destruction f) mineral exploitation."[47]

The next level of Brunhes' instructions appeared in two lists of subjects, one titled "Photography," the other "Cinema," drawn up in 1913 as a general guide for his photographers and cameramen.[48] Apart from a shared core of topics (such as human types), the subjects that only the photographers were asked to take were not surprisingly organized according to a spatial thematic (house types, interior and exterior decoration, highways, roads, gardens, courtyards)—in other words, subjects suited to the long exposure time required by the autochrome process. The topics that appear only on the cinema list were organized by a temporal and generally anthropological thematic (religious ceremonies, individual and group prayer, burials, marriages, dances, housing construction, food preparation). These two lists mirror, in no uncertain terms, the two types of visual emphasis that characterize the "aesthetic of the view." According to Gunning, they are a descriptive focus on space and place across a succession of views (such as a film shot from the front and the side of a train), and a temporal focus on processes and activities across time (such as a film of a wall or a building being pulled down). Even though Brunhes' two lists are structured, at least at the point of shooting practices, according to a technologically determined opposition, when placed together in their intended multimedia context they form a relationship of interdependency that speaks to the autochromes and films' common heritage in the nonfiction "aesthetic of the view."

We need, therefore, to resist distinguishing between the autochromes and the films according to their ontological spatial and temporal features. For one thing, Brunhes' understanding of space was temporally inflected. While considering "the spatial *esprit*" to be the core of geography, Brunhes also reconfigured space according to "the coexistence of facts—even contradictory—*even from different time periods*—on the same plot of land on our planet's skin."[49] Far from being dominated by a static, painterly aesthetic, Brunhes' images also incorporate an understanding of space that opened the way to framing each image as a slice across different time periods and as a potential fragment within an arrangement of contradictory facts. Furthermore, if his temporally inflected concept of space allowed for diachrony in the seemingly immobile autochromes, a closer look at Brunhes' original photographic series also reveals a level of dynamism *between* the images. Even without considering their relation to the moving pictures in the Archive, dynamism was an immanent dimension of many autochrome series. A large portion of them were shot as series that mimicked or anticipated continuity editing conventions (such as cutting into space in a temporally linear progression) then developing in fiction film.[50]

In addition, as demonstrated repeatedly in his lectures, the autochromes were intended to manifest one of the most important themes in human geography: the "perpetual mobility" of geographical phenomena as different as houses, races, costume, and rituals.[51] Each of these categories was understood by Brunhes to be in a state of Bergsonian "becoming" resonant of a wider condition of modernity in which "[e]verything around us is in a state of change" and "nothing is really stable."[52] Temporal (and not just spatial) succession was thus an important component of many of the otherwise immobile, discontinuous autochrome series. Inversely, much of the filming respected the integrity of a slow temporal continuum that reveals the proximity and possibly remediation of the autochrome process's unhurried time. Moreover, in their unedited and fragmented form, Kahn's filmed views actually structurally resembled the unattached and cutout nature of photographs. Brunhes' seemingly opposed photography and cinema lists thus actually constructed reality in a hybridized, open-ended, intermedia appropriation of the world.

LEARN HOW TO SEE

In line with the view aesthetic, Brunhes' illustrated lectures and those given by the other scientist associated with the Archive, the biologist Dr. Jean Comandon (discussed in chapter 7), emphasized the photographic or cinematographic camera as a new tool for seeing and displaying the world in all its visual curiosity. Armed with the latest technologies of vision, Brunhes and Comandon were the latest participants in what Émile Zola called, in reference to the late-nineteenth-century scientific naturalist tradition, "the slow conquest of the unknown."[53] However, where Comandon's time-lapse and microcinematographic views conquered what was invisible to the human eye (the germination of a bean, blood cells), Brunhes focused upon the unknown within what was already visible. He stressed that human geography was not driven by "the ambition to discover on the earth phenomena which have never been seen before" (such as the "hitherto unknown facts" initially fetishized by Lévi-Strauss), but rather its role was to perceive already known phenomena "under a particular light."[54] Far from adhering to some naïve fascination with just looking, Brunhes and Kahn were united in their desire to learn how to see the ordinary and the banal with new eyes. In fact, Brunhes warned his operators before they left on their missions that they must "know how to see, learn how to see."[55] Meanwhile, the only advice Kahn gave James Dickinson, a recipient of one of his Autour du Monde travel grants, was to "keep your eyes open," a message whose visual imperative anchors the central dictum of Kahn's only signed text, *Des*

Droits et devoirs des gouvernements (1918): "To see . . . to predict [. . .] To predict . . . is to know" ("Voir . . . prévoir [. . .] Prévoir . . . c'est savoir").[56] And even though Comandon focused on technologically expanding rather than retraining human vision, his contribution to Kahn's documentary network was also indebted to an appreciation of the cameraman as a new educator of sight. In 1953 in an article titled "Knowing How to Look," Comandon argued that the cameraman's "noble mission" lay in the "art" not simply of passively "seeing" but of actively "knowing how to look; and show."[57] Thus, instead of being a natural, unchanging habit, the practice of "just looking" underwent a complex reeducation (philosophically associated with Bergson's critique of perception) within the diverse experiments with vision conducted in the Kahn Archive.[58]

TECHNICIANS AND ARTISTS OF THE EVERYDAY

This articulated urgency around acts and modes of seeing and looking in the Kahn Archive is inextricably connected to the importance of the categories of the typical and the ordinary in human geography. Brunhes stressed that "what should capture the attention of the cameramen more so than the exceptional was essentially the familiar type, the everyday, man in his lifestyle, in his rural or urban activities, in or in front of his house, with the tools of his trade, dressed for work or festivities."[59] He thus instructed his cameramen to look for "the familiar type" and "the everyday" in order to build up a stock or sample of not only classifiable but comparable views, while at the same time acknowledging that the "unique representative type" was in fact an abstract concept that could be found "nowhere on this earth."[60] The end goal was not a static inventory of essential types (whether architectural, geographical, or human) but a dynamic genealogy of their formation over time. What Brunhes wanted them to focus on as they constructed photographic and film views resembled a sort of proto-structuralist relation between the type and type-variant (a classificatory dialectic at once indebted and resistant to the positivist roots of human geography). The idea behind this comparative thrust was that new truths (and a new order) might emerge from old familiars (and the old disorder). For Brunhes, the type provided an abstract means for accessing the usually invisible, albeit in plain sight, value of the everyday: "The type is, in short, the anonymous agglomerate, that which the tourist does not note, that which does not distinguish itself from anything else, but precisely because of which recalls and expresses all the others and consequently has a high geographical value."[61] Once again, the perceptual encroachments of tourist industries appear as the rival to scientific knowledge. And just as Lévi-Strauss struggled to distance his own structuralist "tale" from the "platitudes" and "commonplaces" of the commercial traveler's account, so too did Brunhes three or so decades earlier strive to distinguish his privileged everyday from the picturesque obviousness cherished by the "tourist," who was of course, the *ur*-consumer of the view aesthetic.[62]

Anti-touristic discourse aside, human geography's nondeterministic approach to geographical reality was not simply promoted at an abstract level. It shaped the *laissez-faire* directions Brunhes gave to Kahn's cameramen. Beyond their instructions to view the world with the eye of an amateur human geographer, Kahn's cameramen were also given an uncharacteristic amount of freedom (compared to their commercial counterparts) to shoot what they thought was important.[63] After a meeting in May 1912 with the cameraman Stéphane Passet, Brunhes reported to Kahn:

[I]t is preferable that the indications I gave Monsieur Passet were meant to serve as inspiration; in my mind they were of the order of general advice, intended to help us coordinate travelers in different parts of the world into a common enterprise, but it goes without saying that this advice *wasn't intended as a sort of restrictive law*. Monsieur Passet must always have an *open eye* and take everything that seems *of interest to him*; the more he displays a considered *initiative*, the more we will be happy with his services.[64]

A few months later, Brunhes reemphasized the trust he held in his cameramen in a letter in which he advised Passet that "so as not to complicate your preoccupations I am not sending you any further plans, just continue to do what you are doing."[65] Brunhes' trust seems to reflect a generous willingness to encourage the cameramen's participation in shaping the raw material to be collected for the Archive. In the instructions he gave them for filling out the index cards (*fiches*) (fig. 2.1) intended to document the date, place, operator, and subject of each photographic and cinematographic shot, he even urged that in describing their subject they should "not be afraid to develop the idea which made them choose such and such a subject."[66] Displaying the Vidalian school's opposition to deductive determinism (a characteristic of human geography applauded by later Annales historians), Brunhes advised the cameramen that "even if your interpretation is later perceived to be *inexact*, it will be helpful to have noted your first impression."[67]

Insofar as Brunhes encouraged the Archive's cameramen and photographers to pursue their curiosity and note their impressions along the way, he was promoting a method, or more correctly anti-method, that was intended to challenge the "restrictive law" of deductive reasoning. Brunhes encapsulated this challenge in the brave claim that "[o]ne can be scientific without being systematic."[68] Reflective of this credo, his anti-systematic approach to scientific methodology relied as much upon feeling (inexact impressions) as it did upon reason (facts).[69] The methodological training given to Kahn's cameramen thus also bore a striking resemblance to the relatively new and equally idiosyncratic practice of anthropological fieldwork elaborated by Bronislaw Malinowski according to the cultivation of what Anna Grimshaw describes as a form of vision "built around the notion of anthropological understanding as an intuitive and uniquely personal moment of insight"

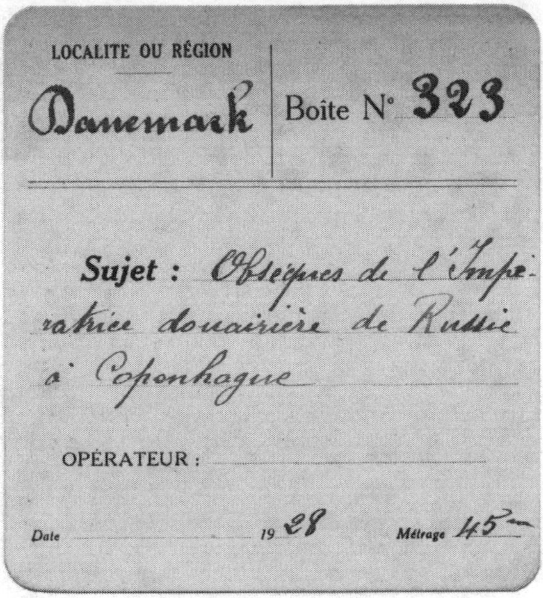
LOCALITE OU RÉGION
Danemark
Boite N° 323
Sujet : Obsèques de l'Impératrice douairière de Russie à Copenhague
OPÉRATEUR :
Date 1928 Métrage 45m

FIGURE 2.1
A typical index card used by Kahn's cameramen with space for the place, date, cameraman, film length, and subject. (MAK)

in which "the fieldworker had to learn to 'see', [in order] to penetrate beneath the surface appearance of things."[70]

Given the considerable trust Brunhes placed in the cameramen's skills and "first impression[s]," it is understandable why he described them as "technicians *and* artists."[71] His respect for them also appears in his lectures, where he often refers to the photographers in a collaborative sense, or points out the aesthetic dimensions of their work.[72] Although the films made for the Archives de la Planète, like the documents in most archives stamped with a scientific aura (such as Alphonse Bertillon's police archives of criminal portraits), were intended as *anonymous* contributions to a collectively produced project, the anonymity of Kahn's autochromes and films was never enforced. Human geography's embrace of what the Polish cameraman Boleslas Matuszewski called the "natural curiosity" of his trade meant that even those Kahn films which were not "signed" by well-known scientists (like Dr. Comandon) or missionaries (Father Francis Aupiais) were and still need to be viewed according to the nonsystematic outcomes of individual cameramen's efforts to keep their eyes open to the impressions, curiosity, and initiative of a subjective, as much as objective, nature.

AN ARCHIVE OF NONFICTION FILM GENRES

Having established the general relevance of the view aesthetic and human geography to the background production of Kahn's films, I now want to consider the more specific stylistic relevance of nonfiction genres of the period. One of the earliest models for nonfiction filmmaking appears in the Kahn film titled *Billancourt: Sortie des usines Renault, 1917* (cameraman unknown).[73] Depicting a mass of workers streaming toward the camera as they leave the Renault factory in Boulogne-Billancourt (not far from Kahn's villa), the film (fig. 2.2) unmistakably recalls the local subject matter, immobile framing, and single-shot length of earlier "factory gate" films, of which the Lumières' *Sortie d'usine* (1895) is probably the most famous. The liminal passage from work to leisure was also a topic that Kahn's cameramen (like the Lumières') filmed several times, and the focus upon an anonymous collective in the form of a crowd portrait reappears regularly in their urban-oriented work.[74]

Affiliation with the Lumière tradition is also evident in the Kahn cameramen's immersion in the ebb and flow of daily life, which distances their films from the earlier Edison kinetoscopes that were peopled with decontextualized performers characteristic of what Charles Musser has described as a "fantastic space *removed* from daily life."[75] To be sure, social performance is part and parcel of any human activity recorded via overt (as opposed to covert) forms of filming and is thus present to a certain degree in all the Kahn films. Moreover, there are also literal performers and performances of "traditional" culture in the Kahn films, particularly those shot in the colonies (from dancers in Algeria and Lebanon, to betrothal and

FIGURE 2.2   Footage of workers leaving the Renault automobile factory, titled *Billancourt: Sortie des usines Renault, 1917* (cameraman unknown). (MAK: frame enlargement 120134)

funeral ceremonies in Cambodia and Dahomey) but also others in rural France (of Catholic pilgrimages in Breton and impromptu bullfights in the Camargue). Yet unlike the Black Maria studio backdrop of the decontextualized Edison performers, Kahn's films of literal performances emphasize the context and environment—human geography's milieu—of the unfolding act.

One of Dutertre's 1909 films in Beijing is dominated by this interplay between a local milieu and a deliberate staging of everyday events. In *Échange de salutations traditionnelles* [*Exchange of Traditional Greetings*] the exterior door of a courtyard facing onto a Chinese street opens just seconds after a man briefly emerges from the interior (probably to verify his cue to exit onto the street).[76] The semistaged drama continues on cue as a variety of people pass in front of the door from left and right, stopping to greet each other or buy some article exactly opposite the location of the camera. This film seems to have been set up in much the same way as those Lumière films that were characterized by the prearranged rather than unexpected unfolding of daily life (such as *Sortie d'usine*, *L'Arrivée d'un train à la Ciotat* [1895] or *Démolition d'un mur* [1896]). Ironically, Dutertre's film also literalizes, albeit in a single-shot, non-narrative form, one of Grierson's descriptions from 1939 of documentary as "the drama of the doorstep."[77] But, as with the attention to composition and an apparent arrangement of social actors in the Lumière films (or any number of filmed or enacted ethnographic performances from the fin-de-siècle in which daily life was packaged into a series of repeatable tableaux), the orchestrated low drama of Dutertre's film is less important than the implicit desire to capture and validate, as both spectacle and document, view and fact, a familiar local event unfolding *in situ*.

What such filmed performances also share is a "natural" arc of temporal succession in which a staged or found pro-filmic event or operation (Grierson's derided "doing or process") unfolds in an uninterrupted fashion. Whether this event is the orchestrated ritual of greetings performed on a Chinese street, cremation ceremonies in Delhi or Cambodia, or a sailor having his tooth pulled on a fishing vessel off the coast of Newfoundland (to take just four examples from the Archive)—the unbroken passage of time constituted one of the most commonly used structural determinants both of the Kahn films and of single-shot nonfiction films in the first two decades of cinema.[78] Among the many Kahn films reflective of this tendency for temporal continuity is Lucien Le Saint's footage of a 56-second view of a sunset over the Tyr cemetery in Lebanon, a film that mobilizes time-as-spectacle, that is, the actual continuous unfolding of the sun setting, as the structural backbone to a seemingly undramatic shot.[79] Although the Kahn films are less likely to bookend the events recorded with choreographed opening and closing gestures (as in the prearranged and quasi-theatrical opening and shutting of the Lumière factory gates), aesthetic dimensions are still apparent within their low-key drama. For example, when viewed alongside the show-stopping attraction of Brunhes' autochrome projections of sunsets, in which the image's long exposure imprints a form of temporal passage into the otherwise still spectacle of light and color, Le Saint's film of a sunset over the Tyr cemetery exemplifies the period's screen culture aestheticization of an outwardly nonaesthetic experience, that of time itself.

If the structural patterning of apparently artless recording describes one dimension of the above films, the crucial nexus between early cinema and the increasingly available experiences and representations of travel forms another. After all, as already mentioned, the tourist is one of the primary spectators of the view aesthetic, and with titles like *Water-spa towns of central France 1926, Cairo's European town 1925,* and *Jerusalem, the Wailing Wall 1925,* it is clear that many Kahn films were shot through the touristic frame of the film travelogue. One of the most persistent and popular of early cinema genres, the commercial travelogue usually strings together a series of often mobile views of either foreign or local noteworthy sites in order to provide a form of vicarious tourism for Western spectators.[80] Contrary to Brunhes' instructions to avoid tourist sights, there are films in the Kahn Archive that supply postcard-like views of sensational and curious highlights, from films of swirling dervishes in Turkey, wrestling competitions in Mongolia, and alpine train rides in Switzerland, to tours of the markets of Tunisia, and a boat ride along the Ganges.

In stark contrast, however, to the more stereotypical travelogue films are those in the Archive that disclose a more intimate, "behind-the-scenes" access to the European colonial world including footage of colonial prostitutes and street "griots" in North Africa and Roger Dumas' films from 1927 of the Maharajah of Kapurthala's garden tea party.[81] In the latter footage Indian ladies smoke cigarettes as the English Viceroy enjoys the fireworks spectacle, their proximity revealing a negotiation of domestic intimacy between colonial and indigenous elites that was crucial to both British and French colonial ideology. Meanwhile, reflective of the disintegration, rather than consolidation, of colonial power, the films of North African street storytellers document an indigenous form of oral narrative central to the rise of anticolonial nationalist sentiment and culture. If such films move into the domain of the anthropological, others in the Kahn Archive claim a more direct connection with ethnography. Although none of the Kahn cameramen were trained in the field of ethnography, Father Francis Aupiais did attend classes taught by the leading figures in the field (Lucien Lévy-Bruhl and Marcel Mauss), a fact that gives weight to the claim that the films Frédéric Gadmer shot under his guidance for the Archive in 1929–30 in Dahomey can be considered the first ethnographic research films in France.[82]

The Kahn Archive extended its exploration of life beyond social and anthropological domains to the biological and botanical in its scientific films. Moreover, the twenty or so heavily intertitled films that Dr. Comandon produced in his Boulogne laboratory that Kahn financed from 1926 to 1930 did not resemble, but were actually a highly emulated model for, the noncommercial, nontheatrical variety of scientific films of the period. But, as I will discuss in chapter 7, Comandon's influence went beyond the pure research field. His earlier work for Pathé (from 1908 to 1923) helped to define the popular scientific film genre in France. Thus, despite its aloofness from commercial film culture, the collection of films in the Kahn Archive still reveal (and in the case of Comandon's films, helped to shape) some of the major conventions characterizing French nonfiction genres of the teens, from the formal patterning and fascination with the flux of daily life in the early Lumière-style actualities to the eternal *autour du monde* travelogue model with its obvious colonial inflections, and from the pure research film (whether biological or ethnographic) to the popular scientific film.

On the one hand, the similarities between Kahn's films (made after the Archive officially began in 1912) and key pre-documentary genres (all elaborated before 1912) point to the relatively unchanging nature of nonfiction conventions from 1895 to around 1914.[83] On the other hand, one can detect a stylistic shift between earlier and later Kahn films reflective of the transformations in nonfiction conventions that appeared by the mid-1910s (especially as a result of the First World War). Most early Kahn films are dominated by static and horizontally framed street-level shots, usually lasting a couple of minutes, of passing everyday life. By contrast, footage shot after 1918, particularly by Lucien Le Saint (a former actuality cameraman for Gaumont) and Camille Sauvageot, reveals the influence of formal advances made in actuality and narrative film production.[84] Strictly speaking, postproduction editing (including the insertion of intertitles) was not done on many of the films, aside from those intended to illustrate Brunhes' courses.[85] Yet even some of the "unedited" footage in the Kahn Archive reveals a rudimentary attempt to create a three-dimensional sense of space with traces of motivated framing, multiperspectival shots, and organized shooting sequences. Whether or not such traces of stylistic intervention and spatio-temporal composition are adequately defined by the concept of "*le montage mental*" or implicit in-camera editing, a seemingly deliberate arrangement of shots (demarcated by the use of camera stoppages during the shooting and resonant of professional practices of multishot actualities of the time) occurs in at least several films in the Archive beyond the obviously edited ones.[86]

More support for the argument that traces of documentary storytelling lie dormant within Kahn's unedited footage appears in the instances where information on the film development card (*fiche de développement*) not only supports an explicit intention to edit but also harnesses that reorganization of shots to an obvious nationalistic narrative, typical of the propagandistic application of documentary film in the First World War.[87] This is the case, for example, with the film development *fiche* of March 13, 1919, submitted by Le Saint, which contains a list of thirteen shots he had taken of the postwar ruins of Reims, one of the most severely damaged and symbolically charged cities in northeastern France.[88] On the back of the *fiche*, beneath the handwritten heading "Editing order of Reims film," Le Saint has constructed a new sequence for the original shots that produces an implicit narrative of French redemption and German reparation. Even though unedited rushes dominate the Archives, there is therefore evidence of editing and storytelling conventions in at least some of the work done by Le Saint, and others by Sauvageot, which confirm the presence of an inchoate story-based mode of documentary filmmaking in the Archive that pulls the films away from the non-narrative "aesthetic of the view." If we cannot know for sure why only some footage was edited, it is at least significant that it was a particularly nationalistic subject matter—the destruction and reconstruction of a French spiritual landmark, the Reims cathedral—that aroused in Kahn's cameramen the desire to narrate, rather than merely describe, the nation.

"PREMATURE RUINS" OF DOCUMENTARY FILM

The evidence of in-camera and postproduction editing in a small number of Kahn's films raises the issue of their connection to an emerging rather than already existing tradition of nonfiction filmmaking, namely, the feature length, story-based, and editing-dependent model of nonfiction film associated with Griersonian documentary. If documentary film proper comes into its own only toward the end of the Archive, that does not mean Kahn's films have nothing in common with what Bill Nichols has described as documentary's murky origins in the science-spectacle dualism of photographic realism, divided between the evidentiary allure of objective truths and the exhibitionist attractions of early cinema. Nor does it mean Kahn's films evolved in isolation from documentary's more formative, postwar influences that Nichols has categorized according to the additional intertwining codes of narrative structure, modernist fragmentation and poetic experimentation, and rhetorical persuasion.[89]

Kahn's frequent references to the "documentation" function of his universalist project and Brunhes' equally evidentiary-based attitudes toward film and autochrome photography as "new processes of technology and science" provide two examples of the Archive's association with foundational documentary discourses of photographic realism.[90] Meanwhile, the multifaceted emphasis upon modes of seeing, showing, and describing, ranging from human geography's focus on direct observation and Brunhes' lecturing style to the instructions he gave to cameramen and photographers, situate the films within the nonfiction genres of the "cinema of attractions." Indeed, if viewed as discrete films (rather than filmed views, facts, or documents), it could be argued that Kahn's films contain, albeit in a nascent form, elements of what Nichols has defined as the four major modes that documentary filmmaking followed after its inception in the 1920s: the observational, the interactive, the self-reflexive, and the expository.[91] As should be evident, however, from

the above exploration of the influence of human geography and the "view" aesthetic upon the Archive, it is clearly an early version of the *observational mode*, with
its tendency, as Nichols puts it, to "take paradigmatic form around the exhaustive
depiction of the everyday" and the "representation of typicality" that comes closest
to encapsulating the documentary style of Kahn's films.[92]

In addition to finding common ground with the early documentary tradition in
science, spectacle, and observation, several features also align Kahn's project with
the Griersonian direction that Anglo-American documentary took by the thirties.
Just as Grierson himself recognized that his idea of documentary "was not basi-
cally a film idea at all" (he had chosen film merely because it was "the most convenient and most exciting" medium available for "spreading civic education"), so
too was Kahn's interest in film nonexclusive and inseparable from a wider (and
not necessarily optimistic) interest in the media of mass communication.[93] The
world of facts (whether geographical, biological, philosophical, or social) Kahn and
Brunhes gathered did not begin and end with the film frame, or for that matter
the autochrome plate. It also included that other modern form of communication,
the mass daily press. Indeed, several of Kahn's fourteen publications were entirely
dependent upon a scrapbook-like collage of articles culled from the world's daily
newspapers. After the last frame of a Kahn film there was, therefore, always the
first page of one of Kahn's bulletins or information about the next meeting of one
of his forums for debate. Moreover, members of the "Boulogne community" usually
frequented and participated in more than one of Kahn's enterprises, leading to a
sense of continuity (although not necessarily narrative in nature) between the otherwise discontinuous sites and media of his documentary utopia.[94] Furthermore,
although Kahn was uninterested in implementing film as a medium of mass communication, and his documentary network was significantly more elitist than Grierson's state-funded General Post Office or Empire Marketing Board Film Units,
he shared the Griersonian attraction to a liberal humanist project of education
from above.

Yet the elitism that characterized the limited exhibition environment at Kahn's
property was not matched within the subject matter of his films. At the level of
content, many of Kahn's films included the people (urban workers, fishermen,
cameramen) who were also chosen to become the everyday heroes (for often very
different political reasons) of international documentary film movements of the
twenties and thirties. Not surprisingly, given their *anthropo*-geographical impetus, Kahn's films also display the "commitment to exploring the lives of 'ordinary'
people" that joined documentary film to scientific ethnography of the period.[95] For
example, Le Saint's 1922 extensive filming of the fishing expeditions off the coast
of Newfoundland (*La Pêche à la morue, Neuve-Terre*) not only salvages a dying premodern practice, but brings home the theme of man against nature and "the high
bravery of upstanding labor" (Grierson) that dominated Flaherty's *Nanook of the*

FIGURE 2.3   Lucien Le Saint posing with a codfish on mission in Newfoundland for the filming of the soon-to-disappear cod fishing expeditions. (Lucien Le Saint, 1922 [MAK: frame enlargement])

North (1922), reappeared in *Man of Aran* (Flaherty, 1934), and influenced other formative works of the British documentary film movement such as Grierson's *Drifters* (1929).[96] The footage of Le Saint joking around with the fishermen as he transforms the huge cod into a hand puppet in an antic copied from a fisherman he had also filmed (figs. 2.3 and 2.4) suggests, if not the anthropological practice of participant observation, then at least evidence of camaraderie and intimacy (rather than antagonism and distance) shaping the cameraman-subject encounter.[97] Similarly, if Le Saint's diary from the fishing expedition does not make any connections between his gesture of handing over the camera to his subjects with anything resembling reverse ethnography, his entries do reveal how closely he lived with the fishermen during the three-month-long voyage, detailing the emotional, health, and safety difficulties of their "rough" job.[98]

In addition to displaying his interest in the subjective dimensions of recording, Le Saint's willingness to place himself before the camera also indicates the wider appreciation of the ordinary heroism of "men with movie cameras" that appears in the Archive's diverse "tributes" to the usually invisible *chasseurs d'images*. The elevation of the cameraman as a fond (and perhaps found) object of documentation in the Kahn Archive is in no way comparable to the self-reflexive revolutionary responsibility imputed to the cameraman as "kinok-pilot" in Vertov's *Man with a*

FIGURE 2.4   Fisherman posing with codfish, Newfoundland. (Lucien Le Saint, 1922 [MAK: frame enlargement 97927])

Movie Camera (1928).[99] Still, these brief self-reflexive moments do reveal a respect for the difficulties and dangers of location-based shooting that Le Saint and his colleagues knew only too well, as well as a proud awareness back home that the labor of filming presented a new attraction upon the stage of modern urban life.[100]

And if the Archive anticipated British and Soviet documentary movements' interest in the daily heroism of the ordinary worker ("Long live the ordinary mortal, filmed in life at his daily tasks!" wrote Vertov), it also did so in its depiction of that rival hero of international documentary film from the twenties and thirties—the city.[101] In this respect, the Archive's survey of Paris (to take the most recorded city) resembles an unconscious repository of the filmed fragments that comprised the "city symphony," a film genre characterized by a musically orchestrated cross section of daily life in a big city. Although the "city symphony" genre developed across politically and stylistically divergent modes, from René Clair's *Paris qui dort* (1923), Alberto Cavalcanti's *Rien que les heures* (1926), and Jean Vigo's *À Propos de Nice* (1929), to Walter Ruttmann's *Berlin, Symphony of a Great City* (1927) and Vertov's *Man with a Movie Camera* (1928), it was united by a quest to replicate through montage (and sometimes music and sound) the new rhythmic and temporal experiences of modern urban space, in a manner that often depended on rearranging shots of discrete moments to conform to the loosely linear trajectory of a day in the life of a city.

However, even though the Archive privileges the topos of the city in defiance of human geography's typically rural bias, the planetary scale of Kahn's project pushes its films more in the direction of what I call the *atlas symphony*. Admittedly more a tendency than a genre, atlas symphony films attempt to encompass—through some combination of cartographic representations, aerial cinematography, superimpositions, and juxtapositional visual (and sometimes sound) montage—the entire planet.[102] Their scope is global rather than local. An example of the atlas symphony is Walter Ruttmann's *Melody of the World* (1929), a promotional film for a transatlantic liner company that visually scans the world in a series of universalizing juxtapositions made up from a global smorgasbord of "slice of life" views. As a film that "flung the whole earth onto the screen in a jigsaw of visual images and sounds" (to use Bazin's description), *Melody of the World* serves as a hypothetical distillation of the Kahn project and its affinity with the atlas symphony.[103] The fact that Ruttmann's loosely humanist vision supported a promotional campaign should not detract from the connections to be made between it and Kahn's noncommercial project. For there is a sense in which Kahn's internationalist ideology is interwoven with the border-free demands of capitalist globalization that the atlas symphony tendency strives to visualize harmoniously. A further similarity between *Melody of the World* and the Kahn Archive appears in Ruttmann's harmonization of the diversity of the globe through a blandly comparative application of montage editing. Ruttmann's editing even resonates with the classificatory and comparative thrust promoted by Brunhes. Indeed, several of the themes that underpin Ruttmann's humanist use of globally comparative juxtaposition—bridges, practices of prayer, agricultural exploitation of the earth—mirror the subcategories by which Brunhes classified, arranged, and exhibited the photographs that he used to illustrate all three editions of his *La Géographie humaine* (1910, 1912, 1925), while other themes in the film (sport and fairground rides) also appear across Kahn's films.

Ruttmann's at once overelaborate and simplistic formalism (the eyes of a woman superimposed over the portholes of a ship) was ultimately antithetical, however, to the formal incompleteness and interpretive open-endedness that characterize the majority of Kahn's films. Any comparison with the city or atlas symphony genres, among other montage- or narrative-driven documentary forms, must ultimately be qualified by the acknowledgment that Kahn's films remained in the form of rushes rather than edited film. Although it is often helpful to imagine the Kahn footage as potentially edited shots, it is more correct (if more challenging) to remember that the raw footage constituted the final, rather than intermediary, product of the Archive's conception of film. It is arguable whether we can even refer to Kahn's films as shots in the conventional sense of the term (that is, as incomplete parts of some future edited whole), given that the majority were intended as discrete visual facts rather than editing-destined shots. Their meaning adhered therefore in their fragmented state rather than a potential narrative rear-rangement in a film sequence.

Given the Kahn films' fragmentation, it is tempting to compare his footage to amateur films (the documentary mode Bazin valorized in opposition to commer-cial travel films) because they both conjure the "premature ruins" of some unfin-ished master film.[104] Indeed, from the perspective of edited film, Kahn's films may look undone, even suggesting the documentary form in decay. The comparison, however, is ultimately limited. Kahn's films did not fall into fragments; they were supposed to look and remain undone. And if incompletion was their original "fin-ish," completion was intended for them but only in the form of an autochrome, bulletin, or discussion, not an argument-driven sequence of shots.

NO MORE THAN "LITTLE DAILY DOINGS"

Grierson's critique of those types of film deemed "lower" than the "higher" catego-ries of true documentary is worth referring to again in full:

> The little daily doings, however finely symphonized, are not enough. One must pile
> up beyond doing or process to creation itself, before one hits the higher reaches of
> art.[105]

In addition to revealing Grierson's infamous mistrust of the city symphony's poten-tially modernist decadence of montage, his prescription for the art of documentary is important because it argues against the descriptive, piecemeal accumulation of cinematic facts. In this regard, his definition of documentary also harbors a level of anxiety toward the stray signification of the everyday echoed in Lévi-Strauss's own fear of "trivial circumstances and insignificant happenings." The faithful recording of "little daily doings," the humble stuff of all those "lecture films" characteristic of early nonfiction film in general and the Kahn films in particular, is "not enough" to make a *film documentaire* into a documentary. Compared to the expository model of documentary now most associated with Grierson's ideal, the majority of Kahn's films lack any internal argumentative structure and remain unincorporated into any wider persuasive, poetic, or realist narrative. If what is at stake, as Phil Rosen has suggested, in the "conversion" from document to Griersonian documentary, is the task of "controlling documents"—that is, adapting the "pure presence and pure (*unfinishable*) chronicle" of amassed facts into the "internal sequenciation" of narrative elaboration—then the Kahn films testify to the recalcitrant status of the view-cum-document within the slow and uneven shift to documentary film in France.[106] For the Kahn films, the "little daily doings" were for the most part more than enough.

Certainly, the Kahn films were supposed to incite analysis, comparison, and juxtaposition but only in an extra-filmic (within discussion and use with the other textual documents) or inter-filmic situation (between the documents) and not as an extension of the experience of viewing the single film in isolation. Additional support for the idea that extra-filmic narratives may have existed for Kahn's films (much as they did for the autochromes as seen in Brunhes' lectures) appears if we position the fourteen bulletins as the missing script to the Archive's often inexplicable views. At the same time, this reading needs to be counterbalanced by the fact that these bulletins apparently failed to reach their constituency. These hopeful messages in a bottle arrived too late to be of any immediate relevance, leaving their sender and his urgent letters to the world stranded on his Parisian island of facts. Even if we account for these extra-filmic contexts, which might have also included spoken lecture accompaniment, we are still left short of any overarching controlling narrative logic underpinning the flow of discontinuous evidence ebbing around the "Boulogne community" in the form of fragmented, unfinishable, and indeterminate filmed facts.

The Kahn project may have thus combined a "descriptive mode based on the act of looking and display" (typical of the view aesthetic) with the fact-gathering mode of the document, but it stopped short of articulating those view-documents to the argument-motivated documentary (of either the Griersonian or Vertovian models).[107] Kahn's films remained (to borrow a phrase of Brunhes' daughter) the raw material for a sort of "sampling" of reality, rather than the end product of conclusive evidence that was the model for the later, problem-solving expository documentary mode.[108] In this regard, striking though it may seem, Kahn's sampling loosely resembled Vertov's "impetuous survey of visual events" (which itself bears quite specific similarities with Brunhes' classifications).[109] Yet as a collection of mostly unedited footage, it did not go so far as Vertov's ultimate goal—the engineering of that survey into the "decoding of life as it is" via the highly selective and organizational capacities of the cameraman and camera in service to the "great craft of montage."[110] Although Kahn's Archive and Vertov's "factory of facts" shared a fact-oriented, indexical-based understanding of film footage, for Vertov the filming of facts was supplemented by a whole series of operations—"Sorting facts. Disseminating facts. Agitating with facts. Propaganda with facts. Fists made of facts"—that may have been dreamed of but were never realized for the majority of Kahn's films.[111]

Unlike all of the above documentary projects, the Kahn Archive was primarily based on raw footage and was defined by the stockpiling of discrete visual documents of the sort that would be deemed insufficient by the evolving Griersonian discourse of documentary film. Given these radical differences, additional models and rationales are needed for understanding the nonsystematic and non-narrative inventorial logic of Kahn's films. I would like to end this chapter by examining another relevant model of French documentary—that provided by Jean Vigo in response to his own version of a city symphony, the film *À Propos de Nice* (1929). In opposition to what he (like Grierson) saw as the facile objectivity of the newsreel, Vigo promoted his documentary optic with reference to the intentionally hybrid "documented point of view" ("*le point de vue documenté*").[112] We might also describe this optic through the protean terms of the view-cum-fact. Combining the subjective with the objective, the poetic with the factual, the witness with the observer, the immersive with the distanced, and the particular with the general, Vigo blurs even further the already vague distinctions between the aesthetic and the scientific in the French visual tradition of the "view" and the "fact." It is this exact willingness to mix the roles of poet and observer that Brian Winston claims (albeit without reference to Vigo) differentiates the French tradition of documentary (typified by "the impressionistic filmed essay" favored by Vigo, and later Georges Franju, Alain Resnais, Chris Marker, and Agnès Varda) from the British (modeled more on the "sociological public education text").[113]

Going even further, I would also link this combination of the objective with subjective, and classificatory rigor with amateur curiosity, to another feature of the French modernist tradition of documentary filmmaking, namely its innovative affinities with naturalism (and descriptive excess, both literary and sociological) rather than realism (and action- and character-motivated narrative).[114] True to the melodramatic excesses of Zola's naturalist novels (which often threaten to overcome the scientific sobriety promoted by his commentaries on literary naturalism), Vigo exaggerated objectivity as much as subjectivity within his hybrid optic. As related by Boris Kaufman, Vigo insisted that his "documented point of view" should [be visualized by a militant method of filming diametrically opposed to the disclosed witnessing of early nonfiction forms: "to take by surprise facts, actions, attitudes, expressions, and to stop shooting as soon as the subject became conscious of being photographed."[115] And in an effort to attain a more authentic portrait of daily life, which had once again succumbed to convention by the mid-1920s, Kaufman stated that he and Vigo consciously rejected the "picturesque" and "commentary or subtitles" in favor of relying on "purely visual means."[116]

Vigo's championing of fly-on-the-wall observation, pointed social critique, and to a lesser extent a non-narrative attention to the purely visual, would seem to separate his documentary idea from that of Kahn's cameramen. And yet the Kahn films, made by cameramen who were artists as well as technicians, educators of vision as well as chroniclers of contemporary history, do share Vigo's preference for the personal, idiosyncratic view, as well as his emphasis upon non-narrative visual description and curiosity. Given the freedom afforded by the supple anti-systematicity of Brunhes' method, they also pushed "just looking" beyond impassive neutrality and clinical distantiation. On the other hand, they depart from Vigo (and his preference for the hidden camera) in their comfort with (or normative adjustment to) the unhidden camera and disclosed witnessing. Unlike Vigo (or Vertov for that matter), the Kahn cameramen were not "obsessed with a desire for visual impartiality" and unlike Grierson they were not beholden to the definition of the documentary impulse as a narrative "desire to make drama from the ordinary."[117] Neither the hidden camera nor the hidden script defined their approach to actuality. At this decisive fork in the path of documentary film's journey, Kahn's cameramen depart ways with their socially radical contemporaries and look toward other future recorders of daily life who would be unconsciously or consciously swayed by the subjective, the curious, and the intuitive in scientific inquiry. This future trend would appear in the involuntary return to the self aroused by a Chopin melody in Lévi-Strauss's *Tristes Tropiques* and, most importantly for French documentary, the voluntary courting of the "Other" as filmmaking participant in Jean Rouch's cross-cultural dialogic film practice, aptly described by Rouch as embodying the seemingly impossible perspective of "an intimate distance."[118]

To be sure, Kahn's documentary practice might be just as distant from Vigo's definition of social documentary as it was from Grierson's. But the complex approach to actuality folded into Vigo's notion of the "documented point of view" introduces a French twist in the idea of documentary (exemplified in Rouch's "intimate distance") that is crucial for understanding the importance of both a modernist *and* seemingly anti-modernist strain in the Kahn films and the French documentary tradition. The immediate discursive history to Vigo's statement encompasses film critics and filmmakers like Colette, Louis Delluc, Jean Epstein, Fernand Léger, and Germaine Dulac, whose own writings on the connections between the everyday, documentary, and film occupy that space in between the "aesthetic of the view" and the "documented point of view" that Kahn's films also inhabited. Epstein summarized this crossover aesthetic in his desire to link together the objective and subjective.[119] All participants in a diffuse cinematic debate with the status of daily life, these strange bedfellows (the cinematic avant-garde and Kahn) bring to light the unexpected proximity of the aesthetically radical elements of the modernist avant-garde and the seemingly conservative nature of documentary projects like Kahn's. Notwithstanding their divergent aesthetic and ideological proclivities, they shared a zealous faith that film, and especially (though not exclusively) nonfiction film, held the key to reacquainting humanity with the estranged nature of modern daily life. Above and beyond conflicts about what type of filming was best suited to this task, these diverse participants in documentary film culture were preoccupied with *new* forms of looking and an underlining desire (reflective of, as I will soon show, Bergson's influence on film) to rupture and renew habitual perception. The particularity of this generation's visual fascination with documentary was encapsulated in 1930 when Jean Dréville claimed that in "[d]issecting the world in which we live, documentary cinema exposes everything which ordinarily goes unnoticed."[120]

CONCLUSION

This chapter has argued that Kahn's films occupy a transitional space between pre-documentary and documentary film. They straddle, on the one side, a heterogeneous prewar film tradition characterized by the "aesthetic of the view" and based on individual shots often loosely organized into a succession of views generally displaying a discrete place or process to a curious observer; and, on the other side, a postwar genre based on a tightly edited arrangement of shots in the service of a pronounced argument or narrative dependent for its appeal upon film's evidentiary claims rather than visual attractions. Daily life was a privileged object at both extremes of this documentary spectrum, and it dominated their midway point in the maelstrom of diverse modernist encounters with nonfiction film in the twenties.

Entering this midway point from a slightly different angle from modernist filmmakers like Vertov, Epstein, and Vigo, the Kahn Archive and its particular interest in the everyday was guided by Brunhes and Kahn's urgent sense of the need to see the familiar with new eyes and materialized in their encouragement of the cameramen's own casual curiosity. These influences resulted in an Archive that is just as much about the questioning of the everyday (as the unseen within the surface) as it is about its confirmation (as the familiarity of the surface). It should not come as a surprise then that some of the most striking films in the Archive are of views usually occluded from the conventional historical, social, and biological eye (see respectively the footage shot only by the Kahn cameramen of the 1920 Congress at Tours, films of colonial brothels, and Dr. Comandon's microscopic films).[121] Wielding the technological advances of the autochrome's "truly modern documentation" (due to its unprecedented reproduction of color) and the cinematograph's ability to "record moving phenomena *with a precision which had been previously implausible*," the Archives de la Planète set out to bring order to the classificatory mania of positivist determinism as well as the observational frenzy and descriptive excesses of literary and scientific naturalism.[122]

Ultimately, however, much like the Chopin melody that upstaged Lévi-Strauss's scientific triumph, the Archive's obsessive quest for positivist order left it all the more vulnerable to new forms of disorder. Especially apparent in the cinematic domain, these carriers of disorder bore the residual or reinvigorated traces of an unmanageable vision that had always haunted scientific inquiry and that was also typical of the three-dimensional and color *excesses* of stereographic and autochrome views. Additionally, the cultivation of the individual cameramen's intuition meant that Kahn's films were motivated by the pursuit of the general geographic view as well as a commitment to the everyday detail that defies classification. The Kahn cameramen's willingness to pursue the recalcitrant facts of naturalism (which Lukács described as the arbitrary, accidental, and fortuitous details that must be excised from realist narrative) is what ultimately tipped the balance in their films away from narrative order to descriptive disorder.[123] In this sense, the entire Kahn project inherited the excessive traits of Zola's literary naturalism, while also magnifying them because of the even more wayward filmic contingencies of what Theodor Adorno called, in reference to the medium's Zola-esque potential, an aesthetic of "radical naturalism."[124] Thus if the stubbornly unedited Kahn footage may seem out of step with the Vertovian montage-derived ethos of making "fists with facts," in its relentless stockpiling of history's detritus it acquired the spirit (if not the form) of that assault, transforming familiar realism into radical naturalism. Where Vertov's mainstream spectators supposedly wanted to "flee from the humdrum, from the 'prose' of life," Kahn's project, with its surfeit of radical naturalism, forced a confrontation with exactly what this audience fled from in horror, the everyday.[125]

Finally, it we wish to understand the untranslatable and forgotten language and logic of the Kahn films, we need to be careful about reading them retrospectively, as descendants or harbingers of already known or future versions of nonfiction film. Released from the injunction to awaken the Kahn films *from* their sleep by tracing how they conform to recognizable patterns within nonfiction film's evolution, one is free (following Foucault's prescription for an anti-historicist enunciative analysis) "to follow them *through* their sleep," attending to the "forgotten, and possibly even destroyed" context of their emergence, thus allowing for the eclectic experimentation of the Kahn project to rise to the surface.[126] As part of research into the new field of human geography, conducted at a time when related disciplines like anthropology were still renouncing film, and as part of a unique test in archival practice, at a time when the major historiographical shift in France depended upon a questioning of the nature of the historical archive and the definition of primary sources, the Kahn films constituted a multifaceted experiment in cinematic meaning. As I will endeavor to show in the following chapters, the horizon of experimentation that comes into view once we resist reading the Kahn films as immature, unsophisticated, and unfinished documentary films also includes the Archive's destabilization of conventional history, the films' incorporation of new modes of historicity associated with newsreels, and the project's multifaceted affinities with both avant-garde and scientific film's dissection of the everyday. However, the most profound if immaterial dimension of the Archive's experimental nature, the clue that might allow us to follow rather than waken them from their sleep, is its relationship with that body of thought responsible for the early twentieth century's most far-reaching critique of familiar positivism, namely, Bergsonian philosophy. Moreover, as the era's preeminent philosopher of time and memory, it is to Henri Bergson that we now turn in order to investigate why the phrase "world *souvenir*"—or, following the French translation, "world memory"—is such a suitable label for the Kahn Archive.

THE COUNTER-ARCHIVE OF
CINEMATIC MEMORY

BERGSONISM, *LA DURÉE*, AND THE EVERYDAY

Photography must, therefore, return to its true duty, which is that of handmaid of the arts and sciences.... Let it save crumbling ruins from oblivion, books, engravings, and manuscripts, the prey of time, all those precious things, vowed to dissolution, which crave a place in the archives of our memories.

CHARLES BAUDELAIRE (1859)[1]

And the photography of all this had taken place within the archives of his memory, archives so vast that he would never look into most of them, unless they were reopened by chance, as happened with the shock of the pianist this evening.

MARCEL PROUST (1895–1900)[2]

Memory, as we have tried to prove, is not a faculty of putting away recollections in a drawer, or of inscribing them in a register. There is no register, no drawer; there is not even, properly speaking, a faculty [of memory].

HENRI BERGSON (1907)[3]

IN THE FIRST DECADES of their emergence, photography and film inspired artists and intellectuals to debate their implications for a diverse range of aesthetic, scientific, and philosophical issues. Underlying many of these debates was the impact of these new recording devices upon conceptions of memory. Both Baudelaire's infamous diatribe against photography and Bergson's equally renowned denunciation of *photographie animée* centered on the association of the new media with a debased if professionally useful form of memory. Proust's related literary inquiry into photographic and cinematographic understandings of memory, whose first stirrings we find in the above fragment from his unfinished novel *Jean Santeuil*, would eventually coalesce into *Remembrance of Things Past*, shaping it into what literary historian Richard Terdiman calls a "three-thousand page condemnation" of everything the mechanically precise media had to offer.[4] Via a detour through

Bergson's notion of pure memory, Proust (whose cousin married Bergson in 1892) labeled that photographic-like, impoverished, and shallow access to the past "*mémoire volontaire.*"

In their different levels of unease with modern technologies of reproduction, Baudelaire, Bergson, and Proust shared the assumption that photography and film's memory was inauthentic precisely because it was *archival*. Capable of an endless accumulation, storage, and retrieval of mathematically exact views of the past, photography, and especially film, seemed to realize the dream of total spatio-temporal recall so cherished by late-nineteenth-century historicism. But they did so, according to these three anti-archival commentaries, at the expense of the aesthetic or the "intangible and the imaginary" (for Baudelaire, "The Salon of 1859," 297), *la durée* or the indivisible continuity of life (for Bergson), and the involuntary pull of true memory (for Proust). Returning to this debate with archival memory in "The Painter of Modern Life" (1863), Baudelaire reframed the issue as the struggle between a misguided "determination to see everything, to forget nothing" and a more enlightened resignation to the more authentic, albeit incomplete "flash[es]" of the past.[5]

Baudelaire's disdain for modern media may seem more surprising than Bergson's because the poet championed the modern in art (understood as the "quest of the ephemeral, the fleeting forms of beauty in the life of our day" to be found in "the trivial" and "daily changing of external things").[6] In distinct contrast, Bergson has more often been imagined (even though he partly inspired seminal modernist encounters with temporality by Proust, James Joyce, and Virginia Woolf, to name a few) as a figure with his eyes shut tight to modernity—a figure, one might say, philosophically at odds with Kahn's scopophilic command to "keep your eyes open."

More recently, the question of Bergson's relation to modernity and memory, telescoped into the issue of whether in fact his philosophical work is "in sympathy with cinema," has become one of the key topics in what Fredric Jameson has referred to as the "Bergsonian revivals" rippling through the humanities.[7] The Bergson-cinema debate hinges upon conflicting interpretations of a selection of his writings, most notably the last chapter of *Creative Evolution* (1907), but also the earlier *Matter and Memory* (1896) and *Laughter* (1900), in which the philosopher's antipathy toward the cinematographic illusion is arguably on display. This recent cinematic turn to Bergson was lead by Gilles Deleuze's attempts to appropriate the philosopher for a counter-history of the Western philosophical tradition, a move intent on retrieving his work from the "philosophical ghetto" of turn-of-the-century vitalism to the philosophical limelight of poststructuralist difference.[8] A central element of Deleuze's proudly perverse reading was his claim that, "Even in his critique of the cinema, Bergson was in agreement with it."[9] Deleuze ventured this paradoxical assertion because he assumed that the potential of Bergson's thoughts on cinema was prematurely stunted by the "primitive" limitations of early cinema—characterized by spatially "fixed" and "immobile" views.[10] Without access to the post-1980s renaissance in early film studies, Deleuze should not be blamed for misrepresenting this period of cinema as spatially fixated and temporally challenged. The more important issue is that, for Deleuze, Bergson's lack of faith in the cinema of his time did not mean he would not have approved of a future, more sophisticated cinema of time (read montage cinema, and in particular what Deleuze characterized as the post–World War II time-image cinema).

Deleuze's assertion that Bergson's thought is central to a comprehension of cinema's temporal and philosophical potentialities is not as new or radical as it appears and was recognized in various forums in Bergson's own lifetime. As I will show in this and subsequent chapters, Bergson himself gave an interview to a journalist in the early teens about the cinematic relevance of his philosophy, and a few years later some of the most important film critics in France (including Émile Vuillermoz and Marcel L'Herbier) waged a debate on this very issue. In the late thirties, going against the tide of a general backlash against the vitalist philosopher, Walter Benjamin (in the essay "Some Motifs in Baudelaire" [1939]) retrieved from Bergson's philosophy a crucial "clue" for theorizing the "decline of aura" in modern technologies of reproduction like photography and film.[11] These testimonies alone are warning enough to be skeptical about Deleuze's unqualified claim that early cinema provided an infertile context for Bergsonian philosophy. In fact, the opposite is more correct.

In order to fully appreciate the fertile exchange between Bergsonism and the cinema of his time, we must account for his most significant yet overlooked involvement with the medium of film: his association with the Archives de la Planète. Having outlined the concrete background to the Archive in the last two chapters, I now pursue the more immaterial traces left by the encounter between Bergson and Kahn upon the project. Given the philosopher's critique of archival memory and Kahn's championing of his Archive as a world souvenir or global memory bank, the contentious issue of film's access to memory is central to my interpretation of the two men's encounter. For it is undeniable that at first glance the Kahn Archive seems like an affront to everything Bergson stood for. Indeed, one must ask why a philosopher who inaugurated what Martin Jay calls one of the most damaging "frontal attack[s] on [Western] ocularcentrism in modern French philosophy" might be even remotely involved with the hyper-optical ambitions of Kahn's globally roaming eye.[12] In answering this question, I will delineate two ways in which Bergson haunts the Kahn project and vice versa. The first path of inquiry will require me to explain how Bergson's distrust of the mechanical aspects of modern everyday life (related to his suspicions toward the cinematograph) can be thought alongside Kahn's visual stocktaking of early-twentieth-century ordinary culture. The second path of inquiry will lead me to explore how a philosopher who was notoriously suspicious of the cinematograph's false reality, and derisive toward the notion of memory-as-archive, came to exist in the same orbit as a first-of-its-kind film archive that outwardly resembled a visual warehouse for the world. Underpinning this exploration is my new interpretation of a counter- (rather than anti-) archival strain in Bergson's theory of memory, which I then compare with theories of the archive by Kracauer and Foucault.

Without claiming that Kahn's films are the illegitimate children of Bergson's enigmatic affair with cincma, their very existence reminds us of the widespread and often idiosyncratic offspring of the philosopher's thought. Moreover, the films point to a less intolerant account of cinema and the everyday than is usually assumed in his writings. The Bergsonian heritage of Kahn's films also discloses a significant point of contact between the Archives de la Planète and avant-garde film culture. Beyond pursuing the question of whether or not Bergson's thinking is in sympathy with cinema, in this chapter I am just as concerned with exploring the sympathies *and* antipathies that arise as we try to understand the Archives de la Planète from the perspective of Bergson. In other words, for all the unquantifiable nature of Bergson and Kahn's relationship, my readings find inspiration in the Bergsonian dilemmas, fantasies, and potentialities posed rather than necessarily solved by the Archives de la Planète.

THE PHILOSOPHER AND THE MILLIONAIRE

It was in the late 1870s that Kahn, who had recently arrived in Paris from Alsace, hired Henri Bergson, then an unknown teacher of philosophy also living in the capital and separated from his family, to train him for the grueling *baccalauréat* exams. There began a unique friendship that continued until Kahn's death on November 14, 1940, followed by Bergson's less than two months later. Although much separates this odd couple, two related factors unite them. They both chose their French national identity—Kahn by staying in France after the 1871 option to leave, and Bergson (whose father was Polish Jewish and mother Anglo-Irish Jewish) by doing the same once his family moved to London. Second, they both died at the lowest point in their country's defense of their right to French nationality.

Kahn's deep admiration for his former "Maître" was especially evident in the development of his multifaceted *ouevre*.[13] An article in one of Kahn's publications, the *Bulletin de la Société Autour du Monde*, acknowledged in 1931 that Bergson was "at the root of" the Société Autour du Monde.[14] Louis F. Aubert, one of Kahn's travel grant recipients, even claimed in a 1928 issue of that journal that it was well known amongst travel grant awardees that Bergson gave his imprimatur to the Autour du Monde fund, and that "his tone of voice" was recognizable in the core of the instructions handed to them before they departed on their missions.[15] In addition, Bergson was the only person privy to the early plans for the Archives de la Planète; he was called on to suggest an appropriate scientific director for the Archive; he was described in 1931 (in a speech heard by Kahn and Bergson's wife and daughter) as Kahn's "personal friend" and "mentor"; and he was one of the few people Kahn remained in contact with after losing his fortune in the early thirties.[16] Yet perhaps the most telling testimony of Kahn's esteem for Bergson appears in what is left of the banker's personal archives. Reticent on every other respect of his life, they speak clearly of his relationship with Bergson in the form of a correspondence with the philosopher between 1879 and 1893 that he preserved carefully. Kahn's personal archiving of his early relationship with Bergson—these curious whispers between a banker and philosopher—constitutes the most intimate of the diverse supplementary archives nestled inside the Archives de la Planète.

Broaching the subject of Bergson's attitude toward Kahn is more difficult, especially given that in his will the philosopher strictly forbade the posthumous publication of any unapproved personal documents.[17] Piecing together his opinion of Kahn is only made slightly less difficult with access to the above-mentioned correspondence, since it dates back to the period (1879–1893) prior to Bergson's celebrity status and Kahn's reputation as a "bizarre man of money."[18] These difficulties aside, it is clear that in his younger years Bergson was a confidant of Kahn's and in his more mature years an interested if slightly skeptical observer of his diverse humanist projects. Bergson was not only privy to the germination of Kahn's plans, but he was willing to pull his weight when it came to securing institutional status for the Archive. Not one to usually participate in the administrative affairs of the Collège de France, where he held the Chair in Philosophy since 1900, Bergson made an exception when it came to showing his support for Brunhes during the election of the Chair of Human Geography in 1912.[19] However, Bergson's most public display of his respect for Kahn's missions came in the form of a speech he was asked to deliver on the occasion of the twenty-fifth anniversary of the Société Autour du Monde. In that address from 1931 Bergson claimed that if the "spirit of Geneva," materialized in the League of Nations, had not succeeded in giving body to a "human society" based on the veneration of "the international mind," then Kahn and his "Boulogne community" had at least prepared its "soul."[20] Coming from a man who had devoted so much effort to the League of Nations and whose last major philosophical book, *The Two Sources of Morality and Religion* (1932), might be described as a requiem for the pacifist bent of "the international mind," this was high praise indeed.

Still, alongside his sympathy for Kahn's commitment to the good of humanity, there is also evidence that Bergson considered Kahn a curious figure. Jean Guitton, a close friend of Bergson, suggested that the philosopher "viewed Albert Kahn's chimerical projects with gentle irony."[21] A consummate diplomat, Bergson clearly found it in his interests to keep his ironic attitude to himself. Perhaps this was because he knew that Kahn could provide him with many favors, as seen in the regular requests Bergson made to Kahn, ranging from help in seeking employment for himself, his brother, and at least two of his students (Jacques Chevalier and Charles Péguy), to asking for advice on whom to marry.[22] Given the sensitivity of such requests, Bergson clearly trusted Kahn, as the letters repeatedly state, with "the greatest discretion."[23]

To be sure, Bergson's frequent requests reveal how comfortable he and Kahn had become with each other and Kahn reciprocated in kind with all sorts of requests, ranging from boxes of matches from London and the address of a Parisian fencing master to the procurement of a skeleton.[24] The earlier letters of the two young men also contain shared expressions of faith in each other's future successes, constant concern for each other's health, fond references to their respective family members and mutual acquaintances (their brothers were also friends), and confidential exchanges relating to their personal and professional frustrations.[25] Although it seems doubtful that their relationship remained on such casual and constant terms once Bergson's eminence as a philosopher soared with the publication of *Matter and Memory* in 1896 and the professorship at the Collège de France in 1900, and Kahn's success as a banker rose with the founding of his own bank in 1898, from their early correspondence it is uncontestable that they once shared an informal, mutually supportive, and even intimate friendship.

BERGSONISM

Although Bergson himself never played a direct role in the Archives de la Planète and his philosophy (according to Chevalier) may not have "particularly interested" Kahn, it is clear that he galvanized Kahn's community. In 1928 Louis F. Aubert claimed that "at Boulogne, Bergson is more than a [philosophical] system: he is a man, he is a *maître*;" the latter referring to the fact that many in that community were his former students.[26] Thus despite the measured skepticism and personal distance Bergson maintained in public toward Kahn's projects, Bergsonism formed one of the major intellectual sources behind the Archives de la Planète.[27] By the term *Bergsonism* I am referring to the then contemporary *popularization* of the philosopher's works, which brought that complex and contradictory web of anti-Cartesianism, antirationalism, anti-mechanism, and intuition to the fore across a wide range of cultural, political, scientific, and cinematographic debates that shaped early-twentieth-century French modernity.[28]

If the renovation of geography by Jean Brunhes was just one of the many disciplinary evolutions which rode the wave of Bergsonism, there are several other direct ways in which Bergsonism left a visible mark upon Kahn's projects.[29] The universalist spirituality and pacifist rhetoric that infused Kahn's wider mission and buttressed his intentions to use film as a tool of peace and international cooperation overlapped with Bergson's role as a central figure in the internationalist movements of the postwar years. It was during this period that Bergson's teaching, and to a lesser extent his philosophical works, took a backseat to his public commitments. For example, in 1917 the philosopher was enlisted on a semiofficial diplomatic meeting to convince the American president Woodrow Wilson of the moral justifications for entering the war, and in 1921 he resigned from his post at the Collège de France in order to dedicate himself to his writing and his work for the League of Nations. Between 1922 and 1925 he led one of the technical organizations attached to the League of Nations, the International Committee for Intellectual Cooperation (ICIC), whose distinguished members included several other guests of Kahn's "Boulogne community": Albert Einstein, Marie Curie, Thomas Mann, and Paul Valéry.

Although Kahn's Archive had no direct affiliation with the League of Nations, his projects resembled unofficial ambassadors for the liberal version of "internationalism" favored by the League and its various organizations that developed after the First World War. The Société Autour du Monde, whose mission was summarized by one member as "the preservation of peace and the furtherance of mutual understanding," looked a lot like a miniature version of the ICIC, whose own goals Bergson described as the pursuit of science and the "fostering of high ideals of brotherhood, human solidarity and peace among men."[30] As for the Archives de la Planète, one could argue that it resembled in spirit, if not fact, the International Institute for Educational Cinema, one of the offshoots of the ICIC. The origins of the Kahn Archive may have predated the high point of internationalist education film movements, as well as other global archiving projects such as Mundaneum (a world library conceived by the internationalist bibliographer Paul Otlet and designed for the city of Geneva by Le Corbusier, though never built), but it clearly shared their liberal humanist vision of global knowledge sharing, creating, as Bergson himself claimed, a home in exile for the battered "spirit of Geneva."[31]

Internationalist motivations aside, the most concrete traces of Bergsonism in Kahn's project appear in the rare testimonies of people who knew Kahn and in the few extant documents he signed.[32] In an interview with Kahn as late as 1938 we learn that he continued to have "long philosophical discussions" with his "intimate friend" Bergson on a regular basis.[33] Just over a decade later, in a rare biographical essay on Kahn, Alain Petit introduced Kahn as "the first student of Bergson" and argued that the "imprint" of the philosopher's thought upon the banker was decisive, even suggesting that Kahn conceived of his "works" in decidedly Bergsonian biological terms, as the interconnected cells of a vast network.[34]Additional evidence of the conception of Kahn's projects as a biological network also appears in the 1933 document titled "Nos Fondations" (Our Foundations) that Kahn sent to members of the French government and which was intended to account retrospectively for all of his projects—at that stage jeopardized by the loss of his fortune. The text invokes Bergsonian vocabulary—*synthesis*, *organicism*, and *creative whole*—to describe the relationship among the elements of Kahn's network.[35] Read alongside Bergson's earliest definition of *durée réelle* in *Time and Free Will* (1889), "Nos Fondations" permits us to understand how the separate parts of Kahn's *oeuvre* were conceived as an indivisible and organic whole that materialized Bergson's idea of a "mutual penetration, an interconnection and organization of elements, each one of which represents the whole, and cannot be distinguished or isolated from it except by abstract thought."[36]

If it is challenging to decipher Kahn's syncopated writing style bereft of full sentences or a logical structure, "Nos Fondations" does make sense as a banker's vision of Bergsonism. Given that there was a Bergsonism of the political right and left, a Bergsonism of the aesthetic establishment and the avant-garde, and even a Bergsonism for French pioneers in advertising psychology and cellular theory, it is not so strange that there might be a Bergsonism for financiers, especially those of a utopian persuasion.[37] Not that Kahn used it to explain the market. Rather, in a last ditch effort to account for his creations, he calls upon the *Maître's* terminology (mobility, matter, intuition, action, intellect), twisting and contorting Bergson's classical syntax into the language of an apocalyptic archivist, producing a furious amalgam of lists, statements, capitalized headings, subheadings, frustrated ellipses, and parenthetical remarks.[38] Beginning with brief, almost cryptic, descriptions of his organizations, "Nos Fondations" culminates with a restless summation of the impending "anarchy" that threatens both the cosmic order and the success of his life works. Typifying anxieties expressed by many French elites toward mass culture and abstraction in general, Kahn pointed to "*machinisme*" (8) as the major threat to the Bergsonian conception of life. He accuses the mass media—radio, *sound* cinema, and the press—of being sources of "false mentality"; shakes his finger at the modern woman's "uniform dress," "modified body," and "standardized smile" (9); and ends by invoking the bleak horizon of the early 1930s also glimpsed in Bergson's *The Two Sources of Morality and Religion* (1932): "a Humanity threatened by dehumanization" (9).[39] Interpreted sympathetically, Kahn's text reveals a prophetic if misdirected awareness of the threats developing within French society of the early thirties—not from a foreign mass culture but from homegrown antirepublican, nationalist, and fascist tendencies. Read in a less sympathetic light, the text also demonstrates the trouble Bergsonism confronted when its key concepts, like *élan vital* (creative impulse or living energy) and *la durée* (lived or experienced time), were applied to the external and collective, rather than the internal and individual, world. The difficulty of this confrontation explains why Kahn's quasi-apocalyptic rhetoric is infused with the speculative cosmology typical of the philosopher's later works like *The Two Sources of Morality and Religion*, whose goal (according to Sanford Schwartz) was nothing less than "the spiritual emotion that awakens us to the brotherhood of all mankind."[40]

Given Kahn's vitalist rage against the modernity of war, mass communications, and gender transformation, it is tempting to read Kahn's films as attempts to capture the indivisible time of *durée réelle*, and to claim that their pursuit of local daily life within the cracks of an otherwise homogeneous and mechanized urban land-scape corresponds to a deeply conservative quest for the *élan vital*. To support this supposition, one might claim that in their resistance to the elisions of editing and their preference for uninterrupted location shooting, Kahn's cameramen approxi-mated Bergson's *durée réelle* (time as human awareness experiences it, as opposed to the abstracted, divisible, measurable time of positivist science). By extension, one might therefore argue that Kahn's films vaguely anticipate André Bazin's own Bergsonian privileging of deep focus, long-take cinematography as the best hope for a "cinema of *la durée*" that respects the integrity of the spatio-temporal con-tinuum and ambiguity of reality.[41]

In addition to the problematic presence of editing in some of the films, what must caution us from pursuing the idea that Kahn's films somehow materialize the continuity of *la durée* is that they focused just as much on newly emerging rhythms, ruptures, and experiences specific to modernity as on the inevitable dis-appearance of more traditional modes and practices of human activity. Likewise, the respect for durational continuity in their shooting practice went hand in hand with the ultimately fragmented and discontinuous nature of the Archive's accu-mulated documents. Tradition and modernity thus do not exist in opposition in Kahn's films, but as coextensives. Therefore, before we can delve deeper into the relationship between daily life (as reconfigured in Kahn's films) and *la durée*, we will need a new understanding of Bergson's key concept. The first step of my revi-sionary reading of duration is, therefore, to question the supposedly absolute op-position between *la durée* and the *machinisme* of daily life and to reevaluate the reduction of duration, in Theodor Adorno's critique, to "the undifferentiated flow of life" from which the "dialectical salt" of history has been "washed away."[42] Wed-ded formally to the "flow of life" continuum associated with prolonged durational shooting (and the realist film theories of Bazin and Kracauer), Kahn's films also contain the interfering grit (history) of the everyday.

BERGSON AND THE EVERYDAY

One of the reasons Bergson's works became so popular during his own lifetime rested on his belief that "even in its most profound analyses and highest synthe-ses, philosophy should speak the language of the everyday."[43] Later critics of Berg-son (like Georg Lukács, Theodor Adorno, Max Horkheimer, and Henri Lefebvre) would have been amused at this gesture to the vernacular and the practical world, coming as it did from a philosopher whose eyes and ears seemed to be closed shut (as Benjamin argued) to the "inhospitable blinding age of big-scale industrial-ism."[44] *Creative Evolution* offers us one of many poses of Bergsonian withdrawal figured as a retreat from the visual exterior to the embodied interior:

> I am going to close my eyes, stop my ears, extinguish one by one the sensations that come to me from the outer world. Now it is done; all my perceptions vanish, the material universe sinks into silence and the night. I subsist, however, and cannot help myself subsisting. I am still there, with the organic sensations which come to me from the surface and from the interior of my body, with the recollections which my past perceptions have left behind them—nay, with the impression, most positive and full, of the void I have just made about me. (*CE* 278)

Yet even though Bergson is regularly asking us to close our eyes in his philosophical texts, he never loses sight of the everyday, understood as the result of accelerated capitalism upon that "outer world" of daily life.[45] First and foremost, Bergson felt that the radical difference of his age resided in the newness of "big-scale industrialism." In *Creative Evolution* he predicted that in thousands of years to come "the broad lines of the present age" would be defined not by wars and revolutions but by the impact of "the steam-engine, and the procession of inventions of every kind that accompanied it," the depths of whose "shock" in the domain of "human relations" humanity was just beginning to feel (*CE* 138–39). Although he might have amended this definition after 1918 to include the shocks of mechanized warfare, Bergson was always responding to, and not simply trying to escape (as Lukács argued), the transformed nature of the world around him.[46]

Bergson's drive to make philosophy answerable to concrete reality was not only evident in his engagement at the broadest level with the major cultural struggles of his time (between positivism and spiritualism, scientific and religious humanism, secular republicanism and Catholic nationalism, patriotism and universalism); it also operated at the micro-level in the choice of examples used in his philosophical texts. Bergson regularly clothes his arguments in what he would have referred to as "the ready-made garments" (*CE* 48), or familiar conceptual appeal, of modern visual and recording technologies—not only the cinematograph, but photography, the moving panorama, the kaleidoscope, the phantasmagoria and magic lantern dissolving views, the stereoscope, and even the phonograph.[47] If Bergson himself acknowledged his overdependence on the metaphorical applicability of some of these philosophical toys (*CE* 306), his familiarity with them indicates more than a brief exposure to the urban distractions of modernity, which he seems to have preferred over more sedate provincial alternatives.[48]

Bergson stated explicitly the connection between his philosophy and one particular attraction of Parisian daily life, the cinema, in the interview he gave to Michel Georges-Michel published in the newspaper *Le Journal* in 1914 (fig. 3.1).[49] The topic of the interview, not coincidentally, was the relevance of cinema to philosophical inquiry. As a prelude to his discussion of that topic, Bergson claimed that

> The philosopher must keep abreast of events happening in the outside world [*des événements de la vie extérieure*]. Anything new that I have been able to bring to phi-

losophy has always had a base in experience. In order to write my book *Matter and Memory*, I studied for five years hundreds of cases of memory loss while interviewing aphasiacs; I consecrated ten years to biology before undertaking *Creative Evolution*.

He might also have added that in order to write *Time and Free Will* (1889) he had immersed himself in neuro-psychiatric research on hypnosis, suggestion, and ideodynamism.[50] Thus, in contrast to the received image of Bergson as the philosopher who blinkered the outside world in his pursuit of the "inner life," he actually understood himself to be forging a new philosophy that rejected abstract speculation in favor of a basis "in experience," lived reality (particularly of time), and the events of *la vie extérieure*.[51] Of particular interest to our discussion is the explicit cinematic content of Bergson's experience of the outside world:

> I first went to the cinematograph several years ago. I was a witness to it from its beginnings. It is obvious that this invention, the complement of still photography, can suggest new ideas to the philosopher.

Leaving aside for the moment a discussion of the "new ideas" cinema suggested to Bergson, it is clear that he regarded himself as a keen observer and thinker of this recent invention. The curiously empiricist attachment to eye-witnessing that Bergson (a staunch critic of positivism) displayed in the newspaper interview appeared even more bluntly in his earlier claim that all his arguments could be tested by what he referred to as "the observation of everyday life" (*MM* 112).

If the empirical evidence of *la vie extérieure* made up one neutral layer of Bergson's multilayered everyday, then his second more condemnatory invocation of the everyday appears in the form of a *veil of inauthentic experience* that separates us from true life.[52] For Bergson everyday experience in the industrial age, whose shocks society was only beginning to comprehend, was characterized by the hegemony of spatial categories and the dwindling of emphatic temporal experience. Bergson saw this situation as the deplorable outcome of the mathematicizing tendency of Enlightenment rationality, materialized by the late nineteenth century in the increased rationalization and mechanization that fueled both industrial capitalism and positivist science. Typifying an enslavement to the "functions of abstraction, generalization and reasoning," capitalism and science had succeeded in consolidating the spatialization of time, evident, for example, in their ability to measure, carve up, and consume time with the aid of technologies like the chronometer (a favorite nemesis within Bergson's texts).[53] The modern spatialization of time ultimately drove a wedge, for Bergson, between the space of conscious or mechanical thought (always divisible) and the time or duration of memory (always indivisible). At a more general level, the spatialized grid through which life, language, and perception operated under ordinary circumstances thus became the default object of critique in all of Bergson's works.

FIGURE 3.1   Michel Georges-Michel's interview on the topic of cinema with Henri Bergson in the daily newspaper *Le Journal*, February 20, 1914, 7. (Association pour la conservation et la reproduction photographique de la presse, Paris)

A foundational example of Bergson's examination of spatialized time appeared in *Matter and Memory* when he distinguished between the expansive and formless temporal quality of duration (time lived through) and what he called "time in general" (*MM* 206). The minimal temporal quality of the latter, he argued, characterized "daily experience" where "the exigencies of life" (*MM* 208) control our consciousness, and where in order to survive we take in the ceaselessly mobile world around us in the pictorial form of "quasi-instantaneous views" (*MM* 209). These automatic, snapshot-like incisions (obviously a reference to chronophotography) enable us to slice through and immobilize the flow of life "[i]n just the same way [as] the multitudinous successive positions of a runner" (209) might be captured in serial photography. Bergson then compared this mechanically precise representation of temporality with a second, nonmechanical vision of time, one in which the separated successive views of the runner "are contracted into a single symbolic attitude, which our eyes perceive, which art reproduces, and which becomes for us all the image of a man running" (209). Once again, maximizing his reference to an everyday uneventful occurrence—a man running—Bergson seems, at first, to equate the precontracted state of the instantaneous photographic views of the runner (whether understood as separately framed as in a Muybridge study or multiply-enclosed on a single plate as in a Marey chronophotographic study) with a more diminished if mechanically exact reality. In contrast to these scientifically irrefutable slices of time, the contraction

of separate views "into a single symbolic attitude" (209) typical of the human eye
or the artist's brush appear to be more superior, if not quite attaining the level of
duration, in his estimation.

What needs emphasizing here is the automatic and arbitrary nature of the instantaneous views of the runner that reflect the mechanically standardized matrix
of "homogeneous space and homogeneous time" (*MM* 211). Indifferent to reality's
ceaseless mobility, these snapshots of time originate in "[t]he glance which falls *at
any moment* on the things about us" (*MM* 209).[54] Operating in a slightly less abstracted and disinterested space, the human or aesthetic eye condenses real duration into "a single symbolic attitude" (*MM* 209) producing a portrait of time reflective of a more invested framing (rather than arbitrary surveying) of the moment
at hand. Nonetheless, it too is trapped in the prison of the everyday—a fortress of
homogeneous time cut off from the ungraspable plurality of real duration.

As it emerges from these diverse treatments by Bergson, everyday life bears the
outline of an abstracted and reified condition, that life-negating realm that would
be taken up in divergent ways by Georg Lukács and Martin Heidegger.[55] However,
in addition to these two invocations of the everyday—the first a more neutral reference to the historical events of *la vie extérieure*, the second a more negative reference to space-enslaved, life-denying forces—Bergson also offers a more utopian
version. This third everyday has the potential to reconnect or produce an exchange
with its opposite, the nonmechanical unpredictable realm of creative (as opposed
to mechanistic) evolution. Never expansively treated, Bergson's third everyday
does nonetheless appear when he makes it clear that the purpose of his philosophy
was not merely the diagnosis but what he calls the transformation and transfigura-
tion of "everyday life."[56] It is during such moments that we can discern the outline
of an attempt to fashion the everyday as the site of both alienation and dis-alien-
ation, and the catalyst for life-affirming and life-denying forces.

This was the side of Bergsonism that would also provide a model for diverse
utopian reflections on the everyday that would resurface in the work of Benjamin,
Lefebvre, and much later, Deleuze. More to the point, it was also the aspect of
Bergsonism that French film critics of the late 1910s and 1920s debated over. In
other words, what was ultimately at stake, especially for the film avant-garde, in
Bergson's two theories of perception mentioned above (the "any moment" versus the "privileged" moment) was the degree to which they imply the camera and
human-aesthetic eye in opposition or interpenetration with each other, and, concomitantly, the extent to which both the camera and human-aesthetic eye were
positioned irrevocably as opposites to duration.

A relevant place to unravel these Bergsonian definitions of the everyday is in
those references to the quotidian that emerge in his more formal philosophical
commentaries on the cinema. In the final chapter of *Creative Evolution*, Bergson
introduces one of the most sphinx-like analogies of modern philosophy. He as-

serts that the "mechanism of our ordinary knowledge is of a cinematographical kind" (*CE* 306); meaning that everyday human perception and the film camera (in its recording *not* projecting capacity) operate in a similar manner by dividing reality into individual views or frames, which even when reanimated or projected only produce an illusion of the true experience of reality-as-movement and time-as-indivisible.[57] For Bergson, the mind and the photographic-based film camera function according to a conceptual, abstract, and spatializing "habit," defined by a regrettable dependency on "tak[ing] stable views of the instability," flux, and irreducibility that make up the authentic condition of life, or what Bergson calls "duration" (*CE* 303).

Here and elsewhere, Bergson's key word for invoking the unthinking, repetitive essence of the everyday is "habit." He goes on to define habit as that which mechanically and automatically orders our life, that which we are unable to separate ourselves from (what Siegfried Kracauer would refer to as a clinging "skin"), that which we do unconsciously and involuntarily; in short, the perceptual bent of our "customary knowledge" (*MM* 186).[58] Bergson conceives of the everyday as a survival space where standard perception is on call, constantly answering the utilitarian "needs of practical life" (*CE* 210) in a condition of servitude doomed to contort "pure duration into space" (*MM* 185).[59] Summarizing the position of his three major texts in a lecture given at Oxford in 1911, Bergson asserted:

> it is in *spatialised time* that we *ordinarily* place ourselves. We have no interest in listening to the uninterrupted humming of life's depths [that we are open to once we close our eyes and withdraw from consciousness]. And yet that is where real duration is.[60]

Figured within the terms of a pro-aural and anti-ocular bias (which we have heard echoed across the accidental shock of memory aroused by Levi-Strauss's Chopin melody and Jean Santeuil's pianist), Bergson puts forward a critique of ordinary experience (and by implication the cinematographical representation of reality) as that which we *see*, suffer, survive, and live through, without ever really *looking* at. This habitual, accustomed eye is barred from that intensified sense of vision Jean Comandon intended in his own Bergsonian privileging of *regarder* (to look) over *voir* (to see).[61] In contrast to the experience of spatialized time in which we see but do not look, duration signals a conscious withdrawal from the "ordinary, *everyday*, good and necessary concerns of human living" into an experience (analogous to certain forms of aesthetic production and chance encounters with forgotten memories) which "the habits more adapted to ordinary living tend to block."[62] Accordingly, duration implies a sense of time endured rather than time measured.

Contrary to the dominant criticism in the 1930s of the conception of duration as a philosophy of experience totally divorced from the "necessary concerns of human living," Bergson's writings actually constituted an engaged response, rather than a naïve and idealist reaction, to the transformation of modern daily life by mechanization, industrialization, and mass mediation. Missing from the 1930s critiques of Bergson as a bourgeois idealist is the possibility that in his philosophy, the everyday, understood as the habitual and repetitive condition of quantitative homogeneous similarity, is never entirely the opposite of duration, understood as the singular, unrepeatable, experience of qualitative heterogeneous difference.[63] If, as I argue in chapters 6 and 7, early French film theory's encounter with the everyday in the 1920s demonstrated the cinematic falseness of this opposition, that is because Bergson had already done so philosophically. He even opens the fourth cinematographical chapter of *Creative Evolution* by heading off potential critiques of *la durée* with his intention to define more precisely "a philosophy which sees in duration the very stuff of reality" (*CE* 272). We can also hear him responding to his critics in the 1911 Oxford lectures when he warns that "to break away from practical life" (as his concept of *la durée* clearly proposes) does not mean "to turn one's back upon it" (*PC* 254). In short, what on the surface appear to be opposites (*la durée* and the everyday) in Bergson's thought actually operate as counterpoints capable of interaction and complementarity.

Typical of the 1930s turn against Bergson, Walter Benjamin (following Max Horkheimer and echoing Mikhail Bakhtin's earlier criticism) condemned the lack of historicity and contingency in the notion of duration, castigating it as a facile evasion of death.[64] At the same time, Benjamin (like Bakhtin) was also sensitive to the residual grit of salt, "the stuff of reality" that remained in *durée*.[65] He clearly understood that the milieux of the everyday and duration, or to use the Proustian opposition of his own argument, voluntary and involuntary memory, were not mutually exclusive.[66] Benjamin may have asserted that Bergson (like Baudelaire) shut his eyes to the obvious signs of modernity, but only to emphasize how this gesture of refusal enabled the philosopher to more forcefully register the "spontaneous after-image" of his modern environment.[67] We should recall that Bergson himself described the experience of after-images in the opening of his 1901 essay "The World of Dreams." Associating them with the "*visual dust*" (*WD* 24) of everyday life, the grit of the real lodged in the eye of the dreamer, Bergson invoked after-images as the shadow of history that persists in the experience of duration. Supporting Benjamin's more sympathetic approach, these comments allow us to see how Bergson may have broken away from practical life and history, but was far from having turned his back on them completely.

Another of Bergson's overlooked comments regarding duration's relation to its supposed blind spot, the "prey of time" (to invoke Baudelaire), will be helpful here. If for Bergson, an impoverished scientific perception of objects rests on "the idea that time does not bite into them," then, he contends in *Creative Evolution*, "real duration" is not that which denies time's destructive drive; it is that "which gnaws on things, and leaves on them the mark of its tooth" (*CE* 8, 46). Far from being drained of historical temporality or cleansed of the grit of everyday contingency, duration's flow does in fact mix with the eroding eddies of time reflective of life lived and endured. Bergson's stance of withdrawal should therefore not be reduced to an anti-modern conservative reaction to the radically altered experience of daily life during this period. Rather, it symbolizes an attempt to *think alongside and through* that transformation and in particular the "procession of inventions of every kind that accompanied" the new visual experiences and perception of life *and* death in an age of large-scale industrialism, consumer capitalism, and mechanical reproduction.

As made apparent in the *Le Journal* interview and the more well-known commentary in *Creative Evolution*, the cinema (the theatrical exhibition site) and the cinematograph (the actual apparatus) were crucial components of the modern everyday environment to which Bergson was responding—in that Benjaminian, eyes-wide-shut dialectical manner. And if habit connoted the everyday, that element of experience as inseparable from us as our skin (as Kracauer would have it), then the camera, as so many film critics of the late teens and twenties would argue, was one of modernity's exemplary technologies that responded to and negotiated this ordinary experience. Film not only glided along the surface of reality but picked away at the edge of the epidermis of daily life. At this point it is crucial to stress that Bergson never condemned unequivocally the cinematograph when he posited its analogous relationship to the cut-and-paste habits of everyday perception. Rather, the point of his cinematic invocation was to posit a tendency, in order then to suggest that this conceptual leaning toward spatialization and immobilization of both the cinematograph and our ordinary thinking patterns can be unmade. And if that which blocks habitual perception can be unblocked, then the radically non-habitual vision unleashed by the camera would have a central role to play in this perceptual release.

Far from rejecting outright the cinematographical model of perception (representation and thought), Bergson actually pursued a more conciliatory direction, suggesting that we must learn to "reverse the bent of our intellectual habits" (*CE* 314). Recovering contact with "the other half of the real" (*CE* 343) with which we have lost touch is realizable for Bergson not outside but only within a new orientation of our intellectual habits and ordinary perception. This is why it has been said that Bergson's overarching philosophical goal was to think backwards.[68] The applicability of this goal was not limited to philosophical discussions. For if Bergson was claiming that the ordinary, conventional, and default hardwiring of the film camera and our perceptual faculties can and indeed need to be reoriented, then this claim also offered what in many ways became the defining goal of the French film avant-garde of the twenties. Just because the camera is a machine, these critics suggested, does not mean film cannot be thought nonmechanistically. Following Bergson's anti-mechanistic command, these critics resisted reducing the cinematograph to its physico-chemical mechanisms and remained open to exploring the potential interpenetration that it posed between matter and life, and seeing and looking.

FILM AS THE "VISUAL DUST" OF HISTORY

As film critics of the late teens knew well, Bergson's engagement with the mechanized dimension of modern experience existed well before the cinematographic imaginary of *Creative Evolution*. Bergson's interest in the interpenetration of daily life and mechanicity also appears in an earlier and more accessible text, *Laughter* (1900).[69] In that work he turned to an investigation of laughter as a common reaction that powerfully registers the infiltration of everyday life by the immobilizing forces of mechanicity. Understood in its most expansive sense, laughter for Bergson represented a response to a perception of the "deflection of life towards the mechanical" (*L* 82). In its more specific embodied sense, the philosopher argued that laughter was aroused by the troubling superimposition of the inanimate over the animate: "The attitudes, gestures and movements of the human body are laughable in exact proportion as that body reminds us of a mere machine" (79). Laughter, one might say, emerged out of the after-image produced when two views, of life and *machinisme*, were superimposed over each other. The perceptual tension of two images held at once in the eye is important here. For comedy was not to be found in merely any situation where the body becomes rigid, resembling either a "puppet" or a "machine" (two of Bergson's favorite examples), but in those in which the human body appears simultaneously to give the "impression of a living being" and the "impression of being a thing" (80, 93).

We laugh, therefore, when there is a sudden temporary rupture in the normal state of affairs and life deflects toward, without entirely succumbing to, the mechanical. Comedy thus records the threatening contamination of the living (flux, movement, continuity) by qualities usually attributed to the dead (rigidity, stillness, discontinuity). If it should now be obvious that cinema, as the era's premier location for the living-dead or the "deflection of life toward the mechanical," was a prime site of this contamination, in the more explicit focus of *Laughter* Bergson was ultimately arguing that laughter is a protective mechanism, a therapeutic engagement with a deeply embedded and historically attuned consciousness of alienation. Bergson does not reduce laughter (or by implication cinema) to a response to the comedic; rather, he analyzes it as a condition that registers at the level of the body our most intimate and innate fears of living in a mechanized society. The same might be argued for his thinking on the cinematograph, which ultimately offers to bring together the organic and the inorganic within a new combination of vital matter.

Bergson's broader engagement with the everyday, as well as his more specific understanding of laughter (and by implication film) as the dreaded superimposition of the living upon the dead, may be brought to bear on a film from the Kahn

FIGURE 3.2   Footage of public urinals, titled *Paris: Vespasienne sur les grands boulevards,*
Octobre 1913 (cameraman unknown). (MAK: frame enlargement 102695)

Archive titled *Paris: Vespasienne sur les grands boulevards, Octobre 1913*. Typical
of the earlier tendency that we find in the Archive for statically framed yet dynamically unfolding, uninterrupted shots of modern urban life, the footage is also representative of the most culturally transgressive views in the Archive. Negotiating the
broader instructions to focus on what remained unseen within the familiar, Kahn's
cameraman (in this instance unknown) records a site and practice that provided
an informal street spectacle structured around visibility and invisibility, the public
and the private: the routine of men waiting outside or using one of the public toilets
(*vespasienne*) that open onto the street in Paris (fig. 3.2). As with all of Kahn's films,
the footage of the *vespasienne* solicits multiple interpretations. It might be read as
a cinematic version of the classificatory obsession intent on filing away every corner
and human type of the capital's architectural and social body since the mid-nineteenth century; or a social reform document intended to praise these relatively new
monuments to modern public hygiene; or a particularly striking example of the
mode of disclosed witnessing pervasive in early cinema. As valid as these and other
readings are for understanding the representational and intertextual dimensions
of the film, the question I want to pursue here is how the *vespasienne* footage, and
in particular its performance of disclosed witnessing, might be placed in dialogue
with Bergson's discourse of laughter, mechanicity, and the everyday.

Once the men in the public toilet catch sight of the camera positioned opposite them, thereby allowing the mechanical gaze to enter their field of consciousness and perception, they take their eyes off the matter at hand and stare back. In a transition typical of the ubiquitous return of the camera's gaze in early cinema, the men in the *vespasienne* shift from being caught truly unaware to acknowledging the inescapability of their being filmed. When they notice the camera they stiffen and become transfixed amidst the flow of their ordinary actions because of the unexpected interruption of the mechanical into their previously unconscious gestures. One of the reasons that this film stands out from the miles of sober footage in the Kahn Archive—proven by the fact that it was perhaps the first Kahn film to be resurrected after thirty-five years or so of sleep in the compilation documentary *Paris 1900* made by Nicole Védrès in 1947—concerns the laughter it arouses across time. Present-day viewers often laugh at the film not only for the more lighthearted reason of catching men in a compromised position, or the more weighty feeling that one is watching a raw and uncensored fragment of the history of daily life as it was actually lived. In addition, we laugh, according to Bergson, because we witness in the few minutes of footage the "deflection of life toward the mechanical"—because the return of the gaze, that most auratic and animating of spectator interpellations, is here accompanied by restraint and immobility, a deadening fixity. To paraphrase Bergson, "the very litheness of the bodies seems to stiffen as we gaze, and the [stage] actors themselves seemed transformed into lifeless automata" (*L* 83). Watching the film one is wedged between the experience of Bergson's key categories, mobility and stasis, those two states that the multimedia Kahn Archive constantly puts into play. Just when we thought we were alive, responding with laughter to the presence of the past, death creeps in. The unsettling suspension of the men's action, these intimate pauses in the surrounding flow of life on the street, is felt in countless other Kahn films in which children and adults become momentarily trapped in the headlights of the camera's vision, both delightfully and horrifically transfixed. In such films, the stiffened milieu of habit and the intuitive flux of becoming are disturbingly intermingled in the unique industrial choreography rehearsed in any number of cameraman-subject encounters.

The recognition of the camera, however, does not always produce these dehumanizing transactions whereby the living is contaminated by the dead. Many other films in the Archive also tremble with life as a result of the penetration of the animate by the inanimate that occurs with the sudden (rather than constant) acknowledgment of the camera. In these latter films, this enervation reverses the passage from mobility to stasis, and the shock of the camera seems to breathe life into a previously lifeless and dehumanized milieu. For example, in one of several shots of Parisians queued in breadlines common during the postwar economic depression of the early 1920s, the repetitive formation of the queue—in its linear spatialization of time, a social emblem for the Bergsonian alienation of the modern everyday if there ever was one—is broken when a young woman notices the camera shooting from behind and then breaks out momentarily into a spontaneous jig before she exits with her provisions frame left.[70] Here the interruption of the camera into the deadening routine of a specifically gendered rendition of daily life is cause for a reversal of habit, a momentary celebration if not escape or resistance.[71] The nameless woman's spontaneous reclamation of place from the planned order and anonymity of space also presents another of the Kahn Archive's humble homages (mentioned in chapter 2) to the equally anonymous man with the movie camera. The demarcation between duration and habit, continuity and discontinuity, authentic and inauthentic experience is not enforced but blurred by the witnessing presence of the camera. The important point is that the footage is not a literal representation of ideal duration, but an animation of the conception of duration as the unpredictable becoming of time released from within the supposedly hostile "cinematographic method."

Read in terms of the indeterminate, archival after-life into which Kahn's films moved after their original "life," Kahn's footage leaves space for a range of virtual possibilities between the historically contingent instants in which the film was shot and re-viewed over fifty years later. André Bazin and Kracauer literally occupied this interpretive space at different points when they viewed and wrote about *Paris 1900*'s archival footage, which included Kahn's film of the *vespasienne*. Bazin used it as an opportunity to connect film's virtuality to its tragic track with the destructive and preservational aspects of time, while Kracauer turned to it to illustrate the historically critical shudder that accompanies the default laughter aroused by outdated photographs and films.[72] Continuing certain themes of the Bergsonian debate with cinema, both critics intuited from the after-life of a scrap of Kahn footage that if film mattered historically it was because it involved a matter of life and death.

Summarizing Bergson's cinematically inflected circuit of thought, his student Jacques Chevalier wrote that "the human intellect, in fact, only feels truly at home among inanimate objects; it is only really satisfied when it is able to translate things, by a cinematographical method, into manageable signs, into fixed signs—[...] into magnitudes which are measurable, in short, into quantity."[73] I have shown, however, that the broader intent of this classic Bergsonian diagnosis in general runs in the opposite direction, aiming to rehouse our intellect, to unmake our habits, and settle into a new abode of perception and reception. Implicit within this remaking of habit is a deepening and widening of our usually blinkered vision. Ironically what Bergson doesn't seem concerned about (but what his philosophy, with its inclination to think *not just about but through* the cinematograph and other inventions, unleashes) is the radical potential of the contingent once released from within film's otherwise leveling, "any moment" survey of the real. As many commentators and critics noted, however, film's new accounting of the world of views, facts, and documents did not convert the medium's unframed details into "manageable signs" (as Baudelaire hoped might be done with photography by limiting its application to the functional needs of those who collect views and facts: the traveler, the naturalist, the archivist). Instead, film's photographic-based positivist survey of the world released a new counter-positivist or counter-archival disorder of signs all of its own—what Benjamin called the "unruly desire" aroused in the eye of the beholder of photography's indexical plenitude.[74]

Glimpses of this disorder appear in the visible disruptions posed by the acknowledged camera in the above examples. In its capacity for excessive documentation and in its interruption into the spectacle of urban living, the new disorder released by the cinematograph's mechanistically blasé "any moment" instigated a sort of house-moving of the mind. Like intellect (and language), the film camera may superficially operate with "measuring tape in hand" (CE 215)—think here of those "kilometers of film" to which the Journal du Ciné-Club reduced the Kahn films or, similarly, the Archive's ledger book, which tabulates each foot of film—but that did not mean that what it recorded only amounted to a quantifiable stock of parceled views. After all, as Bergson claims in Matter and Memory, "our daily life" is far from being spatially or temporally impregnable and is always susceptible to the "rift" of "our past psychical life" which may "slip in its image" (MM 95) into the otherwise preordered habitual arrangement of the present. For all their negative associations, habit and its attendant terms (the everyday and cinematographical thought) are for Bergson unstable, volatile, and permeable conditions.

The significance of the disclosed camera in the above two films moves beyond that which it records and preserves in the representational realm—that limited relation to the past that Bergson would define, as I discuss in the next section, as archival memory—and rests upon the way in which its acknowledged presence opens up passages of exchange between habit and duration, between what is repeatable and what is unreproducible. In such moments we also witness the knotting together of two of Bergson's temporal nets for catching the everyday, nets in which the key debates of film criticism from the twenties would become entangled: the "any moment" of photographic-based instantaneous recording and the "privileged moment" of the human or aesthetic eye (CE 330). Of course, the inevitable encounter between these two moments, in the actual experience of the human eye in conjunction with other senses in front of the cinema screen, is what Bergson leaves out for the most part, and what the film critics of the late teens and early twenties will explicitly address.[75] In other words, the above readings of Kahn's films respond to the point at which the any-moment of the film's automatic recording capacities finds itself interlaced with the singular privileged moments and contractions of the human eye across time. These interpenetrations do not issue exclusively from the belly of the camera (what Bergson calls the cinematograph "in a neutral state"); rather, they speak to what goes on in front of the screen in the multivalent web of reception and perception, punctured by the spatial and temporal "rifts" within Bergson's own time and across time (as suggested by Bazin and Kracauer's responses to *Paris 1900*).

These film readings also serve well as an indication of the status of textual analysis in this book, as they depend upon two approaches. First, they acknowledge the open *and* shut nature of Kahn's films. His fragmented footage always points to a beyond—the overwhelming remainder of examples in the Archive that mock the fantasy of analytical completion while offering the virtuality of constant becoming. Although always rooted in visible fixed determinants of time and space, Kahn's films always break free from historicism's chronological, narrative drive. Second, the readings display a Proustian preference for mining the accidental and casual details and shocks in the film's surface. Yet far from constituting an "anything goes" attitude to film interpretation or an attempt to disclose some secret, marginalized unsaid of Kahn's films, these two approaches entail being sensitive to their dominant discursive specificity, that is, their unique nature as archival films. For unlike ordinary commercial films, films made for an archive have no original privileged moment of interpretation; reception remains an eternally virtual and deferred (rather than an already known) element of their futurocentric condition.

BERGSON AND COUNTER-ARCHIVAL MEMORY

The full import of Bergson's ideas upon the Archives de la Planète cannot be gauged, therefore, at the level of the single film (or for that matter the single frame). We need to move beyond the individual documents to the wider framing of the project—its archival motivation—and back to Bergson's earlier work in *Matter and Memory* to grasp the Archive's relation to a broader crisis in the archival mediation of a relation to the past.

Although there is no master catalogue that lists or organizes the entire film collection in the Archives de la Planète, most of its films belong to series whose topics were probably conceived as the offspring of Kahn's headline view of the world and Brunhes' geographical classificatory matrix. Certainly, at first glance, nothing could seem further from the terrain of Bergsonian philosophy than an attempt to record life according to the prearranged, "ready-made" (*CE* 48) categories of newspaper headlines or spatially dominated geographic classifications, least of all films that belonged to series with topics as unphilosophical as prostitutes, public toilets, boulevard construction, marriage parties, street parades, religious festivals, and children's entertainment. Moreover, Bergson's anti-spatial, anti-mechanistic conception of memory appears to be exactly what the Archive opposed. Where Bergson mocked the idea that memory could be put away in drawers or inscribed in a register, the Kahn Archive proudly reduced the past to fragments of photographic-based media, stored in boxes and tabulated in registers, ready for access via mechanical animation.

Paradoxically, with chapter titles like "Of the Selection of Images for Conscious Presentation," "Of the Recognition of Images," "Of the Survival of Images," and "The Delimiting and Fixing of Images," one might be excused for mistaking *Matter and Memory* for a treatise on the practices of archiving visual media.[76] Yet far from legitimating the growing archival applications of photography in the domains of medical diagnosis, criminal detection, anthropological typing, and other disciplinary practices of the state in the late nineteenth century, *Matter and Memory* is the work in which Bergson built his philosophical reputation for arguing against the notion of the brain as an archive that stores and catalogues memories as though they were photographic-like documents saved from the ravages *of time* and rendered available for consultation *at any time*.[77] True to his own rhetorical habits, Bergson begins his attack with the critique of another bad habit:

> We are so much accustomed to reverse, for the sake of action, the real order of things, we are so strongly obsessed by images drawn from space, that we cannot hinder ourselves from asking where memories are stored up. We understand that physico-chemical phenomena take place in the brain, that the brain is in the body, the body in the air which surrounds it, etc; but the past, once achieved, if it is retained, where is it? (*MM* 148)

At the basis of this skepticism toward the memory-as-archive model (exemplified in Proust's description of the vast photographic "archives of [Santeuil's] memory") is Bergson's ongoing questioning of our default tendency to perceive reality in spatialized terms and thus to pose the wrong question—"where is it?"—in relation to the past and memory. He thus rails against the misguided quest "to *localize* past or even present perceptions," to search for "an abiding *place*" or "a *region* in which memories congeal and accumulate" (*MM* 151, 125, 126).[78] Although he never engages in a discussion of actual archives, they are the dominant after-image of his argument, which is consistently housed in the vocabulary of archival topography—"storehouse" (*MM* 74), "depositories" (130), "receptacle" and "warehouse" (148). Conventional stocktaking sites posit for Bergson the opposite of memory's true place of residence, a place that is nowhere but in time, or if somewhere, closer to what the later Proust of *Remembrance of Things Past* describes as a "void."[79]

Bergson is equally distrustful of the archival metaphor in *Creative Evolution* in which he opposes the idea that "our remembrances are stored away as inert imprints" and decries the tendency of perception to "store up" what amounts to "only snapshots of the changing reality" (*CE* 317). Interestingly, just as Kahn was establishing his Archive, Bergson was still exercising his archival complaint in "Perception of Change" (1911). There he decries the brain and perception's drive to "classify," "label," and "categorize," in order to reveal the abstracted manner in which inauthentic memory works—"by storing [certain parts of the past] away in a kind of box" (253, 261). The words that Bergson supplies to describe this erroneously imagined place (the brain) in which memories are stored should leave us in no doubt as to his rejection of the possibility of capturing and locating true memory through a quasi-archival framework.[80]

If there is indeed an archival after-image in Bergson's work, the documents he draws on to flesh out that metaphor do not resemble those of conventional paper archives but rather those of the newer photographic or film archives (the latter on the verge of emerging, as we will see in the next chapter, just as *Matter and Memory* was being published). In addition to rejecting the archive-brain metaphor, he attacks the common understanding of perception as "a kind of photographic view of things" (*MM* 38) that is then developed in the brain and stored for future reference in an ever-expanding mental archive. This model of memory, as a sort of filing cabinet of the mind, ignores the permeability and constantly evolving cross-referencing that goes on between the supposed interior (the past) and exterior (the present) of the archive. The filing cabinet's metal compartmentalization denies the mental "rifts" between our psychic life and the present. For Bergson, "there is no [present] perception which is not full of memories" (*MM* 33), and "the photograph, if photograph there be, is already taken, already developed in the very heart of things" rather than in the developing laboratory of our minds (38). In other words, the photograph precedes what it captures because reality is always already subject, "in the very heart" of its being, to the spatializing and immobilizing of photographic development. Likewise, our brains do not develop an image of that reality since they are part and parcel of that reality.

In all of Bergson's struggles with memory the model of the archive lingers. But instead of rejecting the archive altogether, Bergson posited what I call a *counter-archival reconceptualization of memory*. He resituates memory from the warehouse of the brain to the "virtual state" (*MM* 240) of the organism or body, a counter-archival non-site still tethered to the accumulated but *unrecollected* past "which acts no longer but which might act" (240) by inserting itself into the present. If memory, in its most habitual archival mode, works by sifting, sorting, and selecting from the always present past in response to the action- and future-oriented needs of the present, then in its counter-archival mode memory has access, unmotivated by any practical function, to the archive's unrecollected, out-of-circulation, virtual plane of perception.[81] The counter-archival, therefore, posits a type of memory at home, rather than at war, with forgetting. In contrast to what Deleuze (in his book on Foucault) decries as "the brief memory inscribed in . . . archives" and limited by a causal, successive temporality "that comes afterwards and is the opposite of forgetting," the counter-archival expands memory's parameters into a deeper and longer period of time.[82] To use Deleuze's language, the counter-archival *doubles* the present, rendering it "endlessly forgotten and reconstituted," its "fold" always merging with the potential newness of its "unfolding" (107). Although Deleuze's distrust of the archive in its conventional sense recalls Bergson, both philosophers theorize memory within and against a not entirely jettisoned model of the archive that allows the possibility of archiving otherwise.

For Bergson, memory is not preserved in archival-like individual documents, but in what he calls, in a rhetorically counter-archival move, "images," those non-realist and nonidealist emanations traceable only to "an existence placed halfway between the 'thing' and the 'representation'" (*MM* 9). Unlike "symbols," which for Bergson refer to mediations such as language, these so-called "images" (of which the body is a central example) are nonlinguistic and nonrepresentational. Neither mirroring the outside world (as in realism) nor existing only in our mind's eye (as in idealism), Bergson's "images" intentionally confuse expectations of the empiricist and the metaphysician. They provide Bergson with a Trojan horse for invading the Cartesian mind-body, subject-object, perception-representation dualism and for countering the writing-based mnemonic foundations of the conventional archive. "Images" thus appear as the appropriate target of a newly de-ocularcentrized eye. Likewise, the self for Bergson is no longer the seat of a personal archive of memories but a decentered point amongst a dispersed universal continuum of images. To paraphrase Bergson, the archive, if there can be an archive, is actually not confined to the brain. It stretches over multiple interrelated planes in which our brains are just one level and in which the past is never fully restored but constantly adapted to the needs of the present.

So how does memory operate in the dispersion of the subject-object divide in which it is the body rather than the brain that remembers? Remembering that the Kahn Archive is not just a storehouse of the present but of the *everyday* present, it is crucial to delve even further into *Matter and Memory* as this is where Bergson articulates one of his key contributions to a theory of the everyday in his understanding of how the ordinary practices of "habit" register our most embodied relation to the past. Bergson characterizes "habit" as a "passive" or inferior type of memory that registers a past that never ceases to exist in the form of unconscious motor responses—in other words, "the remembrances that we evoke . . . [that] are always linked in some way to our present activity" (*WD* 36). These activities refer to those acquired habits that unconsciously get us through our daily routines, saving us from having to relearn a lesson taught long ago every time we know not to touch a burning flame. For Bergson the everyday habit is thus a subordinate form of memory that "acts our past experience, but does not call up its image" (*MM* 151).

On the surface one might posit affinities here with Sigmund Freud's more deterministic unearthing of habits of everyday speech, such as slips of the tongue and malapropisms, and their displaced and distorted relation to the psychic past as examined in *The Psychopathology of Everyday Life* (1901). Like that text, *Matter and Memory* was in part a response to studies of memory loss, particularly in those types of aphasia involving the partial loss of linguistic faculties. Both theorists of

memory were also interested in perception or consciousness as a selective and limiting process akin to the practice of archiving, a practice understood—as Deleuze
and Jacques Derrida will emphasize respectively vis-à-vis discussions of Michel
Foucault and Freud—as being grounded as much in forgetting and destroying as in
remembering and preserving.[83] Bergson shared Freud's belief that the past never
ceases to be ("The whole series of our past images remains present within us" [*MM*
95]), but he was not interested in interpreting or restoring psychic meaning to the
seemingly insignificant marginalia of gestures or speech. Nor did he centralize the
operation of repression, which stipulates that certain documents in the archive of
the unconscious are taken out of circulation, until further notice.[84] Rather, Bergson
framed habitual experience not as a text to be read but as a depletion of memory,
a sort of phantom limb of true experience, persistently twitching with recollection
but forever cut off from any real or emphatic connection to the past.

In one of Bergson's central examples of this type of memory, elaborated in his
second chapter's discussion of the recollection of a "lesson learned by heart" (motor
memory), we have "all the marks of a habit," because the lesson, once remembered
whole, contains "no mark which betrays its origin" (*MM* 80). Activated by practical
exigencies of "everyday experience" (86), this type of habit-memory "is part of my
present, exactly like my habit of walking or of writing; it is lived and acted" (80).
Bergson then delineates a second type of memory found in the psychological recollection of each successive reading or stage that went into the process of the lesson
learned by heart. In contrast to memory-as-habit, independent recollection is non-
habitual because it "is like an event in my life; its essence is to bear a date, and,
consequently, to be unable to occur again" (80). This unrepeatable type of memory
adheres "in the form of memory-images, [that is], all the events of our daily life as
they occur in time; it neglects no detail; it leaves to each fact, to each gesture, its
place and date" (81, 80).

At this point of his argument, Bergson seems to offer two types of memory,
learned recollection and spontaneous recollection (83). The first appears via repetition in the form of "motor mechanisms which make use of [the past]" (88) in
an impersonal manner that fixes upon the general; the second occurs in "personal
memory-images" which "picture all past events with their outline, their color and
their place in time" (88). Unlike the first type of habit-based memory—"seated in
the present," "looking only to the future" (82)—memory as independent recollection fixes upon the singular and the past. If at this stage of his argument a hierarchy
seems to order these two manifestations of memory—the *automatic* recognition
required of habitual memory appearing to be inferior to the *attentive* recognition
required for independent recollection (98)—then in his third and fourth chapters
both will be categorized together under the rubric of homogeneous thought and
contrasted to a third type of memory, pure memory. The hallmark of pure memory
is that it remains unrecollected, virtual, and heterogeneous; it points to the preservation of the past in and for itself. By the end of *Matter and Memory*, Bergson has

thus provided us with a pluralistic reformulation of memory that resembles more of an overarching elasticity (*MM* 104)—able to shrink and expand, according to the demands placed upon it in the present—than a stock of discrete, fixed, localizable documents stored in an archival area of the brain. This supple, indeed living, form of memory is what I term *counter-archival*; it unlocks the heterogeneous potential already within the archival framing of memory.

Although *Matter and Memory's* theory of memory is actually tripartite, its ultimate distinction between a homogeneous (or objective, fragmented, discontinuous, repeatable) and heterogeneous (or subjective, unfragmented, continuous, and unrepeatable) memory continues to underline the two types of knowledge outlined in *Creative Evolution*: cinematographical thought (which is spatial, conceptual, and quantitative) and intuitive thought (which is temporal, durational, and qualitative). The important point to stress, however, is that Bergson offers both motor memory and contemplative memory as extremes of memory. In other words, far from operating separately, "in normal life they are interpenetrating" (*MM* 155), producing a situation of coextensivity and interdependence that also implies the potential irruption of the one type of memory (and thought) into the other. The result is that we will often find ourselves experiencing the intermediate "mixed states" (93) between different planes of memory; we will be customarily split between the experience of the conscious automaton and the human who dreams his/her life instead of living it (155).

As mentioned in my previous reevaluation of the opposition of the everyday and duration, Bergson's dualisms do not signal a negation, rejection, or escape from the inferior category (of perception to memory, of space to time, of the archive to the "image," of passive memory to pure memory, of cinematographical thought to intuitive thought). Rather, they are a call to reverse the habitual tendency of that category. Keeping Bergson's open-ended approach in the foreground, it is now easier to appreciate how his protest against the cinematograph is not an attack upon film *tout court*. Instead, it is a selective critique of certain aspects—reducible to the illusion that "we can think the unstable by means of the stable" (*CE* 273)—of the camera's (and normal human perception's) photographic-based, spatially bound, movement-additive *method*, which by no means condemns our ability to think or mobilize the cinematographical method otherwise.

Similarly, if Bergson rejects the idea that memories reside in a place, he never suggests that the past simply disappears. Just as his philosophy is not antirationalist or irrationalist but counter-rationalist, expanding the supplementary element of Enlightenment rationalism, so too is his theory of memory not anti-archival but counter-archival as it still works within the idea of the self comprised of an endlessly accumulating past. In fact, like Freud, Bergson asserts the preservation of the past as an infinitely increasing stock of memories: "I believe indeed that all our past life is there, preserved in its most intimate details, that we never forget anything, and that everything which we have felt, perceived, thought and willed since the first stirrings of our consciousness lives on indestructibly" (*WD* 37).[85] In his faith that the past is guaranteed to protect even the most insignificant incidents, Bergson may not be relying upon the spatial safety of the archival metaphor, but he is surely still within the temporal catchment area of that metaphor as a place safe from the destruction, if not the bite, of time. Indeed, one could argue that his idea of habitual perception, as echoed in the chapter titles of *Matter and Memory*, resembles in its constant effort of selection the painful labor of forgetting (what Derrida will diagnose, with reference to Freud, as a *mal d'archive*) that is at the heart of both memory and the everyday (rather than ideal) labor of the ordinary archivist, who "at every instant . . . must choose and at every instant exclude" (*WD* 49) documents seeking safety from the tempests of time.

Even if Bergson rejects the traditional model of the archive to explain memory, his substitute metaphors for explaining this new decentered, noncausal, elastic conception of memory direct us to the more recent infrastructure of a modern form of archiving. Thus, unlike Freud, who in 1925 reaches for the premodern mystic writing pad to describe the operation of memory, Bergson draws upon the latest mnemonic devices from his contemporary machine era.[86] In addition to the invocations of snapshot photography in *Matter and Memory*, he compares the brain to a "central telephone exchange" (30) and an "electric circuit" (104); the work of adjustment required for the practice of memory to the "focusing of a camera" (134); and the relation between body and spirit to two types of railway intersections (222). In these examples the philosopher is not simply thinking about but thinking through the surface of industrial capitalism and finding in the multiple networks of its communication, transportation, and media technologies new models for understanding memory. Similarly, when he is thinking through modern photographic archives he is not rejecting outright the archive as a model for memory but challenging the conventional image of the historicist archive as an exhaustive, inflexible prison of the past. In other words, he is imagining a counter-archive—not a literal oppositional place so much as a new direction in the thinking of memory (and potentially history) conjured under the influence of radically new mnemonic technologies like photography and film. Thus, if on the face of it photography and film simply expanded the false, historicist illusion of total recall, when imagined within a counter-archival logic they appear to also reconfigure matters of memory according to the rifts, voids, and disorder of a radically new type of history.

COUNTER-ARCHIVAL THEORISTS OF MEMORY: BENJAMIN, KRACAUER, AND FOUCAULT

Two of Europe's key cultural critics of modern media, Benjamin and Kracauer, opened their eyes even wider and longer than Bergson's onto photography and film's relation to the model of an archive-like memory. Their work is central to pursuing the ambivalences within Bergson's engagements with photography and film and drawing out what I mean by the counter-archival implications of his theory of memory as it pertains to modern media in general and the Kahn Archive in particular. Of equal importance, if we want to consider the long shadow cast by Bergson's theory of memory upon the practice of history, is the work of Annales historians (to be investigated in chapter 5) and, more significant for this chapter's discussion, the work of the last century's most explicit counter-archival theorist, Michel Foucault.

Although Benjamin was inspired by how Bergson connects passive to pure memory, he disagreed with the assumption that the switch between the two forms of experience could be triggered at will. Benjamin thus parted ways with Bergson over the issue of whether access to pure memory was the result of voluntary or involuntary mechanisms. For Bergson there is a permanently open access to the true reflection of experience contained in the *élan vital* or *la durée*. Rejecting this model, Benjamin sided with Proust's revision of Bergson's distinction between pure (accessed via attentive contemplative perception) and impure memory (accessed via spontaneous and automatic perception). Benjamin thus claimed that it is only through the passive mechanisms of *mémoire involontaire* (such as the shock of the pianist in *Jean Santeuil*, the chance effect of the taste of a madeleine, the "tiny spark of contingency" buried in an old photograph, or the "optical unconscious" of photography and film) that this weightier recognition of time associated with an "auratic mode of experience" can be reached.[87] Benjamin's privileged notion of experience (*Erfahrung*) is thus posited in opposition to Bergson's notion of *durée*, on the basis that duration, as a voluntarily accessible condition, is drained of contingency and death. Most importantly, for Benjamin, Bergsonian duration is a category that is ultimately "estranged from history."[88] The immediate purpose of Benjamin's interrogation of Bergson in "Some Motifs in Baudelaire" was to introduce his discussion of technologies of reproduction like photography and film as devices that—even more than other "data of the [modern] world" such as newspapers—"extend the range of the *mémoire volontaire*."[89] Quoting Baudelaire, he claimed that in their "perpetual readiness" to expand the global stock of visual information, photographs assume the status of the "archives of our memory."[90]

One of the film critics who strongly influenced Benjamin's discussion of *mémoire volontaire* and *mémoire involontaire* was Kracauer.[91] In his seminal essay "Photography" (1927), Kracauer compared the infinite accumulation of photography and film in the modern era to the formation of a "central archive" (62). Hinting at the unnatural catastrophe posed by this new global storage of visual documents, he also compared this archive to a "blizzard" of images that blanket our mediated and mental environments, and most importantly to a "flood of photos [that] sweeps away the dams of memory" (58), leaving us adrift on a sea of uncontainable, incomprehensible, and indiscriminate data. Like those earlier and later "historians" of the archive, from Baudelaire and Boleslas Matuszewski, to Marc Bloch, Fernand Braudel, and Henri Lefebvre (who will be discussed further in the next two chapters), Kracauer seemed to suggest that due to its uninterrupted coverage of events, the mass media archive could only ultimately offer the diminished experiential capacities of voluntary, conscious, and official memory.

On the surface, therefore, Kracauer's attitude toward modernity's "central archive" was skeptical, particularly given its resemblance to the stockpiling tendency of conventional historicism. Earlier on in the essay, he critiques the historicist fantasy of an exhaustive temporal-spatial continuum, then points to the media's "central archive" to illustrate this fantasy, noting that "never before has an age been so informed about itself" (58) yet so disconnected from true understanding. This withdrawal from active experience into archival passivity was epitomized by the way in which "photography merely stockpiles" (52) the elements of history (reducing time to space) rather than confronting those elements' meaning (as might happen through the *interpenetration* of time and space made possible by film editing's "capacity to stir up" and actively rearrange the "inventory of nature" [62]). Although never directly referenced, Bergson's categories of memory hover over the first section of the essay when Kracauer makes a distinction between the memory-image and photography. The memory-image (somewhat like Bergson's pure memory) is associated with the "unforgettable" (51, 54) as it "outlasts time" (53) and issues from a relation to the past that is nonutilitarian and "arbitrary" (50). Unlike the exhaustiveness of photography's record, memory's records are fragmentary and "full of gaps." On the other hand, photography (somewhat like Bergson's impure memory) is "associated with the moment in time in which it came into existence" and the spatial continuum of historicism (54). By the end of the essay, however, the polarization between memory and photography is less of an opposition than a potential interpenetration, especially when expanded to include the photographic-based medium of film.[92] Much like Bergson's critique of the memory-as-archive model, Kracauer's protest against photography thus stops short of outright condemnation and leaves space for reengaging new forms of history that emerge from the counter-positivist possibilities of film, and in particular, I would add, the film archive.

Benjamin and Kracauer's positions regarding memory and modern media thus recall Bergson's earlier incomplete opposition to the model of the archive-as-memory. I have argued that Bergson was not completely inhospitable to a new sort of counter-historicist archive, especially if his thought is pushed to account for (as any knowledge of his connection to the Kahn Archive obliges us to) the possibility of film-as-archive. Beneath Bergson's surface antipathy to the positivist, empiricist, mechanical, and spatializing tendencies of memory, movement, and knowledge— embodied respectively in the figures of the archive, the apparatus of the cinematograph, and the experience of habitual perception—there exists another Bergsonism open to reinventing positivism, that is, a Bergsonism of the counter-archive. It is with the intention of reengaging Bergson at his limits that I position the Kahn Archive as a creatively empiricist response—if not a solution—to these and other Bergsonian problematics. By reading the Kahn Archive as a creative response I am emphasizing that it was by nature radically experimental in the Deleuzian sense of that term. In other words, it engaged an empiricism open to the poetics of positivism and a naturalism open to the unfamiliarity of the familiar.[93]

Another of Bergson's rebus-like descriptions of memory types is illustrative here for its hypothetical application to the idea of an archive of films as a counter-archive of memory:

> To call up the past in the form of an image, we must be able to withdraw ourselves
> from the action of the moment, we must have the power to value the useless, we must
> have the will to dream. Man alone is capable of such an effort. But even in him the
> past to which he returns is fugitive, ever on the point of escaping him, as though his
> backward turning memory were thwarted by the other, more natural, memory, of
> which the forward movement bears him on to action and to life (MM 83).

Reconceived as a counter-archive, the Kahn Archive actualizes the extremes of this tug and pull between two types of memory; stretched between the visions of the dreamer and the utilitarian, it is both an idiosyncratic collection of seemingly useless and uneventful views that have meaning only at the level of the personal, and an arsenal of potentially useful facts that have meaning only at the level of some universal design. The outcome of this struggle to capture and freeze the present in representations is a withdrawal from memory defined as the fully recollective plenitude of the past (the fantasy of positivist historicism), and a turn toward a new form of cinematic memory (the dream of the counter-archive) connected to an always "fugitive" prior moment that is cloaked in the "evanescent" eyes-wide-shut uncertainties of film's ghostlike presence (MM 87, 145).

The full historiographical potential of Bergson's counter-archival revision of memory can only be fully appreciated, however, in connection with the most extensive counter-archival theory of history, Foucault's *The Archaeology of Knowledge* (1969). If it is uncertain whether we can extend Bergson's frequent anti-archival references to a direct critique of textual (let alone filmic) documents as sources for history, it is certain that these references rest upon a profound inquiry into the foundational mechanisms of representation itself. The aftereffects of Bergson's critique of representation can still be felt in the equally devastating "questioning of the document"—the historical representation *par excellence*—that opens Foucault's attack upon positivist history in *The Archaeology of Knowledge*.[94] The full impact of that critique occurs once Foucault's initially gentle probing of the historical document expands into an overwhelming anti-authorial, anti-originary, anti-interpretive, antihumanist inquisition into the sacred site in which documents are preserved, the archive.

In chapter 5, "The Historical *a priori* and the Archive," Foucault inaugurates a counterintuitive invocation of the term "archive" (similar to Bergson's catachrestic use of the word "image"). He uproots the word from its commonsensical meaning as the safe-keeper of history's documents, thereby rejecting the quaint notion of the archive as the place that "collects the dust of statements that have become inert once more, and which may make possible the miracle of their resurrection" (129). Hijacking the previously sacred status of the site for historical practice, Foucault then refashions the "archive" for a new type of history ("archaeology") that does not imply "the search for a beginning" (131), but that paradoxically gives birth to a new definition of the archive as "first the law of what can be said, the system that governs the appearance of statements as unique events" (129). No longer the resting place of a culture's origins and no longer capable of being brought to life by the skills of historians trained to hear and interpret whispers from the grave, Foucault's archive refers to the unquestioned, omnipresent, and anonymous regulations that govern the occurrence, survival, and modification of knowledge as such; the archive is that which "differentiates discourses in their multiple existence and specifies them in their own duration."[95] Even if we were tempted to try, Foucault's archive could not be described exhaustively because it is from within its "rules that we speak"; "it is that which, outside ourselves, delimits us" (130). To analyze the archive, therefore, would mean to inhabit the "border or time that surrounds our presence, which overhangs it, and which indicates it in its otherness" (130), that is, according to a new historical methodology open to a model of memory based on discontinuities, ruptures, and difference. Paradoxically described as being invisible yet not hidden (109), Foucault's archive could thus only truly come into view when and where its true meaning, power, is made manifest.

Despite the obvious distances that separate Bergson from Foucault (not the least being the former's interest in continuity and creativity and the latter's interest in discontinuity and power), there are significant affinities. Just as Bergson denies memory is stored in an archive-like brain, Foucault resists the idea of history stored in the archive defined as "the library of all libraries" (130). In addition, just as Bergson sees memory as a context-specific and constantly evolving response to the past, so too does Foucault frame his archive between the determinism of the past and the open-ended freedom of the present/future, that is, somewhere "between tradition and oblivion" (130), where the "general system of the formation and transformation of statements" can be analyzed as they change over time ("in their own duration"). Furthermore, both thinkers are clearly attracted to the in-between states of perception and vision, materialized for Bergson in the eyes-wide-shut world of the phantasmagoria (*WD* 22) and for Foucault in the invisible but not hidden enigmas of the archive (and panopticon).

But the real bridge between the two philosophers, as Deleuze intimated, appears in their opposition to the idea of memory (and by implication, history) as a search for origins. An implicit critique of historicism (that foreshadows a poststructuralist revision of history) nestles in Bergson's attack upon the archival metaphor of memory. When he refutes the "hypothesis of a brain wherein mental states may dwell in order to slumber and to awaken" (*MM* 107) as well as the conventional understanding of memory as that which progresses from the present to the past, Bergson is also potentially mocking the late-nineteenth-century idea of archival-based historical research, rooted in the fantasy of a permanently on-call resurrection of the past. Indeed, if we substitute *archive* for brain and *history* for mental state in the above citation, we have in a nutshell Foucault's criticism of conventional historicism in *The Archaeology of Knowledge*.[96] We can also discern the imminent counter-historicist leaning of *Matter and Memory* in how its broader argument with memory ultimately implicates that discipline, history—and its attendant handmaidens museums, libraries, and archives—that Foucault (in "Of Other Spaces") pinpointed as the major obsession of nineteenth-century Western modernity.

Like Bergson, Foucault also critiqued the concept of the archive. Although he never labeled it counter-archival, Deleuze understood well the counter-archival direction in Foucault's thinking as already suggested above in his claim that Foucault's history was opposed to archival or "brief memory." In an even more pointed reference, Deleuze summarized Foucault's affront to archival thinking in the first line of his essay on *The Archaeology of Knowledge*. There he announced, half-gleefully, as if to an audience of jaw-dropping historians: "A new archivist has been appointed."[97] Deleuze's choice of the word "new" rather than "anti" signals Foucault's arrival as a counter-archival rather than anti-archival thinker. Unlike conventional archivists, the "new archivist" works on statements rather than documents, dispersions rather than subjects, lines of emergence rather than secret meanings and hidden origins. Most importantly, it is in reference to Foucault's rejection of the historicist cult of origins that Deleuze mentions the traces of a Bergsonian conception of memory. Certainly, the statements that make up Foucault's regulatory archive of the said resemble, according to Deleuze, the "building up of a stock of provisions" that may be "preserved, transmitted or repeated" like documents in an ordinary archive. But these statements break free from the conventional model of the archive because their discursive accumulation "replaces notions of origins and return to origins." In this regard, Deleuze concludes, Foucault's anti-authorial reconceptualization of statements resemble "Bergsonian memory."[98]

"THE FIRST STUDENT OF BERGSON"

It is entirely appropriate that the only films of Bergson that exist in the Archives de la Planète, all shot in 1917, would be staged in Kahn's botanical heterotopia. For in addition to being one of the most frequently filmed locales in the Archive, the gardens were the literal and symbolic backdrop to Kahn's more public endeavors.

Members of the League of Nations not only met on the paths that weaved through Kahn's Japanese, French, and English gardens, but also worked at a global diplomatic level for the spirit of international cooperation already growing there in botanical form. Bergson was, of course, the prize flower of Kahn's internationalist landscape.

As portraits of Bergson, the films are emblematic of the philosopher's ambivalent approach to cinema that I have been investigating in this chapter (which is itself connected to his intimate yet ironic relationship with Kahn). The first film, staged according to a pseudo-voyeuristic scenario, captures Bergson walking with a companion along the path of Kahn's rosary by using the ruse of the hidden camera, partially concealed in the rose bushes. The second film consists of a medium shot of Bergson standing alone in the rose garden posing and talking casually to the cameraman, who struggles to keep him in the frame (fig. 3.3). Both films are oddities, to say the least, within an Archive of films that normally flaunt the visibility of the camera and the professionalism of the cameraman. And yet the hidden camera in the first reflects more than a sensitive awareness of Bergson's publicly expressed discomfort with being filmed (and archived).[99] The philosopher's personal unease with the camera was magnified to obsessive proportions in Kahn's already-mentioned camera-phobia. It is in Kahn's exaggerated mimicry of a Bergsonian idiosyncrasy that we find our final clue to understanding the philosopher's influence upon the Archives de la Planète.

FIGURE 3.3 Henri Bergson in the rose garden on Kahn's Boulogne property, June 1917 (cameraman unknown). (MAK: frame enlargement 87670)

From one perspective, it would seem appropriate that history left it up to the outsider, the "bizarre man of money," to do what the venerated philosopher could never have done with his ideas, that is, to risk (with all the bravado of a venture capitalist) the materialization or at least approximation through film of a philosophical vision.[100] In a certain way Bergson himself foresaw Kahn's ability to take such risks. On May 14, 1886, he wrote to his friend from what he describes as the "monotonous" provincial life of Clermont-Ferrand just as he was about to hand in his dissertation (which would become *Time and Free Will*) to the Sorbonne. As usual, Bergson stresses how busy he has been: "You see that I don't have the time for *flânerie*, and yet . . . I am sure that I work less than you. When I think of all you are capable of doing in a limited time, I envy you."[101] A less flattering—though none the less sympathetic—reflection on Kahn is quoted by Jacques Chevalier, who recalls the philosopher's opinion of the banker's mission (to facilitate "the coming together of minds and facts") in the following terms: "a little simple, but in the end not so absurd."[102]

These unofficial fragments suggest a way of reading the Bergson-Kahn relationship as one that continually harked back to the pedagogical nature of its early years when Bergson attended so scrupulously—line by line, as the earliest correspondence makes clear—to the formation of his student's thinking *habits*. The teacher-student nature of their early correspondence issues from the demands of an intimate and rigorous pedagogical exchange whose traces are evident, on the one hand, in the lessons, corrections, praise, and advice of some of Bergson's letters, and on the other hand in the nervous erasures that pattern Kahn's letter drafts. As many commentators have since noted, Bergson's pedagogical method was rooted in assisting the student not to passively read and believe but to actively "repeat the experiment."[103] His method of teaching thus put into practice his philosophical rejection of the lesson learned by heart in favor of the lesson learned by having the student solve the problem for her/himself, opening onto the principle that, "True freedom lies in a power to decide, to constitute problems themselves."[104] This is a repetition to be sure, but with a difference. In the Archives de la Planète, Kahn, who was once referred to as the "first student of Bergson," was indeed repeating the experiment and solving the problem with a difference.[105] The result? "A little simple" perhaps, "but in the end not so absurd."

That is not to say that Kahn materialized what Deleuze saw as the radical cinematic potential of Bergson's ideas. For as I have emphasized already, the Kahn Archive is an experiment that must be as antithetical to as it is revealing of the potential of the philosopher's ideas on cinema, the everyday, and memory. What my exploration of the Kahn films hopes to show is that, *pace* Deleuze, it is more useful to return discussions of Bergson to early cinema than to try and rescue him from it. In this chapter, I have therefore resisted arguing that Bergson was a visionary whose thoughts would come to fruition in future cinema or that his philosophy thinks the un-thought of cinema, showing us what the cinema would look like once "the shot stop[ed] being a spatial category and bec[a]me a temporal one."[106] For if Deleuze wanted above all to argue that Bergson's critique actually speaks beyond what it responded to—that is, the technical limitations of film in his time—and anticipated a cinema that would emancipate the viewpoint through editing techniques such as the flashback, alternation between first and third person points of view, the mobile camera, and use of deep space, then it is equally important to recognize that Bergson's philosophy also speaks of, through, and to the cinema and the world he actually knew. As I will explore more fully in chapter 7, Kahn's Archive was undoubtedly a part of Bergson's cinematic consciousness, itself a component of the *vie extérieure* on which all his philosophy was based. Without wanting to claim that Kahn's films inspired Bergson to see the future of cinema, or that they finally reveal the hidden screening room of Bergsonian philosophy's enigmatic fascination with the cinematograph, Kahn's films confirm how relevant the philosopher's work was to the broad spectrum of experimentalism—from the Kahn Archive to early avant-garde film theory—within French cinema culture of the period. In short, if Bergson was strategically in favor of closing his eyes to modernity, I am interested in investigating what it would mean to read the Kahn films as the "image" delivered to those eyes once opened.

To pursue this line of thinking is to take seriously the other dimension to Deleuze's claim that Bergson was ahead of himself in what I suggest is a counter-archival and counter-historicist tendency in Bergson's critique of memory. For all their affinities, where Bergson's and Foucault's counter-archival theories of memory differ is that Bergson's reflects the rupture of a cinematographically stamped early twentieth century. In contrast, Foucault's theory of the archive resists that distinction, invested as he is in an overarching differentiation between the temporal *esprit* of the nineteenth century and the spatial *esprit* of the twentieth century.[107] What *The Archaeology of Knowledge* thus voluntarily avoids (and his essay "Of Other Spaces" brushes up against) is what Bergson's philosophy involuntarily collides with—the early twentieth century's most striking reconfiguration of space and time, the film archive.

To return Bergson to early cinema does not imply a simple restoration of origins. Rather, it liberates the diverse Bergsonian discourses of French film culture, returning the philosopher to a cinema fascinated by time, movement, memory, the archival, and everyday life. Additionally, to return Bergson to early cinema allows us to see how the films and the logic behind the Archives de la Planète contain a possible model of the camera's capacity to think backwards, to reengage mechanicity, to reanimate habitual experience, and to reinvigorate the uneventful; in other words, to discover a cinematic rapprochement between *la durée* and history. Finally, to return Bergson to the cinema of his time and of time itself is also to foreground an exchange between film theory and film culture at its limits. Bergson was not a film theorist or even critic, and Kahn was barely mentioned in French cinema culture of the time. However, the relationship between Bergson's philosophy and Kahn's research offers a noncanonical and unconventional variant of the interdependence of the discourses and practices constituting film culture in France in the late teens and early twenties. I will now turn to a key topos within that exchange—the concept and practice of the film archive.

"NO MORE WRITTEN ARCHIVES, ONLY FILMS"

EARLY DISCOURSES AND PRACTICES OF THE FILM ARCHIVE

This simple ribbon of exposed celluloid not only constitutes an historical document, but a piece of history, a history that has not vanished and needs no genie to resuscitate it. It is there, scarcely sleeping, and like those elementary organisms that, living in a latent state, revive after years given a bit of heat and moisture—it only requires, to reawaken it and relive those hours of the past, a little light passing through a lens in the darkness.

BOLESLAS MATUSZEWSKI (1898)[1]

Education by means of the cinema is encyclopedic and incoherent, and that makes it eminently modern.

RENÉ DOUMIC (1913)[2]

IN AN ARTICLE FROM 1910, one of the early literary prophets of cinema, the poet Guillaume Apollinaire, came face to face with the inability of traditional storehouses of knowledge to acknowledge film when he made what appeared to be a shocking request at France's foremost library, the Bibliothèque Nationale.[3] Apollinaire attempted to access the library's film-related documents stored somewhere at the venerable rue de Richelieu institution (just a few doors up from Kahn's bank at 102 rue de Richelieu), only to discover he was the first person to have ever requested them. As it turned out, the collection (which included scenarios, sample film frames, and paper prints) could not be consulted because it had not yet been processed according to standard bibliographic conventions. The librarian was not yet equipped, she explained, to catalogue or make them available to the public.[4] Thus, fifteen years after the first public projections of film, and twelve years after

Boleslas Matuszewski's defense of film as a valid source for history, one of France's most significant institutions for the preservation of knowledge still considered film to be a recalcitrant document—a record resistant to the norms of epistemological classification, application, and circulation.

In order to understand the challenges posed by film we must return to the broader mnemonic concerns of the period in which it emerged. The late nineteenth and early twentieth century witnessed an obsession with the possibilities and limitations of modern media as memory devices. For example, the array of technologies for safeguarding the memory of the present, which Siegfried Kracauer described as the "optical inventory" of photography, cinema, and mass-distributed newspapers, were also seen to be memory's enemy, a dilemma Walter Benjamin connected to the exponentially "increasing atrophy of experience," that is, the perceived inability to really know, encounter, or register that present.[5] Commentators on the new media's implications for memory like Kracauer and Benjamin thus diagnosed a crisis in modern memory caused by the paradoxical coexistence of cultural amnesia and hypermnesia; in the one column of that period's bookkeeping we note a memory deficit, while in the adjacent column a memory surplus.

As we saw in the preceding chapter, the archive, as a metaphor for human memory and a site of application for new mnemonic technologies like photography, also came under indirect attack during this period by artists and philosophers alike. In striking opposition to this anti-archival trend, one of the most persistent predictions employed in the first decade of cinema prophesied that films would constitute the archives of the future. This prediction was a reflection of the widespread early application of film's positivist and utilitarian tendencies. As a result of these uses, film history (according to Noël Burch) took a "detour" during its early years through non-narrative experimentation before it settled on the path toward narrative hegemony.[6] These early distractions from film's future narrative path included not only the "quasi-scientific attitude" (*Life* 18) that Burch is keen to claim for the Lumières, but also the collection and storage of information about daily life that was put to both disciplinary and seemingly benign uses in scientific research, educational appropriations, and national-colonial projects. The difference of early cinema, one might thus argue, was linked in part to the archival-inventorial web within which film's memory of the everyday was often caught.

This chapter claims that cinema's "detour" through inventorial applications constituted a defining moment rather than a temporary stopover in the evolution of film history and theory. Early cinema's anti-illusionist and scientistic tendency (to use Burch's words) stamped the film medium with a long-lasting archival proclivity that continued into the teens and twenties, as seen in Kracauer's relegation of film to an "inventorial optic."[7] This archival drive was especially active in the observation and classification of everyday life where it directed filmic representation more toward the threatening disorder of what Theodor Adorno called "radical naturalism" than the aesthetic regularity of "familiar realism."[8] In other words, if this archival tendency posed a threat (as Burch argues) to naturalistic illusionism (*Life* 23), it also tapped into the excesses that had always been a part of literary and scientific naturalism's hyper-descriptive affront to realist narrative.

Early hopes for film's archival future flew in the face of the Lumières' fear that cinema had no future without quite succumbing to the hype of Charles Pathé's declaration in 1900 that cinema would be "the Theater, the Newspaper and the School of tomorrow."[9] Most importantly, the film-as-archive prediction seemed to imply that the memory crisis could be solved (rather than exacerbated) by film's superior capacity for recording, storing, and reviving the past with the unprecedented advantage of kinetic verisimilitude. However, as seen in Apollinaire's encounter at the Bibliothèque Nationale, by the 1910s these earlier fantasies regarding film's archival compatibility had failed to come to fruition.

This chapter explores why and how film was imagined as inheriting an archival mission. Several questions will guide this inquiry into the extent to which the concept and practice of the archive was simply updated or radically remade in the age of cinema. First, what discourses predetermined or set the stage for the understanding of film as an archive? Second, how did these discourses (film's rivalry with the written book key among them) eventually coexist with the newly developing discourses of film as entertainment and film as art in the teens? And third, how did one of the world's first film archives, the Archives de la Planète, situate itself in relation to these discourses and in particular to the dominant model for record storage, the historicist archive?

The expectation that film would capitalize on its unique archival properties took many forms. For some commentators, it meant that the film reel resembled a sort of time capsule or time machine, literally a place or object in which time is stored for future reference, marking the indexical, irrefutable, and reproducible trace of past events as they unfolded in duration.[10] For others it referred to the more specific aspiration regarding film's ability to refashion and reform visual-based archives (from the perspective of an age-old bias toward written documents that had, as Apollinaire learned, barely changed even since the advent of photography). In addition to bearing the potential to transform the official realm of state and scientific archives, there were still others who incorporated film into new fantasies of unofficial vernacular archives such as the novelty of moving-picture family albums imagined in a 1917 article titled "Les Archives familiales."[11] Shadowing these optimistic film-as-archive discourses, a countercurrent of commentators emerged who were more troubled than enthused by film's counter-archival potential for endless chronicle, unmanageable detail, unhealthy curiosity, and a pathological surfeit of memory. Whether for or against the film-as-archive discourse, one theme underpinned these diverse expectations—the articulation of the concept of the film archive to the newly professionalized domain of history.

ARCHIVAL FEVER IN FILM CULTURE OF THE 1910s

By the 1910s, Matuszewski's promotion of nonfiction film as an authentic archival source for future historians had become a common topic in the French cinema press. In 1911 in the film industry journal *Le Courrier cinématographique*, Morgan Fredy revived Matuszewski's 1898 pamphlet in order to demonstrate how far behind France was in recognizing and exploiting the "historical, documentary, and pedagogical" value of film.[12] Whereas phonographic archives had already become a reality at the Paris Opéra and the City of Brussels Archives had begun "a collection of films of contemporary history," the French cinema industry, complained Fredy, still lacked an analogous archive. Two years later, the director of another pioneering film magazine, *Ciné-Journal*, reported with some embarrassment that France, the "country of progress," had even fallen behind Egypt in the use of film as a source for historical archives.[13] Thus by 1912, when Kahn's Archive had already officially begun, the early expectations for film as an archival tool of history as outlined in Matuszewski's 1898 manifesto were still invoked by representatives of the French film industry as a worthy though unrealized goal.

It is telling that Fredy cites Matuszewski because the film-as-archive discourse of the early 1910s manifested itself in two approaches, both of which can be found in the latter's pamphlet "A New Source of History." The first of these depended upon the invocation of film as a superior epistemological tool intended for the rational betterment of humanity by facilitating the gathering, collecting, and disseminating of knowledge about the near and far with an unparalleled speed and accuracy. Contrary to the dominant concern regarding the loss of oral or lived memory in the age of cinema, Matuszewski had argued that film would be able to "verify oral tradition" (12), putting an end to the subjective discrepancies of human witnesses. Film would also be a superior archival source, Matuszewski claimed, because its "mathematical exactitude" (13) would render obsolete the "lines of vague description in books" (7) upon which education was based. Presaging by two years the Polish cameraman's claims regarding film's positivist applications, this time from the perspective of racial science, the physician Dr. Félix-Louis Regnault looked forward to the time when film, color, *and* sound would converge to revive the past, and the "archives of the future will no longer be made up of boring writings."[14] Similarly, as we have already seen in chapters 2 and 3, Jean Brunhes' human geography not only promoted film as an exact "tool for scientific research" concerned with life, but did so with the intention of supplanting the inexact, out-of-date, descriptive limitations of geographical textbooks.[15]

Alongside these utilitarian hopes for cinema as a superior archival force, a second less celebratory approach appears in the discourse. Matuszewski had also alluded to it in the margins of his otherwise optimistic bid for the first French film archive, where he briefly reflected upon film's dangerously "indiscrete" tendency to capture in its all-encompassing survey of reality those minor and unofficial events that usually do not occur where the (photographic) camera or history "expects" them.[16] If film was to become, as Matuszewski hoped, the archive of the future, then that archive would be defined not only by records of official history, but by those depicting a counter-archival history open to the unexpected, unexceptional, and fleeting traces of the present.

Before discussing how these two directions in the archival conceptualization of film (as an at once superior archive and a counter-archive) materialized in various projects, including Kahn's, we need to reinsert them into the network of major film discourses of the mid-teens to mid-twenties. According to film historian Richard Abel, the first of these discourses spoke of film as an educational force; the second primarily perceived film as a scientific tool and product of industrial invention; the third understood film as a mass spectacle or popular entertainment; and the fourth, and most radical for its time, invoked film as a new art form.[17] By the early teens, the dominant discourses legitimating the cinema in France arguably remained those that promoted film as an educational or scientific instrument. In other words, the tradition of thinking about film in a non-narrative (though not necessarily anti-narrative) mode was still dominant, even though this was the period in which we see the commercial expansion of film as a narrative-based entertainment form (especially with the influence of the evolution of the Hollywood classical style of storytelling around 1917).

To be sure, the scientific-educational discourse on film boosted self-interested industry efforts to legitimate cinema in reaction to the opposing disdain leveled at it by the French cultural establishment of the early teens. No doubt overreacting to the equally exaggerated "school of crime" arguments about the dangers of screen spectacles, pro-cinema commentators often reached for a utopian rhetoric to justify their medium.[18] This optimism found outlets in two dominant claims: film's potential as a superior epistemological tool, and film's status as the new *visual Esperanto* that could bring about what the critic Yhcam called the "universality of peoples."[19]

Thus, in spite of a continuing fear in the 1910s that fiction film in particular was corrupting the moral fabric of French society, the institution of cinema strengthened its claim to being a democratizing and universalizing tool of instruction. Members of the nascent film educational movement of the period argued that the medium's pedagogical value was particularly promising where *observation* was a key method of learning, as in the natural sciences and disciplines like geography, the latter having already successfully incorporated photography and magic lantern projection into its teaching practice.[20] Yet even though the scientific context was used to legitimate film, and notable figures like Dr. Jean Comandon were making research breakthroughs with the aid of film, most scientists of the time (Brunhes among them), as well as educators, would not have considered film *alone* as a valid form of evidence.[21] As can be gauged from the scientific luminaries he stacked on the Archive's honorary committee (Bergson, Vidal de la Blache, and the Dean of the Faculty of Sciences at the University of Paris, Paul Apell), Kahn was obviously more than aware of the intellectual risk he took in basing his Archive on a medium still considered to be a disreputable form of popular distraction in 1912.

The scientific pretensions Kahn nurtured for his film Archive went hand in hand with its humanist dimensions or what he called its goal of facilitating a "new orientation" for humanity.[22] Such great expectations for film within a scientific-humanist framework were not as eccentric as they might sound today and belonged to a much wider ideology of euphoric cosmopolitanism animating film culture during this period. When, in 1912, the critic and future filmmaker Abel Gance predicted that, "We are journeying toward a new synthesis of the human spirit, toward a new humanity so a new race of man can appear . . . [whose] language will be the cinema," he was driven by the same utopian visions for the cinema that Kahn's Archive began to put into practice that very year.[23] Within cinema cultures across Europe and America, the teens witnessed the proliferation of discourses that rhapsodized about film's global destiny, speaking of it as "a sort of visual language comprehensible in all countries," capable of uniting humanity, and spreading (as Gance wrote) "its faith throughout the world."[24]

One of the most popular analogies invoked to describe film's universal appeal resided in its similarity or superiority to the book. The widespread notion that "film is the book destined to be read by all the world" directly aligned the medium with the traditionally print-based institutions of the archive and the library.[25] Nonetheless, there was often a competitive tone to the comparison. For example, France's national library became a common target of resentment among those promoting the cause of film archives and the value of film as a source for history.[26] In 1923 the music and film critic Émile Vuillermoz substantiated his petition for a Cinémathèque Nationale by asserting the difference between books and film: "We have a Bibliothèque Nationale where all the aspects of our interior life are conserved; let us preserve for the future the reflections of our exterior life by creating a Cinémathèque Nationale."[27] Vuillermoz recognized that, in contrast to the "interior life" conserved in novels and fiction at the Bibliothèque Nationale, films were unconsciously archiving a new type of nongraphic, nonfiction history based on the previously unvalued surface appearances and fleeting experiences of our contemporary "exterior life." Both the guiding metaphors of film-as-universal-language and film-as-book, in addition to the more specific claims regarding film's affinity for external actuality, would inform the Kahn Archive in its conception as a force for international rapprochement, in its comparison (by Kahn and Bergson) to the global book of Descartes' *Grand Livre de l'Homme*, and in its mission to capture daily (especially street) life all over the world. In this respect, it could be argued that Kahn merely tried to elevate to a scientific level the populist idea of film as democratic language that flourished internationally in the teens.

FILM AS THE POSTHUMOUS LIFE OF THE PRESENT

Typical of so many celebrations of film as a democratizating disseminator of knowledge, Louis Haugmard's 1913 essay on the cinematograph's aesthetic compared the cinema to a "vivid universal newspaper."[28] Yet unlike earlier users of the newspaper metaphor such as Charles Pathé, Haugmard also recognized film's *superiority* to the ephemeral newspaper because of its indexical qualities as a medium preserving the material impressions of past events. Echoing Matuszewski's characterizations of film as a living "piece of history" or a dormant organism waiting to be revived, Haugmard claimed that film not only mirrored the reality of its audience's daily lives in the present but carried forward the durational unfolding of that reality into the future. In Haugmard's words, film "resurrects reality, prolongs it, and gives to the ephemeral an unlimited posthumous life" (84). In addition to eternalizing the fleeting, film became the afterlife of the present.

Like many other commentators, Haugmard also connected film's resemblance to a living fragment of history with the idea of the archive.[29] Yet in doing so he moved beyond Matuszewski's more modest position by arguing that film not only resembled an archive and could be integrated into present archival practices, but was destined to replace archives as they were then known:

> No more written archives, only films. Memorable events, diligently catalogued and classified, will be deposited in stores of human motion. There we will find the "pressings" of public life, the "preserves" of the past, though scarcely exempt from falsification. (84)

To be sure, Haugmard's tone was ultimately more apocalyptic than celebratory, as seen in his prediction that cinema's "disquieting" (78) and "infinitely dangerous power" (83) symbolized "the end of a race" (85), and more specifically, a threat to history's immunity from "falsification." Still, his prediction that film would replace written archives assumed an equation between the written and filmed document. Describing film as "facts [that] are photographed" and a "form of notation by image," Haugmard thus viewed both written and filmed records as discrete pieces of data capable of being "diligently catalogued and classified" (83). Although for Haugmard film could never reveal the "intellectual and interior life of man" (a fact that Vuillermoz praised) and would always be subject to claims of falsification, it seemed destined to house "the 'preserves' of the past" (84).

The reading of film as a superior graphic medium and source for archives marked a trend which in France found its busiest spokesperson in Victor Perrot and his indefatigable campaigns to promote film as a "new Writing" destined to transform history.[30] As early as 1911 he proclaimed:

> The cinematograph is history written in a language that everyone can comprehend; to sum up it is a universal writing that refers back to the ideogrammatic writing of the first ages of the world, but is more perfected, more rapid. It is the stenography of history, readable by all.[31]

In contrast to Haugmard's pejorative recognition that film heralded "the triumph of simplification" (83), Perrot offered a more confident celebration of film's democratic or shorthand version of history. Others like Clément Vautel had been even more extreme about the historical value of film, going so far as to claim that "the cinematograph is a historian."[32] Giving a certain degree of proof to the assertion were attempts to employ film as a tool (or at least ersatz book) for archival research, as occurred with the machine called the "bibliophote," a precursor to microfilm that was able to film and project the pages of books and manuscripts.[33]

Although professional historians were far from using projected films as new sources for history, film's unique "document"-like connection to history, and in particular a history of the everyday, continued to be heard into the late twenties. In response to a 1927 survey questioning the need for a Bibliothèque du Film and the possibility that film might be "the only book of tomorrow," Jean Valmy-Baysse, the secretary general of the Comédie Française, replied that "the document is the very expression of the everyday life of a civilization," and that the occasion "to enrich a people with all that might help materialize its memories for those who come after" by preserving such documents must never be passed over.[34] He then went on to claim that "the document *par excellence*" of today was in fact not the novel, the photograph, or the newspaper, but film, the essential record of modern daily life that his generation was entrusted to bequeath to the next.

The promotion of film as a visual document or fact cut from the fabric of social life functioned to align film with the sober realms of objective truth and useful knowledge rather than the more questionable entertainment sites of pleasure and curiosity.[35] This legitimating strategy reflected the desire to attach respectable credentials to the cinema while tapping into an awareness (either celebratory or anxious) of the archival properties of the medium. We can often see this occurring when the urgency of this discourse pushed the rhetoric away from the sober realm of secular rationalism it was courting and back in the direction of excess, magic, and quasi-religiosity it was trying to leave behind. It has even been claimed that a sort of "cinematic messianism" subtended much film criticism of the late 1910s and early 1920s, as exemplified in the critic and filmmaker Jean Epstein's survey of the 1924 film horizon: "[n]ow we are approaching the promised land."[36]

It was, however, the would-be archivist, Victor Perrot, who expressed his devotion to the medium in the most explicit of religious metaphors. In 1920 Perrot styled the climax to an article calling for the conservation of film by literally comparing the *cinémathèques* of the future to the risen-from-the-dead biblical figure of Lazarus: "[Once the films come to life like Lazarus] the Cinématographe will say: 'I am the Resurrection and the Life . . . he who believes in Me, though dead, will live; and he who lives and believes in me will never die!'"[37] Far from being an extreme and isolated precedent for André Bazin's definition several decades later of cinema as "change mummified," Perrot's biblical invocation of film's ability to outdo time and death typified the hyperbolic rhetoric that film's unprecedented indexical capacities aroused in critical debates of the teens.[38] Indeed, in a striking precursor to Bazin's famous description, and just one year after Perrot's plea, Epstein wrote in 1921 that because of cinema's affinity for contemporary everyday life, "today's reality [would be] preserved for eternity by art. Embalmed in motion."[39] Closely on his heels, the critic Ricciotto Canudo breathed new life into the film-as-Lazarus trope in 1923 by combining it with the film-as-universal-language metaphor. He argued that film was not simply copying but "reinaugurating the entire experience of writing," especially through its ability "to arrest the fleeting aspects of life" *and* "to renew the representation of life itself," thereby accomplishing "the triumph over the ephemeral and over death."[40] Where writing could only register the outline of fleeting events, film could embody and revive them in all their durational and disorderly plenitude.

"ENCYCLOPEDIC *AND* INCOHERENT"

In one respect, the diverse reflections upon film's potential as a superior source of history merely applied to film what Baudelaire had wished for photography in 1859, that is, to limit the medium to a strictly utilitarian and nonaesthetic function as a mnemonic aid restricted to serving the "archives of our memories."[41] Underlying both Baudelaire's false apologia for photography and the later tendency to see film as a superior tool of instruction, we can discern, however, the need to control (and not just celebrate) the excessive potential in photographic media's "stupendous capacity" for "precise evidence" (Canudo).[42] It is partly in recognition of the "dangerous" and "disquieting" (Haugmard) transgressions of early cinema's imprecise and chaotic evidence that several film historians and theorists have recently distinguished that period's mode of representation from the later, more regimented perceptual codes of narrative-based cinema.[43]

Following these recent arguments, one might contend that if during the early cinema period the film image remained, metaphorically speaking, unarchived (that is, unregulated by strict spatio-temporal codes of narration and editing), then by the late teens it was well on its way to being archived, albeit unevenly. By the same logic, it could be said that the Kahn Archive, with its implicit understanding of films as ordered, classifiable, and comparable documents, resembled the non-narrative equivalent to classical Hollywood cinema's metaphorical "archiving" of film information. In other words, the classificatory scaffolding (admittedly exterior rather than interior to the films) in Kahn's Archive can be compared to the grammar of classical film conventions that aimed to discipline film language through the regulatory classifications of continuity editing, psychological motivation of character development, and causal and linear plot construction.[44]

Adherence to the rules of continuity editing was, however, by no means the only way French film culture of the 1910s tried to contain cinema's lingering excesses—those qualities of temporal contingency and wayward naturalism that I term *counter-archival*. Anxiety over the excessive visual information in film—whether understood in the semiotic sense of a form that was "encyclopedic *and* incoherent" (Doumic; my emphasis) or in the evaluative sense of a form open to the socially inflected representation of "immoral, licentious, or sensual spectacles"—always undermined the more naïve positivism that buoyed the film-as-archive predictions.[45] Matuszewski's two manifestos from 1898 (the second titled "Animated Photography: What It Is and What It Should Be") in fact can be read on one level as the recognition and attempted management of the anxiety associated with film's radical rather than familiar naturalism.[46] In "A New Source of History" he celebrates films that emerge from and speak to a sober "curiosity" (in "slices of public and national life") while in "Animated Photography" he criticizes those that cater to what he called (in reference to the controversy surrounding the public reception of Dr. Eugène-Louis Doyen's surgical films) an "unhealthy curiosity" aroused by the more defamiliarizing visual indiscretions of vivisection.[47] That Matuszewski might just as well be describing the attraction of Émile Zola's self-professed literary surgery upon the human and social body reminds us of the tendency for invasive curiosity within naturalism's observational frenzy.[48]

An "unhealthy curiosity" also creeps into "A New Source of History" as the other side to official history, where events find their way into the historical record due to what Matuszewski describes as the essentially "indiscreet" nature of the cameraman's "instinct" and "natural curiosity."[49] Thus, if the cinema was indeed, as Matuszewski's pamphlet claimed, the new source of history, then this did not bode well for the master discipline of the Third Republic. The camera's natural talents for chronicling modern life could also be exploited for causes less noble than scientific history or science in general. As Yuri Tsivian has shown, scientific advances like X-rays and the microscope ushered in a "new era of universal voyeurism" that—when applied to film—compounded conservative fears that there was something in "the very nature of the medium that suggested intrusion, indecency, [and] violation of privacy."[50] Once the camera's X-ray–style vision migrated out of the laboratory and onto the streets in films like Kahn's footage of the *vespasienne*, a transgression occurred that threatened to give access to the more "indiscreet" applications of the camera's scientificity and historicity and reclaim the medium for the lower levels of the popular and the mundane, the fairground and the fantastic, the flâneur and the detective.

During the period in which Kahn launched his Archive, fiction film was also recognizing the camera as a threat to domestic order. In Louis Feuillade's *L'Erreur tragique* (1913, Gaumont) a husband is led to believe his wife is having an affair after seeing her captured accidentally in a film with another man who turns out to be her brother. The husband's intention to use the film as evidence to prove his wife's infidelity—a conventional subject for domestic melodramas of the period—was not as far-fetched as it sounds.[51] Expressing the extremes of his own zealous promotion of film, as well as direct knowledge of the disciplinary uses of the first photographic archives, Matuszewski himself envisaged "a system of cinematographic *fiches* [index cards]" for the police that would exist "alongside anthropometric *fiches*," heralding a new world order of surveillance in which there would be a camera on every corner.[52] It is not just Kahn's film of the *vespasienne* that might lead us to believe Matuszewski was not so far off. Just one year after the release of *L'Erreur tragique*, *Le Journal* reported that the Paris Police Prefecture was already using film to train policemen in the detection of "the most habitual types of criminals."[53]

Shifting the debate to the aesthetic terrain, Canudo argued in "The Birth of a Sixth Art" (1911) that the threat of film's informational surplus resulted from its identity as a "mechanical mode of expression."[54] In this essay Canudo was primarily concerned with questioning whether film could be defined as an art. His answer is instructive for the purposes of my discussion of the continuing recognition of film's wayward naturalism, not because he finally decides that cinema "is not yet an art" (echoing the messianic patience of early film criticism), but because he went on to explain that the reason for film's nonaesthetic status resided in its resemblance to a disorderly and automatic inventory of reality.[55] Echoing Baudelaire's and Bergson's complaints, Canudo felt that film was limited by "the condition that prevents photography from becoming an art," that is, "it lacks the freedom of choice peculiar to plastic *interpretation*" due to the all-inclusive, impersonal, nonhuman, nonselective, nonhierarchical, any-moment-whatever nature of the camera-eye's arbitrary scan of reality.[56] The problem resides precisely in the film image's resistance to being entirely controlled or stylized, its evasion of the traditional aesthetic filters of "choice and elaboration" (62). Transposed into the terms of archival practice in which choice, exclusions, and discernment are essential, film's automatic inclusiveness presents a counter-archival disruption of aesthetic norms. Furthermore, the mechanical reproducibility of the film image—its essential nature as a "*copy* of a subject" (61) susceptible to infinite duplication—differed radically from the unique, non-reproducible aura of the conventional work of art, and betrayed (according to Canudo) the medium's participation in that wider modern malaise (which Kracauer and Benjamin would also align with modern mass media), namely, an "excess of documentation" (62).

Although earlier efforts to reign in cinema's "excess of documentation" might be read into the Lumières' and Méliès' cataloguing and classifying of views, attempts to regulate the film experience intensified in the teens.[57] In 1912 Yhcam put forward a proposal for a "general classification system" that attempted to systematically categorize the functions, genres, and audiences of cinema with the intention of disciplining the film experience and ensuring that the cinema program "correlate[s] with the public to which it is addressed."[58] Yhcam not only extended the descriptive range of Méliès' earlier categorization of cinema views but magnified the classificatory drive underpinning the latter's taxonomy. In his endeavors to streamline the eclecticism of the typical film program, we can also detect the intent to control the chaotic, undisciplined range of film genres, functions, and audiences.[59] This same article offered further proof of a conservative campaign to restrain the potential amplification of nonutilitarian details that lay dormant beneath the veneer of film's documentary surface. For example, Yhcam suggested that cinema theater managers should treat all types of screen enlargement, from the increasingly used close-ups to the magnifications involved in popular scientific films (such as those being made at the time by Dr. Comandon for Pathé), with "the greatest discretion" (73), and should accompany them (as indeed Comandon would) with precise information about the degree of enlargement so as to prevent audience confusion.[60] In recognition of the nonstandardized, eclectic nature of film programming, René Doumic argued in 1913 that even though most screenings began with the instructive "object lesson" in the form of an actuality film, they inevitably devolved into a state of disorder and discontinuity. The "serious" façade of the opening newsreel was subsequently undermined, Doumic claimed, because "incoherence [was] essential to cinema programs."[61] And yet, far from wanting to restrain the cinema's at once "encyclopedic and incoherent" counter-archival potential, Doumic embraced this duality as a sign of its unique reflection of modernity. What we thus discern in these commentaries upon the cinema's challenge to traditional standards of perception, art, representation, and knowledge is the reversal of Bergson's association of the cinematograph with conventional everyday perception. Instead, these critics reveal a cinema that regularly suspended the habitual, in all its aesthetic and epistemological forms.

THE ARCHIVE AS THE LABORATORY OF HISTORY

Considering film's multiple challenges, it is surprising that Kahn was willing to venture into the unknown territory of actually creating a film archive intended to control the cultural and experiential disorder wrought by modernity. Faced with these challenges, which epistemological and practical models influenced the logic and structure of the Kahn Archive and to what extent did it move beyond or transform these underpinning influences? The pull exerted upon the Archives de la Planète by the Matuszewskian model of the film archive as a resource for history cannot be underestimated.[62] Given history's status as the official "discipline of memory" (Terdiman) recently professionalized according to a scientific application of archival primary sources, it is no surprise that Matuszewski provided the title "A New Source of *History*" (my emphasis) to his 1898 blueprint for the creation of a centralized film archive, thereby designating history as the noble subject to which the "first" film archive would serve as handmaiden.[63] Central to Kahn's project and Matuszewski's manifesto was a positivist conception of the archive, one crucial to the French banker's need for scientific legitimacy and the Polish cameraman's courting of "History." In comparing the Kahn Archive to other film archives of the period we must, therefore, begin with the most common definition of the term *archive*, defined in the late nineteenth century as a scientifically organized depository for documents of interest to future historians. For even though the Kahn Archive was officially associated with the new discipline of human geography, one of its central legitimating strategies was to align itself with the older discipline of history for which archives had only recently become essential. In short, the ideal model to which the Archives de la Planète (and to a certain extent, all turn-of-the-century archives) aspired was the positivist historical archive.

In France, the notion of the archive as "the indispensable laborator[y] of historical research" was a modern invention of the mid-nineteenth century.[64] Before this period the word *archive* connoted different things: the king's depot of official documents, the storehouse of juridical evidence, the governmental "*arsenal d'administration*," the treasures of imperial conquest, or the eclectic work of the amateur collector.[65] The more fixed modern concept of the archive dates back to the establishment of the Archives Nationales in 1790, an institute founded upon a revolutionary call for equal access to official records. These noble origins, however, were followed by the French revolutionary and Napoleonic periods when archives became associated with "sites of contest and intrigue."[66] It was not until well into the nineteenth century that the nation's archive emerged as a site of scientific and sober work, indeed, the principal workshop for writing history. The factors contributing to the scientific renovation of the archive included the elaboration of cataloguing and indexing systems intended to organize written state documents; the establishment in 1821 of the École des Chartes (the oldest institution in Europe specializing in archival sciences); and most importantly, the privileging of the discipline of history under the Third Republic as a means to awaken "the soul of the nation" after the defeat of the Franco-Prussian War in 1871.[67] This governmental initiative was integrally connected to the rise of the *école méthodique* or the methodical school, which rooted the production of French history between 1880 and

1930 in the scientific application of "rigorous techniques concerning the inventory of sources, [and] the criticism of documents" based in state archives.[68]

In short, our commonplace idea that an essential activity of historians is to "engag[e] with documentary evidence, collected together in a particular kind of place" called the archive, only came to be universally promulgated and accepted at the end of the nineteenth century.[69] In turn, the new professionalizing dependence upon archival sources had direct consequences for the type of history produced. It further entrenched the bias toward written sources and the history of political events and the bias against non-written sources and the history of everyday life.[70] In addition to this preference for political history, the scientific archive brought with it a new dream. If the fantasy of speaking with the dead epitomized the Romantic archive of the French historian Jules Michelet, then that of collecting the world's documents in one place—what Michel de Certeau described as "the dream of a totalizing taxonomy" of the world—epitomized the later scientific historicist archive.[71]

It was no coincidence then that Bergson's critique of the memory-as-archive metaphor and other people's predictions regarding film's archival capacities—the former opposed to and the latter supportive of the myth of the archive as a site of unmediated access to the past—were gaining momentum by the turn of the century just as France found itself at the forefront in scientific archiving practices. Archivists were held in the highest esteem—even considered to be national heroes—within government circles.[72] It is not an exaggeration to claim that to be an archivist in the Third Republic was to be on the frontlines of the battle for the modern French nation-state.[73] No wonder then, that the recently arrived Polish immigrant Matuszewski would look to the institution of the history archive as the perfect site from which to launch his film archive in France.

Although Brunhes' qualifications guaranteed a solid reputation for the Archives de la Planète, it was the association with the model of the scientifically organized archive, as conceived by historians of the *école méthodique* like Charles-Victor Langlois and Charles Seignebos, that vouched for the seriousness of Kahn's unorthodox Archive. Kahn's photographers and cameramen actually underwent a form of archival training that revealed the connection between historicist research and its offshoot in the newer forms of iconographical archiving. Brunhes taught them a variation of the most basic and essential of archival practices perfected by the *école méthodique* of history, namely, the index-card system (*le système des fiches*).[74] Kahn's cameramen were instructed to fill out a *fiche* indicating the date, place, and subject of what they filmed (fig. 2.1). As already discussed in chapter 2, every shot captured for Kahn's Archive was supposed to be supplemented—in theory—by a written document produced in the field and based on direct observation. In addition to registering the basic spatial and temporal coordinates of each autochrome or film, the cameramen were also encouraged (according to Brunhes' instructions) to note down their initial thoughts on the subject matter. When the cameramen returned from their missions, this combination of objective and sub-jective information was then transcribed into the photographic and film registers back in Boulogne. Although no detailed explanations for this method remain, it is reasonable to suggest that the intention behind such a system was similar to the intention (vis-à-vis written documents) behind the historian's use of the *système des fiches*—to give order to the often indecipherable meaning or excessive detail automatically featured in the potentially incoherent and infinite descriptive reg-ister of each autochrome and film. The difference between the incorporation of *fiches* into writing-based and photographic-based archives, of course, resided in the extent to which the latter posed new challenges to systems of ordering and classifying information.

In its reliance upon the written supplement of the *fiche* to anchor each visual document, the Kahn Archive, at least in its production mode, resembled one of the pioneering systems of photographic cataloguing: Alphonse Bertillon's vast archival apparatus for criminal identification established at the Paris Police Prefecture in the 1880s.[75] Consisting of highly detailed *fiches*, Bertillon's police archive was di-rectly motivated by the social regulation of deviance figured in the physical body of the criminal.[76] In contrast, the written *fiches* in Kahn's Archive bore no explicit dis-ciplining relation to the flow of human bodies, spaces, and events captured in the net of each frame, but they did set out to discipline the body of the photographic and cinematic image.

The Archive's incorporation of the *fiche* might thus be compared to a classic call to regulate descriptive excess in the literary domain: Georg Lukács' efforts to tame the recalcitrant detail of the literary naturalist mode in the essay "Narrate or Describe?" (1936). He argued there that it was the organizational duty of true or "realist" narrative to contain the "filler" of descriptive excess.[77] For Lukács, nar-rative legibility was threatened by the uncontrollable infinity of "[a]n arbitrary detail, a chance similarity, a fortuitous attitude, an accidental meeting" that was typical of the quasi-photographic dimensions in the novels of a naturalist writer like Zola.[78] In an analogous context, Brunhes (whose human geography descended directly from a naturalist obsession with the observation of man and his environ-ment) imagined that if the images in the Archives de la Planète were also made legible by a written supplement that provided evidence of their date, place, and subject matter, they could be easily analyzed, manipulated, and compared in the future like the documents of any scientifically organized archive.[79] As individual films, they might resemble the descriptive views of Zola's fiction, but as *archival* films semiotically anchored by a textual document, they accrued the potential sta-tus of historical narrative.[80] In this sense, the archival logic that underpinned the production of textual supports for Kahn's films was intended *ideally* to function as realist narration did for Lukács, that is, as a controlling and elevating device, much as Matuszewski's film archive was supposed to function as an "uplifting monumental historiography devoted to the moral education of the citizen and the celebration of the nation."[81]

However, at the same time as ensuring their cultural legibility, the archival logic supposedly controlling Kahn's films at the level of the *fiche* could never entirely protect itself against the counter-archival virus carried by Lukács' arbitrary detail. Just as the most restrictive anthropometric and classificatory photographic practices of the late nineteenth century fell prey to the counter-archival disorder and illegibility that haunted taxonomic systems, so too would Brunhes' desire to transform the image into a stock of quantifiable and comparative data, especially given the infinite informational chaos of film, constitute a losing battle.[82] More importantly, this battle was also consciously offset or undermined from within by Brunhes' explicit interest in the stray, casual detail.

A LIGHT THAT ILLUMINATES SPACE AND TIME

Notwithstanding the force of these counter-archival tendencies, the more conventional aspects of the *école méthodique's* model of the archive also appeared in other features of Kahn's Archive. For example, one of the central principles of the more positivist factions of the *école méthodique* rested upon a new calling for history: to predict and manage the future through the rational and highly detailed examination of documents from the past. Positivist historians of the late nineteenth century claimed their goal was to "research the laws which preside during the development of the human species" in order to "at once reconstitute the past and predict the future."[83] What Krzysztof Pomian has called the *futurocentric* aspect of the positivist archive was summarized by one of the many respondents to Matuszewski's 1898 pamphlet.[84] Commenting favorably upon Matuszewski's claim for film's potential as a new source for history, the pseudonymous journalist Thomas Grimm warned: "It is important that all the arts [including film] converge *to control* and ensure the veracity of this precious science History, thanks to which the present can, by studying the past, *prepare for the future*."[85]

Kahn inherited both the utilitarian and utopian aspects of the positivist's dream of total knowledge. The desire to discover the universal laws of the world (what he called "life's path and the universe's functioning principles") in order to organize a better future for humanity, particularly after the atrocities of the First World War, was a central concern of Kahn's documentary projects and runs like a mantra through his *Des Droits et devoirs des gouvernements* (1918), particularly in its insistent, ocularcentric command "To See–To Predict–To Know" (*Voir–Prévoir–Savoir*).[86] Not surprisingly, Kahn was also described as "a man who does not content himself with living in the present and who applies himself, not only to divine tomorrows but what's more to determine [and] to prepare for them."[87] And in one of Kahn's rare descriptions of the Archive, he referred to it as a "documentation" project devoted to "directly recording, by means of film and color photography, activities suited to illuminating the development of life, and testimonies always ready to radiate, everywhere, ongoing activity to the benefit of future Humanity."[88] At the heart of this need to control the future was Kahn's war-driven fear of the unpredictability of the present. Voiced in a rage against the forces of what Kahn regularly abbreviates as "chance," this fear of unpredictability also appears, albeit in different forms, in Bergson's rejection of the purely contingent "any moment" and in Lukács' suspicion toward the "arbitrary detail."[89]

If the Archives de la Planète was built as a sort of dam against the forces of chance, film clearly held a privileged role to play in Kahn's positivist and utopian belief in the scientific value of observation and the transformative power of the recorded fact once delivered into the hands of a guiding elite:

> In order to decipher the meaning of life, and appreciate the origin and import of events, facts offer a powerful, irresistible, and incorruptible language. As an inexhaustible haven for providing information, they project incessantly a light that illuminates space and time.[90]

Of all his funded media, it was film, a form that literally embodies that "light which illuminates space and time," that was most suited to fulfilling Kahn's goal of establishing a safe haven for the world of facts in an "incorruptible" medium. Underpinning Kahn's vision of an "inexhaustible haven" of information and his expectations for film's role as a modern tool of enlightenment was the humanist and pacifist ideology of at least one branch in the evolution of the modern archive, the one that would develop in response to the destruction of state archives in the First World War and the literally murderous archives of the Second.[91] It was the same ideal— of establishing or protecting vast knowledge banks dedicated to what Bergson called a "common world experience"—that motivated the Belgian internationalist and bibliographer Paul Otlet (and "bibliophote" inventor) in his diverse efforts to increase access to global knowledge through the creation of a "world library" intended to foster peace and tolerance.[92] The humanist rationale for this archiving tradition resurfaced in the post–Second World War era when Charles Braibant, then director of the Archives Nationales, situated the institution he headed within the tradition to which Kahn's Archives de la Planète aspired, one "centered on the avatars of the great human desire for peace, since the Quarantaine du Roi up until the League of Nations, the UN and UNESCO."[93] Although there are good reasons why today we more commonly associate archives with tools of state oppression, it is just as important to recognize the alternatives in the history of archives that have explicitly resisted this definition.

FROM THE WORLD LIBRARY TO THE SOUND ATLAS

The Kahn Archive clearly drew upon the utilitarian, enlightenment, humanist, and utopian aspects of the combined positivist and historicist model of the archive. Yet it also belonged to a continuum of archiving practices across diverse modern media. Beginning with the notion of film archiving in a loose sense, we could suggest that the most obvious antecedent to Kahn's mission to send cameramen around the world to catalogue everyday life was the Lumières' global film enterprise of the turn of the century. However, if the Lumières' global production schedule may have inspired Kahn, it would have only done so in a vague way as Lumière film production had ended by the time the Archive began in 1908.[94] Furthermore, although the origins, and indeed demise, of Kahn's project lie in the profit and risks of capitalist speculation, expansion, and investment, unlike the Lumières' commercial enterprise the Kahn Archive was never intended to make a profit. Therefore, if the Lumières' cataloguing of the world does not provide the model for Kahn's global film archive of daily life, what other modern archival projects predated or existed alongside the Archives de la Planète?

A global cinematic archive may not have been available to Kahn when he embarked on establishing his Archive, but as my earlier reference to Bertillon's police archives suggests, there were many photographic-based archival models to draw upon. A clue to the Kahn Archive's relation to such projects appears in one of the most common titles used in the Kahn film ledger—the category "Vieux Paris."[95] The phrase *Vieux Paris* refers to the recording of Old Paris in the tradition of the Commission Municipale du Vieux Paris, the institution established around 1897 to protect and document the historical heritage of the capital after the damage wrought by Baron Haussmann's radical modernization projects.[96] Eugène Atget, probably the most well-known photographer to have filled requests for the Commission, may have boasted to them in November 1920 that "I possess all of Vieux Paris," but it was those lesser known visual chroniclers of Paris, Kahn's cameramen, who first applied the possession of a systematic visual documentation of "Vieux Paris" to the medium of film.[97]

Aside from their interest in "Vieux Paris," an even more important overarching feature joins Atget and Kahn's documents, namely, their adherence to an archival logic. The reason many of Atget's views of Paris looked so uncannily "empty" (as Benjamin famously put it), deserted as they were of human presence, is because they originally functioned as public records of topographical and architectural, not anthropological, traces.[98] Their initial "incomplete" look was intentional and was supposed to be supplemented in the future when they would be used by clients like antiquarians, artists, and set designers not interested in the messy interruptions of contemporary human figures upon the eternal stage of "Vieux Paris."[99] In other words, the *archival* context of the Commission's requests formed the basis of Atget's style of unadorned documentation. Whatever else we might read into his images, the "primacy of the abstract catalogue" seems incontestable in Atget's *oeuvre*; he was guided in his choice of subjects and the ordering of his work by the need to fulfill the orders of an overarching archival directive.[100]

Although the archival impulse was noncommercial and even more explicit in Kahn's as opposed to Atget's documents (where it was attached to the profit motivations of his profession as a stock-image provider), the incomplete nature of the Kahn footage and the intentionally unfinished look of Atget's images reflect the archival, user-focused destinies of both projects. However, Kahn's cameramen did not share Atget's preference for empty street scenes abstracted from historical time. On the one hand, such a distinction is perhaps not worth mentioning. The motion picture technology obviously drew them to movement and crowds in order to fulfill Kahn's goal of tracking the "look, modes and practices" of human *activity* and Brunhes' interest in "the rhythms of life." On the other hand, their obsessive attention to the random occurrences, gestures, and movements that breathe life into the city street indicate the influence of a different tradition of photographic encyclopedism, that which existed in the world of science and education.

In contrast to Atget's commercial archive, the more didactic end of the photographic archive spectrum in which images were collected *en masse* for intra-scientific research dates back to proto-cinematic forms such as the vast serial photographic studies of human and animal motion by Eadweard Muybridge, Étienne-Jules Marey, and Félix-Louis Regnault. All worked toward the ideal of a "positivist program for the constitution of archives" based on the photographic and filmic study of movement.[101] Although less associated with the form of the archive, the proto-ethnographic films made by the anthropologists Alfred Cort Haddon and William Baldwin Spencer in Australia also contributed to this tradition. Their films point to the crucial nexus between anthropology's "salvage paradigm" (to save and record primitive cultures before they disappear) and film's potential application as a positivist source of evidence and preservation regarding supposedly "dying" cultures.[102] A more explicit Eurocentric archival motivation appeared in the institutionalization of fieldwork and participant observation promoted by Bronislaw Malinowski in the 1920s. Malinowski divided the world into those who have written archives (the West) and those who do not (nonliterate oral-based societies), thereby supporting a hierarchy between archives as the houses of history and the "field" as the laboratory for the "imponderabilia of the everyday."[103] Writing in 1922, Malinowski argued that it was the ethnographer's duty to redress this imbalance, by "collecting concrete data of evidence" and "drawing general inferences" from "all that is permanent and fixed" in the daily life of the tribe, in effect cataloguing (as Lévi-Strauss went on to do) the everyday life of the Other for the purposes of expanding the knowledge archive of the West.[104] Although Kahn's cameramen filmed their own countrymen as much as they did colonial subjects or foreigners, their curiosity-driven filming and note-taking (which in the case of Albert Dutertre, Lucien Le Saint, and Stéphane Passet included diary writing) situates them at least on the amateur edges of the new archivally aligned ethnographic practices of fieldwork and participant observation.

If Kahn's Archive was not the only project to appreciate film's value as a haven for "dying cultures," nor was it the only one to recognize the historical or educational significance of film's capacity to salvage the nascent but ephemeral daily culture of urban modernity. In a 1913 report supporting the city's intentions of beginning a film archive, Paul Flobert, the secretary general of Les Amis de la Bibliothèque de la Ville de Paris, emphasized the urgent need to "conserve these fugitive fragments" of Paris that appeared in actuality films.[105] At a time when the material face of the city was changing more rapidly than ever, preserving footage of Paris acquired an ever more material and, during the war, nationalist urgency. Coupled with the already established mania for encyclopedic practices, this preservational ethic in France produced arguably the most developed network of film archiving efforts in the world.[106]

A decade later, an article calling for the creation of the Archives Nationales du Cinéma came even closer to invoking the encyclopedic mission behind Kahn's Archive. In terms that echo Brunhes' 1913 description of the Archive as "a sort of true picture of life in our age," the author of the 1924 article imagined a film collection that "would be an immense *tableau vivant* of the existence of our country which would be forever reflected across the future centuries."[107] Although a national film archive would not be established in France until 1969, a range of smaller film archives did exist during the 1910s and 1920s. The Kahn Archive resembled these other archive-related film efforts, especially those that produced their own documents, rather than collecting them from other sources. These included the collection of nonfiction films created for the Encyclopédie Gaumont (1913), the Section Photographique et Cinématographique de l'Armée (1917), the Ministère des Colonies (under the aegis of the Agences Economiques from 1918), and to a lesser extent, the Musée Pédagogique (1921), the Cinémathèque du Ministère de l'Agriculture (1923), as well as the institution that was the culmination of Flobert's and others efforts, the Cinémathèque de la Ville de Paris (1925).[108] Most importantly, unlike the second wave of film archiving, which gathered momentum in the mid-thirties with the creation of national-based film collections (like Stockholm's Filmsamfundet, Berlin's Reichsfilmarchiv, New York's Film Library at the Museum of Modern Art, London's National Film Library, and Paris's Cinémathèque Française), the first wave of film archiving (to which the Kahn Archive and the above projects belonged) all privileged the documentary rather than the aesthetic value of film.[109]

The closest relative of the Kahn Archive, however, was not even a film archive. The project that inspired both the model and name of Kahn's Archives de la Planète was in fact a phonographic archive called the Archives de la Parole. Described by the musicologist and director of the Phonotèque Nationale Roger Dévigné as "a true national sound Encyclopedia of languages, dialects, popular traditions and old songs of France," the Archives de la Parole was created by the linguist Ferdinand Brunot in 1911 at the Sorbonne with funding and equipment by Émile Pathé (whose more well-known film company originally produced phonographs).[110] During the early teens it was often referred to in the cinema press as a benchmark for what ought to be accomplished in the area of film archiving.[111] It is thus not surprising that Brunhes and Kahn were actually in contact with Brunot.[112]

Kahn's Archive also shared the encyclopedic ambitions of the Archives de la Parole, which Brunot variously described as a "sound atlas," "sound Museum," and "printing press for sounds."[113] But the real point of convergence between these two projects appears in their shared desire to enrich the national *patrimoine* by drawing attention to the usually overlooked significance of everyday life, within the framework of a quasi-anthropological approach to culture. Very much the inheritor of the late-nineteenth-century folkloric movement in France, Brunot pursued what de Certeau would characterize as the study of the everyday rooted in an "internal exoticism."[114] Mirroring in reverse the quest to capture difference that was being pursued by his anthropological colleagues in the colonies, Brunot traveled to the remotest parts of France in a truck loaded with recording equipment in order to capture, in the home field, sonic vestiges of a rural culture deemed to be on the brink of extinction. Ironically, the threat to rural cultures came from the same technologies trying to save it. As one reporter noted, it was the standardizing and nationalizing "diffusion of the French language," promoted, in part, by film intertitles, that was leading to the demise of local dialect.[115] Reflecting upon how the Archives de la Parole was established to manage this threat—"when the precious vestiges of our history [dialects and patois, vocal traditions and songs] continue[d] to disappear"—Roger Dévigné wrote of "the importance of these sound monuments, which can equal in value, if they are *scientifically collected*, other monuments of stone and marble that the centuries have bequeathed to us and that we conserve with pride."[116] Brunhes' description of the Archives de la Planète's goal, "to capture and conserve the facts of the planet which are going to die," struck a strikingly similar note to Brunot's goal for his own archive written two years earlier—to "go first toward what is going to disappear."[117] Brunot's sound archive thus provided Kahn and Brunhes with a reputable positivist model (note Dévigné's reference to the "*scientifically collected*" sound documents) with which to reinvent the archive by expanding the notion of nationally significant historical evidence to include nonwritten sources, new media technologies, and, most importantly, the daily culture of ordinary people.

THE UNIQUENESS OF THE ARCHIVES DE LA PLANÈTE

Far from being the eccentric invention of a reclusive millionaire, the Archives de la Planète thus belonged to a widespread trend in France—articulated in reference to the historicist model of the archive—to mobilize film and other modern technologies of recording as archival media. Nevertheless, vital differences separated the Kahn Archive from the related projects detailed above, not least the fact that its films were noncommercial, nontheatrical, and noncirculating. Although a small selection of Kahn's films were regularly screened on his property for invited guests, and one instance has come to light of a film being loaned, the majority of the films remained out of circulation from day one of their existence.[118] As a result of their noncirculating status, the Kahn films lie outside conventional understandings of film as a recording medium intended for projection close to the original time of recording. In its deferral of the moment of projection, the Kahn Archive thus reached for the preservationist futurocentrism of a time capsule. "Do not disturb," rather than "handle carefully with gloves," was the command under which these films existed.

Moreover, in stark opposition to the democratizing ethic of access that inspired the revolutionary origins of the French archive, Kahn's films belonged to an archive devoted to the idea of intentionally confiscated fragments of history. Although we can learn much by speculating about the sizeable if closed audience to whom a selection of these films were screened, all explorations of their exhibition context must account for the fact that what Kahn's audience's saw was a sneak preview of some future film with an imprecise release date.[119] In short, Kahn's films were intended more for our eyes than theirs. Thus, if during the course of the Archive's operative years its films remained mostly unwatched, and, perhaps more importantly, unwatchable—due to their non-edited form that removed them from contemporary expectations of commercial actualities and travelogues of the time—this perhaps was precisely the point: they were not meant to be watched in their own present.

The deferral of the Kahn films' reception forces us to consider even more striking differences between the Archives de la Planète and other archival-related film projects of the era. First, the Archive actually sits uncomfortably alongside those enterprises that were united by a scientific application of film. For instance, although the Kahn Archive undoubtedly shared Marey's and Regnault's positivist zeal for description and classification, the Kahn films were not stored in archives for the purpose of being "examined repeatedly, frame by frame" by either scientists or the general public.[120] In fact, the only person who seems to have had the opportunity to repeatedly view the films was Kahn himself, whose name is the most frequent entry in the projection register (fig. 7.3). Second, the Archive may have resembled the French Army archive or the film service of the Ministry of Colonies in that it produced, rather than purchased, its own films, yet unlike both it was never intended as an organ of nationalist-imperialist propaganda. Third, though the Kahn films existed in the orbit of an elite pedagogical network they were never destined for use in school education, as were the films at the Cinémathèque de la Ville de Paris and those belonging to the Encyclopédie Gaumont. Fourth, unlike Brunot's sound archive, which mainly focused on rural France, or the Colonial Ministry films, which were dominated by the need to make the colonies visible to the French, or Gaumont's cinematic Encyclopédie, which by 1929 was stuck in a time warp in which the Great War and the following economic and social upheavals seem to have never occurred, the Kahn Archive paid as much if not more attention to urban life, the metropole, and postwar social issues as it did to rural life, the colonies, or the war.

In other words, in spite of the conservative and nostalgic regionalism of Brunhes' outlook, Kahn's cameramen were just as dedicated to tracing the emergence of modern France. Furthermore, unlike the above projects, Kahn's cameramen regularly updated and refilmed subjects in a sort of perpetual stocktaking of the present, which is why one can find serial recordings of certain topics, places, or practices. Finally, even though Kahn's project definitely found a model in the Archives de la Parole, it resisted that project's attachment to a single medium (phonography) or a single institution (the Sorbonne).[121] And though many famous dignitaries were filmed for the Archive, Kahn, unlike Brunot, would never have compared his project to a "Pantheon."[122] If it did contribute to the wider aim behind all of Kahn's projects (as described by Henri Bergson), to fulfill the wish of "eminent men from all countries, especially those who nurture the dream of a better and organized humanity," it did not consider those same eminent men to be the privileged subject of its films.[123] The flip side to its privileging of ordinary people on the screen was its intention, typical of an early-twentieth-century intellectual fascination with the everyday, to promote an exclusively elite reception context in front of the screen. Thus unlike the "Sound Pantheon," the Archives de la Planète was never meant to arouse public curiosity. And if famous people were filmed at Boulogne, it was mostly for their own pleasure as many of these films seem to have been given to their subjects as personal gifts from Kahn.[124]

Kahn's approach to the film Archive also differed from both the early advocates of film archives, such as Matuszewski, and subsequent proponents like Victor Perrot (who along with Léon Riotor and Flobert spearheaded the campaign for the establishment of the Cinémathèque de la Ville de Paris in the teens and early twenties) in that it was more ambitious on a technological, internationalist, and utopian level. And unlike Auguste Rondel's textual-based film library (the first in France to systematically collect scenarios, stills, posters, reviews, and books on contemporary film and the history of cinema), Kahn's archival passion was not aroused by the desire to conserve the history of film culture as a theatrical and commercial form of art and entertainment.[125] Most importantly, the Archives de la Planète was far more dependent than these related plans and versions of film or film-related collections on its self-conscious identity as an archive of everyday life.

ARCHIVE *VOLONTAIRE*

Finally, although the Archives de la Planète followed the example of the positivist archive, in its attempt to set up a model of scientific deduction through the index card system, it also diverged from Langlois and Seignebos' concept of the historicist archive in several respects. In order to trace these divergences, it will be useful to consult Langlois and Seignbos' definition of the archive that still prevailed in the early 1960s when the former director of the Archives Nationales, Robert-Henri Bautier, offered the following distinction between archives and collections:

> The notion of "*fonds d'archives*" is totally opposed to that of a "collection": a col-
> lection—that of a museum . . . is constituted after the fact [*après coup*], according
> to certain necessarily subjective criteria, in order to respond to certain tastes, to
> chance purchases, gifts, bequests. In contrast, documents are deposited in archives
> exactly in the manner in which the sediments of geological layers form, progressively,
> constantly.[126]

Bautier and other like-minded pre-Foucauldian historians of the archive believed in the neutrality of original sources as inviolable depositories of "truth" at the expense of admitting the political dimensions of the cataloguing and sorting procedures through which historical documents are preserved.[127] For Bautier, archives (unlike collections) are not manufactured, they are simply deposited and later unearthed. Following Bautier's definition, archives do not develop according to the "subjective" and "chance" interventions of humans and history; rather, they seem to grow organically with the same slow, almost invisible and inevitable progression that produces in nature "sediments of geological layers." Consequently, their historical value and appeal only emerges retroactively in their second life once the documents have been mined from their original context (usually as state records) and brought into the public domain of the archive with the intention of eventually being consulted by historians. As Bautier argues, the "document from the archives is thus not conceived from its origins as . . . having a historical importance" and in their original context "they are not destined for public curiosity."[128] In other words, despite Bautier's organicist rhetoric, his definition makes it clear that the unnatural processes of abstraction and decontextualization—reflective of the document's submission to an *après coup* logic—are essential processes in the production of the archival document.

Though earlier and more contemporary advocates of a historical-based film archive, such as Matuszewski and Flobert, followed the historicist model of Bautier's idea of the archive—as a collection of already-made and retrospectively salvaged documents—Kahn's Archive diverged radically from this model. His primary aim, we should remember, was not to preserve already-made films or rescue gems from cinema's geological substrata but to make entirely new films, or more correctly, fragments of films, deliberately intended to be documents in an archive. Thus, unlike Benjamin's favorite urban archivist—the *chiffonnier* who reconfigures consumerism by reworking the material detritus of capitalist exchange, kneading new life into discarded and outdated refuse—Kahn reconfigures the production (of history) by doing away with the original circulation of the document from which its archival afterlife is conventionally abstracted.[129] He does away with the event (*coup*) that the archival document was meant to follow (*après*). Put simply, Kahn's fragments of film did not just find their way into an archive after having lived a life somewhere else; his films were born in an archive. Consequently, they transgress the law, as described by Carolyn Steedman, which stipulates that "nothing starts in the archive, nothing, ever at all, though things certainly end up there."[130]

Magnifying the anxious impatience of Kahn's desperation to do away with time (reflected in his frenzied writing style, his noted irritation with the present, and most grandiosely, his camera-phobic aversion to being personally ensnared by film's temporal web), the Archives de la Planète treats the present as though it was already historical. It approaches the contemporary with all the respect usually saved for the imperiled detritus of the past. Contrary to conventional archives that are shepherded by those who come after the original life of its documents, Kahn's Archive was not retroactive but anticipatory; it was, in short, a voluntary rather than involuntary film archive. From their conception, Kahn's films brazenly courted the future and were always identified as "having a historical importance." And unlike the majority of films from this period, Kahn's were deliberately made to travel to the future where their meaning awaited them. The futurocentric single-mindedness of the Archive places a particular historical pressure on Kahn's films, forcing them to bear openly the "unknowable weight" that Jacques Derrida argues the concept of the archive carries, subject as it is to the "movement of the promise and of the future no less than of recording the past."[131]

Measured against Bautier's definition, however, the Archives de la Planète would thus have to be categorized as an unnaturally evolving archive. In contrast to the archival ideal of history in the raw, deposited in the form of unpublished, found records, the documents in the Kahn Archive are as cultivated and artificially composed as their owner's collection of English, Japanese, and Mediterranean landscapes, or, to take an even more pertinent example, Dr. Comandon's time-lapse studies of flowers blooming. Unlike the mythical historical archive discovered by chance or rescued heroically from the ravages of time, there is nothing haphazard or natural about how Kahn's Archive came to be. Whereas other archives were seen as virgin sources to be penetrated by the newly trained army of scientific historians, the Kahn Archive distinguished itself as a blatantly constructed and manipulated archive. Instead of passively waiting for history to happen in some other medium and then collecting its traces, the Kahn Archive seized the impatient curiosity of the camera and manufactured history. It thus denaturalized Bautier's definition of the archive as that which forms naturally over time. Consequently, it unwittingly placed in question the myth of the ideologically neutral archive as an institution intended to passively reflect and collect rather than intervene with and shape history. Furthermore, comprised as it was of documents which were *always already* archival, having never lived in any original context prior to the Archive in the outside world, the Archives de la Planète does not satisfy that nostalgic desire to find, possess, and "return to the authentic and singular origin" that Derrida claims is central to Western obsessions with archiving.[132] The Kahn Archive may have courted archival orthodoxy from day one of its existence, but it also thwarted that goal by promoting invention not unmediated truth, willful recording not passive inscription, and repetition not singular authenticity.

The Kahn Archive did, however, uphold that other key feature of the modern archive as defined by Bautier, namely, the goal of exhaustiveness and indivisibility based on the principle of respect for the provenance and *"fond organique"*—the organic whole of the collection.[133] Kahn and his collaborators kept everything they recorded and left the films (aside from the small amount that were edited) in the original state in which they were shot. Unlike Gaumont and Pathé, who as commercial companies understood their commodity to be edited film rather than raw footage, from its inception the Kahn Archive privileged the rushes as the essential form around which the film collection was based.[134] Although this does not mean that everything shot by Kahn's cameramen exists today, it does suggest that Kahn had a profound respect for the indexical value and spatial-temporal integrity of raw footage. Moreover, the rawness of the Kahn footage also aligns the project with the essential object of the historicist archive: *unpublished* documents. Unlike libraries, which traditionally store and circulate published texts, and unlike the earliest national film archives that emerged in the thirties and aimed to save the *fiction* film heritage, the Kahn Archive was deeply faithful to the traditional understanding of an archive as the site for nonfiction, unpublished fragments or *documents inédits*. Kahn's Archive thus conformed to the Bautier model in its respect for the organic totality of the collection and in its singular adherence to the original length of the rushes and the privileging of unpublished documents, yet departed from the Bautier model in that the films were made intentionally as documents with historical and pedagogical value.

If the voluntary nature of the Kahn documents posed an indirect threat to Langlois and Seignebos' concept of the archive, the Kahn Archive's de-privileging of the written document as the sole source for archival evidence posed a more serious threat. Notwithstanding the growing acceptance of film as an educational tool (particularly for younger children), Kahn's decision to include moving images in his Archive was daring, especially for a project seeking approval from the Sorbonne and the Collège de France. Even though so-called men of science like Félix-Louis Regnault tried to promote the research use of film in the early teens, and the birth of fieldwork in anthropology during Haddon's 1898 Torres Strait Expedition had been accompanied by film, it was still deemed untrustworthy as a medium for providing objective scientific evidence.[135] As for biology, Dr. Comandon himself recalled how the first screenings of the films he made in the Pathé laboratory at Vincennes (where he began working in 1908) caused him to be derided as a "profane figure" by some of his scientific colleagues.[136] Boldly (or naively) disregarding these academic reservations about film and photography's status as archival sources, and many years ahead of the state's efforts to archive film, Kahn grafted the late-nineteenth-century notion of the historical archive with its exclusive focus on the written document onto the new media of a twentieth-century archive.[137]

Yet, as I have been suggesting at different points in this chapter, in forcing a confrontation between traditional history and modern mnemonic technologies, a confrontation that echoes Bergson's intervention into the memory-as-archive metaphor and foreshadows Foucault's interrogation of the document, the Kahn Archive risked exposing the fabrication of the myth of the archive as a repository of objective truth where documents lie dormant, waiting to be roused. Kahn's documents were never "put to sleep" like the documents entering a conventional archive; they entered the world asleep (if not quite stillborn). But even more crucially, what was at stake in his gamble on film was the very epistemological status of his documents, that is, whether they resembled unique originals or (to invoke Canudo's assessment of film) merely "*cop[ies]* of a subject."[138] Even though the early film archival theorist Matuszewski tried to instill the "aura" of the authentic original into his model of the film archive by stressing the importance of safeguarding the film negative, the technically reproducible nature of the medium, as Benjamin would famously argue, had disturbed the notion of the unique and authentic original (art work or document) forever.[139] This also meant that film could never be a new source for the type of late-nineteenth-century "scientific" history that privileged original sources following the influential example of German textual-based philology.[140] Furthermore, even though Matuszewski noted how difficult (in comparison to photography) it would be to touch up and distort the "truth" of film via frame-by-frame manipulation, there were very few scientists who were prepared to depend on film alone as their single source of objective evidence.

Finally, shadowing the more triumphant predictions regarding film's ability to store and preserve the fleeting and the ephemeral was the recognition of the material fragility of the celluloid nitrate medium itself. As early as 1897 one commentator impressively estimated in *La Nature* the butterfly-like lifespan (in projected time) of a single film frame to be "one-and-one-third seconds."[141] And in a related comment made by Yhcam in the teens that ties film's fragile material temporality to an archival context, film's tragically ironic talent for preserving the momentary eventfulness of uneventful life takes another turn in his contemplation of the "ephemeral life" of most films.[142] Thus, at least eight decades before Derrida described the condition of "archive fever" (the death-driven twin to the origins-driven "archive desire"), the diagnosis was perhaps already being made in reference to the self-immolating fatalism that haunted modernity's outwardly perfect medium of preservation, namely film. If for Derrida the Freudian unconscious provided the purest "example it seems of archiving *otherwise*," the above commentators and the Kahn Archive suggest that the other major discovery of the turn-of-the-century, film, presented an even more applicable and extreme alteration to the concept of the archive.[143]

PERROT AND POSTERITY

Whether due to its uncharacteristic respect for the integrity of unedited film footage or its apparently advanced system for storing sensitive nitrate film, Kahn's Archive did appear on the radar of one of the most active pioneers in the early effort to archive film in France, Victor Perrot. Perrot's personal archives, which detail the decades-long struggle to establish the Cinémathèque de la Ville de Paris, reveal that his interest in Kahn's Archive began as early as 1914 and persisted until at least 1953.[144] In 1920, as part of preliminary research into how one might establish and maintain a film archive, Perrot wrote to a number of relevant figures, including Louis Lumière, the French Army Archives, and Albert Kahn. His letter to Kahn is worth quoting in full:

> The Commission du Vieux Paris is presently occupied with the matter of the conservation of *films historiques*. As the vast future of this "new Writing" interests me particularly, I have been charged with writing up a report on this question. Having known for years you have been far ahead of the public authorities—which have still done nothing—when it comes to the collection of numerous *films documentaires*, allow me to benefit from your experience in asking you to let me visit at an hour most convenient to you.[145]

Aside from the flattering recognition of Kahn's achievements and the display of Perrot's continuing reference to film as a "new Writing" for history, the letter indicates that his primary interest lay in learning how to run a film archive. In a letter dated February 23, 1921, that he received from a secretary to Kahn, Perrot in fact received information on such film archiving practices as how to store the precious nitrate negatives.[146] This letter also indicates that, following Perrot's earlier request, Kahn's secretary was in the process of cataloguing all the films in the Archive that might be of interest to the Commission du Vieux Paris.[147] Perrot thus seems to have expressed an interest in buying copies of the Kahn films that dealt with Paris.[148] Perhaps because it entailed a "huge job," in the end Kahn's secretary does not appear to have furnished that filmography to Perrot, but he did provide him with the length of films relating to Paris—"30, 000 meters."[149]

Perrot's engagement with the Archive is revealing on several counts. First, it suggests further connections between Atget and Kahn's visual archives because the Commission du Vieux Paris was the same organization to which Atget sold many of his photographs. Second, the correspondence shows that even by 1920, a ready-to-hand comprehensive catalogue of the Kahn films did not exist, point-ing to the failure of the Archive to conform to systematic scientific models of ar-chiving.[150] Perrot's request at the Boulogne property seems to have met a similar fate to that made by Apollinaire at the Bibliothèque Nationale a decade earlier, which indicates at the least the continuing challenge posed by the sorting, cata-loguing, and communicating of filmic as opposed to print-based documents, even within a self-styled film archive. Third, the correspondence with Kahn's "amiable secretary" suggests that Kahn may have been accommodating to external interest in his Archive but only up to a point.[151] For it is well known that Kahn did not want his films to be distributed in conditions outside his control; this probably explains why the purchase of Kahn's Parisian films by the Cinémathèque de la Ville de Paris never took place.

Most importantly, this brief exchange led to Perrot's stepping in to ensure in 1934 that Kahn's films were saved from destruction and included in the sale of his properties to the Département de la Seine.[152] Perrot's efforts were probably helped by the increased sense of urgency around film preservation in the early 1930s fol-lowing the shift to sound in the French industry, which caused the destruction of countless silent films and consequently heightened the appeal for film preserva-tion in general—an appeal that culminated with the establishment in 1936 of the Cinémathèque Française. That does not mean, however, that Kahn's films nar-rowly escaped being orphaned in response to the importance of Kahn's original intention—to use film as a tool for international cooperation—nor because they appealed to the fiction film bias of the Cinémathèque Française. Rather, they were saved from the flames because two decades after his original encounter with them, Kahn's films still inspired Perrot's cherished dream: to recognize nonfiction films as a valid "Source of History."

On a different note, the survival of Kahn's films also marks a pivotal moment in the archival meaning of the Archives de la Planète. The 1934 sale of the collection signals the rebirth of the Archives de la Planète as a more traditional *après coup* archive.[153] Nearly entirely decontextualized and abstracted from their primary context as tools in the struggle for international peace and cooperation and from their original counter-archival logic, the Kahn films fall into a more conventional, archival slumber from 1934 onwards.[154] The only reminders of their first deeper sleep, the gardens in which they still remain rooted.

CONCLUSION

One of the many respondents to Matuszewski's proposal for an archive for films of historical interest took the opportunity to predict that "in a few years time chairs of history would all be occupied by simple magic lantern operators."[155] In personally funding the first Chair of Human Geography and ensuring it was given to a geographer who was enlisted to direct an Archive based on the projection of autochrome slides and film, Kahn indeed succeeded by 1912 in installing a camera into an academic Chair of Geography, if not of History. Although in many respects the Kahn Archive carved its own path, it also reflected a widespread recognition of film's unique historicist archival capacities that dated back to the beginnings of cinema. This chapter has been concerned with tracing the common desire to wed film to an archival context across a range of discourses and actual projects in France that negotiated figuratively and literally the positivist and counter-positivist archival properties of film, especially as they related to the idea and discipline of history.

Film emerged in the wake of the golden age of the print-based positivist and historicist archive. Although commentators were ready to imagine the first film archives as superior versions of print-based records offices, they were less able to confront how films reconfigured the concept of the archive altogether. Thus, the first intimations of film's counter-archival tendencies did not amount to an active opposition to the archive. Indeed, many early film archive efforts continued in the tradition of the print-based archive. Nonetheless, their film rather than print-based documents meant they simultaneously enacted and contested, reinstated and dissolved traditional archival principles. More than any other such project, the Kahn Archive allows us to think about film as a counter-archival force. The Archives de la Planète illuminates the general properties of the medium not conducive to positivism—its propensity for anarchic disorder, visual excess, arbitrary details, nonoriginal evidence, and unhealthy curiosity—alongside its own more specific counter-positivist leanings. Beyond the Archive's privileging of nonsystematic rather than systematic science, these tendencies included its preference for a private rather than publically accessible and state-centered notion of the archive, for documents that were stylistically and subjectively stamped rather than clinically anonymous, for visual information that was nonhierarchizable rather than easily classifiable, for an incomplete and fragmented rather than comprehensive and edited notion of film evidence, and for a voluntary rather than involuntary conception of history.

For all its positivist ambitions, Kahn's Archive ultimately presented both the apotheosis and contestation of the historicist archetype of the archive. Consequently, its films magnify the tensions within the medium's archival identity. On the one hand, they show how film was envisaged as the perfect archival document, "a very humble servant" of history, and indexical referent or material trace of a past event.[156] On the other hand, the films, and their relation to the wider Archive to which they belonged, also disclosed this dream's shadow within the unexpected contours of a counter-archival project, one characterized by film's uncontrollable capacity to automatically and indiscriminately record anything that passes in front of the camera's unblinking gaze, and the Archive's ability, through the deliberate manufacturing of documents, to produce, rather than simply store, fragments of contemporary history.

The Archives de la Planète thus contributed in a pioneering way to the history of French archiving practices (and of film in particular) while also disrupting the traditional concept of the archive as a naturally occurring textual depository of history. If the Kahn Archive provided the one exception to France's failure to bring to fruition the spirit, if not the actual substance, of Matuszewski's vision, then it also showed that film was not simply a more accurate or new source of history as usual. The Kahn Archive suggested an entirely different approach to history, one made possible through film's archival imperative and its potential for being (as Doumic put it) at once "encyclopedic and incoherent."

Far from validating Bergson's contempt for the archive-as-memory metaphor, the Archives de la Planète disrupted preconceived conceptions of the archive and its associated discipline, history, in line with the philosopher's own counter-archival reimagining of memory. Furthermore, rather than being confined to the early cinema period, film's archival drive continued to sidetrack the medium's safer destiny with familiar realism well into the era of narrative-dominated cinema, and especially in reference to its affinity with the invisible, neglected, or elusive dimensions of contemporary daily life. In short, what we begin to see from the varied discourses and practices focused on film-as-archive is that the new medium destabilized the concept of the archive and out of that destabilization emerged new forms of representing and thinking memory and history's relation to the everyday. These new modes of historicity included that nonfiction genre most preoccupied with the history of the present, actualities, and extended to the appropriation of film's unique temporal registers by the school of history that succeeded the *école méthodique*, that founded by the early Annales historians.

THE "ANECDOTAL SIDE OF HISTORY"

TEMPORALITY, FILM, AND ANNALES HISTORIOGRAPHY

> *Les grandes événements historiques* do not all have the same importance: there is the battle of the Marne and the boxing match. However, it is the boxing match, which, if one thinks about it, will open the secret door of the archives of tomorrow—cinematographic archives.
>
> PIERRE HUMBOURG (1933)[1]

> If we are so often disappointed [with conventional actualities], the reason is this: events are of two kinds: there is the blockbuster event—sudden and important; and then there is the slow-burn kind of event, which evolves as the days go by and whose true meaning becomes clearer only with time. The striking event and the subtle event.
>
> GERMAINE DULAC (C. 1936)[2]

BEYOND ITS PHOTOGRAPHIC CAPACITIES, film's arrival on the cusp of the twentieth century introduced for the first time the means for recording, storing, and reproducing motion—in other words, events as they unfolded in the fullness of time. Seizing upon the archival possibilities of this revolution in the recording of kinetic phenomena, Kahn and his collaborators adapted the positivist model of the nineteenth-century archive by incorporating into it the media of the twentieth century. As a result, they ended up mounting a threat to that model by virtue of the manifest counter-archival tendencies in film and the latent instability within the positivist archival enterprise itself. Riding the wave of interest in the 1910s for diverse utopian applications of film, while pursuing its own idiosyncratic experimentalism, the Kahn Archive ignored warnings regarding film's unsuitability as an archival source of historical or epistemological evidence. Unconcerned that it provided (to borrow Jacques Derrida's appraisal of psychoanalysis) "an archival documentation where the 'ordinary historian' identifies none," the Archive thwarted as much as it courted historicist archival ideals of speaking with the dead and cataloguing exhaustively.[3] Film's counter-archival properties—its propensity for capturing excessive detail, inciting unmanageable curiosity, suspending habitual modes of memory and perception, and most importantly, automatically collecting that which was usually overlooked or suppressed in the official archive, such as the minor events of social life that Boleslas Matuszewski described as the "anecdotal side of History"—elicited both anxiety (as discussed in the last chapter) and fascination (as we will discover in the next chapter). In this chapter, I explore the temporal specificity of anecdotal history in Kahn's films in light of cinema's archival instability and the increased historiographical weight given to the everyday in the interwar period.

An overarching question guides this exploration: did the Kahn films' gravitation toward anecdotal history—where the white heat of "grand historical events" (*grandes événements historiques*) is ignored in favor of the "slow burn" of more uneventful daily occurrences—challenge or merely mirror the general perception of nonfiction film's affinity with historical evidence? As the closest cinematic relative to Kahn's films, commercially programmed actualities, with their chaotic juxtapositions of the "boxing match" and the "battle of the Marne," provide the background to this discussion. In the foreground will be an attempt to situate Kahn's films in relation to the major shift within French historiography during the interwar period, that is, from the *école méthodique* (discussed in the last chapter) to the emergence of the Annales school of history led by Marc Bloch and Lucien Febvre, the two historians who in 1929 founded the journal *Annales d'histoire économique et sociale* in which the Annales methodology emerged.

Kahn's Archive bore affinities not only with what Lynn Hunt has described as the "initial anti-establishment" and post-positivist practices of the first generation of Annales historians but also with the work of the second-generation Annalist, Fernand Braudel.[4] I will be reading Kahn's films alongside Braudel's categorizations of historical temporality that he carved out between the "two poles of time, the instant and the *longue durée*"—the latter category formulated in affinity with Claude Lévi-Strauss's structuralist uncovering of a deep, almost unconscious time.[5] These extremes of temporality (much like Bergson's extremes of habitual and pure memory) are helpful for thinking about Kahn's films for a number of reasons. They build upon Bloch's earlier distinction between the "momentary convulsions" and "the most lasting developments" of history, in addition to recalling that distinction made by the film theorist, filmmaker, and actuality producer Germaine Dulac in her own division of history according to the "sudden" "striking" event and the "subtle" "slow-burn kind of event."[6] Although Dulac was thinking exclusively about newsreels, her cinematic rendering of "two poles of time" (as Braudel would have it) signals a key theme in French film theory. It reappears, for instance, in the ontological division André Bazin put forward in 1945 between the photographic embalming of the instant (or moment) and the cinematographic embalming of time (and change).[7] Bazin's distinction is doubly significant because it is also a revision of the Bergsonian vacillation between photographic stasis and cinematographic mobility that influences all of the above historians' and film critics' conceptions of time.

Yet in viewing Kahn's films through the grid of Braudel's 1950s temporal classifications, I am not especially interested in narrating a teleological history that points forward to the ways in which nonfiction films like Kahn's and fiction films would eventually be used as sources of historical evidence by French professional historians such as Marc Ferro (a third-generation Annales scholar) in the 1970s.[8] Nor will I be focusing on the diverse narrative filmmakers, from Jean Renoir in the 1930s to Chantal Akerman in the 1960s and 1970s, who arguably incorporated an Annales sensibility to the temporal duration of everyday life into their films.[9] Rather, my concern, as the reference to Dulac's comments indicates, is with the way in which nonfiction film in the first four decades of its evolution presented a model for challenging the temporal, narrative, and thematic biases of traditional historicism. Of particular importance as we try to understand this challenge is the need to unearth the outlines of a philosophy of history—conceptualized between the contradictions and correspondences of *la durée* and the *longue durée*—in Bergson's counter-archival theory of memory.

BERGSONIAN HISTORY

It is curious that as a philosopher of memory and time Bergson did not apply himself to a theory of history. After all, history was the official discipline of memory. Furthermore, Bergson's conceptual adversaries—mechanical time, positivist science, and the spatializing metaphor of memory—all impacted the idea of history during his lifetime. For example, mechanical time, or what Bergson referred to as the "imaginary homogeneous time" of perception (*MM* 207–208), is clearly analogous to traditional historicist time in that it divides, immobilizes, and condenses into "differentiated moments" what exists in reality as "enormous periods of an infinitely diluted existence." The analysis of memory attached to the Bergsonian critique of mechanical time also runs counter to the rationalist chronology of history's linear time line. Where the latter traditionally marks a regression from the present to the past motivated by a search for origins, Bergson's memory moves from a "progression from the past to the present" (*MM* 239). It involves a time line that disrupts chronology, producing, as Richard Terdiman puts it, an account of events that is "tangled and folds back on itself," in the process losing sight of any original point of reference.[10] In addition, behind Bergson's critique of the model of the brain as a storehouse of archival-like documents is an implicit rejection of the encyclopedic mentality that was so crucial to the Enlightenment, and in particular

to the notion historians took from it that knowledge could be classified and accessed with mechanical precision—as though it were already given in preexisting
categories.

But if Bergson did not explicitly address history, he did broach the subject indirectly. For in addition to rejecting a mechanistic view of the universe, he also
rejected a teleological perspective of events (what he called "finalism").[11] For Bergson, the problem with finalism (a key tenet of the scientific history that underpins
the Kahn Archive's futurocentrism as discussed in the last chapter), and by implication a narrative of history that is exclusively magnetized toward some future
determination (or by the equally mistaken mechanistic determination of the past),
is that it "holds in front of us the light with which it claims to guide, instead of putting it behind" (*CE* 39). A present harnessed by the future or the past, according
to Bergson, is a depleted present in which *"all is given"* (*CE* 37), in other words,
a present devoid of chance and life. Given Bergson's critique of the memory-as-
archive metaphor, positivist science, the reign of homogeneous space, and the pre-
dictive capacity of rationalist inquiry, it is not surprising that his theory of memory
opened up new perspectives onto historical reality and time for the young historians—the early Annalists, chief among them—of his era.[12]

In the final pages of *The Historian's Craft* (1941), one of those early Annalists'
most extensive treatments of the philosophy of history, Bloch made the connection
to Bergson explicit when he concluded that

> Human time will never conform to the implacable uniformity or fixed divisions of
> clock time. Reality demands that its measurements be suited to the variability of its
> rhythm, and that its boundaries have wide marginal zones. It is only by this plasticity
> that history can hope to adapt its classifications, as Bergson put it, "to the very con-
> tours of reality": which is properly the ultimate aim of any science.[13]

Without giving up on the quest to make history a science, Bloch nonetheless
pinned his critique of *école méthodique* historicism (associated with Charles-Victor
Langlois and Charles Seignebos, two key figures in the field) upon its inflexible
conception of time, cut to fit the "uniformity" of science rather than the constantly
changing "variability" of life as defined in Bergsonian philosophy. Displaying the
same disdain for the mechanicity of "clock time" that is a staple of Bergson's own
anti-chronometric thinking, Bloch also expressed sympathy for the philosopher's
promotion of heterogeneity while translating it into a spatial interest in expanding the socially "marginal zones" of history. But Bergson's counter-archival logic is
most evident in Bloch's effort to adapt (rather than reject outright) history's conventional classifications. Not surprisingly, a central target of Bloch's reform was
the clearinghouse of historical classifications, the archive.

As part of their transformation of historical practice, Bloch and Febvre expanded the definition of the historical archive to include "non-written documents,
involuntary testimonies (archaeological remains, statistical series, etc)" and icon-

ographical material.[14] Although the first-generation Annales historians did not embrace film as a source for history (probably due to its voluntary, mechanistic, excess of information), film provided them with a model for nonlinear memory, as exemplified in Bloch's traumatic memory of trench warfare described in terms of a damaged, discontinuous film.[15] Moreover, other visual media played a foundational role in their expansion of the notion of historical documents beyond written records, privileging new types of source material such as "old maps, place-names, ancient tools, aerial surveys, [and] folklore."[16] The profound role that the visual played in Bloch's practice of history continued in the vital importance accorded to "observation and the visual image" including (as I will return to in chapter 8) the use of aerial photography in his teaching and his texts.[17] Very much in line with the promotion of vernacular observation by Kahn and Brunhes, Bloch trained his pupils to appreciate that "the most important tool for historical research was 'the eyes,'" while nearly all of his major works employed images as historical documents.[18] Although voluntary testimony, or what Bloch called the "intentional" evidence of history (state and official records), would always be crucial, historians (he contended in the early 1940s) had come to "place more and more confidence in the second category of evidence, the evidence of witnesses in spite of themselves" as a result of the Annales school's expansion of the contents and concept of the archive.[19]

The Annales historians' commitment to new forms of *involuntary* evidence reflected their desire to study local ways of life and the *longue durée* in a manner that revealed their influence by Vidal de la Blache (Jean Brunhes' teacher). Febvre explicitly outlined the connections between the new history and human geography in *A Geographical Introduction to History* (1919). He admitted there his indebtedness to the Vidalian interpretation of nature's effect upon society. Far from buttressing positivist claims, the Vidalian worldview taught Febvre that nature forms "an imperceptible and complex interference, the results of which slowly accumulate" according to "a gradual and continual process."[20] Reflecting upon the foundational *post-positivist* impact Vidal de la Blache had upon French history, the philosopher Paul Ricoeur more recently claimed he was the first "to react against the positivism of historicizing history and to give meaning to the notions of setting, lifestyle, and everydayness."[21] Although Vidal de la Blache and Brunhes' nondeterminist appreciation of *milieu* would undergo a degree of ossification in the second generation of Annales historians, in particular through Braudel's triadic stratification of historical time, its earlier incarnations, both in the Archives de la Planète and the first texts of the Annales historians, still left room for the "anecdotal history" and the irreducible level of the *événement*.[22] Indicative of their antiestablishment origins, their broadening of the concept of the archive, and their interest in human geography, the early Annalists promoted a model of history that intersects with Kahn's films; in other words, a counter-archival history open to non-written

sources, opposed to the privileged status of political or biographical history, and
told from the perspective of everyday life—a terrain Febvre associated with "the
innumerable and *especially unclassifiable* activities of humans."[23]

Regardless of the intersections that may be posited between Annales historiography and Kahn's films, the Annales historians did not offer any straightforward
praise for film. The unspoken problem with film for these historians, of course,
lay in its suspicious amenability to the *école méthodique*'s positivist and archival
applications. As discussed in the last chapter, the methodical school that typified
French history of the *fin-de-siècle* was dominated by a new legitimation of archival
research. Following Bloch's own opposition to that school, Braudel critiqued the
école méthodique for its enslavement to the "ideal of history 'in the raw'" exemplified by a new limited style of chronicle that "followed the history of events step by
step as it emerged from ambassadorial letters of parliamentary debates."[24] What
Braudel shared with Bloch in this Bergsonian-related critique of positivist (cinematic) history was an opposition to knowledge based upon a seemingly exhaustive,
but ultimately historically limited and passive, accumulation of causally connected
micro-data.

Of crucial importance here as we try to unravel Bergson, Bloch, and Braudel's
affinities with the Kahn project is that all three men turned to the memory devices
of modernity—especially photography and film, but also newspapers—to illustrate
the paucity of historicism's endless chronicle. Bergson reached in *Creative Mind*
(1934) for the example of the exhaustive photographic survey ("Were all the photographs of a town, taken from all possible points of view, to go on indefinitely
completing one another, they would never be equivalent to the solid town in which
we walk about"); Bloch used the example of the "mere photograph" to criticize the
model of a "mechanically complete reproduction" of events that is flawed (unlike
the selective narrative of the historian) due to its random and passive imprint of
reality; while Braudel's bad object appeared in the record of events typified by the
chronicle or daily newspaper: "this mass [that] does not make up all of reality, all
the depth of history."[25]

As we have already seen, however, it was Siegfried Kracauer who expressed this
suspicion toward modern media's capacity for historical memory most extensively.
In his 1927 essay on photography, written around the same time that the found-
ers of the Annales school, Bloch and Febvre, were waging their attack upon late-
nineteenth-century historicism, Kracauer argued that, "Historicism is concerned
with the photography of time. The equivalent of its temporal photography would
be a giant film depicting the temporally interconnected events from every vantage
point."[26] Kracauer's vision of a "giant film" that would survey events from every
temporal and spatial vantage point, exhausting their slightest significance, offers
an explicit critique of the potential cinematic translation of nineteenth-century
positivist historicism that lay nascent in Bergson, Bloch, and Braudel's own anti-

media commentaries.[27] This potential was realized in the Kahn Archive, which accomplished, if nothing else, a fragmented global version of Kracauer's "giant film."

THE LEDGER BOOK OF TIME

Echoing Braudel's complaint about the archival cult of history in the raw, Allan Sekula has claimed that, "For historicism, the archive confirms the existence of a linear progression from past to present, and offers the possibility of an easy and unproblematic retrieval of the past from the transcendent position offered by the present."[28] While this may be true (in theory) of late-nineteenth-century historical scholarship still entranced by visions of an unmediated scientific access to the past, in terms of their actual activity in the archives historians questioned as much as they confirmed the notion of history as a science (rather than history as art or literature). As Bonnie Smith has shown, for all the neutral and clinical aura of the late-nineteenth-century archive, these workplaces were spoken of by historians in extremely passionate and even gendered terms, using a "language of love, obsession, and, more particularly, fetishism," all of which "unwittingly raised doubts about the truth that historians claimed to find in intense study of a document."[29] "Each discovery," Langlois and Seignebos apparently exclaimed in response to finding an untouched document in a dusty archive, "induces rapture."[30] In recognition of the passions swelling within these mausoleums to the document, Smith ultimately claims that "scientific history was not driven by the noble dream of objectivity alone but rather by objectivity *and* the fantastical."[31]

Leaving aside for the moment Kahn's own deeply personal obsession with his project, and the fantastical world in which some of his films were viewed (to be discussed in chapter 7), the Kahn Archive contains (at the levels of inception, production, and reception) significant traces, beyond the films, of this irregular pulse of desire in the supposedly lifeless body of French positivism. One indispensable text in which to unravel the contradictory relationship between the pure, positivist ideal of the archive and the messy reality of the day-to-day functioning of the Archives de la Planète is the Archive's handwritten ledger that tabulates the empirical production data pertaining to each film (fig. 5.1). This information includes cameraman, date, film length, film title, and the positive and negative copies of the film. But like so much else in Kahn's Archive, the ledger is incomplete. Listing only the films shot by Lucien Le Saint and Camille Sauvageot from 1919 to 1931, it provides us with a different sort of anti-systematicity within the Kahn Archive than that suggested by Brunhes' anti-methodology (mentioned in chapter 2). Yet even in this partial inventory, the ledger's precisely tabulated columns harbor a condensed if somewhat cryptic blueprint of the contradictions—between the particular and the general, the singular and the universal, the eccentric and the typical, the incomplete and the exhaustive, the obsessive and the rational, the casual and the causal—underpinning the scientific pretensions and counter-archival outcomes of Kahn's project.

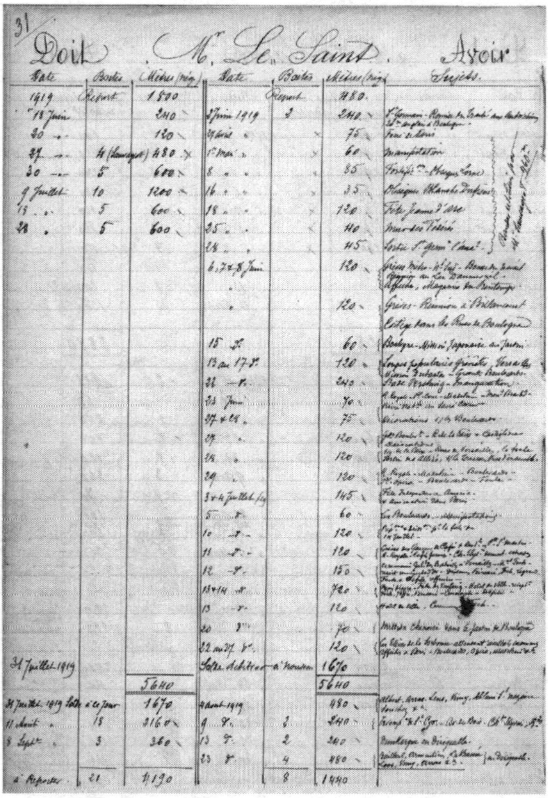

FIGURE 5.1

A page from Lucien Le Saint's entries in the Archive's film ledger book. (MAK: *ADLP Film Register*, 1919–1931)

One of the reasons the ledger is so interesting is that it truly reveals Kahn's hand in that it adheres to the general principles of double-entry bookkeeping. Signaled clearly by the columns marked "debit" and "credit," each ending in a "balance," the ledger book is in fact the unmistakable tool of a banker's archive. It also reflects the banking mentality—of endless acquisition and stockpiling underpinned by forms of power indicative of what Sekula calls an "aggressive empiricism"—that underwrites all archiving projects.[32] In her analysis of the practice of double-entry bookkeeping, Mary Poovey has suggested that with its harnessing of numerical particulars to a general claim resting on the virtue of a state of balance, it emerged as a key exemplar of the "epistemological unit" that she calls the "modern fact."[33] For Poovey, the modern fact is a unit "whose existence is almost impossible to document" (xiii). In stark contrast, for Kahn, whose various projects were devoted to the production of knowledge based upon (what Poovey calls) the "noninterpretive data collected about observed particulars" (xv), the documentation of modern facts was a realizable goal worth devoting one's life and fortune to.

It is important in this respect to note that although the ledger is functionally intended to track the amount of film negative and positive used and produced by his cameramen, this accountancy practice did not ultimately serve the logic of quantifiable profit. The "commodities" Kahn produced, his filmed facts or "documents," existed outside the capitalist exchange system that had originally funded them, that commercial cinema of the time was enmeshed in, and that would eventually be responsible for closing down the Archive (with the loss of his fortune due to the 1929 crash). It was only in 1934 when the films were sold with the property that they entered the capitalist system of exchange and the conventional afterlife of the decontextualized archival document for the first time. Certainly, during their first, short life before being sold, Kahn's films were intended to accrue capital— only it was cultural and historical, rather than financial capital.

The ledger book, however, is not made up only of numbers. To the right of the sober columns of debit and credit, it also contains what Poovey considers to be the antithesis to the objective register of numerical representation—descriptions— that appear in the form of titles given to the footage, presumably by the cameramen following their notes on the *fiches*. Two of three temporal categories—as defined by Braudel's tripartite elaboration of historical times in the preface to his 1949 history of the Mediterranean—emerge from the descriptive content of the titles.[34] They include examples of what Braudel would disparagingly lump under the category of *histoire événementielle*—the infinite roll call of official history ("Anatole France's funeral," "King of England in Paris," "Locarno Conference") and daily life ("marriage parties leaving the photographers," "signposts for pedestrians") that together resemble the cross-section of reality extending from a newspaper's headlines to its *fait divers* section. In contrast to the "individual time" of *histoire événementielle*, what Braudel defined as the midlevel "social time" is present in those films that depict events of a more cyclical and repetitive nature ("Jeanne d'Arc Fête," "elections in Paris," "strike of the Citroën company," "crowd at the arrival of the Tour de France," "Sunday working-class market"). Unrepresented in the ledger book, however, is Braudel's third type of historical temporality, the *longue durée* or long-term history that ticks to a clock that is so slow it resists being humanly measured or quantified. Nonetheless, where the structural and comparative dimensions of slow time emerge in the ledger book is in the frequency with which titles and topics are repeated across the years. There, in the virtual and invisible realm of the meta-archive, we glimpse a history whose meaning becomes clearer only within the projected range and indeterminacy of long time.

In addition to the actual examples of individual and social time and the more virtual indications of the *longue durée*, a range of subtopics seems to organize the titles in the ledger. Not surprisingly, these subtopics include travel ("Cilicia-Syria-Palestine voyage," "voyages to devastated regions [from the war]"), types of view ("views of Paris from air balloon," "sunsets on the Seine," "Paris in the fog," "evening lights on the boulevards," "clouds and the Arc de Triomphe," "solar eclipse"), and technical information ("Pathé camera test with view to sell," "new Agfa film test," "camera accident—film derailed"). If such titles perfectly illustrate Brunhes' appreciation of his cameramen as "artists *and* technicians," they also allow us to see the looseness of the Kahn Archive's scientificity in those descriptions that exceed Brunhes' classificatory categories all together. These include titles focused on death, as in the footage titled "cadavers in the trenches," "disappearance of the morgue," and "return of the aircraft debris of the pilot Garros," in addition to others characterized by a home-movie style relation to events, for example in the footage of Dutertre's son (fig. 1.7), Kahn's dogs, the removal of a tree from the Boulogne garden, or Brunhes' funeral (in 1930). Scanning the ledger's entries, one cannot help but be jolted by how the film of Kahn's dogs appears just above the momentous state funeral procession of the Socialist Jean Jaurès, or how the Chateaux de la Loire were shot on the same day as one of many condemned houses in Paris awaiting to be demolished ("Number 15, Dutertre Place; house which threatens to cave in"). Rather than a systematic form of documentation, what we have here is the anti-systematicity of what Poovey describes as "a catalog of observed but unrelated particulars."[35]

To be sure, such discordant juxtapositions, gauged at the level of the inventorial arrangement of the ledger book, were unintended and might be found in any number of list-based documents. What interests me at this stage of my argument is not so much how such enigmatic titles indicate the ever-present intervention of the private, subjective, and marginal in the construction of this, and no doubt all, archives. Of more importance is that, as Michel Foucault demonstrated (with inspiration from Jorge Luis Borges's apocryphal Chinese encyclopedia) in his preface to *The Order of Things*, we find the curious anomaly that exceeds taxonomical classification disturbing because it undermines all order.[36] Not coincidentally, it was the disturbing juxtapositions of Borges's fictional encyclopedia, the sheer incongruity implicit in the placement of *this* next to *that*, which first inspired Foucault to use the term *heterotopia* before he applied it to actual sites.[37] What is thus worth emphasizing is how the ledger book's division between enumeration and description, numbers and titles, is repeatedly transgressed, with information tending toward the irreducibility of the particular rather than the universality of the general. In other words, although the ledger is established to offer a quantifiable calculation of film stock, the numbers just don't add up; there is no sum meaning that records the heterotopian (im)balance of those film titles.

And where the Kahn ledger's positivist system of notation undermines order, so too do its films. The ledger thus displays as much as it tries to contain the conflict between the systematic generalizable knowledge that the modern fact yearns for and the chaos of unrelated observations that its cinematic analog seems to devolve into even before the point of projection. In contrast to the historicist order of Kracauer's "giant film," the textual form of the ledger harbors the potential to unravel into all sorts of unintended configurations that any extensive viewing of Kahn's

films only magnifies. Rendering all information equivalent and thus interchangeable, the Archive's ledger levels the high and the low, the sacred and the profane,
reducing all to the common denominator of the fact or document unhinged from
narrative or causal order. In its disregard for hierarchies and its spatial organization, the ledger flattens and quantifies much like the cinematographic method (in
Bergson's view) reduces flux to discrete images. Remaining outside the neat lines
and calculations of the ledger was what Bergson called *durée* and what Braudel
would reconfigure as the perpetually invisible remainder of individual and social
time, the *longue durée*.

A SOURCE OF *NEW* HISTORY

If Kahn's films were unwittingly pioneering a new form of history writing between
the poles of Bergsonian memory and Annales history, what was their connection
to the more official cinematic chroniclers of contemporary history, the commercial
newsreels? The Archive began just as modern French newsreel production was
consolidated in the form of filmed news journals established by Pathé (in 1908),
then Gaumont (in 1910), followed by Éclair and Éclipse. Further evidence of the
shared history between Kahn's films and the commercial actualities even appears
on film in the many instances where both enterprises were filming the same subject at the same time. Consequently, commercial cameramen often accidentally appear in Kahn's films, particularly in those of newsworthy events where the shooting space would have been limited.

When they share a focus on the singular events of official history, Kahn's films
and the commercial actualities capture the headline-grabbing, short-term attractions of Braudel's *histoire événementielle*. Other Kahn and Gaumont films also
exist within the somewhat slower, group-focused temporal order of social history. For example, the films of Saint Catherine's Day celebrations (the patron saint,
among others, of single women) or the Lent Mardi Gras parades (fig. 6. 2) belong
to an almost ritualistic coverage of popular and religious *fêtes* whose cyclical and
semisacred nature lent a "slowly rhythmed" pattern (to use Braudel's description
of the mid-level temporal order of social time) to the otherwise frenetic pace of
modern daily life in Paris.[38] And finally, in their implicit cyclicality grounded in
continuity and an eternal return of certain archaic social substructures and patterns, these *fête* days also contain, if only at a meta-textual level, the temporally
weighted data of daily life essential to Braudel's privileged historical temporality—
the *longue durée* of centuries—whose true significance can only be accessed at the
deep, almost geological and atemporal substrata that continues beneath the surface distractions of *histoire événementielle*.

Before applying Braudel's categories too closely, however, the issue of the cinematic specificity of Kahn's or Gaumont's "documents" must be addressed. The ques-

tion here is not if films could become a new source of history (as Boleslas Matusze-wski hoped), but whether film implicitly involved a source or model of *new* history. The distinction becomes more apparent when we recall that Matuszewski openly promoted the former, but only hinted at the latter. A crucial factor determining the newness and difference of film as a model of history rests upon the excessive, un-ordered, and nonhierarchical nature of the medium's information (exemplified by the cluttered frame of early single-shot actualities but also glimpsed in the unruli-ness of the Kahn Archive's ledger book). The medium's counter-archival excesses appears in countless examples from the Kahn and Gaumont collections of what film historians note to be one of the essential characteristics of actuality-related genres, namely, the eruption of accidental and secondary details into the primary focus of the camera frame.[39] In terms of evidentiary value, film's unintentional de-tails provide that type of historical proof that Bloch called "the evidence of wit-nesses in spite of themselves."[40]

The automatic registering of unexpected and uncontrollable incidentals took many forms but none more common, visible, or written about than the acknowl-edgment of the presence of the camera by those being filmed.[41] These diverse forms of camera acknowledgment interpellate a new form of history that becomes even more pronounced with Kahn's films due to their self-conscious archival aspi-rations. While comparable to the subject who looks at the camera in actualities or "local" films (who, in the latter instance, could expect to see herself/himself on the screen close to the original time and place of filming), the subject who looks at the camera in the Kahn footage gazed across a much longer *archival* stretch of time. Moreover, unlike conventional actualities that have acquired across time an invol-untary, evidentiary value, Kahn's films always looked history squarely in the face (even though history may not have been quite ready to register their gaze).[42]

Although Kahn hired at least one former Gaumont cameraman, and even turned to Pathé and Gaumont to supplement his collection when it came to parts of the planet missing from his Archive (such as Britain, Australia, New Zealand, Mexico), the archival basis of his films distinguish them from the commercial actu-alities.[43] For one thing, there is evidence that Kahn directly opposed, "from above," as it were, the actuality mode of observation as a model for his films. He rejected not only the application of one actuality cameraman (because he thought his work would be too "commercial") but also Brunhes' initial suggestion to use Gaumont cameramen during filming missions for the Archive.[44] Furthermore, the Kahn cameramen operated as if oblivious to the competition that drove companies like Pathé and Gaumont to shoot, develop, and screen subjects as fast as they could. Often in step with the frantic pace of the newspaper dailies, the commercial film-ing-screening process was sometimes executed within the span of a single day.[45] The production and distribution pace of Kahn's films—a large proportion of which were still negatives in 1934—bore no relation to this hectic commercial schedule.[46]

Kahn's films existed in a unique archival continuum whose potential longevity (cut short by the crash of 1929) reached for the nearly beyond time aloofness of Braudel's *longue durée*. Made solely for the sake of an archive, and not determined by the presentist limits of commercial appeal, the films were free to take their time with history. Thus, while the Kahn films and the commercial actualities often had similar subject matter and stylistic traits, they were separated entirely by divergent temporal patterns within their reception contexts. For instance, although both film enterprises returned annually to shoot certain topics, they invoked this cyclical motif in very different ways. Take, for example, the films of a religious festival, Easter Sunday in Bethlehem, filmed by both the Kahn and Gaumont cameramen. In the case of the Gaumont films, which would have been screened in Paris not long after being shot in Bethlehem, we can presume that the annual repetition of the film's subject matter and the relative simultaneity of events depicted on the screen with events experienced by the spectators actually conditioned the cinema hall experience as a sort of globally and religiously inflected "imagined community."[47] And what print capitalism and the newspaper were to the nineteenth-century national community, "screen capitalism" was becoming to the more transnationally imagined, cinematic communities of the early twentieth century.[48] To be sure, Kahn's network was also geared toward an internationally imagined community, albeit one which hoped to use a global elite to elevate the mass ceremony of print and screen capitalism. But the cyclical mode functioned differently in Kahn's films. Camille Sauvageot's *La Basilique de la Nativité à Bethlehem* of 1925 was not meant to be screened as a devotional aid or religious commemoration for a paying public. Rather, it was intended to be consulted, perhaps along with the other film of the same title shot by Le Saint six years before from the same position of the same events, some time after the recording of events in accordance with the comparative dictates of the Archive's future use.[49] We can only imagine how many films might have been shot of this event, and how many chances for comparison among chronologically separated but spatially simultaneous documents might have been made, if the Archive had continued well beyond 1931.

Their voluntary and purposeful archival identity also explains why Kahn's films nearly always have a detailed level of information (place, day, year) attached to them in the form of their titles. This detail is missing from the commercial actualities whose own time-boundedness (to the depiction of a newsworthy event of the day or a ritual celebration) meant (at least in the short term) a brief financial distribution life rather than a potentially infinite archival life. In the Kahn Archive, the purpose of serial recording thus had little to do, *at least in theory*, with supplying a steady stream of commodities feeding a paying consumer's short-term interest in the blips of *histoire événementielle* or the equally time-sensitive limits of the communal and emotional experience of annually watching the film among a group of like-minded religious participants (midterm social history). Rather, in the Kahn Archive the *original* purpose of filming singular or annual events, within and across different countries, resided in the production of historical sources of the present for the future.

BONSAI TIME

The Kahn Archive most radically reoriented such a hypothetical archival function in the way its filmed documents deviated from the norms of written documents. Unlike the latter, Kahn's films resist legibility and interpretation, mostly because they still followed the turn-of-the-century, single-shot model of actualities. Far from entirely dying out or succumbing to the drive for internal narrativization that shaped classical Hollywood fiction film and commercial actualities of the late teens, the earlier actuality mode, characterized by films that captured and catalogued—without necessarily ordering and narrating—views of the familiar and near as well as the strange and far, continued in Kahn's films. The Archive reveals the continuing appeal of film's potential for the infinite, discontinuous cataloguing of events, the unabashed acknowledgment of the camera, the decentered indeterminacy of meaning, the lack of focus within the frame conducive to an unharnessed gaze in the spectator, and the fascination with mundane occurrences. But the Kahn films' most striking affinity with *earlier* rather than contemporaneous newsreels lies in their adherence to the spatio-durational integrity of single-shot filming. In their preference for relatively uninterrupted and open-ended shooting, Kahn's films resume the temporality of earlier actualities, adhering to a decidedly slower rhythm than their commercial counterparts.

Although not necessarily ensuring some purer, more authentic version of reality, the Kahn films' noncommercial and archivally destined context provided the impetus for his cameramen to focus on unconventional events and scenes, and in a manner that was uncharacteristic of the newsreel view of the world that they so often rub up against. Central to this divergence was a more patient appetite for cataloguing and gathering the unfolding evidence of the present within documented views conceived as *complete fragments of duration* rather than *incomplete unedited shots*. Even when the Kahn films reveal impatience with natural time (most spectacularly in Dr. Comandon's time-lapse films of beans germinating or flowers blooming), they are also paradoxically the inextricable product of and testament to an extreme patience with the normally invisible passage of slow events (involved in the actual recording duration). Embodying this fascination with slow, botanical time is the corner of Kahn's property that he treasured most—the bonsai garden—where the deferred pleasure of archival time underpins the imperceptible growth of miniature trees.

THE EVENTFULNESS OF *HISTOIRE ÉVÉNEMENTIELLE*

Several features thus distinguish Kahn's films from the commercial actualities that they superficially resemble: their attraction to the less sensational, uneventful occurrences of daily life; their overarching affinity for an archival temporality that stretches toward the *longue durée*; and their devotion to durational shooting and non-edited fragments of film. Given these features, it would appear that Kahn's films managed to go deeper than Braudel's shallow *histoire événementielle*, which he understood as the traditional history of "great men" (political, military, and diplomatic meetings; marches, defeats, and victories). In contrast to the superficial distractions or "the thousand explosions" of *histoire événementielle*, the Kahn films that are dominated by the undramatic stuff of anonymous daily life provide the potential documents for the sort of history Braudel narrated according to the calming, patient continuum of the *longue durée*.[50] Characterized by a tempo that "almost borders on the motionless," or to be more precise, a "semi-stillness," Braudel's *longue durée* resembles the deep almost forgotten sea that exists beneath the constantly moving waves (analogous to the single semi-still photographic frame that underpins the film strip).[51] As such, Braudel's *longue durée* betrays an affinity not only with the social and cyclical subject matter of so many Kahn films but also with the slow tempo and rhythm that distinguished them from the actualities. This is not to equate the centuries-long time span of Braudel's *longue durée* with the relatively long—if only by a matter of seconds when compared to newsreel shots— duration of the Kahn footage, but to suggest that in the attempt by Kahn's films and Braudel's history to capture the unconscious history of everyday life, both are animated by an articulated opposition to the sensational blips and discontinuities of current events. The arbitrary cut into time, marked by an edit in the film (for the Kahn cameraman) or the event in the short term (for Braudel), signals for both a kind of death or at least a denial of history's less visible or striking continuities.

Much as Bergson's *durée* came under fire for evading history and death, Braudel's *longue durée* was criticized for evading the political (and with it, the history of rupture, change, and revolution) and seeking refuge in the ideological conservatism associated with continuity, stasis, and "immobile time."[52] The critique of continuity leveled at Bergson and Braudel ignores, however, the possibility that continuity and discontinuity (movement and stasis, expansion and ellipsis) actually coexist in their work. Likewise, film's propensity to cut up time did not imply a stark opposition to durational shooting but was matched by the latter's equally troubling ability to accumulate time continuously and endlessly. Deceptively solid in their mathematical precision, like the Archive's ledger, Kahn's films ultimately betray the unbalancing force that accompanies fragmented, discontinuous filming as well as excessive, continuous recording.

It would therefore be incorrect to associate Kahn's films exclusively with the *longue durée*. After all, many Kahn films—particularly when taken in their entirety—conform to another of Braudel's definitions of *histoire événementielle* (provided in his 1958 essay "History and the Social Sciences"). For Braudel, the infinity of singular events that make up *histoire événementielle* take on the character of a choking and "delusive smoke [that] fills the minds of its contemporaries."[53] They need to be treated warily by the historian as their flame, their underlying source, "can scarcely ever be discerned" due to the limited, fleeting moment in which they are captured. At issue for Braudel is not the content but the temporality of such events, which is compromised because it is too limited by the present; it is "proportionate to individuals, to daily life, to our illusions, to our hasty awareness," and above all to the time of "the chronicle or the daily paper" (28). Like the common newspaper that Bloch rejected in preference for unintentional evidence (and that in a similar vein Henri Lefebvre would also reject), Braudel condemns *histoire événementielle* because it "offers us all the mediocre accidents of ordinary life" (28).[54] Reading somewhat like the titles from a newsreel program—"a fire, a railway crash, the price of wheat, a crime, a theatrical production" (28)—ordinary life, fished out from the temporal surface of *histoire événementielle*, can never give us the underlying "depth of history." Thus, while Braudel's work is conventionally understood as opposing traditional political history and promoting the historicization of everyday life from the perspective of the centuries-long time span, in this foundational essay daily life and political events, minor and major history, exist side by side in a condition of temporal brevity associated with "the time of the chronicle and the journalist" (28).[55] History registers daily life at different speeds. Likewise, daily life in Kahn's films is not stamped exclusively by the *longue durée*, but also by the temporal flashes of *histoire événementielle*. Given that the Archive possibly had a global scrapbook of newspaper headlines as its textual origin, it is hardly surprising that some Kahn films also betray a temporality wrapped up in the moment, carried away by the quick breath of presentist excitement or anxiety.

Free from the pressure to deliver the expected highlights of the day's events to a paying audience, Kahn's cameramen were thus given the opportunity to shoot more (initially) uneventful happenings. Le Saint filmed, for instance, the only known footage of the 1920 Congress at Tours, a seemingly run-of-the-mill meeting of socialists that did not attract the commercial actualities. But what occurred that day was anything but ordinary. Amounting to one of the most important political events of the interwar period, the meeting gave birth to the schism in the Socialist Party that would lead to the eventual creation of the first French Communist Party and, by most accounts, leave France's left wing divided for at least another fifty years.[56] As an exemplary "piece" (as Matuszewski would put it) of what will become *histoire événementielle*, the film also captures the significance of randomness,

FIGURE 5.2   Evidence of police retaliation (note the raised baton lower left) at a May 1st demonstration, Paris 1920. (Camille Sauvageot and Lucien Le Saint [MAK: frame enlargement 73307])

discontinuity, and flux that Braudel's critics' argued the *longue durée* denied. The curiosity that enabled Kahn's cameraman to record the random—whether attributable to historical prescience, sheer luck, or Kahn's directives—did not end with the capture of the Congress of Tours. Kahn's Archive, for instance, remains one of the only sources for film footage of workers and Communist Party demonstrations during the twenties in France.[57] This footage includes accidental evidence of baton-wielding police retaliation caught "at the margin of a close-up" (to invoke Kracauer's cinematic description of a counter-teleological privileging of history's blind spots) within at least one of Kahn's May Day films (fig. 5.2).[58]

If the impatient spirit of journalistic reportage animates this aspect of Kahn's films—capture everything, as much as you can, right now, before it vanishes or changes—this urgent goal of all-inclusiveness was subject to a much slower rhythm at the point of shooting. As already suggested, Kahn's films were shot within a context of comparative patience, length, and duration that speaks to the overarching indeterminacy of archival time. Running beneath the agitated surface of the films and in contrast to the fragmented nonlinearity of the final mass of unedited documents is the calming continuity of cyclical return that so often reappears across the films at the level of overarching themes (such as festive holidays). Thus, the Kahn films were always subject to being dragged down by the weight of slow time even when buoyed along with the foam of history's restless surface.

We are now in a better position to see how the film of the Congress at Tours is a record of an exchange between emergence and continuity, the instant and duration. It records the unpredictable moment of rupture (the creation of the French Communist Party) *and* the familiar expectancy of the genre of a political meeting. The film embodies the multiplicity and plurality that is at the crux of Braudel's understanding and narration of social time—"this living, intimate, infinitely repeated opposition between the instant of time and that time which flows only slowly" (26). The central conflict in Braudel's description of social time rehearses Bloch's own Bergsonian opposition to the abstracted, homogeneous, chopped-up time of scientists. Rejecting mechanical time, Bloch favors "this real time [which] is, in essence, a continuum" and yet is "*also perpetual change.*"[59] Thanks to, rather than despite, their present-ness (whether figured in another political meeting or a *fait divers* occurrence), the Kahn films restore a positive, open-ended eventfulness (if not the actual chronological duration of the *longue durée*) to Braudel's depthless *histoire événementielle*. In Bergsonian terms, they interpenetrate habit with duration, and continuity with change, offering what Bloch describes succinctly as the superimposition of the stable historical "continuum" on "perpetual change." Translated into the concerns of film theory, we have what Jean Epstein describes as a reality "embalmed in motion" and what Bazin will resurrect as "change mummified."[60]

It is useful here to analyze a Kahn film choked by the distracting smoke of *histoire événementielle*. The sequence of dignitaries entering the first meeting of the Conseil de la Société de Nations (League of Nations Council), on January 16, 1920, provides a view of history, to return to Matuszewski's terms, exactly where we, the camera, and perhaps historians of the time would "expect it," in "public and national slices of life" (fig. 5.3).[61] Indeed, in his own critique of the "blizzard of photographs" comprised of modern illustrated newspapers and newsreels, Kracauer used the example of a League of Nations meeting to make the point that "never before has an age been so informed about" yet "known so little about itself."[62]

The Kahn footage from January 1920 offers, however, more than an illustration of the "temporal continuum" of positivist historicism that Kracauer argued found its match in the "spatial continuum" offered by mass-mediated photography.[63] Kahn's cameraman (in this instance unknown) did not only film an event; he filmed, as in many other instances, the filming of an event. By positioning his tripod directly opposite the row of commercial actuality cameramen capturing the same event, the Kahn cameraman deliberately or unwittingly brought into focus much more than the official rationale for this shot. Two background stories compete for our attention in this roll call of diplomatic VIPs, as we notice that, one by one, the commercial cameramen, bobbing up and down on the waves of *histoire événementielle*, lose interest in the primary event as they become distracted by the arrival of other dignitaries and other news stories offscreen left. In contrast to the intermittent attention of their colleagues' cameras, the Kahn cameraman

FIGURE 5.3   First meeting of the council for the League of Nations, Paris, Quai d'Orsay.
(Camille Sauvageot, Jan. 16, 1920 [MAK: frame enlargement 127059])

remains patiently cranking at the same location, gathering images that his commercial colleagues shut their eyes to. Although he does not simply leave the camera
running (rather, he stopped shooting after the entrance of each dignitary), he does
shoot all of the minor as well as major players in this drama, patiently documenting what Pathé and Gaumont would likely have considered excessive, marginal, or
secondary.

Interpreted from an empiricist perspective, what the Kahn cameraman provides is valuable evidence of the temporal differences between the daily filming
practices of commercial and noncommercial cameramen. Gaumont and Pathé
cameramen were trained to edit the endless flow of daily events into concise newsworthy segments. And the world was adapting at an unprecedented speed to being
shaped for the cameras, or "conceived and grasped as picture" as the philosopher
Martin Heidegger would put it in a somewhat different context.[64] The increasing
conformity of reality to the limited attention span of the camera's gaze appears in
the codification of previously uneventful moments (such as the entrance of dignitaries) into photo-opportunity events accompanied by their own set of recognized
behavioral gestures: buttoning up one's suit, standing to attention, or shaking
hands in an unnatural frontal position.[65]

Just as Kahn's cameramen were often out of step with the commercial cameramen in regard to the spaces they deemed worthy of recording, they also differed
from their colleagues in relation to the temporal rhythm of their shooting. The
patient pace of their shooting was almost anachronistic if not intentionally oppo-

sitional in this era of fast American editing. Shooting according to the exhaustive (and, it must be added, exhausting to watch) schedule of a long duration, Kahn's cameramen expanded the temporal borders of the momentary rush of *histoire évé-nementielle*. Placed in front of the lens of the commercial cameramen, these same events would be packaged and abbreviated according to the commercial determinants of the actuality mode of production. By contrast, the Kahn cameraman's recording on that day of the distraction of the commercial cameramen, as well as all that they refused to shoot as a result of their distraction, also allowed him to capture that sense of time (associated by Kracauer with boredom) that is rationalized out of existence in the commercial actualities.[66] Far from dominating the film, however, this empty time rubs up against the more occupied space of eventful time. In the interweaving of continuity and change, convention and innovation, the film manifests the interdependency between the long and the short term, carving a new route to history signposted by the interplay (rather than opposition) of structure and event.

WHERE THE CAMERA AND ORDINARY HISTORIAN LEAST EXPECT IT

Even when focused on noteworthy events, Kahn's films delivered the vision of a new type of history of the everyday. The difference of this history was half-glimpsed in what Matuszewski characterized in 1898 as "the beginnings of action [and] unexpected facts which hide themselves from the photographic camera" (with its fixation upon the frozen moment) but which make themselves potentially available to the cinematographic camera with its infinite accumulation of moments in time, or continuity in change.[67] Characterized as contingent, indeterminate, and endless, this is the type of reality Kracauer described (in his posthumously published book *History: The Last Things Before the Last*, which recalls many of his writings from the 1920s) as "the half-cooked state of our everyday world"—the semi-raw, unfinished condition of daily experience that he argued was the privileged object of both the camera and history.[68] Writing around the same time that Kracauer wrote *History* (albeit without the focus on photography and film), Michel Foucault also formulated an interest in cultivating "the details and accidents that accompany every beginning" within the new type of history he called "genealogy."[69] Although Kahn's films were made a half-century earlier, they were contemporaneous with Kracauer's Weimar writings and are not so distant from the ideas underpinning his and Foucault's later theories. Sanctioned by Brunhes' encouragement of an antiscientific and postdeterministic faith in casual curiosity, Kahn's films contain much that belongs to what Kracauer called the "lost causes" of history and what Foucault sought to uncover "in the most unpromising places, in what we tend to feel is without history."[70] By witnessing the immediate prehistory of an event in those precious moments before the anecdotal or random occurrences of social life solidify into the more conventional and thus forgettable blips of *histoire événementielle*—that is, before the either/or dance of chance, contingency, and historic opportunity freezes into change—films such as that of the Congress at Tours stage the possibility of a history of the present in all its flux and random becoming. Thus, despite Kahn's fear of chance and the contingent, and in spite of his desire to predict the future with his documents, his Archive is a monument to unpredictability and change as much as it is a haven for predictability and continuity.

Well before the Kahn Archive, in his 1898 manifesto "A New Source of History," Matuszewski was the first to acknowledge the camera's proclivity for history's effects rather than its origins:

> Without doubt historical effects are always easier to seize than causes. But the two shed light upon each other; these effects brought into the broad daylight of cinematography will cast bright flashes of light upon causes lying in their shadow.[71]

He also acknowledged that film "does not give history in its entirety," and that it could at best offer only a limited, selective, and incomplete survey of events. Perfect for chasing the aftermath of events across the surface of history within the space of what Émile Vuillermoz called "exterior life" (*la vie extérieure*), the camera, according to Matuszewski, was less obviously successful in illuminating history's interior causes. But where Vuillermoz's championing of film's exteriority opposed the private interiority of novels and fiction, Matuszewski was keen to claim for film an interiority understood as the public underlying causes of history. Always the promoter, Matuszewski thus argued for the potential of film's record of effects, once "brought into the broad daylight of cinematography," to "cast bright flashes of light upon causes lying in their shadow." At first glance, we may recognize here an attempt to reconcile film's depthlessness, its preference for the superficial "blizzard" of history, with a deeper version of events. Supporting this legitimating strategy is Matuszewski's desire to accord the "simple ribbon of exposed celluloid" the honor of becoming one of the "privileged source[s] of History"—a worthy servant to the causal and chronological narratives traditional history of the period required. Writing during the heyday of scientific, origins-obsessed, archival-based history devoted to causal laws of explanation, Matuszewski argued accordingly. He therefore reasoned that film was endowed with the ability to help the historian faced with an infinite series of events to "cast bright flashes of light" upon their origins and causes, or, to use the similar, albeit mocking words of Foucault, "to rediscover the flash of their birth."[72]

Although Matuszewski was understandably pandering to turn-of-the-century scientific history, his hyperbole ultimately undermines the cinematograph's "mathematical exactitude" (13). Let us recall that his defense of film actually issues from the personal experiences of Matuszewski the cameraman—introduced in his text with the cue "[a]nd here I ask modestly to enter the picture" (17)—rather than from any anonymous principles of objectivity.[73] What he goes on to tell his dear readers is the story behind how he used his own actuality footage to settle a minor (but potentially disastrous) diplomatic dispute of the turn of the century. The film that he shot during the September 1897 visit of France's president to St. Petersburg was used to disprove the allegation circling at the time that President Félix Faure had shown disrespect to the Russian flag during his official state visit. And yet the most significant thing about Matuszewski's film is not that it provided a convincing example of film's potential as positivist evidence by uncovering the truth behind that false allegation. Rather, its importance issues from the suggestion— barely disclosed in the only footnote to Matuszewski's text (present in the March version but edited from the April version of the pamphlet)—that film had the potential to capture and elevate the "whole anecdotal side of History that henceforth escapes the imagination [*fantaisie*] of [future historical] narrators."[74]

The recognition of the dangerous element of film's "anecdotal" history was echoed by one of the many newspaper respondents to Matuszewski's pamphlet.[75] Even more explicit than the Polish cameraman regarding film's threat to traditional history, this respondent worried: "it's the death of legend, this flower of history [the cinematograph]. It is the great man captured in his petty details and small moments; there will be no more great men for the cinematograph, no more so than their man-servants."[76] Twenty-seven years later, in another call for the state to create a "legal depository of film" in order to preserve the historical value of actualities, the specificity of film's historicity was again attached to its "anecdotal" tendencies: its ability to "permit our descendants to relive the slightest events [*les moindres événements*] that marked the life of their ancestors."[77]

But it was not only conservative film promoters who were validating the anecdotal. As exemplified by the rise of the Annales school, professional historians were also becoming more interested in vernacular history. In fact, Kahn's travel grants funded the young historian Eileen Power, whose social and economic history shocked the establishment with its opposition to what she called the "Card Index historicism" of traditional history.[78] Rejecting the *système des fiches* model of history (discussed in the last chapter), Power privileged a gendered perspective of the past viewed from "the kitchens of History."[79] The Archives de la Planète elevated to a new level film's already predetermined, "anecdotal" intrusion into history's Panthéon. We have already seen how this reversal of history as the sacred space of great men and great deeds (that is, Braudel's *histoire événementielle*) was enacted in the film shot in 1913 on the Parisian *grands boulevards* of men entering and leaving a *vespasienne*.[80] In the furtive glances of the men toward the camera, this film reveals a subject aware of being watched even during his most private moments; a subject of interest to a new historical eye that Kracauer might have called camera-history; a subject of interest even "in his small moments" or while participating in the "slightest events." Instead of documenting official history, or what

Matuszewski called the domain of "meetings of Heads of State," what such a view provided evidence of, at least as it would have been filtered through the eyes of the anti-cinema establishment of the early teens, was the potential for film to uncover the usually "censored" dimensions of the everyday—the "indiscrete," tawdry, and anecdotal view of history from the kitchen sink, or in this case, public urinal.

In promoting the film strip as a sort of flashlight onto history's hidden causes, Matuszewski was arguing just as Kahn would have wanted him to, that is, for the application of the filmic document to the utilitarian context of a cause-effect logic. Nonetheless, Matuszewski's and Kahn's efforts leave us not so much in the light of film's revelations but somewhere in the dark, stuck in the permanent obscurity of Matuszewski's "shadow," that unpredictable void of "lost" causality and origins (which, as we have seen in chapter 3, Deleuze offers as a bridge between Bergson and Foucault) that borders the more recognizable outline of "effects" captured by film. As the first French film theorists would explain, something more than easily detectable causes and origins lie within the shadow of film's accumulation of sur-face "effects."

One of those film theorists was Germaine Dulac. Best known for her experi-mental work of the 1920s, Dulac was also an indefatigable promoter and admirer of nonfiction film. Her deep interest in the historical potential of nonfiction film came to a head between 1932 and 1935 when she directed France-Actualités, a newsreel company associated with but editorially independent from Gaumont.[81] Her writings dealing with the specific historical value of actualities intersect with the humanist dimensions of the Kahn Archive ("classes and races meet in the cin-ema without intermediaries . . . humanity rises above its individual characteristics: as the sight of other human beings brings understanding, it helps destroy hostil-ity"), the spirit of civic uplift within Griersonian documentary ("cinema is the great modern educator of society"), and the more general perception typified by Victor Perrot's rhetoric of the newsreel as "a machine for writing history."[82] Underpinning all of these appeals, however, was Dulac's interest in the radically new forms of everyday memory posed by contemporary newsreels and their often unpredictable and indeterminate significance for the future film archive of history.

In place of conventional newsreels dominated by the "blockbuster" view of events, however, Dulac hoped to promote an avant-garde reformulation of the newsreel. Three related features (all dominant in the Kahn Archive) were central to her interest in the historical potential of the newsreel: their foundation in the unspectacular content and repetitive temporality of everyday life (their ability to go behind "the official face of historical tradition" and reveal "the intimate details of the life" of foreign peoples even at the risk of appearing "boring" by filming the same thing "repeated over and over"); their eclectic and chaotic archiving of con-temporary events in which "the trivial follows on the heels of the momentous"; and their ability to capture for history events "the importance of which has not immediately been grasped."[83] Ironically, just as Dulac was announcing in 1932 that "film is, in fact, the living documentary of history," the Archives de la Planète, a project that had devoted twenty years to fulfilling this mission with little recognition from the French cinema culture, had just come to an end.[84]

Films in the Kahn collection of events that usually "hide themselves from the photographic camera" occupy the shadow of history that reaches from Matuszewski's pamphlet to Dulac's commentaries on newsreels. They stake out a space and time of history whose coordinates could not be traced through what Bergson would see as the spatializing abstraction of the camera's gaze, let alone by the chronological fixation of the traditional historian's linear timelines. Instead, these films' off-the-map compass of events—their ability to record future-oriented fragments of the present, whether in the premonitional mode of the Congress at Tours film or the intensely presentist mode that marks all of their expansive interest in contemporary life—marked a terrain that could only be discovered by what Matuszewski referred to as the "indiscrete" yet "natural curiosity" (9) of a new form of cinematically inflected historical consciousness.

FROM INSTINCTUAL TO ANONYMOUS HISTORY

Without wanting to romanticize the agency of history's marginal actors, we cannot understand the shadows nestling in these films without reference to the "instinct" of Kahn's cameramen. As an early spokesperson for these usually faceless and nameless recorders of history, Matuszewski understood the subtle room for maneuver open to the cameraman on the street: "Authorized in somewhat official circumstances, he will contrive to slip unauthorized into others, and most often will know how to find the occasions and places where the history of tomorrow is unfolding" (9). Kahn's cameramen not only shared with their commercial counterparts this type of "instinct" for future history, for capturing what will appear in tomorrow's newspapers, but combined this instinct "from below" with the order "from above" to pursue and to value the events of unauthorized and unofficial history less likely to be found in commercial actualities or the front page of newspapers: men urinating, people reading posters on the streets, a man sweeping the gutters, prostitutes soliciting clients, a woman doing laundry on the banks of the Seine.

Still, if we recognize that Kahn's films and the Matuszewski manifesto challenge the notion of anonymous history, we cannot deny that the peculiar historical value of much nonfiction film depends on its authorless aura. Evidence of the Kahn cameramen's singular "curiosity" therefore coexists with the anonymous dimensions of their films. In their unsigned original context, they therefore conform to a type of historical document that satisfies one of the few methodological goals shared by Braudel and Foucault, namely that of uncovering the "anonymous rules governing collective practices" and "displacing the individual 'subject' from history."[85] The exact nature of the challenge that Braudel and Foucault posed to individual-based *histoire événementielle* as a result of their different interest in anonymous documents can be gauged by remembering that the authorless aspect of Kahn's films was one of the factors that made them unthinkable as documents for historians of the early twentieth century.

The third-generation Annales historian Marco Ferro focused on just this issue in explaining the impossibility of early-twentieth-century historians using film as a source of history, given their investment in the print-based archive and in a hierarchical corpus of sources and archives. Leading this procession of documents were the "prestigious state archives—holding manuscripts or printed matter and unique documents—which expressed the state's power," followed by newspapers, legal and legislative texts, and ending with the anecdotal—"biographies, sources of local history, and traveler's tales."[86] He goes on to claim that one of the reasons film (even newsreels with their obvious evidentiary appeal) could never have been taken seriously by historians was because they were anonymous, unsigned, and unauthored. Without an author, Ferro asks, "How could historians refer to the image or even quote it?"[87] From the perspective of conventional historians of the time, Kahn's films were totally unacceptable as historical evidence: they were non-written, non-original (in the sense of being copies), and in their uncontrollable, unsystematic mass of visual information, nonhierarchized. But perhaps most problematic of all, they were, in spite of Brunhes' praise for his cameramen, anonymous. Put simply, Kahn's films were as far as one could get from the written traces left by famous men. Indeed, Ferro has argued as much in the first documentary devoted to Kahn, *L'Héritage d'Albert Kahn* (René-Jean Bouyer, 1978), in which he states that Kahn's footage differs from actualities of the period because, rather than focusing on famous individuals and a glorified view of the Republic, they turned primarily to faceless collectives and the unofficial history of the nation. Although Ferro does not go as far as this, he might also have noted that Kahn's films disturb the three idols of history—the political, the individual, and the chronological—that the Annales school eventually toppled and replaced with a new idol, that of the everyday.[88]

THE "BLIZZARD" CLEARS

If the modern archive of photography and film haunts Bergsonian philosophy and Annales historiography as an irredeemable *and* redeemable figure, it appeared center stage for cultural critics like Kracauer (and Benjamin) who were devising new models of history beyond the linear narratives of conventional historicism. As mentioned in chapter 3, Kracauer clearly recognized in his "Photography" (1927) essay that photography and film's negative attributes, their positivist, inventorial leanings—the qualities that make them resemble a "central archive" (62)—paradoxically made them redeemable for new forms of (counter-archival) history. What seems to have captivated Kracauer about film's archival drive was not only that it produced an automatic survey of life. Rather, film's blanket coverage of events meant that it also had the capacity to expose from within this "blizzard" of positivist information the outlines of what he calls (in *Theory of Film*) "alien patterns": critical perspectives upon daily life that emerge out of the discontinuous and fragmented views that constitute the modern mediascape.[89]

Moving beyond Kahn's individual films and refocusing on their archival determinations, what "alien patterns" of daily life can one discern from the fragmented aggregate of the Kahn Archive's visual blizzard? If the entire Kahn Archive cannot avoid being read as a response to a general crisis of memory—whereby rapid urban change and the resulting pressure to forget were accompanied by equally rapid technologies for recording change and inciting recollection—then the spatio-temporal vortex of this crisis was felt nowhere more forcefully than in its films of the capital. In three series of films shot between 1924 and 1926—whose overarching theme, one could claim, is the memory of modern Paris—the Kahn cameramen obsessively recorded the construction *and* destruction of key Parisian sites. Although at other times they focused on conventional picturesque views of the capital (for example, in the color film experiments shot in the late twenties under the title "Picturesque Corners of Paris"), they seem most interested in the vacillating existence of specific urban topoi that were central to the articulation of early-twentieth-century Paris. On three separate occasions they recorded the dismantling of the huge Ferris Wheel that remained from the 1900 World Exposition; on at least fifteen occasions, they shot the demolitions needed for the continuation of the Boulevard Haussmann between 1924 and 1926; and at least five times they captured the construction of the 1925 Exposition des Arts Decoratifs.

Taken together, these series illustrate perfectly the limitations of the camera's access to Bergson's pure memory. They are confined by a preference for quantitative rather than qualitative difference, and hampered by a tendency to substitute the "common denominator" (Bergson, *MM* 202) of the sample for the irreducible moment of true memory. In their repetition (each film forms part of a series) and singularity (each film has a date and place), these films also demonstrate two aspects of the camera's servitude to habitual memory: first, they favor a history responsive to the utilitarian demands of the present; and second, their sense of the past as endless accumulation ensures detail at the expense of understanding. This latter type of exhaustive documentation that underpinned the Archive's survey of Paris is exactly what Bergson, Kracauer, and Bloch find troubling in their references to mechanically complete reproduction. Even if we were to arrange Camille Sauvageot's views taken for the Archive on January 10, February 6, and April 7, 1922, in a chronological sequence so dear to historicism—the "temporally interconnected events from every vantage point" that made up Kracauer's "giant film"— we would still not have an experientially or historically meaningful rendering of the dismantling of the gigantic wheel.[90] Kracauer repeated this critique of the positivist urge behind documentary-style reportage and photography in *The Salaried Masses* (1929) when he argued that, "A hundred reports from a factory do not add up to the reality of the factory, but remain for all eternity a hundred views of [a] factory."[91] What Sauvageot's more or less random succession of views amount to is what Bergson called the "parceling of the real" (*MM* 183) and what Kracauer identified as the modern mania for "the reproduction of observed reality."[92]

In addition to the serial-like shooting schedules of the Kahn cameramen, the use of diverse forms of media in the Archives de la Planète (capturing movement through the cinematograph, color and detail through the autochromes) further enforces the impression of the project as a voluntary, cumulative, and all-encompassing record of reality fueled by the manic drive for recorded observation derided by Bergson, Kracauer, Bloch, and any number of other skeptics of historicism. Believers in the representational dream of total reality, Kahn and Brunhes assumed that by combining photography and film they were increasing our comprehension of reality.[93] And yet while neither Kahn nor Brunhes would have ever subscribed to Kracauer's deduction regarding the hundred views of a factory (that "[r]eality is a construction"), the ultimately mosaic-like archival destiny of the Archives de la Planète's fragments of film attests to Kracauer's nonrealist comprehension of the real.[94] Each film in the Kahn Archive is not just a document on the present state of reality, but a document-in-the-making, subject at the level of its inevitable archival evolution to a becoming whose ultimate actualization is deferred to the undetermined demands of the future. The mosaic of the Archive's documents is, therefore, always subject to a process of "arrangements and rearrangements," not only of fixed options (like the vision one finds in a kaleidoscope), but unknown choices (like the undetermined hands dealt in a deck of cards).[95] And if the Archive's capacity for mosaic-like assemblage sounds similar to John Grierson's definition of the documentary form proper ("arrangements, rearrangements, and creative shaping [of natural material]"), in fact, what we see here is further evidence of how the predominantly non-narrative recalcitrance of Kahn's documents refuse the order and coherence that is the ultimate goal of that Griersonian editing: a "finality (beyond space and time) to the slice of film."[96] Moving us a little closer to the Bergsonism of Gilles Deleuze's analysis of cinema, the Archive then becomes a mobile assemblage of images (a figure suited to the unedited, fragmented, and open-ended nature of the Kahn films) and a living process in time (like memory) in which each film is contingent, specific, and evolving rather than bound by a spatially organized representation of time.

Whether viewed from the perspective of Bergson or Kracauer's counter-positivist distrust of a photographically based survey of reality, Kahn's films still fail to return us to the "solid town" of Paris. It is perhaps more fruitful to suggest that each spatially repetitive series presents the cinematic approximation of Braudel's lifelong goal as a writer of history—"to show how time moves at different speeds" that coexist when examined in one cross-section of space.[97] To pursue such a reading would be to recognize that the footage of the dismantled Ferris Wheel recalls the 1900 World Exposition where it was first erected as a God-like eye overseeing what was then imagined to be Paris's predestined role (taken up by Kahn) of leading humanity into a more rational, peaceful, and just century. In a similar collision of different times, Kahn's cameramen shot the expansion work on the Boulevard Haussmann on the same days they filmed the equally controversial clearing of the "zoniers." Those communities of ragpickers and tradespeople (famously photographed by Eugène Atget and filmed by Georges Lacombe in *La Zone, au pays des chiffonniers* [1928]), who lived near the old fortifications of Paris's periphery, came to symbolize for Benjamin (following Baudelaire) a new materialist practice of history that worked upon the edges and debris, rather than the boulevards and monuments, of the capitalist cultural landscape. Crisscrossing Paris's new axes and old peripheries, Kahn's cameramen visually chronicled the spatial and temporal instability of modernity in the space of a single day, where Paris's monuments to progress came face to face with the other side of "creative destruction." No sooner had Kahn's cameramen shot the construction of the 1925 Exposition des Arts Decoratifs, where Le Corbusier presented his vision of the house as a machine for living, than they were back to film its being torn down. Other days saw them documenting additional fault lines of modernity. Their films of boulevard construction depict the detailed outline of former buildings etched onto the remaining walls like sun photography writ large, while others show the temporary walls surrounding construction sites plastered over with the monumental but flimsy façades of advertising posters. Together, these films combine what Bergson described as the multi-rhythmed nature of time (*MM* 207) and what Bloch called in his own rendition of short- and long-term history as "the momentary convulsions and lasting developments" of time.[98]

When viewed abstractly, Kahn's Archive seems to have treated memory as though it were a measurable quantity. Viewed up close, however, we can see that the Kahn cameramen were not simply recording, tape-measure in hand (to invoke a Bergsonian image of quantified reality [*CE* 215]), the aggregate of a new Paris of progress or the remains of a "Vieux Paris" of preservation. They were very much focused on those disaggregated moments and places in which the past remains and out of which the new is blasted—bringing forward an image of the city in constant flux (Bloch's "permanent change"), suspended between processes of building and leveling, continuity and discontinuity, conservation and emergence of both architectural and social structures.

As a monument to voluntary memory (surface appearances, exterior life, *histoire événementielle*) and to the spirit involved in keeping one's eyes on the world pinned open, Kahn's Archives de la Planète superficially embraced everything that supporters of involuntary memory (from Freud, Proust, Bloch, and Braudel, to Kracauer and Benjamin) mistrusted. At the same time, it opened up the possibility that the meaning and full import of its documents could only partially be known in the present; that our ability to understand or truly experience the reality of the present was unreliable given what Bergson understood as the self-interested instrumentalism or what Braudel understood as the presentist limitations of our essentially distracted relation to the present. Altogether, this tendency to misunderstand the present—to *see* it passively rather than *look* at it actively—made the gathering of its outcast and fragmented views even more necessary (as Dulac well knew) for the deferred involuntary encounters promised by the future reckonings of archival time.[99]

Kracauer (like Dulac) ultimately cherished the historical value of this gathering of the neglected. If his opening position in the photography essay is that "in order for history to present itself, the mere surface coherence offered by photography must be destroyed" (52), by the end he suggests that photography and film do more than stock the "central archive" (62). They have the capacity to puncture the archive's façade of historicist order and liberate the more meaningful if temporary incoherence of true history's "alien patterns."[100] The essay concludes close to the suggestions made in *The Salaried Masses* that history's true image appears in the aggregate pattern or "mosaic" that might emerge from these fragments of photographic reportage "on the basis of comprehension of their meaning."[101] Kracauer's essay thus finally suggests that it was film's archival impulse, its ability to collect automatically the surface data of daily life, that gave it the potential to spark the more historically radical encounters with involuntary memory. For Kracauer (as for Bergson), the devices of passive memory could indeed serve as the base for new forms of modern memory. By providing, according to Kracauer, a home for the world in fragments, film channeled its archival complicity and everyday affinity in the direction of a counter-archival, counter-historicist practice. In other words, the camera's and history's ready provision of "an opaque mass of facts" about everyday life enabled rather than hindered their relationship with new forms of memory, leaving behind the nineteenth-century "premise that history is a continuity unfolding in homogeneous time."[102] In light of this more positive intimation of film's archival complicity, we can now see how Kracauer's "giant film" symbolizes, like the Kahn Archive it resembles in fragments, the critique and reformation of the medium's positivist tendency.

If the archive equated to historicism in late-nineteenth-century historical scholarship, it is clear that by the 1930s a diverse set of intellectuals from Bloch to Kracauer were in the process of unbalancing this equation. Those closer to the world of actual film archives were also undertaking a revision of the historicist archive, from Jean Vignaud's prediction that cinema heralded the replacement of "dead history" with "living history" and Laure Albin-Guyot's assertion that "cinema is the only memory able to transmit faithfully the history of the world," to Dulac's support for film's status as "the living documentary of history."[103] Where the late-nineteenth-century archive boasted of its status as the laboratory of history, the nascent film archive of the twentieth century posed a much more radical site of experimentation with history. In short, what we see by the 1930s is not just a promotion of film as a new archive but a recognition of film's particular counter-archival suitability as the memory of modernity.

CONCLUSION

Even though Bergson never dealt extensively with the topic of history, he set the horizon for the younger postwar generation's far-reaching reformation of the philosophy of history by deconstructing contemporary conceptions of memory and time and dethroning a mechanistic and teleological view of the world. For Bergson, photography and film transformed the terms and potentiality in which his philosophy of time was conceptualized. For Bloch and Braudel, writing within the intellectual footprint left by that Bergsonian potential, photography and film transformed the terms in which their theory of historical time was conceptualized. Were we to imagine what a Bergsonian history would look like, we would encounter the postwar relationship between film and the Annales school, with the Archives de la Planète—based in the human geography that was foundational to Bloch and Febvre—providing an exemplary experiment within this film-history laboratory. As suggested in the readings I have done in this chapter, a Bergsonian history would posit a negotiation rather than an outright opposition to cinema, much as the Kahn films' primary attention to the "most lasting developments" of the day mark an intersection with rather than detour from the "momentary convulsions" of *histoire événementielle*. It would be a history that revolutionized the parameters of the "document," now inextricably bound to the camera as a probing witness and record of modern daily life whose testimony was defined as much by its involuntary as its voluntary evidence. It would bring together involuntary and voluntary mechanisms of perception, pure memory, and habitual memory. And finally, as a result of this flexibility, a Bergsonian history would have to move against an understanding of events based in linear and temporal causality.

In addition to embodying a form of Bergsonian history, the Kahn Archive inherited the turn-of-the-century expectation that film was destined to record the ephemeral and forgotten components of modern experience and elevated it to the level of a pseudoscientific mission. Instructed to capture the transformation of early-twentieth-century daily life as it escaped from an agrarian and community-based model of living into an urban and technologically mediated one, Kahn's cameramen went in search of nascent life ("the beginnings, initial movements [and] unattended facts"), often guided by random curiosity. To be sure, they regularly headed in the direction of the *histoire événementielle* of tomorrow's headlines. Yet by traveling toward those signposts of official history armed with the culturally leveling eye of the camera and the patience of archival rather than newspaper time, they were inevitably brought into contact with a more informal and unauthorized history of everyday practices. As a result, their films produced as much as they discovered the modern everyday. Although Kahn's original aim was conservative, commemorative, and nostalgic, to record and store that which was passing, his project ended up capturing and in a sense constructing just as clearly that which was emerging. Consequently, it is very difficult to distinguish evidence of continuity and stasis from that of discontinuity and rupture in the Kahn films. It was precisely in this overlapping area, where the *longue durée* and *histoire événementielle*, temporal duration and brevity, are superimposed, only to reveal the disappearing and emerging dimensions of history, that the general coordinates of a specifically modern and cinematic everyday emerge, and that something resembling the multiple rhythms of historical time impress themselves upon the project.

The Kahn Archive did not gravitate haphazardly toward the everyday. Within the Archives de la Planète, the camera's involuntary and automatically exhaustive inventory of the present went hand in hand with a voluntary effort to augment film's relation to the anecdotal. Ultimately, however, neither the camera, the individual cameraman, Bergson's philosophy, Brunhes' geography, nor Kahn himself were solely responsible for the Kahn films' pervasive attraction to minor history. Rather, it was the archival context of their filming that allowed Kahn's cameramen to boldly pursue the infinite levels of particularity common to the everyday. Even though the drive to include everything in the Kahn Archive was restrained by the vague aspiration for academic rigor that underpinned the classificatory logic of Brunhes' human geography, as I have already argued, far from enforcing an impersonally positivist approach to the production of documents, Brunhes' influence actually swayed the Archive back in the direction of instinct, the subjective, the casual, and the anti-systematic. This constant tension within the Kahn Archive was compounded by the equally contradictory archival qualities of film as a source of both indexically verifiable and potentially indeterminate data, and as a model for complete and incomplete memory. If we want to engage, however, with the most explicit explorations of film's affinity with history and the everyday, we need to turn to Dulac and her colleagues, those early film theorists, critics, and filmmakers from the late teens and twenties (so crucial to Kracauer's later theorization of the centrality of the everyday to film) for whom film was always the primary rather than secondary object of inquiry.

SEEING "FOR THE FIRST TIME"

THE REDISCOVERY OF THE EVERYDAY IN
EARLY FRENCH FILM THEORY

I simply carried out on two living bodies the same analytical examination that surgeons perform on corpses.

ÉMILE ZOLA, PREFACE TO THE SECOND
EDITION OF *THÉRÈSE RAQUIN* (1868)[1]

Here it is: 80 percent of the clients and objects that help us to live are only noticed by us in our everyday lives, while 20 percent are seen. From this, I deduce the cinematographic revolution is *to make us see everything that has been merely noticed.* . . . The dog that goes by in the street is only noticed. Projected on the screen, it is seen, so much so that the whole audience reacts as if it discovered the dog.

FERNAND LÉGER (1922)[2]

If the film were to give itself up to the blind representation of everyday life, following the precepts of, say, Zola . . . the result would be a construction alien to the visual habits of the audience, diffuse, unarticulated outwards. Radical naturalism, to which the technique of film lends itself, would dissolve all surface coherence of meaning and finish up as the antithesis of familiar realism.

THEODOR ADORNO (1951)[3]

IT COULD BE ARGUED that the films made for Kahn's Archive were "little spoken of" (as the brief notice in *Journal du Ciné-Club* put it) not because they were irrelevant or totally unknown but because French film culture simply had not yet formulated a language to comprehend the unique ambitions of Kahn's archival project.[4] This is perhaps why the notice mistakes an archive for a museum. Alternatively, the *Journal du Ciné-Club*'s disavowal of the project's archival context and its more correct description of the films as *films documentaires* do suggest two discourses according to which the Kahn films did in fact make sense. Beyond their affiliations with Bergsonism and Brunhes' human geography, we have already examined two cinematic languages in which Kahn's films can be comprehended:

the archival context of film's relation to historicity, and the actuality and documentary traditions of filmmaking. In this chapter, I focus on another discourse central to understanding the broader cinematic landscape (typified by the *Journal du Ciné-Club*) to which the Kahn films belong, namely, that of early French film criticism. The Kahn Archive and early French film theorists of the ciné-club movement shared, albeit with different goals, a discursive and experimental investment in film's affinity with what Siegfried Kracauer called—in *Theory of Film*, a book in explicit dialogue with many of the key French film critics of the 1920s—"life in the form of everyday life."[5]

But as Kracauer's recollection (in *Theory of Film*) of his first experiences at the cinema shows, film's affinity with life did not refer to the medium's ability to simply witness or reproduce faithfully the ordinary side of reality. Rather, it referred to the medium's deranging appeal, its potentially radical rearrangement of the way in which we perceive everyday reality.

> I was still a young boy when I saw my first film. The impression it made upon me must have been intoxicating, for I there and then determined to commit my experience to writing. To the best of my recollection, this was my earliest literary project. Whether it ever materialized, I have forgotten. But I have not forgotten its long-winded title, which, back from the movie house, I immediately put on a shred of paper. *Film as the Discoverer of the Marvels of Everyday Life*, the title read. And, I remember, as if it were today, the marvels themselves. What thrilled me so deeply was an ordinary suburban street, filled with lights and shadows which transfigured it. Several trees stood about, and there was in the foreground a puddle reflecting invisible house façades and a piece of the sky. Then a breeze moved the shadows, and the façades with the sky below began to waver. The trembling upper world in the dirty puddle—this image has never left me.[6]

Kracauer's acknowledgment of the permanent impression early cinema made upon him hinges upon the transforming, rather than realistic, nature of film's relation to the "ordinary." He recalls how the film's transfiguring and trembling mediations drew the eye beyond the surface to the "invisible" where intoxication imbalances an otherwise sober street scene. These primal cinematic encounters lead Kracauer to embrace the medium's post-positivist aesthetic, which, true to the scientific looseness of Zola's naturalism, encompassed the naturalistic and the fantastic in a cinema of unadorned facts and technologically mediated effects. If Kracauer was later to find examples of this unrestrained naturalism in films like Jacques Feyder's *Thérèse Raquin* (the 1928 adaptation of Zola's 1867 novel), his boyhood friend Theodor Adorno was also drawn to the cinematic relevance of the extremes of Zola's passion for the real.[7] In *Minima Moralia*, Adorno turned, albeit more briefly, to film's unrestrained representational attraction to everyday life, describing the potential of its post-positivist aesthetic with the term "radical [as opposed to familiar] naturalism." Like Kracauer, whom he aptly described as a "curious realist," Adorno also connected this nonrealist reserve to film's capacity to rupture the "surface coherence" of its superficial inventorial optic and release "alien" perspectives of our everyday environment.[8]

Kracauer and Adorno's reflections upon film's capacity for an *alternative* unnatural realism speak to the undeclared possibilities of Kahn's own Zolaesque survey of daily life and the major preoccupation of early French film theory, namely, the vacillating appeal of everyday life between the poles of familiar verisimilitude and radical naturalism. A reconsideration of the legacy of French naturalism is thus central to understanding how early film theory cannot be reduced to another example of modernism's dread of the everyday.[9] Building upon the discussion in chapter 2 of the importance of human geography's postdeterminist life-milieu template and Kahn and Brunhes' broad instructions to the *boursiers* and cameramen to *see differently*, I am interested here in that post-positivist strand of early French film theory that rejected familiar realism (based on narration, character-centered action, and events) and embraced unfamiliar naturalism (based on excessive description, observation, and details). Central to this new optic was a hyper-naturalist gaze that combined the penetrative and exhaustive observational habits of the surgeon and ethnographer.

The counter-archival qualities I have so far been discussing and attributing to Kahn's films here find a parallel in film criticism's Bergsonian distrust of optical realism. In place of a standard witnessing of reality, the poet Blaise Cendrars argued, film supplied "evidence" of a different (what I call counter-archival) order—proof of a world "which has never been seen before."[10] With a view to mapping out the common ground between the Kahn Archive and early French film theory, while also pointing to the latter's forgotten influence upon the supposedly familiar realism of Kracauer and Bazin's film theory, this chapter investigates a pivotal moment in the evolution of "the medium's primordial concern for actuality."[11] It traces this evolution across three contexts: the influence of the First World War and the emergence of a post-humanist perspective; the proliferation of a post-positivist realism (or radical naturalism) within early film theory, particularly visible across certain themes (the surgical or ethnographic gaze and the trope of reborn vision) and tensions (the animate versus the inanimate, life versus death, human versus milieu) aroused by nonfiction and fiction film alike; and finally, moving to the most solid bridge between the world of Kahn and the cinephiles, the impact of Bergsonism in film criticism debates.

Early cinema's naturalist tendency went beyond clichéd associations with everyday life such as the medium's reflection of the lives of ordinary working men and women. It extended to the medium's capacity to collect contingency—what Dai Vaughn alludes to as the "invasion of the spontaneous" or what Mary Ann Doane recognizes as the camera's ability "to record indiscriminately" or "to accumulate a hoard of uncataloguable details"—which presented an anti-illusionist threat to bourgeois norms of naturalist representation.[12] As described by Noël Burch, the threat of early cinema's inventorial impulses was ideologically recuperated in what he called, using a variant of the Lazarus trope, the "Frankenstein complex," that is, the bourgeois desire to wed film to "the mythology of victory over death" in the "realization of a perfect illusion of the perceptual world."[13] Drawing on the implications of early cinema's radically different modes of reception and presentation (as described by Burch and other historians), Doane has made the additional claim that early cinema's relation to an unrationalized temporality became compromised with the shift in the 1910s to a more standardized mode of representation, narration, and film reception associated with the classical Hollywood style.[14] In a related analysis that also privileges actualities as the *ur*-form of early cinema's otherness, Phil Rosen claims that "commercial cinema passed [in its early years] through a brief period when its status as document was dominant, and then stabilized enough to make the status of the image as explicit diegesis the mark of dominant filmmaking."[15]

These diverse explorations of early cinema's anti-aesthetic instability—whether associated with scientific anti-illusionism (Burch), temporal contingency (Doane), or excessive detail (Rosen)—ultimately suggest that this threat would be regulated and codified by the late teens as a part of the move to harness the eye of the audience and make the film image more legible by means of narrative, continuity-based editing, and feature-length films screened in permanent cinemas catering to middle-class audiences.[16] On the contrary, however, far from disappearing, film's radically naturalist tendency for anti-aesthetic, non-narrative disorder reemerged resiliently, not only within a project like the Archives de la Planète or the continuing appeal of nonfiction film, but within the ascendant American narrative films that began to have such a profound influence upon film critics' explorations of the everyday by the late 1910s. The high stakes of these critics' insights reflect how their revised naturalism still registered the submission to capitalism and industrialization by which Georg Lukács defined traditional naturalism's (as opposed to realism's) worldview.[17] At the same time, the radically naturalist dimensions of these critics' depictions of film's encounter with modernity signaled less a relationship of total capitulation than ongoing negotiation of the daily effects of capitalist mechanization. As the most devastating expression of early-twentieth-century modernity's encounter with mechanization, the First World War provided a benchmark in the process of this negotiation, both for the Kahn Archive and the first independent French film critics.

"HUMANITY COULD VANISH"

Under the pressure of German occupation in 1941, the writer and pioneering film critic Colette ruminated upon the newly attentive disposition of young Parisians toward their usually overlooked surroundings:

They leaf through a marvelous "Paris ancien" [book], raise their eyes and, aston-
ished, recognize it all around them. They make contact with a past which they renounced from ignorance, a capital where they were born but which they do not even
look at; they are moved by the thought that it might have perished without their ever
having truly loved it.[18]

This was the second time Colette negotiated wartime Paris, and her description of
the war's incitement of an urgent state of awakened vision echoes hers and others'
experiences—cinematically mediated—of the First World War. That earlier war
had similarly forced Parisians to encounter on a daily basis the fragility of what
had seemed permanent, the transience of what had been taken for granted, and
the sudden visibility of what they had previously "not even looked[ed] at." For
French film critics, this general condition of perceptual reawakening was experienced in a heightened way due to the cinema's talent for making us see things
"for the first time." Almost as defamiliarizing and disorienting as the war itself, the
cinema enabled a contact with the previously "renounced," uninvestigated, and impermeable surface of everyday phenomena. Reading through the film criticism of
Colette and her peers, we sense that without the cinema a whole museum of everyday artifacts—telephones, cars, revolvers, typewriters, ticker-tape—the ready-to-
hand, modern versions of "Paris ancien" monuments "might have perished without
[our] ever having truly loved [them]."

The heightened sense of civilization's impermanence also led to the enlistment
of Albert Kahn's Archives de la Planète during the war to document Paris according to the preservational dictates of the "Vieux Paris" category (or "Paris ancien,"
as Colette calls it). One of the reasons for this alliance had to do with the massive
destruction of France's cultural heritage during the war. As we have glimpsed in
the Kahn Archive's serial filming of key topoi under erasure in modern Paris, the
destruction of parts of the French capital has often been accompanied by heightened preservation efforts, with photography and film playing a major role in the
nineteenth- and twentieth-century manifestations of this paradox. Just as Baron
Haussmann's violent destruction of much of Paris's medieval architecture during
the Second Empire (1852–1870) led to compensatory "monuments" in the form
of vast photographic surveys of what had been effaced, so too did the devastation
wrought by the Great War stimulate an equally reparatory investment in technologically based modes of documentation and memory, all leading to the supplanting of the material with the immaterial.[19] Even though Paris was barely touched in
comparison with the northeastern cities that underwent near total destruction like
Arras and Reims, the war still incited an unprecedented pressure to employ every
recording medium available to document the potentially threatened capital. Indeed, one of the major rationales behind the operations of the Kahn Archive during the war was to record in detail the destruction of buildings and cities so that
they might be repaired and restored in the future.[20] The new phenomenon of total

war brought with it the threat of total destruction, which in turn engendered the response of an equally totalizing and reconstructive conception of the archive.[21]

Kahn's Archive was not, however, just motivated by a nostalgic turn to the past or a nationalistic focus upon the aftermath of the catastrophe but was also interested in the full documentation of the war itself. The Archives de la Planète covered all stages of the war, from its nascent forebodings in the Balkan conflict, which formed the topic of Jean Brunhes' inaugural class at the Collège de France in 1912 and the site of his first mission, to the day-to-day life of soldiers at the front, along with the scenes of material destruction and human loss and trauma which followed these events. Unlike other encyclopedic film or photographic projects such as the Encyclopédie Gaumont or Atget's documentation of Paris, the Kahn cameramen confronted rather than lamented the transformation of the modern world wrought by that catastrophic event.[22] And just as its cataclysmic events inspired his mentor Bergson to relinquish his teaching duties at the Collège de France in order to take on the semiofficial diplomatic mission of convincing President Wilson to join the war, so too did it lead Kahn, for the first time, to put pen to paper publicly with the publication in 1918 of his only signed publication, *Des Droits et devoirs des gouvernements*.

A crucial if rather cryptic source for deciphering Kahn's personal philosophy (much like his text "Nos Fondations"), the 81-page pamphlet was written with the urgency of anti-German and antiwar sentiment characteristic of those years while also intimating the leanings of a pacifist internationalism that would emerge after the war in the Wilsonian idealism of organizations like the League of Nations. Following Bergson's own highly charged analysis in 1915 of the origins of German "brutality" in the "machine" of Prussian militarism and industrialism, and reflecting Kahn's personal relation to one of the major French justifications for the war (that is, the desire to retrieve the "lost provinces" of Alsace-Lorraine), *Des Droits et devoirs des gouvernements* identified the German people with an "*esprit* which is not that of the race of men" (4).[23] Kahn's ultimate message, nonetheless, is one of peaceful international organization, and the need to fight against the real enemy, the anarchic forces of "arbitrariness and chance" using a "permanent organ of collective foresight" envisaged along the lines of a "Federation of Nations" (9, 10). Kahn clearly understood his Archive as part of this fight against chance. Reconsolidated under the wartime premonition that "Humanity could vanish" (18), Kahn's already impatient gathering of the present acquired an even more apocalyptic urgency.

For Kahn, as for so many others, the war was experienced as a violent overhaul of the Western humanistic tradition, a transformation that he strikingly likened to a "storm which shakes the earth and touches every creature, not having left intact a single human fiction" (24). Photography and film's witnessing of this event contributed greatly to Kahn's and others' perceptions of the war as an unprecedented assault upon humanistic norms. And though Kahn was no doubt safely ensconced in his Boulogne villa during the worst of the atrocities, his cameramen and photographers brought home images to their boss from the very eye of that storm.[24] Although the more graphic of these images would never have reached mass distribution even had they existed in a commercial context, the central role that photography and film played in the war changed forever the public's perception and representation of war and violence.[25] More specifically, it brought to the surface the apprehension of film's particularly exploitable relationship with everyday life. For example, one of the ways in which the French Army's weekly newsreel, the *Annales de la Guerre*, and the commercial actualities packaged an increasingly unpopular war to the French public was by prioritizing the filming of day-to-day life at the front. Thus alongside the more traditional films of military marches, diplomatic meetings, and medal ceremonies, or those with a more limited distribution such as the films that dealt with the topic of psychic traumatism, the Army produced a series of films defined by their "anchorage in the everyday."[26]

The filming of the daily life of soldiers at the front was clearly guided by the propaganda mission to maintain support for the war by emotionally and ideologically "bringing it home." Instead of representing the newer and unfamiliar military domain of trench warfare, barbed wire, and poison gas, or the actually uneventful and boring nature of the infamously protracted war, they presented film viewers with the more familiar activities of cooking, eating, and cleaning. In this manner, the depiction of a conventionalized and domesticated everyday became a means for the ideological interpellation of patriotic subjects. The public, however, did not automatically consent to this propaganda. For if the war provoked a boom in the production of actuality films and reinforced—at least in the official rhetoric of government circles—film's status as an "impassive witness" and "impartial observer" of history (as one contemporary put it), such developments were met by a growing recognition that films of life at the front were filtered through the lens of official censorship.[27] Official censorship was stricter for film than photography and for films viewed by civilians than by soldiers, who were given a freer reign to represent and view the graphic brutality of war and "unidealized views of daily life" at the front in their trench cartoons and newspapers.[28] The cinema thus became a strategic battleground for the harnessing of citizens to the nation through the depiction of a shared daily reality that served to suture over the mutual alienation felt between the urban viewers and *poilus* (as infantry soldiers were known) on the screen.[29]

HISTORY BITES

Whereas the Army's nonfiction films featuring the daily life of soldiers may have domesticated the foreignness of the war, fiction films seemed to have produced a different relationship to the everyday, making the familiar and the near seem strange and distant. An article by Colette, titled "Cinema" (1918), published before the end of the war, illustrates film's tendency to disconnect viewers from their daily lives.[30] Against the backdrop of a depleted consumer landscape, in which sugar, bread, and gasoline shortages were the norm and "artificial light" and "bright colors" had become glaringly absent from the streets as well as people's clothes (45), Colette argues the cinema exceeds quenching the "thirst for superfluity that torments human beings deprived of necessities" (44). It has the capacity, she suggests, to restore to the audience the "luxury"—amidst scarcity and alienation—of feeling human again through the screen display of material abundance. At the same time, however, filmed décor acquires a defamiliarizing function, rupturing the surface of realist excess on the screen and highlighting the drab emptiness of the Parisian stage outside. While Colette specifically mentions Cecil B. DeMille's *The Cheat* (1915) with its depiction of oriental décor and excessive American consumerism as a film that fulfilled the public's material desire for luxury, she then adds (in a transition characteristic of the period's fluid viewing practices across fiction *and* nonfiction films) that "the finest flower of cinema" appears, however, not in melodrama but in the naturalist drama of the popular scientific film.

> I have seen "documentaries" in which the hatching of an insect, the unfolding of a butterfly outside its chrysalis, set the fairytale quality of stage illusion before our eyes and, thanks to photographic enlargement, open to us the forever-mysterious world where [Jean-Henri] Fabre lived.... Oh, that is the thing itself, luxury, magnificence, fantasy! The feathery and irised material of a butterfly's wing, the palpitations of a minuscule bird, the vibrating bee and its tiny hooked feet, a fly's eye, the flower whose image has been captured on the other side of the world, unknown waters, and also human gestures, human looks brought to us from an unknown world—that is it, that is the thing, inexhaustible luxury! Patience: it will be known at last. (45–46)

Colette's shift from fiction to nonfiction film is accompanied by her displacement of "luxury" from the consumer's world to that of the naturalist's. Whereas she earlier imputes to film the ability to bridge the distance between screen and audience reality by providing spectators with the memory of material affluence (in Paris), she now discerns in the distant and "unknown world" of the popular scientific and educational films a new type of compensation. Far from confirming the dry, realistic world of positivist instruction, the "finest flower[s] of cinema" surprise with the pulsating life and "fantasy" within scientific visual description.

These short documentaries emerging from the "forever-mysterious world" of Fabre—the famous entomologist whose works supplied Kahn's bedtime reading—not only magnify film's ability to record the near and the familiar (through, for example, the process of enlargement that can deliver to us the "fly's eye"); they also offer the possibility of a reconciliation between the furthest points of the globe. In the cinema's capacity to furnish images of nature "captured on the other side of

the world" and of "human gestures, [and] human looks brought to us from an unknown world," Colette imagines a means of overcoming the absence at the heart of
modern alienation, brought to a head by the experience of the war and embodied
so palpably in the subordination of the human eye to the superior eye of the camera. In those "human looks brought back to us," the cinema, Colette suggests, finds
a way of looking back at us too. In other words, the cinema is "rehabilitate[d]" (16)
for Colette thanks to film's potential to return, unexpectedly, the gaze of the human
spectator.

Colette's article is a testament to how the cinema (of both American fiction
and European nonfiction films) intensified and mitigated the experience of alienation within daily life that the war brought about. If neither *The Cheat* nor popular
scientific films were depicting the horrors of the war straight-on, and if censorship was doing everything it could to depoliticize public entertainment, Colette's
spotlight on (what Henri Lefebvre would call) the "genuine reverse image" of war's
reality—the allure of foreign luxurious props and the wonder of the secret life of
insects on the screen—taps into a much wider critical interest in the defamiliarizing "after-images" left by the cinema during the war.[31] Her glimpses into film's
redemptory potential should thus not be read as an escape from the harsh realities of the war. Instead, they point to the connections between the two seemingly
irreconcilable spaces of the war front and the home front, a connection that soldiers, who often named their trenches after city streets, knew only too well.[32] The
luxurious excess that her 1918 audiences found in the cinema betrayed an uncanny
foundation in violence and destruction in a manner that suggested, as much as it
denied, the reality of the ongoing war: "Only the cinema spends, wastes, destroys
or miraculously builds, mobilizes hordes of extras, rips embroidered cloth, spatters
with blood or ink thousand-franc dresses" (45).

The uncanny reverberations of the front echoing across films shot on location
during the war in Paris explain why *Les Vampires* (Louis Feuillade, 1915–16) was so
important to the future surrealists.[33] Filmed on Paris's eerily abandoned wartime
streets, *Les Vampires* provided another cinematic passage between the front and
the home front. In an article looking back from 1951 to his and his friend Jacques
Vaché's unorthodox moviegoing practices while on leave during the war, surrealism's leader André Breton touched on this spatial confusion when he pinpointed
the appeal of the crime series in their "power to disorient."[34] As for their temporal
disorientation, this is to be found in a dialogue Breton wrote with Aragon in 1929
between two characters named Time and Eternity in which the latter declares in
the midst of a debate on the value of cinema:

> It is in *Les Mystères de New York*, it is in *Les Vampires* that one ought to look for the
> *true reality* of the century. Beyond fashion, beyond taste. Come with me. I will show
> you how one writes history.[35]

FIGURE 6.1   Men reading posters advertising reruns of Éclair's prewar crime series *Zigo-mar* in front of the Cinema Plaisir, rue de la Roquette, Paris 1917. (MAK: Black-and-white reproduction of color autochrome A014056)

Looking beyond the surface content of the series, in defiance of their positivist information or their supposedly uneventful place in the endless parade of *histoire événementielle*, the surrealists remembered these films for their counter-archival writing of early-twentieth-century history. Rooted in the cinema's ability to defamiliarize and displace the spectator in an uncanny rather than simply realist encounter with the space and time of contemporary Paris, the serials were imprinted, to apply Bergson's line of thought, with the teeth marks of film's durational bite. A unique trace of this bite appears in the encounter between the soldier's eye and the film serial on the virtual battlefield of Paris captured in a Kahn autochrome from 1917 (fig. 6.1). Showing a soldier on leave standing outside the Grand Cinéma Plaisir reading the big-as-a-screen posters advertising reruns of Éclair's prewar detective serial *Zigomar* (Victorin Jasset, 1911–12), the autochorme is a condensed expression of Breton and Aragon's insights into film's spatio-temporal enfolding and unfolding of there and here, then and now. Where *Les Vampires* originally depicted a space shadowed by the ghostly presence of the war, *Zigomar* offered a prior memory of that space bleached with the oblivion of prewar innocence. Yet the memory of the "innocent" serial was now also irrevocably tainted by the war, dominated as its narrative was by the repeated death and revival of its antihero, the master criminal Zigomar. Once the serials themselves were revived and reviewed a couple of years or a decade after their original screenings, they depicted a relation to the past not dictated by the limited, utilitarian demands of the present. Never simply endowed with a comforting reversible passage of time, the serials were impressed with the destructive aspect of film's temporal relation to memory. In short, they reinserted into film's durational utopia a reminder of what the soldier transfixed before the *Zigomar* poster really saw—unfinished death.

WAR AND THE ASSAULT UPON "INCORRUPTIBLE OBJECTIVITY"

Colette's recognition of the camera's redemptive capacity to return the human gaze in American fiction films and popular scientific films and the surrealist's discovery of the secret history of the twentieth century in French crime serials were symptomatic of a larger crisis in the status of the bourgeois humanist subject within representation and documentary evidence precipitated by the First World War. By all accounts, the war brought about an irreversible devaluation of the philosophical and aesthetic foundations of Western humanism, fought as it was in the name of bourgeois civilization yet over the dead bodies of 1.3 million French soldiers (3.4 percent of its population, 54 percent of whom were peasants).[36] As Kahn himself put it, no "human fiction" remained intact under the force of this assault.[37] In response to the thoroughly changed nature of daily life and the new "cruel gaze" of technologies available for representing it, film criticism also registered a radically different emphasis on the everyday explored across cinema's assault upon traditional perception and aesthetics.[38] In a variation of the discourse on the cinema as a democratic language, Louis Delluc (who was released from war duty due to weak health) argued that parallel to "the war [which has] upset everything," film caused an upheaval in the concept of traditional art, declaring to "the most cultured Latin types that they can admire something which has nothing to do with classical studies."[39] The foundation of this upheaval, as Delluc and many of his peers argued, lay in film's nonhuman, photographic, mechanical base and its purported capacity, as Kracauer put it, for "incorruptible objectivity."[40]

Echoing these assessments from within the military domain, Camille Bloch, the Inspector General of Archives and Libraries, marshaled the advantages of film's identity as a "purely mechanical process" in May 1918 in order to authenticate the historical value of the Army's films as positivist documents that were far superior to any human-made record.[41] In contrast to this archival-related instrumentalist interpretation of film's objectivity, Delluc pointed to the modern and mechanical dimensions of the medium so as to highlight the way in which it was redefining the parameters of art, perception, and by implication, the historical record. Delluc understood that far from being the sixth art, as Ricciotto Canudo claimed, the cinema had no place at all among the traditional arts. Film had transformed the very notion of the aesthetic in accordance with its contribution to the increasing reconfiguration of daily life by machines. Delluc thus opened the way for a new generation of filmmakers, critics, and commentators to explore how film redefined (sometimes to the point of outright negation) art *and* evidence.

The aesthetic and perceptual critiques implicit in this redefinition cannot be divorced from the context of the historical rupture of the war. In their dependence upon industrial technology and their implicit critiques of classical humanism and traditional aesthetics, the cinema and war were (as suggested by Colette's blood-spattered dress mentioned above) intricately connected. Without claiming that the events of 1914–1918 produced avant-garde film criticism, we can assert that they profoundly shaped the insights into film developed by members of the diverse post-war cinematic avant-gardes who had served in the war, including Blaise Cendrars (whose right arm was amputated), Fernand Léger, Louis Aragon, Léon Moussinac, André Breton (who served as a stretcher-bearer), and Guillaume Apollinaire (who received a head wound and died of the Spanish flu in November 1918).[42] Central to these artists' experience of the war was a rethinking of the nature of film beyond its familiar evidentiary skills.

But contrary to the Army's instrumentalist faith in the pure objectivity of film, the war in fact punctured film's status as superior evidence. To begin with, the material limitations of the bulky and heavy camera equipment largely precluded the capturing of battle scenes (except in the very few films shot with the portable Aero-scope camera).[43] For this, the lighter instantaneous black-and-white photographic still cameras were needed. Moreover, it is likely that commercial audiences felt free to question a film's veracity due to common knowledge of propaganda and censorship restrictions in all forms of popular entertainment, from the songs sung in the *cafés-concerts* to the musical revues performed at the music halls.[44] Much as persistent credibility problems haunted the press throughout the war, there is also evidence to show that audiences did not necessarily expect unmediated truth when they watched war footage.[45] Even the Army's *Annales de la Guerre* series regularly used fiction film conventions. These did not just take the form of filming recon-structed combats or military maneuvers but also extended to the filming of staged scenes depicting the daily life of soldiers.[46]

The war thus subjected the reputed inviolability of the camera's evidentiary power to a broad range of scrutiny. On the one hand, conservative commentators expressed dissatisfaction with the "raw reality" of the actualities and called for the use of fictional devices so that the films might have a more explicit and propagan-distic "moral effect" upon the audience.[47] On the other hand, audiences were re-ported to have responded to certain scenes shot by cameramen—who in fact risked their lives in the process—with cynical cries of "It's faked."[48] Some soldiers even re-called attending public screenings while on leave only to be shocked by "the disappointment of civilian spectators with the few visible traces the battle of the Marne had left on the landscape."[49] In short, the war placed severe pressure upon the public and artistic perception of truth and led to a crisis of representation as well as civilization. No wonder the surrealists would look elsewhere than official war films for the history of this period. And if the war's affront to representational objectivity was felt across literature and the arts, it posed an even more pressing challenge to film—a medium that was intertwined with the war's own industrial mechanicity yet still wedded in many ways to more traditional standards of aesthetic realism.

It was out of this struggle over film's traditional and modern applications that postwar film theory emerged. Film's connection to the everyday was reconfigured, much as it would be redefined in film criticism, as a transformative rather than mimetic relationship. Film did not just record, it revealed; film did not just archive history, it produced a counter-archive of history. Thus even though the commercial and Army newsreels endeavored to create a sympathetic bond with the French public through the depiction of an everyday life common to both, what they could not help delivering in their news from the front was the disturbingly unfamiliar nature of "life as usual" at the front. The shocking effect produced by the insertion of the ordinary into the extraordinary was delivered in a more direct manner in the disturbing images that began to filter onto French screens toward 1918: the threatening nihilism of apocalyptic landscapes where there had once been picturesque French countryside; the affront to human decency in footage of dead German soldiers where there had once been an abstract enemy.[50] In summary, the war enhanced the awareness that cinema's relation to daily life went beyond the depiction of *la vie telle qu'elle est* ("life as it is") to encompass film's ability to turn the ordinary inside-out, provoking critics to take a scalpel to the seemingly benign metaphor of film-as-life.

BEYOND FAMILIAR REALISM

As Colette's early film criticism makes clear, many of the postwar critical and creative film innovations were inspired by the diverse nonfiction genres (scientific films, exploration and educational films, industrials, travelogues, actualities or newsreels) that were loosely grouped beneath the term used to categorize Kahn's films—*films documentaires*. Indeed, the educational alibi provided by nonfiction films had been crucial in winning over not only middle-class mothers but French intellectuals and literary figures to the "sixth art" during the mid-teens, when it was still associated with the low end of the cultural spectrum. Consequently, the conversion of cinema's brave new prophets transpired not through the popular crimes series like Éclair's *Zigomar* or Gaumont's *Fantômas* (Louis Feuillade, 1913–14), nor in response to the more highbrow Film d'Art productions, but instead through the seemingly more pedestrian world of nonfiction film.[51]

Aside from rejecting outright the irredeemable theatrical films, the cinephiles did not however distinguish too strictly between fiction and nonfiction preferences as it was the multivalent nature of the film experience itself, regardless of origins in truth or fiction, that aroused their devotions. This is perhaps why, even though American films posed a major threat to the postwar French film industry, the French film critics fell without resistance under the spell of American cinema.[52] These critics, including Colette, Delluc, Émile Vuillermoz, Jean Epstein, and the young surrealists Philippe Soupault and Aragon, thus may have entered the temple of cinema via a devotion to nonfiction, but their full conversion occurred through a cult-like absorption in American fiction films such as Cecil B. De Mille's *The Cheat* (1915), Charlie Chaplin (or Charlot, as the French called him) comedies, and the William S. Hart westerns.

As formative as these cinematic *coup de foudres* were, it was only with the expansion of a truly public and independent discourse on cinema in the mid- to late teens that the first "new wave" (as opposed to the second of the 1950s) of French film criticism began to gain momentum.[53] By 1925 the pluralism of this discourse on film had distilled into a set of somewhat distinct groups, ranging from those who approached cinema from the mainstream narrative, realist, or documentary positions, to those more associated with the so-called "impressionist," avant-garde, and (anti-avant-garde) surrealist positions.[54] Although it would be futile to distinguish too neatly between these often overlapping groups, two broad arguments underline their attempts to articulate cinema's relation to the material world of daily life, or what the music and film critic Vuillermoz referred to as *la vie extérieure*.[55] Put simply, the first rejected film's connection to modern daily life while the second embraced it. Both arguments, however, stemmed from the default assumption that film, as the first truly industrial art form capable of reproducing motion and reviving time, held a historically unprecedented role in shaping and making palpable the transformed spatio-temporal experience of modern daily life. Film could enable audiences not only to see anew what they had formerly overlooked in traditional life but to see more clearly what was radically different about the modern world.

As Kracauer recalled in *Theory of Film*, the objects of cinema's revelations were both common and uncommon. Early films invited audiences to notice the "slightest incidents of the world about us"—such as waves, clouds, facial expressions, or leaves dazzling with their "flashlike transformation of matter"—while simultaneously emphasizing the medium's perceptual correspondence with the new temporal acceleration, spatial fragmentation, and violent shocks of crowds, travel, traffic, war, and machines that characterized the modern landscape.[56] Kracauer distilled the effects of the medium's unique address when he argued that, for better or worse, film was destined to puncture our habitual indifference to the everyday "things [which] are part of us like our skin."[57] Awakened from their blindness to the everyday, film critics of the 1920s (Kracauer among them) evangelically militated on behalf of film's mission to make us "know [the everyday] with the eye" of the camera. For those most eager to break with the audience's visual habits, as Adorno suggested, this meant redirecting the camera-eye to the extreme of an even more radical sort of "blind representation of everyday life." Surrendering to the "blind" (meaning automatic, arbitrary, nondiscriminatory) quality of film's grab at the world, the French film critics paradoxically experienced a rebirth of vision. They believed that, beyond providing a copy of what already lay before our eyes, film retranslated perception through the visual language of modernity. In short, as Aragon put it, whether you were for or against it, cinema had to be understood as a phenomenon "deeply of its time."[58]

The first body of criticism to evolve in response to the recognition of film's of-the-moment-ness rejected the medium's excessive connection to all that was modern and sought for other older contexts in which to integrate the cinema. Belonging to this more conservative group were critics like Canudo (at least in his early phase) and Paul Souday, for whom the challenge of cinema was to overcome its connection to the mechanical and the inhuman. One way to do this was by humanizing the film apparatus. Souday thus suggested that what is "exciting [about film] is not so much the external and banal aspect of reality—whatever automatically strikes any retina or lens—but its atmosphere, its life, its soul, what is perceptible only through the direct and mediating presence of a somewhat refined sensibility."[59] Life, for Souday, marked the opposite of chance. Therefore, if film was redeemable it had to side with an anti-arbitrary conception of life. In striking contrast, film's attraction to the contingent (whose photographic base Delluc recognized when he described the "upsetting" aesthetics specific to the medium's translation "of life by chance") is precisely what Kracauer (directly quoting Delluc's ideas on photography) would later highlight in his equation of film with life.[60] For Souday, however, film's affinities with chance, its inclination to depict "whatever automatically strikes any retina or lens," presented a barrier to the superior force of the artist's hand and signaled the downfall of the medium's potential as art. If the most generous dimensions of this criticism sought to imbue film with a civilizing Bergsonian interiority, another strand sought to transcend altogether film's pact with alienation. Thus, even as it championed film as the "symbol of modern life," Canudo's "Birth of a Sixth Art" (1911) betrayed a nostalgic longing for a premodern past prior to alienation in which "all men [could] forget . . . their isolated individuality."[61] To sum up, these anti-modernist positions hoped to control the unmanageability of film's "upsetting" aesthetic by subsuming film into traditional aesthetic criteria.[62]

In contrast, the second more radical group of critics generally accepted that cinema was embedded in the increasingly mechanized and alienating relations of modern life and were receptive rather than resistant to film's magnetic attraction to "the external and banal aspect of reality." Aroused rather than repelled by the cinema's foundations in the material and mental structure of the modern industrial era, these writers welcomed the fact that film made us confront the "isolated individuality" of life in the early twentieth century and suggested that the medium's uniqueness lay precisely in its fragmentary, indeterminate, and disordered perspective on contemporary reality.

As early as 1913, the writer and journalist Louis Haugmard saw that the attractions of the everyday delivered by the camera were above all ordinary and fleeting: "the conventional value of certain gestures" or the allure of "ephemeral events."[63] This renewed fascination with the commonplace and contemporary, and this recognition of the eventfulness of the seemingly uneventful, were stimulated by the camera's predilection not only for the subject matter of a banal gesture but, more importantly, for the complex temporal web in which these ordinary movements and events were caught. Elevating the stakes of film's unique temporal qualities, Delluc claimed that cinema's superiority over the other arts, including its forebear photography, resided in its ability to transport us to "the profound beauty of the *passing moment*."[64] That film's preservation of moments in time was itself threatened daily by material erasure, due to the equally "ephemeral life" (as the critic Yhcam noted) of its nitrate base, added another dimension to what Bazin would later call film's *tragic* relation to everyday time.[65]

Even further from the idea of film as capturing the fullness of the past in any positivist sense was Delluc's assertion in his essay "Photography" (1920) that photography's unique attraction to the everyday resided not so much in the surface content of what it recorded—"the gesture one was intending to fix," he tells us, is "never exactly" what enchants one when viewing the photograph (or film)—but in the "secret unconscious" of time deposited in the photographic instant.[66] As a photographic-based medium, film inherited this "secret unconscious" of the passing rather than strictly instantaneous moment. In other words, to use Marc Bloch's terms, film encompassed a continuum that was also perpetual change, a durational capacity that also had (to invoke Bergson) a historical bite.

Typical of the more concrete efforts to situate film's connection to the everyday was Delluc's influential claim that film was the chronicler *par excellence* of the city street—a site that later theorists of the everyday, from Kracauer and Henri Lefebvre to Maurice Blanchot and Michel de Certeau, would consecrate as the quintessential location of European urban experience.[67] In a comment that also intersects with Kahn's desire to use film to "capture life, there where it exists, on the streets," Delluc claimed in a 1917 review championing American cinema that film had "the new force of modern poetry, the real thing, what you glimpse on the street, in a sign, in a color, everywhere and incessantly."[68] Responding to this request for the "real thing," Epstein demanded in his typically quixotic fashion, "I want films in which not so much nothing as *nothing very much* happens."[69] For Epstein, the

diminished drama and humble contents of this anti-abstract yet still-representa-
tional "nothing very much" were typified by the street movements of a crowd or "a
man walking, any man, a passerby."[70]

In many respects such meditations upon the "street," "the passerby," and the
"crowd" merely reflected the incorporation of the cinema into an older realist tradition whose commitment to representing the new reality of urban conditions
"from below" (to use Edgar Degas' words) dates back to the endeavors of painters
like Degas and Édouard Manet and writers like Zola in the nineteenth century.[71]
Indeed, the earliest version of Delluc's interpretation of cinema's responsibility toward the real, expressed in his preference for natural landscapes, untrained actors,
and exterior shots, worked through the prism of a painterly and realist aesthetic.[72]
He refined, however, this quasi-ontological alignment between film and the real in
the early twenties through a more emphatic relation to the "modern." In a statement that encapsulates French criticism's enchantment with cinema's inextricable
(though not necessarily realist) correspondence with the material and technological specificity of early-twentieth-century life, and its unrivaled suitability for depicting the contemporary world, Delluc went as far as claiming that, "Because it is
modern, the cinema should *only* concern itself with modern things."[73]

NOTICING VERSUS SEEING

Although the word *modern* meant different things to different groups, Delluc's
proselytizing reminds us that for a significant sector of France's avant-garde it referred specifically to the mechanized technology from which the camera was made
and on which its eye should be trained. Before avant-garde filmmakers actively
produced a modern "machine aesthetic," to use Léger's phrase, they happened
across it (as Epstein and Léger noted respectively) in film "fragments" and "rare
moments scattered among various" non-modernist fiction films, such as the scenes
depicting the frenzied speed and mechanical universe of the train in Abel Gance's
La Roue (1921–22).[74] In addition to inspiring Léger's own analysis of cinema's
ability, with extreme close-ups, "to make us *see* everything that has merely been
noticed," Gance's film stimulated experiments with the abandonment of narrative
and the exploration of the material specificity of filmic form.[75] As with Colette's
counter-intentional reading of documentary shorts, or Delluc's discovery of photography's "unconscious," here too the intended plot and informational surface of
the film were beside the point.

These critics tapped into the way in which perceptions of the world were
changing due to the visual reconditioning offered by specific cinematic techniques.
If critics like Vuillermoz were comfortable asserting that documentary film offered
the most "faithful witness of our daily existence," the more experimental filmmakers and critics preferred redirecting the camera's evidentiary range.[76] They

offered less traditionally realistic testimonies to the camera's capacity as witness by experimentally combining the specifically cinematic innovations of fiction film (faster rhythmic editing, close-ups, unusual angles) with those appropriated from scientific and physical educational films (from micro to fast and slow-motion cinematography).

This merging of fiction and nonfiction techniques produced diverse experiments, ranging from the antinarrative and fractured observational aesthetic of *Le Ballet mécanique* (Fernand Léger, 1924) and the use of superimpositions and fast and slow motion in the subjective sequences of *La Souriante Madame Beudet* (Germaine Dulac, 1923), to the inclusion of the worm's-eye, slow-motion view up women's skirts in the satirical *À Propos de Nice* (Jean Vigo, 1929). But the most visible evidence of the cross-pollination between documentaries and avant-garde films occurred in the literal citation of scientific films by members of the avant-garde. Germaine Dulac, for instance, included microcinematographic film footage in the opening of *La Mort du soleil* (1921) and also borrowed and recontextualized central subjects and techniques from the popular scientific canon in the time-lapse sequences of flowers blooming in *Étude cinégraphique sur une arabesque* (1929) and beans germinating in *Thèmes et variations* (1929). The frequency with which writers from the teens and twenties described the epiphany experienced while watching time-lapse films of flowers blooming or beans germinating alone indicate the impact of these films' new techniques of perceptual expansion.[77] Originating in scientific applications allied to naturalist description, time-lapse and microcinematography became associated in the eyes of the cinematic avant-garde with an alternative, more radical type of naturalism capable of extracting the hidden underside to film's otherwise familiar reality. Whether used "innocently" as part of the research agenda of a scientific film or for narrative effect in a fiction film, spatial magnification and temporal manipulation would prove central to this generation's theoretical and practical articulation of film and the everyday.

Advances in the manipulation of speed and scale of the camera's vision also expanded the parameters of film's synthesizing capacities as a universal visual language. The camera could not only conquer global and cultural difference discovered in far and foreign lands. It could also uncover that which was near and familiar yet undetectable to the naked eye (such as flowers blooming, insects flying, or cells regenerating), or simply beneath the habitual radar of the human gaze (a common dog that we are made to *see*, as Léger writes, rather than simply *notice*). In a 1919 article that reveled in the simultaneity of experience created by film's utopian perception, Cendrars evoked the thrill *and* danger of the camera's antinarrative capacity to witness a reality no longer merely *noticed* but *seen*:

> There is a new direction. From this point of view, arbitrarily, the cinema has given man an eye more marvelous than the multifaceted eye of the fly. A hundred worlds, a thousand movements, a million dramas occur simultaneously within the field of

this eye. Emotion: they don't know where it is anymore. The tragic unities are out of place.[78]

Cendrars' celebration of this "new direction" in perception welcomed film's departure from classical aesthetics as a result of its (and in particular nonfiction and modernist films') irreversible displacement of the Aristotelian "unities" of place, time, and character. Albert Kahn's own invocation of what he also called a "new direction" for humanity, which would in part be facilitated through film's ability to act as a force of rapprochement between culturally divided and politically opposed peoples, issued from a similar (albeit aesthetically disinterested) faith in cinema's ability to unify.[79] In response to the chaos of the war, the twenties thus witnessed two antithetical visions of film's capacity for synthesis: the dream of uniting the globe through cinema's universalist tendencies, and the nightmare of an excessive and destabilizing simultaneity of vision embodied in an "eye more marvelous than the multifaceted eye of the fly." With its globally roaming eye, Kahn's Archive may have leaned more heavily toward the utopian vision of the former, but it also encompassed the disturbing dimensions of film's capacity to "abolish the bondage of time and space," most notably in its own collection of pioneering microcinematographical films by Jean Comandon.[80]

SEEING THINGS "FOR THE FIRST TIME" IN AMERICAN FICTION FILM

Cendrars illustrated his claim that film had the capacity to undo the anthropocentric and spatio-temporal tragic unities by invoking a time-lapse nonfiction film in which the "life of the flowers [rather than the characters] is Shakespearean" (183). He was, however, just as aroused by the "unexpected mystery" (183) lurking in fiction film. The "evidence," as he called it, for cinema's new nonanthropocentric orientation appeared just as forcefully "in a banal film made in Los Angeles" (183) as it did in the more expected terrain of fast- or slow-motion films. The point that must be stressed here is that Cendrars' and others' apprenticeship in film appreciation through nonfiction film directly influenced their subsequent response to the American fiction films that flooded the French market during and after the First World War.[81] Although they were also concerned with French and European fiction film, the cross-pollinated reception of European nonfiction *and* American fiction films is what distinguished their particular take on cinema's relation to the everyday. Responding to nonfiction and narrative films in a perversely integrated loop, French film critics' pluralistic viewing practices reflect the porous boundaries between fact and fiction and the lack of standardized exhibition and reception modes during this period. Moreover, it suggests that their earlier schooling in the unintentional pleasures, thrills, and dangers of nonfiction film trained them, as it were, to read narrative films in a non-narrative way. This training not only influenced their modernist films but reflected the now forgotten importance of nonfiction and American fiction films to the evolution of early modernist film theory. In other words, we cannot reduce the effect of scientific films of the period to their purported educational impact just as we cannot limit the impact of cult American films like *The Cheat* to their ability to export American consumerist ideology or teach the principles of Hollywood continuity editing.[82]

Central to the French critics' non-narrative, nonfiction style of reading American films was the expression of a rebirth of sight and the discovery of a new everyday. In contrast to early cinema's supposedly descriptive affinity for the everyday, often ascribed to its mirroring of the audience's daily lives or its realistic capturing of the flux of modern life (busy streets, new forms of transport), the transitional fiction films of the late teens were appreciated more for their *revelatory* relationship to the everyday, that is, their ability not only to represent but pierce (with the help of film's quasi-scientific vision) the surface calm of *la vie extérieure*. As Delluc made clear, it was the "secret unconscious" of these films (rather than their advanced editing techniques) that attracted the critics. Reflective of this shift in film interpretation, a more self-conscious conceptualization of the relation between film and the category of the everyday began to develop in film criticism.

In one of the most striking bids for film's status as the modern guardian of the everyday, Delluc argued that the reason film "suddenly makes you think art is useless" is because in those moments when it transgresses being a "median term between stylization and transient reality" it "reveals something beyond art, that is, life itself."[83] Not surprisingly, the films that brought Delluc to this conclusion were a mixture of travelogues, Charlie Chaplin, and Sessue Hayakawa (the star of, among others, *The Cheat*) films. Progressing beyond the traditional aesthetic values of the eternal and the fleeting, the life that film reveals for Delluc is a rediscovered *everyday* life, experienced anew through the cinematic "beauty of chance" in concert with the skills of cameramen who have moved beyond noticing and "learned how to see."[84] Refuting the pejorative interpretation of *durée*, this was not life as an undifferentiated flow from which pain, suffering, and death had been extracted. On the contrary, it signaled life infused with "melancholy" and "suffering," leaving any measure of beauty left to it "painful" (139).

Continuing Delluc's emphasis on film's new approach to life, Epstein argued that through cinema a "new reality is revealed, a reality for a special occasion, which is untrue to everyday reality just as everyday reality is untrue to the heightened awareness of poetry."[85] Far from suggesting that this "new reality" transcended or negated the banal and repetitive character of modern daily affairs, Epstein (and other film critics such as Léger) specified that filmic reality, in its purest moments, brought a "heightened awareness" to the material ordinariness and uneventfulness of everyday surfaces, objects, gestures, and appearances. Again echoing Delluc's focus on the painful beauty of cinema, Epstein described these extreme arbitrary moments (typical of what he meant by *photogénie*) of film viewing as intermittent, surgically precise "spark[s]" of emotionally charged experience that "affect me the way needles do."[86]

The post-positivist inflection of French critics' fascination with American cinema reappeared in Léger's 1922 essay on *La Roue* in which he acknowledged that the aesthetic rupture posed by cinema was particularly visible in American films— "cowboy plays, Douglas [Fairbanks], [and] Chaplin's comic genius."[87] Their primary narrative content, of course, was secondary. What interested Léger was the films' relatively new use of the *"infinite* realism of the close-up" to isolate fragments of the body or highlight particular objects for purposes beyond narrative motivation or familiar psychological realism. Jean Cocteau also responded to the close-up as a technique for facilitating a magnified attention to the familiar: "On the screen, enormous objects become superb. A sort of moonlight sculpts a telephone, a revolver, a hand of cards, an automobile. We believe we are seeing them for the first time."[88]

If the machine aesthetic that defined the close-up enabled what Léger described as the "rebirth of a world," at least for those "who will have eyes to see," Cocteau also interpreted the technique as enabling a visual rebaptism of the object world.[89] His semimystical encounter with specifically cinematic techniques such as the close-up or "moonlight"-ing effects and their ability to make us see things as though we were opening our eyes "for the first time" marked a common thematic in film criticism. If the theme found its most extreme cinematic example in Aragon's desire for a sort of visual "virginity" before the screen, it also had a literary heritage.[90] As Fredric Jameson has argued, the nineteenth-century realist novel had "the task of producing *as though for the first time*" the modern "life world"—the "newly quantifiable space of extension and market equivalence, the new rhythms of measurable time, the new secular and 'disenchanted' object world of the commodity system, with its post-traditional daily life and its bewilderingly empirical 'meaninglessness' and contingent *Umwelt*."[91] Once the everyday had become conventionalized in literature by the end of the nineteenth century, film critics believed that cinema inherited this claim to produce the most profound reflection of modern reality. By the late teens, however, it was clear that the relationship between film and the everyday was not merely one of reflection but of revelation. Film would not merely emulate literary realism but generate a new "infinite," counter-habitual realism. As Epstein suggested, the experience of film's counter-habitual gaze may have had little to do with conventional naturalism, but it had everything to do with the "new nature" of "another [modern and mechanized] world."[92] In this respect, the hyperemotive rebirth of vision experienced by the early French film theorists as they navigated the foreign landscape of the screen's new nature had its contemporary parallel (much like the instruction to learn to see given to Kahn's cameramen) in anthropological fieldwork, then being revolutionized due to a new notion of cross-cultural understanding based upon the cultivation of an "innocent eye" feeling its way through the strange sights of "primitive" cultures.[93]

The future surrealist Aragon embodied this penetrative, ethnographic optic when he turned to the new world waiting to be discovered in American films. In them he witnessed the power to rearrange the overly familiar inventory of "screen objects" and reveal new "menacing or enigmatic meanings."[94] In "On Décor" (1918), his first published piece of writing, he suggested that the attraction of cinema lies in its ability to conjure a type of "modern magic" from the "really common objects" found in old American adventure films (such as the Pearl White crime and adventure serials of a few years before) or current Chaplin films.[95] The specifically "modern" magic Aragon had in mind had little to do with film's realism. Rather, much like Léger and Epstein's invocation of a new realism that was "untrue to everyday reality," Aragon's equation of film with magic implied a medium that delivered "[s]omething more than the exact representation of life" (167). His interest in the close-up, therefore, stems not from its codification in continuity editing patterns (that is, in what a film like *The Cheat* might teach), but from its ability to tap into the transformative potential lying dormant within the habitually overlooked. The meaning of the close-up for Aragon was then in its ability to reconfigure our conventional perception of things, to allow us, for example, to count the number of eyelashes on a man's eye, thereby making us see the eye in a radically alien light—as an assemblage of quantifiable abstract parts.[96] By the same antirealist measure, film's "superhuman, despotic power" was not to be found in the kind of "faithful reproduction of a nature [that] the Thomas Cook Agency" produces in film travelogues, but, rather, in yesterday's adventure films "that speak of daily life" or Chaplin's latest slapstick comedies that illustrate the "struggle between the external world and man" (166, 167).

Although he did not share Colette and Delluc's admiration for travelogues and exploration films, Aragon continued their critical interest in "the feelings that transport us" (166) in front of the screen. In other words, whatever the fetishized screen objects of these cinephiliac transportations—Delluc's "telephone," Epstein's "revolver," Colette's single eyelash, Cocteau's automobile, Léger's "polished fingernail," Cendrars' "watch chain," or Aragon's "typewriter"—they all shared an apprehension of cinema's capacity to break through common habits of perception via an intense spectatorial mode in which (as Cendrars noted) "attention is fixed" and passions unleashed.[97] Epstein expanded upon the nature of this perversely disciplined yet emotionally unrestrained visual attention in his 1927 essay titled "Art of Incidence" ("*Art d'événement*"):

> Among tokens of reality, banality is the least relative. This meticulous, deep-seated, dissected, intensified, itemized, applied banality will lend the cinematic drama a

startling depth of humanity, an immensely enhanced power of suggestion, an unprecedented emotive force.[98]

Ironically, it was film's Zolaesque positivist heritage—its hyper-observational,
autopsy-style presentation of reality that enabled the penetration of the usually
impermeable surface of ordinary material culture—which then, in turn, allowed
the medium to bypass the rational and positivist separation between spectator and
screen, in the process liberating the disturbingly post-human, affective dimensions
of what Delluc called the "sensitivity of things."[99]

Underpinning the cinema's power to sensitize the object world was its capacity to transfer human qualities onto inanimate objects. This explains, for Aragon
and others, the strong appeal of Chaplin's slapstick, which with its often riotous
reversal of the normal order of things, transformed dead matter into living things
and inversely made "each person [look like] a dummy whose starting-handle must
be found" (167). In its abundance of machinelike humans and humanlike objects,
slapstick staged a de-anthropocentric world that was both "untrue to everyday reality" (Léger) yet truer to a deeper reality that spoke of the body's discomfort and
out-of-placeness amidst an increasingly mechanized environment. But slapstick,
of course, was not the only genre in which this transference occurred. Cendrars
extended his appreciation of the camera's ability to reveal "material so tragically
impregnated with humanity" from the decontextualizing fragmentation of the material world offered in any fiction close-ups (such as "a watch chain that resembles
a man's temples") to the revelation of "depths sensitized" in the microcinematographic natural world of popular scientific films.[100]

Epstein encapsulated film's ability to awaken the inertia of the object world
when he wrote of the camera's "animistic" qualities. Paradoxically, this insight into
film's soul was underpinned by his and other critics' perception of the camera as a
mechanical rather than human register of reality, one that was, as Epstein put it in
anticipation of Kracauer and Adorno, "*alien* to the human sensibility."[101] Described
as an "eye gifted with inhuman analytic properties," the camera, for Epstein, enabled a sort of perceptual estrangement comparable to the unsettling and uncanny
vision one receives of oneself when caught off-guard looking into a mirror.[102] Epstein ultimately suggests that at its maximum acuity film is this alienating, unflat-
tering mirror. Moving beyond a nostalgia for the traditional humanist subject, his
and others' postwar insights into the newly estranged human-milieu relationship
welcomed the screen's deserted streets, the magical décor, or the menacing close-
up as so many signs-of-the-times. Delivered in the blink of the camera-eye, they
offered anti-portraits of a truly modern and therefore decentered subject, at least
for those capable of seeing rather than simply noticing the transformed nature of
the world around them.

BERGSONISM AND FILM CRITICISM

Given Bergson's prewar reputation as the preeminent philosopher of chance and the unofficial muse of diverse aesthetic revolutions in literature and art—from Filippo Marinetti's Futurist manifesto (1909) to Pablo Picasso's cubist painting—it is hardly surprising that he should find a place in the postwar debates that raged around the newest cultural form, film, nor that the more specific ambivalences of his commentaries on the cinematograph were also recognized in his own time by France's leading film critics.[103] Indeed, a postwar Bergsonism underpins the central themes I have been tracing in French film criticism: from film's ambivalent negotiation of the traditional borders between the animate and inanimate, the human and nonhuman, to its post-positivist and antihumanist ability to rupture perceptual habits and unleash the disorder of chance in a medium alienated from normal aesthetic conventions. Film critics, especially those who were trying to legitimate cinema, eagerly engaged the cinematic thoughts of the most famous philosopher of their day. Furthermore, far from assuming Bergson was an anti-cinema philosopher, these critics argued he was *the* philosopher of cinema, as exemplified in Vuillermoz's assertion in 1917 that "the art of *cinégraphie* will be Bergsonian or it will not be!"[104]

As explained in chapter 3, our contemporary anti-cinema reading of Bergsonism depends on two overgeneralized assumptions: Bergson believed film was only capable of reproducing the illusion of life and that consequently any conception of memory that resembled film was entirely misconstrued. In his book on interwar memory in France, Daniel Sherman rehearses the latter claim in arguing that Bergson implied that the "eye of the camera epitomized a misconception of memory as localized, a set of images that the mind has captured as though on film, rather than a combination of such images, bodily sensations, and less palpable intuitions."[105] Far from devaluing the idea of memory as a localized "visual archive," Sherman then argues that the Bergsonian reformulation of memory as "a combination of such images, bodily sensations, and less palpable intuitions" had "the paradoxical effect [in the postwar years] of strengthening the hold of a visual conception of memory" (14). While I support Sherman's claim that the visual became even more emblematic of memory in the immediate postwar era (with the Archives de la Planète providing a classic instance of this phenomenon in addition to Sherman's examples of war narratives, battlefield tourist guides, and museum displays), I would emphasize, however, that it was often a radically counter-habitual type of vision that was at stake.

Those critics on the front line of analyzing that technology most associated with the observational immediacy of the visual—film—operated in the postwar context of the Bergsonian debate outlined by Sherman. Several of them, including Delluc, Vuillermoz, Marcel L'Herbier, Epstein, Élie Faure, and Antonin Artaud, mobilized elements of Bergsonism to argue that film was eminently suited to tapping into new truths and forms of temporality and memory. Most importantly, they located these new truths within rather than beyond mechanical and everyday reality. In their diverse explorations of cinema's radical reformulation of art, they shared an appreciation of film's ability to break through what Marcel Proust described in Bergsonian terms as the "heavy curtain of habit."[106] Sometimes they were definitely more interested in pursuing a more traditional Bergsonism through film's potential access to an inner, individualist, subjective world pulsating with vitalist becoming. Dulac, for instance, described the close-up as delivering "the inner" and "intimate life of people or things," while Epstein reflected upon the same technique as one that animates "inert objects" with a "vital import" and an "intensified sense of life."[107] At other times, however, these and other film critics took Bergsonism to more radical conclusions, especially when exploring the interpenetration of duration and habit by applying the qualities of *la durée* and the *élan vital* to the exterior, objective, material world.

Emblematic of the more traditional approach were those critics who seized upon the obvious applications for film in Bergson's philosophy. This tendency appears in the writings of several critics who applied Bergson's *Laughter* (1900) to an analysis of film's objectifying tendencies during the First World War. For example, in a discussion of Charlie Chaplin from 1916, Jacques Dyssod turned to Bergson's "penetrating analysis" of laughter.[108] Summarizing Bergson's main thesis, Dyssod understood laughter as emanating from "the brusque passage from life to automatism," a passage that he sees materialized on the screen, not surprisingly, in the slapstick performances of Chaplin with their machinelike contortions of human movement. Contributing to the Bergsonian context in which Chaplin was understood, Epstein went so far as recalling that his first encounter with Charlot in 1914 left him with a distinct awareness of the "Bergsonian essence of this comic."[109] In an article in *Le Film* from 1918, another commentator ("A.R") demonstrated how the cinema was replete with examples of the Bergsonian definition of laughter as "the mechanical plastered onto the living."[110] Claiming an innate relation between the cinema and Bergsonian philosophy, and by implication film practice and theory, the critic argued that "the cinema has intuitively rediscovered the theoretical definitions of the philosopher." "A.R" also suggested that the original terms of Bergson's theory of laughter should even be expanded in order to include the complementary type of laughter that ensues when the "living is plastered onto the mechanical." Suggestive of the world of objects with a mind of their own that people Chaplin's slapstick films, this expansion of Bergson's theory in the direction of the inanimate plastered onto life finds itself writ large in the surreal apparition Kahn's cameramen filmed during a Lenten parade of a giant Charlot float—a fitting papier-mâché monument to the popular and intellectual appeal of the comedian's sly critique of modernity (fig. 6.2). As this and other critics knew well, the

FIGURE 6.2   A Charlie Chaplin float at the Lent festival, Paris. (Camille Sauvageot, March 11, 1920 [MAK: frame enlargement])

implications of Bergson's philosophy for understanding the inverted hierarchy be-tween humans and their *milieux* were not exhausted by the superficially comic effects of anthropomorphism in trick or slapstick films.[111] At the root of the comic appeal of objects acting like humans was a deadly serious reflection of the pres-sures of technological modernization.

In addition to these scattered Bergsonian references, a more focused debate on the relevance of his philosophy was launched in the October 10, 1917, installment of Vuillermoz's weekly article on cinema for the newspaper *Le Temps*. There he argued that Bergson's theory of art—based on the desire (as Vuillermoz put it) "to enter into immediate communion with things and ourselves"—could and should be applied to film.[112] Vuillermoz seized on this description because its focus on the issue of *milieu*—that peculiarly French obsession with the relationship between humans and environment—held such special relevance to cinema. Detecting the same multilayered reaction to cinema in Bergson's writings that Deleuze would focus on some sixty years later, Vuillermoz even claimed that Bergson was "un-consciously" speaking of the cinema when he wrote that we will have attained an experience of true art when "[o]ur eyes, aided by our memory, will cut out of space and fix in time inimitable images."

This defense of cinema as a Bergson-approved art was attacked just two days later by Paul Souday's swift retort in which he recoiled at the suggestion that cinema, "a mechanical copy" of reality, might be considered an art in Bergsonian terms.[113] Citing with familiar ease from the pages of *Laughter* and *Creative Evolution*, he argued that the experience art (unlike cinema) brought us face to face with was the "reality that we don't habitually see" (10). Not surprisingly, Souday enlisted an anti-modern, anti-everyday reading of Bergson in support of a notion of art that solicits a reality and an experience that eludes the "common man" as effectively as it shuns "the mechanism of photography or the cinema" (10).

In the climax to this debate, the budding filmmaker L'Herbier launched his own nascent theory of film in an essay titled "Hermès and Silence" (1918). He agreed with Vuillermoz's general conclusion, affirming that cinema enacts Bergsonian philosophy's "desire to elevate the soul over the mind" and to promote intuitive over conceptual thinking (149).[114] He parted company with Vuillermoz, however, on the issue of whether the cinema, in its present form, could be considered an art in the strict Bergsonian sense. L'Herbier suggested that cinema's status as "the art of the real" meant it was antithetical to the Wildean ideal of art as a lie as it was wedded to recording "as faithfully and truthfully as possible, with neither transposition nor stylization and through means of exactitude strictly its own, a certain phenomenal truth" (150). Like Souday and many other critics before him, L'Herbier concentrated on film's mechanical nature, arguing that its resemblance to a "mere printing press of images" (150) that churned out the subject-less anonymity of "bare fact[s]" ensured its status as the "opposite of an art" (151). Unlike Souday, however, he still promoted the cinema as a potential conduit for the *élan vital*. Typical of the more conservative uptake of Bergsonism in film criticism, his ultimate aim in emphasizing the "phenomenal truth" of film's images was to rescue the cinema from the "thick naturalism" (153) then suffocating that truth and to restore it to its fundamental Bergsonian "aspiration[s]" (149).

Not all critics invoked Bergson's philosophy to legitimate the cinema as a traditional art (of the present or the future). A second group, which included Epstein, Faure, and Artaud, was more concerned with reconciling Bergsonism with, rather than rescuing it from, the cinema. Contra Souday, they found in Bergson's description of art—the realm "we don't habitually see"—an encapsulation of film's disfiguration of familiar reality. This third group of critics pursued the potential of Bergsonian anti-positivism and anti-mechanism within the aesthetically hostile terrain of a cinema of "hard fact[s]" and "thick naturalism" (L'Herbier), a cinema, that is, typified by techniques that magnify beyond all functional purpose our observational powers into time and space across the screens of both scientific and fiction films. Theirs was a cinema drawn to what Lukács, in another condemnation of Zola's naturalism, called the "mechanical average" of the everyday.[115] By no means voicing Kahn's vision of cinematic "hard facts," these critics did, however, speak from within a parallel cinematic world defined by a new Bergsonian nature revealed by the camera's nonhuman eye. Constitutive of this new realism were the non-narrative attractions of nonfiction and fiction film and the modern reconfiguration of the human-milieu dialectic found within them.

In contrast to literal translations of naturalism, for example in the work of André Antoine, the work of critics like Epstein was deeply enmeshed with a more mechanically attuned naturalism of the early twenties modernist avant-garde.[116] Their perverse positivism is evident in Epstein's incongruous description in his essay "Art of Incidence" (1927) of the camera's ability to extract an affective, humanist potential from the alienated landscapes of film's "dissected, intensified, itemized, [and] applied banality." In addition to reflecting his own background as a student of medicine, the laboratory aura of Epstein's autopsy of reality recalls Zola's proclaimed surgical approach to his literary characters while also drawing out the repressed fantastical excess within the works of the father of French literary naturalism. With one foot planted firmly in the field of scientific cinema, and the other in the field of aesthetic creativity, filmmakers like Epstein (and Dulac and Léger) expanded the purview of naturalist observation through a panoply of techniques specific to the camera, such as rapid editing, superimpositions, fast and slow motion, and split-screen effects. But their attraction to cinema's scientific nature was balanced by a Bergsonian skepticism toward conventional scientific knowledge. Thus, even though cinema was the product and pure example of the conceptual thinking typical of positivist science—in 1924 Epstein wrote "the Bell and Howell [camera] is a metal brain"—by the mid-twenties it was also, for these very same reasons, that mindset's only possible critique.[117]

Another former medical student, the art historian Élie Faure, also recognized that film was bound up with yet not enslaved by "the most accurate scientific apparatus" of the time (263)—the camera. In a 1922 essay dominated by a Bergsonian acceptance of the post-painterly and anti-theatrical dimensions of (especially American) cinema's "radically new" and "unknown art," he focused on movement in conjunction with temporal and spatial manipulations as being essential to the medium's *cineplastic* appeal.[118] The camera's tradition-less aesthetic of chance flaunts its appeal for Faure in the unmistakably Bergsonian way in which film "varies and winds in a continuous movement" that produces "the constantly unexpected things imposed on the work by its mobile composition, ceaselessly renewed, ceaselessly broken and remade, fading away and reviving and breaking down, monumental for one flashing instant, impressionistic the second" (261). And in a direct invocation of Bergsonian philosophy, he argued film actually modifies "our idea of the duration of time" because in its ability to insert the temporal unfolding of a past event into our present spatial arrangement, "the cinema incorporates time in space" (265). Rather than reducing time to space (Bergson's primal fear), Faure argued that through the cinema "time really becomes a dimension of space" (265).

By the late twenties Epstein had arrived at an even fuller expression of film's ambivalent identification with positivism (and historicism). Pointing to the multiple accidental effects that follow from slow or accelerated motion, he argued that the cinema acts as a catalyst for the viewer to experience directly nonlinear time and the true disorder of the "chronology of the human mind" in which "fragments from several pasts take root in a single present" and "the future erupts through the memories."[119] Without directly referring to Bergson, Epstein here rehearsed the philosopher's key cinematic complaint—that the fullness of the present will always elude mechanical reproducibility. He even paraphrased Bergson's ideas—"Time is invention or it is nothing at all" becomes "The present is an uneasy convention"— and acknowledged the latter's reformulation of memory as the eternal presence of the past in the present.[120] Epstein went on to argue that even though the present "eludes the chronometer" and escapes all forms of standard measurement, "the cinema is the only art capable of depicting this present as it is," that is, as a convention, just one perspective upon the temporal openness of reality onto the past and future. The capacity of cinema to depict the present "as it [truly] is"—that is, as a temporal construction open to the future and past—was exactly why Aragon and Breton believed *Les Vampires* (rather than, say, the National Archives) guarded the secret true history of French modernity.

In 1933 the actor, poet, and theorist of theater Antonin Artaud pushed the point even further, invoking this new anarchic take on the Bergsonian framework in his own analysis of film's essential relation to the chaotic realms of chance and contingency:

> What can be said under these conditions [in which film's vision is ruled by the arbitrariness of the machine] is that insofar as the cinema is left alone in the presence of objects, it imposes an order on them, an order which the eye recognizes as valid and which corresponds to certain external habits of the memory and mind. The question that arises here is whether or not this order would continue to be valid if the cinema tried to carry the experiment further and offer us not only certain rhythms of habitual life as the eye or ear recognizes them, but those darker, slow-motion encounters with all that is concealed beneath things, the images—crushed, trampled, slackened, or dense—of all that swarms in the lower depths of the mind.[121]

In the correspondence between filmic reality and "external habits of the memory and mind," Artaud is clearly referring back to the analogy in *Creative Evolution* that the "mechanism of our ordinary knowledge is of a cinematographical kind." However, just as Epstein and Faure recognized but moved beyond the camera's machine essence, so too did Artaud intuit film's mechanical norm as a limit begging transgression. Although he ultimately reverted to the pessimistic reading of Bergson's equation ("the cinema remains a fragmentary, . . . stratified, and frozen conquest of reality"), what lies beneath film's "epidermis" for Artaud is a distinctly surrealist version of duration—not the "uninterrupted humming of life's depths" to which Bergson had argued ordinary life is deaf, but instead the "crushed" and "trampled" underworld that haunts "the lower depths of the mind."[122] Artaud was typical of the more radical film critics who used Bergson to understand their fascination with film's capacity to turn its back on, or at least disorientate, its straightforward recording and evidentiary capacities. In doing so, they liberated a range of counter-positivist revelations from within film's metaphorical archiving of the everyday.

CONCLUSION

However distant the Kahn Archive was from the cinephiliac world of the first generation of French film critics, both shared a cinematic concern with daily life translated through Bergsonian philosophy. Given their investment in exploring film's ability to make us see anew the everyday, they remind us that film's relation to the everyday became even more visible during the transitional period in which Hollywood narrative film began to dominate. The potential for shock that nonfiction film possessed since the early cinema period not only continued but also shaped the reception of those supposedly more restrained American narrative films, and in turn contributed to the hybrid attractions and pleasures of the avant-garde's own films. In dialectical tension with the more conservative and didactic invocations of film as an archive of historical sources or scientific knowledge, critics who contributed to this counter-archival tendency in film criticism that I have explored in this chapter emphasized and celebrated film's indeterminate, unmanageable, and unfinished survey of modern reality.

Revealing the enduring and often contradictory influence of Bergsonism, early French film theory borrowed the philosopher's ideas to speak to the transformed nature of postwar aesthetics while also relying upon them in the continuing appeal of more traditional prewar aesthetic debates. Together, the diverse critics discussed above explored a Bergsonian-inflected postwar cinematic landscape and drew a new map of that terrain plotted according to the dialectic of the familiar and the revelatory. Most often inspired by viewing cinematic spatial and temporal manipulations, they traced the points of interpenetration between duration and habit, emphatic looking and sightless seeing, the "privileged moment" and the "any moment" whatever. These critics took to the new postwar cinematic environment as surgeons-ethnographers-naturalists exploring with scalpel, magnifying glass, and notepad in hand a foreign yet also uncannily familiar world. Central to this new camera-assisted perceptual revolution was a nonanthropocentric vision of the world that cast a relativizing, pseudoscientific gaze across the human-milieu and fiction-nonfiction hierarchies. Through their exploration of film's suitability for registering the overlooked dimensions of life (the contemporary, the ordinary, the fleeting, the nonhuman, and death), these critics prepared the way for imagining how cinema configured the everyday as a space not of enclosure but of temporal and historical possibility, that is, in a place between the *longue durée* and *histoire événementielle*.

Their preoccupation with the camera's intensified vision of ordinary objects should therefore not be reduced to an obscurantist and ahistorical interpretative preference for reading films against the grain of their narrative or historically specific denotations. Rather, their fixed attention delivered an understanding of film grounded in the new effects of historicity that Breton and Aragon hinted at in their recollection of *Les Vampires*, prompted by the medium's revelatory encounter with the present. Thus, if the aesthetic revelations of "slow-motion encounters" were what was on Artaud's mind when writing about film's ability to arouse the "lower depths" of his imagination, the temporal patience of these encounters also matched the unflashy, non-historicist temporality that drew Dulac to the "slow burn" kind of event found in common actualities. And just as the Kahn films were exploring the temporal and spatial coordinates of an "anecdotal history" of the present, so too were French film critics mapping out their own contribution to a specifically cinematic—and by extension everyday—version of history. To be sure, Kahn's cameramen and French film critics approached the everyday from very different angles. They both produced, however, cinematic experiments in "applied banality" (as Epstein called it) within laboratories dedicated to researching film's modern contagion—the everyday.

This chapter has also shown that the post-positivist naturalism of these critics' approach to cinematic reality did not entirely leave behind the classic themes of literary naturalism (the struggle of social classes and obsessive passions) exemplified in Zola's quest to document France's natural and social history. The radical naturalism of film critics' writings took up key elements of literary naturalism (the surgical, the sordid, the antiheroic, the fantastic, and the laboratory-style gaze upon humans in their environment) while refiguring them according to a different scale, that of cells not streets, of eyelashes not mines, of bodies in front of as well as on the screen, of a history of the present not just the past. Most significantly, for its influence upon French documentary, radical naturalism also departed from the didactic determinism of traditional naturalism (which plays such an important role in Griersonian documentary). In the French documentary tradition the informative and reformative dimensions of literary naturalism and social documentary thus took second place to other attractions (also present if repressed in the official rhetoric of Zola or Grierson) by giving free reign to "dissolve all surface coherence of meaning" on the screen. In the next chapter I will explore the intersections between the cinematic experiments with the everyday undertaken by the Archives de la Planète and film criticism by discussing the actual reception of Kahn's films. At the center of this intersection is Jean Comandon's biological laboratory at Boulogne—a cinematic counterpart to the naturalist novel as experimental laboratory of the everyday.

ILLUMINATIONS FROM
THE DARKENED "SANCTUARY"

RECEPTION OF THE KAHN FILMS

We must strive to see in order to see, and no longer to see in order to act.

HENRI BERGSON (1907)[1]

Just as a stroller leans down to get a better look at a plant, an insect, a pebble, in a sequence describing a field the lens must include close-ups of a flower, a fruit, or an animal: living nature. I never travel as solemnly as these cameramen. I look, I sniff at things, I touch.

JEAN EPSTEIN (1921)[2]

Clearly it is another nature which speaks to the camera as compared to the eye.

WALTER BENJAMIN (1936)[3]

NO CONTEMPORARY DESCRIPTIONS of the actual film screenings on Kahn's Boulogne property have come to light. Nonetheless, the outlines of a typical screening can be reconstructed from the memoirs of Jean Brunhes' daughter, Mariel Jean-Brunhes Delamarre, and from the extant projection register that provides the date, film titles, and names of audience members for every screening from March 18, 1921, to June 29, 1950. After having had a light lunch, a tour of the gardens and their color portrait taken, the personal guests of Kahn or the Société Autour du Monde, as described by Delamarre, would have "penetrated" the small projection room, which resembled a darkened "sanctuary."[4] There, they would watch a program of typically three to seven films from the Archive in the company of between three and sixty people, and usually in the presence of Kahn himself. This might be their first and only visit to the Archive (as with the English writer

Rudyard Kipling) or it might be their second or third visit (as with the Indian poet Rabindranath Tagore or the financier Baron Edmond de Rothschild).

This chapter sheds more light on the intersections between the Kahn Archive and the cinematic avant-garde by highlighting the actual material patterns and possibilities of film reception within Kahn's screening room. In order to explore the correspondences between Kahn's order to "keep your eyes open" and Fernand Léger's desire *"to make us see everything that has been merely noticed,"* I will reconnect Kahn's films—in particular those made by the pioneering biologist Dr. Jean Comandon, as well as other actuality-type films made by his cameramen—with the few "film" people who came in contact with them (the philosopher Bergson, the author and film critic Colette, and the cofounder of the Cinémathèque Française and filmmaker Georges Franju).

Any consideration of the topic of reception and the Kahn films must begin by recognizing that the films departed radically from standard conceptions of commercial film consumption. They were not screened for profit, nor did they have a use-by date on them (as commercial actualities did). Above all, they were not intended for public consumption, but only for a select invited audience, and as I have previously emphasized, most of them were not screened at all but reserved for the future appointments of archival time. The Kahn films thus raise difficult questions. What do films mean when they are not screened or watched? What does documentation do when it is not communicated? What sort of evidence resides in an unwound reel of film? What is a message when it is not received? What is an archive when it is not open to public access? Keeping these questions in mind, my readings of Bergson, Colette, and Franju's encounters with Kahn's films open onto a speculative and unintentional side of the Archive that may move beyond its original objectives but that nonetheless speaks to the indeterminate and unforeseeable quality inherent in the films' future orientation as archival documents.

By using the above interactions as case studies for the hybrid and impure reception context of nonfiction films, I deepen my investigation into the post-positivist naturalism that helped shape early French documentary traditions. The focus in this chapter thus shifts from the everyday of urban modernity (explored in the last chapter) to the everyday of nature (a flower blooming, a cell dividing). This shift is motivated by the question: why does Kahn's Archive of everyday life even contain scientific films? Far from representing some ideal opposite to the everyday of the modern machine age, Comandon's studies of biological and botanical life, as the most natural *and* unnatural films in the Kahn Archive, reveal a dialectical relation in the Archive's (and ultimately early film theory's) interest in the everyday, poised between the organic and the mechanical, life and death.

I have already suggested that those film critics interested in a cinematic everyday beyond verisimilitude favored the trope of a rebirth of vision. Here I explore how this obsession with new forms of vision—epitomized in Jean Epstein's claim that never before has there "been an emotive process so homogeneously, so exclusively optical as the cinema"—was accompanied by an interest in multisensorial reception that paradoxically arose out of naturalism's heightened observational modes.[5] Walter Benjamin intuited this expansion of the visual sense when he wrote in *The Arcades Project* of the importance of the "tactile," arguing that with "the recent *turn away from naturalism*, the primacy of the optical that was determinate for the previous century has come to an end."[6] At issue in these transgressions of film's positivist borders of vision was an alternative approach to the photographic base of its habitual perception, one that did not oppose so irreversibly the cinematic specificity of *photogénie* to its common object of disavowal, photography.

To be sure, as argued in the previous chapter, the avant-garde film critics always had a skewed, impure appreciation of nonfiction films that respected neither intentionality nor genre divisions, and Epstein was no exception. Refusing to follow the picturesque and "recommended points of view" in Pathécolor newsreels or travelogues, Epstein instead dared to fall in love with what was "natural" and "indigenous" to the camera's modern optic: shop windows, cafés, ordinary gestures, a fair, the dust of automobiles.[7] This counter-archival cinephilic gaze rerouted the "solemnity" of the newsreel or travelogue's guided tours in favor of a more spontaneous, sensorially distracted, and optically expanded access to modern nature. Following in the footsteps of Epstein's reevaluation of the "natural" and those other critics from the twenties whose bifocal responses to fiction and nonfiction films celebrated the potential of film's technical effects once released from narrative motivation, Benjamin argued that it was the camera's infinite capacity for "swooping and rising, disrupting and isolating, stretching or compressing a sequence, enlarging or reducing an object" that confirmed that "it is another nature which speaks to the camera as compared to the eye."[8] A nature different, that is, from the observational limitations of naturalist description or narrative realism; in short, a camera-nature. As previous film critics' discussions of these nature films had already made clear, what was at stake here was a technologically interpenetrated "second" nature in which our everyday world's anchorage in space and time no longer applied. Paralleling the concern with the everyday in French film criticism of the period, the Kahn Archive's obsession with sight was by no means bound to a straightforward scientific notion of objective evidence or familiar realism. Thus, if the functional equation of seeing "in order to act" guaranteed the Archive's traditional status as a utilitarian visual archive, the Bergsonian challenge of seeing "in order to see" suggested its more radical status as a pragmatically functionless yet perceptually purposeful counter-archive.

PENETRATING THE DARKENED "SANCTUARY"

Kahn's films may have been projected far from Paris's boulevard cinemas or small specialized *salles* favored by the ciné-clubs, but they had several features in common with both exhibition spaces. Many Kahn programs catered to the continuing commercial popularity (often associated with early cinema audiences) of "local" films, figured in those screenings which featured films of Parisian sites and events or audience members in the Boulogne gardens. Comandon's biological studies were also "local" films of a type (albeit of flora and cells rather than humans), in that they were projected very close to the site and time of filming. Paradoxically, the visible status of the "local" in the screenings on the Boulogne property reveals a parochial side to the Archive's otherwise global pretensions.

The Kahn programs also bear some resemblance to the small preplanned screenings of the ciné-club movement of the twenties. The Archive's projection register suggests that programs were tailored to the specific interests of the small audiences, and that they often took on the informal intimacy that was also a feature of the close-knit ciné-club gatherings.[9] Moreover, far from being a totally isolated "sanctuary," Kahn's screening room actually belonged to an alternative, off-the-map network of projection venues operating in the Paris region that accommodated the appetite for entire programs of short nonfiction films after the commercial cinemas had abandoned them in the twenties in favor of the feature-length *grands films documentaires*.[10]

Among diverse exhibition contexts, perhaps the most revealing through which to understand the Kahn screenings is that of scientific film research. At first glance, the intimate projections at Boulogne appear to have little in common with the purely scientific model for viewing films as research tools as put forward in Brunhes' description of the Archive as a source of global comparative study. This is because the scientific model of film reception rarely existed in a pure form. The absence of any clear line between popular scientific films and their more research-oriented counterparts appears in the career trajectory of Comandon, whose major work before he was funded by Kahn was done for the commercial company Pathé between 1908 and 1923, and who himself wrote about the fluid boundaries between popular, pedagogical, and research films.[11]

The intersection of popular and scientific film reception appears vividly in an issue from 1914 of *Je Sais Tout* (a popular science and mechanics magazine) devoted to "The Scientific Conquests of Cinematography."[12] The magazine opens with an illustration captioned "The cinematograph at the Académie de Médecine (fig. 7.1), which likely refers to one of Comandon's first screenings following the controversial inaugural projection on October 26, 1909, at the Académie de Sciences of his research films made at the Pathé Vincennes laboratory.[13] In contrast to the gloomy, poorly illustrated and attended natural science lectures of the 1920s recalled by Claude Lévi-Strauss, the *Je Sais Tout* illustration depicts a 1914 hall packed with *savants*, either sitting in rows of desks or standing in the central aisle, watching beneath the proscenium arch of the theater a screening of microscopically enlarged cells. The caption informs us that the film is one of Dr. Comandon's microcinematographic explorations of the "struggle against red blood corpuscles by sleeping sickness microbes." Viewed from the back of the auditorium, the men of science gaze

FIGURE 7.1
Illustration depicting the
screening of a Jean Comandon film for the article "Les
Conquêtes scientifiques du cinématographe" in the popular
science magazine *Je Sais Tout*
(May 1914): 624.

studiously at the film, several of them standing, straining, like Epstein before nature, to get closer to the "world filled with an extraordinary vitality" unfolding
across the screen.

A few pages on from this illustration is a double-page spread depicting another
Comandon film but in a very different light (fig. 7.2). Twenty-four frames of Comandon's film of the metamorphosis of a dragonfly—from its origins in a cocoon
to the moment it is about to take flight—were reproduced in three rows of eight
across the two pages, so that, as the accompanying text points out, one can "read"
and "study" the film "from left to right and from top to bottom" like so many words
in a book.[14] These "lines" of film emphasize in a more explicit manner the textual
and scholarly mode in which such films were being visually quoted, if not always
literally studied. Although at the beginning of his research career Comandon did
apparently use a frame-by-frame analysis of his films, and even published film
frames as part of his findings, it is doubtful that the practice of publishing and
arranging frames in the *Je Sais Tout* manner was customary.[15] Rather, it is more
helpful to imagine that the translation of the actual film reel into a readerly, graphic line in *Je Sais Tout* marks the culmination of the pedagogically utopian expectation that film would become the "only book of tomorrow."[16] In addition, the reme-

diation of the film-frames-as-text served to regulate the excessive and wayward appeal of ostensibly scientific images when projected in front of an audience—an appeal clearly on display in the previous illustration of scientists transgressing lecture hall decorum by getting up out of their seats to take a closer, *hands-on* look at Comandon's film. Even though a frame-by-frame analysis of ultra-microscopically enlarged cells enabled Comandon to "conduct precise research into the quantity of Hemokones contained in blood," the supplementary quality that is clearly missing from the printed frames and that dominated both the scientific *and* emotive attraction of these films when projected was, of course, that of *movement*.[17]

Whether or not the *Je Sais Tout* printed frames represent an accurate portrayal of scientists' research use of film, between the lines of those horizontally contorted film frames that have been drained of the lifeblood of movement we detect that which they disavow—the potentially disorderly essence of the experience of film once projected in a collective setting. It is the unmanageable excess accompanying enlarged motion pictures that required the managing supplement presented in the linear arrangement of film frames on a page. The *Je Sais Tout* article thus stages a contest between the positivist evidence and post-positivist arousals of the scientific film. The opponents in the struggle emerge from the discursive space between the left-to-right graphic translation (and pacification) of the film frames and the illustration of the aroused scientists in the auditorium.

FIGURE 7.2 Double-page illustration of frames from a slow-motion film for the article "Les Conquêtes scientifiques du cinématographe" in *Je Sais Tout* (May 1914): 630–31.

What can this discursive struggle tell us about the reception of Kahn's films? A group reception shaped by a similar battle between film's positivist claims on evidence and its counter-positivist arousals also characterized the projection of documents from Kahn's Archive. In spite of Brunhes' claim that they were research objects of "consultation and comparison," Kahn's films were not researched frame by frame as in the second illustration of *Je Sais Tout*, nor read from left to right as the conventional textual documents of an ordinary archive.[18] Rather, they were projected in front of an audience. A collective, as opposed to an individual and contemplative style of reception, was clearly fundamental to the Kahn Archive as a whole. Given that the color autochrome process could not be successfully printed and necessitated projection for maximum effect, a group reception also must have been intended for the autochromes from the Archive's inception.[19] Moreover, if repetitive viewing was intended for the documents, Kahn seems to have been the only "ideal" user of the archive. As the regular appearance of his name in the projection register suggests (fig. 7.3), Kahn was the only person to view the films repeatedly in accordance with their purported function as objects of comparative research. Finally, the autochromes that were projected beyond the Boulogne "sanctuary" in Brunhes' lectures at the Collège de France were open to the general public, including women, and not limited to the mostly male academic world of students or professors. In other words, audiences more diverse than the narrow scientific community may have come into contact with at least the autochromes in the Archive. The loud applause that followed Brunhes' projections of the color autochromes at the Collège de France and the Sorbonne, together with his own praise for Kahn's cameramen and photographers as "technicians *and* artists," reveal even further the exhibitionist and aesthetic appeal of the Archive's scientific documents.[20]

University lecture halls were not the only sites beyond the Boulogne screening room in which a small percentage of Kahn's documents circulated. Although Kahn was adamant that his films not be loaned, even for charity, there was at least one screening in a forum not directly aligned with Kahn's community: a meeting of the Union de Femmes Juives pour la Palestine (Union of Jewish Women for Palestine).[21] Furthermore, there was in fact an unofficial precedent for certain documents from the Kahn Archive to leave the Boulogne property. The film ledger notes for instance that several films were copied and sent to members of the "Boulogne community."[22] Meanwhile, all guests who sat for their color portrait received a copy of the autochrome as a gift. Thus, a small number of films and all of the autochrome portraits became part of a dispersed, informal, and now largely untraceable circuit of distribution and exhibition. That many documents produced for Kahn were subsequently transformed into souvenir-like mementos reveals the existence of not just another archive beyond the official Archives de la Planète but the status of his Boulogne villa (the central eye of the Archive) as a destination unto itself, an event worthy of record and remembrance. The Archive's shadow

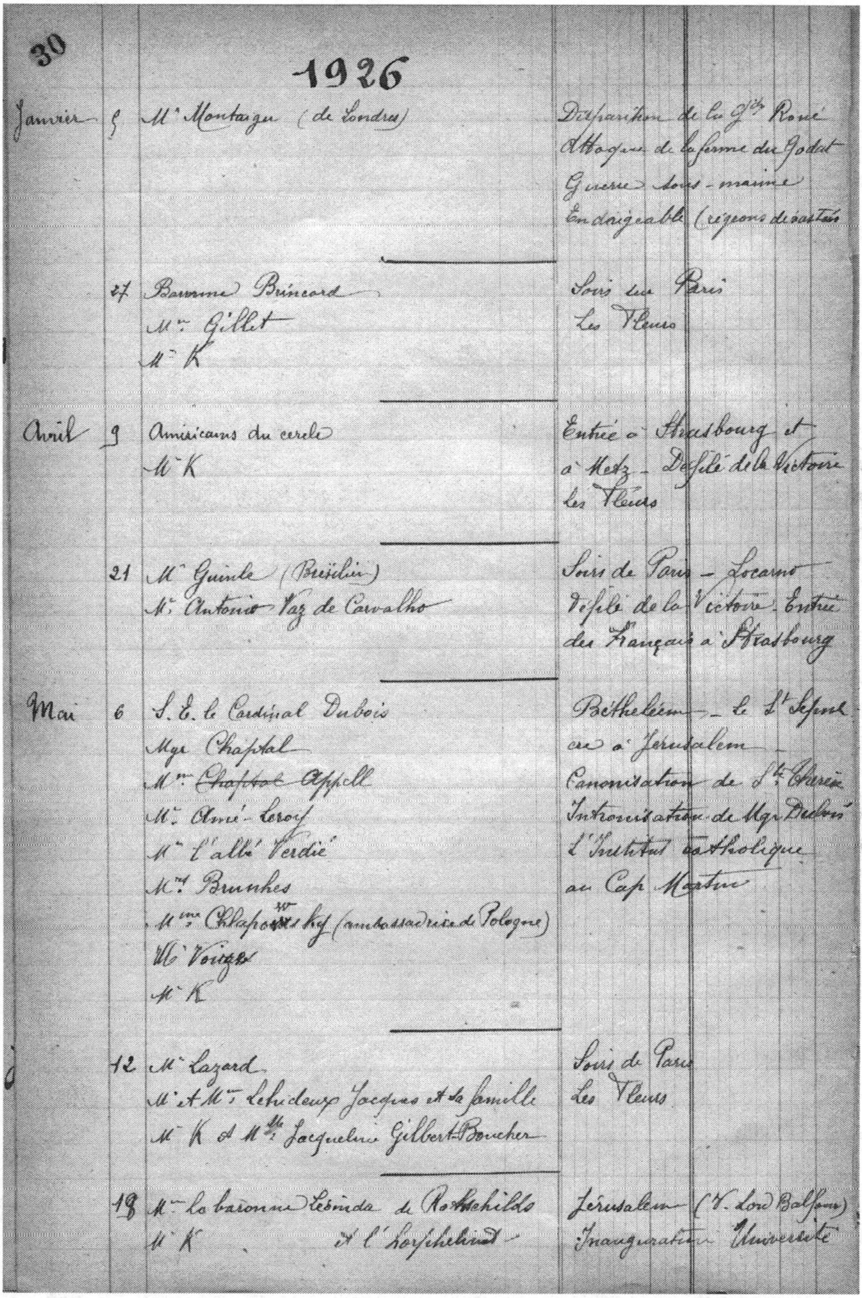

FIGURE 7.3   A page from the Kahn Archive's film projection register showing the frequency of "Mr. K" at the screenings. (MAK: *ADLP Projection Register*, 1921–1950)

life as an intimate family album of the globally dispersed "Boulogne community" becomes even more apparent once we recall the domestic ordinariness in the films of Dutertre's son, Kahn's dogs, and a playful flower fight filmed among Japanese royalty on his property in Cap Martin.

Above and beyond the lofty ideals of international cooperation and understanding that Kahn's films were supposed to facilitate, the above evidence suggests that they were also clearly appreciated as entertaining, memorable, and moving spectacles. Indeed, it seems that the aesthetic attractions of color, light, and movement, more so than the educational appeal of information, narrative, and argument, structured the experience of the Kahn screenings at Boulogne. Of the 833 autochrome slide projections (organized around 75 subjects) and the 555 film screenings (organized around 173 subjects), the most popular thematic, aside from the subject of the impact of war on everyday life in France, was the display of color, light, and other technical wonders of the camera. Films showcasing these themes included the time-lapse microcinematography of Comandon and various "studies" (*études*) shot by the Kahn cameramen themselves.

, The foregrounding of visual pleasure was particularly evident in the films of Paris's monuments, which were framed not as architectural evidence (as the official "Vieux Paris" category implied) but as spectacles for the eye. The cameramen's interest in magnifying the spectacular and particularly cinematic attraction of certain views of monuments appears in their studies of "Clouds and the Arc de Triomphe" and "Lights on the Champ de Mars," as well as in the color films devoted to, among other sites, the Opéra, the Panthéon, and the Place de la Concorde.[23] Like the opening and closing shots of René Clair's La Tour (1928), which focus on a shifting cloud pattern against the immobile monolith of the Eiffel Tower, the Kahn film "Clouds and the Arc de Triomphe" also uses the iconic power of the monument as an occasional excuse to appreciate the perceptual wonders of the camera's ability to capture the ephemeral passage of cloud movements. And in another convergence with the avant-garde's guidebook to Paris, Kahn's cameramen also fell under the spell—like the surrealists—of solar eclipses as natural wonders of light and dark that transformed the whole of the Parisian sky into a blackened screen, and the city into an open-air cinema for half-blinded spectators.[24]

It was this interest in the technical innovations and visual attractions of nonfiction film, shared by wider popular and avant-garde audiences alike, which would have animated Kahn's screening room filled with ministers, financiers, professors, students, princes, philosophers, and poets. But the most convincing evidence of this passionate enthusiasm for vision itself (as I will discuss shortly) appears in the fact that the most consistently screened film between 1921 and 1935 was Comandon's lusciously hand-painted, time-lapse flower study *Épanouissement de Fleurs*. Indeed, actual reception seems to have been dominated by the Comandon scientific films right up until the end of the Archive. In 1931, at the twenty-fifth anniversary celebration for the Société Autour du Monde, color autochromes and "scientific cinema" were projected, "which made," according to one eyewitness, "a strong impression on our visitors."[25]

The evidently impressive nature of Comandon's pioneering films raises an important question. How did a collection of films devoted to everyday life and including fast motion and microcinematographical biological studies manage to escape the attention of the French film avant-garde of the twenties? After all, as we have already seen, key members of this group (like Epstein and Germaine Dulac) were often inspired by the radically new aesthetic and historical models to be found in scientific films and actualities precisely like those in the Kahn Archive. All of the cinematic techniques that transported these critics to the experience of visual rebirth were being experimented with in the Kahn Archive. In the borderless range of the Archive's gaze, from the microcinematography of Comandon's blood cells to the bird's-eye views over the bomb-ravaged Reims cathedral, the Kahn films managed to offer both the enchantment of the "fly's eye" view of the world as well as the thrill of "tak[ing] a tour of the world in a few hours" that drew popular audiences to the travelogues' armchair voyages.[26] Beyond the immediate world of the Parisian cinema scene, Kahn's Archive also shared, with efforts as different as Dziga Vertov's "Kino-Eye" practice, the International Institute for Educational Cinema, or Dulac's promotion of actualities in the 1930s as the resource of a new type of history, the aspiration to change the world through film's acute observation of daily life. Considering these connections with currents in French and international avant-garde film, it is striking that the Kahn Archive remained in virtual obscurity.

There was, however, a small community of people, some of them well known in the world of cinema, who were acquainted with those screenings on the Boulogne property. The Archive's somewhat underground renown surfaces in the introduction given by the noted autochromist Léon Gimpel to a slide presentation of the Kahn autochromes in 1931, on the occasion of the twenty-fifth anniversary of the Lumière color process. One of the only times that Kahn's documents were shown outside their limited official network, to an audience including Louis Lumière himself, Gimpel referred to Kahn as the "creator of the *famous* Archives de la Planète."[27] With a view to exploring how those semisecret documents could possibly be called "famous," I now want to investigate the first of three scenes in which a well-known film figure penetrated Kahn's screening room.

BERGSON IN FRONT OF THE SCREEN

As shown in the last chapter, Bergson's scattered commentaries on the cinematograph punctuated the spectrum of French critical discourse on the cinema in the interwar years, inspiring a range of interpretations and applications, which together reveal an early recognition of the openness and fecundity of the philoso-

pher's cinema-thought equation. If these often diametrically opposed critics might
have differed in their interpretations of Bergson's relevance to cinema, they would
have all agreed that the primary cinematic question for the philosopher revolved
around the issue animating the *Je Sais Tout* scientists, that is, whether film represented merely the illusion (as stable, immobile parts delivered through abstract
time) or the true essence of movement and life (as an unstable, mobile whole delivered through multivalent time).

Bergson's tendentious critique of the cinema was intricately connected to his
appreciation of the scientific *and* popular fascination with the recording of movement and time in pre- and early cinema.[28] His awareness of cinema's transformation of ordinary motion into an extraordinary event (already discussed in chapter
3 in relation to *Matter and Memory*) appears in the types of movement and the
choice of film he used to discuss the limitations of the cinematographic method in
Creative Evolution. He begins his critique of the conventional attitude of human
perception (soon revealed to be "cinematographical") by comparing it to a "trick"
("*artifice*") that "manages to solidify into discontinuous images the fluid continuity
of the real" (*CE* 304, 301). To illustrate the point he places his philosophical microscope over the same mundane specimens that would later obsess Epstein, Dulac,
and Benjamin, that is, the perception of movement involved in natural evolution
(from flower to fruit, larvae to nymph, nymph to insect) as well as human motion
(involved in eating, drinking, or the simple movement of an arm).[29] He then shifts
to possible representations of the movement of a marching regiment, first considering treatments of this subject by shadow puppet and magic lantern projections,
then moving to the example of a *projected* film ("on a screen a living picture") (*CE*
304–305). Much like the instantaneous images of the runner from *Matter and
Memory*, Bergson's stock examples are clearly derived from Muybridge's or Marey's
motion studies as well as early cinema programs in which military parades were
a common sight. What these projected films ultimately prove for Bergson is the
abstraction of scientific time or "movement in general" (*CE* 305) rather than the
true aspect of movement as duration or "the inner becoming of things" (*CE* 306).
In other words, the film frame may successfully box movement and represent time
flown, but it cannot deliver, even when projected via the movement mechanism
within the apparatus, a true representation of time *flowing*, that unstable, irreducible and formless passage between two points of a movement.

Building on his earlier critique of the arbitrary and automatic "any moment"
type of vision (*MM* 209), he then mocks the Marey-like quest to divide movement
to infinity. Scientists, he implies, may strive to record "the smallest discernible
fraction of a second" (*CE* 301), yet they will still never be closer to capturing the
true passage of movement that escapes the abstracted transition "between any two
snapshots" of that movement (*CE* 307–308), much like the smoke that always escapes the clapping hands of the child trying to crush it.[30] No matter how convinc-

ing the illusion, for Bergson, we can never understand the true mobility of reality through a cinematographical rendition since "rests placed beside rests will never be equivalent to a movement" (*CE* 312).

Bergson's commentaries upon film's relation to movement and time had implications that extended well beyond the technical limitations of early cinema and whatever sources he may have had access to in formulating the mind-cinema analogy. Contrary to Deleuze's assertion that Bergson would not have had the opportunity to perceive the camera's multivalent temporal capabilities, Bergson did in fact witness what it looked like to carry the experiment of film's essential affinity with movement and time (to paraphrase Artaud) beyond its early naturalist satisfaction with capturing the "rhythms of habitual life."[31] This witnessing occurred on Kahn's property. On June 26, 1921, Bergson, accompanied by his wife and daughter, viewed six films. The first of these, Dr. Comandon's film titled *Les Fleurs* (most likely the time-lapse, hand-colored film of flowers blooming still extant in the Albert Kahn Museum), would have offered the philosopher (as I will explain in detail below) one of those cinematic "encounters" that Artaud argued contested the normal temporal-spatial chronology of events captured by the camera.[32] Like Colette and the other invited guests who viewed the Kahn films, Bergson most likely chose the films he wanted screened, and may well have selected *Les Fleurs*—a mechanically aided yet natural spectacle of plants moving as they grow within a condensed time frame—in order to reflect further on issues of vitality, movement, and time.

In his final book, *The Creative Mind: An Introduction to Metaphysics* (1934), a collection of essays in which he self-consciously reengaged the foundational philosophical questions of his career, Bergson returned to the cinema of temporal manipulation similar to the sort he viewed in Boulogne in 1921. Resuming his stance in *Creative Evolution*, he argued that no matter how much we speed up the film, the representation it produces still eludes the essential reality because of the cinematograph's "weakness to divide up the film image by image instead of grasping it in the aggregate."[33] While recognizing the efforts of scientists, from Marey to Comandon, in the fields of chronophotography and time-lapse microcinematography to reveal astonishing evidence previously undetectable by the human eye, Bergson remained convinced that they were still inadequate "tricks" that veiled the underlying reality of indivisible continuity. In fact, *Les Fleurs* might have convinced Bergson even further of the photographic-based inadequacies in the medium's representation of movement and time due to that film's hyper-dependence upon the camera's temporal tricks. At their core, in these and other complaints Bergson seems to suggest (much as film critics of the time) that if only film could break free from the weight of its photographic base it could transcend the spatial limitations of framed time.

Yet even if he himself did not acknowledge it, Bergson's philosophy permits a different evaluation of *Les Fleurs*. As suggested in chapter 3, Bergson's recognition of a limitation or a habit, such as the camera's tendency to glide over the surface, to frame or trick time, is never purely negative; it is always more a calling to move beyond or even reverse the limitation. Indeed, as discussed in the last chapter, many critics were already responding to this Bergsonian imperative to move beyond the camera's deficiencies. To differing degrees, they resisted simply condemning the positivist and mechanistic aspects of film's photographic origins and acknowledged that the slippery arbitrariness of photographic recording itself was responsible not only for film's affinities with death but death's reversal in chance, contingency, and the secret life of things. Furthermore, many of these critics (especially Colette, Epstein, and Dulac, further discussed below) encountered the surface of the cinematic representation as a threshold that beckons the eye to go beyond passive seeing, and even beyond the eye to the other senses.

In light of the success such critics had in theorizing the reversal of film's positivist tendencies, we must recall that in the final chapter of *Creative Evolution* Bergson did not freeze his argument at the point where the cinematograph stands in for the universal abstractions of conceptual thought. Later on in the chapter he makes a second, mostly overlooked yet crucial qualification through a distinction between "snapshot views" or "the Forms, which the mind isolates and stores up in concepts" like successive "moments gathered along the course of time" (317) and the cinematographical effect of "Forms [that] are no longer snapshots taken of change, [but] are its constitutive elements, [and] represent all that is positive in Becoming." Film may be made up of snapshots, of frames of "motionless eternity" representative only of an "artificial reconstruction" or "symbolical expression" of time. Nonetheless, in those spaces between the "any moment" and "privileged moment" (*CE* 330) of this perceptual modality, that is, between film's anonymous survey and its individualized eye-pricks (to invoke Epstein's needle metaphor), Bergson allows, without explicitly illustrating, the thinking of film as *approximating* an opening onto duration.[34] If Bergson had already outlined a space between the mechanical and human eye when he aligned the "privileged moment" with the "unforeseeable nothing which is everything in a work of art" and whose "*sprouting and flowering*" (*CE* 341; my emphasis) resemble the work of nature, then *Les Fleurs*, the flower-blooming film he viewed on Kahn's property in 1921, realized and even transgressed the potential of that virtual interstitial site.

More informal reflections upon cinema given in his interviews with journalist Michel Georges-Michel further contradict our received notion that Bergson denounced film's diminished access to duration.[35] In the *Le Journal* interview with Georges-Michel in 1914, Bergson recalled how "[a]s a witness to its beginnings" he had realized that cinema "might be able to assist in the synthesis of memory, or even of the thinking process."[36] Again alluding to the distinction between photography (the material basis of the celluloid strip) and projected film, or put differently, the medium's tendency and the reversal of that tendency, he said that,

"Immobile, [film] is in a neutral state; moving, it is life." Like so many other *savants* of his time, including Dr. Comandon (whom he must have known through Kahn), Bergson cited the well-known motion study of a horse to prove the limited benefits of film's predecessor, still photography. He described how the first fast-exposure photographs of horses galloping revealed that contrary to conventional expectations enforced by figural painting, in reality all four legs of the horse leave the ground in mid-gallop.[37] The split-second advances of instantaneous photography may have inspired in the short term a revolution in the painting of horses, now stamped with what Bergson calls a post-photographic "mathematical exactitude," but only at the expense of beauty and the more general "impression of truth" given to the human and artistic eye in those privileged moments. It was that more general, mathematically imprecise "impression of truth" that film, Bergson continued, was capable of restoring, even we might add, from within the scientifically precise world of a time-lapse film. Early French film theory arrived in the wake of this post-positivist restoration of a new impression of truth discovered in the machine eye. Reflective of the Bergsonian framing of their cinematic debates, these critics grappled with the paradoxes of film's scientifically aided yet imprecise impression of truth, its photographically based yet moving impression of time, and eventually they produced a revised cinematic reconciliation between Bergson's "any moment" and the "privileged moment."

The full potential of the Bergsonian redemption of film that animated the first stirrings of French film theory can only be gauged when we attend to Bergson's little-known, more optimistic invocations of photography, the most striking of which occurs in the essay "The Perception of Change" (1911). There he opposed the contractions and condensations of both the "any moment" and the "privileged moment" to a general enlargement of vision that occurs when artists or poets ask our eyes "to see more than they see."[38] In this context, he discussed the *undeveloped* "photographic image," in order to illustrate the as yet invisible, chance revelations of an enlarged, indeterminate, sense of vision whose experiential possibilities move beyond the image's intended content. These possibilities are also extended to film in another essay published in *Creative Mind*, titled "The Possible and the Real." Here he invoked the cinematographic film "prior to its unrolling" as an example of predetermined conceptual thinking and a state of knowledge "calculable in advance."[39] Immediately afterwards, however, he qualified this denunciation of the unrolled film in a manner that enables us to see an analogy between it and the undeveloped photograph. The qualification occurred when he points to the reversal of prearranged knowledge in the eruption of the new implicit in the unrolling of the film due to that process's essential relation to the "indetermination" of time (posited by Delluc as the photograph's "unconscious" and by Kracauer as the photograph's "shudder").[40] Thus, if in the abstract logic of the apparatus, film still represented the contracted rationalization of conceptual thought, it is clear that by the 1910s Bergson had become more willing to acknowledge film's capacity for an enlarged sense of vision because he recognized the experiential indeterminacies (the "unforeseeable nothing[s]" he wrote about in *Creative Evolution*) that accompany film's life beyond the apparatus, that is, as projected images on a screen.

Bergson explained at greater length the lesson he learned *at the cinema* (as he himself located it) in Georges-Michel's second publication of their interviews in 1926. Reflecting upon the initial aesthetic rupture posed by photography, when Théodore Géricault's imprecise impression of a gallop was updated by Degas' technically correct gallop, Bergson confessed that, "Cinematography taught me that Géricault's vision was the apparently exact vision. . . . And from that you can imagine what a philosopher could apply himself to deducing from the apparent exactitude and from the real exactitude."[41] The example of instantaneous photographs of a galloping horse was used in *Creative Evolution* to illustrate the distinction between the flattening equivalence of "any moment" and the "flash" of a "privileged moment," that is, between the superficial advances of modern science figured in the "complete recording" (*CE* 332) of movement by instantaneous photography and the deeper, albeit condensed and schematic "truth" registered by the human eye.

Two points are crucial to stress here: first, even though the second category seems to be closer to the experience of duration, both cases partake of the "same cinematographical mechanism" of extracting and isolating views from among an otherwise continuous flow; and second, that if we are to read the two categories back into the discussion of the runner in *Matter and Memory* (208–209), both belong to the inferior experience of a consciousness controlled by the exigencies of daily life as opposed to the superior experience associated with a withdrawal from everyday consciousness. Nonetheless, as we have seen above in the open-ended examples of the undeveloped photograph or the unrolled film (both marked positively by the unforeseeable immanence of their virtual unraveling in archival time), the durational can emerge out of these two bases of modern media. Far from fixing duration in opposition to the cinematographical method or habitual experience, after *Matter and Memory* Bergson actually expanded the attributes of duration to include a potentially positive sense of an enlarged cinematographical vision of the everyday. In doing so he also enabled a rapprochement in his own thinking between duration and habit, the qualitative and the quantitative, the artistic and the scientific, the temporal and the spatial.

SCULPTURE, DANCE, CELLS

If Bergson did not spell out this rapprochement, there were others who materialized it from within scientific and aesthetic fields. In his own 1922 retelling of the galloping horse experiment, Dr. Comandon explained that even though Géricault's galloping horses were scientifically incorrect, they produced a more artistic and therefore truthful impression because they "represent to the eye not what is, but what the eye believes it sees."[42] Then following Bergson (whom he quotes) and paraphrasing the period's most famous sculptor of movement, Auguste Rodin, Comandon also argued that the cinematograph, in contrast to the fixed immobility of photography, "gives us [the] possibility of marking passages" of movement albeit dependent upon the optical trick of "what the eye believes it sees."[43] Edging toward a more sympathetic appreciation of the illusion of movement in film than was customary for a scientist, Comandon hints at an awareness of the cinematograph's alternative aesthetic potential.

Not surprisingly, Bergson himself had referred to Rodin in the 1914 *Le Journal* interview. Cinema, unlike photography, was able to accomplish "the impression of truth," he claimed, much as the sculptor had succeeded in capturing motion "by basing the phases of a movement in different parts of the figure that he models." What Rodin's sculptures managed to represent, much like film, was a "generalized field of movement" (akin to Bergson's "impression of truth").[44] Bergson and Comandon's reference to the cinematic methods of Rodin is not mere conjecture, for the sculptor himself spoke of this connection in the film journal *Le Cinéma* that same year.[45] Echoing Bergson's argument, Rodin reasoned that as a "[s]cientific image in which time is rudely suspended," a photograph fails to capture true reality in which "time does not stop," whereas "by the movements and variety of its *tableaux* the *cinématographe* is a school which artists ought to frequent" because "Art is movement, Art is life." Accordingly, the sculptor suggested, film was the art of movement and life.

These three renowned commentators on film's unique relation to movement and time—Bergson, Comandon, and Rodin—were all key luminaries of Kahn's "Boulogne community." Kahn not only collected Rodin's works but also invited him in 1897 to the Wagner festival at Bayreuth and made him (like Bergson and Comandon) an honorary member of the Société Autour du Monde.[46] The sculptor also shared Kahn's passion for all things Japanese and apparently resumed his acquaintance with the dancer Ohta Hisa (better known as Hanako) at a performance in Kahn's gardens directed "under the aegis" of the American dancer Loïe Fuller in 1907.[47] As Tom Gunning has suggested, "one would be hard put to conceive of a better image of Bergson's contrasting, new, dynamic understanding of duration than the dances of Loïe Fuller," whose serpentine movements and billowing gowns, accompanied by a "shifting phantasmagoria of color," were a common and regularly copied attraction on the European avant-garde circuit as well as the screens of early cinema.[48] Choreographed against the backdrop of the constantly evolving Kahn gardens, Fuller's serpentine dances of change and becoming present a striking superimposition of Bergsonian expressions.

Whether or not Bergson also witnessed Fuller's presentations of the art of motion in the Kahn gardens in 1907, what we can say, at the least, is that his commentaries on the cinematograph were neither made in a metaphysical vacuum, nor limited by the "primitive" state of film, nor constrained by an outright denunciation of cinema. On the contrary, Bergson's idea about film developed in response to what he himself spoke of (in the interviews with Georges-Michel) as the contingencies of his *vie éxterieure*, characterized by the interest of the masses as well as the elites in what Georges-Michel called "these entertainments [such as the cinema] which hold such an important place in modern life."[49] The more elite dimension of Bergson's cinematic *vie éxterieure* comprised potential encounters with people like Rodin, Kahn, Comandon, and Fuller, as well as private screenings of state-of-the-art time-lapse films on Kahn's property—in other words, a unique network of pioneering scientists and avant-garde artists inspired in different ways by film's quasi-scientific experimental relation to the everyday, movement, and time.

Yet it was the most frequently screened films on Kahn's property, those by Comandon, that provided the purest visualizations of Bergsonism. Reflective of his research into cellular biology, a field that provided the practical background to the myriad impulses of life examined in *Creative Evolution*, Comandon's ultra-microcinematographic studies literally brought into visibility slices of life teeming with vitality (as *Je Sais Tout* put it). Comandon's cinematography "of the infinitely small" (as one magazine put it in 1909) succeeded in traversing the barriers between the visible and invisible, turning the human body inside out in a manner analogous to Bergson's rearrangement of the subject-object divide.[50] In other words, Comandon materialized what the philosopher himself had previously only imagined as the "'imponderable' within" (*CE* 8). His experimentation with the basic spatio-temporal technology of the cinematograph and his more specific films of plant growth and cell division (all metaphorically central to *Creative Evolution*, which was published just a year before Comandon began his film research at Pathé) externalize and project onto a screen the "'imponderable' within" life; they think the unthinkable, separate us from the skin (as Kracauer would have it) of our everyday attachments, and elevate the debased status of "cinematographical thought" to a new philosophical level.

Working within the intellectual space opened up by this Bergsonian cinematographical-philosophical nexus, it is perfectly understandable why Epstein gave the title "The *Photogénie* of the *Imponderable*" to a 1935 essay in which he argued that, "There is a philosophy of the cinematograph as there is a philosophy of every thing."[51] Comandon's films converged with early film theory's fascination with the camera's ability to reveal, with the help of microcinematography and time-lapse, the previously invisible dimensions of nature's daily life: from the infinitesimally small (splitting cells) and the unbearably slow (beans germinating, flowers blooming) to the normally unthinkable (plants swaying in tune to the passage of time). The unforeseen revelations of cells and plants offered by this new thinking machine or "metal brain" (as Epstein put it in a clear valorization of Bergson's cinema-thought metaphor) did not rest exclusively upon magnification of scale but, even more shockingly, on the revelation of movement as imminent to the ceaselessly changing evolution of life.[52] There was no longer such a thing as still life, even in a photograph. In Comandon's cinematic revelation of incessant movement within cells previously immobilized in static diagrams, we see not only the visualization of Bergsonian duration as incessant, indivisible becoming, but literal evidence of cinema's interpenetration with duration. Although other scientists like Alexis Carrel also materialized Bergsonian philosophy via biological films, Comandon's proximity to Bergson along the figural and literal paths that joined Kahn's biological laboratory and screening room presents the most direct example from the period of the philosopher's cinematographical impact and reach.[53] Given their expression of a scientific faith in explaining and expressing all of life in terms of mechanical processes, Comandon's films may appear to represent everything that Bergson wanted to rescue life from. But in the experiential space of the actual screening room, a very different response to these films emerged. Even more than accomplishing a limited biological representation of the vitalist "concept of life," they embodied a challenge to cinematographical referentiality by opening the doors to what Kracauer called, in *Theory of Film*'s treatment of the dreamlike mode of the film spectator, a "reality which transcends the anemic space-time world of science."[54]

"UNFORGETTABLE SPECTACLES"

A relevant exploration of this transcendence occurs in the film criticism of another of Georges-Michel's interviewees who also happened to be a visitor to the Kahn screening room, Colette.[55] In her unique accounts of popular scientific film reception we find the transcendence of science's usurpation of life. Paradoxically aided by the genre's quantitative study of microscopic or time-lapse dependent movement, spectators experienced these films according to a Bergsonian qualitative drift, or what Kracauer described as a "kind of reality which eludes measurement."[56]

Contrary to anti-cinema and anti-ocular diatribes of the time (which ranged from the cinema as a "school of crime" panic to the eyestrain scare), vision was only one of the senses being addressed by the cinema. A seminal illustration of cinema's multisensorial arousals appears in Colette's account of a young audience's reception of a popular scientific film of germinating beans screened at the Musée Galliera in 1920 and originally published in a collection the same year under the title *Everyday Adventures*.[57] Setting the stage for a typical defense of educational films, she begins her analysis by mentioning the hazardous effects of a detective and crime series upon a young viewer, noting that "the beating of his heart, [and] the shifting of his eyes, replace thinking" (60). Situating the film experience in a seemingly pre-symbolic realm of physical intensity, Colette's criticism of fiction film would seem to fit in neatly with the dominant opinion of cinema as a moral peril capable of inciting dangerous behavior among the more impressionable members of the audience (typically identified as children, but also women and the working class).

But a contradiction shortly arises in Colette's opposition to the hyper-stimulation of the Feuillade-like films of sensational violence and action that "leave the child gasping as though from a respiratory arrest" (60). Instead of highlighting the sedate rationalism of nonfiction film, her subsequent praise for educational films rests upon an appreciation of their even more emphatically physical and kinetic mode of spectator engagement. After having viewed a geographical tour of France and then a slow-motion study of seagulls in flight (most likely a Lucien Bull film), the young audience witnessed another of cinema's "incontestable miracles" (59):

> A little later, the speeding up process recorded the germination of a bean, the birth of its searching rootlets, the greedy yawning of its cotyledons from which, darting its snake head, the first shoot burst forth. . . . At the revelation of the plant's purposive, intelligent movement I saw children get up and imitate the prodigious ascent of a plant climbing in a spiral, circumventing an obstacle, groping at its stake. "It's looking, it's looking!" cried an impassioned small boy. He dreamed of it that night, and I too. These dreams are not forgotten and excite a hunger to learn more. We desire for our children and ourselves, we desire, after the poor workings of one's imagination, the extravagance of reality, Nature's unrestrained fantasy; we desire the fantastic fable of the germination of the pea, the marvelous story of the metamorphosis of a dragonfly and the explosion, the forceful expansion of the lily-bud, half-open at first with its long mandibles on a somber swarm of stamens, an avid potent process of flowering, at sight of which a little girl said quietly, rather scared: "Oh, a crocodile!" (61)

In short, the time-lapse films of peas germinating and flowers blooming incite the very feelings of "painful pleasure" and thoughts of "self-preservation" (61) that Colette claimed the children had experienced in front of the more objectionable and threatening action films. Far from instilling in the children a "hunger to learn more," it appears that the cinema's superiority in the field of education resided in its nonintellectual or prelogical sensory and affective appeal, in the camera's ability to transport audiences to unforgettable experiences rather than memorized object lessons. The children experience the film, that is, in a state of active fascination rather than passive comprehension. The cause of this fascination is not information, narrative, or argument, but the interbreeding of science and dreams as figured in the startling image of a "plant's purposive, intelligent movement" (fig. 7.4). Where Colette had earlier on in the review expressed a Bergsonian distrust of photographic memory in her concerns that "teaching by films makes the child a mere *storehouse* of images and encourages the atrophy of every sense except the visual" (60), she now reveals the cinema to be a collective space teeming with Bergsonian vitality in which the stimulation of nonvisual senses such as bodily imitation channel film viewing into unforeseeable, counter-archival experiences and memories.[58]

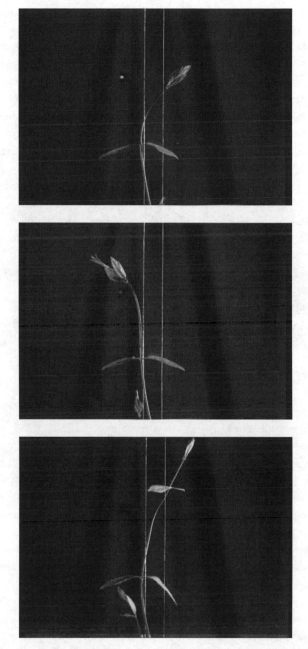

FIGURE 7.4   The upward-reaching dance of a growing honeysuckle from *La Croissance des végétaux* (Jean Comandon, 1929), a time-lapse plant study filmed on Kahn's property that resembles the one that so stimulated a young audience as discussed in Colette's review of popular scientific film. (Les Documents Cinématographiques, Paris)

If Bergson was learning from the cinema by just attending, Colette promoted a style of film criticism that learned as much about film from watching the audience as it did from watching the films. Colette includes herself in the enduring force field of this film experience, admitting that "I too ... dreamed of it that night." In other words, she was just as interested in what happens after the screening as what happens during it. In full recognition of how films stimulate memory and senses other than sight—within an at once subjective and collective, individual and social world of "unrestrained fantasy"—Colette suggested that the "dreams" (or "spectacles" as *féeries* is sometimes translated) such as those featured on the Galliera screen would "never [be] forgotten."[59] In making such a claim she was, of course, not only referring to the persistent memories of the children. Colette herself requested to revisit this unforgettable spectacle when she scheduled a very similar if not identical film during her visits to Kahn's Boulogne screening room. On September 9, 1921, the projection register for the Kahn Archive notes that "Mme. de Jouvenel" (who became known by her patronym "Colette" only in 1923) watched three films. Among them was the same film Bergson watched, *Les Fleurs* by Comandon. It is also highly probable that Comandon was the filmmaker behind the popular scientific films viewed by Colette and the children at the Musée Galliera in 1920 (the same venue where in 1924 Comandon and Germaine Dulac would participate in a conference on cinema).[60] Less than four months after her first visit to Kahn's villa, Colette returned and had her color photographic portrait taken with her beloved bulldog (fig. 7.5), and came back once again five months later to watch *Les Fleurs*.

What was it about the Comandon films that drove Colette to seek them out again, to the extent of tracking them down in a screening room that was not open to the public and that was not known by any of the professional cinephiles who so admired her film criticism?[61] Although Comandon's *Les Fleurs* did not belong to the Brunhes-directed Archives de la Planète, its repeat screening (the projection register shows that Kahn himself viewed it at least twenty times) provides a crucial clue to the reception context of other films from the Archive. *Les Fleurs* was typical of the popular scientific genre of nonfiction films from the teens. Indeed, in 1910 Gaumont launched its popular scientific catalogue on the back of colored flower studies.[62] Unlike the "pure" research films that Dr. Comandon produced in a laboratory on Kahn's property from 1926 to 1930, including those dealing with topics such as tuberculosis bacteria, sleeping sickness, and another titled *Germination des Fleurs*, the flower film that Colette watched contains no intertitles aside from the opening brief quantification of the film's distortion of natural speed and the common (not botanical) name of each flower. Even though Comandon himself was invested in promoting a clear distinction between the use of cinema for scientific popularization and the use of cinema as a "laboratory instrument," he would have been well aware that many popular scientific films were simply reworked

FIGURE 7.5
Mme. Henry de Jouvenal
(Colette), taken during her
visit to Kahn's Boulogne
screening room. (*Photo*:
Roger Dumas, January 2,
1922 [MAK: black-and-
white reproduction of color
autochrome])

research films (minus the intertitles) and that many so-called scientific films were not made by scientists at all.[63] Nonetheless, what Comandon would have referred to as research films characteristically contained more detailed visual or graphic information (in the form of, for example, lengthy intertitles or the inclusion of a clock indicating the passing of actual rather than viewing time).[64] As Comandon himself explained to a meeting of the *Congrès du cinéma éducatif de Paris* in 1931, such information was crucial in the context of an educational setting such as a university in order to promote standards of legibility and limit the threatening potential of the cinematic image as autonomous spectacle. The threat and curtailment of film's ability, as Comandon put it, to *"dérange* the lesson," is precisely what was on display in *Je Sais Tout's* image of the aroused audience followed by the visual quotation of horizontal film frames.[65]

At the same time, Comandon was also open to appreciating the deranging appeal of scientific film. In his writings, especially those intended for an avant-garde audience such as the essay Dulac commissioned from him titled "Les Possibilités artistiques de la cinématographie" (1927), Comandon openly promoted the unpredictable *dérangement* of perception experienced when people watched his films.[66] Although this potential for perceptual disturbance existed in even the most research-oriented of his films, *Les Fleurs* surrenders (in no small part due to the additional attraction of color) to the unrestrained aesthetic excesses of the scientific film. The film is clearly neither an advanced scientific film nor one intended for educational purposes. Technologically speaking, the hand-colored process featured in the film was anachronistic by the early twenties, and the film in many ways contains the charm of the recently outmoded.

In contrast to the unavoidable informational content of a "pure" research-oriented scientific film, *Les Fleurs* privileges other attractions that issue from a more direct and unmediated stimulation, within the experience of a succession of color, repeated forms, compressed time, and accelerated movement. As the color spectrum shifts from violet bellflowers and yellow honeysuckle to blue irises and pink peonies (fig. 7.6), accompanied by a pattern of movement that rhythmically folds back on itself as each flower repeats and begins anew the upward and outward generic cycle of the opening bud, the viewer is treated to an unrestrained display of the "artistic possibilities" that lay waiting to be unfurled (like Bergson's unwound film reel) within Comandon's scientific experiments. The spectacular dimensions of the otherwise instructional element of the film is also apparent in the deliberately staged botanical drama structuring each time-lapse sequence, which never depicts the wilting of the flower but always ends climactically, suspended in the unnatural eternity of a fully bloomed flower, captured in a state that keeps death, unnaturally, at bay.[67] Shameless promoter of the lush life of film, *Les Fleurs* recalls the exhibitionary impulses of the "cinema of attractions" and the avant-garde shocks and sensations into which that earlier film mode was morphing during this period, just as much as it references the more solemn research conventions of the scientific film.[68] In a review from 1921 that reads as though he had just visited Kahn's experimental landscape of cinematic attractions, Delluc described the hybrid scientific/avant-garde appeal of Comandon's flower studies when he wrote of "these giant lilies or colossal roses which bloom in front of us in thirty seconds like brutal fireworks and sometimes like the flying multicolored skirts of Loïe Fuller."[69]

Delluc's analogy came to life in the entertainments staged on Kahn's property, which, as already mentioned, provided the backdrop to a unique Bergsonian mise-en-scène of gardens, Fuller dances, and time-lapse flower films. Well before the surrealists and André Bazin after them granted the scientific films of Jean Painlevé a cult-like status for their oneiric dimensions, Delluc, Colette, and other film critics expressed being captivated by the animistic and dreamlike properties of Comandon's popular scientific films in which plants and cells spoke to viewers from a world in which the laws of habitual communication, perception, and causality had been suspended.[70] These critics' worshipping of the biological and botanical stars of Comandon's films may have preceded the establishment of the surrealist canon. Yet their responses indicate Comandon's films produced the exact kind of "profane illumination" that Benjamin associated with the later work of the surrealists.[71]

FIGURE 7.6   Images of a peony rose blooming from *Épanouissement de Fleurs* (Comandon, date unknown), one of the most regularly screened films on Kahn's property. The colored film resembled the type that inspired Louis Delluc to compare them to Loïe Fuller's
dances. (MAK: black-and-white reproduction of original hand-colored film)

Central to their revelatory promise was the pseudoscientific "solemnity" (as Epstein would put it) out of which the illuminations arose.

Unlike the overtly infantile, oneiric, and illogical world of Émile Cohl's animation films, for example, whose inversions of reality were ready-made for children and surrealists alike, Comandon's films were primarily rooted in fact, thus rendering their passage from everyday reality to the fantastic all the more abrupt.[72] This also resulted from the fact that Comandon's films of the natural world—the result of laboratory-controlled temporal and spatial manipulation—were more staged and choreographed, and thus *unnatural*, than any trick or animated film. Their jarring quality is magnified even further in light of their overall relationship to the Archive's other films shot *en plein air* of the human life-world. At the opposite end of the spectrum to these latter films, the Comandon films uncover a reality that is exaggerated, magnified, and untrue to normal perception. Falsity and artifice are at the core of their alternative evidentiary status as they pushed beyond film's original pact with familiar realism into a post-objective, post-positivist reconfiguration of the everyday. Breton described the cinema's unique ability to inhabit the critical passage between "waking and sleeping" by noting that, "A *superdisorientation* is to be expected here, not from the transference of a normal act from everyday life to a place consecrated to *another* life, which it profanes, but between the 'lesson' the film teaches and the manner in which the person receiving it disposes of it."[73] In other words, cinema's bridge between the everyday and the fantastic operated as a two-way street, welcoming spectators to another world separate from normal reality while at the same time shuttling them back—bearing profane lessons—in the direction of external reality and everyday life. Colette's Galliera audience may have been made up of minors, but in their counter-rationalist mode of responding to the fast- and slow-motion films we witness a major indication of audiences' encounters with the radical disposability (as Breton puts it) of film's surplus semiotic value.

Other viewers recognized the surplus of signification in these films. As early as 1914, in the same issue of *Je Sais Tout* discussed above, a doctor compared Comandon's microcinematographic views of white corpuscles to "serpents" that incited in him an "emotion whose intensity" was close to "terror."[74] Comandon's films, produced and distributed commercially by Pathé up until the early 1920s, also had their fans among the recently converted cinephiles.[75] In 1922, Vuillermoz—a friend of Colette's—compared them to "fairy tales," and five years later he continued his inquiry into the "gripping phantasmagoria" contained within these studies of cellular activity, describing one film as a "twelve-episode *ciné-roman* [film serial] of phagocytosis."[76] Further highlighting their relationship to the Feuillade-type detective serials and the Fabrean tradition of anthropomorphic descriptions of the natural world, the 1925 issue of the *Illustrated Encyclopedia* claimed that Comandon's biological studies enacted a drama as "fascinating as the most complicated detective films."[77] Colette's "humble audience" was, therefore, hardly idiosyncratic in its imaginative ability to see "marvelous stories" and "fantastic fables" within Comandon's non-narrative scientific recording of the life of a flower. The children responded to the factual world of the plant-growth film with the same physical intensity as they did to the threatening spectacle of a fiction crime series. Inversely, the more mature writer for the *Illustrated Encyclopedia* experienced within Comandon's biological films the complex twists and turns of the detective series.

Between a doctor describing white corpuscles as "serpents" and children mistaking germinating peas and flowering irises for crocodiles and other unnamed creatures captured in the quintessentially terrifying pose of "looking back," we see evidence of the continuing centrality of shocks and sensations in the experience of cinema. These experiences continued even in the so-called transitional era, when films in France were becoming dominated by the more contained and narrative-focused classical Hollywood cinema style. More specifically, they also survived in environments as seemingly inhospitable as Kahn's screening room, where, in addition to ministers, philosophers, and doctors, we should recall that school-age children were also sometimes present in the audience.[78] In Colette's portrait of film reception, moreover, we can detect the return of those qualities of aesthetic and melodramatic excess evoked by stereographs and color photographs—the irrational, the visceral, the bodily—that the organizers of the Kahn Archive had tried to repress.[79] Beyond the Kahn Archive, the continuing impact of cinema's supposedly earlier modes of attraction reflects the Zolaesque combination of the sensationalist and the scientific, the melodramatic and the mundane, that characterized the lively exchange between French documentary and avant-garde practices.

EYES (EARS AND BODIES) ON THE SCREEN!

From the perspective of the history of film theory, Colette's article illustrates the significance of children's forms of spectatorship and scientific films' rich formal inventiveness for the cinematic avant-garde, perhaps demonstrated most extensively in the writings and films of Dulac. Dulac's definitions of and contributions to "pure" cinema—defined by her as the "art of movement and of the visual rhythms of life and the imagination"—crystallized around written and filmed references to the impure domain of popular scientific cinema, including bean-germinating and flower-blooming films of the kind Colette viewed on Kahn's property.[80] Indeed, her conference talks from the 1920s were often illustrated with Comandon films.[81] She also solicited from him an article on aesthetics and scientific film for the first and only issue of the magazine *Schémas*, and several of her lectures made reference to the unique mode of multisensory synesthetic reception displayed by children as they watched Comandon's plant films. Illustrating the innate multisensorial dimensions of Comandon's scientific films, Dulac recalled in a mid-1920s lecture how on viewing one of his time-lapse flower studies a child screamed out "it's marvelous, one can hear with one's eyes."[82] In addition to the sense of hearing aroused by these silent films, Dulac also seems to have been struck, like Colette, with their capacity to tingle the sense of touch as evoked in the Galliera children's mimicry of plant movement. This is most visible in one of three pure cinema experiments Dulac made in 1929, *Thèmes et variations*, in which close-ups of a ballerina's spiraling arms are intercut with time-lapse images of beans germinating—the human movement of arms appearing to touch and mimic (across the cut) the visual rhythm of nature's dance in a striking reprisal of the Galliera children's imitation of plant growth.

If childlike modes of reception provided Dulac with avant-garde inspiration, children's defiance of films' intentional message also dovetailed with the surrealists' *anti*-avant-garde hopes for cinema to arouse the "revolutionary pleasures" (Robert Desnos) nestled between the waking and sleeping hours of everyday life.[83] In 1917 the surrealist-to-be Louis Aragon used the "emotive concentration" of children in his article "On Décor" (1917) to illustrate how cinematic techniques like close-ups and time-lapse can yield unintended eddies of association that flow beneath the seemingly impenetrable surface of ordinary objects, moving against the current of their everyday function: "Poets without being artists, children sometimes fix their attention on an object to the point where their concentration makes it grow larger, grow so much it completely occupies their visual field, assumes a mysterious aspect and loses all relation to its purpose."[84] At a general level, Aragon's analysis is representative of the counterintuitive model of spectatorship that the cinephiles fostered during this period, which regularly fixated upon incidental cinematic details at the expense of any narrative or editing grammar of cause and effect. More specifically, Aragon's comments tapped into the different type of spectatorial literacy among children noticed by Colette and Dulac. In contrast to the solemn literacy of those horizontal lines of film frame published in *Je Sais Tout*, here is a more playful visual competency literally *in touch* with the filmic image. As alluded to in Epstein's multisensorial "I look, I sniff at things, I touch," in this haptic extension of visual experience, sensuous correspondences between perceiver and perceived seem to be triggered when the spectator's sensory field is occupied—as a result of film's scientific capacities—to saturation point.[85]

These flashes of expanded perceptual enchantment that allow us to move beyond the intended content—to see what was never filmed—evoke what Benjamin meant by the "mimetic faculty": those experiences expressive of "an archive of nonsensuous similarities, of nonsensuous correspondences" between humans and the world.[86] Benjamin may not have included film reception among the experiences in which the "mimetic faculty" (otherwise in decay in the modern world) might be resurrected, but he did point to the survival of that faculty (beyond his key example of language) in the imitative habits of children's play. As a form that addresses the body as well as the brain, the cinema was primed for the arousal of both sensuous and nonsensuous similarities.[87]

It was Colette, not Benjamin, however, who explicitly explored both the common and uncommon idea of mimicry in cinema. In her 1914 review of the South Pole expedition film, *The Scott Expedition* (Herbert Ponting, 1912–13), she described the more typical, mechanistically mimetic nature of film viewing when spectators copied the lurching movement of the camera as they "leaned forward" in their chairs "toward the salty waters" while watching images shot from the side of a boat.[88] Instead of positioning the film as an exclusively visual attraction to be admired or contemplated from a distance, her review registered a medium that invited multisensorial participation and unforeseeable responses.

Colette moves more in the direction of Benjamin's notion of "nonsensuous" (meaning non-semiotic and noninstrumental) mimesis related to forms of corporeal reproduction in the Galliera review. The excessive reactions, such as the boy's "it's looking, it's looking," go further than merely expressing a giddily enthusiastic involvement with the screen illusion. The boy's misreading of a plant for an entity capable of looking back at him exaggerates to terrifying proportions pre-documentary films' mostly benign tendency to mimic the camera's uncensored act of looking. Beyond these playful instantiations of mimicry based on physiological identification, which would also include the children's bodily imitation of the germinating bean, the Galliera audience also experienced, if we read Colette carefully, a more nightmarish and self-implicating version of the return of the gaze.

The boy's cry of "it's looking, it's looking" and the girl's vision of a crocodile are particularly unsettling because their incitement can be traced back to a nonhuman source. As Roger Caillois would suggest in his analysis of mimicry in the insect world, "Mimétisme et psychasthénie légendaire" (1937), the practice of bodily imitation in insects reflected not the functional instinct for self-preservation (as in the conventional understanding of camouflage) but the "instinct of abandon" (what Colette calls in the Galliera review "painful pleasure" [61]), involving an apprehension of the permeable and thus always threatening boundaries between self and milieu, and by extension self and other.[89] Read through Caillois's analysis, what the Galliera audience underwent in their liberation from the classical distinctions between auditorium and screen was the experience of the human body as "no longer the origin of coordinates, but a point amongst others . . . dispossessed of its privilege, and . . . no longer knowing where to put itself" (108). In other words, exactly what Comandon meant by the deranged lesson. This experience of bodily abandonment and the transgression of borders between the self and other, human and nonhuman, also recalls Bergson's theory of laughter and the related condition of de-anthropocentrism—the dethroning of the formerly privileged human to a humble coordinate or mere "point amongst others"—that Colette and other film critics alluded to as they tried to come to terms with the radical newness of the film experience.

In addition to invoking flower-blooming films as the first real examples of "pure cinema," Dulac also argued that in these plant studies the "barrier between things and us" no longer existed.[90] Delluc, too, had been particularly keen to emphasize

how moving images might renegotiate the barriers between the nonhuman ("vegetation or everyday objects") and human world.[91] Anticipating Caillois's account
of the de-anthropocentrizing precondition for mimicry, Deluc's description of
film's ability to make palpable the "sensitivity of things" concomitantly suggested
the medium's insensitivity to humans: "This prior dimension of things [which the
camera magnifies] *diminishes* the character of the actor, the human element. He
himself is no more than a detail, a fragment of the material that is the world."[92]
Léger clarified even further the positive potential of film's reversal of the hierarchy
between humans and things by arguing that *La Roue*'s ability to eliminate "the
human object as the traditional focus of the cinema" (by having its "leading character" be a train) in effect liberated a new type of spectatorship based on emphatic
seeing rather than merely noticing.[93]

Delluc was aware that by intensifying the confrontational aspect of the camera's new perspective on humans and things, indeed by transforming humans *into*
things, film was complicit in, and thus especially suited to exposing, modernity's
reifying tendencies. Although his vision of cinema's essential relevance for the
modern relationship between "men and things" was largely inspired by the exotic
everyday objects and heroes of American films, he, like Colette, extended this interest to the camera's depiction of "vegetation" or the natural world. The diverse
tactile, haptic, and mimetic modes of reception incited by nature films, all of them
in different ways reflective of cinema's appeal to the body, evoke the nonutilitarian
experiences Bergson meant by a type of seeing "in order to see" rather than in order
to act. In the Galliera audience's unrestrained reception, Colette thus detected a
possible reanimation of the supposedly dead-end relationship that a conservative
reading of Bergsonism posed between technology and humans, the inanimate and
animate, stasis and mobility, mechanicity and life, merely noticing and emphatic
looking. Ultimately, for critics like Colette and Delluc, the potential payoff for cinema's reifying tendencies—"to make us all comprehend the things of this world as
well as force us to recognize ourselves"—was too great to risk losing.[94]

THE "SHUDDER" OF FILM'S HISTORICITY AND
THE ARCHIVE'S LAST AUDIENCE

The "primitive" or infantile modes of reception noted by Colette and other critics
anticipated the surrealists' hopes for cinema to tap into the unconscious depths of
daily life. Childlike responses were revelatory for the surrealists because they at-
tested to another universe with potentially revolutionary energies lying dormant
within the everyday attractions—narrative or scientific—of the cinema. According
to Benjamin, what distinguished the surrealists from earlier fans of the fantastic
was their understanding that the decisive moment of "revolutionary experience"
can be penetrated "only to the degree that we recognize it in the everyday world,

by virtue of a dialectical optic that perceives the everyday as impenetrable, the impenetrable as everyday."[95] No matter how resistant to meaning the everyday world appeared, it contained the key to unlocking for Benjamin a critique of capitalist modernity. In other words, it was not enough to revel in the abandonment of order inside the cinema; its potential for derangement (to invoke Comandon's words) had to be brought to bear upon the perceived-but-not-known, noticed-but-not-seen, visible-but-overlooked spaces of daily life outside. This is why films that employed spatial and temporal manipulation were so important to Benjamin because they transgressed the safe haven of the cinema house, attaching dynamite, as he put it, to the "familiar objects" and "commonplace milieus" of our ordinary life.[96]

The surrealists also understood, however, that the explosive illuminations they "found" in cinema could be manufactured through their own highly orchestrated modes of resistant reception. For example, by jumping from cinema to cinema with a "scorn for timetables," they engineered a deliberate disorientation of the chronometric linearity of the standard exhibition context and were able to create, in transit, in their heads, their own *ad hoc* compilation film.[97] Additionally, their preference for watching films in auditoriums that were in a state of "decay" or located in the unfashionable *faubourgs* allowed them to remap commercial cinema's profit logic by tapping into the critical power of the recently outdated and marginalized, as though they were picking over the ancient ruins of capitalism while also reinvesting in the fresh ruins of early cinema.[98] Within the realm of film practice, too, they aimed to precipitate this revolutionary potential by means of unnatural juxtapositions or "profane illuminations," some conjured through the literal appropriation of scientific film fragments, as in the opening footage of scorpions in Luis Buñuel's *L'Âge d'or* (1930).

These collage-like practices were, in part, the product of the open exchange between documentary and avant-garde film cultures that so many filmmakers profited from during the 1920s. If Kahn's screening room provided an informal outpost for such exchanges, the more formal venues were the "temples of cinema" like the Studio des Ursulines where Parisian cinephiles came to worship and preach in the twenties.[99] Their screening programs were highly creative, juxtaposing the recent works of Epstein or Léger with scientific films and "fragments" from early cinema.[100] These fragments included not only the newly canonized Lumière and Méliès films, or the recently rediscovered serials (like *Les Vampires*, *Les Mystères de New York*, and *Zigomar*, whose rerun is captured in a Kahn autochrome [fig. 6.1]). More surprisingly, these avant-garde programs also featured run-of-the-mill prewar newsreels.

If the appeal of scientific films and detective serials to a group of experimental filmmakers should by now be clear, why the interest in these obsolete scraps of film actualities? Kracauer's essay on "Photography" (1927) provides an important explanation. The recently outdated prewar actualities contain the simultaneously "comical and terrifying" power that Kracauer attributed to photographs from the "recent past:" that is, an ability to mock the viewer with the revelation that "this detritus was once the present."[101] Not confining his analysis to still photography, Kracauer claimed the alienating "shudder" evoked by the recently outdated also appeared in a "drastic fashion" in the "pre–World War I films screened in the avant-garde 'Studio des Ursulines' in Paris" in the twenties. Put simply, the "shudder" produced by the prewar actualities, much like that Aragon and Breton received from *Les Vampires*, was historically charged. The seemingly innocuous, ghost-like newsreels "conjure[d] up anew a disintegrated unity" that allowed the audi-ence to imagine a "different organization" of the present social order by means of a de-habituated perspective upon "[t]hose things [that] once clung to us like our skin."[102] Once films became unstitched from the naturalized fabric of the present, they enabled (Kracauer suggests) viewers to think the unthought, in this instance, not of science or biology but of history, namely the non-inevitability of the present economic state of things.

One actual member of the Studio des Ursulines audience, the filmmaker René Clair, also remembered the mid-1920s screenings as a Bergsonian mixture of deadly seriousness in which the actualities and dramas from the recent prewar past "made most of the audience double up with laughter and led others to some useful reflections."[103] Just as Kracauer gives us a glimpse of the possible content of these "useful reflections" in his claim that the old newsreels had the potential to shock the audience into an awareness of the fragility of the present economic order of things, Clair concludes his recollection of the Ursulines screenings by highlight-ing the economic underpinnings of cinema's temporal paradox—a medium born to "defy time" yet simultaneously condemned to "live under the sign of [temporal] relativity" due to the inevitable turnover required by its capitalist industrial struc-ture.[104] This is why (according to Kracauer) outdated films, themselves capitalist castoffs, could make audiences confront the looseness with which "our property [Kahn's included] still clings to us today."[105] Whether Kahn or any of his guests ever felt such a shudder as they watched slightly outdated actuality-type films from the Archive is impossible to know. What is more certain, however, is that it was the instability of that economic system, in the form of the 1929 stock market crash, that caused Kahn to lose his fortune, and that brought real time to bear upon the atemporal utopia of his Archive.

Perhaps it was in search of orchestrating such an encounter with outdated non-fiction film that the surreal-inclined filmmaker *and* archivist Georges Franju came to view Kahn's films fifteen years after the official end of the Archive.[106] The third to last entry of the Kahn projection register, for May 28, 1946, notes that a Mr. Fran-ju watched three films by Camille Sauvageot filmed in the 1920s for the Archive: *Queue at the working-class soup kitchen, Paris's Villette cattle market,* and *Queue in front of a working-class soup kitchen.*[107] The Villette market footage focuses on the massive iron and glass abattoir in the northeast of Paris, and in particular on the cattle auctions held there, while the footage of the working-class soup kitchen focuses on long lines of hungry unemployed waiting to be given a meal. Although by 1946 the Kahn films were no longer being regularly screened, Franju probably came to know of them through Henri Langlois, with whom he had cofounded the Cinémathèque Française in 1936 and who would be enlisted to help preserve the Kahn collection during the 1950s.[108] Franju's visit to Boulogne thus to some extent retraced the footsteps of that earlier film archive advocate, Victor Perrot.

More interesting, however, than how Franju got access to the "sanctuary" is the manner in which he may have rechanneled the "shudder" of Kahn's films. In keeping with the collection's identity as an Archive and his own professional profile as a film archivist and a budding filmmaker with a poetic-political interest in the documentation of Paris, Franju may have used the Kahn collection to do some preliminary visual research for his first postwar film, *Le Sang des bêtes* (1948), a quasi-surrealist documentary on the slaughterhouses of Paris's northern and southern fringes, particularly the one at Villette. The film Franju made two years after his visit to Boulogne, however, bears little obvious resemblance to the comparatively idyllic documentation of the cattle markets in the Kahn films. An extreme display of the repressed violence in naturalism's surgical attention to the social world, *Le Sang des bêtes* removes Lautréamont's proto-surrealist vision of an umbrella and sewing machine on a dissecting table out of the nineteenth-century salon and grafts its critical perspective onto the literal and allegorical slaughterhouses haunting France's immediate postwar post-collaboration years.[109] Aided in no small part by the commentary written by Jean Painlevé (a great admirer and professional peer of Dr. Comandon), Franju juxtaposes beauty's brutality and violence's banality in his dissection of the various methods by which the abattoir workers calmly slaughter livestock, just one metro stop away from bourgeois dining tables—the everyday barely protected from the butchery of its myths.

If the "profane illumination" of *Le Sang des bêtes* did indeed begin in the ruins of Kahn's "sanctuary," Franju thereby actualized one aspect of the Archive's counter-archival potential that I have been arguing was a central if mostly dormant effect of its logic. He was neither the first *nor the last* to respond to the dormant "shudder" in Kahn's films.[110] Where Colette's children acted out film's arousal of the mimetic faculty, Franju channeled the "archive of nonsensuous correspondences" contained in Kahn's films into *Le Sang des bêtes*'s flashes of (human, post-Holocaust) flesh that profanely illuminate its otherwise mundane documentation of (animal) carcasses. Although radically different, the Kahn Archive and Franju's film both harbor a critical relation to the overriding archival, historical, and documentary dimensions of their respective projects. Kahn's Archive, with its combination of indeterminacy and order, and modes of reception balanced somewhere between play and pain, the body and the eye, pleasure and knowledge, avant-garde provocation

FIGURE 7.7   A film of one of the many Parisian flea markets. (Lucien Le Saint, October 3, 1920 [MAK: frame enlargement 102575])

and scientific research, sensuous and nonsensuous correspondences, overturned the supposedly straightforward evidentiary status of film as document. Similarly, Franju undermined the abstracted rationality of his instructional documentation of slaughtering practices by sandwiching it between mock romantic and picturesque opening and closing sequences whose surreal disassociations ultimately work to reveal slaughter at the center of, although geographically and morally invisible to, mid-twentieth-century Parisian society. It is precisely in recognition of the film's perverse "togetherness of pleasure and slaughter" (a direct reprisal of the "comical and terrifying" dualism from his 1927 photography essay) that Kracauer argued in *Theory of Film* that *Le Sang des bêtes* "casts deep shadows on the ordinary process of living," revealing through its sudden glimpses into death the "dread of the abyss that is everyday life."[111]

The Kahn Archive and Franju's film were both invested in the desire to document the present from sites and senses usually deemed marginal to capitalist modernity. In addition to the liminal space of the slaughterhouse, *Le Sang des bêtes* captured other peripheral Parisian areas previously documented by Kahn's cameramen, most notably the flea markets (fig. 7.7), those pilgrimage sites for the surrealists where outmoded objects found a second life in commodity culture's counter-archive. To be sure, Breton and other surrealists were culturally slumming it when they went to the flea markets in search of "*objects* that can be found nowhere else" whereas Kahn's cameramen went there to record *social practices* (noncapitalist consumption) essential to working-class daily life in the 1920s.[112] Despite their different motivations, as counter-archivists of modernity both gravitated toward the city's unofficial exchange economies.

The flea markets depicted in the Kahn films of the 1920s also had a material connection to cinema's counter-archival circuits. They were an important source for the pioneering film collectors who purchased (two *sous* for every ten meters) and saved the discarded heritage of French film culture.[113] Feeding the first official film archives, the flea markets thus provided a counter-archival evasion from the capitalist exchange network that dominated the film industry and inevitably shut down Kahn's Archive. Franju's meeting with the Kahn footage reminds us that the spirit of this escape, of rescuing used and outdated fragments of film, was revived as one of the major motivations of postwar French experimental documentary film practice based on the recontextualization, either literal or metaphorical, of old film footage. Exiles from of an alienated history, these fragments of footage thus became the source for new types of cinematic historicity.

CONCLUSION

No matter how much Kahn believed his Archive could mobilize a faith in the power of science and technology to control the irrational forces of chance and arbitrariness, his films were still susceptible to arousing unpredictable "flash"-like revelations. In fact, it was their primary focus on aspects of reality understood to negate any element of surprise—the conventional, the expected, the habitual, all that appears insignificant, blank, and noncommunicative, dead to history and blind to change—that made them particularly fertile sources for the cinema's penetration of the everyday. As for the Kahn footage that may have literally or retrospectively penetrated habitual reality's outer skin (from Comandon's scientific films to Sauvageot's cattle market films), the "profane illuminations" Bergson, Colette, or Franju found in them did not necessarily contradict their pure scientific or documentary context. After all, the immediate scientific rationale for the Archive—human geography—emerged from a radically "impure" post-positivist discipline, while the immediate setting for those screenings, Kahn's property, hosted a continuum of avant-garde-related spectacles and celebrities.

Rather than being aberrations, the three screenings explored in this chapter, by Bergson, Colette, and Franju, in conjunction with the *Je Sais Tout* illustrations, speak to a larger constellation of counter-archival experiences of film. Indebted to while also challenging the empiricist tendencies of its photographic base, film's counter-archival capacities reflect the medium's openness to the aesthetic derangements within scientific representations of movement and time, the bodily emphasis that follows from of an enlarged extrasensory vision, and the chance involuntary revelations of historical flashes. Cinema offered the possibility of entering a universe liberated from natural and historical causalities where germinating beans took on the appearance of crocodiles, a telephone (viewed in close-up by Delluc) could transform into a towering Parthenon, and a rerun of a prewar newsreel could trigger an awareness of the fragility of the postwar social order.[114]

Together, Bergson, Colette, and Franju's brief encounters with the Kahn screening room also reveal an alternative culture of visual pleasure (and horror) that operated across the fiction and nonfiction film spectrum and alongside the more codified attractions of stars and genres. Their rendezvous with Kahn's films also introduce the critical element of aesthetic pleasure, play, and chance into the supposedly regulated space of the archive. In addition, they signal the presence of a radically naturalist cinematic gaze that tied nonfiction to avant-garde films in an exchange that forms one of the forgotten unions of French modernism. As the chief mouthpiece for this exchange, early French film theory evolved within this counter-positivist experience of film inherited from Bergsonism's unfinished business with cinema. Unwilling to bemoan the medium's mechanistic "method" (in the Bergsonian sense), early film theory still sought to align the film experience with "a reality which eludes measurement" (Kracauer) but regularly collides with impressions, albeit fleeting, of truth. Ironically, it is at this limit to quantifiable representation that we find the true affinity between Kahn's empiricist project and Zola's earlier but equally ambitious, hyper-documentary literary archive, the Rougon-Macquart series of twenty novels that he subtitled "the social and natural history of a family under the Second Empire." If this comparison rings true, however, then a central annex for the Archive's study of the national family of the Third Republic remains to be examined in the colonial laboratory known as Greater France.

THE AERIAL VIEW

HUMAN GEOGRAPHY, COSMOPOLITANISM, AND COLONIALISM

> Let us go up some hundreds of yards above the earth in a balloon or an aeroplane, somewhat after the fashion envisaged by the Swiss geologist [Eduard] Suess at the beginning of his great book *The Face of the Earth*. Then, ridding our mind of all knowledge of man, let us try to see and note the essential facts of human geography with the same eyes and in the same way as we discover and disentangle the morphological, topographical, and hydrographic features of the earth's surface. From this imaginary vantage-point what shall we see? Or, better still, what are the human facts that a photographic plate would register just as well as the retina of the eye?
>
> JEAN BRUNHES (1910)[1]

> Our senses are our prison, their limits the bars of our human cage. One day it may be otherwise: the whole world may be as clearly visible to my eyes as the room in which I am writing. Extension of vision and with it of sympathy, that is what one wants; but to discover the way to it is as difficult as finding the path which leads to truth itself.
>
> B. IFOR EVANS (1928)[2]

IF THE MICROSCOPIC VIEW provided a privileged vantage point for rediscovering the everyday in early French film theory, then its opposite, the aerial view, held a similarly privileged role in the rediscovery of the earth for human geography. In the above passage from Jean Brunhes' major work, *Géographie humaine* (1910), he summons his readers like a latter-day Jules Verne to accompany him on an "imaginary" ride above the earth, where the "facts" of human geography will *for the first time* appear fully to the human eye, or "better still," to the "photographic plate." Much like the visual revolution announced by microcinematography and timelapse explored in the previous chapters, a break in habitual perception—expressed in B. Ifor Evans's (one of Kahn's grant recipients) desire to transgress the sensorial limits of the "human cage"—also accompanied the cultural impact of the actual rather than imagined aerial view. Indeed, the new abstract potentialities of aerial photography have long been associated with the birth of utopian and dystopian modernist perspectives, from the reduction to pure form within cubist painting, the expansion of the aesthetics of violence with the Italian futurists, and the mathematical abstractions of the Russian Suprematists, to Siegfried Kracauer's critique of the reifying image of mass gymnastics "from above," and László Moholy-Nagy's photographic preference for the liberatory aspects of the overhead view.[3] As for the aerial imaginary within the realm of motion pictures, the assemblage of cockpit, camera, and machine gun barrel has become an equally emblematic figure in the intertwined history of technologies of vision and destruction, cinema and war.[4]

I return in this chapter to my book's opening assertion that for all its global pretensions the Kahn project harbored anxieties about the imperialist dimensions of modern travel. Focusing upon the convergence between modern travel and the survey-and-control logic of colonialist expansion and appropriation that underwrites Brunhes' and Evans' God's-eye visions, I situate the aerial view—with its ability to deliver Michel Foucault's "unimpeded empire of the gaze"—as a hyperbolic reference point in this intersection of technologies of vision and apparatuses of power.[5] The aerial view lent itself to both disciplinary and humanist applications, from its development in military intelligence during the First World War and its mobilization as the privileged visual tool of Brunhes' human geography to its utopian appeal in early film theory and inspirational role in the emergence of the Annales perspective on history. Most importantly, these shards of aerial views and discourses I will be examining offer the fitting material through which to produce our final kaleidoscopic image of the Kahn Archive: its relation to interwar imperial culture.

The aerial perspective must be read not in isolation but in conjunction with its spatial twin, the microscopic view. To highlight the connection between the aerial and microscopic views, I will figuratively edit certain Kahn films so that we transition from the miniaturizing to the magnifying perspective, using travel narratives written by the grant recipients and published in Kahn's *Bulletin de la Société Autour du Monde* to help make the cut from the distanced to the more immersed view of culture. This approach brings into play the benefits of the macro- and micro-view for historical methodology as implied in the work of Siegfried Kracauer and Michel Foucault, who both suggested that the history of the everyday is best located when viewed across these extreme perspectives.[6] Shuttling between both literal and metaphorical views from above, below, and indeed within the national body, this chapter's journey highlights the sexual, racial, and gender dynamics of the Kahn Archive's connection to French colonialism.

Although aerial vision would appear to have little in common with the enclosed, boxed-in world of the archive, the connections between the world-encompassing view and the archive's "dream of a totalizing taxonomy" of the world (as Michel de Certeau put it) also deserve exploration.[7] This connection appears clearly in an im-

portant milestone in the history of French archiving, which occurred in 1913 when
Charles-Victor Langlois, then director of the Archives Nationales, scaled back on
his goal of a single archive containing every document of concern to French history. Instead, he substituted this dream of document centralization with the idea
of a single warehouse of catalogues that would create an ideal "vantage point" from
which all archive materials from around the world could be surveyed.[8] If Kahn's
property provided a photo-cinematographic version of Langlois' vantage point, the
God's-eye views of his aerial cinematography delivered the most extreme visualization of the archival dream of a world captured in a single glance.

As a type of view reminiscent (particularly when used for reconnaissance missions) of Foucault's panoptic model of the omniscient gaze (located in "eyes that
must see without being seen"), the aerial view also highlights the Archive's relation
to that other Foucauldian emblem of power: the model of the archive as an epistemological technology of discursive regulation and control.[9] In a highly influential
appropriation of Foucault for the understanding of the European imperial imaginary, Edward Said argued that the discourse of Orientalism did not just originate
in the lust for "land or profit or rule" that dominated the expansionist phase of European imperialism from 1815 to 1914.[10] More importantly, the "textual attitude"
(41) of Orientalism was prepared in imperialism's complementary location—the
"library or *archive* of information" (42) that extended to literary, scientific, and
aesthetic texts, which over the centuries elaborated a "unifying set of values proven
in various ways to be effective" (84) in explaining the Oriental to the Westerner.[11]
Said's definition of Orientalism "as a set of constraints upon and limitations of
thought" (42) regarding the West's knowledge of the Orient clearly borrows from
Foucault's invocation of the archive as an apparatus for the regulation of knowledge. Regardless of the differences between Foucault and Said, what is at issue for
both is the notion of an archive without walls that exists before statements and
utterances are allowed to emerge.[12] As Foucault explains, before it is the house of
history, "[T]he archive is first the law of what can be said."[13]

Where Said, or perhaps more correctly the appropriation of Said's argument,
moved beyond Foucault's original invocation of the archive was by grafting its earlier discursive instantiations from *The Archaeology of Knowledge* onto Foucault's
later, more blatant analyses of the power-knowledge nexus, in particular that of
Discipline and Punish (1975). The archive without walls posed by Foucault's *The
Archaeology of Knowledge* thus underwent a renovation in the phenomenal wake
of Said's *Orientalism* (especially in the field of visual and, more specifically, photographic studies). What emerged (much to the surprise of Foucault and Said) was
the more intractable and generalizable hybrid of what we might call the *panoptic
archive*, an archive walled in by the oppressive architecture of the all-seeing, all-
knowing, and invisible eye of the panopticon.[14] Lost in this theoretical mutation,

in which the more general monolith of visual panopticism came to swallow the specific histories of diverse archives, was Foucault's warning to always question the self-evidence of the visible.

As a result of this conflation of the archival with the visual, and space with power (in the critical cross-pollination of *The Archaeology of Knowledge* and *Discipline and Punish*), film ironically became subject to that exact type of evidentiary transparency that Foucault the anti-empiricist had set out to attack (summed up in *The Archaeology*'s introductory "questioning of the *document*") in his elaboration of the archive as discourse.[15] Paradoxically, a theory intended to challenge the obviousness of the (visual) document ended up supporting it. Once the self-evidence of the panoptic archive model is accepted, it is but a small step to condemning vision altogether as "being complicitous in the complementary apparatuses of surveillance and spectacle [like photography and cinema] so central to the maintenance of disciplinary or repressive power in the modern [colonial] world."[16] According to this logic, it becomes axiomatic that Kahn's triangulation—"to see, to predict, to know"—sews vision, control, and knowledge to a rationale tailor-made to the Foucauldian "empire of the gaze."[17]

As important as the Saidian appropriation of the Foucauldian archive was, particularly for reconciling the Eurocentrism of Foucault's universal archive to the shadow of its colonial "others," this chapter questions the now naturalized hold of the hybridized panoptic-archive upon the study of visual documents connected to colonial archives.[18] My rethinking of the Foucauldian model of the archive provides the last example of this book's counter-archival investigations. My critique addresses the following concerns: what happens when the two Foucauldian archival paradigms—the archive without walls and the disciplining, state-bound, panoptic-archive—are placed in contact with an archive bound by the walls of a garden and characterized by an undisciplined, privately funded, and nonsystematic production of knowledge? What happens when the Foucauldian model of the archive, elaborated upon the monument of the written document, confronts a radically different record, the filmed document, or the implicit cosmopolitanism of the quest for an empathetic (as B. Ifor Evans put it) rather than disciplinary extension of vision? What happens when a model based on the power of invisible surveillance meets films dominated by the display rather than masking of the European gaze? What happens when Foucault's theory of seeing without being seen encounters the Bergsonian theory of seeing in order to see? And how, ultimately, does the Foucauldian model deal with a discourse as hegemonic yet inconsistent as French colonial ideology?

In addition to offering a new reading of Foucault's archive, this chapter engages recent debates in French colonial history and cinema history concerning the ambivalent relationship between colonial ideology and a range of previously deemed neutral cultural domains, from disciplines of knowledge, such as anthropology, geography, and history, to forms of popular culture, such as postcards, colonial ex-positions, and motion pictures.[19] Films are a particularly easy target of denuncia-tion in a project aimed at proving the complicity of the representational realm in the relationship between colonialism and culture. This is especially true for films from the early cinema period in which voyeurism is still unmasked and there for all too see (unlike in viewing relations of the classical Hollywood cinema in which voyeurism becomes naturalized, for example, through the interdiction against ac-tors looking at the camera). As undeniable as the evidence is of early cinema's ob-jectionable heritage, it is not enough to reveal the racist imagery in early films if we want to understand how discourses of racism evolve and mutate over time once offensive images, individuals, and indeed colonialism itself are, at least on the sur-face, a thing of the past.

Recent work in early cinema and photographic studies that has challenged the assumption of a perfect alignment between colonial ideology and visual cul-tures has stressed the need to move beyond a utilitarian and expressive notion of the relationship, without letting go of the undeniable ideological involvement of film and photography as legitimating components of the European colonial visual regime. At the core of these works is a debate about the limits of film as colonial evidence. Refusing any easy resolutions, these works prefer to recognize the opacity of the colonial-film interaction rather than bask self-righteously in the assumed transparency of a predetermined connection between colonial discourse and filmic text.[20] More often, however, the bond between colonialism and culture (film, human geography, philosophy) has been cast in one of the following ways: as a "self-enclosed and self-sustaining archive" of colonial discourse; an interlock-ing network of indirect social regulation; an interpenetration of unwitting par-ticipants; an imperfect alliance; or a site of ideological contradiction and slippage that recognizes the inconsistencies of colonial discourse.[21] Whichever method is used to finesse the relationship, it is undeniable that the colonial enterprise of France's Third Republic, which was by no means popularly accepted in the late nineteenth century, increasingly depended upon the domain of culture for its sup-port, legitimation, and reproduction. The Kahn Archive is an especially challeng-ing case study for any possible reconfiguration of the colonialism-culture equation, not only because of the explicit role of geography, cinema, the archive, and cultural anthropology in the project but also because of the now almost unquestionable postcolonial association of archives with state regulation and control.

GEOGRAPHY, COLONIALISM, COSMOPOLITANISM

Even though the Kahn Archive was not directly aligned with French colonial pro-paganda, its financial origins in South African mines and Japan's colonial incur-sions in China and Taiwan embedded it in the global colonial culture of its time.

The colonial substratum of the Archive appears across a range of evidence, including the importance of colonial diseases within Dr. Jean Comandon's research agenda; the anomalous presence in the Archive of one fiction film (*Amours exotiques*, 1925), directed by a pioneer in the field of colonial cinema, Léon Poirier (who also directed the Citroën-sponsored *La Croisière noire* [1925]); and the broader careers of certain cameramen who occasionally worked for or contributed to the Archive's stock (from Jules Gervais-Courtellemont, a popular orientalist and photographer, and Léon Busy, a colonial officer in Indochina who had offered his services to Kahn, to Paul Castelnau, a geographer who also participated in the Citroën expeditions). Finally, there is also the uncensored colonial and racist attitudes of some Kahn cameramen toward their subjects, and indeed, of Bergson himself, who conflated "African savages" with children.[22]

An even more instrumental connection to the colonial domain appears in the execution of several "missions" attached indirectly to the Archives de la Planète that were aided by national-colonial enterprises such as the Michel Clemenceau mission to Afghanistan, the Charles Michel-Cote mission to Ethiopia in 1920 (both organized by the French government to survey the potential for building railways), and Father Francis Aupiais' ethnographic and religious mission to Dahomey in 1929–30 (cofunded by the Société des Missions Africaines de Lyon). This loose evidence of colonial affiliations also includes footage in the Archive of the anticolonial writer Albert Londres, as well as the projection of Camille Sauvageot's films of the first Jewish University in Palestine to a pro-Zionist women's congregation—a screening that marks a rare exception to Kahn's no-loan policy on his films.[23]

But the most substantive colonial affinity in the Kahn Archive is its grounding in the discipline of geography. Kahn's films did not emerge from a disciplinary vacuum and must be accounted for within a history of geography that goes back even further than the Vidalian rupture of the 1890s, just as the men who shot them need to be positioned alongside those other "soldiers of modernity"—the intrepid explorers, zealous missionaries, and land-hungry colonists—who contributed to the murky scientific origins of modern geography.[24]

Historians and cultural theorists of geography, from David Livingstone and David Harvey to Edward Said, have shown that far from being a disinterested science, the production of geographical knowledge in France during the late eighteenth and early nineteenth centuries was inextricably bound up with Napoleonic militarism and government.[25] The yearly output of "maps by the thousand, memoirs by the hundred, and atlases by the dozen" that were produced by Napoleon's corps of *ingénieurs-géographes* as a "sort of living archive for the expedition" were instrumental in solidifying the pact between cartography and conquest and in satisfying the strategic and bureaucratic services of the state and the nationalist demands of an imperial civilization.[26] For Said, the spatial abstractions of power, figured in the cartographical parceling out of the world into East and West, the

Orient and the Occident, as well as the more banal and daily distinctions between spaces that are "ours" and spaces that are "theirs," together formed the powerful "imaginative geography" upon which the intertwined destinies of orientalist ideology and European territorial expansion flourished.[27]

Geography was one of the master discourses that allowed European culture, as Said argued, "to manage—and even produce—the Orient politically, sociologically, militarily, ideologically, scientifically, and imaginatively during the post-Enlightenment period."[28] By the end of the nineteenth century, France was a leader in geographical discourse with more geographical societies than any other country.[29] In contrast to the first Paris Geographical Society of 1821, which had merely promoted overseas exploration, the geographical societies of the late nineteenth century tied exploration to conquest, resulting in strong connections with the colonial lobby, the emergence of the distinct fields of commercial and colonial geography, and the rise of the "militant geographer."[30]

Human geography developed at the tail end of the territorial "carve up" that characterized the expansionist phase of late-nineteenth-century French imperialism. Like most of his peers, Brunhes' teacher Vidal de la Blache was a supporter of colonial enterprise, but the mode of geography he founded did not serve colonial needs as directly as the more utilitarian schools of geography.[31] Nonetheless, Vidalian human geography provided fertile ground for the crucial alignment between geography and national identity. Vidal's valorization of the French rural landscape dovetailed with the rise of preservationist discourses that encompassed landscape painting (for example, of the Barbizon school) as well as more ideologically conservative turns to "the soil" associated with the French regionalist movement.[32] Furthermore, although not in direct service to colonial policy, human geography did embrace another dimension of geography's late-nineteenth-century imperial identity, its association with the "global thinking" paradigm of cosmopolitanism.[33] An 1884 article from the Paris Geographical Society's journal pointed to this association by arguing that geography's obligation "to know the earth and to conquer it" had rightfully developed into the "philosophy of the planet."[34]

Cosmopolitanism might seem at odds with geography, given that the former (at least in the Kantian version that underpinned the Boulogne community's postwar devotion to the League of Nations) is wedded to the supranational, the general, and the universal, while the latter is embedded in the regional, the local, and the particular. Cosmopolitanism's subject is the world citizen; human geography's is a local "type." Yet, as David Harvey has argued, "geographical and anthropological knowledge play a crucial, though often hidden, role in defining what any cosmopolitan project might be about in theory as well as in practice."[35] In other words, cosmopolitanism depends on the regional stability of the local, which in most cases translates into the geopolitical level of the nation, from which to launch its supposedly disinterested and altruistic claims to the international. In plain terms, behind every "citizen of the world" lurks a market-hungry capitalist or self-confident nationalist.

The planetary ambitions of Kahn's Archive were underwritten by French national ideals, which is why the Archives de la Planète might more correctly be called the Archives of the *French Colonial* Planet. Likewise, the discourse of cosmopolitan internationalism that so animated the Boulogne community barely veiled the underlying competitive relations between France, Germany, and Britain that characterized the early twentieth century. Herman Lebovics has argued that the apparent inconsistency between universalism and nationalism (which also implicates that between cosmopolitanism and geography, and liberal republicanism and colonialism) has always been a structuring principle of French national identity. If modern French national ideology attached itself to a "universalist pluralism that has set it off from other nations and yet has marked it as the special seat for the hopes of humankind," then the Kahn community is a classic twentieth-century locus for maintaining the perception of France (to appropriate Lebovics' words) as the "second home of humankind."[36]

Indeed, it would be difficult to find a location more worthy of the title, the "heartland of cosmopolitanism," than Kahn's Boulogne property, where, in addition to welcoming a Who's Who of the world's intellectual and artistic elite, Kahn's crew of gardeners cultivated a landscape of nationally thematized gardens.[37] In the exemplary heterotopian instance in which the soil of the sixteenth arrondissement nurtured a re-territorialized Japanese, English, and Vosgian *paysage*, we have the botanical embodiment of a particularly French cosmopolitan ideal in which local and "imaginative geography" are literally inseparable. The gardens attempted to resolve botanically the overriding contradiction between the universalism of cosmopolitanism and the regionalism of geography that distinguished the Archive's ideology. Ultimately, however, far from successfully resolving that contradiction, the garden's transnationalism provided a further expression of Kahn's own troubled relation (given French distrust of the cosmopolitanism of the "wandering Jew") to the nation.[38]

"WHAT IS THE NATION?"

The self-characterization of geography as a form of global thinking also extended beyond its association with cosmopolitanism to Brunhes' promotion of the discipline as the master science of all human knowledge. Nonetheless, for all its claims to being an overarching universal discipline, human geography's first monographs were defined by their regional focus, and the films that most clearly display Brunhes' influence are of areas, like Brittany, at the core of the regionalist revival in France. Not surprisingly, members of the political right were interested in the renaissance of regionalist-based ethnographic and folkloric studies that rooted a conservative construction of "True France" in the essentialist terrain of rural life.[39] The anti-urban and anti-industrial bias of the Vidalian geographical *Tableau of France* thus intersected with the warning from the right of "disappearing peasants and threatened regionalism."[40] Far from inhabiting the margins of French right-wing discourse, regionalism by the late 1920s was the "quasi-official doctrine" of postwar reconstruction, and the reactionary invocation of "the return to the soil, anti-urbanism, [and] the questioning of technology" had even caught up with the modernist avant-garde.[41] The interwar period in France thus witnessed a regionalism in art, painting, and architecture that celebrated the vernacular landscape and the French peasantry, all the while denigrating as modern and foreign "all things urban and industrial."[42]

Brunhes himself privileged the vernacular house as a primary classification in his comparative approach to human geography, a privileging that Patricia Morton has interpreted as evidence of the way in which architecture was used by French social scientists during the interwar period to evaluate a society's evolutionary status.[43] Offering a contrasting picture, however, to this interpretation, is Brunhes' explicit statement in the second (1912) edition of *Human Geography* that his book was a reaction *against* the national-colonial bias of previous geographic works that had emphasized the "superior rights of this or that race, or this or that empire."[44] Brunhes also parted company with his teacher Vidal de la Blache in the importance he ascribed to the urban and modern alongside the rural and the traditional, a tendency that pushed his work—especially in its experimental application by Kahn's cameramen—"towards taking seriously the inner working of social life rather than concentrating solely on [Vidalean] naturalized *genres de vie*."[45] Although there is a sense in which Kahn's Archive domesticated the machine aesthetic of cinema when training its eye on local agrarian culture, its visual documents focused just as much on modern life. We should thus be careful about assuming that the Archive was guided by a narrowly nostalgic attitude to traditional culture. For example, when Kahn's cameramen filmed the 1925 Exposition des Arts Décoratifs et Industriels Modernes in Paris, they were probably just as attracted to Le Corbusier (a participant in at least one of Kahn's forums) and Amédéé Ozenfant's gift to high modernism (the Pavillon de L'Esprit Nouveau), as to the pavilions of regional France that included model French villages from the reannexed provinces of Alsace and Lorraine.

Like many interwar intellectuals, particularly those in the natural and social sciences, Brunhes had been enmeshed in debates concerning race and the origins of national identity that were forged under the particular national-colonial pressures of the First World War and its aftermath. His wartime lectures at the Collège de France were often driven by all-embracing questions such as "What is race?" "Who are the French? Who are the English? Who are the Germans?" and most crucially, "What is the nation"?[46] The answer that Brunhes consistently produced, with the aid of human geography and the autochromes from the Archives de la

Planète, was that "race is often no more of a reality than the word *nation* or the word *country*."[47] Brunhes' nondeterminist approach to geographical reality (all part of a wider Bergsonian distrust of mechanical rationalism and causality) thus also extended to his questioning of what he described as dangerously "dogmatic ideas" about race.[48] To be sure, he did not entirely reject but repositioned the category of race, much in line with broader scientific evolution of the period, according to a cultural-environmentalist rather than biophysical conception of race.[49] Still, his conception of race and the nation as fluid and evolving entities existed in direct contrast to the essentialist orthodoxy of the political right and the fixed categories of physical anthropology. As Brunhes argued in a book he published in 1930 titled *Races*, the idea of a "single and indivisible" France (that was so sacrosanct to the right) was in fact a myth as the French were made up of a number of subethnic groups.[50] And as for national affiliation, that "mysterious connection" which unites "societies as *mixed* as ours," Brunhes warned in an earlier lecture that it might seem strong during the galvanizing time of war, but it was always the fragile product of a "mobility of cohesion."[51]

Brunhes delivered that lecture at a fraught period of the war in 1917, when the news of mutinies among French soldiers was a topic of much concern. He chose this particularly fragile period in national cohesion to argue that the ephemeral quality of national identification was subject to a daily plebiscite. In other words, national identification is not innate, but the product of everyday negotiations: "This feeling of cohesion between the men who live in the same territory is nearly variable daily, like the price flows at the Stock Exchange."[52] Much like his conception of race, there was nothing eternal, essential, or unchanging about national character or identification for Brunhes. Again, this does not mean that his generally culturalist conception of race and the nation implied a radical deconstruction of those categories; his invocation of unity-in-diversity resembled, for example, the argument used in the 1920s to bolster the conservative True France policy.[53] Nevertheless, the support Brunhes showed for mixed, mobile, and contingent conceptions of race and the nation posed a threat to the interwar conservative idea of "Frenchness." More specifically, the essentialist logic of that French nationalist ideal rested upon criteria that his Jewish employer Kahn (who had also written of the importance of "variety" over the dangers of "uniformity" posed by Germany) could never hope to satisfy.[54]

READING THE FACE OF THE EARTH IN
HUMAN GEOGRAPHY AND FILM CRITICISM

If two of the most debated categories of his time, race and the nation, were clearly related to the facts Brunhes was gathering for the Archive, how and from what perspective did he register what he himself described as their fleeting features? The answer can be found in Brunhes' pioneering use of aerial photography in the multiple editions of his magnum opus, *La Géographie humaine*, which fully demonstrates his early embrace of advanced photographic technology and his preference for techniques of display over documentary-like narration (discussed in chapter 2).[55]

Written just before the Great War, *La Géographie humaine* opens with Brunhes alluding to the importance of the aerial or airborne perspective as "a general *glance over the earth* [which] reveals an entirely new and very abundant set of surface phenomena: there are towns and railways, cultivated fields and quarries, canals and irrigation tanks and salt-pans; and here and there, in particular, there are masses or groups, of varying density, of human beings."[56] Aerial photography made this impossibly casual "glance over the earth" technologically exact and infinitely reproducible. The result for human geography was phenomenal—it rendered lengthy verbal descriptions of the landscape (which had been the mainstay of physical geography) redundant, thus elevating cartography to a more precise scientific level. Secondly, its long sought-after, oblique bird's-eye view of the world enabled one of the central analytical perspectives of human geography to come into focus, namely, the perception of the earth in physiognomic terms (that is, as an expressive *surface* whose meaning could be read like a face). Although a conceptualization of the earth in physiognomic terms predated modernity, it was only with the development of airborne photography (originally with the aid of balloons, dirigibles, kites, and even pigeons, and later with the help of airplanes) that the impulse to perceive the earth as an expressive skinlike surface finds an objective correlate.

In a letter written to one of Kahn's cameramen, Stéphane Passet, after their initial meeting, Brunhes summarized human geography as "a general classification of all the facts of the surface through which man's activity and ingenuity are transferred onto the skin [*épiderme*] of our planet."[57] What the actual bird's-eye view disclosed to Brunhes (which centuries of panoramic maps and city prospects only hypothesized) was a radically relativist scan of the earth, in which the monuments of physical geography (mountains, rivers, and ravines) stood side by side with the monuments of humans (railways, irrigation tanks, bridges, houses, roads). Beneath the modern gaze of the mechanized skies, human works and humans—"themselves [now reduced to] surface phenomena" (19)—could henceforth be considered as geographical data, while traditional geographical features of the surface of the earth could be analyzed as expressions or even "living organisms" (21). Most importantly, in its determination to avoid being "simply an encyclopedic description of people and places" or a "deterministic interpretation of man-nature relationships," human geography specifically distanced itself from a model of geography based in "philosophical generalization" or bookbound "archival research."[58] Instead, it transformed the earth itself into a readable text (hence the literalism invoked by Kahn's and Bergson's references to the Archive as "the book of the world") and a living archive. And if human geography understood the

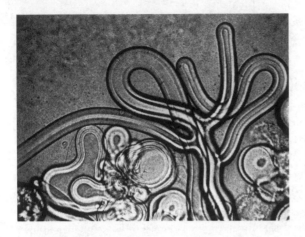

FIGURE 8.1
Image of nerve fiber cells
from Jean Comandon's microcinematographic film *Figures
myéliniques* (1929). (MAK:
frame enlargement)

earth as a surface imprinted over the *longue durée* by the text of human activity,
it is only with the aerial view that the suitable perspective appears from which to
record and decipher documents from the planet's living archive.[59]

The macroscopic views of Brunhes' aerial imagery formed the perfect comple-
ment to the other collection of documents funded by Kahn that epitomize the
"aesthetic of the view": Dr. Jean Comandon's microscopic films. Where Brunhes'
images glided across the earth's skin, Comandon's films continued the Archive's
fascination with travel by penetrating beneath human skin. In his microscopically
enhanced films of blood circulation or nerve fiber cells (fig. 8.1), a pioneering voyage to the interior of the body was made that allowed viewers to see themselves as
if for the first time and experience the human body as a foreign landscape.[60] By
contrast, Brunhes' geographical explorations were less interested in revealing what
the human eye could not see than in looking afresh at what was already humanly
visible. He was primarily concerned with privileging the overlooked complexity of
the surface, rather than the more mysterious unknown interiors of the globe or
human body.[61]

Of course, the challenge to normal perception implied by the aerial photograph
(which Brunhes hints at in his quick substitution—noted in this chapter's opening
epigraph—of the human for the camera eye) became most apparent at the point of
interpretation, especially once the image was enmeshed in the maze of military reconnaissance. Far from merely reinforcing the photographic myth of direct contact
with the real, aerial photography introduced a readerly and interpretive relation
to the earth's surface as a highly encoded text. No longer a matter of just looking
from above, meaning in the aerial photograph is embedded in the complexities of
decipherment attached to a newly trained eye. This interpretive relation to photography was particularly acute with high vertical aerial photographs that issue from
a perspective entirely alien from our habitual lateral viewing positions, resulting

in a flattened, geometricized, and inhuman transformation—rather than mimetic reproduction—of reality.

THE AERIAL VIEW FROM THE ANNALES
SCHOOL TO EARLY FILM THEORY

One person perfectly positioned to grasp the new training of the eye that was needed to interpret aerial images was the Annales historian Marc Bloch, who was an intelligence officer during the second half of the First World War. Film was not the only visual technology that influenced the evolution of this historian's craft. Anecdote has it that Bloch's vision of a new more comprehensive and holistic approach to history was inspired by the vantage point of an aerial view.[62] Thus, if the new aerial optic allowed Brunhes to literally transform the landscape into a book to be read and interpreted, according to a hermeneutic in which, as one historian of geography has put it, "the terrain took the place of the book, text, and *even the archive* of the historian," then in many ways Bloch became this historian of the earth-as-archive.[63] But the aerial perspective was not the sole determinant of Bloch's historical optic. Bloch's vision of history was formed from above *and* from below—that is, across the experiences of seeing the earth via aerial photography and living beneath the soil's surface in trenches, the latter offering him access to a deep, almost archaeological view of landscape that was productive of a long-term view of history.[64]

This link between the young historian and the established geographer regarding their attraction to the dialectic of the view from above and below is not so surprising given human geography's influence upon the early Annales school. More striking is that the link between the aerial and trench views also organized a critical axis within film criticism and theory of the interwar years and beyond. Indeed there are several areas of overlap between French film criticism and human geography. Both shared an interest in film's unique contribution to the human-milieu debate. The question of environment was crucial to the naturalist heritage and obsession with direct observation of everyday life in early cinema and human geography. It underwent, however, a post-positivist rethinking in early French film theory and Brunhes' human geography, both of which emphasized film's ability to provide an unfamiliar perspective on the ordinary relations between man and his environment (whether natural or material). For Louis Delluc, the cinema was a medium fixated on "men and things" whose destiny lay in its ability to renegotiate this classical binary: "to make us all comprehend the things of this world as well as force us to recognize ourselves."[65] Brunhes, too, was interested in the camera's ability to deliver—from the sky or from the earth—a completely modern map of the geographical interrelation between "men and things." If Delluc and Brunhes believed this new perspective could result from the camera's simple recording of found locations and real people, for Jean Epstein as for Dr. Jean Comandon it emerged out of the particularly non-naturalistic spatio-temporal innovations of the camera as expressed in close-up, time-lapse, slow motion, and microcinematography. Thus, between Brunhes' macro- and Comandon's micro-focused approaches to representing natural phenomena in the Archive, we span the two poles of early French film theory's perspectives on the everyday. Where these two poles lined up was in their emphasis on the camera's ability to rescue the everyday from the conventions of the picturesque or the exotic, and to return to it the richness of the unjustly denigrated surface *événement*.

We are now better positioned to understand how the macro and micro positions also map out a heterotopian relation to the everyday that runs through the Kahn Archive and early film theory. For within the already "Other" space of the cinema, these two extremes of magnification and miniaturization evoke an additional heterotopian quality due to their heightened "contestation of the space in which we [normally] live."[66] Untrue to, yet still based in, everyday reality (much like Foucault's definition of heterotopian spaces), macro and micro views are not necessarily radical alternatives to an otherwise repressive system of cinematic spaces (codified, for example, by the regulations of continuity editing). Rather, as counterviews to everyday perception they bring together seemingly incompatible sites and thereby encapsulate the fleeting, disorienting, and often fantastical experiences that grounded the French film critics' exploration of the cinema (and Foucault's definition of heterotopia) as a space where juxtapositions are intensely felt.

Further affinities between film criticism and human geography are evident in Delluc and Epstein's emphasis upon a *nondeterminist* interpretation of the relationship between "men and things." Vividly aware of how cinema expressed modernity's often brutal reconfiguration of man and his environment, Delluc's promotion of film's capacity to make us "comprehend . . . things" and "recognize ourselves" nonetheless held out hope for the cinema's power to mediate inventively the alienation of humans and the material world in industrial-capitalist culture. A nondeterminist approach to representing reality was also central to Epstein's attempt to deconstruct the chronological causality that dominated film narrative by the early 1920s. In a challenge to the proponents of narrative or mainstream cinema, Epstein argued that in the true cinema, "There have never been stories . . . only situations, having neither head nor tail; without beginning, middle or end, no right side or wrong side; they can be looked at from all directions; right becomes left; without limits in past or future, they are present."[67] Released from spatial and temporal coordinates of traditional perspective and historicist narrative, Epstein's *ur*-cinematic form (these floating "situations" in which nothing very much happens) directly resembles the abstracted liberty of the aerial or microcinematographic views, those images "that can be looked at from all directions." Not coincidentally, floating situations (as opposed to narrated facts) also serves well as a description of the pre-documentary quality of Kahn's films.

The third shared insight promoted by human geography and film criticism concerns film's potentially antihumanist de-privileging of an anthropocentric perspective. In place of the traditional aesthetic view of the world that posited man as the measure of all things, film presented a visually democratic survey of the human-milieu topos from the exact perspective delivered to Brunhes from his imaginary balloon above the earth, that is, one from which we have "ridd[en] our mind of all knowledge of man." If in the domain of human geography this meant that man was now just one among many geographical facts, in the discursive field of film criticism it translated, as Delluc put it, into the depiction of man as "no more than a detail, a fragment of the material that is the world."[68] As Kracauer's later citation (in *Theory of Film*) of Delluc's above comment makes clear, film had the power to destabilize the sacred hierarchies between man and the natural or material world, in the process de-privileging the anthropocentric perspective of traditional aesthetics.[69]

On the other hand, the camera's ability to animate the previously inanimate could also result in a reinvigorated and expanded anthropocentrism. Brunhes gives voice to the anthropomorphizing results of the aerial view in the caption to one of thirteen aerial photographs presented in the 1925 edition of *Géographie humaine*, in this instance shot from above a train terminus in Metz-Sablon: "A circulation knot, tight fibrous 'muscle': Metz-Sablon train-shunting yard" (fig. 8.2).[70] Continuing, to a certain degree, his teacher's predilection for "humanized landscapes," Brunhes' depiction of a densely technological landscape as a fibrous, sinewy muscle humanizes the foreign, almost abstract view (thus reversing the dehumanizing tendency of Comandon's microscopic view of nerve cells that resemble aerial images of roadways).[71] Ultimately, however, the manner in which Brunhes collects the evidence with which his geography would be able to compare and equate "urban centers" with "living beings" produces an image that is as potentially alienating as it is purportedly comforting.[72] Overlaying an organicist map across the inorganic urban terrain, Brunhes negotiates his encounter with the transformed face of the modern planet by attempting to reconcile a humanist and post-humanist, nostalgic and revolutionary, view of modernity.

But the most striking point of convergence between film criticism's reflections upon the camera's tendency to reveal the personality of things and human geography's desire to treat the surface of the earth as a physiological expression took shape in the shared trope of the "face of the world." In this figure we see the overlapping of the old and the new. Vidal de la Blache's humanized landscape meets the camera's anthropomorphized material and natural world. The collapsing of the macroscopic and microscopic tendencies morphs into the dialectic of the face as

FIGURE 8.2 (ABOVE AND OPPOSITE)   Aerial photograph captioned "Traffic junction resembling a muscle with close-packed fibers: The marshalling-yard of Metz-Sablon" (Jean Brunhes, *La Géographie Humaine*, vol. 3 [illustrations], 3d ed., 1925: 135).

world, and the world as face. Delluc also suggested the doubling of landscape (*paysage*) and face (*visage*) in 1917 in his search for a decidedly modern beauty in the cinema: "Pure beauty, which I now demand and always find in natural landscapes, is sometimes synthesized in a gesture, a face, a talent."[73] A few years later in the article "Magnification" (1921), the landscape-face trope returns in Epstein's intoxicating celebrations of the close-up, in which he describes the face-filled screen as a topographical and climatic vortex. In Epstein's facial meteorology, the

enlarged visage has become a place marked by a force that "ripple[s] beneath the skin," a screen-terrain on which "shadows shift, tremble, [and] hesitate" and "seismic shocks begin" and where a "breeze of emotion underlines the mouth with clouds."[74] The face filmed in close-up is at once human and geographic, particular and universal, home to surface undulations and violent depths. This convergence is expressed in what is arguably Epstein's most concise definition of *photogénie* (or film specificity) when he describes film as the "most powerful medium" capable of showing us "the face of the world."[75] Chosen out of the vast range of mobile views available to him, Epstein points to the potential view from an airplane as the most "modern" of the camera's perspectives, equal to, though in inverse scale from, the radical "magnification" of the close-up. These are, then, the two sides to Epstein's human geography of cinema, the close-up of the face and the extreme long-shot of the aerial view. The deformation and deviation of meaning that results from the foregrounding involved in the magnified perspective is the flip side to the effect of backgrounding or miniaturizing that occurs in the aerial view. Thus, in the cinema's potential to juxtapose incongruous spatial scales there resides one of the central factors in early film theorists' heterotopian experience of cinema.

COLONIAL CLOSE-UP

It is no coincidence that the actual face that Epstein describes is the same face that sends Delluc into a rhapsody in "Beauty in the Cinema"—that of the Japanese actor Sessue Hayakawa. Just as the aerial view was underpinned by militaristic surveillance, the close-up was underwritten by the racial phantasms of French colonial anxiety. The abstracted reading of Hayakawa's face as the blank screen of the Other passively receptive to Western projections of awe and fear could not have been so easily accomplished if Hayakawa had been Indochinese (and therefore more intimately implicated in French colonial anxieties) instead of Japanese. And if the poetry of the close-up was hardly racially innocent, neither was the aesthetic appropriation of its more magnified relative, cellular microphotography. Romy Golan has shown how microphotographic images adapted from the biological sciences were used during the thirties to impart a regressive organicism to furniture design, reclaiming the formerly modernist material of "metal and glass under the taxonomy of nature."[76] She also claims that the use of enlarged microscopic cell structures by Le Corbusier and Fernand Léger in their pavilion at the 1935 Brussels International Exposition was not immune to the racial contagion of biological and cellular discourse, displayed in the promotion of eugenics by the biologist Alexis Carrel, who like many on the right during this period of escalating racialism vis-à-vis French identity found inspiration in elements of Bergsonian philosophy that were "ripe for distortion."[77] Reminding us of the dialectics of scale so crucial to the experience of actual travel, we here see the dystopian side of early film theory's heterotopian attraction to the virtual voyages that cinema offered between the magnification of the near and the miniaturization of the far.

Similarly, whereas Vidal's human geography had originally set out to capture humanized landscapes, the aerial reinvention of human geography by Brunhes seldom resulted in flattering portraits of the earth (just as he did not answer his questions regarding race and the nation with comforting essentialist certainties). In the most extensive example of aerial-based imagery that exists in the Archive, the films taken by Lucien Le Saint in 1919 from the side of a dirigible over the battlefields of northern France and the devastated towns of Arras and Reims, we are presented with the portrait of a ravaged earth, scarred and wrinkled from the trenches, bombings, and destruction of the war.[78] Summoning the new humanism afforded by this God-like view of the world, Brunhes' proto-environmentalist depiction of the consequences of human exploitation of the earth as a "form of murder" suddenly acquires a more literal meaning when attached to Le Saint's postwar views.[79] To put it more simply, human geography not only placed the human at the center of geographical inquiry but also inhumanity at the center of modernity.

Le Saint's footage of a devastated northeastern France ends with a flight over the comforting permanence of Paris's monuments. But even here, safely "home," the postwar surveillant visuality that would now always accompany the aerial view delivers an unsettling vista of potential impermanence. The film may celebrate Paris as survivor of the past, but its eye from the sky also looks toward Paris as target of future airborne invaders. Back on earth, Kahn's cameramen were taking a much closer look at the changing social and racial landscape of the present. Shot in 1917, the footage titled *Prostituée devant une maison close* (Prostitute in front of a brothel) depicts a woman negotiating with two French soldiers, one white, the other black, in the street entrance of a lower class Parisian hotel (fig. 8.3) before she alerts them to the presence of the camera.[80] The footage of the "shady hotel" (as the film ledger describes it) provides evidence—in addition to other films of flea markets, urinals, and street sweepers—of how often Kahn's cameramen were distracted from the imperial vistas that had been so deliberately carved around the capital's monuments during Baron Haussmann's modernization of the city.[81] If Le Saint's aerial footage made Haussmann's Paris visible in all its repressive as well as spectacular order, this ground-level film, positioned on a side street forgotten by Haussmann's bulldozers, highlights the more intimate and embedded focus upon the evolving social landscape. It evokes a sort of anthropology of the interior and the contemporary (rather than the exterior and the past) that accompanies the Archive's seemingly ahistorical view from above. The film was shot during the same year Brunhes questioned the solidity of French national identification, that is, at the height of a conflict that saw unprecedented anxiety regarding the transformation of traditional gender and colonial roles due to the opportunistic recruitment and heightened presence, often in close proximity, of both French women (particularly in the munitions factories) and colonial men (in the workforce and on the battlefields).[82] The film's triangular structure of French female prostitute, black colonial soldier, and white French soldier thus witnesses, not from afar but up close and personal, the wedge of sexual relations introduced into a complex urban encounter of race, gender, and class. Played out on the artificial stage of the war's temporary loosening of relations between white women and black men, and white men and black men, Kahn's film also implicates the future in the unfinished

FIGURE 8.3   Film of a Paris brothel: *Prostituée devant une maison close* (cameraman un-known, 1917). (MAK: frame enlargement 139926)

business of the metropole and colonies' intertwined destinies, as hinted at in Brun-hes' comments on the "mixed" nature of France.

BETWEEN THE *TEXTE CONNU* AND THE *LIVRE DU MONDE*

The war's disclosure and exacerbation of the fragility of hierarchies underpinning the three categories of race, class, and gender (emblematized in the Paris broth-el film) contributed in the postwar decade to an unprecedented racialization of French national identity.[83] Thwarting the goal of universal cooperation and ra-cial equality that Kahn's travel fund was supposed to achieve, the twenties saw a tighter articulation of race and French national identity. This shift in conceptions of national identity was accompanied by a range of developments that included the strengthening of nationalism and of biological concepts of the nation; an in-creasing concern regarding the disappearance of rural France (by the mid-1920s the balance between the rural and urban population was about to tilt in favor of the city for the first time); a stricter attention to the role of French women in the regeneration of the race after the demographic depletion of the war; a rejuvenated anti-Semitism; and a virulent attitude of revanchism toward Germany.[84]

    Underpinning all of these developments was the transition to a new colonial policy based on the notion of association rather than assimilation. Although both forms of policy coexisted, it is generally recognized that during the interwar period official colonial policy (epitomized by the writings of Albert Sarraut) moved away from an understanding of the colonized as an inferior object in need of civilizing to a seemingly more "enlightened" and "humanist" recognition of the colonized as a subject (although never citizen) of cultural difference.[85] No longer relying so exclusively upon the need to convert or eradicate the difference of the colonial Other, the reformulated colonial policy was accompanied by a revised discourse of the extended family of Greater France (comprising approximately 100 million people) that now embraced the notion of unity in diversity. The economic backbone of this evolution lay in the "shift in emphasis from conquest to *mise en valeur* [economic development], and from unlimited to limited exploitation"; in other words, a policy that focused on respecting and learning more about the cultural context of the colonial other also fed expediently into the need to exploit and manage more efficiently the natural and human resources of the colonies.[86]

As frequent travelers to and from France's colonies, instructed to combine an instrumentalist approach to travel as a provider of useful knowledge with a utopian longing for intercultural comprehension, Kahn's grant recipients (*boursiers*) were well positioned to express these contradictions of empire. Indeed, Kahn's travel fund had been established with the express intention of having the nation's future teachers confront the incompatibility of textbook knowledge with actual life on the ground. Having successfully met Kahn's scholarship challenge, F. Bernot defined travel in his 1914 report as a "precious object lesson" capable of teaching us from the "*livre du monde* [book of the world]" once we had found the courage to abandon "*le texte connu* [the familiar text]" of conventional scholarly knowledge.[87] In his self-conscious allusion to the broader textual archive of cultural knowledge about the Other, Bernot comes close to anticipating what Said calls "the pre-existing Orientalist archive."[88] The *texte connu* of France's orientalist imaginary—in its intertwined popular, literary, and military permutations—hung like a weight upon Kahn's beneficiaries as they set out to unburden themselves from it in the supposedly more authentic and unmediated encounter with the "book of the world."

Another Kahn *boursier*, Félicien Challaye (who would become a noted anticolonialist and pacifist of the interwar period) drew a more blunt connection in his 1920 report between travel's object lessons and the specific economic functions to which they should be put in his plea to "future traders" and "industrialists" to "not forget the immense clientele that the innumerable populations of Asia and Africa offer you."[89] In Challaye's advice to his own *lycée* students to study "the needs" and "tastes" of the "yellow" and "black" races (54), the economic destiny of Kahn's humanistically motivated world voyages is unapologetically on display. Aware of the economic benefits of more sympathetic cross-cultural understanding, Challaye understood that the noble documentation he had been funded to gather was intended to produce not a more sympathetic understanding of the Other (particularly when that Other was a colonial subject), but a transvaluation of the Other into a potential consumer with untapped desires. Echoing Lévi-Strauss's travels in *Tristes Tropiques*, the *boursiers'* voyages resulted not so much in a more truthful understanding of the Other as in a more "useful" understanding of the self. And at a time of dangerous geopolitical reconfiguration, when France was beginning to feel increasing economic competition from Germany and Great Britain, as well as emerging resistance from her own colonies, it goes without saying that that "self" was always a stand-in for the French nation.[90] Proving the limits of the cosmopolitan myth, Bernot argued that while travel can allow one to appreciate more fully "the bonds of international solidarity," it ultimately made one "clearly aware of national sentiment" (235). He thus finally described travel as a "good teacher since it teaches the most important of all the virtues of the mind: to doubt oneself in order to be more sure of oneself" (236).

FOUCAULT'S BOAT

The justifications for travel elaborated in the *boursier* reports expressed the Archive's panoptic but humanist goal of an empathetic "extension of vision." Read, however, in light of the specific places to which Kahn's cameramen directed the Archive's gaze, such as the Paris brothel, these travelers' explorations "of other spaces" remind us that the boat Foucault chose to exemplify heterotopias was not just any boat.[91] It is in fact a boat traveling between what were for Foucault the most extreme forms of heterotopias—brothels and colonies. Behind the more official "academic" itineraries of Kahn's films, another sexual trade route emerges that is crucial for understanding France's interwar colonial history and all its attendant anxieties of race and national identity. This shadow market is especially significant for understanding several Kahn films of women shot in the mandates and colonies of Indochina and Lebanon.

As with the film of the Parisian *maison close*, I will approach those of colonial women first from the particular perspective of the distanced vantage point before moving to a more intimate view. This time, the aerial view's terrestrial parallel, the horizontally sweeping panoramic view, provides the necessary perspective. No other shot in the Archive displays more forcefully how the camera was used to approximate spatially Langlois' textual ideal of total archival coverage than the 360-degree panorama over the Temple of Angkor Wat shot in Cambodia in 1921 by Léon Busy (fig. 8.4). The colonial officer's technically exhibitionist shot confirms the camera's ability to function like the invisible, unreturnable, sovereign eye of the panoptic-archive—an anonymous, removed, and distanced horizontal glance suited to a reading of the earth as a living archive. This seamless scan of the ruins is set up to admit no interruption, resistance, or intrusion. Even the two human presences in the film—the individual men who walk away from the camera at opposite ends

FIGURE 8.4   Beginning of 360-degree panorama of the Angkor Wat temple façade in Cambodia. (Léon Busy, February 1921) [MAK: frame enlargement])

of the temple's central axis around the 90- and 270-degree points of the shot—seem to have been intentionally included in a symmetrically orchestrated and non-confrontational pose of retreat rather than return. Viewed in this context, the film's gaze resembles that of an all-powerful and benevolent viewer of France's imagined imperial terrain, one in which the French were able to fashion themselves as the deserving, if geographically displaced, heirs to Angkor Wat—the modern rescuers, custodians, surveyors, and readers of the remnants of Cambodia's once glorious civilization.[92]

Resonant with the new spatial codes of associationist policy, the panoramic shot thus encompasses a respectful, distanced, preservational approach to the native monuments of stone. The other end of the spectrum to the ethics of spatial distance appears when the Archive zooms in to a closer view of the living native in Busy's film *Scène de déshabillage, Tonkin* (Undressing scene, 1921), in which a Vietnamese girl demonstrates the intricacies of her traditional dress, or rather undress. The film features a young woman removing and then putting back on her clothes (fig. 8.5). In that she has clearly been directed to go through the motions of her daily dress routine, the woman is meant to satisfy the same fascination with the registering of ordinary movement and ritual featured in Eadweard Muybridge's chronophotographic studies. However, where Muybridge's "women" were professional exhibitionists, appearing like magicians' assistants against the grid of their artificial backdrops, Busy's girl is offered *en plein air* as a purer, more anthropologically authentic vessel of the beauty of everyday ritual.[93] Where clothes in the Muybridge studies were merely included, like so many other props, as "superfluous detail," in the Busy film, clothes, transposed into the desexualized realm of costume, supposedly become the primary object of interest.[94]

Scène de déshabillage, Tonkin is a striking anomaly in the Kahn Archive, not least because of the full, if brief, nudity it features, but even more so because the film was purposely shot out-of-focus, perhaps to absolve itself from the titillating appeal of the subject matter. Even though the film is formally dominated by the out-of-focus surface, what it clearly brings into focus is a self-consciousness regarding the pornographic potentialities of the scientific ethnographic gaze. Busy's addition of the out-of-focus visual veil inscribes an unmistakably artificial texture in the otherwise natural surface of the film, forcing us to notice what we are not supposed to be doing, that is, staring voyeuristically. The film blatantly combines intention for respect and distance (hallmarks of the policy of association) with an unavoidable voyeuristic aspect that is in fact heightened rather than negated by the bashful curtaining effect. The partly hidden nature of Busy's documentation thus serves to incite the act of seeing and thus increases the film's attraction as a visual display. Here we perhaps see a transitional moment between the unmasked

FIGURE 8.5   Image from a film titled *Scène de déshabillage, Tonkin*, shot intentionally out of focus, of a Vietnamese woman undressing. (Léon Busy, 1921) [MAK: frame enlargement])

voyeurism of early cinema and the more encoded and masked voyeurism of classical Hollywood viewing relations, except the transition is not quite complete, the masking too literal and visible to be naturalized. The film's anthropological alibi (the descriptive representation of traditional dress) is in a permanent state of coming undone. Neither pure anthropological document nor pure pornographic spectacle, the film displays the uncertain vacillation of visual evidence as it arouses the two gazes—that of the exposed and hidden voyeur—simultaneously.

The few films in the Archive containing nudity bear obvious affinities to the realm of popular semipornographic colonial imagery. Although the young women who cheekily flash their breasts in Camille Sauvageot's 1920s footage of Casablanca's prostitution quarter perform very differently from the unsmiling costume specimen in Busy's film, both films literally animate a parallel visual culture of postcard poses of colonized women (especially from North Africa) in various stages of undress.[95] Regardless of their differences and the extent to which prostitution is an explicit or implicit part of their documentation, both films satisfy Kahn's mission to replace the *texte connu* with the more authentic encounters offered on location by the *livre du monde*.

Whatever anthropological pretext veils the above films is stripped away in the most extensive films of prostitutes in the Kahn Archive, shot in Beirut by Lucien Le Saint in 1919 on the occasion of the official inauguration of the French mandate in the Levant by the new High Commissioner, General Henri Gouraud.[96] The more official views within Le Saint's footage of Gouraud welcoming what he called France's newly "adopted children" of Lebanon and Syria provide further evidence of narrative-associated, in-camera editing in the Archive (again motivated by obviously nationalistic events).[97] As for the heterotopian itinerary of this journey that began with footage aboard the boat that carries Gouraud and his officials to the Levant, it is only fully completed once we enter the more unofficial terrain of Le Saint's 1919 films of a Beirut brothel. The filming begins with a static shot of a courtyard of a modest house that appears to be like any other. Within a few seconds, a woman and a man in uniform exit the interior and stand before the camera, the soldier kissing the woman while remaining in an awkward frontal pose staged clearly for the camera. A subsequent shot in the same location shows another woman establishing the tone of casual reciprocity in this encounter between the Western gaze and the colonized female by quickly giving the finger to the cameraman. Le Saint resumes cranking the camera on a scene that goes much further than the animated postcard films discussed above in giving us access to the "real" promised by the *livre du monde*. Now Le Saint's stationary camera is angled toward the wall of a half-shadowed lane, against which the soldiers and prostitutes continue their performance of cultural contact as rough play (fig. 8.6). Untypical of his generally durational style of shooting, Le Saint starts and stops his filming several times in this location, perhaps due to the lane's more public exposure or the

FIGURE 8.6   Film of Beirut prostitutes cavorting with soldiers, titled *Prostituées devant des maisons closes* (Lucien Le Saint, November 21–25, 1919 [MAK: frame enlargement 110 675])

obviously bad light. Distinguished by an unusually candid depiction of relations between occupying soldiers and "native" prostitutes, Le Saint's footage ends with a strangely calm long shot of the *maisons closes* taken from the street.

This unique footage embodies the complicated relationship the Kahn films have with both the nineteenth-century positivist archive of historical evidence and the late-twentieth-century's postcolonial critique of that archive. Exemplary of the latter critique, Said's *Orientalism* posited the archive—whether understood in the abstract as the regulatory site for discourse or understood literally as a store-house for governmental records, or a combination of both—as a central enabling technology of imperialist expansion and cultural domination. If the positivist archive functioned as an arbiter of historical proof and authenticity while its relative, the generalized colonial archive (including geographical surveys and the diverse genres of colonial cinema), functioned as a guide to colonizable space, it is very difficult to determine the exact "truth" of the evidence or the precise directionality of power in the spatial relations encoded in Le Saint's film.

One might argue that the film reflects unequivocally early cinema's complicity with nationally, racially, and sexually executed campaigns of domination—that what is being symbolically displayed in this film is Western technology's participation in the submission of another non-European space to the neocolonial dictates of the Treaty of Versailles (an event also filmed by Kahn's cameramen). The occa-

sion for the brothel film was of course the simultaneous cartographical carving up
and parceling out of the invented nation-states of Lebanon and Syria to France as
a mandated territory authorized by the League of Nations following the wartime
collapse of the Ottoman Empire. Perhaps there is no more obvious evidence in the
Kahn Archive of the collusion between cinema and oppression, vision and objectification, than in the films of colonial prostitutes and other women in voyeuristic
contexts. If such a reading allows the prostitutes to partly emerge from the darkness of cinema's colonial history, it still leaves them within the shadow of their
more immediate historical past. The women in Le Saint's films are most likely sur-
vivors of the great famine of 1915–1918 when between 150,000 to 300,000 Lebanese died amid rumors about the food blockades against the Lebanese by the Otto-
mans, British, and French.[98] Particularly traumatic for the female population, the
famine was accompanied by the fear of dishonor reflected in the common stories
that circulated of "girls who traded their virtue for food from soldiers."[99] Although
not totally beyond the constrictions of a shame culture, Le Saint's film captures an
exchange that marks a trading of victimhood for survival.

This footage, along with the few other films of brothels in the Archive (such
as the one in Paris discussed above), might also be read in conjunction with the
topics being discussed at Kahn's Comité National d'Études Sociales et Politiques
(National Committee of Social and Political Studies). In the late twenties these
topics included "public hygiene in France," "[the] social plague" of prostitution,
and "the social peril" of syphilis, the latter a topic on which Comandon's research
focused.[100] In the context of France's ongoing anxiety about its low birth rate, particularly vis-à-vis Germany's and Britain's, such a debate, hinging upon the connections between the Parisian and the colonial brothel, cannot be ignored. Its
immediate relevance for the Kahn film of Beirut prostitutes appears in what Elizabeth Thompson has described as "the aggressive regime of health regulation for
prostitutes" that was undertaken in the Levant shortly after the establishment of
the French mandate. After the 1921 outbreak of venereal disease among French
troops, "prostitutes, dancers, and singers were required to register with police,
carry identification cards, work in designated brothels (*maisons de tolérance*) and
submit to twice-weekly medical exams."[101] Following Foucault's discussion of panopticism, in which the medical examination is a key technique in the invisible and
consensual operations of modern power, Le Saint's film literally merges a knowledge of the body with a body of knowledge, thereby transforming "the economy of
visibility into the exercise of power," at the point "where the codified power to punish turns into a disciplinary power to observe."[102] To invoke Bergson's vocabulary,
the films provide a literal example of seeing in order to act.

Both readings of this film, as evidence of the camera's oppressive and social
reformist tendencies (connected respectively to film's geographical and documentary applications), are valid. And yet we are still left short of pinpointing the exact

nature of the evidence contained in the film. One of the reasons that it is difficult to establish this film as evidence of any sort is because, contra the generalizable experience of panopticism in which the effective functioning of power depends on "eyes that must see without being seen," here the subjects to be seen look back, again and again, in a repetitive agonistic loop of attraction and repulsion.[103] As we have already noted with other films (of the men in the *vespasienne*; the commercial cameramen and their cameras at the League of Nations meeting all staring back at the Kahn cameraman; Le Saint performing the puppet trick for the camera; or Kahn himself waving his finger at his cameramen), when the camera's gaze is returned, either by a human or mechanical eye (of another camera, that is), the illusion of power supposedly maintained by the invisible and objective eye of the camera and (by the process of identification) the spectator is compromised. Le Saint's camera is so often engaged by the prostitutes and the soldiers, sometimes in a joking and casual way (a woman waves at the camera), at other times in an aggressive and imploring way (a soldier grabs the breasts and buttocks of one woman, then thumps his groin into her from behind while the woman tries to free herself), that far from resembling anything like an invisible eye, it takes on the role of a participant (but no less exploitative) observer. Following in the footsteps of Brunhes' lecture style, Le Saint combines what Georg Lukács claimed were usually separated (in written narrative): the witnessing of naturalist observation with the participating of historical action.[104] The involved look animating this sequence is the exact opposite of the removed and invisible gaze of the panoramic surveys over Angkor Wat by Busy. As a result of Le Saint's involved observational mode, it seems that the cameraman, his camera, and the implied spectator in Boulogne (not to mention the historically displaced spectator) are as much under the microscope in this sequence as the biological "threat" of the colonial prostitute.

Even if one can still assert that the prostitutes are the only real objects in this film, it would be incorrect to assume that their actions can be interpreted transparently, especially given the staged nature of this entire sequence. They may not be in control of the filming, but they are anything but docile specimens placed beneath the microscope of an archival gaze or, for that matter, easy targets for an interpretive method that claims to read meaning off the physiognomic surface of the image. There remains something unclassifiable about their always half-obscured performance. They alternate between coyly rejecting the soldiers' offensive advances, bashfully smiling for Le Saint and provocatively showing disrespect with their mock military salutes. By claiming the film retains a level of opacity that blocks my previous readings, I am not simply granting these women some measure of dignity which the prying of interpretation, no matter how well intentioned, inevitably abuses. Rather, I am suggesting that the intimate and perhaps invasive films should be read with the same attention to their opacity (that is, their challenge to representational norms of transparency) as the abstracted, distanced, and highly encoded aerial views of French topography.

Where elevation and distance in the latter translate the landscape into a body of previously inaccessible yet still encoded information, proximity and camera-acknowledgment in the former translate the body (literally of the woman but also metaphorically of the film) into a landscape of equally encoded epistemological and hermeneutic desire. Just as the unnatural perspective of the aerial image must be decoded in a process that is never complete, so, too, do these seemingly exploitative films demand an awareness of film's nontransparent relation with power, vision, and knowledge. The ledger used by Kahn's cameramen may indicate the exact date, place, and subject of each meter of this sequence, but the drama it captures between submission and resistance, functional seeing and nonfunctional looking, personal recollection and historical forgetting, conjures the "imagined community" of Greater France as a space and a race internally divided and antagonized; unbalanced and unaccounted for within the neat divisions of the ledger's stocktaking of the present.[105]

If Busy's panorama over Angkor Wat conditions viewers to see functionally—that is, to view Other spaces as places to be explored and inhabited by Europeans—then Le Saint's films collapse the safe, distancing techniques of the panorama into an uneasy display of intimacy and proximity in which exploration is revealed as being always already coupled with penetration. The shot is no longer about the wondrous display of the camera's controlling panoramic capacities. The wonder on display here is of a more pedestrian nature; it is that the camera (answering Boleslas Matuszewski's desires for a camera on every corner) is even there in the shadows of history's laneways. Unlike the distanced and highly composed panorama over the Angkor Wat ruins shot by the colonial officer Busy, Le Saint's footage presents an altogether different vision of the French nation's history as peep show. More in line with Busy's modestly blurred striptease, Le Saint also combines discretion and indiscretion. No matter how many other shots exist in the Archive of General Gouraud officiating over the inauguration of France's protectorate of Lebanon, it is this other scene that discloses the conventionally obscured connections between what Ann Laura Stoller has described as "the broad-scale dynamics of rule and the intimate domains of implementation," which operate most palpably "in the banal and humble intimacies of the everyday."[106] In this sense, Le Saint was faithfully following the principle rule of Brunhes' geographical vision, to remain "in *intimate* contact with the facts."[107]

The unbalancing supplement of this intimacy spills over into the women's addresses to the camera. These diverse forms of camera acknowledgment bear the weight of a new form of history enacted by people not only aware of, but in (eye-) contact with, their observers and recorders. They therefore disrupt the Foucauldian carceral architecture of "looking without being looked at" and the model of history that grounds his panoptic theory of modern technologies of power. The visibility of the supposedly invisible Western gaze ends up loosening the purportedly panoptic grip of visual regimes within colonial modernity. In other words, what was supposed to produce a seeing in order to act incites a seeing in order to see. We cannot agree fully, therefore, with Foucault's assertion that the democratization of descriptive attention in the modern world, which has made it possible for "the everyday individuality of everybody," not just of the privileged few, "to be looked at, observed, described in detail" and stored in archives, has resulted in a situation in which archival records are "no longer a monument for future memory, but a document for possible [for example, police] use."[108]

For although archives sustain history in a hegemonic sense through the ideological violence of inclusion, exclusion, and repetition, the Kahn Archive's use of a medium characterized by a tendency to store too much and descend into disorder creates the possibility for perspectives previously unnoticed by history to be released in the form of memory shards if not monuments. Neither abstract Woman as victim-object, nor real Woman as sovereign-subject, the women in Le Saint's footage (figured as memory shards) refract power as a simultaneously invisible and visible play. If Le Saint's film of prostitutes participates in the regulatory archive (posed by Foucault) of French racial regeneration, it just as coherently reveals the incongruities that Foucault also admitted existed in archival documents which reflected the limitations of the archive's capacity to regulate knowledge and memory.[109] Further instances of the Archive's unregulated memory appear in Sauvageot's 1926 footage of traditional itinerant storytellers, or griots, on Moroccan streets. Ostensibly another example of quaint local types, the storytellers were of course popular oral disseminators of anticolonial discourse central to the fueling of Moroccan nationalism. Sauvageot's and Le Saint's films illuminate the blind spots of the history of the nation (France, but also Lebanon and Morocco) where the rational, finite, and utilitarian logic of the classifiable document meets the threatening, open-endedness of the unclassifiable remainder in a visual field where seeing in order to see discloses the undisciplined evidence of vision itself rather than the irrefutable proof of visible evidence.

UNINTENDED OBJECT LESSONS AND
THE "OTHER" COUNTER-COLONIAL EXPOSITION

The Kahn Archive questioned as much as it promoted, and contested as much as it confirmed the colonial ideology of the period. The Archive's ambivalent relationship to colonial discourse extended to the granting of travel scholarships to several recipients who queried both Western imperialism and universal humanism. Although Félicien Challaye clearly supported the belief that Europeans "must understand and practice the essential responsibility of the white race toward other races," he also admitted that "unfortunately" whites have "too often abused their power in order to exploit yellow and black people."[110] Providing further evidence of the imperial self-consciousness of some of Kahn's *boursiers*, B. Ifor Evans, a British citizen, admitted to a very different emotion than the one Marlowe expresses in response to maps in Joseph Conrad's *Heart of Darkness*. Evans claimed that even before embarking on his journey, "I was a little ashamed of all the countries marked red in the school atlases."[111] His travel *récit* is even more uncensored than Challaye's in its skepticism toward the Kahnian ideal of knowing the common, *everyday* Other through the unmediated contact of travel: "One meets the fussy people and at times the important people, the financiers, the social reformers, and the politicians. . . . But it was the *ordinary* man that I missed. . . . More particularly it was the women whom I did not see" (66; my emphasis). To be sure, Challaye never negates the superiority of the white race in calling for the end everywhere to "these abuses and crimes" of colonialism (54). Furthermore, his approach is typical of the collusion of antiracism and pro-colonialism during the period of colonial humanism. Likewise, Evans is not arguing for the return of those countries marked red to self-determination. Nonetheless, their conclusions indicate the ways in which travel, experienced as the collision of the distanced (macro) and immersive (micro) views, and the encounter between the "known text" and the "book of the world," produced bad object lessons for Kahn's belated emissaries of the French and British empires.

Given its express purpose of turning the colonial world into a spectacle via the technique of miniaturization and the attraction of an Autour du Monde experience, it is highly fitting that some of the last films shot for the Archives de la Planète were of an event that marks the ideological apotheosis of both French "exhibitionitis" as well as the "aesthetic of the view," namely the Exposition Coloniale Internationale of 1931.[112] The Exposition is also illuminating as a reminder of why the Archive collapsed. For in many respects Kahn's interwar dream of a film archive upholding peace and mutual understanding was doomed not only by the stock market crash and the coming of sound technology (which ended the hope for film as a universal visual language). Even more damaging was Paris's Colonial Exposition and its associated anti-imperial protests that interrupted forever the benevolent myth of a Greater France that Kahn's Archive had indirectly supported.

In many ways the 1931 Colonial Exposition is the expositional, albeit more explicitly colonial, analogue of the Kahn Archive.[113] Both participated in what Walter Benjamin described as the collective fantasy—associated, as his friend Kracauer knew well, with the aerial view—of the "world in miniature."[114] Just as the soil of the sixteenth arrondissement cultivated the artificiality of Kahn's world landscape, so too on the other side of Paris did the Bois de Vincennes provide the soil for another unnatural outgrowth of the global imaginary in the form of an impossible boulevard lined with architectural simulations of the colonial world. That these simulations were often larger or smaller versions of the originals places the whole Exposition in line with the magnifying and miniaturizing extremes of film techniques discussed above.[115] The Exposition's spatial manipulations thus fulfilled

Ifor Evans' desire to make the whole world "as clearly visible to my eyes as the room in which I write."

Travel, whether virtual or actual, pleasurable or utilitarian, or a combination of both, was also central to the "world souvenir" metonymy of the Archives de la Planète and the Exposition. Much as Brunhes invoked Jules Verne in his geographical ride above the earth, so too did the Colonial Exposition promote itself as a "voyage around the world in one day."[116] Where Busy's 360-degree panorama surveyed the real Angkor Wat temple with the invisible panoptic eye, as if preparing for sovereign ownership of all that lay before it, the Kahn cameraman's film of the temple's replica, shot on site at the Colonial Exposition, delivers on that promise. In the film, the Exposition's visitors lay claim to the temple, literally climbing its outer balustrades, supposedly on their way to embracing the *idée coloniale* the fair's organizer—General Hubert Lyautey, another visitor to Kahn's villa—was desperate to inculcate.

And yet, as similar as the Archive was to the Exposition, it was also radically different. Instead of facing outward toward public exposure, the Kahn Archive was turned protectively inward in a conscious rejection of the masses. Furthermore, where the Archive had tried, however naively, to use film to capture the real world on location, the Exposition produced a film-set–like replica of the world. And instead of being characterized by the intentional impermanence of all expositions (their plaster façades so emblematic of the planned obsolescence of the commodities they promoted), Kahn's project was rooted in the intentional permanence of the Archive.[117] The Archives de la Planète was civilization's bunker, not its shopwindow.

Despite its mesmerizing promotional appeal and status as the interwar mass object lesson for the French colonial enterprise, the Colonial Exposition, as revealed by the concurrent highly critical Surrealist Counter-Exposition, also represented an anxious monument to France's failure to secure a popular base or consolidate a coherent imperial order.[118] If the Counter-Exposition is a well-known if admittedly small indication of the cracks in the French Empire's façade, I would like to close my journey through the Archive by gesturing to an analogous, if entirely censored, challenge to official colonial policy that emerged from Kahn's enterprise.

The films in the Archive that most directly anticipate ethnographic film—those of fetishistic vodoun culture in Dahomey (Benin), West Africa—were shot between December 1929 and June 1930 under the supervision of Father Francis Aupiais, a priest attached to the Société des Missions Africaines of Lyon. The two sets of edited and intertitled films he made in collaboration with Kahn's cameraman Frédéric Gadmer (*Le Dahomey chrétien* and *Le Dahomey réligieux*) resulted in his near ex-communication and the banning of the second set of films (on Dahomeyan religious practices) from the Colonial Exposition of 1931 (where it was supposed to be screened) under the orders of none other than the head of the Missions Africaines and the President of the Republic. The Catholic Church protested that his work, in which he compared African vodoun and Christian rituals, threatened to inaugurate a sort of reverse anthropology viewed from the perspective of a "primitive" and "heathen" people.

Even in an era of so-called enlightened colonial policy in which the French government itself was promoting respect for cultural difference over the older ideology of the civilizing mission, the superior status of French civilization could not bear equivocation in official quarters. To incite an anthropology of France itself—whether offered in Aupiais' framing of African religious rituals as analogous to Catholic rituals, Brunhes' question "What is a nation?," Le Saint's films of soldier-prostitute relations, or the *boursier* reports that speak back to Kahn's belief in the universal citizen—entailed denying the center its invisibility, in the process contesting normative cultural, racial, and technological hierarchies.

If the Colonial Exposition provides a fitting denouement to the Archives de la Planète, then the curtain only truly falls, however, with the death of Kahn in November 1940, just a few months after the Nazi invasion of Paris in June. In many ways, the Colonial Exposition and the Nazi invasion, apogees of French colonial and German National Socialist triumphalism, drag the Archive forward into the intertwined traumas of decolonization and collaboration. Earlier films in the Archive, of Macedonian refugee camps and Greek refugees leaving Turkey in 1913, had already registered the pull of Europe's future of forced migrations, mass annihilation, and ethnic cleansing. Viewed on the slope of this temporal slide, Aupiais' nascent expressions of cultural reciprocity and Sauvageot's films of anticolonial storytellers may hint at the inevitability of autonomy and self-representation for France's external Others.[119] But another fate was being planned for France's internal Others, foreign as well as French Jews. Similarly, while the swan song of Bergsonian philosophy—*The Two Sources of Morality and Religion* (1932)—ends by invoking the battered spirit of the League of Nations as an avatar of a future in which hostility between nations would give way to universal brotherhood, in Fascist circles variants of vitalist philosophy were being appropriated to destroy that dream.

The quest for racial and biological "purity" in both French and German nationalist enterprises also conspired to reinvigorate the practice of archiving in a manner that must have forced an incredulous Kahn to glimpse the horrors (that his own Archive had tried to oppose) of the near future. Even taking into consideration the relevance of a conservative ethnic element in Brunhes' rural-focused typologies, we must distinguish the Kahn Archive from the state-sanctioned ethnographic surveying that was established in postwar Germany. This latter revitalized classificatory drive came to a head in the expanded function of the archive's racist uses in National Socialist Germany in the form of "a systematic ethnographic and racial archive" that resulted in the sort of statement made by one archival administrator in

1936: "There is no racial politics without archives, without archivists."[120] Just two
months before the death of that other European archivist, Albert Kahn, the Nazi
ordinance of September 21, 1940, demanded all Jews identify themselves to police
stations. Although it is not known if Kahn presented himself, we do know Bergson
was granted but refused exemption, insisting on lining up at the Paris Prefecture of
Police to register as a Jew just a couple of months before his own death.[121] Beginning October 3, 1940, with the signing of Vichy's first Statut des Juifs by Marshal
Philippe Pétain, French civil servants began compiling for the Germans a census
of Jews in the Occupied Zone, using as their major tool a photographic-based archive, the infamous *fichier juif* card file.[122] The meticulously color-coded central-
ized archive proved an indispensable tool in the subsequent roundup, beginning
July 1942, of Jews for deportation to concentration camps and death.

CONCLUSION

_____

TOUTE LA MÉMOIRE DU MONDE:
COUNTER-ARCHIVAL TENDENCIES BEYOND KAHN

What will it look like, this culture that emerges from this new cinematographic deluge?

VICTOR PERROT (1953)[1]

[Fernand] Léger dreamed of a monster film which would have to record pains-takingly the life of a man and a woman during twenty-four consecutive hours: their work, their silence, their intimacy. Nothing should be omitted; nor should they ever be aware of the presence of the camera. "I think," he observed, "this would be so terrible a thing that people would run away horrified, calling for help as if caught in a world catastrophe." Léger is right. Such a film would not just portray a sample of everyday life but, in portraying it, dissolve the familiar contours of that life and expose what our conventional notions of it conceal from view—its widely ramified roots in crude existence. We might well shrink, panic-stricken, from these alien patterns which would denote our ties with nature and claim recognition as part of the world we live in and are.

SIEGFRIED KRACAUER (1960)[2]

SIEGFRIED KRACAUER'S RECOLLECTION of Fernand Léger's 1931 dream of a "monster film" in which every single moment of a day in the life of a couple would be recorded without their knowledge presents a dystopian version of the quest to archive everyday life that motivated Albert Kahn's Archives de la Planète.[3] This book has explored the two extremes of film's archival longing for the everyday as figured literally in the Archives de la Planète and conceptually in the discursive context engendering Léger's "monster film." At one extreme this desire expected to unite humanity through a multimedia visual inventory of daily life. At the other end of the scale it aimed to awaken humanity to a new everyday by forcing an intense visual confrontation with our "conventional" surroundings through film's capacity—via excessive, indeterminate, and "alien" evidence—to "dissolve the familiar contours" of life and make us question our ties to "the world we live in and are." Neither Kahn's utopian goal (derided by Henri Langlois in the late 1930s as a "World Memory [*Mémoires du Monde*]" docu-fantasy) nor Léger's horrifying nightmare of a cinematic surveillance that sees all and forgets nothing was fully realized during the interwar period.[4]

To be sure, these two examples hardly exhaust the cinematic archival imaginary during this period, which Kracauer himself contributed to, most explicitly in his metaphorical references to the "giant film" of historicism and the "central archive" of modern media in the "Photography" essay from 1927.[5] Film's ability to capture the terrain of life we usually "conceal from view"—the unremarkable space and time of "work," "silence," and "intimacy"—had elicited both wonder and dread since the beginning of cinema and well into the thirties. Léger's vision of film-as-invisible-surveillance (so manifestly different from the overt shooting style that dominates early nonfiction film) was echoed in László Moholy-Nagy's reference in 1925 to another "unnerving" film, this one made of "a man daily from birth to his death."[6] Meanwhile, those other utopians, Dziga Vertov and Jean Vigo, who were trying to live rather than simply dream this cinematic imaginary, took a different approach by promoting the critical potential of the hidden camera as the key to unmasking the social façades of everyday life.

Like the above utopian filmmakers, Kahn the utopian archivist was intimately acquainted with failure. But instead of emphasizing the unsuccessful fate of his project, my investigation of the Archives de la Planète has sought to contribute to what Thomas Elsaesser has called an "archaeology of all the possible futures of the cinema" by finding within those projects that "failed" new perspectives—such as the counter-archival tendencies in film—on those which prevailed.[7] I have, therefore, been less interested in showing how the Kahn Archive fell short of the nineteenth-century fantasy of archiving the planet than in teasing out how it manifested the evolution of that dream under the specific pressures of twentieth-century modernity, including the perception and experience of accelerated time, the proliferation of technologies capable of managing and manipulating that acceleration, and most importantly, the reconfiguration of the concept, technologies, and ideal object of the archive (itself a spatial technology for managing time). In order to illuminate the imprint of these and other pressures of modernity, I have read the Archives de la Planète as an intermediary experiment involving Bergsonian philosophy, on the one hand, and the interwoven destinies of human geography, Annales historiography, early film theory, and colonial ideology, on the other. At the heart of this experiment lay the possibilities and limits of film's affinity with daily life and the archive.

The tentative and unfinished nature of the Archives de la Planète reflects its status as a transitional project that looked back to the eighteenth and nineteenth centuries while embarking on a discovery of the twentieth. If Kahn's Archive inherited the Encyclopedists' desire for totalizing knowledge, it also operated in the colonial tradition of the adventurer-geographer's mission to map and conquer the infinite variety of the world. At an ideological level, Kahn's project brought together the neocolonialism of the Treaty of Versailles with a secularized messianism and then filtered both into a vision of history as the sum of a culture's neglected fragments and a universalist perception of cinema as the new *visual Esperanto*. Standing somewhere near, although never quite in the center of these historical eddies was Kahn himself, a sort of Captain Nemo with a camera, caught between shunning the world and furtively storing it in rows of shelves hidden within a semi-secret garden on his Boulogne property. As much as the Archives de la Planète represents a major discursive shift in the conception of modern memory and history, I have also suggested that Kahn's obsessive collecting must be read in-between the historic bookends of individual and collective loss—of Alsace Lorraine in the Franco-Prussian War, of his personal fortune in 1929, and of the attempted historical effacement of French Jewry after 1940. That the administrative path leading to the Holocaust was paved with archives, while its aftermath has given rise to a "massive archive of survivor accounts that is without precedent," speaks tragically to the shifting fate of the archive in the twentieth century as a site for the destruction and preservation of memory.[8]

At the theoretical level, this book has also claimed that the 1920s marked a watershed moment in the theorization of the everyday, particularly within the domain of French film criticism and from the perspective of its belated impact upon realist film theory. For Louis Delluc the medium's radical departure from other art forms meant that film could not be reduced to the median term between art's traditional extremes of "stylization and transient reality."[9] Instead of striking a compromise between aesthetic permanence and impermanence, film, for Delluc, actually adopted a new object, "life itself." Film's affinity for life, however, was cast in a post-positivist form, moving beyond the imitation of life to the transformed nature of everyday life. Rather than simply applying Bergsonian vitalism to film, I have understood Delluc's equation of film with life to refer to the medium's unique purchase upon the experiential and material specificity of modern everyday life. This reading depends on my claim that Bergson's philosophy and its uptake in French film criticism leaves room for the interpenetration of habit (the "any moment" and the "privileged moment") and duration (nonutilitarian vision and memory, nonchronological temporal multiplicity). Far from dying out by the end of the decade, the early French film critics' explorations of film's intermingling of habit and duration would find another outlet in the so-called realist film theory of Bazin and Kracauer.

Given the intensity of the discourse on film and the everyday during the 1920s, it is not surprising that the decade marked a repressed if not entirely forgotten period for France's preeminent theorist of the everyday, Henri Lefebvre. Then a member of the radical Philosophes group, Lefebvre was known to parade a tortoise named "Creative Evolution" around on a leash at the Sorbonne in defiant mockery of Bergson's still powerful if soon-to-be loosened grip on French institutions of learning.[10] This was also the period when Lefebvre had a brief but crucial fling with surrealism through his friendship with Tristan Tzara, whose understanding of the everyday he later attacked in the first volume of his *Critique de la vie quotidienne* (1947). However, as the Lefebvre of the 1960s would finally concede, it was the surrealists and dadaists who most strongly displayed the anarchic dimension within the widespread impulse to archive everyday life in the 1920s, a rediscovery that made possible his own eventual conjoining of "critical utopianism with the analysis of everyday life."[11] Moreover, the 1920s also came back to haunt Lefebvre forty years later in the form of his subtle rapprochement with Bergson, which augured a return to the outmoded philosopher that became more explicit in work from the 1970s by Michel Foucault, Gilles Deleuze, and Félix Guattari.[12]

But it was Deleuze alone who claimed that film had a central role to play in this return to Bergson. My history of the Archives de la Planète thus provides a vital annex to Deleuze's theories because the Archive was conjured not only in proximity to Bergson the man but under the influence of a profound Bergsonian-related critique of positivism. If the Kahn Archive was indebted to scientific rationalism and an abiding faith in an educated elite and the forces of progress, it was also attracted to the mystical, creative, and experimental edges of positivism traveled by Bergson. Without Bergson, we cannot truly understand how Kahn built his Archive over the then-recent ruins of the epistemological, mnemonic, and technological concept of the archive, or how the Archives de la Planète acquired the overreaching status of a baroque version of the archive.

If there is a counter-archival potential in all archives, that tendency was magnified in the Kahn Archive by the provocation to positivist order posed by film. The concept of the archive that Kahn's project challenged was also actively confronted between the wars by avant-garde movements, the Annales school of history, and various cultural and sociological surveys, within and beyond France. This period witnessed an explosion of interest in collecting and cataloguing the facts and fragments of ordinary culture, what Kracauer, in his own "sociological archive" from that period, called "the dust of everyday existence."[13] This archival impulse appears in projects as different as Marcel Duchamp's ready-mades; the New Objectivity photographic movement in Germany; the photographic inventory of everyday Paris shot by the Séeberger brothers for Hollywood set designers in the late twenties; Georges Bataille's ethno-surrealist magazine, *Documents*; the U.S. Farm Security Administration's photographic archiving; and that nationwide, pseudo-scientific anthropology of the interior that fed the archival gargantuan of Britian's Mass Observation movement. Such projects reveal how Kahn's vision of looking for history where one does not always "expect" it, as Boleslas Matuszewski had put it in 1898, had really just begun by the time the Archive closed its ledger books in the early 1930s.

Positioned alongside these alternative archivists of the everyday, Kahn's films reveal an unexpected connection to the surrealists' multifaceted attack upon the core epistemological unit of the archive: the "document." Kahn's cameramen, the surrealists, and the first generation of French film collectors—all of them unofficial archivists of the present—constructed a story of modern Paris told from the margins, in the anecdotal, uncatalogued or forgotten documents to be made of or found in the city. Aside from the flea markets, one of the most frequented of those marginal spaces were the nineteenth-century arcades (also photographed by Kahn's autochromists). Iron and glass counter-archives of modernity, the arcades provided a *frisson* from the recent past as Louis Aragon testified to in *Paris Peasant* (1926), just as many of them were being threatened with destruction by the completion of the Boulevard Haussmann (filmed in detail by Kahn's cameramen). The endangered older arcades like the Passage de l'Opéra (where Bergson sent Kahn to find a fencing master) became the focus of one of the most elaborate instances of a counter-archival form, Walter Benjamin's intentionally fragmented and dreamlike history of modern Paris, *The Arcades Project*.[14] A textual montage of citations, commentary, and images, Benjamin's unfinished counter-positivist history was collected mostly from Paris's Bibliothèque Nationale, that institution which in 1910 had denied Guillaume Apollinaire's curiosity in film. Ironically, the same institution two decades later indirectly supported the *Arcades Project* as a work heavily influenced by the idea of film as a counter-archival technology, one capable of recording *and* reordering the given configuration of social reality, producing a mosaic-like assemblage that would "carry the montage principle over into history."[15] While this book has partially aligned Kahn's films (with their predominantly non-edited, non-narrative, and durational form) with an anti-modernist refusal of montage, it has also disclosed the radical implications of an aesthetic of temporal continuity. Additionally, it has recognized that the future-oriented pull acting upon Kahn's mass of dormant and disordered film fragments inevitably solicits the discontinuous methodology of montage for their awakening from archival slumber.

Beyond its affinities with the above alternative archival obsessions, the Kahn project was buttressed by an equally important geographical commitment to the everyday that also made its presence felt in film theory and documentary film practice. The camera's attraction to what Brunhes called the earth's "epidermis" reappeared in Kracauer's claim in *Theory of Film* that the medium's representational uniqueness lies in its depiction of a reality that "cling[s] to the epidermis of things" (206). In a sentence that brings together three of the central topoi of Brunhes' human geography—the face, the street, and the house—and which might have been penned by the geographer, Kracauer presents a portrait of an urban-human landscape patterned by the interpenetration of matter and human: "intimate faces, streets we walk day by day, the house we live in—all these things are part of us like our skin, and because we know them by heart we do not know them with the eye" (53). Once again, the camera is offered as the means of capturing that which normally "escape[s] our attention in everyday life" (53). For Kracauer, as for Brunhes, it was the camera's ties to the familiar and the immediate (or what Bazin—another film theorist indebted to geographical, scientific, and Bergsonian categories—would call the "*continuum* of reality") that heralded the discovery of a new topography of the everyday.[16] Furthermore, this discovery was also motivated, for Kracauer, by a certain cosmopolitan drive. He found in films, particularly those which "explore the texture of everyday life" across the myriad milieux of "place, people, and time," the means by which cinema could "virtually make the world our home" (304). To be sure, such a statement was intended to redeem the borderless imperialism of early cinema's track with geography. Yet it also harbors an impulse to wrest a more local and humble world from other-worldliness, to inhabit the home-made-of-film that Kahn's Archive yearned for in so many ways.

Regarding the future of documentary film beyond the Kahn Archive, one could argue that human geography remained the guiding discipline for all documentaries focused on the relationship between people and their environment. There were both negative and positive responses to this geo-humanist influence in French documentary film. One of the most explicit incorporations of human geography from the interwar period—Luis Buñuel's *Las Hurdes*, a 1933 ethno-surrealist film about Spain's minority Hurdanos community which was based in part on the anthropo-geographical work of the French geographer Maurice Legendre—questioned the ethical dilemma of documentary film's ethnographic instincts. Where Buñuel critically mimicked the conventions of fieldwork, exhaustive description, and humanistic empathy that underpinned anthropo-geographical scientific inquiry, Bazin invoked human geography more sympathetically in the next decade as the explicit descriptor for the humanist commonality between *Farrebique* (Georges Rouquier, 1946) and *La Terra Trema* (Luchino Visconti, 1948).[17] Alternatively, it was clearly the *radically* naturalist, non-anthropocentric potential within human geography that resurfaced (with echoes of Louis Delluc) in Bazin's praise for the aesthetic of Italian neorealism as one in which "[m]an himself is just one fact amongst others."[18]

If both the conservative and radical dimensions of human geography continued to influence the practice and theory of French documentary filmmaking, a new direction emerged in the postwar years due to the intensified creative preoccupation with the counter-archival potential of old footage. Alongside his better-known theories of media ontology and neorealist aesthetics, Bazin explored the counter-archival qualities of film often in response to diverse nonfiction form (newsreels, amateur, compilation, and scientific films). Bazin argued that film's potential subversion of positivist evidence was magnified by filmmakers' exposure to what Victor Perrot (in an article from 1953) described as the unprecedented "cinematographic deluge" of the contemporary mediascape. On the one hand, this situation brought about for Bazin (as it had for Kracauer in 1927) the nightmarish prospect of "total history" glimpsed in the newsreels' endless chronicle of events.[19] On the other hand, Bazin repositioned film's archival potential in a more positive light with his regular references to another "dream," that of the Italian screenwriter Cesare Zavattini—"to make a ninety-minute film of the life of a man to whom nothing ever happens"—as the ideal of cinema's essential duty to the "continuum of reality." And yet, fulfilling Léger's predictions, Bazin still ran in horror from that ideal's apotheosis—the "filmic monster" (as Bazin called it in an uncanny repetition of Léger's characterization) of exhaustive continuity conjured by Visconti's proposed trilogy of films beginning with *La Terra Trema*.[20]

Bazin's flight was not, however, representative of an unequivocal rejection of film's counter-archival qualities. He had, after all, already championed a more sympathetic version of film's horrors in Nicole Védrès' "monstrously beautiful" compilation film *Paris 1900*.[21] Watching Védrès' reassemblage of old fiction and nonfiction film in 1947, he found himself reacting positively to film's spatio-temporal blanketing of history when he argued that old footage rehabilitated from archives had the potential to reveal the "tear" (242) in film's otherwise seamless historicist fabric. For Bazin, it is this tear that unstitches the archival image's ties to positivist objective history, which in turn allows the "specifically cinematographic tragedy"—the medium's Janus-faced identity as "a machine for regaining time all the better to lose it"—to be fully exposed and experienced.[22] Although I understand that Bazin's tear may have been more severe in the midcentury, given (to appropriate Léger's words) the "world catastrophe" of the Second World War, I have argued in this book that the tragic split (alluded to in my introduction) from which it emerges and the shudders that it aroused were already visible in the first decades of cinema.

In addition to rethinking the status of the everyday, geography, and the archive in film history and theory, this book has reclaimed Bergsonism as a foundational context for the evolution of early French film criticism and as a belated influence upon realist film theory, particularly at its counter-archival, anti-positivist, and counter-representational edges. Given the swiftness with which Bergson became unfashionable in the interwar years, one can understand why the at times quasi-mystical musings of the Bergsonian-influenced early French film theorists were hastily cast aside. Yet these early Bergsonian affinities clearly reemerged in the work of Bazin and Kracauer. The championing of "concrete duration" that underpins Bazin's defense of Italian neorealism returns us to probably the most extensive and provocative attempt to reconcile the cinema with Bergsonism before Deleuze.[23] Indicative of his adaptive appropriation of Bergsonism, Bazin celebrated and reclaimed what Bergson deplored, film's ability to carve time and "the event up into still smaller events and these into events smaller still, to the extreme limits of our capacity to perceive them in time" as the essence of Italian neorealism's identity as "a cinema of 'duration.'"[24] And of particular interest to this book's concerns is that Bazin's Bergsonian provocation issues from his alignment of cinematic duration with a newly eventful everyday. As Bazin argued, "it is a matter of making 'life time'—the simple continuing to be of a person to whom nothing in particular happens—take on the quality of a spectacle, of a drama."[25]

As for Kracauer, his direct indebtedness to the vitalism of Georg Simmel, if not Bergson, accounts for the dominant refrain of *Theory of Film*, that film has a particular affinity with a "flow of life" rendition of the everyday.[26] In addition, Kracauer invokes his film-skin metaphor using a Bergsonian vocabulary of the everyday. Much like the skin we live in, the faces, streets, and houses of our familiar environment are invisible to us because they inhabit "the blind spots of the mind" that "habit" (53) prevents us from seeing, but that the film camera forces us to confront. The confrontational nature of film's affinity with the everyday was critical for Kracauer. Opposing the cliché that film offered an escape from the everyday, Kracauer held that at its deepest film could, in fact, bring us face to face with that which the everyday denied, namely death. Its ability to make "visible what is commonly drowned in inner agitation" (58) turned the body of reality inside out, exposing the normally interior pulse of *durée* to the cold assessment of *la vie extérieure*. Reinvoking the enlarged, non-habitual sense of vision that Bergsonism bequeathed to early French film theory, Kracauer argues that film "keeps us from shutting our eyes to the 'blind drive of things'" (58), changing us from passive spectators to active witnesses of reality's autopsy. Running through the lingering Bergsonism of Kracauer's (and perhaps even more so Bazin's) film theory is that set of tensions that also joined the Kahn Archive to the dominant themes of early French film theory—those between photography and film, stasis and mobility, death and life, order and unpredictability.

These tensions also speak to how the Archives de la Planète anticipates a pervasive theme of modern and postmodern twentieth-century art—the questioning of the archive as a mode of collecting, sorting, and storing the vastness of all the world's (visual) memory. Although it existed outside the context of modern art, Kahn's Archive is directly related to that field through its counter-archival experimentation. As a cipher for issues of repetition, encyclopedism, juxtaposition, and official and unofficial memory, the archive has become an unexpected muse of twentieth-century art and art history, from the document context of Eugène Atget's photographic archiving of Paris and the transhistorical montage of Aby Warburg's *Picture Atlas*, to the inventorial logic of Robert Rauschenberg's silkscreen series and the collecting mania of Christian Boltanski's and Susan Hiller's installations.[27] The affinities between Kahn's Archive and this general archival obsession in twentieth-century art are numerous. In August Sander's photographic series from the 1920s of Germans posed formally in their everyday milieux, we see the same detailed anthropological attention to man and his everyday environment that dominates the Kahn autochrome and film collection; in Gerhard Richter's catalogue of "Illustrious Men," as in his more famous *Atlas*, an ongoing encyclopedic work of approximately 4,000 photographs, ranging from found amateur photographs to journalistic and advertising photography, we see the same devotion to the unedited and anonymous document of everyday life and the same tendency toward an orderly but open-ended collection; and in Andy Warhol's "time-capsule," just one of six hundred boxes of junk the artist obsessively hoarded and filed away during his life, we see a similar (albeit ironic) faith in the future value of the previously undervalued.

Although it was a one-of-a-kind experiment in archival film production, the Archives de la Planète also anticipates diverse directions that "post-archival" filmmaking has taken since the Second World War. For a wide range of filmmakers the archive has become a literal site of investigation itself—from Alain Resnais' *Toute la Mémoire du monde* (1956), an essayistic rumination upon the wisdom and folly of global memory as figured in a mock industrial documentary of Paris's Bibliothèque Nationale, to Bill Morrison's *Film of Her* (1996), a creative archaeology of the erotics underpinning the Library of Congress's paper print collection, and Uriel Orlow's *Inside the Archive* (2000–2006), a video installation exploring the interpenetration of the present and the past and space and time through the world's oldest Holocaust archive, London's Wiener Library. The archive has also become a methodological inspiration for experimental film practice (from Resnais' *Nuit et brouillard* [1955] to the more recent autobiographically inflected multimedia collage-archives of Jonas Mekas, Chantal Akerman, and Chris Marker) and a fecund material and conceptual source for diverse appropriations of used, found, orphaned, stolen, or faked footage.

The attraction of an archival paradigm for rethinking film practice, theory, and history has increased substantially in the past two decades. This is due to a number of interrelated developments: the evolution of digital technologies with their promise of infinite storage, ease of manipulability, reproduction, access, and borderless distribution; the heightened attention to preservation and access in national and "minor" audiovisual archives around the world; the renaissance in early cinema studies; and the intensification (to the point perhaps of normalization) of avant-garde and experimental film praxis based on the reemployment of "archival" images. Of course, the repurposing of either found or famous footage has been a mainstay of diverse modes of film practice throughout the twentieth century, from Esther Shub and Jospeh Cornell to Ken Jacobs, Hollis Frampton, Morgan Fisher, Bruce Connor, Abigail Child, Chick Strand, and Peter Tscherkassky, to name a few. But an even more self-conscious relation to that global cinematic archive referred to in Kracauer's "blizzard," Langlois' "*Mémoire du Monde*," and Perrot's "deluge" appears in a range of more recent intentionally subversive invasions into the archive (either literally, symbolically, or conceptually). This work is internationally diverse, and includes film, video, digital, and installation artists as different as Yervant Gianikian and Angela Ricci Lucchi, Péter Forgács, Barbara Lattanzi, Joana Hadjithomas and Khalil Joreige, and Uriel Orlow, as well as distinct methodological approaches, from the invented archives and/or archive searches of Cheryl Dunye, Marlon Fuentes, Waalid Raad, Luis Ospina, and Gregorio Rocha, to the reappropriation of literal archival images in the work of Harun Farocki, Daniel Eisenberg, Gustav Deutsch, Peter Delpeut, and Bill Morrison. Differences aside, this broad archival turn in moving-image practice reflects a fixation with picking at the frayed edges of Bazin's tear, resulting in the reinvention of the archival film tradition beyond its positivist tendencies. All of these artists aim consciously to puncture the aesthetic, formal, and ideological surfaces of and separations between nonfiction and fiction film, the past and the present, collective and personal memory with the aid of a critical gaze sharpened by a retrospective awareness of the political unconscious *and* creative potential of the archive as it once was and is now being reinvented.[28] No longer unwelcome poachers of the archive's secrets, artists of diverse media are now more often invited curatorial collaborators in the archive's remaking. Interestingly, the Kahn Archive has not yet opened its film reels to artists' desires. In this regard, *Counter-Archive* has been intended as a textual harbinger of the inevitable visual remaking of the Kahn Archive, whose appropriation is only a matter of time.

Ironically, as attempts by artists and scholars to reuse the often forgotten history of film imply a deconstruction of the historicist methodologies of the nineteenth-century archive, one of the most important developments in official history in late-twentieth-century France sought to abandon the archive (print as well as film) altogether. In his promotion of a history based on symbolic monuments rather than monumental documents, the third-generation Annales historian Pierre Nora excluded an analysis of film—central, in my opinion, to any understanding of modern France—from the past half-century's most epic excavation of French memory, the multivolume *Lieux de mémoire* [*Realms of Memory*].[29] In the introduction to that well-known project, itself worthy of the title *lieu de mémoire*, Nora made a distinction between two types of remembering that he explicitly traces back to the Bergsonian mnemonic crisis: a modern and impoverished memory which tends to reside in sites or places that he names the *lieux de mémoire* and, on the other hand, the *milieux de mémoire*, the collective and embodied, immediate and spontaneous lived experience of memory within a tradition-bound community that modern memory had all but replaced.[30]

For Nora, the major offence committed by modern memory, particularly flaunted in its enshrinement in professional history of the late nineteenth century, is that it is "first of all archival" (8). In permanent exile from the "settings in which memory is a real part of everyday experience" (1) and cut off from the ties that bind (as connoted by that Vidalian-loaded word *milieu*), modern archival memory "relies entirely on the specificity of the trace, the materiality of the vestige, the concreteness of the recording, the visibility of the image" (8). Invoking a negative version of the film-skin metaphor, Nora writes that archival memory resembles "a thin film of current events" (2). It is so enslaved to the "sifting and sorting" (2) of empiricist traces that it is never actually free to remember. Individualist and compensatory, mediated and distanced, modern voluntary memory emerged, for Nora, in reaction to the loss of memory in history (2). Just as the science of archives got under way with the rise of professional history and the development of more advanced techniques for recording, storing, organizing, and distributing documents, the pressure to forget and the impossibility of remembering increased. Due to this inversion of the traditional order ("The less memory is experienced from within the greater the need for external props" [8]), Nora argues historians relocated and found their alternative archive, not in written documents where events are studied but in symbolic monuments where sites are studied between living memory and dead history.

Nora's archival complaint of the more recent fin-de-siècle was, of course, nothing new. In it we hear echoes of Baudelaire, Bergson, Bloch, Kracauer, and Braudel's reservations about the voluntary nature of the conventional archive and modern media. Nora's archival complaint also helps us to recognize the Archives de la Planète as an exemplary compensatory monument, or *lieu de mémoire*, to the early-twentieth-century memory crisis. At the same time, far from falling prey to Nora's dead-end judgments regarding modern archival memory, I have argued that film reformulated a counter-archival memory due largely to its affinity with, rather than alienation from, everyday life. If, as compensatory reactions to the loss of immediate embodied memory and the inadequacies of positivist history, all *lieux de mémoire* are built from the ruins of archival memory, then film was always counter-archival. It may have promised a new superior archival age, but it delivered a profound challenge to—without entirely overthrowing—traditional archival logic.

Nora, of course, was reacting to the archive glut of the late twentieth century in which official record depositories often welcome not only filmic and audiovisual documents but those belonging to any entity, no matter how insignificant. To Nora's mind, the late-twentieth-century archive is indulgent, excessively inclusive, dangerously private, and, from the perspective of someone wanting to rejuvenate national history, internally divisive. By implication, part of the danger of the contemporary archive is its everyday omnipresence. For others, such as the filmmakers mentioned above, the condition that most concerns Nora—to each person a statelike archive or, to each filmmaker *toute la mémoire du monde*—has been embraced in a more experimentally positive light.

Whether viewed from the perspective of the archivist or artist, the historian or culture jammer, the institution or the individual, the meaning of the archive is undoubtedly once again in flux. The real question, however, remains the extent to which the new media's archival obsessions with the everyday offer opportunities for different forms of counter-archival memory. Looking back from our own period of archival utopia characterized by the Internet's realization of Kahn's attempts to build multimedia global information networks, we should recall that Kahn was warehousing the present in a period of archival rarity, prestige, and deficit; a period, in fact, before the era if not the dream of a film archive. Unlike Kahn's, our near post-celluloid horizon is no longer best described by the prediction of "No more archives. Only films," but rather by that of "No more films. Only archives." Following Nora and the new access-for-all reinvention of major state archives, we might also notice that in those archives there are no more historians, only artists. Amidst the digital turn to immaterial databases and the accelerated flows of transnational information and images, the quest to collect and preserve not just the past but the refuse of the present has lost none of its attraction although perhaps some of its historical urgency. After all, Kracauer's media "blizzard" fades in comparison to the instantly renewable deluge of today's audiovisual mediascape. From the bottom-up and top-down knowledge and surveillance utopias of Wikipedia, Google Books, and Google Earth, and the personal auto-archiving of Facebook and MySpace, to the infinite preservation of ephemeral cultures in YouTube, the Way Back Machine, eBay, and the Internet Archive—all of them, in their own way, archives of the planet—it may seem that nothing need ever be lost, or forgotten, again. No object, image, document, thought, or feeling need ever remain unarchived. And yet, access and loss, not to mention willful destruction, still represent avenues of political control; selection and choice are still indispensable to any encounter with the global archive. Forgetting (in both its repressive and productive senses) is just as crucial as it ever was to the practical management of remembering in an age of mnemonic instantaneity and overload.

In keeping with the trend for immediate access, the Musée Albert-Kahn has recently installed an entirely digital viewing facility for visitors interested in the autochromes and films. Quite different from the previous analog setup, today one can instantly sift and sort through the visual records and a wealth of contextual information in the new multiscreen viewing stations, now safely protected from the distracting foliage beyond by a separating wall that displays behind glass a selection of the original autochrome boxes. Finally, perhaps the Archives de la Planète has acquired the status of a traditional archive. Yet, while cleaned of the clutter of history, Kahn's Archive continues to collect the digital dust of the everyday.

APPENDIX

Cameramen and photographers who worked for the Archives de la Planète

CAMERAMEN

LE SAINT, LUCIEN (1881–1931): *ADLP*, 1918–1923 (France, Lebanon, Syria, Turkey, Austria, Belgium, Germany, Switzerland, Newfoundland). He worked as a newsreel cameraman before 1914 for Gaumont, from May 1917 to March 1918 for the Service Cinématographique de l' Armée, and from 1925 to 1929 for Pathé-News.

SAUVAGEOT, CAMILLE: *ADLP*, 1919–1932 (France, Poland, Belgium, Turkey, Malta, Monaco, Germany, Egypt, Switzerland, Italy, Morocco). He also served as the color cameraman for Jacques Tati's *Jour de fête* (1946).

THIBAUD(T): *ADLP*, 1919–1931 (mainly France). He was essentially a printer in the photographic laboratory on the Boulogne property.

CAMERAMEN AND PHOTOGRAPHERS

BUSY, LÉON (1874–?): *ADLP*, 1914–1920 (Ceylon, Egypt, Djibouti, Tonkin, Vietnam, France, Greece, Turkey, Bulgaria). He was a colonial official and an accomplished amateur photographer (even receiving recognition from the Société française de photographie). Wanting to contribute to the *ADLP*, he contacted Jean Brunhes directly.

DUMAS, ROGER (1891–1972): *ADLP*, 1920–1931 (France, Italy, England, Switzerland, Japan, India, Germany). Began as a portraitist and photographic colorist.

In 1937 he perfected a color film process with Georges Grosset and Roger Marx called Dugromacolor which was put on the market in 1949 without success.

GADMER, FRÉDÉRIC: *ADLP*, 1919–1932 (Syria, France, Switzerland, Belgium, Turkey, Thrace, Prussia, Germany, Canada, Iran, Iraq, Afghanistan, Algeria, Holland, Dahomey, Tunisia).

PASSET, STÉPHANE: *ADLP*, 1912–1919, 1929–1930 (China, Mongolia, France, Turkey, Morocco, Greece, Bulgaria, India, Holland).

OCCASIONAL CAMERAMEN AND PHOTOGRAPHERS

CASTELNAU, PAUL (?–1944): Geographer and photographer. Worked for the Service Cinématographique de l'Armée during the war and for Kahn from 1917 to 1919. Participated in the Citroën-sponsored expeditions filmed in *La Traversée du Sahara en autochenilles* (1923) and *La Croisière noire* (Léon Poirier, 1925).

CHASTENET, GEORGES AND BERNARDEL: Contributed to the Archive's war documentation between 1915 and 1917.

DUTERTRE, ALBERT: Cameraman, photographer, and chauffeur, 1908–1909. Worked for the Service Cinématographique de l'Armée, January to July 1919.

GERVAIS-COURTELLEMONT, JULES: Autochromist and well-known orientalist. 1909–1910. (Algeria, Tunisia).

MIGNON, MADELEINE AND MARGUERITE MESPOULET: Teachers and recipients of the Autour du Monde travel grant who took a series of autochromes during their trip to Ireland between May and June, 1913.

NOTES

INTRODUCTION

1. Kracauer, "Photography," 62–63.
2. Bazin, "*Paris 1900*," 242. All translations from the French are my own unless otherwise noted.
3. Ibid.
4. I use the capitalized Archive throughout the book to refer to the Archives de la Planète and lowercase *archive* to refer to archives in general.
5. See cover of this book for an image of the original autochrome boxes.
6. Matuszewski, "Une Nouvelle Source de l'histoire" (Apr. 1898). Matuszewski also published a slightly different version of the pamphlet in March 1898. Hereafter, all page references in the text to this pamphlet refer to the April 1898 original unless otherwise noted.
7. The reference to "anecdotal History" comes from the first version of the essay published in March 1898. See Matuszewski "Une Nouvelle Source de l'histoire" (Mar. 25, 1898), 11n1.
8. *Le Radical* (Dec. 30, 1895), cited in Jeanne and Ford, *Le Cinéma*, 14–15.
9. For a similar account in *La Poste* that focused on the camera's vitality ("It is life itself, it is movement captured as it happens") and in particular its ability to capture humans "in their movement, in their action, in their ordinary gestures" with such lifelike effects that "death will cease to be absolute," see Jeanne and Ford, *Le Cinéma*, 15.
10. For this definition of poetic realism's aesthetic, see Andrew, *Mists of Regret*, 20.
11. Vertov, "Kino-Eye," 71; and Breton, "Manifesto of Surrealism," 9.
12. After Kahn's financial ruin in 1936 the Département de la Seine took over his collection and his vast Boulogne property, which is still managed today by the Département des Hauts-de-Seine as the Musée Albert-Kahn (MAK).

13. For information on Kahn's cameramen and photographers, see the appendix.

14. Although no original and complete filmography of the Archive exists, extant original textual documentation concerning the films includes a film projection register; production ledger books; film development slips; and for the autochrome collection an autochrome ledger book. For further details on these textual supplements, see Le Bris, "De l'Image," and Hervé, "Exposition d'une collection." The Archive also contains a smaller amount of films presumably edited by the cameramen from the rushes, films bought from Gaumont and Pathé by Kahn to supplement his stock, and edited films recently produced by the MAK from the rushes for exhibition purposes. See *Panorama des collections Albert Kahn*, 8.

15. Though the museum has regular exhibitions based on the autochrome collection, the films are less frequently projected. For the proceedings of the first and only conference devoted to Kahn's films (held in December 2000 at the Institut Jean Vigo in Perpignan, France), including my essay "Archives ou contre-archives?," see *Les Cahiers de la cinémathèque: Revue d'histoire du cinéma* 74 (Dec. 2002). For my other publications on the Archive, see my essays in *Film History* 13.2 (2001) and in Ruoff, ed., *Virtual Voyages*. Continuing the historical neglect of Kahn's film, the 2007 BBC documentary on Kahn focused primarily on the autochromes.

16. For works that reference or explore Kahn's project, see Sadoul, *Histoire générale du cinéma* 2:402; Borde, *Les Cinémathèques*, 37–38; Sorlin, *Le Fils de Nadar*, 186; Piault, *Anthropologie et cinéma*, 19–21; Rony, *The Third Eye*, 80–82; Ponte, "Archiving the Planet"; Gunning, "Before Documentary," 19–20; Rohdie, *Promised Lands*; Winter, *Dreams of Peace and Freedom*, 13–27; Bloom, *French Colonial Documentary*, 163–76; and Castro, "*Les Archives de la Planète*."

17. Kracauer, *History*, 199.

18. The phrase "treasures from the American film archives" is the title of a series of DVDs of restored films produced by the U.S National Film Preservation Foundation. On the term "orphan films," see Streible, "The Role of Orphan Films"; and on the term "unseen cinema," see Posner, *Unseen Cinema*.

19. For some of the recent work focused on these alternative forms of cinema, see Hertogs and De Klerk, eds., *Uncharted Territory*; Griffiths, *Wondrous Difference*; Toulmin, Popple, and Russell, eds., *The Lost World of Mitchell and Kenyon*; Peterson, *Education in the School of Dreams*; and Ishizuka and Zimmermann, eds., *Mining the Home Movie*.

20. Borges, "Museum: On Exactitude in Science," 325.

21. Unlike the Archives Nationales or the Bibliothèque Nationale, the Musée Albert-Kahn is not organized as an open research facility. As its name suggests, it is primarily a museum (to an archive), whose identity is also inextricably connected to its location in the original Kahn gardens. Given issues of access I cannot claim to have seen or read every visual or textual document pertaining to the Archive that exists in the MAK.

22. See Braudel, "History and the Social Sciences," 27.

23. Kracauer, *Theory of Film*, 304.

24. For the classic treatment of daily life in seventeenth-century Dutch painting, see Alpers, *The Art of Describing*; and for an overview of the important status of "the particularity of everyday life" in the eighteenth-century realist novel's shift from the collective to the individual, see S. Stewart, *On Longing*, 4.

25. Lefebvre, *Everyday Life in the Modern World*, 30.
26. See Simmel, "The Metropolis and Mental Life"; Lukács, *History and Class Consciousness*; Lefebvre, *Critique of Everyday Life*, vol. 1, and *Everyday Life in the Modern World*, 29.
27. See Sandberg, "Effigy and Narrative," and V. Schwartz, *Spectacular Realities*, 11.
28. Foucault, *Discipline and Punish*, 187–91.
29. For discussions of these three extraordinary-ordinary photographic or cinematic moments, see Rice, *Parisian Views*, 3–6; Gunning, "New Thresholds of Vision," 86–91; and Vaughn, "Let there be Lumière," 65.
30. See Delluc, "Beauty in the Cinema," 137.
31. Kracauer, *Theory of Film*, 7.
32. Rifkin, *Street Noises*, 67. For further examples of this rhetorical caution, see Langbauer, *Novels of Everyday Life*, 2; Highmore, ed., *The Everyday Life Reader*, 1; Margulies, *Nothing Happens*, 24; and Schilling, "Everyday Life," 23.
33. See Baudelaire, "The Painter of Modern Life," 403; Bergson, *Matter and Memory*, 80; and Malinowski, "Proper Conditions for Ethnographic Work," 143.
34. See Foucault, ed., *I, Pierre Rivière*, 203–207; Highmore, ed., *The Everyday Life Reader*, 3; and Margulies, *Nothing Happens*, 27.
35. Lefebvre, *Everyday Life in the Modern World*, 32.
36. See, among others, Kaplan and Ross, *Everyday Life* (Special Issue of *Yale French Studies* 73 [1987]); Auslander, *Taste and Power*, 1–28; Felski, "The Invention of Everyday Life"; Schilling, "Everyday Life"; and articles in *New Literary History* 33.4 (Autumn 2002) and *Cultural Studies* 18.2–3 (Mar.–May 2004).
37. Kracauer, *Theory of Film*, 72.
38. For works that redress the neglect of Kracauer, see Hansen, "Introduction," in Kracauer, *Theory of Film*, vii–xlv, and *The Other Frankfurt School*; and for Bazin, see P. Rosen, *Change Mummified*, 3–42, and Margulies, ed., *Rites of Realism*. For further revisions of the bias against realist film theory of particular significance due to their interest in 1920s French film criticism, see Ray, *How a Film Theory Got Lost*, 1–14, and Aitken, *European Film Theory and Cinema*, 2, 69–90, 162–202.
39. Among the many books that deal with the everyday dimensions of film exhibition and reception, see Koszarski, *An Evening's Entertainment*; Gomery, *Shared Pleasures*; and Waller, ed. *Moviegoing in America*.
40. For just some of the key works pertaining to the social experience of moviegoing in the first decades of the twentieth century, see Ewen, "City Lights"; Mayne, "Immigrants and Spectators"; Carbine, "'The Finest Outside the Loop'"; Hansen, *Babel and Babylon*; Rabinovitz, *For the Love of Pleasure*; Kuhn, *An Everyday Magic*; and J. Stewart, *Migrating to the Movies*. For exceptions to the relatively untheorized invocation of the everyday by film scholars, see Margulies, *Nothing Happens*, and Gaines, "Everyday Strangeness."
41. Friedberg, *Window Shopping*, 7. For an overview of work by Friedberg, Bruno, and Hansen that highlights their conception of film viewing "as a function of everyday life," within what she attributes to a "counterapparatus theory," see C. Russell, "Parallax Historiography," 555. For some of the key studies of early cinema from the perspective

of modernity, see work in my bibliography by Gunning and Hansen as well as Bruno, *Streetwalking on a Ruined Map*, and Friedberg, *Window Shopping*.

42. For her influential analysis of cinema in terms of a vernacular aesthetic, see Hansen, "The Mass Production of the Senses."

43. Amidst the vast body of work which treats everyday life as an essential component of Western and non-Western modernity, the nation-state, and/or colonialism, see B. Anderson, *Imagined Communities*; Bhabha, "DissemiNation: Time, Narrative, and the Margins of the Modern Nation"; Appadurai, *Modernity at Large*; Chakrabarty, *Provincializing Europe*; Stoller, *Race and the Education of Desire*; Harootunian, *History's Disquiet*; and Auslander, *Taste and Power*. For analyses that focus on the interpenetration of terror, torture, and the everyday, see Ross, *Fast Cars, Clean Bodies*, 71–122, and Ries, "Anthropology and the Everyday," who also offers a critique of the Eurocentric bias of theories of the everyday.

44. In bridging Kracauer's writings from the 1920s with those from the 1960s, I am building on Miriam Hansen's historicization of his work. See Hansen, "Introduction," in Kracauer, *Theory of Film*.

45. Kracauer, *Theory of Film*, 55.

46. Lefebvre, *Critique of Everyday Life*, 35 and *Everyday Life in the Modern World*, 16. Significantly, late in life Lefebvre acknowledged his own repressed debt to the intellectual context of the 1920s. See my "Conclusion" (this volume).

47. Kracauer, "Photography," 55.

48. See Dulac, "Cinema at the Service of History: The Role of Newsreels" (c. 1936).

49. See Bazin, "*Paris 1900*."

50. For the first phrase, see Fredric Jameson cited in Nichols, "Documentary Film and the Modernist Avant-Garde," 593–94; and for the second, see Vertov, "Kino-Eye," 66.

51. Foucault, "Of Other Spaces," 22.

52. See Foucault, *The Order of Things*, xix.

53. For a both personal and historiographical meditation upon the archive (and in particular the juridical Archives de la Bastille held at the Bibliothèque d'Arsenal in Paris) that was influenced by the work of her sometime collaborator Foucault, see Farge, *Le Goût de l'archive*; and for another intervention into archival theory from the perspective of the personal, see A. Kaplan, "Working in the Archives."

54. De Certeau, "L'Espace de l'archive ou la perversion du temps," 6; see also *The Writing of History*, 69–77.

55. Derrida theorized this supplementary condition of the psychoanalytic archive as the "*mal d'archive*" or "archive fever" which functions according to the destructive principles of the Freudian death drive. See Derrida, *Archive Fever*, 12.

56. For works that rely on Foucault for theorizing and historicizing the photographic archive and vision in general, see Tagg, *The Burden of Representation*; Sekula, "Reading an Archive" and "The Body and the Archive"; and Crary, *Techniques of the Observer*. For a historical overview of the archive and photography of the everyday, see J. Roberts, *The Art of Interruption*, esp. 72–97.

57. See Krauss, "Photography's Discursive Spaces," 298. And for a study that returns one of the classic bodies of modern photography, that of Eugène Atget, to its archival context,

while distancing itself from the more abstracted tendencies of Foucault's notion of the archive, "if only because it brushes over the specific little archives," see Nesbit, *Atget's Seven Albums*, 17.

58. See Steedman, *Dust: The Archive and Cultural History*. For critiques of the Foucauldian model for photographic theory, see Tagg, *The Burden of Representation*, 6–7, and Kember, "'The Shadow of the Object,'" 206–207.

59. Sekula, "Reading an Archive," 446. For an example of a book that incorporates the problem of the gaps in the early cinema archive in a theoretically creative manner, see Bruno, *Streetwalking on a Ruined Map*.

60. See Sekula, "The Body and the Archive," 16–18.

61. For use of the phrase "media fantasies," see Tsivian, "Media Fantasies and Penetrating Vision," 82.

62. For illuminating works that rely on a more abstract rather than material invocation of the archive in relation to film, see C. Russell, *Experimental Ethnography*, 238–72; Doane, *The Emergence of Cinematic Time*, 22–30, 82, 101–105, 220–23; and Lippit, *Atomic Light*, 1–34.

63. Derrida came closest to addressing the film archive in his 2001 interview with Antoine de Baecque and Thierry Jousse titled "Le Cinéma et ses fantômes."

64. See Kracauer, *Theory of Film*, 18–20.

65. Kracauer, *History*, 122. For a striking resemblance to Kracauer's big-small methodology, see Foucault "Nietzsche, Genealogy, History," 89.

66. Foucault, *Archaeology of Knowledge*, 123.

1. WORLD SOUVENIR: "MR. K" AND THE ARCHIVES DE LA PLANÈTE

1. Anon., "Echos et informations: Un musée du cinéma," *Le Journal du Ciné-Club* 38 (Oct. 1, 1920): 2. For detailed contextualizations of this journal, see C. Gauthier, *La Passion du cinéma*, 14–121, and Abel, ed., *French Film Theory* 1:195–223.

2. The interview with Kahn was conducted for an article in the journal *France-Japon*. See *Albert Kahn: Réalités d'une utopie, 1860–1940*, 62 (hereafter, *AK*).

3. Kracauer, *Theory of Film*, 304.

4. I will use the French word *oeuvre* to connote Kahn's works, not only because it was often used in contemporary accounts, but because its connotations extend beyond the aesthetic to an understanding of "works" as a person's deeds and undertakings.

5. Amidst the vast literature on the history of travel, much of it concerned with the ambivalences associated with its transformation in the modern period (broadly characterized in the oppositions between and within the pre-1850s concept of travel versus the post-1850s concept of tourism), see Urry, *The Tourist Gaze*; C. Kaplan, *Questions of Travel*; C. Williams, ed., *Travel Culture*; and Green, "The Comparative Gaze."

6. Kahn also appears in a group photo of Japanese and French businessmen taken in 1908 in which he literally struggles against having his face photographed. See Baud-Berthier, "Le Métier de la banque," 125. Kahn's reticence to draw attention to himself as the benefactor of so many different organizations should be understood in the context of

the Jewish tradition of anonymous philanthropy, in addition to being read as a survival tactic employed by many wealthy French Jews during this period. On this issue, see Jean-Brunhes Delamarre and Beausoleil, "Deux Témoins de leur temps," 98.

7. Nord, *The Republican Moment*, 245.

8. See Kahn, *Des Droits*.

9. See Coeuré and Monier, "De l'Ombre à la lumière."

10. Kahn's essential biographical data has been uncovered thanks to the work done by researchers at the Musée Albert-Kahn. Aside from *Albert Kahn: Réalités d'une utopie, 1860–1940*, other relevant works published by the museum include *Paris 1910–1931: Au travers des autochromes et des films de la Phototèque-cinémathèque Albert Kahn*; *Jean Brunhes: Autour du Monde, regards d'un géographe/regards de la géographie* (hereafter, *JB*); *Les Archives de la Planète*, vols. 1 and 2; and *Panorama des Collections Albert Kahn*.

11. The most comprehensive biographical account of Kahn appears in *AK*, 17–54 and 107–131.

12. Caron, *Between France and Germany*, 12–13.

13. Ibid., 10, 128.

14. Bloch quoted in Fink, *Marc Bloch*, 1.

15. For the origins to Kahn's fortunes and dealings in Japan, see *AK*, 106–131.

16. See *AK*, 62.

17. Nord, *The Republican Moment*, 65, 81, 86. An important element of this reconciliation between Jewish identity and French national identity was the revision of the messianic idea into a more universalist and secular mission concerned with the "spiritual redemption of all humankind" (Caron, *Between France and Germany*, 8). In this regard, one might align Kahn with secular messianism. For an analysis that does so, see Ory, "Albert Kahn dans l'histoire," 391 (see also ch. 5, note 99).

18. Fink uses this phrase to describe Marc Bloch's family. See Fink, *Marc Bloch*, 14. On Kahn's family and youth, see Beausoleil, "Les Années Marmoutier"; and on the difficult issue of how to interpret his family's decision to stay in Alsace once it had been annexed, see Naquet, "Au delà d'un Alsacien patriote." For more detailed histories of Alsatian Jews and their complicated relation to French national identity, see Caron, *Between France and Germany*, and Hyman, *The Emancipation of the Jews of Alsace*.

19. The Vosgean forest was nearly entirely decimated in the December 1999 storms that hit Paris.

20. Kahn quoted in Thein, "Un Jardin japonais à Paris," 383.

21. Kahn quoted in ibid.

22. Unless noted otherwise, the following testimonies come from the film *L'Héritage d'Albert Kahn* (René-Jean Bouyer, 1978); Petit, "Le Premier Élève de Bergson"; and the CD-ROM *Albert Kahn et le Japon, Confluences*. For the most concentrated collection of portraits of Kahn, see the testimonies published on the occasion of the twenty-fifth anniversary of the Société Autour du Monde in *Bulletin de la Société Autour du Monde* (June 14, 1931).

23. See Jean-Brunhes Delamarre, quoted in *JB*, 99.

24. De la Blache, quoted in Jean-Brunhes Delamarre, "Jean Brunhes," 102.

25. Petit, "Le Premier Élève de Bergson," 426.

26. Ibid., 429.

27. See Coeuré and Worms, eds., *Henri Bergson et Albert Kahn: Correspondances*, 68; and *AK*, 62.

28. Baldensperger, quoted in Beausoleil, "Albert Kahn et son oeuvre," 10.

29. For reference to the "mission" statement used to describe his first project, the Autour du Monde travel fund, see *AK*, 141. For reference to the phrase "invention without a future," purportedly attributed to Louis Lumière, see Gunning, "New Thresholds of Vision," 71.

30. For Borel's description of Kahn's "final goal," see *Bulletin de la Société Autour du Monde* (June 14, 1931): xvii.

31. See *L'Héritage d'Albert Kahn*.

32. Original instructions for the travel grant, quoted in *AK*, 141. The grants were eventually opened to students from Britain, the United States, Japan, Germany, and other European countries.

33. See Adler, "Origins of Sightseeing," 16, and *AK*, 64.

34. *AK*, 140.

35. Ibid.

36. This description was made by J. W. Manhardt, who represented Germany for the Kahn travel foundation. See *Bulletin de la Société Autour du Monde* (June 14, 1931): xiii. The cosmopolitan ideology was mirrored in the speech by André François-Poncet, who argued that the *boursiers* were meant to return from their trips "more intelligently national and more resolutely international." See François-Poncet, xx.

37. For more information on the Société Autour du Monde, see AK, 237–41.

38. Speech by M. Roustan, *Bulletin de la Société Autour du Monde* (June 14, 1931): viii.

39. See chapter 7 for a fuller exploration of film reception on Kahn's property.

40. Brunhes' external use of the Archive included an annual lecture illustrated by the autochromes and delivered in the Sorbonne amphitheater. President Poincaré attended one of these lectures on February 26, 1925. See Anon., "Les *Archives de la Planète* sont présentées au Président de la République."

41. For Bergson's laudatory invocation of the phrase "Boulogne community" to describe Kahn's projects, see Bergson, "Letter from Henri Bergson," iv.

42. For more information on the publications funded by Kahn, see *AK*, 211–16.

43. For further details on the Centre de Documentation Sociale, see Coeuré, "Les Centres de Documentation Sociale, 1920–1940," in *AK*, 201–209.

44. *AK*, 208. See also Jay, *The Dialectical Imagination*, 30, 38. Jay also notes that further support for the Frankfurt School in Paris came from Bergson.

45. For an overview of Comandon's contribution to scientific film as well as a list of the films he made for Kahn, see Thévenard and Tassel, *Le Cinéma scientifique français*, 43–47. After the demise of Kahn's fortune and the closure of the laboratory, Comandon was able to transport his laboratory to the Institut Pasteur, where he worked from 1933 to 1970. See Isabelle Do O'Gomes, "Le Cinéma scientifique," 187. Equally important cinematic supplements to the Archives de la Planète include the films made by Father Francis Aupiais in colonial Dahomey (present-day Benin) between 1929 and 1930; a series of tests (with color film) and experiments (filming clouds and eclipses) carried

out by Kahn's cameramen; a range of commercial actualities purchased by Kahn to supplement the gaps in the Archive's global coverage; and some miscellaneous items that made their way into the collection, such as an incomplete copy of Léon Poirier's *Amours exotiques* (1925).

46. On Kahn's gardens, see *AK*, 97–105; Molinier, *Jardins de villes privés*; and Bullot, *Jardins-Rébus: Histoires de trois jardins remarquables*.

47. Foucault, "Of Other Spaces," 24. Subsequent references to this essay are cited in the text.

48. In addition to the famous Boulogne gardens, Kahn also established a similar one at his villa in Cap Martin in the south of France. Kahn also owned properties in Normandy (France) and Carbis Bay (Cornwall, England).

49. Indeed, beneath the hills of the original Alpine garden were the materials taken from the demolition of buildings on rue Lecourbe, while behind the planting of the huge fir trees lies the story (captured on film) of a midnight transportation that had required cutting the wires of nearby tramway lines. See Molinier, *Jardins de villes privés*, 162–63.

50. Foucault makes this connection between heterotopias and travel even more explicit in arguing that the twin site to the museum and its "accumulation of time" occurs in sites linked to "time in its most flowing, transitory, precarious aspects" ("Of Other Spaces," 26), such as fairgrounds on the outskirts of cities, and vacation villages. As one of the primary exhibition sites of early cinema, fairgrounds also provide another important cinematic allusion within Foucault's inventory of heterotopian sites.

51. On diverse traditions of collecting and representing the world, see Defert, "The Collection of the World" and Jacob, *The Sovereign Map*.

52. For a critique of the oppositions between the figure of the traveler and the tourist, see Strain, *Public Places, Private Journeys*, 4–5, and Risse, "White Knee Socks Versus Photojournalist Vests."

53. For works focusing on cinema's relation to the emergence of modern travel industries, see Kirby, *Parallel Tracks*; Strain, *Public Places, Private Journeys*; and essays in Ruoff, ed., *Virtual Voyage*.

54. See *AK*, 59–72. See speech delivered in 1909 at Waseda University by Count Okuma, cited in *AK*, 61.

55. *AK*, 60.

56. In addition to those travel accounts published in the *Bulletin de la Société Autour du Monde*, I have also been able to locate several accounts by non-French recipients published in the form of reports to the Albert Kahn Travelling Fellowship board. See, for example, Randerson, *Report to the Trustees*; Dickinson, *Report to the Trustees*; and Power, *Report to the Trustees*.

57. See Kahn's interview with A. Thein, "Un Jardin japonais à Paris," 382.

58. E. Antoine, "Mon Voyage Autour du Monde: octobre 1912–août 1913," 113.

59. Kahn, *Des Droits*, 39; and Bergson, "Letter from Henri Bergson," iii.

60. For more on Kahn's photographers and cameramen, see the appendix.

61. Stereographs comprised pairs of photographs capable of producing the illusion of depth for an individual when viewed through the hand-held optical device known as a stereoscope.

62. Pellerin, *La Photographie stéréoscopique*, 14–16. On the importance of the appellation "views," see Krauss, "Photography's Discursive Spaces," 291–92. For further elaboration of the significance of the category of the "view" to early cinema, see chapter 2. For additional overviews of the history of stereographs, see Richard, "Life in Three Dimensions," and Strain, *Public Places, Private Journeys*, 74–86.

63. On the Vérascope Richard, see Pellerin, *La Photographie stéréoscopique*, 26, and Wing, *Stereoscopes*, 171–84.

64. For analyses of the desire for authenticity in tourism and its connections to modern alienation, see Strain, *Public Places, Private Journeys*, 4–5, 8–9, 23–27.

65. Williams cited in *AK*, 219.

66. For Dutertre's quote and a sample of his stereographs, see *Albert Kahn et le Japon*. For the second pejorative reference to the picturesque made by Edmond Eggli, a Kahn travel grant recipient, in 1908, see Eggli, quoted in *AK*, 151.

67. On commercial stereographic applications, see Pellerin, *La Photographie stéréoscopique*, 21–24.

68. For reproductions of these images by Dutertre, see *AK*, 69.

69. For reproductions of these images by Dutertre, see *AK*, 70, 72.

70. *The Steerage*'s mythic status as an icon of the American migration story ignores the reality behind the image: the photo actually captured migrants leaving New York for Le Havre. See Koetzle, *Photo Icons*, 134–41.

71. For more on the status of "types" in anthropological photography and early ethnographic film, see Edwards, "Ordering Others"; R. Roberts, "Taxonomy"; and Griffiths, *Wondrous Difference*, 113–16.

72. On the physiologies tradition, see Benjamin, *Charles Baudelaire*, 35–41; Le Gall, *Atget, Life in Paris*, 25–28; and M. Cohen, "Panoramic Literature and the Invention of Everyday Genres."

73. On Atget's *petits métiers* series from 1899–1901, see Le Gall, *Atget, Life in Paris*, 7–106, and Nesbit, *Atget's Seven Albums*, 33.

74. For more on this shift, see Strain, *Public Places, Private Journeys*, 49–73. On the different types of anthropometric photography in the nineteenth century, see Edwards, "Ordering Others," 54–68, and Griffiths, *Wondrous Difference*, 93–109.

75. See stereograph by Dutertre, N1065 (MAK).

76. For a treatment of an indigenous fascination with Japanese types, see Harootunian, *History's Disquiet*, 118, 126–34, and *Overcome by Modernity*, 178–201.

77. For a classic example of the traditional positivist gaze, see Hyppolyte Taine quoted in Kracauer, *Theory of Film*, 5: "I wanted to reproduce the objects as they are, or as they would be even if I did not exist."

78. Vertov, "The Factory of Facts."

79. Foucault, *The Archaeology of Knowledge*, 126–31. For further discussion of the Foucauldian model of the archive, see chapters 3, 5, and 8 (this volume).

80. For key engagements with the archive in photographic discourse, see Sekula, "Reading an Archive"; Krauss, "Photography's Discursive Spaces"; Tagg, *Burden of Representation*; and J. Roberts, *The Art of Interruption*, 72–97. On the appropriation of Atget's photographs for an art history approach to photography, which privileges artistic intention and stylistic evolution over larger, nonaesthetic forces animating the produc-

tion of his work, see Krauss, "Photography's Discursive Spaces," 294–95. In her reposi-
tioning of Atget's photographs away from an art history approach toward that domain's
"aesthetic Other," the document, Nesbit argues that the proper context for Atget's work
is "not the public exhibition of Salon painters and galleries but the field of the archive
and the printed page." See Nesbit, *Atget's Seven Albums*, 9.

81. On Bertillon, see Sekula, "The Body and the Archive."

82. For other examples of archival films contemporaneous to Kahn's, see chapter 4. Although "pure" archival filmmaking projects are rarer than post-archival ones, important recent examples include the anthropological Human Studies Film Project (founded in 1975 as the National Anthropological Film Center at the Smithsonian Museum
in Washington) and the videotaped oral testimony project of the Shoah Foundation
Institute for Visual History and Education (initiated by Steven Spielberg in 1994 and
now preserved at the University of Southern California).

83. Two of his French grant recipients, Marguerite Mespoulet and Madeleine Mignon,
would photograph Ireland for the Archive in 1913, while one of their British counterparts, Eileen Power, would go on to become a pioneer in women's social and economic
history.

84. See Pellerin, "Les Lucarnes de l'infini," 29.

85. Pellerin, *La Photographie stéréoscopique*, 16, 83.

86. Crary, *Techniques of the Observer*, 126.

87. De Margerie, reprinted in *JB*, 91.

88. Emphasis added.

89. Kahn paraphrased in letter from de Margerie to Brunhes, reprinted in *JB*, 92.

90. Brunhes quoted in *AK*, 73; for more on Brunhes' appreciation of the advantages of film,
see *JB*, 134.

91. *JB*, 92.

92. See *JB*, 93.

93. For evidence of Brunhes' photographic expertise, see Brunhes, "La Question du format," and "Un Nouveau Procédé de reproduction." He also counted among his friends
"Mr. Gaumont" (presumably Léon Gaumont, the pioneer filmmaker and director of the
second largest film company in France, who would eventually supply the Archive with
film equipment after difficulties were experienced with the first Pathé camera). On the
connection to Gaumont, see *JB*, 92.

94. See *JB*, 60. This period also marked a high point in the related cartographical quest to
draw up an international standardized map of the world. See L. Brown, *The Story of
Maps*, and Heffernan, "The Politics of the Map in the Early Twentieth Century."

95. For these citations and an overview of the Social Catholic movement in France, see
Beale, *The Modernist Enterprise*, 104–144, 107, 113, 172. On the role of Social Catholicism in Brunhes' life, see also *JB*, 42–45.

96. Brunhes, "Ethnographie et Géographie humaine," 32.

97. For a detailed overview of this shift in the discipline of anthropology and its attendant
forms of representations, see Strain, *Public Places, Private Journeys*, 23–24, 49–73.

98. Kahn, *Des Droits*, 23.

99. See [*Visit of Rabindranath Tagore to Boulogne gardens*] (Sauvageot, Aug. 10, 1920). For all references to Kahn's films I use the italicized title provided by the MAK, followed by the cameraman (if known) and the date.

100. Foucault, *Discipline and Punish*, 189.

101. Only codified in 1910 in Brunhes' *La Géographie humaine: Essai de classification positive, Principes et exemples* (1910; 2d ed., 1912; 3d ed., 1922), human geography was by no means an established science or discipline at the time.

102. See *AK*, 190, and *JB*, 197.

103. For evidence of connections between events depicted in Kahn's films and his bulletins, see the film *Le Quinzième Bulletin d'Albert Kahn: l'année 1920* (Conseil Général des Hauts-de-Seine/MAK, 1995). See also Le Bris, "Le Quinzième Bulletin, résultat d'une hypothèse."

104. Kahn, quoted in Petit, "Le Premier Élève de Bergson," 426.

105. For contemporary variants on the cinema-newspaper metaphor, see Depriel, "À la Gloire du Cinéma," 61, and Haugmard, "The 'Aesthetic' of the Cinematograph," 80.

106. See Lefebvre, *Everyday Life in the Modern World*, 1, and Braudel, "History and the Social Sciences," 28.

107. For a cultural history of France in the 1930s whose methodology is modeled upon a more empathetic account of the multiplicity of the newspaper's heterogeneous access to the history of daily life, see Andrew and Ungar, *Popular Front Paris*, 8–14.

108. On Gervais-Courtellemont, see Devos, "À Travers le Monde," and Boulouch, "Le Miracle des couleurs," 42.

109. On the Gervais-Courtellemont autochromes in the Kahn Archive, see Boulouch, "Le Miracle des couleurs," 47; and on the single film in the Kahn Archive (probably shot in Algeria or Tunisia between 1909 and 1911) that has also been attributed to Gervais-Courtellemont, see Devos, "À Travers le Monde," 26, 34.

110. Wood, *The Art of the Autochrome*, xiii, 1.

111. Ibid., xiii. Although prints could be made from autochromes, they were costly and rare. On this point, see Boulouch, "The Documentary Use of the Autochrome in France," 143.

112. For a citation of autochrome exposure times based on a contemporary manual that estimated 20 seconds for a shot *en plein air* and 240 seconds for a studio photograph, see Boulouch, "Le Miracle des couleurs," 55. For analyses of Kahn's autochromes, see Boulouch, "The Documentary Use of the Autochrome in France," 143–45, and Wood, *The Art of the Autochrome*, 51–53.

113. The privileging of the autochromes over the films is a dominant feature of the first non-French documentary on the Kahn Archive, the nine-part BBC series conspicuously titled *Edwardians in Color: The Wonderful World of Albert Kahn* (2007).

114. See Bazin, "The Myth of Total Cinema," 20, 22.

115. See Gunning, "New Thresholds of Vision," 93–94.

116. See Burch, *Life to Those Shadows*, 16, and Gunning, "New Thresholds of Vision."

117. Brunhes, "Ethnographie et Géographie humaine," 39.

118. See ibid., 38.

119. Benjamin, "Little History of Photography," 518–19, and "The Work of Art," 104–105.

120. Wood, *The Art of the Autochrome*, 2, 37.

121. Ibid., 29.

122. See ibid., 5–6.

123. On the difficulty of interfering with the autochrome image during development, see ibid., 33, 36.

124. Brunhes, "Ethnographie et Géographie humaine," 38.

125. See ibid.

126. My invocation of the categories of the souvenir and collection is indebted to the work of Susan Stewart, *On Longing*, xii, 152–62.

127. Ibid., xii, and Steedman, *Dust*, 80.

2. FROM PRE-DOCUMENTARY TO DOCUMENTARY FILM IN THE KAHN ARCHIVE

1. Lévi-Strauss, *Tristes Tropiques*, 18–19. Subsequent references to this work are cited in the text.

2. Bazin, "Cinema and Exploration," 155–56.

3. Nichols, "Documentary Film and the Modernist Avant-Garde," 584; Vigo, "Towards a Social Cinema," 62. For another theorization of the evolution of nonfiction forms dependent upon an elaboration of the shift from the concept of the document to the documentary, see Rosen, *Change Mummified*, 225–64.

4. Malinowski cited in Grimshaw, *The Ethnographer's Eye*, 47.

5. See Worms, "Agir en Homme de pensée," 118.

6. Jean Brunhes, "Ethnographie et Géographie humaine," 38.

7. On the significant intersections between the discipline of anthropology (of Malinowski and Radcliffe-Brown) and documentary film (of Flaherty and Grierson), see Grimshaw, *The Ethnograher's Eye*, 44–56.

8. Gunning, "Before Documentary."

9. In comparing Kahn's films to Grierson's documentary ideas I am, of course, aware of the inconsistencies within and the differences between Grierson's official proclamations and the diversity of film practices apparent in the movement most associated with his name, 1930s British documentary. The work of the filmmaker and cofounder of the Mass Observation movement, Humphrey Jennings, is exemplary of this gap between discourse and practice. Indeed, although Kahn's films do not conform to Grierson's canonical definitions of documentary, especially those bent on distinguishing between "higher" and "lower" forms of documentary (see Grierson, "First Principles of Documentary," 82), I suggest in the conclusion that significant connections can be drawn between Kahn's Archive and Jennings's Mass Observation archive. See also Amad, "Cinema's Sanctuary," 155.

10. Grierson, quoted in Rotha, *Documentary Film*, 70. For revisionist analyses of Grierson's canonical definition of documentary, see Winston, *Claiming the Real*, 11–14; Gunning, "Before Documentary," 11–12; and Nichols, "Documentary Film and the Modernist Avant-Garde," 592–93, 599–607.

11. Grierson, "First Principles of Documentary," 81–83. Although Grierson recognizes the French "first used the term" *documentary* (81), he incorrectly limits the French term to exotic travelogues. On the multiplicity of genres intended by *film documentaire*, see Cosandey, "Some Thoughts on 'Early Documentary,'" 39. *Actualités* or newsreels were understood to be a different category than *film documentaire*. See de la Bretèque, "Les Actualités filmées françaises," 3.

12. For some of the works characteristic of these revisions, see Schlüpmann, "The Documentary Interest in Fiction," 33–36; Veray, "Fiction et 'non-fiction' dans les films sur la Grande Guerre de 1914 à 1928," 235–36; Gunning, "Before Documentary," 22; T. Lefebvre, "'Scientia': Le Cinéma de vulgarisation scientifique"; Griffiths, *Wondrous Difference*; and Peterson, *Education in the School of Dreams*. For important collections on early nonfiction film, see Hertogs and De Klerk, eds., *Nonfiction from the Teens: The 1994 Amsterdam Workshop* and *Uncharted Territory: Essays on Early Nonfiction Film*; and special issues of *1895*, 18 (Summer 1995); *Cahiers de la Cinémathèque* 66 (July 1997); *KINtop* 6 (1997); *Film History* 13.2 (2001); and *The Historical Journal of Film, Radio, and Television* 22.3 (Aug. 2002).

13. Pure and abstract film would have to be excluded from the avant-garde's and documentary's shared concern with verisimilitude and everyday reality.

14. Grierson, "First Principles of Documentary," 83; Nichols, "Documentary Film and the Modernist Avant-Garde," 583.

15. Brunhes, "Ethnographie et Géographie humaine," 38.

16. Buttimer, *Society and Milieu in the French Geographic Tradition*, 44.

17. Brunhes, "Ethnographie et Géographie humaine," 29.

18. Brunhes, "Lecture: 27 March 1916," 10. Typed transcripts of Brunhes' lectures at the Collège de France consulted at the Musée Albert-Kahn.

19. Paul Mantoux's review of Brunhes' major work, *La Géographie humaine*, cited in Brunhes, "Ethnographie et Géographie humaine," 29.

20. Brunhes, *Human Geography* (Abridged Edition, 1910; hereafter, *HG*), ed. Mariel Jean-Brunhes Delamarre and Pierre Defontaines, trans. Ernest F. Row, 36.

21. Brunhes, *HG*, 21.

22. On the reticence within anthropological circles to incorporate film as a pedagogical tool, see Grimshaw, *The Ethnographer's Eye*, and Griffiths, *Wondrous Difference*. For more on the history of the connections between anthropology and cinema, see Rony, *The Third Eye*, and Piault, *Anthropologie et cinéma*.

23. Robic, "Jean Brunhes," 109.

24. See Delmeulle, "Le Monde selon l'Encyclopédie Gaumont," 31, and Bernard, "Le Record du monde cinématographique," 219.

25. Brunhes, "Ethnographie et Géographie humaine," 38. For similar expressions of faith in cinema by Regnault and Comandon, see respectively Regnault, "Les Musées de films," and Comandon, "Le Cinématographe instrument de laboratoire."

26. Letter from Emmanuel Jacquin de Margerie to Brunhes, cited in *JB*, 92.

27. For the ethnographic dimensions of human geography's interest in costume, see Brunhes, "Ethnographie et Géographie humaine," 39. For an example of how Brunhes analyzed the details of traditional costume, see Brunhes, "Lecture: 10 February 1913."

28. Brunhes, "Ethnographie et Géographie humaine," 39.

29. For example, in one of his lectures on Albania, after having projected an autochrome he alerts the audience to the fact that, "It was not us who put those breeches on the car there; we have too much of a concern for science to add such details." See Brunhes, "Lecture: 20 December 1913," 3.

30. See Laurvik, "The New Color Photography" (1908).

31. For an example of the distrust of photography, see Matuszewski, "Une Nouvelle Source de l'histoire," 12.

32. For an example of the use of the word *views* in a cinematic context, see Méliès, "Cinematographic Views."

33. Grierson, "First Principles of Documentary," 81–83.

34. Ibid., 87.

35. Gunning, "Before Documentary," 15–16.

36. See Grierson, "First Principles of Documentary," 87, and Gunning, "Before Documentary," 19. Of course, the pervasive appeal of "just looking" that appears in countless one-shot travelogues, actualities, and scientific films from the first two decades of cinema was not exclusive to cinema. The cinema provided an auxiliary outlet for the range of impulses trained through a focus on display and visual curiosity in other key practices (of travel, consumerism, and colonialism) and sites (morgues, museums, department stores, military parades) of modernity. On cinema's relationship to a broader continuum of visual sites and practices, see Gunning, "The Cinema of Attractions" and "'The Whole World Within Reach'"; Friedberg, *Window Shopping*; and V. Schwartz, *Spectacular Realities*.

37. Vertov, "The Birth of Kino-Eye," 41; Vigo, "Towards a Social Cinema," 63.

38. For the footage of a woman shielding her face from the camera, see *Restaurant Populaire, Jardin des Tuileries, Paris* (Sauvageot, Jan. 1920).

39. Mendibil, "Deux 'Manières,'" 155. The early cinema historian André Gaudreault has also used the French term *monstration* to characterize the non-narrative, exhibition-based qualities of early cinema genres. See Gaudreault, "Film, Narrative, Narration" and "Theatricality, Narrativity, and 'Trickality.'"

40. For one of Lukács' key treatments of literary naturalism, see "Narrate or Describe?"

41. Although the text of the lectures does not indicate exactly which autochromes were being displayed, it does note when they are being projected with the word "Projections."

42. See Altman, "From Lecturer's Prop to Industrial Product," 62, and for further elaboration of the impact of the "lecture logic" upon the exhibition context of early cinema in the States, see Altman, *Silent Film Sound*, 55–76.

43. See Brunhes, "Lecture: 20 December 1913" and "Lecture: 27 January 1913."

44. Lukács, "Narrate or Describe?" Lukács' distinction will be returned to in following chapters in which I focus on the presence of a *radically* naturalist aesthetic in the Kahn films, French film theory, and the French documentary tradition.

45. Delamarre, "Preface," in Jean Brunhes, *HG*, 7.

46. On the popularity of sunsets and sunrises as a topic for autochrome projections of the period, see Boulouch, "Le Miracle des couleurs," 47, 51.

47. See *AK*, 190.

48. See *JB*, 202–203.

49. Brunhes cited in *JB*, 104 (my emphasis).

50. For reproductions of autochrome series that display a temporal progression, see *JB*, 149, 210–11; and *Villages et villageois au Tonkin: Autochromes réalisées par Léon Busy pour les Archives de la Planète*, plates 11–12.

51. See *JB*, 254.

52. Brunhes, *HG*, 20.

53. Zola, "The Experimental Novel," 186.

54. Brunhes, "Ethnographie et Géographie humaine," 32.

55. Brunhes, quoted in *AK*, 30.

56. Kahn, *Des Droits*, 9. Note that all these verbs contain the verb "to see" (*voir*).

57. Comandon, "Savoir Regarder,'" 6.

58. Not surprisingly, Comandon's article quotes Henri Bergson's idea of the "cinematographic evolution of thought." See chapters 3 and 7 for further explorations of the Comandon-Bergson relationship.

59. Brunhes quoted in *JB*, 202.

60. Brunhes, "Lecture: 10 February 1913," 4.

61. Brunhes quoted in *JB*, 179.

62. On the connection between the view aesthetic and the tourist, see Gunning, "Before Documentary," 15, 23.

63. For contemporary references to the restrictions on commercial actuality cameramen during the teens (the first coming from the diary entries relating to the work that one of Kahn's cameramen, Lucien Le Saint, did for Gaumont), see Le Saint, "Les Grands Reportages de Lucien Le Saint," and Hugon, "Hints to Newsfilm Cameramen." I consulted French transcripts of Le Saint's diary made available on the Internet by his grandson Olivier Le Saint under the title "Les Grands Reportages de Lucien Le Saint."

64. Letter from Brunhes to Kahn, May 15, 1912 (Brunhes archives, MAK [my emphases]).

65. Brunhes, quoted in Delamarre, "Jean Brunhes," 104.

66. Brunhes, cited in *JB*, 216.

67. Ibid. (my emphasis). For an example of the praise for human geography's anti-determinism by the Annales historian, Lucien Febvre, see Buttimer, *Society and Milieu in the French Geographic Tradition*, 77.

68. Jean Brunhes, *Races*, 14. The non-systematicity of human geography was a target for its most vehement detractors, the Durkheimian school of French sociology. See Buttimer, *Society and Milieu in the French Geographic Tradition*, 76.

69. To be sure, as Zola noted in his excursus on the experimental method in medicine pioneered by the physiologist Claude Bernard, feeling and intuition always had a part to play in scientific methodology. See Zola, "The Experimental Novel," 182–83.

70. Grimshaw, *The Ethnographer's Eye*, 45, 53, 119. I will explore the incorporation of this anthropological "innocent eye" as it intersects with the scientific and documentary dimensions of the visionary logic of early French film theory in chapters 6 and 7.

71. Brunhes quoted by Delamarre, "Jean Brunhes," 104 (my emphasis).

72. For example, see Brunhes' praise for the photographer Auguste Léon during his lecture of December 20, 1913, 1.

73. Throughout this book when referring to a Kahn film I rely on titles provided by the MAK.

74. See Aubert and Seguin, eds., *La Production cinématographique des Frères Lumière*, 214–15. For other "factory gate"-style footage and crowd portraits in the Kahn Archive, see *Sortie des usines Farman, 1918* (1918), *Allemagne, La Ruhr, Usines Krupp, sortie des ouvriers* (Sauvageot, Oct. 1923), and *La Mi-carème, les reines à l'Elysée, aspect de la foule* (Le Saint, Mar. 3, 1921).

75. Musser, "At the Beginning," 26 (my emphasis). For further elaboration of the differences between Edison and Lumière films, see Gunning "New Thresholds of Vision," 74–81.

76. See *Chine, Beijing, Ville Tartare: Échange de salutations traditionnelles* (Dutertre, Jan. 25–28, 1909).

77. Grierson quoted in *Grierson on Documentary*, 18.

78. See *Déroulement d'une cremation, Cambodge, Phnom Penh* (Léon Busy, Feb.–Mar. 1921) and *Indes: Province de Delhi, Les crémations* (Roger Dumas, 1914). On structuring principles in early single-shot films, see Deutelbaum, "Structural Patterning in the Lumière Films," 300, and Belloï, "Lumière and His View."

79. See *Liban: Cimetière de Tyr* (Le Saint, 1919).

80. On early travelogues and travel films in general, see Peterson, *Education in the School of Dreams*, and the essays in Ruoff, ed., *Virtual Voyages*. Of course in the early cinema period, travelogues were more likely to be single-shot films.

81. See *Indes: Garden Party at Kapurthala* (Dumas, Nov.–Dec. 1927). The films focused on prostitutes will be discussed in chapter 8.

82. See Bernard Dupaigne, "Preface," in Balard, *Dahomey 1930*, vi.

83. On the issue of early nonfiction film's static evolution when compared to the rapid evolution in narrative film from the same period, see Gunning, "Before Documentary," 12–13, and Uricchio and Rutten, "Le Film de non-fiction français," 230. For more on the differences between early and late films in the Kahn Archive, see Leclerq, "Albert Kahn et le cinématographe"; Leclerq-Weiss, "Introduction au cinéma des opérateurs Kahn"; and de la Bretèque, "Albert Kahn, d'un certain regard sur le monde."

84. For a brief reference to Le Saint as a Gaumont actuality cameraman, see Delmeulle, "Le Parent pauvre? La Pratique du documentaire chez Gaumont," 49–51.

85. See for example the film on religious pilgrimages in Brittany, *Locronan, La Grande Troménie* (Sauvageot, July 1929). In the opening shots of *Locronan*, a geographically motivated movement into space (also often apparent in Brunhes' autochrome series) is cartographically literalized via the insertion of a map on which Locronan is situated, followed by a general view of the village and then closer shots of the central church. For an analysis of *Locronan*, see Loussouarn, "La 'Géographie' des vues Albert Kahn."

86. The film archivist at the MAK, Jocelyne Leclerq-Weiss, has argued there is an implicit attempt to edit in the shooting sequence of the three shots that make up *Restaurant populaire, Jardin des Tuileries, Paris* (Sauvageot, Jan. 1920). See Leclerq, "Albert Kahn et le cinématographe," 76–77. On the issues of implicit montage, editing-in-camera, and camera stoppages, see Gaudréault, "Les Traces du montage dans la production Lumière"; Bottomore, "Shots in the Dark—The Real Origins of Film Editing"; and Gunning, "Before Documentary," 13.

87. Although they were not filled out uniformly, the development *fiches* (which only date from 1918 and seem to have been intended as guides for the technicians who developed the film) usually list the cameraman, title, date, and order of what they had shot. The development *fiches* are different from the official *fiches* (fig. 2.1) that were to be filled out on location. In addition to these two types of *fiches* there was also the *Livre de Compte* or film stock register. For more on the extant textual documents supporting the Kahn films, see Le Bris, "De l'Image et de son identification," 35–36, and Hervé, "Exposition d'une collection," 37–38.

88. See "fiches de développement," no.27–28 [MAK].

89. For Nichols's delineations of the evolution of documentary film, see Nichols, *Introduction to Documentary*, 82–98, and "Documentary Film and the Modernist Avant-Garde."

90. Brunhes, "Ethnographie et Géographie humaine," 38.

91. Nichols, *Representing Reality*, pp. 32–75.

92. Ibid., 39–40.

93. Grierson, "The Documentary Idea," 106.

94. For instance, many of the speakers at the Comité Nationale d'Études Sociales et Politiques were invited to the Société Autour du Monde lunches.

95. Grimshaw, *The Ethnographer's Eye*, 30. Grimshaw, like Roberts, argues that the more radical edges of this representational turn to ordinary people would be co-opted by the state in the interwar period. See also Roberts, *The Art of Interruption*, 58, 60, 36.

96. Grierson, "First Principles of Documentary," 89.

97. On the controversial and exploitative side to Flaherty's so-called participant observation while filming *Nanook of the North*, see Rony, *The Third Eye*, 109–119.

98. For an example of his attention to the difficulty of life aboard the fishing boats, see Le Saint, "Les Grands Reportages de Lucien Le Saint," Newfoundland diary entry for Thursday, May 25, 1922.

99. Vertov, "The Birth of Kino-Eye," 19.

100. Le Saint's diary refers regularly to the dangers and difficulties encountered in his filming career. Additional examples of cameraman self-reflexivity in the Kahn Archive include footage taken during a Lenten carnival of a camera-shaped Pathé float inside of which a Pathé cameraman is seen filming Kahn's cameraman, as well as footage of commercial cameramen at a League of Nations meeting (discussed in chapter 5).

101. Vertov, "Kino-Eye," 71.

102. In addition to *Melody of the World*, films (or more correctly elements in films) I have in mind in proposing the "atlas symphony" tendency, which can be found across avant-garde, commercially sponsored, and colonial-inflected production units of the first half of the twentieth century, include *Rien que les heures*; *La Croisière noire* (Léon Poirier, 1925) and *La Croisière jaune* (Léon Poirier/André Sauvage, 1934), both sponsored by Citroën; and *The Song of Ceylon* (Basil Wright and Walter Leigh, 1934), sponsored by the GPO Film Unit and the Ceylon Tea Propaganda Bureau. For more recent examples of "atlas symphony" films, see *Koyaanisqatsi* (Godfrey Reggio, 1983), *Baraka* (Ron Fricke, 1992), *Megacities* (Michael Glawogger, 1998), and *World Mirror Cinema* (Gustav Deutsch, 2005), to name a few.

103. Bazin, "Cinema and Exploration," 155.

104. Ibid., 162.

105. Grierson, "First Principles of Documentary," 82, 87.

106. Rosen, *Change Mummified*, 234, 240, 244.

107. Gunning, "Before Documentary," 22.

108. Delamarre, "Preface," in Jean Brunhes, *HG*, 5.

109. Vertov, "Kinoks: A Revolution," 20. A drive to organize observation according to spatial, temporal, and thematic categories that is similar to Brunhes' appears in Vertov's writings. In "Kino-Eye," for example, he suggested that "initial observation" can be organized into three categories: "observation of a place," "observation of a person or object in motion," and "observation of a theme." See Vertov, "Kino-Eye," 70.

110. Vertov, "Kino-Eye," 66.

111. Vertov, "The Factory of Facts," 59. Although Vertov respected the need for footage to be appended by an "information supplement" held in what he referred to as a "film archive," he did not believe such information needed to be included in the film itself because "[e]very instant of life shot unstaged, every individual frame shot just as it is in life with a hidden camera, 'caught unawares,' . . . represents a fact recorded on film, a film-fact as we call it." See Vertov, "The Same Thing from Different Angles," 57.

112. Vigo, "Toward a Social Cinema." Not coincidentally, Vigo's optic was organized through the lens of his cameraman, Boris Kaufman, the brother of Dziga Vertov.

113. Winston, *Claiming the Real*, 183. Although Winston's differentiation exaggerates the representativeness of the post–World War II French documentary tradition, neglecting to factor in, for example, the significant role of state-sponsored propaganda and educational film (for example in the colonies) in interwar France, it does highlight the prevalence of an idiosyncratic and personal strain in the French documentary tradition.

114. Although literary naturalism was of course a subcategory of realism, my differentiation between the two follows Georg Lukács' distinction in the essay "Narrate or Describe."

115. Kaufman, "Jean Vigo's *À Propos de Nice*," 78.

116. Ibid., 78–79.

117. For the characterization of Vertov, see Vaughn, "*The Man with the Movie Camera*," 57, and Grierson cited in *Grierson on Documentary*, 18.

118. See Rouch, *Ciné-Ethnography*, 267. Moving beyond France, the other major documentary project of the interwar period that also participated in this subjective intrusion into the scientific was Britain's Mass Observation movement from the 1930s, with Humphrey Spender's photographs and Humphrey Jennings' films providing key visual satellites to that mostly writing-based archive.

119. Epstein, "Magnification," 237.

120. Dréville, "Documentary: The Soul of Cinema," 42.

121. See the 55-second sequence "Congrès national socialiste pour la IIIème Internationale, Tours, du 25 au 30 décembre 1920" in the film *Le Quinzième Bulletin d'Albert Kahn: L'Année 1920*.

122. Brunhes, "Ethnographie et Géographie humaine," 38–39 (my emphasis).

123. Lukács, "Narrate or Describe?" 115.

124. Adorno, *Minima Moralia*, 141–42.

125. Vertov, "Kinoks: A Revolution," 19.

126. Foucault, *Archaeology of Knowledge*, 123.

3. THE COUNTER-ARCHIVE OF CINEMATIC MEMORY

1. Baudelaire, "The Salon of 1859," 297.
2. Proust, *Jean Santeuil*, 898. Left unfinished in 1900, Proust's autobiographical work *Jean Santeuil* was first published posthumously in 1952 (in a novelistic state) and again in 1971 (in a more fragmentary state).
3. Bergson, *Creative Evolution (CE)*, 4.
4. Terdiman, *Present Past*, 234. On the issue of Bergson's influence upon Proust, see Terdiman, *Present Past*, 190, 199, 209, 274. For the claim by Pierre Clarac that the "shock of the pianist" passage represents one of the earliest invocations of Proust's more positive category of memory, *mémoire involontaire*, see Proust, *Jean Santeuil*, 1100.
5. Baudelaire, "The Painter of Modern Life," 407.
6. Ibid., 435, 393.
7. Jameson, "The Theoretical Hesitation," 273. For the first phrase see Douglass, "Bergson and Cinema: Friends or Foes?" 209, and for more reflections upon this debate, see Douglass, "Deleuze's Bergson: Bergson Redux"; Doane, *The Emergence of Cinematic Time*, 170–80; and essays in *MLN* 120 (2005) and *SubStance* 114 (2007).
8. See Mullarkey, "Introduction," *The New Bergson*, 3.
9. Deleuze, *Cinema 1: The Movement-Image*, 58.
10. Ibid., 3.
11. See Benjamin, "Some Motifs in Baudelaire," 111, 147. For an example of the 1930s critique of Bergson, see Max Horkheimer, "On Bergson's Metaphysics of Time."
12. Jay, *Downcast Eyes*, 186 and 191–208.
13. For an example of a letter in which Kahn continues to refer to Bergson as his "Maître" or teacher, see letter draft from Kahn to Bergson of August 1886 in Coeuré and Worms, eds., *Henri Bergson et Albert Kahn: Correspondances*, 75 (hereafter, *HBAK*).
14. See footnote in Bergson, "Letter from Henri Bergson," iv.
15. See Louis F. Aubert, "Henri Bergson," 14.
16. See *JB*, 91–93, and M. Roustan, "Speech," viii. For the testimony of Kahn's secretary Paul Ducellier in which he recalls how even as his employer was approaching eighty he would have to drive him to visit Bergson at the nearby Villa Montmorency, see the film *L'Heritage d'Albert Kahn* (René-Jean Bouyer, 1978).
17. See Chevalier, *Entretiens avec Bergson*, ii–iii.
18. For the source to this description of Kahn, see Beausoleil, "Albert Kahn et son oeuvre," 10. The first decade of the twentieth century marked the peak of Bergson's celebrity with his lectures at the Collège de France, drawing record crowds of eager listeners, women chief amongst them, standing outside straining to hear.
19. See *JB*, 92–94.
20. Bergson, "Letter from Henri Bergson," iv.
21. Guitton quoted in an interview with Jeanne Beausoleil in *JB*, 107.
22. For these and other requests from Bergson to Kahn, see *HBAK*, 77–79, 88–89, 93, 94; and Letter from Bergson to Kahn (June 5, 1889) (MAK). In the case of Chevalier, Berg-

son's request took the form of an idea for constituting at the Collège de France a philo-sophical version of the Archives de la Planète tentatively referred to as "*les archives du monde moral*." See Chevalier, *Entretiens avec Bergson*, 77, 82. Although Bergson had suggested he contact Kahn, Chevalier noted that the philosopher was not particularly confident Kahn would agree because he had "a strict principle of only funding works which he had initiated himself." For correspondence between Bergson and Péguy that refers to Kahn, see Bergson, *Mélanges*, 630, 827.

23. See *HBAK*, 89. For similar expressions of trust in Kahn, see *HBAK*, 79, 86.

24. See *HBAK*, 96, 99–100, 102–103.

25. For instance, Bergson complains not just about being overworked in the provinces but also shares his fears of paralysis after not being able to write during an exam; Kahn expresses his dissatisfaction with the world of business and his secret desire to pursue a different "ideal"; Bergson complains about the monotony of his life as a provincial teacher; and Kahn mocks the Bois de Boulogne "*bourgeoises*." See *HBAK*, 62, 58, 70, 73, 75, 76.

26. Aubert, "Henri Bergson," 13.

27. Chevalier, *Entretiens avec Bergson*, 77.

28. For a comprehensive analysis of the profound impact of Bergsonism in France during this period, see Grogin, *The Bergsonian Controversy*, and Antliff, *Inventing Bergson*. Antliff is careful to map out how Bergsonism meant different things to different politi-cal groups. For instance, in prewar France Bergson was reviled in public by the right for being foreign, anti-classical, romantic and therefore Germanic, while a later critique from the left argued that certain appropriations of Bergson's organicism and nonra-tionalism fed into the Fascist cult of the anti-intellectual, organic, and racially unified nation. For another overview of the contradictory ideological readings of Bergson's key works, see S. Schwartz, "Bergson and the Politics of Vitalism."

29. At least five general features of Brunhes' human geography reveal the impact of Berg-sonism: the reference to a comprehensive, holistic, and ecological view of the world often described through biological metaphors; the opposition to a mechanistically determined interpretation of geography in favor of an understanding of the human-milieu context as in constant flux; the general air of anti-intellectualism and anti-ratio-nalism; the importance of *intuition* in Brunhes' practical advice to Kahn's cameramen; and the promotion of concrete experience and direct observation (as opposed to the ar-chival world of abstract thought, memorized texts, and rote learning) as the foundation to teaching and practicing geography. The history of human geography and Bergsonian philosophy also converged in that they both fell victim to similar criticisms for lacking theoretical rigor and methodological systematicity.

30. See by R. P. Brooks, "Speech," xv, and Bergson, *Mélanges*, 1350.

31. For the original plans, both philosophical and architectural, for Mundaneum, see Otlet, *Mundaneum*. Otlet's world library could be read as a textual analogue to the Archives de la Planète, as it was devoted to "a universal and global spirit deliberately oriented toward the well being and elevation of human society" (7). For more on Otlet, see chapter 4.

32. For an analysis of the most concrete cinematic evidence of Bergsonism in the Archive in Comandon's biological films, see chapter 7.

33. See A. Thein, "Un Jardin japonais à Paris," 383.

34. Petit, "Le Premier Élève de Bergson," 414, and Petit quoted in *AK*, 52.

35. Bergsonian vocabulary is also evident in Kahn's earlier text from 1918, *Des Droits*.

36. Bergson, *Time and Free Will*, 101.

37. On the appropriation of Bergsonism within the new discourse of advertising psychology, see Beale, *The Modernist Enterprise*, 20–30.

38. The following are direct translations with original punctuation of some representative lines from "Nos Fondations": "Fragments: Space, Time; Matter, Force; Beginnings, End; Life, Death; Source, Accomplishment; Rights, Responsibilities (Co-rights), (Co-responsibilities); Liberty (Co-liberty) . . . " (3); "Our attitude—renovated—dictated us, in order to assure, without mysticism, the non-arbitrary development, of Destiny—TO ORGANISE—from HUMANITY—the modalities of—Man—ORGANISED UNITY—Work of Creation" (4). Under the capitalized heading "ACTIVITY HAS A SURVIVAL." Kahn's text continues: "Light . . . Sound . . . will circulate, Cosmic bodies will come together . . . will fall apart or . . . will suddenly disappear. Flowers, fruits will follow one another. Rest, work will alternate . . . " (7).

39. Although the typewritten text of the manuscript refers to "cinema," the French word "*sonorisé*" (meaning sound cinema) has been added in pencil. The manuscript is covered with pencil corrections, and also contains Kahn's signature on the last page.

40. S. Schwartz, "Bergson and the Politics of Vitalism," 292, 301.

41. Bazin, "De Sica: Metteur en Scène," 326 (French original); and "De Sica: Metteur en Scène," 76 (English translation). For further discussion of the Bergsonian dimensions of Bazin's work, see conclusion.

42. Adorno, *Negative Dialectics*, 19.

43. Chevalier, *Henri Bergson*, 55.

44. Benjamin, "Some Motifs in Baudelaire," 111.

45. For other examples, see Bergson, *Matter and Memory*, 92, and *World of Dreams*, 21.

46. On Lukács' critique of Bergson, see S. Schwartz, "Bergson and the Politics of Vitalism," 290, 297.

47. See Bergson, *The World of Dreams*, 22; *Creative Evolution*, 306, 351; and "The Perception of Change," 252, 263.

48. For Bergson's confession to Kahn that "I detest provincial life" and Kahn's concern about "the absence of all distraction *chez vous*," see *HBAK*, 73–74, 57.

49. Georges-Michel, "Henri Bergson nous parle au cinéma," 7.

50. See Silverman, *Art Nouveau in Fin-de-Siècle France*, 89–90.

51. Bergson, "The Perception of Change," 260.

52. Bergson's negative everyday resembles what Lévi-Strauss referred to as the "dross" of everyday routine, "the thousand and one dreary tasks which eat away the days to no purpose." Lévi-Strauss, *Tristes Tropiques*, 17.

53. Bergson, "The Perception of Change," 250.

54. My emphasis.

55. On the connections between Bergson, Lukács, and Heidegger, see respectively Jay, *Downcast Eyes*, 418, and Lehan, "Bergson and the Discourse of the Moderns," 325–27.

56. See Bergson, "The Perception of Change," 248.

57. As Bergson himself notes in *Creative Evolution* (272), he first formulated the comparison of conceptual thought to that of the cinematograph in a course on the "History of the Idea of Time" in 1902–1903 at the Collège de France.

58. See Kracauer, "Photography," 56, and *Theory of Film*, 55.

59. For further characterization of our waking "normal life" as one of struggle and toil, see Bergson, *The World of Dreams*, 49–50.

60. Bergson, "The Perception of Change," 261 (my emphasis). Bergson's two lectures delivered at Oxford in 1911 were later published in the collection of essays *The Creative Mind* (1933).

61. See Comandon, "Savoir Regarder,'" 6.

62. First phrase is from Barden, "Method in Philosophy," 33 (my emphasis); second phrase is Bergson quoted in Barden, ibid., 33.

63. For one of the classic 1930s critiques of Bergson, see Max Horkheimer, "On Bergson's Metaphysics of Time."

64. Benjamin, "Some Motifs in Baudelaire," 144. As explained by Martin Jay, Horkheimer criticized the notion of duration because "to see reality as an uninterruptible flow was to ignore the reality of suffering, aging, and death." See Jay, *The Dialectical Imagination*, 50. On Bakhtin's criticism of Bergson, see Rudova, "Bergsonism in Russia," 180.

65. Although Bakhtin attacked Bergson's conception of the self, arguing that "it is never close to history and eventness" (as Rudova puts it), there is still room to argue that Bakhtin's philosophy of life—"a form of thinking that presumes the importance of the everyday, the ordinary, the 'prosaic'"—bears the unrecognized impact of Bergsonism. See Rudov, "Bergsonism in Russia," 178–80.

66. Benjamin, "Some Motifs in Baudelaire," 144, 113.

67. Ibid., 111.

68. See F. C. T. Moore, *Bergson: Thinking Backwards*.

69. For further discussion of critics' references to Bergson's *Laughter* within a cinematic context, see chapter 6. In what follows, I quote from the English translation of Bergson's *Laughter*.

70. See last sequence of *Paris sur fond de Guerre 1917–1918* (le Centre Départemental de Documentation Pédagogique et le Musée Albert-Kahn, 1987).

71. Although the camera seems to have gone previously unnoticed by the woman, we cannot rule out the possibility that she was always aware of its presence and in the jig was perhaps responding to a cue from the cameraman.

72. Bazin, "*Paris 1900*," and Kracauer, *Theory of Film*, 56–57.

73. Chevalier, *Henri Bergson*, 214–15.

74. Benjamin, "Little History of Photography," 510.

75. For a further elaboration of this argument, see chapters 6 and 7.

76. The counter-positivist bent of Bergson's classificatory chapters reappears in the mock taxonomic rhetoric and structure of Deleuze's two cinema books.

77. For an analysis of the various other theories of memory that formed the scientific context for Bergson's monumental study, see Terdiman, *Present Past*, 194–200, and Matsuda, *The Memory of the Modern*, 79–99.

78. My emphasis.
79. Proust, *Remembrance of Things Past* 3:143.
80. Not surprisingly, when it came to the archiving of his own life, Bergson practiced as he preached and commanded in his will that all his personal files be destroyed. See Chevalier, *Entretiens avec Bergson*, ii–iii. From the perspective of Bergson's will, the Kahn-Bergson correspondence is literally counter-archival, opening up the philosopher's selectively archived legacy to affinities he may not have welcomed. Not coincidentally, Bergson's personal resistance to the archiving of his life may have contributed to the neglect of his philosophy after the Second World War in favor of that of Husserl, Heidegger, and Merleau-Ponty, who all left behind abundant archives. In contrast, the Bergson Archives in Paris, held at the Bibliothèque Jacques Doucet, only contain his personal library. See Lawlor and Moulard, "Henri Bergson."
81. In direct continuity with this tradition, Pierre Nora will describe the inferior mode of history by its "sifting and sorting" archival obsessions. See conclusion (this volume).
82. Deleuze, *Foucault*, 107.
83. Derrida, *Archive Fever*, 11–12.
84. For comparison of Bergson and Freud, see Hughes, *Consciousness and Society*, 124; Cariou, *Lectures Bergsoniennes*, 36–83; Copjec, *Reading My Desire*, 43–56; and Doane, *The Emergence of Cinematic Time*, 45, 61.
85. For Bergson's expression of sympathy for Freud's interpretation of dreams, see *World of Dreams*, 55–56.
86. Freud, "Note on the 'Mystic Writing Pad.'"
87. For Benjamin's distinction between Proust and Bergson, and his reference to the madeleine, see Benjamin, "Some Motifs in Baudelaire," 111, 142; and for the reference to the alienating power of old photographs and the "optical unconscious" of photography and film, see Benjamin, "A Short History of Photography," 510, 512, and "The Work of Art," 117.
88. Benjamin, "Some Motifs in Baudelaire," 144. Benjamin is here invoking Horkheimer's attack on Bergson from 1934. He argues elsewhere in "Some Motifs in Baudelaire" that Bergson's wider philosophy "rejects any historical determination of memory" (111).
89. Ibid., 112, 145.
90. Ibid., 146.
91. On Kracauer's influence on Benjamin, see Hansen, "'With Skin and Hair,'" 455.
92. My understanding of this final shift in Kracauer's argument is indebted to Miriam Hansen's reading of the essay. See Hansen, "'With Skin and Hair,'" 456.
93. See for example, Deleuze's description of Foucault's work post–*Madness and Civilization* (1961) as belonging to a "new positivism" "which in itself is poetic." See Deleuze, *Foucault*, 13, 18.
94. Foucault, *Archaeology of Knowledge*, 6. This initial questioning of the document is central to his critique of traditional historical practice as one that operates erroneously "by a sort of memory that moves across time, free[s] meanings, thoughts, desires, [and] buried fantasies" (123).
95. Foucault, *Archaeology of Knowledge*, 129–30.
96. See ibid., 123.

97. Deleuze, *Foucault*, 1.

98. Ibid., 4.

99. In the 1914 *Le Journal* interview with Georges-Michel, Bergson mentions that he had recently rejected the request to be filmed on the occasion of his election to the Acadèmie Française: "Can you imagine . . . that a film company asked me to pose for them. . . . I refused . . . even though the cinematograph interests me as much as all the other new inventions."

100. Mirroring Kahn's relation to Bergson, I will also argue that the cameramen took Brunhes' human geography where he did not dare to go.

101. See letter from Bergson to Kahn, May 14, 1886, in *HBAK*, 73–74.

102. Chevalier, *Entretiens avec Bergson*, 82.

103. Barden, "Method in Philosophy," 34. See also Worms in *HBAK*, 24–25.

104. Deleuze, *Bergsonism*, 15.

105. Petit, "Le Premier Élève de Bergson."

106. Deleuze, *Cinema 1: The Movement-Image*, 3.

107. See Foucault, "Of Other Spaces," 22.

4. EARLY DISCOURSES AND PRACTICES OF THE FILM ARCHIVE

1. Matuszewski, "A New Source of History," 323. For original in French, see Matuszewski, "Une Nouvelle Source de l'histoire," 11.

2. Doumic, "Drama Review: The Cinema Age," 86.

3. See Pascal Hédégat (a pseudonym for Apollinaire), "Le Cinéma à la Nationale," 1, and Ramirez and Rolot, "Guillaume Apollinaire." Apollinaire also authored a story on this topic titled "Le Rabachis" (1910).

4. Hédégat, "Le Cinéma à la Nationale," 1. For information on the early attempts to store film at the Bibliothèque Nationale (as early as 1897 and later by Gaumont who deposited scenarios from 1906 and by Pathé who deposited scenarios with film frames between 1908 and 1914), see Jeanne and Ford, *Le Cinéma et la presse*, 194–97; Ramirez and Rolot, "Guillaume Apollinaire," 56–57; Toulet, "Avant-Propos," 6–9; and Gauthier, "La Conservation et la consultation des films dans les années 1920," 227.

5. Kracauer, "Photography," 57, and Benjamin, "Some Motifs in Baudelaire," 113.

6. Burch, *Life to Those Shadows*, 11, 17. It is important to point out that Burch's reading of film history resists situating Hollywood classical narrative as the bad object to the good object of early cinema (3).

7. Burch, *Life to Those Shadows*, 13, 17.

8. Adorno, *Minima Moralia*, 141–42.

9. Pathé quoted in Jeanne and Ford, *Le Cinéma et la presse*, 14.

10. For more recent reflections upon discourses related to early cinema's capacities to store and revive time, see Nicolas, "Les Ombres du temps"; Musser, "At the Beginning," 20; Kittler, *Discourse Networks*, 3; and, more extensively, Doane, *The Emergence of Cinematic Time*, 1–68, 206–234.

11. Verhylle, "Les Archives familiales," 7.

12. Fredy, "Les Archives cinématographiques," 5–6.

13. See Dureau, "Les Archives du cinéma," 3, and "Les Films historiques," 3–4.

14. Regnault (from an 1896 article originally published in *L'Illustration*) quoted in Jeanne and Ford, *Le Cinéma et la presse*, 32. For an analysis of Regnault's efforts to establish an "ethnographic film archive as a visualizing technology of the taxonomic ranking of peoples," see Rony, *Third Eye*, 21–76, 48.

15. See Brunhes, "Ethnographie et Géographie humaine," 38.

16. Matuszewski, "Une Nouvelle Source de l'histoire," 8–9.

17. Abel, ed., *French Film Theory and Criticism* 1:xix, 8–22, 97.

18. For typical anti-cinema diatribes, see Jeanne and Ford, *Le Cinéma et la presse*, 132. For a defense of cinema against the "school of crime" debates, see Anon., "L'École du crime."

19. Yhcam, "Cinematography," 77.

20. See Delmeulle, "Le Monde selon l'Encyclopédie Gaumont," 31, and Sentilhes, "L'Audio-visuel au service de l'enseignement," 171–73, 179. For further references to film's suitability as an educational tool for classes based on "visual demonstration," see Ricaud, "Communication de M. Denis Ricaud, Administrateur-Délégué de la Société Pathé Consortium Cinéma," and in the same catalogue, Aubert, "Communication de M. Aubert," 7.

21. See, for example, Jean Benoît-Lévy quoted in Sentilhes, "L'Audio-visuel au service de l'enseignement," 179.

22. "New orientation" is another of the catchphrases that appears in Kahn's *Des Droits et devoirs des gouvernements*, and was also the title of one of his fourteen publications whose preambles are thought to have been written by Kahn.

23. Gance quoted in Abel, "The Contribution of the French Literary Avant-Garde," 33.

24. Flobert, "Les Amis de la Bibliothèque de la Ville de Paris et le Cinématographe," 72, and Gance, "A Sixth Art," 66–67. See also Canudo, "The Birth of a Sixth Art," 60, and Colette's review of "*Civilisation*," 21. On the discourse of film as *visual Esperanto* in the States, see Hansen, "Universal Language and Democratic Culture" and *Babel and Babylon*, 78 and chapters 2, 7, and 8.

25. Ricaud, "Communication de M. Denis Ricaud," 10. In the same exposition catalogue, Léon Riotor, the secretary of the Conseil Municipal de Paris, argued that film "could well replace not nature and man, but the book and the theater." See Riotor, "Communication de L. Riotor," 5.

26. See, for instance, Vautel, "Propos d'un Parisien," and also two responses to the survey on the need for a film library, in *Enquête de René Brunschwik sur une Bibliothèque du Film* (1927), 83 and 85.

27. Vuillermoz, "Cinémathèque."

28. Haugmard, "The 'Aesthetic' of the Cinematograph," 80. Subsequent references to this essay are cited in the text.

29. For an Italian example of this tendency, see d'Ambra, "Il Museo dell'attimo fuggente." Thanks to Francesco Casetti for sending me this reference.

30. Perrot, "Pour le Cinématographe" and "Pour la Conservation des films historiques."

31. Perrot quoted in Léandre Vaillat, "À la Commission du Vieux-Paris."

32. See Vautel, "Propos d'un Parisien."

33. See Hauser, "Le 'Bibliophote' cinématographie livres et manuscripts." The bibliophote was invented by the internationalist and bibliographer Paul Otlet. For more on his efforts to use technology, including photography, cinema, and radio to further universal access to documents, see Françoise Levie, "Paul Otlet et le multimedia." The practice of filming the pages of books can only be understood to be using film as a source of history in the most narrow and utilitarian sense. In fact, it has only been within the last thirty or so years, in France, as well as the United States and Germany, that the broader idea to use film as a source of historical evidence has really been applied by professional historians. See Ferro, *Cinema and History*, 14–46 and 158–65.

34. *Enquête de René Brunschwik sur une Bibliothèque du Film*, 91.

35. For an example of the invocation of film's document-like status from within the fiction film domain, see Feuillade, *"Scènes de la vie telle qu'elle est,"* 54.

36. Epstein, "On Certain Characteristics of *Photogénie*," 318. For the reference to "cinematic messianism," see Heu, "Émile Vuillermoz," 70–71.

37. Perrot, "Pour la Conservation des films historiques."

38. For an earlier invocation of the Lazarus trope (written in response to Matuszewski's pamphlet "A New Source of History"), see Jean Frollo, "Le Cinématographe et l'histoire," 74. For Bazin's reference to "change mummified" and for his own biblical metaphor of film as analogous to the imprinting capacity of Veronica's veil, see respectively Bazin, "The Ontology of the Photographic Image," 15, and Bazin, "Cinema and Exploration," 163.

39. Epstein, "The Senses 1 (b)," 245. Epstein's original reads *"[e]mbaument mobile."* In contrast, for Bazin photography *"embaume le temps,"* but film is *"la momie du changement."* See Epstein, "Le sens, 1b," 92, and Bazin, "Ontologie de l'image photographique," 14.

40. Canudo, "Reflections on the Seventh Art," 295–96.

41. Baudelaire, "The Salon of 1846," 297–98.

42. Canudo, "Reflections on the Seventh Art," 296.

43. See for example, the discussion of the work of Burch, Vaughn, Doane, Rosen, and others in chapter 6.

44. On the evolution of the classical Hollywood style, see Bordwell, Staiger, and Thompson, *The Classical Hollywood Cinema*. For an argument that aligns the disciplining logic of historiography, documentary film, and mainstream Hollywood film, see Rosen, *Change Mummified*, 178, 184.

45. See also Haugmard, "The 'Aesthetic' of the Cinematograph," 83.

46. Matuszewski, "La Photographie animée: Ce qu'elle est, ce'qu'elle doit être." His second pamphlet is a more detailed elaboration of his predictions for the future of film.

47. Matuszewski, "Une Nouvelle Source de l'histoire," 6, and "La Photographie animée," 26.

48. See epigraph for chapter 6 from Zola's "Preface to the Second Edition" (1868), *Thérèse Raquin*, 2.

49. Matuszewski, "Une Nouvelle Source de l'histoire," 9.

50. Tsivian, "Media Fantasies and Penetrating Vision," 86–87 and 95–96.

51. For references to the popular device of the camera-as-evidence plot in films centered on domestic betrayal and other pursuits of evidence, see Gunning "Tracing the Individual Body," 36, and Abel, *Ciné Goes to Town*, 350–53.

52. Matuszewski, "La Photographie animée," 53–4.

53. "Le Cinéma à la Préfecture de police," 7.

54. Canudo, "The Birth of a Sixth Art," 60.

55. Twelve years later, when Canudo was ready to recognize cinema as an art, he did so by distinguishing it from all other arts due to the fact that "its rhythm arises from everyday life." See Canudo, "Reflections on the Seventh Art," 292.

56. Canudo, "Birth of a Sixth Art," 61. Interestingly, it was the exact qualities of film that Canudo opposed—its resistance to being stylized—that Louis Delluc (the critic who took over Canudo's role as the most important film critic of the late teens and early twenties) would in turn embrace as the essential features of film as art. See Delluc, "Beauty in the Cinema," 137. Canudo thus regrets exactly what Siegfried Kracauer will also later celebrate (often using Delluc's criticism) as film's photographic ability to "transmit raw material *without* defining it." See Kracauer, *Theory of Film*, 20 (my emphasis).

57. See Méliès, "Cinematographic Views."

58. Yhcam, "Cinematography," 68.

59. Haugmard refers to the eclectic nature of film programs, with their combination of actualities, comics, educationals, and dramas, as having the unenvious democratizing duty of catering to "every category of spectator and their different tastes." See Haugmard, "The 'Aesthetic' of the Cinematograph," 79.

60. See chapter 7 for further discussion of this topic.

61. Doumic, "Drama Review: The Cinema Age," 86.

62. Matuszewski's pamphlet was even revived on its thirtieth anniversary in an article by Forèze titled "Le Cinéma il y a trente ans."

63. Terdiman, *Present Past*, 31.

64. Bautier, "Les Archives," 1121. For histories of the concept and institution of the archive in France, see Braibant, "Les Archives de France"; Favier, *Les Archives*; essays in *Traverses* 36 (January 1986); Pomian, "Les Archives"; and Milligan, "'What is an Archive?'"

65. Braibant, "L'Histoire, fille des archives," 5.

66. See B. Smith, "Gender and the Practices of Scientific History," 1165–66.

67. Bourdé and Martin, *Les Écoles historiques*, 187, and Fink, *Marc Bloch*, 27–29. On the emergence of modern European archives, see Steedman, *Dust*, x–xi, 69.

68. See Bourdé and Martin, *Les Écoles historiques*, 181–214. The *école méthodique's* reign ends just before the rise of the opposing Annales school of history, discussed in the next chapter.

69. Steedman, *Dust*, x.

70. See Burke, *The French Historical Revolution*, 7. On the few dissenting voices against the hegemony of political history in nineteenth-century French history, see Burke, ibid., 7–9. On previous models of history writing, see B. Smith, "Gender and the Practices of Scientific History," 1151–53, 1166. For Charles Seignobos' regrets regarding his neglect of everyday history, see Seignobos cited in Benjamin, *The Arcades Project*, [N5a, 5], 467.

71. See Tollebeek, "'Turn'd to dust and tears,'" 240–44, and de Certeau, "L'Espace de l'archive ou la perversion du temps," 5.

72. See Braibant, "Les Archives de France," 8–13, and B. Smith, "Gender and the Practices of Scientific History," 1162, 1164.

73. For more on the intertwining of the nation-state and the history of archives, see Fritzsche, "The Archive," 17, and B. Smith, "Gender and the Practices of Scientific History," 1165–6.

74. Bourdé and Martin, *Les Écoles historiques*, 191.

75. For a comparison of Bertillon's system with the composite identification system of Francis Galton ("two poles of [the positivist] attempt to regulate the semantic traffic in photographs"), see Sekula, "The Body and the Archive." Bertillon was the director of the Identification Bureau of the Paris Prefecture of Police, where his photographic system of criminal identification was established in 1883. Sekula ultimately argues that it is the *fiche*, filing cabinet, and archive, rather than any ontological essence of the medium itself, that guaranteed photography's claims to objective realism.

76. For an investigation of the implicit disciplining of colonial bodies in certain Kahn films, see chapter 8. Like other photographic histories focused upon the repressive use of photography in the nineteenth century, Sekula draws upon Foucault's *Discipline and Punish* to contextualize the disciplining and panoptic dimensions of Bertillon's system. See Sekula, "The Body and the Archive," 7–10. On the bind between classificatory practices and photography in the service of disciplinary visual regimes, see R. Roberts, "Taxonomy"; Edwards, "Ordering Others"; and Frizot, "Body of Evidence."

77. Lukács, "Narrate or Describe?" 110.

78. Ibid., 115. Zola himself rejected the comparison of his work to photography. See Zola, "The Experimental Novel," 168.

79. For reference to Brunhes' intentions to make the photographic image readable, see *JB*, 125.

80. As we have seen in chapter 2, a similar move appears in Grierson's elaboration of an ideology of documentary film, whereby he sought to distinguish the mere piling up of facts one finds in early nonfiction film from the arrangement and creative treatment of facts that was essential to documentary proper.

81. For this description of Matuszewski's campaign, see Cosandey, "Some Thoughts on 'early documentary,'" 42.

82. On the issue of taxonomic "slippages" and "uncertainties" in photographic archives, see Edwards, "Ordering Others," 57, 62, 56–59, and R. Roberts, "Taxonomy," 9. Given the autochrome's material amenability to Brunhes' practices of classification (unlike film each autochrome resembled a discrete, bounded document that could be conveniently catalogued), I would argue the films posed more of a threat to contemporary iconographic taxonomies.

83. Bourdé and Martin, *Les Écoles historiques*, 206.

84. See Pomian, "Les Archives," 225.

85. Thomas Grimm, "La Cinématographie historique," 77 (my emphasis). Another respondent to Matuszewski's pamphlet, Jean Frollo, went so far as to claim that thanks to the phonograph and the cinematograph, "history was going to become an exact science." See Frollo, "Le Cinématographe et l'histoire."

86. Kahn, *Des Droits*, 9, and Kahn cited in *AK*, 218.

87. Speech by the then Undersecretary to the Présidence du Conseil, André François-Poncet, *Bulletin de la Société Autour du Monde* (June 14, 1931): xix.

88. Kahn, "Nos Fondations," 2.

89. See Kahn, *Des Droits*, 9. On Bergson's fear of the contingent, see Lehan, "Bergson and the Discourse of the Moderns," 326.

90. Kahn, *Des Droits*, 23.

91. Fritzsche argues that "it was the wars of the twentieth century that dramatically reconfigured the archive because total war posed the question of the survival and definition of the people" and that consequently "[t]otal war thus prompted an expansion of what constituted compelling historical evidence." See Fritzsche, "The Archive," 21–22.

92. See Bergson, "Letter from Henri Bergson," iii. For more on Otlet's multimedia efforts to create a world library, see Levie, "Paul Otlet et le multimédia."

93. Braibant, "Les Archives de France," 10. The Quarantaine du Roi refers to the law that required the King to wait forty days before declaring war.

94. Lumière film production ended in 1905. See Aubert and Seguin, eds., *La Production cinématographique des frères Lumière*, 466.

95. For examples of classic "Vieux Paris" sites filmed by Kahn's cameraman, see opening section titled "Rues de Paris 1913–1924" in film entitled *Paris Vu par les Opérateurs d'Albert Kahn, 1913–1928, Part 1* (Conseil Général des Hauts-de-Seine/MAK, 1982).

96. Baron Georges Eugenè Haussmann, the Prefect of the Seine between 1853 and 1870, was encharged by Napoleon III to modernize Paris, which entailed destruction of large portions of the historic city. For a more detailed history of the Commission du Vieux Paris and the Commission des Monuments Historiques, which she argues "established the archetypes for pictorial documentation in all media," see Nesbit, *Atget's Seven Albums*, 62–75, and Rice, *Parisian Views*, 52–54.

97. Atget quoted in Nesbit, *Atget's Seven Albums*, 62.

98. See Benjamin, "Little History of Photography," 518–19.

99. On the functional explanation for the incomplete look of Atget's photos, see Nesbit, *Atget's Seven Albums*, 35.

100. See J. Rosen, "Atget's Populism," 51.

101. Piault, *Anthropologie et cinéma*, 14.

102. See ibid., 16–19, and Griffiths, *Wondrous Difference*, 127–70.

103. Malinowski quoted in D. Marks, "Ethnography and Ethnographic Film," 340.

104. Malinowski, "Proper Conditions for Ethnographic Work," 143–44. See also Grimshaw, *The Ethnographer's Eye*, 1–31, 44–56.

105. Flobert, "Les Amis de la Bibliothèque de la Ville de Paris," 72–73. For a detailed timeline of all the efforts made to establish an archive for films of historical interest to Paris, see Riotor, "Rapport au nom de la 4ème Commission," 2.

106. For diverse film archiving efforts outside of France, see Sadoul, "Cinémathèques et photothèques," 1172; Borde, *Les Cinémathèques*, 29–51; Bottomore, "'The collection of rubbish'"; and Houston, *Keepers of the Frame*, chapters 1–3. For an example of a film archive in Germany that shared the Kahn Archive's global ambitions, see the discussion of the Encyclopaedia Cinematographica in Uricchio, "The *Kulturfilm*." For the earliest Danish example, initiated by the journalist Anker Kirkeby in 1911 and funded by Ole

Olsen (founder of the Nordisk Film Company), with the intention of recording "living portraits of famous Danes of our time," see Krohn, "About the First Danish Film Archive." And for Britain's oldest film archive begun in 1917 with the establishment of the Imperial War Museum, see Houston, *Keepers of the Flame*, 12–13.

107. Brunhes, "Ethnographie et Géographie humaine," 38, and Anon., "Pourquoi ne crée-t-on pas les Archives Nationales du Cinéma?"

108. For references to these film services, see respectively, Delmeulle, "Le Monde selon l'Encyclopédie Gaumont"; Lemaire, ed., *Les Films militaires français de la première guerre mondiale*; Bloom, *French Colonial Documentary*, 127–31; Sentilhes, "L'Audiovisuel au service de l'enseignement"; Duvigneau and Duvigneau, "Les Archives du Service cinématographique du ministère de l'agriculture"; and De Pastre-Robert and Devos, "La Cinémathèque de la ville de Paris."

109. For a history of these and other national-based film archives, see Borde, *Les Cinémathèques*, 53–69. For two journal issues devoted to the history of film and television archives in France, see Serceau and Roger, eds., *CinémAction: Les archives du cinéma et de la télévision* 97 (2000), and Valérie Vignaux, ed., *1895*, 41 (Oct. 2003), Special Issue on Archives. On the wider history of the film museum, which meshes to a certain degree with the history of film archiving, see Trope, "*Le Cinéma pour le cinéma*," 33–34, and Wasson, *Museum Movies*.

110. Dévigné, "De la Mission des Ardennes," 3. For contemporary accounts of the sound archive, see *Inauguration des Archives de la Parole*, which includes speeches delivered at the archive's inauguration.

111. For direct references to Brunot's archive as a model, see "Les Archives du Cinéma," *Ciné-Journal* (May 3, 1913): 17, and Riotor, "Rapport au nom de la 4ème Commission," 2. Also see "Les Archives de la Parole," *Ciné-Journal* (Oct. 18, 1913): 9.

112. The geographer was invited to attend Brunot's demonstrations at the Sorbonne, and Kahn even placed Brunot on a draft of the list of members he wanted for the Archive's scientific committee. See letter from Brunhes to Kahn (Jan. 11, 1913), Jean Brunhes Archives (MAK), and *JB*, 194.

113. Dévigné, *Musée de la parole et du geste*, 10, 14.

114. De Certeau, "The Beauty of the Dead: Nisard," 121. On the folklorist and regionalist movements in France, see Lebovics, *True France*, 12–50, 135–61.

115. See "Une Application insoupçonnée," (editorial), 4.

116. Dévigné, "De la Mission des Ardennes," 3 (my emphasis).

117. Brunot quoted in Dévigné, "De la Mission des Ardennes," 9; Brunhes, "Ethnographie et Géographie humaine," 38.

118. For evidence of a Kahn film being loaned, see Trebitsch, "Le Robinson juif."

119. See chapter 7 for reception analysis of the Kahn films.

120. Rony, *The Third Eye*, 23.

121. A multimedia predecessor to the Kahn Archive was Jean-Martin Charcot's photographic enterprise at Paris's Salpêtrière Hospital, which included both photography and stereography.

122. Dévigné, "De la Mission des Ardennes," 7.

123. Brunhes, "Ethnographie et Géographie humaine," 38; Bergson, "Letter from Henri Bergson," iii–iv. In this respect, the Kahn Archive also differs from Kirkeby's Danish film archive.

124. The film ledger notes that several copies of such films were given as gifts, including films of Rabindranath Tagore.

125. For a history of the Rondel collection (which today forms the historical basis of the film library of the Département des Arts et Spectacles, previously held at the Bibliothèque d'Arsenal, now at the Richelieu site of the Bibliothèque Nationale), see Toulet, "Avant-Propos," 6–9. On the multiple efforts in France in the teens and twenties to preserve and collect the history of film, see Gauthier, *La Passion du cinéma*, 89–90, 211–33, and "1927, Year One of the French Film Heritage."

126. Bautier, "Les Archives," 1120.

127. Of course, writing in the mid-twentieth century, Bautier developed his definition of the institution over which he presided before the rise within the discipline of history of a poststructuralist suspicion toward the constructed and repressive nature of the archive. For a general history of this development, see Velody, "The Archive and the Human Sciences," and Brown and Davis-Brown, "The Making of Memory."

128. Bautier, "Les Archives," 1121.

129. For a key example of Benjamin's commentary on Baudelaire's *chiffonnier*, see Benjamin, *Arcades Project* [J68, 4], 349.

130. Steedman, *Dust*, 45.

131. Derrida, *Archive Fever*, 29.

132. Ibid., 85; see also 1 and 91.

133. André, "De la Preuve à l'histoire," 29, and Bautier, "Les Archives," 1135.

134. On Pathé's own internal commercial archive, see Schmidt, "*Le Pathé Journal*," 40–42.

135. See Regnault, "Les Musées de films."

136. Comandon, "L'Evolution de la microcinématographie," 491.

137. The French National Archives only officially incorporated film as a source governed by its statute in the 1950s. It would not be until 1977 that the law decreed that all filmic works had to be deposited at diverse sites of the *dépôt légal*, which in 1992 was extended to include all audiovisual works. See Serceau, "Les Archives," 16. Apparently, Henri Langlois was responsible for the lateness of the decree being applied to film. See Kula, "Film Archives at the Centenary of Film," 214–15.

138. Canudo, "The Birth of a Sixth Art," 61.

139. Benjamin, "The Work of Art." This is not to say that the notion of origins is totally alien to film culture for clearly the idea of the definitive version or original negative of a film claimed the status of the unique original. More recently, film archivists have tended to downplay the notion of the definitive version or original print, especially in relation to the notoriously multivalent nature of early cinema. See Usai, *Burning Passions*, 58, 67, and *The Death of Cinema*.

140. Steedman, *Dust*, 9, and B. Smith, "Gender and the Practices of Scientific History," 1166.

141. Anon., "La Vie utile des vues cinématographiques," *La Nature* (1897): 302–303, cited in Usai, *The Death of Cinema*, 5. This is the type of evidence that grounds Usai's asser-

tion, which I would characterize as counter-archival, that "cinema is the art of destroy-ing images" (7).

142. See Yhcam, "Cinematography," 74. Not surprisingly, Yhcam proposed an archival solu-tion—a "library of cinema"—to this problem.

143. Derrida, *Archive Fever*, 64.

144. I consulted Victor Perrot's archives at Paris's Bibliothèque du Film (BiFi). On Perrot's interest in Kahn's Archive, see Perrot, "Handwritten memo on an index card by Victor Perrot dated 1914" and typed letter from R. Joffet to V. Perrot, Mar. 30, 1953 (BiFi:FVP 054), thanking Perrot for an article from the magazine *Cinéopse* regarding the "ciné-mathèque des Jardins Kahn." I have not yet identified the *Cinéopse* article.

145. Typed letter from Victor Perrot to M. Kahn, Oct. 19, 1920 (BiFi: FVP 054).

146. Handwritten letter from Bonnet-Brodart (?) to Victor Perrot, Feb. 23, 1921 (BiFi:FVP 054).

147. Typed letter from Victor Perrot to [M. Kahn?], Feb. 18 1921 (BiFi: FVP 054).

148. Ibid.

149. We know this because in a series of press articles that appeared following the publica-tion of Perrot's report on film archives there are references to the "30, 000 meters" of film in the "Parisian catalogue" of the Kahn Archive. See "Rapport présenté par M. Vic-tor Perrot" (May 26–27, 1922), 12–13; and Anon., "Les Archives cinématographiques et les cinémathèques" (Aug. 11, 1922). For another press report on Perrot's film archive efforts, see "Les Archives cinématographiques de Paris" (Aug. 26, 1922).

150. The Archive's ledger book is more of a production record for the film laboratory than a proper catalogue, and it only contains the films shot by two cameramen.

151. See typed letter from Victor Perrot to [M. Kahn?], Feb. 18, 1921 (BiFi: FVP 054).

152. For evidence of Perrot's knowledge of and involvement in the sale of films, see Perrot, "Handwritten memo titled 'Cinémathèque' and dated Dec. 6, 1934," and "Handwrit-ten memo on an index card by Victor Perrot dated 1914" with an addendum obviously written after 1934 referring to the sale of the Boulogne property and the fact that, "I then asked that the *cinémathèque* be included in the acquisition." The films remained at Boulogne until 1952–53 when they were moved to the Préfécture de la Seine. In 1963, at the request of the Département de la Seine, Henri Langlois transferred the films to the Bois d'Arcy Archives, and then in 1968 he sent the majority of the film negatives to the Boyer laboratories near Nîmes. Today the negatives are stored at the Bois d'Arcy Centre National de la Cinématographie film archives. Using the three textual descriptions of the films (the film ledger, the film development slips, and the catalogue made by the first archivist of the collection, Mme Magne de Lalonde) the Bois d'Arcy CNC was able to make another inventory of the films during their conservation of the Archive that began in 1971. Safeguarding of the nitrate film onto Tri-Acetate took place between 1981 and 1992. Thanks to Jocelyne Weiss-Leclerq of the MAK for this information.

153. Even in this shift, however, the Kahn Archive is anomalous. Unlike most films that only enter the archive once their original commercial life has ended, the Kahn films entered the traditional conception of the archive as a result of their first commercial exchange, that is, being purchased by the Département de la Seine.

154. It is important to note here Henri Langlois' distinction between a film museum and a film archive. The cofounder of the Cinémathèque Française, and sometime "guard-

ian" of the Kahn collection in the fifties, commented in 1976: "film archives that don't understand that they must, first of all, be museums will be cupboards and nothing more" (Langlois cited in Trope, "*Le Cinéma pour le cinéma*," 30). Langlois thus defined the film museum in opposition to the original inaccessible, cupboard-bound aura of the Kahn Archive, implying that a museum has a duty to be publically accessible. It is obviously no coincidence that the Musée Albert-Kahn opened its doors just a few years before Langlois made this distinction. Although the present institutional habitat of the Archives de la Planète in a museum has changed its original function in line with Langlois' logic, this has had more of an impact upon the autochromes (which are regularly the center of exhibitions) than the films (which are usually screened only as a supplement to an autochrome exhibition). The shift from archive to museum in the institutional history of Kahn's documents thus implies a shift from a documentary-history-research context to an art-exhibition-display context.

155. Anon., *Journal des débats* (May 11, 1898), quoted in Matuszewski, "La Photographie animée," 71.

156. Matuszewski, "La Photographie animée," 26.

5. THE "ANECDOTAL SIDE OF HISTORY"

1. Humbourg, "Le Film historique."

2. Dulac, "Cinema at the Service of History: The Role of Newsreels."

3. Derrida, *Archive Fever*, 64. Although the history of psychoanalysis and Freud's archives provide the specific object of Derrida's theory of the archive, his analysis (like Foucault's in *The Archaeology of Knowledge*) also targets the more general object of positivist historical research (based on the "irreplaceable singularity of [the] document"). See also *Archive Fever*, 50, 90.

4. Hunt, "French History in the Last Twenty Years," 209. Regarding the early Annalists' maverick post-positivist research practices, Hunt argues that Bloch and Febvre intended "to create an open forum for interdisciplinary research and to promote concrete, collaborative work that would *not be tied to the 'positivism'* of traditional historical scholarship in France" (my emphasis).

5. For Braudel's reference to two poles of time and Lévi-Strauss, see Braudel, "History and the Social Sciences," 27, 36, 40, 44–45.

6. Marc Bloch, *The Historian's Craft* (hercafter, *HC*), 20.

7. Bazin, "The Ontology of the Photographic Image," 14–15.

8. On French historians' reluctance to consider film a source of history, see Ferro, *Cinema and History*, 23–28.

9. For these claims about Renoir and Akerman, see respectively D. Andrew, *Mists of Regret*, 294–95, and Margulies, *Nothing Happens*, 24.

10. Terdiman, *Present Past*, 8.

11. Lehan, "Bergson and the Discourse of the Moderns," 309.

12. Fink, *Marc Bloch*, 32–33. A fuller exploration of the Bergsonian influence upon historical methodology must account for the work of Maurice Halbwachs, a colleague of Bloch and Febvre's, who was profoundly influenced by Bergson as especially evident

in his posthumous work *On Collective Memory*. See Coser, "Introduction," in Maurice Halbwachs, *On Collective Memory*, 3, 7.

13. M. Bloch, *HC*, 189. Bloch was still writing *The Historian's Craft* (eventually published in 1949) when he was executed in 1944 as a member of the French resistance by the Nazis.

14. Bourdé and Martin, *Les Écoles historiques*, 209.

15. See M. Bloch, *Memoirs of War, 1914–1918*, 89.

16. Joseph R. Strayer, "Introduction" to M. Bloch, *HC*, xi. See also Burke, *The French Historical Revolution*, 23.

17. E. Bloch and Cruz-Ramirez, *Marc Bloch*, 143.

18. Ibid.

19. M. Bloch, *HC*, 61.

20. Febvre, *A Geographical Introduction to History*, 18–19; Vidal de la Blache quoted in Febvre, ibid., 24.

21. Ricoeur, *Memory, History, Forgetting*, 151.

22. For an overview of the second generation of Annales historians, see Hunt, "French History in the Last Twenty Years."

23. For this description of Febvre's understanding of the everyday, see Rebérioux, "Preface," 10 (my emphasis).

24. Braudel, "History and the Social Sciences," 28–29 and 34.

25. Bergson, *The Creative Mind*, 160–61; M. Bloch, *HC*, 144; Braudel, "History and the Social Sciences," 28.

26. Kracauer, "Photography," 50.

27. See ibid. For Kracauer's return to this trope in *Theory of Film* with reference to Fernand Léger, see conclusion.

28. Sekula, "Reading an Archive," 447.

29. B. Smith, "Gender and the Practices of Scientific History," 1169, 1171.

30. Seignebos and Langlois quoted in ibid., 1172.

31. B. Smith, "Gender and the Practices of Scientific History," 1176.

32. Sekula, "Reading an Archive," 446.

33. Poovey, *A History of the Modern Fact*, xiii.

34. In the preface to his major work of history, *La Méditerranée et le monde méditerranéen à l'époque de Philippe II* (1949), Braudel introduced the three levels of historical time that shaped his book via the metaphor of three interpenetrating layers of the sea: the sea's deepest depths symbolized the "quasi immobile" history of "geographic time"; the midlevel sea figured the "slowly rhythmed" history of "social time"; and the constantly changing froth of the waves symbolized the "traditional history" stamped by "individual time." See Braudel, "Préface de *La Méditerranée*," 273–75. In contrast to that work of history, the 1958 essay "History and the Social Sciences" seems more dominated by a distinction between two types of historical temporality belonging to *histoire événementielle* and the *longue durée*.

35. Poovey, *A History of the Modern Fact*, 1.

36. Foucault, "Preface," *The Order of Things*, xv–xxiv, xviii.

37. See ibid., xviii.

38. See Braudel, "Préface de *La Méditerranée*," 274. For the Kahn films on these topics, see *La Sainte Cathérine* (Sauvageot, Nov. 25, 1925) and *Mi-Carême* (Le Saint and Sauvageot, Mar. 3, 1921). The Gaumont newsreel catalogue shows that the Saint Cathérinettes were filmed 1911, 1913, 1920, 1921, and 1924.

39. On accidental details in early nonfiction film, see Veray, "Lendemains de victoire," 12, and Meyer, "Moments of Poignancy."

40. M. Bloch, *HC*, 60–61.

41. For analyses that focus in part upon the look at the camera in early cinema, see Van Dooren and Krämer, "The Politics of Direct Address"; Veray, "La Représentation de la guerre," 20–23; Gunning, "Before Documentary," 15, 18–19, and "'The Whole World Within Reach,'" 39–40; "Griffiths, *Wondrous Difference*, 72–74, 195–203; Belloï, "Lumière and His View"; Hammerton, *For Ladies Only*, 27, 68–71; and Toulmin and Loiperdinger, "Is It You?"

42. On the importance of "the unexpected and the involuntary" disclosures in both actuality and fiction films, see Ferro, *Cinema and History*, 30.

43. *Panorama des collections Albert Kahn*, 31.

44. See *JB*, 185, 197.

45. See Meusy, "La Diffusion des films de 'non-fiction,'" 184, and De Klerk, "A Few Remaining Hours."

46. Information on negatives from a handwritten memo by Victor Perrot titled "Cinémathèque" (Dec. 6, 1934), detailing his visit and informal inventory of the Kahn films.

47. See B. Anderson, *Imagined Communities*.

48. I have appropriated the term "screen capitalism," which he uses in reference to the past quarter century, from T. J. Clark's review of Benedict Anderson's work, "In a Pomegranate Chandelier," 6.

49. *La Basilique de la Nativité à Bethlehem* (Le Saint, Dec. 24, 1919) and *La Basilique de la Nativité à Bethlehem* (Sauvageot, Apr. 1925).

50. Braudel, "History and the Social Sciences," 33.

51. Ibid. For a possible earlier source of the sea metaphor, see M. Bloch, *HC*, 156.

52. For a critique of Braudel's notion of the *longue durée* as an evasion of the "messy" "here and now" of the decolonizing present of World War II France, see Ross, *Fast Cars, Clean Bodies*, 184–91 (quote from p. 190). On the ideological conservatism of Braudel's last works, particularly pertaining to French national identity, see Lebovics, *True France*, 1–2, and P. Anderson, *A Zone of Engagement*, 251–78.

53. Braudel, "History and the Social Sciences," 27. Subsequent references to this essay are cited in the text.

54. See M. Bloch, *HC*, 62; H. Lefebvre, *Everyday Life in the Modern World*, 1.

55. See Burke, *The French Historical Revolution*, 45–47.

56. See the sequence "Congrès national socialiste pour la IIIème Internationale, Tours, du 25 au 30 décembre 1920" in the compilation film *Le Quinzième Bulletin d'Albert Kahn: l'année 1920* (Conseil Général des Hauts-de-Seine/MAK, 1995). For a detailed reading of this Kahn footage, see Cadé, "Le Congrès de Tours."

57. See Tartakovsky, "Les Manifestations de rues dans les actualités," 26.

58. Kracauer, *History*, 216.

59. M. Bloch, *HC*, 28 (my emphasis).

60. Epstein, "The Senses I (b)," 245, and Bazin, "The Ontology of the Photographic Image," 15.

61. Matuszewski, "Une Nouvelle Source de l'histoire," 8, 6.

62. Kracauer, "Photography," 57–58.

63. Ibid., 49.

64. Heidegger, "The Age of the World Picture," 129.

65. Kracauer understood this all too well in his example of the League of Nations picture spread whose central meeting merely "serves as a pretext for showing Mr. Stresemann and Mr. Briand conversing in front of the entrance of the hotel." See Kracauer, "Photography," 57.

66. See Kracauer, "Boredom."

67. Matuszewski, "Une Nouvelle Source de l'histoire," 8.

68 Kracauer, *History*, 58.

69. Foucault, "Nietzsche, Genealogy, History," 76, 80.

70. Kracauer, *History*, 199; Foucault, "Nietzsche, Genealogy, History," 76.

71. Matuszewski, "Une Nouvelle Source de l'histoire," 8.

72. Foucault, *The Archaeology of Knowledge*, 123

73. On Matuszewski and the origins of his two pamphlets, see Mazaraki, "Boleslas Matuszewski."

74. For the original, see Matuszewski "Une Nouvelle Source de l'histoire" (Mar. 25, 1898), 11*n*1. For an English translation, see Matuszewski, "A New Source of History," 324*n*1.

75. Matuszewski collected and published these responses about six months after his "Une Nouvelle Source de l'histoire" in the second appendix to "La Photographie animée" (1898).

76. Matuszewski, "La Photographie animée," 85–86 and 76. The source cited, without date, by Matuszewski is *Le Républicain orléanais*.

77. *Encyclopédie par l'image: Le cinéma* (1925), 38.

78. For the full citation of Power's "famous proclamation" written in defense of the "unnamed and undistinguished masses of people" lost to a history that only praises "famous men," see Berg, *A Woman in History*, 130–39. Not surprisingly, Marc Bloch sought Power as a collaborator on the journal *Annales*. See ibid., 210–21, 251.

79. Power cited in Berg, *A Woman in History*, 139.

80. See *Les Grands Boulevards, Paris, Octobre 1913* (cameraman unknown).

81. Reynolds, "Germaine Dulac and Newsreel: 3 articles and Introduction."

82. See Dulac, "La Portée éducative et sociale des actualités," 204, "Cinema at the Service of History" (c. 1936), and Reynolds, "Germaine Dulac and Newsreel."

83. Dulac, "La Portée éducative et sociale des actualités," 204, and "Cinema at the Service of History."

84. Dulac, *Liberté* (May 18, 1932). On Dulac's brief employment with Gaumont and the discovery of her montage of actuality films titled *Le Cinéma au service de l'histoire*, which illustrates the continuing avant-garde fascination with common newsreel footage, see Borde and Guibbert, "*Le Cinéma au service de l'histoire* (1935)."

85. Hunt, "Introduction," 7. On Foucault's critique of Annaliste and Marxist social history, see P. O'Brien, "Michel Foucault's History of Culture," 25. As for the connections be-

tween Foucault and the Annalists, John Rajchman has argued that Foucault found in Bloch and Braudel "a corrective to one tendency in the philosophy of time in Bergson," that is, "the tendency of putting 'space' on the side of the 'practico-inert' while reserving for time the great questions of project and history." See Rajchman, "Foucault's Art of Seeing," 103. In other words, contra those who critique Bloch and Braudel for spatializing time, Foucault saw in their tendency a corrective to Bergson's excessive antispatiality. For an example of a critique that accuses Bloch and Braudel of committing the Bergsonian offense of spatializing time, see Bentley, "Past and 'Presence,'" 353.

86. Ferro, *Cinema and History*, 25–26.
87. Ibid., 27.
88. Burke, *The French Historical Revolution*, 10.
89. Kracauer, *Theory of Film*, 64. We can find an earlier version of these "alien patterns" in what he refers to as "mosaics" in *The Salaried Masses* (1929), 32.
90. Kracauer, "Photography," 50.
91. Kracauer, *The Salaried Masses*, 32.
92. Ibid.
93. For the cinematic version of this dream, see Bazin, "The Myth of Total Cinema."
94. Kracauer, *The Salaried Masses*, 32.
95. Bergson, *Creative Evolution*, 306.
96. Grierson, "First Principles of Documentary," 83, 87.
97. Braudel, quoted in Burke, *The French Historical Revolution*, 39.
98. See M. Bloch, *HC*, 20.
99. Although I do not pursue it here, it would be worth thinking about Kahn's Archive in relation to the Jewish messianic dimension that subtends the theme of the gathering up of history's detritus within Kracauer's and Benjamin's work, and that is also present in Derrida's treatment of the archive. See M. Hansen, "Benjamin and Cinema," 315, "'With Skin and Hair,'" 455, and Derrida, *Archive Fever*, 36.
100. Kracauer, *Theory of Film*, 64.
101. Kracauer, *The Salaried Masses*, 32.
102. Kracauer, *History*, 46, 199.
103. Vignaud, "L'Histoire vivante"; Albin-Guyot quoted in "Du Cinéma au cirque."

6. SEEING "FOR THE FIRST TIME"

1. Zola, *Thérèse Raquin*, 2.
2. Léger, "*La Roue*: Its Plastic Quality," 273.
3. Adorno, *Minima Moralia*, 141–42.
4. "Echos et informations" (Oct. 1, 1920), 2.
5. Kracauer, *Theory of Film*, 71–72.
6. Kracauer, "Preface," *Theory of Film*, li.
7. On Kracauer's review of *Thérèse Raquin*, see Hansen, "Decentric Perspectives," 67.
8. Adorno, "The Curious Realist: On Siegfried Kracauer."
9. For an example of the argument that modernism holds the everyday, and in particular its gendered associations, in contempt, see Felski, "Introduction," 608–609.
10. Cendrars, "The Modern: A New Art, the Cinema," 182.

11. Kracauer, *Theory of Film*, 73.

12. See Vaughn, "Let there be Lumière," 65, and Doane, *The Emergence of Cinematic Time*, 62–63, 129.

13. Burch, *Life to Those Shadows*, 6, 20.

14. Doane, *The Emergence of Cinematic Time*, 67–68.

15. P. Rosen, *Change Mummified*, 183, 195, 147.

16. For further examples of this argument concerning the harnessing of vision with the gradual shift to a narrative-focused cinema around 1907, see Bowser quoted in Hansen, *Babel and Babylon*, 79; Kirby, *Parallel Tracks*, 70; and Burch, *Life to Those Shadows*, 152–55.

17. See Lukács, "Narrate or Describe?" 118–19, 122–27, and "The Zola Centenary," 90–91. For Lukács, Zola and Flaubert's penchant for observation and description of ordinary and typical events "confused life with the everyday existence" of bourgeois alienation and their descriptive (as opposed to narrative) method was the "inevitable product" of "the continuous dehumanization of social life" ("Narrate or Describe?" 125, 127). The everyday, according to Lukács, is thus what remains of life after it undergoes the onslaught of industrial capitalism.

18. Colette, *Looking Backwards*, 111.

19. See Sutcliffe, *The Autumn of Central Paris*, 179–212.

20. The instrumentalist function of film as a tool of cultural preservation and restoration also provided one of the principal rationales for the establishment of the Section Cinématographique de l'Armée in February 1915, which in January 1917 combined with the Section Photographique de l'Armée (established in April 1915) to form the Section Photographique et Cinématographique de l'Armée (SPCA), the unit with which Kahn collaborated during the war.

21. On the war's transformation of the European archive in general, see Fritzsche, "The Archive," 21–22.

22. See Delmeulle, "Le Monde selon l'Encyclopédie Gaumont," 32–34, and Nesbit, *Atget's Seven Albums*, 193, 202. The impact of the war upon Kahn and his circle appears graphically in the pages of the bulletin published by the Société Autour du Monde.

23. See Bergson, "Speech given to the Académie des Sciences Morales et Politiques," 17. On the role of the "lost provinces" in sustaining support for the war, see L. V. Smith et al., *France and the Great War*, 11, 30, 142.

24. From December 25, 1914, to April 30, 1915, Brunhes, accompanied by Auguste Léon and Georges Chevalier, took four missions in the war zone of northeastern France. See *AK*, 248. For an overview of the towns and topics covered during their war documentation, see *Panorama des collections Albert Kahn*, 15. Le Saint and Sauvageot were both recruited to the Kahn Archive after their period of service as cameramen at the SPCA, from May 1917 to March 1918, and December 1917 to April 1918, respectively. Albert Dutertre also served as a cameraman in the Army from January to July 1919. See Lemaire, *Les Films militaires français*, 243.

25. See Hüppauf, "Emptying the Gaze," 24. For a comparative analysis of photography and film in France during the war, see Veray, "Montrer la guerre." For an international overview of the documentary role of film in the First World War, see Barsam, *Nonfiction Film*, 32–41, and Brownlow, *The War, the West, and the Wilderness*, 1–214; on fic-

tion and nonfiction film during the war, see Dibbets and Hogenkamp, eds., *Film and the First World War*, and Paris, ed., *The First World War and Popular Cinema*; and for works especially focused on France, see Veray, *Les Films d'actualité français de la Grande Guerre*, and Sorlin, "France: The Silent Memory."

26. Lemaire, *Les Films militaires français*, 8, 9; see also Sorlin, "The French Newsreels of the First World War," 513.

27. Armand Verhylle, "Le Cinéma témoigne devant l'histoire," *L'Écran* 8 (May 27, 1916): 2, quoted in Veray, "Fiction et 'non-fiction,'" 236.

28. Daughton, "Sketches of the *Poilu*'s World," 37; Veray, "Montrer la guerre," 235; and Sweeney, "*La Pudique Anastasie*," 8.

29. On the issue of civilians' and soldiers' mutual alienation, see L. V. Smith et al., *France and the Great War*, 104–107; Sorlin, "Cinema and the Memory of the Great War," 13; and Daughton, "Sketches of the *Poilu*'s World," 55, 63.

30. Colette, "Cinema," *Excelsior* (14 May 1918), reprinted as "The French Cinema in 1918" in *Colette at the Movies*.

31. Lefebvre, *Critique of Everyday Life*, 35.

32. On the uncanny connections between the home front and the front, in which the latter is described as a "grotesque parody of a modern city," see Gilbert, "'Unreal City': The Place of the Great War in the History of Modernity," x.

33. For further work on Feuillade's crime series, see Abel, "The Thrills of *Grande Peur*"; and Callahan, *Zones of Anxiety*. The surrealist interest in the series also stems, of course, from its origins in popular literature, its illogical nonlinear narrative, its chaotic threat to moral order, and its surfeit of eroticism in the black-stocking-clad figure of Irma Vep, played by Musidora.

34. Breton, "As in a Wood," 73. For contextualization of this article and more on Vaché, see Hammond, "Available Light," 5, 7, 21; and Ghali, *L'Avant-garde cinématographique*, 348. Vaché committed suicide in 1919. For another surrealist reflection upon *Les Vampires*, see Desnos, "*Fantômas, Les Vampires, Les Mystères de New York*" (1927).

35. Aragon and Breton, *Le Trésor des Jésuites*, extract reprinted in Virmaux and Virmaux, eds., *Les Surréalistes et le cinéma*, 114 (my emphasis).

36. For the statistics, see L. V. Smith et al., *France and the Great War, 1914–1918*, 69–71. Amidst the vast amount of work on the cultural impact of the war, see Fussell, *The Great War and Modern Memory*; Winter, *Sites of Memory, Sites of Mourning*; and Mackaman and Mays, eds., *World War I and the Cultures of Modernity*; and on the connection to film, see Eksteins, "The Cultural Impact of the Great War," and Hüppauf, *War, Violence, and the Modern Condition*.

37. Kahn, *Des Droits*, 12.

38. Hüppauf, "Emptying the Gaze," 27.

39. Delluc, "The Crowd," 162. On Delluc's wartime experiences, also reflected in his novels and poems from the era, see G. Delluc, *Louis Delluc*, 86–93.

40. Kracauer, *Theory of Film*, 7.

41. Bloch quoted in Lemaire, *Les Films militaires français*, 10.

42. On the profound effect of Apollinaire's death upon Cendrars, see Winter, *Sites of Memory*, 18–22.

43. On the difficulties and experiences of war cameramen, see Brownlow, *The War, the West, and the Wilderness*, 1–22, 55–68; and on the Aeroscope, see Brownlow, ibid., 9, 59, 66.

44. On the association of the use of film in the First World War with "the birth of modern propaganda," see L.V. Smith et al., *France and the Great War, 1914–1918*, 53; on direct and indirect censorship of the cameramen, see Sorlin, "The French Newsreels," 508–510; and on censorship of popular entertainments, see Sweeney, "*La Pudique Anastasie.*"

45. L. V. Smith et al., *France and the Great War, 1914–1918*, 34.

46. Veray, "Fiction et 'non-fiction,'" 239.

47. Henri Diamant-Berger, "Le Cinéma aux armées," *Le Film* 116 (June 3, 1918), cited in Veray, "Fiction et 'non-fiction,'" 242.

48. See Anon., "Le Vrai peut quelquefois," *Filma* 17 (Jan. 15–31, 1918).

49. Sherman, *The Construction of Memory in Interwar France*, 43.

50. Veray, "Fiction et 'non-fiction,'" 240.

51. For the influential role of actualities and documentaries in attracting France's cultural establishment to cinema, see Meusy, "La Diffusion des films de 'non-fiction,'" 176–80.

52. For the war's negative effect on French fiction film production, see Abel, *French Cinema: The First Wave*, 7–14. In 1921, 69 percent of the films shown in France were American. See Gauthier, *La Passion du cinéma*, 40.

53. For a more detailed coverage of the newspapers, journals, ciné-clubs, and conferences that made up this intense cinema culture, see Abel, *French Film Theory and Criticism*, vol. 1 (hereafter, *FFT1*), 5–8, 95–97, 195–99; Liebman, "French Film Theory, 1910–1921," 2–4; and Gauthier, *La Passion du cinéma*. And for a reconsideration of the gendered and indeed erotic origins of French cinephilia from the perspective of the actress and wife of Delluc, Ève Francis, see Amad, "'Objects became witnesses.'"

54. For more thorough explorations of the diverse approaches to film in France in the twenties, see Abel, *French Cinema: The First Wave*, and *FFT1*, 199–206; Liebman, "French Film Theory, 1910–1921"; Bordwell, *French Impressionist Cinema*; Ghali, *L'Avant-garde cinématographique*; Kuenzli, ed., *Dada and Surrealist Film*; Christie, "French Avant-Garde Film in the Twenties"; Hammond, *The Shadow and Its Shadow*; A. Williams, *Republic of Images*, 77–156; and Aitken, *European Film Theory and Cinema*, 69–90.

55. Vuillermoz, "Cinémathèque."

56. Kracauer, *Theory of Film*, 28.

57. Ibid., 55.

58. Aragon, "On Décor," 168.

59. Souday, "On the Cinema," 130.

60. For the quotes by Delluc, see Delluc, "Photographie," 33, which is also quoted in Kracauer, *Theory of Film*, 22. For Kracauer's interest in film's indeterminacy, or in other words its photographic-based ability to "transmit raw material without defining it," see *Theory of Film*, 20.

61. Canudo, "The Birth of a Sixth Art," 65.

62. As we have seen in chapter 4, other disciplining discourses hoped to attach the medium exclusively to the realm of education and science or standardize it through the grammar of continuity editing.

63. Haugmard, "The 'Aesthetic' of the Cinematograph," 84–85.

64. Delluc, "Beauty in the Cinema," 137 (my emphasis).

65. See Yhcam, "Cinematography," 74, and Bazin, "*Paris 1900*," 242.

66. Delluc, "Photographie," 33. Delluc's "secret unconscious" is a striking precursor to Benjamin's notion of the "optical unconscious." See Benjamin, " A Short History of Photography," 510, 512, and "The Work of Art," 117.

67. See Kracauer, *Theory of Film*, 71–73; Blanchot, "Everyday Speech," 242–43; and de Certeau, *The Practice of Everyday Life*, 91–110.

68. Kahn quoted in Beausoleil, "Albert Kahn," 14; Delluc, "Douglas Fairbanks," 82 (Delluc is specifically referring to the film *Aventure à New York* [*Manhattan Madness*, Allan Dwan, 1916]).

69. Epstein, "The Senses I (b)," 243 (my emphasis).

70. Ibid., 245.

71. As Linda Nochlin and others have pointed out, a central element of the French realist tradition was a passion for "direct observation and notation of ordinary, everyday experience" within an urban milieu. An example of this passion appears in Degas' notebooks: "No one has ever done monuments or houses from below, from beneath, up close, as one sees them going by in the streets." Degas quoted in Nochlin, *Realism*, 19.

72. For an example of Delluc's predilection for realistic scenes, see his "Antoine at Work."

73. Delluc, "Notes pour moi: *L'Âme du bronze*," 57 (my emphasis).

74. See Epstein, "For a New Avant-Garde," 351, and Léger, "*La Roue*: Its Plastic Quality," 274.

75. Léger, "*La Roue*: Its Plastic Quality," 273 (my emphasis). Léger's dedication to the idea of a cinema without scenarios in *Le Ballet mécanique* (1924; codirected with Dudley Murphy) and René Clair's visual hymn to the geometric mechanics of the Eiffel Tower in *La Tour* (1928) were just two of many films spawned by the decontextualized but highly influential machine aesthetic sequences in *La Roue*. See Léger, "*La Roue*: Its Plastic Quality," and Clair, "*La Roue*." Germaine Dulac also used sequences from *La Roue* to illustrate her lectures on the art of cinema.

76. Vuillermoz, "Before the Screen: Hermès and Silence," 157.

77. For examples of references to plant, bean, and flower-growth films, see Colette, "Cinema" (1920) 61; Dulac, "Les Esthétiques, les entraves, la cinégraphie intégrale," 104; Epstein, "Timeless Time," 17; and Cendrars, "The Modern: A New Art, the Cinema," 183.

78. Cendrars, "The Modern: A New Art, the Cinema," 182–83.

79. *La Nouvelle orientation* was the title of one of Kahn's fourteen publications whose preambles he is thought to have written, and the language of a new direction for humanity fills Kahn's *Des Droits et devoirs des gouvernements*.

80. The phrase comes from Vuillermoz, "Before the Screen: *Les Frères Corses*," 133. For an analysis of Comandon's films, see chapter 7.

81. On the phenomenal impact of American films in France during the teens, see Abel, "The Contribution of the French Literary Avant-Garde," 21–27; Abel, *FFT1*, 95–96; Abel, *French Cinema: The First Wave*, 10–12; Sadoul, *Histoire générale du cinéma* 4:29–70; Jeanne and Ford, *Histoire illustreé du cinéma* 1:78–88; and K. Thompson, *Exporting Entertainment*, 71–74, 85–90.

82. *The Cheat* apparently taught Abel Gance the rules of continuity editing. See Burch, *Life to Those Shadows*, 75.

83. Delluc, "Beauty in the Cinema," 137.

84. Ibid., 138.

85. Epstein, "On Certain Characteristics of *Photogénie*," 318.

86. Epstein, "Magnification," 236. Interesting comparisons might be made here with Roland Barthes' notion of the photographic *punctum*.

87. See Léger, "*La Roue*: Its Plastic Quality," 273.

88. Cocteau, "Carte Blanche," 173.

89. Léger, "The Machine Aesthetic," 54, 56, 57.

90. Aragon, "On Décor," 168.

91. Jameson, *The Political Unconscious*, 152 (my emphasis).

92. Epstein, "The Senses I (b)," 243.

93. Grimshaw, *The Ethnographer's Eye*, 45, 53, 119.

94. Aragon, "On Décor," 166.

95. Ibid., 165–68. For an investigation into the early conceptualization of cinema as modern magic, see R. Moore, *Savage Theory*.

96. For Colette's earlier reference to the close-up's ability to let us count individual eyelashes, see Colette, "They're all going to the cinema," 39.

97. For reference to these muse-like objects of criticism, see Delluc, "Contes du Cinéma: Téléphone," 11; Epstein, "*Le Cinématographe vu de l'Etna*," 134; Colette, "They're all going to the cinema," 39; Léger, "*Ballet mécanique*," 48. The reference to fixed attention comes from Cendrars, "The Modern: A New Art, the Cinema," 183

98. Epstein "Art of Incidence," 413.

99. See Delluc, "Contes du Cinéma: Téléphone."

100. Cendrars, "The Modern: A New Art, the Cinema," 183.

101. Epstein, "On Certain Characteristics of *Photogénie*," 317 (my emphasis). See also Epstein, "Le Regard du verre," 136.

102. Epstein, "Le Regard du verre," 136.

103. On the Bergsonian impact in the aesthetic field, see Antliff, *Inventing Bergson*; Harrison, Frascina and Perry, *Primitivism, Cubism, Abstraction*, 135–40, 231; Silverman, *Art Nouveau in Fin-de-Siècle France*, 307–310; and Crafton, *Émile Cohl*, 112–13.

104. Vuillermoz, "Devant l'Écran," October 10, 1917.

105. Sherman, *The Construction of Memory in Interwar France*, 13–14.

106. Proust, *Remembrance of Things Past* 2:554.

107. Dulac, "The Expressive Techniques of the Cinema," 310; Epstein, "For a New Avant-Garde," 352.

108. Dyssod, "En Marge du cinéma," 668.

109. Epstein, "Amour de Charlot," 150–51. For a later reference from 1932 to the relevance of *Laughter* to Buster Keaton slapstick film comedy, see Dr. E. Horn, "La Philosophie et le film."

110. A.R., "Bergson et le cinéma," 10.

111. On the tendency for anthropomorphism in trick and animation films, see Crafton, *Émile Cohl*, 275.

112. Vuillermoz, "Devant l'Écran," October 10, 1917.

113. Souday, "Les Derniers Prophètes: Bergsonisme et cinéma," 9. For a contemporary report on the Bergsonian debates, see "Les Philosophes à la rescouss," 16.

114. L'Herbier, "Hermès and Silence," 149.

115. Lukács, "The Zola Centenary," 91.

116. The father of theatrical naturalism in France, Antoine was also one of the leading proponents of cinematic naturalism and a frequent adaptor of Zola's work.

117. Epstein, "The Senses I (b)," 242.

118. Faure, "The Art of Cineplastics," 261.

119. Epstein, "Art of Incidence," 413.

120. Bergson, *Creative Evolution*, 341, and Epstein, "Art of Incidence," 413.

121. Artaud, "The Premature Old Age of the Cinema," 123.

122. Ibid., 123, 124.

7. ILLUMINATIONS FROM THE DARKENED "SANCTUARY"

1. Bergson, *Creative Evolution*, 299.

2. Epstein, "Magnification," 237.

3. Benjamin, "The Work of Art," 117.

4. Delamarre, "Jean Brunhes," 105.

5. Epstein, "Magnification," 237.

6. Benjamin *Arcades Project* [H2, 5], 206 (my emphasis).

7. Epstein, "Magnification," 237–38.

8. Benjamin, "The Work of Art," 117

9. For instance, a screening for Cardinal Dubois featured films from the holy land, and Bergson viewed films in the company of his wife and daughter. See *ADLP Projection Register* (1921–1950) [MAK], 3, 30.

10. For a detailed analysis of Paris's nonfiction screening venues, see Meusy, "La Diffusion des films de 'nonfiction,'" 186–88.

11. That Comandon's work only found a conventional scientific home with his position at the Institut Pasteur in 1933 is an indication perhaps of the scientific community's reticence to embrace film during the first three decades of the twentieth century. For Comandon's recognition of the fluid distinctions among different types of scientific films, see Comandon, "Rapport" (1931); and for further analysis of the distinctions between "films de vulgarization, films d'enseignement, [and] films de recherche," see O'Gomes, "Le Cinéma scientifique," 183–89; and Painlevé, "Scientific Film," 161–62. On French popular scientific films, see T. Lefebvre, "'Scientia': Le cinéma de vulgarisation scientifique au début des années dix"; Delmeulle, "Le Parent pauvre? La pratique du

documentaire chez Gaumont au début des années dix," 56–65; and Gaycken, "'A Drama Unites Them in a Fight to the Death.'"

12. *Je Sais Tout* (May 18, 1914).

13. For Comandon's 1932 reference to this event, see Comandon, "L'Évolution de la microcinématographie," 491. For the original 1909 report of the research, see Comandon, "Cinématographie, à l'ultra-microscope, de microbes vivants et des particules mobiles."

14. See *Je Sais Tout* (May 18, 1914): 630–31.

15. For evidence of Comandon's reference to using a frame-by-frame analysis of his film in the lecture he gave at the Académie des Sciences on October 26, 1909, see Comandon, "Cinématographie, à l'ultra-microscope, de microbes vivants et des particules mobiles," 940–41. In another publication from the same year, Comandon's text was illustrated by a series of vertically positioned frames from three of his films. See Comandon, "Cinématographie, à l'ultra-microscope, de microbes vivants et des particules mobiles" (Nov. 22, 1909): 1–3 [plus page of film frames captioned "Pathé frères"].

16. *Enquête de René Brunschwik sur une Bibliothèque du Film* (1927), 18.

17. Comandon, "Cinématographie, à l'ultra-microscope, de microbes vivants et des particules mobiles" (Oct. 26, 1909), 941.

18. Brunhes, "Ethnographie et Géographie humaine," 38.

19. The intention for the documents to be viewed by a group also explains why the stereographs, which could only be viewed for maximum effect with the aid of individually held stereoscopes, were abandoned after the 1908–1909 world tour.

20. See Pierre Deffontaines (a friend and disciple of Brunhes), quoted in Delamarre and Beausoleil, "Deux Témoins de leur temps," 106, and Brunhes, quoted in Delamarre, "Jean Brunhes," 104.

21. For evidence of Kahn's determination not to allow his films to be distributed, even for charity events, see letter from Brunhes to Gouverneur [?], Nov. 16, 1927, Brunhes Archives, MAK. The historian Michel Trebitsch has found that the writer and socialist Jean-Richard Bloch was invited to a meeting of the Union de Femmes Juives pour la Palestine on December 12, 1925, where he screened Camille Sauvageot's films (made for the Archives de la Planète) on Lord Balfour's visit to Palestine for the inauguration of the Hebrew University, which he himself had also attended (independent of Sauvageot). The screening was accompanied by Bloch's own commentary which Trebitsch describes as "militant" in its Zionist support. See Trebitsch, "Le Robinson juif." Trebitsch emphasizes, however, that Bloch's use of Kahn's film should not be read as evidence of a propagandistic function in Sauvageot's films, especially given Kahn's "silence" on his Jewish identity (100–101). Nonetheless, it speaks to the importance of a colonial backdrop for thinking about the Kahn Archive. For more on this issue, see chapter 8.

22. For example, the film ledger indicates that two copies were made of the film *Arrivée de Mon. Tagore au Bourget* "of which one [was] for Mon. Tagore." See *ADLP Film Register* [MAK], 86, 89.

23. See *ADLP Film Register* [MAK], 78–79. Sauvageot's color films, which used the Keller-Dorian process, were shot between 1928 and 1929, and also included scenes from the Southern Alps, a bullfight in Arles, and the town of Les Saintes-Maries de la Mer. See Leclerq-Weiss, "Le Procédé Keller-Dorian," 53–54. The subjects of Kahn's color films

were similar to Gaumont Chronochrome films: flower studies, still life, travel views, and short documentaries. See Meusy, "La Diffusion des films de 'non-fiction,'" 192.

24. See *Paris: Éclipse de soleil* (Sauvageot, Apr. 8, 1921). Films of a lunar eclipse were also taken. See *Boulogne: Éclipse de lune 1921* (Le Saint, Oct. 16–17, 1921). For the famous uncredited use of Eugène Atget's photograph "The Eclipse, Paris, April 12, 1912" (showing a group of Parisians staring at the sky while shielding their eyes) on the cover of a surrealist journal (thanks to Man Ray), see *La Révolution surréaliste* 7 (June 15, 1926).

25. Reported in André François-Poncet, *Bulletin de la Société Autour du Monde* (June 14, 1931), xxi.

26. See Colette, "Cinema" (1918), 45, and Depriel, "À la Gloire du cinéma," 61.

27. Gimpel, "Principe de la plaque autochrome," 178 (my emphasis).

28. This popular fascination with the recording of movement and time appears in early commentaries' preoccupations with the natural and urban movement of the leaves, waves, and crowds in the early Lumière films; the elision of space and time in trick films; the reversal of time in the practice of backward projection; and the mimicking of movement through space in "phantom ride" shots.

29. Benjamin will use such commonplace movements as the starting point for his analysis of the camera's "optical unconscious" in the "Work of Art" essay: "Whereas it is a commonplace that, for example, we have some idea what is involved in the act of walking (if only in general terms), we have no idea at all what happens during the split second when a person actually takes a step. We are familiar with the movement of picking up a cigarette lighter or spoon, but know almost nothing of what really goes on between hand and metal" (117).

30. Of course, Marey did not believe that cinema solved the problem of representing true movement either as it merely replicated rather than advanced upon the human eye.

31. Artaud, "The Premature Old Age of the Cinema," 123.

32. Although it is difficult to match up titles in the projection register with extant films in the Archive, *Les Fleurs* is most likely *Épanouissement de Fleurs* (Comandon, 1926–27), a film probably made by Comandon originally for Pathé but later purchased by Kahn. The projection register also refers to the title *Épanouissement de Fleurs*. However, as the MAK also has another flower film titled *Germination de Fleurs* (Comandon 1926–1929), it is difficult to determine exactly which film Bergson viewed. The important point is that both extant films are time-lapse flower studies by Comandon. The MAK also has a bean-germination film titled *Germination de Graines* (Comandon and de Fonbrune, 1926–27).

33. Bergson, *Creative Mind*, 18.

34. Epstein, "On Certain Characteristics of *Photogénie*," 318.

35. See Georges-Michel, "Henri Bergson nous parle au cinéma," 7, and his later recollection of interviews with the philosopher in which he mentioned the cinema, published in *En Jardinant avec Bergson*, 13–15.

36. Georges-Michel, "Henri Bergson nous parle au cinéma," 7.

37. For Bergson's earlier reference to the horse gallop example, see *Creative Evolution*, 332.

38. Bergson, "The Perception of Change," 251.

39. Bergson, "The Possible and the Real," 224.

40. Ibid.; Delluc, "Photographie," 33; Kracauer, "Photography," 56.

41. Georges-Michel, *En Jardinant avec Bergson*, 13.

42. Comandon, "Le Cinématographe instrument de laboratoire," 12.

43. Ibid.

44. Silverman, *Art Nouveau in Fin-de-Siècle France*, 312. On the connections between Rodin's art and Bergson's philosophy, see Silverman, ibid., 307–311.

45. See *Le Cinéma* (June 26, 1914), cited in *AK*, 53.

46. On the written correspondence between Rodin and Kahn from 1897 to 1917, see Bonhomme, "Correspondances . . . l'art et la philosophie."

47. *AK*, 51. Hanako was a protégé of Fuller's and had performed with her at the 1900 Exposition in Paris. It was also on the occasion of Fuller's performance in the Kahn gardens that Anatole France was introduced to Fuller, an event that he recounts in the preface to her memoirs published in 1908. See A. France, "Preface," in Loïe Fuller, *Quinze Ans de ma vie*, 5. France's recollection of being introduced to Fuller "at a luncheon of the 'Tour du Monde' in Boulogne" is undoubtedly a reference to Kahn's Autour du Monde luncheons.

48. Gunning, "Loïe Fuller and the Art of Motion," 86.

49. Georges-Michel, *En Jardinant avec Bergson*, 13.

50. See "Le Cinématographe des infiniment petits" (interview with Dr. Dastre).

51. See Epstein, "La Photogénie de l'impondérable," 249–53 and 238 (my emphasis).

52. Epstein, "The Senses I (b)," 242.

53. For a treatment of the relations between the biological films of Comandon and Carrel and early film theory, see Landecker, "Cellular Features." Although Landecker deals with the Bergsonian influence upon Carrel, she does not mention the Bergsonian influence upon Comandon (evident in several of his articles) nor the substantial body of films Comandon made within the Bergsonian environment of Kahn's community.

54. Kracauer, *Theory of Film*, 169, 170.

55. See Georges-Michel, *En Jardinant avec Bergson*, 109–123.

56. Kracauer, *Theory of Film*, 170. It is significant for my argument that Kracauer's discussion occurs in the context of his examination of film spectatorship which he connects to dreamlike and childlike modes of perception.

57. See *Aventures Quotidiennes* [*Everyday Adventures*] (Paris: Flammarion, 1920); reprinted as "Cinema" in *Colette at the Movies* (subsequent references in the text are from this volume); and Colette, "Cinema," in *Journey for Myself, Selfish Memories*. The Musée Galliera was the venue for some of the most important conferences on film in the early twenties. In 1924 between May and October it hosted a conference of lectures and screenings titled "Art in the French Cinema," which contained a whole section devoted to educational films. For a contextualization of the 1924 conference, see Gauthier, *La Passion du cinéma*, 74–76, 356–57.

58. My emphasis.

59. As used by Colette in 1920, the term *féeries* would have specifically connoted the early film genre of *féeries* or "multiple tableaux" trick films.

60. Comandon participated in the second part of the *Exposition de l'art dans le cinéma français* conference (devoted to "Educational Cinema"), held at the Musée Galliera in May–June and October 1924. Other film luminaries who participated in this conference, included Germaine Dulac, Léon Moussinac, Marcel L'Herbier, Jean Epstein, and Robert Mallet-Stevens.

61. For a more expansive treatment of the literary and biographical appeal of this film for Colette, see Amad "'These spectacles are never forgotten,'" 141–46.

62. See Delmeulle, "Le Parent pauvre?," 59.

63. Comandon, "Le Cinématographe instrument de laboratoire," 13. On the lack of scientific origins for Gaumont's early scientific films, see Delmeulle, "Le Parent pauvre?," 62.

64. For examples of the more research-oriented scientific films, see *Division du Trypanosome, agent de la maladie du sommeil* and *Phagocytose de bacilles tuberculeux*, two of the nineteen films Comandon produced at Boulogne. For the complete list, see Thévenard and Tassel, *Le Cinéma scientifique français*, 47.

65. Comandon, "Rapport," *Congrès du cinéma éducatif de Paris, 26–30 September 1931, Programme des Séances*, 1–2 (pages unnumbered in program consulted). For further references by Comandon to the need for scientific films to be guided by "sober, objective" intertitles or commentary, see Comandon, "Savoir Regarder."

66. Dulac commissioned Comandon's essay for the first and only issue of the journal *Schémas*. For the typed manuscript of the essay, see Comandon, "Les Possibilités artistiques de la cinématographie."

67. This does not seem to be common for other flower-blooming films that more often show the full life cycle of the flower ending with the wilted bloom.

68. See Gunning, "The Cinema of Attractions."

69. See Delluc's editorial in *Cinéa* (Dec. 2, 1921), 10.

70. On the surrealist-related interest in Painlevé, see the use of stills from Painlevé's films to illustrate the article by Artaud, "The Premature Old Age of the Cinema." For Bazin's interest in Painlevé, see his "Le Film scientifique: Beauté du hasard" (1947). For more on Painlevé, see Bellows and MacDougall, eds., *Science Is Fiction: The Films of Jean Painlevé*.

71. Benjamin, "Surrealism: The Last Snapshot of the European Intelligentsia."

72. For a detailed treatment of the "principle of excess" in Cohl's animation films, and their appeal to children and surrealists, see Crafton, *Émile Cohl, Caricature, and Film*, 268–83.

73. Breton, "As in a Wood," 74–75.

74. Docteur Crinon, "C'est Surtout à la Médecine et à la biologie que le cinématographe a fait de grands progrès," 628.

75. For a contemporary review of Comandon's early films for Pathé, see "Le Cinématographe et la biologie," *Ciné-Journal* (Apr. 5, 1913), 64.

76. Vuillermoz, "La Cinématographie des microbes," *Le Temps* (Nov. 9, 1922), and "La Musique des images," 64. In his column a few weeks after the November 9, 1922, article, Vuillermoz noted how people had been sending him letters asking where they could view the Comandon films as they were not being shown anywhere. See "Quelques Films," *Le Temps* (Nov. 22, 1922).

77. *Encyclopédie par l'image: Le cinéma*, 38; this issue of the encyclopedia was devoted to cinema. For contemporary Russian references to Comandon's films, see Tsivian, "Media Fantasies and Penetrating Vision," 84–85. According to Thierry Lefebvre, prewar popular scientific films were dominated by Fabre-inspired anthropomorphizing tropes, in addition to the incorporation of scientific experiments within the milieu of "everyday practices." See T. Lefebvre, "'Scientia,'" 89. See also Delmeulle, "Le Parent pauvre?," 61–63.

78. For examples of screenings attended by children or students, see *ADLP Projection Register* (MAK), 4, 10, 14, and 18.

79. Gaumont's early colored-flower studies were originally described in *Ciné-Journal* as having a "stereoscopic effect." See Delmeulle, "Le Parent pauvre?," 59.

80. For just one of Dulac's references to bean-germinating films, see Dulac, "Les Esthétiques, les entraves, la cinégraphie intégrale," 104. On Dulac's experimental films from the 1920s, see T. Williams, "Germaine Dulac: Du figurative à l'abstraction."

81. For a typed transcript of a Dulac lecture from around 1926–27, in which she mentions she will be screening a Comandon flower study (*La Germination des plantes à fleurs*) alongside two of her own films, see BiFi: Fonds Germaine Dulac 317 B 21 (sixth of nine talks), 9–10.

82. See BiFi: Fonds Germaine Dulac 317 B 21 (sixth of nine talks), 9–10.

83. Desnos, "*Fantômas, Les Vampires, Les Mystères de New York*," 399.

84. Aragon, "On Décor," 166.

85. This type of visuality resembles what Roger Cardinal more recently has described as "habits of looking which are akin to habits of touching." See Cardinal, "Pausing Over Peripheral Detail," 124.

86. See Benjamin, "On the Mimetic Faculty," 722.

87. For an elaboration of Benjamin's concept of mimesis, see Hansen, "Benjamin and Cinema," 329–32. See also Hansen, "Room-for-Play: Benjamin's Gamble with Cinema."

88. Colette, "*The Scott Expedition*," 16.

89. Caillois, "Mimétisme et psychasthénie légendaire," 118.

90. Dulac, "L'Essence du cinéma: L'idée visuelle," 65.

91. Delluc, "From Orestes to Rio Jim," 256.

92. Ibid. (my emphasis). For his reference to the "sensitivity of things," see Delluc, "Contes du cinéma: Téléphone," 11.

93. See Léger, "*La Roue*: Its Plastic Quality," 272.

94. Delluc, "Beauty in the Cinema," 139.

95. Benjamin, "Surrealism," 182, 190.

96. Benjamin, "The Work of Art," 117.

97. See Valentin, "Introduction to Black-and-White Magic," 97, and Breton, "As in a Wood," 73.

98. See Desnos, "Picture Palaces," 78. On the surrealists' preference for the *faubourg* cinemas and Breton's specific love of *films documentaires*, see Gauthier, *La Passion du cinéma*, 262–63, 269, and 244.

99. The phrase "temple of cinema" is Robert Brasillach's, quoted in Gauthier, *La Passion du cinéma*, p. 249.

100. For the reference to early cinema "fragments," see Gauthier, *La Passion du cinéma*, 140. On the program diversity of the Studio des Ursulines and other specialized screening rooms, see Gauthier, ibid., 140–41, 187, 190–91, 281–85. Dulac's lectures from the 1920s were illustrated with the Lumières' films, Comandon's scientific films, and fetishized sequences from recent "classics" (such as the rapid train montage from *La Roue*). See Dulac's lecture texts archived at BiFi: Fonds Germaine Dulac.

101. Kracauer, "Photography," 55–56. Bergson's theory of laughter is perhaps implied in Kracauer's invocation of the comical.

102. Kracauer, "Photography," 56. Kracauer's use of the "skin" trope will return in *Theory of Film* to describe film's counter-habitual tendencies. See *Theory of Film*, 55.

103. Clair, *Cinema Yesterday and Today*, 104.

104. Ibid. The temporal paradox for Clair lies in the fact that "the cinematograph, a machine for capturing minutes of life, had tried to defy time" yet at the same time, as a commercial product, it had become subject to the contingencies of capitalist time: "time was taking a terrible revenge by speeding up everything relating to the screen." For an interesting analogous reflection upon film's temporal paradox, see Bazin's description of cinema's "tragedy" discussed in the conclusion.

105. Kracauer, "Photography," 56.

106. This was not Franju's last visit to Boulogne. He returned to the botanical, if not cinematic, world of Kahn in his short promotional documentary on Paris's semisecret gardens titled *Paris est une forêt* (1965), in which a shot of Kahn's Japanese garden (which the voice-over commentary notes displays a certain taste for "exoticism") is followed by one of the rosery.

107. The extant Kahn films that most likely correspond to those Franju watched are *Paris marché aux bestiaux de la Villette* (Sauvageot, November 14, 1921), *Miséreux à une soupe populaire* (Sauvageot, February 15, 1927), and *Chômeurs faisant la queue devant une soupe populaire* (Sauvageot, January 20, 1921).

108. He might have also known of the Kahn Archive due to his acceptance in 1938 of the position of executive secretary of La Féderation Internationale des Archives du Film.

109. Most readings of *Le Sang des bêtes* recognize its obvious post-Holocaust, post-collaboration resonances.

110. See reference to Bazin and Kracauer's responses to *Paris 1900* (Nicole Védrès, 1947) in chapter 3 and the conclusion of this book.

111. Kracauer, *Theory of Film*, 308, 310.

112. This description of the "found" world to be discovered in the flea markets comes from André Breton's passage on the Saint-Ouen market in *Nadja*, 52. For an example of a Kahn flea market film, see *Marché aux puces, porte de Clignancourt* (Feb. 17, 1924).

113. See Gauthier, *La Passion du cinéma*, 119–20.

114. See Delluc, "Contes du cinéma: Téléphone," 11.

8. THE AERIAL VIEW

1. Brunhes, *Human Geography* (Abridged Edition), 36 (hereafter, *HG*).

2. See Evans, "Rapport (fragments)," 68.

3. See Kracauer, "The Mass Ornament," 77; and for overviews of the status of the aerial view in modernism, see Saint-Amour, "Modernist Reconnaissance," and Dubois, "Le Regard vertical ou les transformations du paysage."

4. See Virilio, *War and Cinema: The Logistics of Perception*.

5. Foucault, *The Birth of the Clinic*, 46.

6. Kracauer, *History: The Last Things Before the Last*, 122, and Foucault, "Nietzsche, Genealogy, History," 89.

7. De Certeau, "L'Espace de l'archive ou la perversion du temps," 5.

8. See Tollebeek, "'Turn'd to dust and tears,'" 244.

9. Foucault, *Discipline and Punish*, 189.

10. See Said, *Orientalism*, 41. Subsequent page references to this work appear in the text.

11. Ibid., 41, 42, 84. For other references by Said to the word *archive* to describe the discursive framing of Orientalism, see *Orientalism*, 13, 58, 81, 169.

12. For Said's reference to Orientalism as "a sort of imaginary museum without walls," see *Orientalism*, 166.

13. Foucault, *The Archaeology of Knowledge*, 129.

14. For Foucault's critique of the reduction of his work to a binary model of power, see Foucault, "Précisions sur le pouvoir: Réponses à certains critiques." For Said's critique of the ossification of power and the evaporation of possible resistance in the passage from Foucault's *The Archaeology of Knowledge* to *Discipline and Punish*, see Said, "Foucault and the Imagination of Power," 239–45, 240–41.

15. Foucault, *The Archaeology of Knowledge*, 6.

16. Jay, *Downcast Eyes*, 383. For Jay's discussion of the role of the visual in Foucault, see *Downcast Eyes*, 381–416. For an opposing interpretation of Foucault's attitude to vision, see Shapiro, *Archaeologies of Vision*, 294.

17. Kahn, *Des Droits*, 39; Foucault, *The Birth of the Clinic*, 46.

18. For diverse analyses indebted in different ways to Said's work and the articulation of the archive to colonial history and postcolonial theory, see Chakrabarty, *Provincializing Europe*, 42, 101; Richards, *The Imperial Archive: Knowledge and the Fantasy of Empire*; Spivak, *A Critique of Postcolonial Reason*, 198–245; and Shetty and Bellamy, "Postcolonialism's Archive Fever."

19. For an overview of the new colonial French history, see the review article, Sherman, "The Arts and Sciences of Colonialism." For key examples, see Conklin, *A Mission to Civilize: The Republican Idea of Empire in France and West Africa, 1895–1930*, and Peabody and Stovall, eds., *The Color of Liberty: Histories of Race in France*. For texts that deal with cinema in the French colonial context, see C. O'Brien, "The 'Cinéma colonial' of 1930s France"; Ezra, *The Colonial Unconscious*; Slavin, *Colonial Cinema and Imperial France*; Norindr, *Phantasmatic Indochina*; Andrew and Ungar, *Popular Front Paris and the Poetics of Culture*, 299–339; and Bloom, *French Colonial Documentary*.

20. For works of early cinema history that question rather than automatically assume the transparency of the film-colonialism bind, see Gunning, "'The Whole World Within Reach'" and "Before Documentary"; C. Russell, *Experimental Ethnography*, 51–115; De Klerk, "Home Away from Home: Private Films from the Dutch East Indies"; and

O'Shaughnessy, "Poor Propaganda: French Colonial Films of the 1930s." A similarly questioning spirit, applied to the related interactions of universal expositions and Orientalism, and photography and colonialism, appears respectively in Çelik and Kinney, "Ethnography and Exhibitionism at the Expositions Universelles," and Pinney and Peterson, eds., *Photography's Other Histories*.

21. O'Shaughnessy, "Poor Propaganda," 27.

22. On Comandon's hygienic reform films, see Landecker, "Cellular Features," 909, and Bloom, *French Colonial Documentary*, 100; and on Léon Poirier, see Andrew and Ungar, *Popular Front Paris and the Poetics of Culture*, 314–24. According to information from the MAK, Poirier was also a visitor to the Société Autour du Monde, and an incomplete version of his film *Amours exotiques* was purchased around 1925. Castelnau also directed *La Traversée du Sahara* (1923) as well as the 12-part series of short films *Le Continent mystérieux* (1924). For evidence of colonial attitudes by a Kahn cameraman, see Letter from Stéphane Passet to Kahn, February 1, 1913 (from Rabat); Letter from Passet to Kahn, January 21, 1913; and Letter from Passet to Kahn, January 19, 1914 (from Peshawar) [MAK Archives]. For Bergson's reference to "African savages," see Bergson, *Matter and Memory*, 154.

23. See Trebitsch, "Le Robinson juif."

24. Godlewska, "Napoleon's Geographers."

25. Livingstone, *The Geographical Tradition*, 216–19; Harvey, "Cosmopolitanism and the Banality of Geographical Evils," 215–20; and Said, *Culture and Imperialism*, 7.

26. Livingstone, *The Geographical Tradition*, 217, and Said, *Orientalism*, 81.

27. Said, *Orientalism*, 57.

28. Ibid., 3.

29. Aldrich, *Greater France*, 104.

30. See Heffernan, "The Science of Empire"; Godlewska, "Napoleon's Geographers"; Aldrich, *Greater France*, 103–106; and Said, *Orientalism*, 216–19.

31. On the "amnesia" within histories of French geography regarding the colonial context to the formation of the Vidalian school, see Soubeyran, "Imperialism and Colonialism versus Disciplinarity in French Geography."

32. See Ford, "Landscape and Environment in French Historical and Geographical Thought." A law was passed in 1906 to protect landscapes that had an aesthetic interest (127). The father of human geography in Germany, Friedrich Ratzel, developed a theory of geography based on the connection between soil and man that would later be appropriated by the Nazis.

33. Harvey, "Cosmopolitanism," 292. See also Said, *Orientalism*, 215–16.

34. Article cited in Aldrich, *Greater France*, 104.

35. Harvey, "Cosmopolitanism," 274.

36. Lebovics, *True France*, 200.

37. Ibid.

38. We need to remember here the specific context of cosmopolitanism in Kahn's case for it also entailed a negative association with the notion of the "wandering Jew" as a person who was faithful to no place. On this aspect of cosmopolitanism, see Lebovics, *True France*, 20.

39. On the rise of folklore studies in France and its connection to the political struggle over French national identity, see Lebovics, *True France*, 7–8, 135–61.

40. Lebovics, *True France*, 8. On the rural focus in Vidalian geography, see Guiomar, "Vidal de la Blache's *Geography of France*," 187–210.

41. Golan, *Modernity and Nostalgia*, ix, 27.

42. Ibid., 23.

43. Morton, *Hybrid Modernities*, 179.

44. Morton's evidence for the claim comes from Vidal de la Blache's texts, not Brunhes'. See Morton, *Hybrid Modernities*, 182–83; Brunhes, "From the Preface to the Second Edition" (1912), in *Human Geography: An Attempt at a Positive Classification*, x.

45. On Brunhes' redirection of Vidalean thought into environmental social geography, see Philo and Söderström, "Social Geography," 113–14.

46. See Brunhes, "Lecture: Mar. 27, 1916," 12, and Brunhes, "Lecture: Dec. 3, 1917," 14.

47. Brunhes, "Lecture: Jan. 27, 1913," quoted in *JB*, 158.

48. Brunhes, "Lecture: Mar. 27, 1916," 12.

49. For the conservative implications of this turn from the "harder" biologically determined physical conceptualizations of race to the "softer" cultural conception, see Fogarty and Osborne, "Constructions and Functions of Race in French Military Medicine, 1830–1920," 206–209, 225–27.

50. Brunhes, *Races*, 10.

51. See Brunhes, "Lecture: Mar. 27, 1916," 12 (my emphasis), and "Lecture: Dec. 3, 1917," 15.

52. Brunhes, "Lecture: Dec. 3, 1917," 15.

53. See Wilder, "Framing Greater France Between the Wars," 203.

54. Kahn, *Des Droits*, 44.

55. Aerial photographs are more abundant in the 1925 edition, which contains approximately thirteen, than in the 1910 and 1912 editions, which each contain two. The 1947 edition contains eighteen aerial images.

56. Brunhes, *La Géographie humaine* (hereafter, *GH*), 19 (my emphasis).

57. Letter from Brunhes to Passet, May 8, 1912, quoted in *JB*, 201.

58. Buttimer, *Society and Milieu in the French Geographic Tradition*, 44.

59. On the popularity of the metaphor of imprinting in Brunhes' and Vidal's texts, see Besse, *Voir la Terre*, 106–107.

60. See, for example, *Experiences biologiques: Le sang* (Jean Comandon and Pierre de Fonbrune, 1926–1929).

61. See Brunhes, "Ethnographie et Géographie humaine," 32.

62. Thanks to Leora Auslander for first bringing this anecdote to my attention. Marc Bloch's experience as an intelligence officer no doubt helped him to understand sooner than many others the importance of aerial photography for studying lands and their history. See É. Bloch and Cruz-Ramirez, *Marc Bloch*, 143, and also Golan, *Modernity and Nostalgia*, 67. The full *deep* historical import of aerial imagery would emerge in the 1920s and 1930s with the development of aerial archaeology and geology.

63. See Marie-Claire Robic cited in Besse, *Voir la Terre*, 106 (my emphasis).

64. Raulff cited in Audoin-Rouzeau, "Introduction," Bloch, *Écrits de guerre*, 5.

65. Delluc, "From Orestes to Rio Jim," 256, and "Beauty in the Cinema," 139.
66. Foucault, "Of Other Spaces," 24.
67. Epstein, "The Senses 1 (b)," 11.
68. Delluc, "From Orestes to Rio Jim," 256.
69. See Kracauer, *Theory of Film*, 45.
70. Brunhes, *La Géographie humaine*, vol. 3 (illustrations) (3d ed., 1925), 135.
71. For a citation of Vidal de la Blache's phrase "humanized landscapes," see Buttimer, *Society and Milieu in the French Geographic Tradition*, 41.
72. Brunhes, *GH*, 21.
73. Delluc, "Beauty in the Cinema," 138.
74. Epstein, "Magnification," 235.
75. Epstein, "On Certain Characteristics of *Photogénie*," 318. The physiognomic capacity of the camera that Brunhes intuited and Epstein explored was even more explicitly theorized in Béla Balázs's *Theory of the Film* (1945), which privileged the close-up of the face as the essence of cinematic reality. See Balázs, "The Close-Up" and "The Face of Man," and Koch, "Béla Balázs."
76. Golan, *Modernity and Nostalgia*, 92.
77. Ibid., 96–104.
78. See *De l'Aillette à Reims: Les champs de bataille en dirigeable 1919* (Lucien Le Saint, 1919).
79. See Brunhes, *GH*, 39.
80. See *Prostitué devant une maison close* (cameraman unknown, 1917).
81. See *ADLP Film Register* [MAK], 34.
82. Over half a million soldiers and laborers were imported into France during the war. See Stovall, "Love, Labor, and Race," 297.
83. See Conklin, *A Mission to Civilize*, 142–73; Stovall, "Love, Labor, and Race" and "National Identity and Shifting Imperial Frontiers."
84. Stovall, "Love, Labor, and Race," 299; Golan, *Modernity and Nostalgia*, 51; and Conklin, *A Mission to Civilize*, 250–51.
85. For overviews of this colonial shift, see Conklin, *A Mission to Civilize*, 6, 41, 74–77, 174–211. Sarraut was Governor-General of French Indochina from 1911–14 and 1916–19 and minister for the colonies from 1920–24 and 1932–33.
86. Conklin, *A Mission to Civilize*, 41.
87. F. Bernot, "Éloge du voyage," 232. The report was originally addressed to French high school students but published in Kahn's *Bulletin de la Société Autour du Monde*.
88. Said, *Orientalism*, 169.
89. Challaye, "Les Leçons d'un voyage autour du monde," 52. Challaye's total pacifism later led him to support the Vichy regime.
90. During the Archive's existence, resistance in the colonies ranged from the antidraft riots in French West Africa and Indochina in the First World War to the 1925 Druze revolt in Syria, the 1925 Rif War in Morocco, and the 1930 Yen Bay rebellion in Indochina.
91. Foucault, "Of Other Spaces," 24.
92. For his analysis of the central role that the Angkor Wat ruins played in French colonial ideology, see Norindr, *Phantasmatic Indochina*, 5, 18–19, 25–27.

93. On women in Muybridge's studies, see L. Williams, "Film Body," and C. Russell, *Experimental Ethnography*, 66–74.

94. L. Williams, "Film Body," 512.

95. The Archive also contains similar films shot (but not by a Kahn cameraman) in Djibouti in 1920 for the Mission Michel Cote. On North African postcards from the colonial era, see Alloula, *The Colonial Harem*, and Sebbar, Taraud, and Belorgey, eds., *Femmes d'Afrique du Nord*.

96. See "Les maisons closes" in the film *Liban* (Le Saint, 1919). For the more comprehensive filming done in Lebanon, see *Le Levant français: Beyrouth* (1919; Conseil Général des Hauts-de-Seine/MAK). The French mandate in Lebanon marked the culmination of France's centuries-long claim to a protectorate of Catholic and Christian subjects of the Ottoman Empire. The mandate was thus in effect a religious protectorate of the Maronite minority in Lebanon, France's closest allies in the Levant, sealing the "special" historical relationship between them. For a detailed history of the French mandate period in Lebanon and Syria, which she argues operated within a colonial framework, and in response to a crisis of paternity and gender roles in the postwar period, see E. Thompson, *Colonial Citizens*.

97. Gouraud cited in Thompson, *Colonial Citizens*, 40.

98. Thompson, *Colonial Citizens*, 21.

99. Ibid., 21, 25. On rumors of the rape of Muslim women by French soldiers that circulated in anti-French propaganda, see ibid., 47–8.

100. See *Bulletin du Comité National d'Études Sociales et Politiques*, Dec. 5, 1927; Mar. 5, 1928; and Mar. 26, 1928.

101. Thompson, *Colonial Citizens*, 86–87.

102. Foucault, *Discipline and Punish*, 187, 224.

103. Ibid., 189.

104. Lukács, "Narrate or Describe?"

105. See B. Anderson, *Imagined Communities*.

106. Stoller, "Tense and Tender Ties," 831, 843.

107. Vidal de la Blache's description of Brunhes' *Géographie humaine* made in 1911, cited in Brunhes, "Préface de la Troisième Édition," v.

108. Foucault, *Discipline and Punish*, 191.

109. See Foucault, "Lives of Infamous Men," 170–71.

110. Challaye, "Les Leçons d'un voyage autour du monde," 54.

111. Evans, "Rapport (fragments)," 67.

112. For a cultural history of French "exhibitionitis," see Hamon, *Expositions*.

113. Amid the vast amount of work on the 1931 colonial exposition, see Ageron, "L'Exposition Coloniale de 1931"; Lebovics, *True France*, 51–97; Norindr, *Phantasmatic Indochina*, 14–33; Morton, *Hybrid Modernities*; and Golan, *Modernity and Nostalgia*, 114–18.

114. Benjamin, "Fourier or the Arcades," *Charles Baudelaire*, 158.

115. On the out-of-scale proportions of the different pavilions, see Hodeir, "Decentering the Gaze at French Colonial Exhibitions," 242–43; Morton, *Hybrid Modernities*, 206–213; and Golan, *Modernity and Nostalgia*, 115. But according to Hodeir (251*n*26), the Angkor Wat temple was reconstructed to scale.

116. Promotional line cited in Morton, *Hybrid Modernities*, 208.

117. The Musée Permanent des Colonies was the exception to the general rule of impermanence for the 1931 Exposition pavilions. For an analysis of the "cinematographical
effect" of the design of the exhibition, see Hodeir, "Decentering the Gaze at French Colonial Exhibitions," 242.

118. On the Surrealist Counter-Exposition, see Norindr, *Phantasmatic Indochina*, 34–71.
For a history that focuses on the weaknesses rather than the successes of the interwar
French imperial effort, see Thomas, *The French Empire Between the Wars*. In 1935 Al-
bert Sarraut lamented that most of the French remained indifferent about the colonies.
See Aldrich, *Greater France*, 114.

119. Like Challaye, Aupiais would also align himself with the Vichy regime.

120. See Fritzsche, "The Archive," 26–27.

121. For a detailed account of the questions surrounding Bergson's death, such as whether
he died as a result of contracting bronchitis while lining up in freezing conditions at
the Prefecture of Police, and whether he had spiritually if not officially converted to
Catholicism by the end of his life, see Soulez, *Bergson: Biographie*, 271–74.

122. On the controversial fate of the *fichier juif*, see Combe, "Les Fichiers de juifs," and Albert, "Vichy and the Jews: A Past That Is Not Past," 236–38.

CONCLUSION

1. Perrot, "À la Recherche de l'écriture perdue," 10.

2. Kracauer, *Theory of Film*, 63–64.

3. For the original Léger, see "À Propos du Cinéma," 340.

4. See Langlois cited in Mannoni, *Histoire de la Cinémathèque française*, 24.

5. See Kracauer, "Photography," 50, 62.

6. Moholy-Nagy, *Painting, Photography, Film*, 36.

7. Elsaesser, "Après Lumière," 283.

8. Fritzsche, "The Archive," 39.

9. Delluc, "Beauty in the Cinema," 137.

10. Shields, *Lefebvre, Love, and Struggle*, 13.

11. Michael Gardiner on Lefebvre cited in Shields, ibid., 29.

12. Shields, *Lefebvre, Love, and Struggle*, 118.

13. For this description of Kracauer's *The Salaried Masses* (1929), see Mülder-Bach, "Introduction," *The Salaried Masses*, 17. For Kracauer's reference to the "dust of everyday
existence," see *The Salaried Masses*, 93.

14. See Benjamin, *The Arcades Project* [C1, 3], 82 and 871.

15. Ibid., [N11, 4], 476, and [N2, 6], 461.

16. See Bazin, "The Evolution of the Language of Cinema," 37. This essay also provides
evidence of Bazin's frequent use of geographical terminology.

17. Bazin, "La Terra Trema," 41.

18. Bazin, "An Aesthetic of Reality," 38. See Delluc, "From Orestes to Rio Jim," 256.

19. Bazin, "On *Why We Fight*: History, Documentation, and the Newsreel," 188.

20. For references to Zavattini's dream, see Bazin, "The Evolution of the Language of Cinema," 37, Bazin, "De Sica: Metteur en Scène," and Bazin, "*Umberto D*: A Great Work," 67, 76, 82. For his reference to the "filmic monster," see Bazin, "*La Terra Trema*," 45.

21. Bazin, "*Paris 1900*," 241.

22. I intend to explore the terrain set out by Bazin in these writings in a future project on the archival imaginary in post–Second World War French visual culture.

23. Bazin, "De Sica: Metteur en Scène," 77.

24. See Bazin, "*Umberto D*: A Great Work," 81, and "De Sica: Metteur en Scène," 76.

25. Bazin, "De Sica: Metteur en Scène," 76. Bazin's exploration of Bergsonian duration becomes even more explicit in a review of Henri-Georges Clouzot's *The Picasso Mystery* (1956) in which he focuses upon the film's ability to represent the "phenomenon of unpredictability," connecting this quality to the fact that "only film could make us see duration itself." See "A Bergsonian Film: *The Picasso Mystery*," 212–13.

26. For his invocations of the "flow of life," see Kracauer, *Theory of Film*, 164–70.

27. For works related to the role of the archive in contemporary art and culture, see Suzanne Pagé, *Voilà: Le Monde dans la tête* (exhibition catalogue); Schaffner and Winzen, eds., *Deep Storage: Collecting, Storing, and Archiving in Art*; Comay, ed., *Lost in the Archives*; and Enwezor, ed., *Archive Fever: Uses of the Document in Contemporary Art*.

28. For works that reflect upon diverse archival turns in moving-image practice, including found footage compilations, amateur films, structuralist reappropriations, and digital remediations, see Katz, "From Archive to Archiveology"; Hill, "(Re)performing the Archive"; Danks, "The Global Art of Found Footage Cinema"; Russell, *Experimental Ethnography*, 238–72, and "Parallax Historiography"; Zimmerman, "Morphing History into Histories"; Rony, "The Quick and the Dead"; Skoller, *Shadows, Specters, Shards*; and Connarty and Lanyon, eds., *Ghosting*.

29. For the English version of the project, see Nora, ed. *Realms of Memory: Rethinking the French Past*.

30. Nora, "Between Memory and History," 11.

BIBLIOGRAPHY

CORRESPONDENCE, DOCUMENTS, LECTURES, AND JOURNALS CONSULTED AT MAK

ADLP Film Register (1919–1931)

ADLP Projection Register (1921–1950)

Brunhes, Jean: lectures delivered at the Collège de France (1912–1917)

Bulletin de la Société Autour du Monde

Bulletin du Comité National d'Études Sociales et Politiques

Correspondence between Jean Brunhes and Albert Kahn

Correspondence between Jean Brunhes and Stéphane Passet

Correspondence between Henri Bergson and Albert Kahn (1879–1894)

Dutertre, Albert. "Journal de route de mon voyage autour du monde du 13 novembre 1908 au 11 mars 1909," Paris.

Film development index cards [*Fiches de développement*]

Kahn, Albert. "Nos Fondations" (1933) (typed document).

OTHER PRIMARY AND CONTEMPORANEOUS SOURCES

Antoine, E. "Mon Voyage Autour du Monde: Octobre 1912–Août 1913." *Bulletin de la Société Autour du Monde* (1915): 89–116.

Apollinaire, Guillaume. "Le Rabachis" (1910). *Oeuvres complètes de Guillaume Apollinaire*, 485–89. Vol. 1. Ed. Michel Décaudin. Paris: André Balland and Jacques Lecat, 1965.

"Une Application insoupçonnée: À l'Extension des principales langues européenes et en particulier du français et à la reduction des patois" (editorial). *Le Courrier cinématographique* (Sept. 29, 1917): 4.

A.R. "Bergson et le cinéma." *Le Film* 114 (May 20, 1918): 10.

Aragon, Louis. "On Décor" (1916). Reprinted in Abel, ed., *French Film Theory* 1:165–68.

Aragon, Louis and André Breton. *Le Trésor des Jésuites.* Originally published in *Variétés* (June 1929), Special issue on "Le Surréalisme en 1929." Extract reprinted in Virmaux and Virmaux, eds., *Les Surréalistes et le cinéma.* 113–14.

"Les *Archives de la Planète* sont présentées au Président de la République" [BiFi: Fonds Victor Perrot (hereafter, FVP); press clipping].

"Les Archives du cinéma." *Ciné-Journal* (May 3, 1913): 17.

"Les Archives de la parole." *Ciné-Journal* (Oct. 18, 1913): 9.

"Les Archives cinématographiques et les cinémathèques." *L'Étoile belge* (Aug. 11, 1922) [BiFi: FVP 054; press clipping].

"Les Archives cinématographiques de Paris." *Le Petit Niçois* (Aug. 26, 1922) [BiFi: FVP 048; press clipping].

Artaud, Antonin. "The Premature Old Age of the Cinema." *Les Cahiers jaunes: Cinéma* 33 (1933): 22–25. Reprinted in Abel, ed., *French Film Theory* 2:122–24.

Aubert, "Communication de M. Aubert." *Exposition du cinématographe: Section du film documentaire et d'enseignement* (Apr. 1922) 7 [BNF-AS: Rk 583; exhibition catalogue].

Aubert, Louis F. "Henri Bergson." *Bulletin de la Société Autour du Monde* (1928): 13–21.

Balázs, Béla. "The Close-Up" and "The Face of Man" (from *Theory of the Film* [1945]). In Mast and Cohen, eds., *Film Theory and Criticism*, 255–64.

Baudelaire, Charles. "The Painter of Modern Life" (1863). *Selected Writings on Art and Literature*, 390–435. London: Penguin, 1972.

——. "The Salon of 1859" (1859). *Selected Writings on Art and Literature*, 285–324.

Benjamin, Walter. *The Arcades Project.* Trans. Howard Eiland and Kevin McLaughlin. Cambridge and London: Belknap Press of Harvard UP, 2002.

——. *Charles Baudelaire: A Lyric Poet in the Era of High Capitalism* (1939). Trans. Harry Zohn. London: Verso, 1973.

——. "Fourier or the Arcades" (1935). In *Charles Baudelaire*, 157–60.

——. "Little History of Photography" (1931). In *Walter Benjamin, Selected Writings*, vol. 2: *1927–1934*, 507–530. Ed. Michael W. Jennings, Howard Eiland, and Gary Smith. Trans. Rodney Livingstone. Cambridge and London: Belknap Press of Harvard UP, 1999.

——. "On the Mimetic Faculty" (1933). *Walter Benjamin, Selected Writings*, vol. 2: *1927–1934*, 720–22.

——. "Some Motifs in Baudelaire" (1939). In *Charles Baudelaire*, 107–54.

——. "The Storyteller." *Illuminations* (1936), 83–110. Trans. Harry Zohn. New York: Schocken, 1968.

——. "Surrealism: The Last Snapshot of the European Intelligentsia" (1929). In *Reflections*, 177–92. Trans. Edmund Jephcott. New York: Harcourt Brace, 1978.

——. "The Work of Art in the Age of Its Technological Reproducibility" (1936) (second version). In *Walter Benjamin, Selected Writings*, vol. 3: *1935–38*, 101–133. Ed. Michael W. Jennings, Howard Eiland, and Gary Smith. Trans. Edmund Jephcott, Howard Eiland, and Others. Cambridge and London: Belknap Press of Harvard UP, 2002.

Bergson, Henri. *Creative Evolution* (1907). Trans. Arthur Mitchell. New York: Dover, 1998.

——. *The Creative Mind: An Introduction to Metaphysics* (1934). Trans. Mabelle L. Andison. New York: Philosophical Library, 1946.

———. *Evolution créatrice* (1907). Geneva: Éditions Albert Skira, 1945.

———. *Laughter* (1900). Reprinted in Wyle Sypher, ed., *Comedy*, 61–192. Trans. Fred Rothwell. New York: Doubleday Anchor, 1956.

———. "Letter from Henri Bergson." *Bulletin de la Société Autour du Monde* (June 14, 1931): iii–iv.

———. *Matter and Memory* (1896). Trans. N. M. Paul and W. S. Palmer. New York: Zone, 1991.

———. *Mélanges*. Ed. André Robinet. Paris: Presses Universitaires de France, 1972.

———. "La Perception du changement." Lecture presented at Oxford University, May 26–27, 1911. Reprinted in *Mélanges*, 888–914.

———. "The Perception of Change" (1911). Reprinted in Pearson and Mullarkey, eds., *Henri Bergson: Key Writings*, 248–66.

———. "The Possible and the Real." Lecture presented at Oxford University, Sept. 24, 1920. Reprinted in Pearson and Mullarkey, eds., *Henri Bergson: Key Writings*, 223–32.

———. *Le Rire: Essai sur la signification du comique* (1900). Paris: Quadrige/Puf, 1940.

———. "Speech given to the Académie des sciences morales et politiques" (Dec. 12, 1915). Reprinted in *Bulletin de la Société Autour du Monde* 1 (1915): 16–23.

———. *Time and Free Will: An Essay on the Immediate Data of Consciousness* (1889). Trans. Frank Lubecki Pogson. New York: Macmillan, 1910.

———. *The World of Dreams* (1901). Trans. Wade Baskin. New York: Philosophical Library, 1958.

Bernot, F. "Éloge du voyage: Discours prononcé par F. Bernot à la distribution des prix du lycée de Sens." *Bulletin de la Société Autour du Monde* (1914): 231–37.

Bonnet-Brodart (?) to Victor Perrot, Feb. 23, 1921 [BiFi: FVP 054; letter].

Breton, André. "As in a Wood" (1951). Reprinted in Hammond, ed., *The Shadow and Its Shadow*, 72–77.

———. "Manifesto of Surrealism" (1924). Reprinted in *Manifestoes of Surrealism*. Trans. Richard Seaver and Helen R. Lane. Ann Arbor: U of Michigan P, 1972.

———. *Nadja* (1928). Trans. Richard Howard. New York: Grove Press, 1960.

Brooks, R. P. "Speech." *Bulletin de la Société Autour du Monde* (June 14, 1931): xiv–xv.

Brunhes, Jean. "Ethnographie et Géographie humaine." *L'Ethnographie: Bulletin de la Société d'ethnographie de Paris* (Oct. 15, 1913): 29–40.

———. "From the Préface to the First Edition" (1910) and "From the Preface to the Second Edition (1912)." *Human Geography: An Attempt at a Positive Classification*. Ed. Isaiah Bowman and Richard Dodge. Trans. I. C. LeCompte. New York and Chicago: Rand McNally, 1920.

———. *La Géographie humaine: Essai de classification positive. Principes et exemples*. Paris: Librairie Félix Alcan, 1910 (2d ed., 1912; 3d ed., 1925).

———. *Human Geography* (Abridged Edition, 1910). Ed. Mariel Jean-Brunhes Delamarre and Pierre Defontaines. Trans. Ernest F. Row. London: George G. Harrap, 1952.

———. "Un Nouveau Procédé de reproduction appliqué à l'étude et à la representation des faits géographiques: Phototypie stéréoscopique." *Études géographiques* (Jan. 1900): 1–11.

———. "Préface de la Troisième Édition." *La Géographie humaine*, i–xi. 4th ed. Paris: Librairie Félix Alcan, 1934.

——. "La Question du format (en vue des reproductions géographiques photographiques)." *Tourista: Revue pratique de voyages* (Oct. 1, 1903): 139–41.

——. *Races* [documents commentés par Mariel Jean-Brunhes]. Paris: Firmin-Didot, 1930.

Caillois, Roger. "Mimétisme et psychasthénie légendaire." In *Le Mythe et l'homme*, 84–120. Paris: Éditions Gallimard, 1937.

Canudo, Ricciotto. "The Birth of a Sixth Art." *Les Entretiens idéalistes* (Oct. 25 1911). Reprinted in Abel, ed., *French Film Theory* 1:58–66.

——. "Reflections on the Seventh Art" (1923). Reprinted in Abel, ed., *French Film Theory* 1:291–303.

Cendrars, Blaise. "The Modern: A New Art, the Cinema." *La Rose rouge* 7 (June 12, 1919): 108. Reprinted in Abel, ed., *French Film Theory* 1:182–83.

Challaye, Félicien. "Les Leçons d'un voyage autour du monde." *Bulletin de la Société Autour du Monde* (Jan.–Dec. 1919; Jan.–Mar. 1920): 51–57.

"Du Cinéma au cirque: Le Gala de la cinémathèque nationale." *Miroir* (Apr. 8, 1933).

"Le Cinéma à la Préfecture de police." *Le Journal* (Feb. 13, 1914): 7.

"Le Cinéma d'éducation." *Le Journal du Ciné-Club* (Nov. 19, 1920): 7.

"Le Cinématographe des infiniment petits" (interview with Dr. Dastre). *Lectures pour tous: Revue universelle et populaire illustrée* (Oct. 1909): 407–410.

"Le Cinématographe et la biologie." *Ciné-Journal* (Apr. 5, 1913): 64.

Collection phonotèque nationale, Catalogue établi par la Commission internationale des arts et traditions populaires. Paris: Unesco, 1952.

Cocteau, Jean. "Carte Blanche." *Paris-Midi* (Apr. 8 and May 12, 1919): 2. Reprinted in Abel, ed., *French Film Theory* 1:172–74.

Colette [Sidonie Gabrielle]. "Cinema." *Excelsior* (May 14, 1918). Reprinted as "The French Cinema in 1918" in *Colette at the Movies*, 42–46.

——. "Cinéma" (1920). *Aventures Quotidiennes* in *Oeuvres Complètes de Colette*. Vol. 6:424–27. Paris: Le Fleuron, Flammarion, 1949. Reprinted as "Cinema" in *Colette at the Movies*. 59–61.

——. *"Civilisation"* (review). *Le Film* (May 28, 1917). Reprinted in *Colette at the Movies*. 21–23.

——. *Colette at the Movies: Criticism and Screenplays* (1974). Ed. Alain Virmaux and Odette Virmaux. Trans. Sarah W. R. Smith. New York: Ungar, 1980.

——. *Colette au cinéma: Critiques et chroniques, Dialogues des films*. Ed. Alain Virmaux et Odette Virmaux. Paris: Flammarion, 1974.

——. *Journey for Myself, Selfish Memories*. Trans. David le Vay. London: Peter Owen, 1971.

——. *Looking Backwards* [Translation of *Journal à rebours* (1941) and *De ma fenêtre* (1944)]. Trans. David Le Vay. Bloomington: Indiana UP, 1975.

——. *"The Scott Expedition."* *Le Matin* (June 4, 1914). Reprinted in *Colette at the Movies*, 16–17.

——. "They're all going to the cinema." *Le Film* (July 21, 1917). Reprinted in *Colette at the Movies*, 37–39.

Comandon, Dr. Jean [presented by M. A. Dastre]. "Cinématographie, à l'ultra-microscope, de microbes vivants et des particules mobiles." *Compte rendus hebdomadaires des séances de l'Académie des Sciences* 149 (1909): 938–41.

——. "Cinématographie, à l'ultra-microscope, de microbes vivants et des particules mobiles." *Librairie des comptes rendus des séances de l'Académie des Sciences* (Nov. 22, 1909): 1–3 [includes page of film frames captioned "Pathé frères"].

——. "Le Cinématographe instrument de laboratoire." *Exposition du cinématographe, Section du film documentaire et d'enseignement* (Apr. 20–30, 1922): 12–13.

——. "L'Évolution de la microcinématographie." *Revue internationale du cinéma éducateur* 6 (June 1932): 487–94.

——. "Les Possibilités artistiques de la cinématographie" (1927) [BiFi: Fonds Germaine Dulac, 408 B 26; typed manuscript].

——. "Rapport." *Congrès du cinéma éducatif de Paris, September 26–30, 1931, Programme des Séances.* Paris: Société de Matériel Acoustique, 1931.

——. "Savoir Regarder." *Le Cinéopse* 316 (Jan. 1953): 6.

Crinon, Docteur. "C'est Surtout à la Médecine et à la biologie que le cinématographe a fait de grands progrès." *Je Sais Tout* (May 18, 1914): 627–34.

d'Ambra, Lucio. "Il Museo dell'attimo fuggente." *La Tribuna illustrata* (Torino) (May 17–24, 1914): 309.

Delluc, Louis. "Antoine at Work." *Le Film* 75 (Aug. 20, 1917): 5–7. Reprinted in Abel, ed., *French Film Theory* 1:140–42.

——. "Beauty in the Cinema." *Le Film* 73 (Aug. 6, 1917): 4–5. Reprinted in Abel, ed., *French Film Theory* 1:137–39.

——. *Le Cinéma et les cinéastes: Écrits cinématographiques I.* Ed. Pierre Lherminier. Paris: Cinémathèque française, Éditions de l'étoile/Cahiers du cinéma, 1985.

——. *Cinéma et cie: Écrits cinématographiques II.* Ed. Pierre Lherminier. Paris: Cinémathèque française, Éditions de l'étoile/Cahiers du cinéma, 1986.

——. *Le Cinéma au quotidien: Écrits cinématographiques II/2.* Ed. Pierre Lherminier. Paris: Cinémathèque française, Éditions de l'étoile/Cahiers du cinéma, 1990.

——. "Contes du cinéma: Téléphone." *Le Film* (Dec. 17, 1918): 11.

——. "The Crowd." *Paris-Midi* (Aug. 24, 1918): 2. Reprinted in Abel, ed., *French Film Theory* 1:159–64.

——. "Douglas Fairbanks." *Paris-Midi* (June 1, 1918). Reprinted in Delluc, *Cinéma et cie: Écrits cinématographiques II*, 81–83.

——. "Editorial." *Cinéa* (Dec. 2 1921): 10.

——. "From Orestes to Rio Jim." *Cinéa 31* (Dec. 9, 1921). Reprinted in Abel, ed., *French Film Theory* 1:255–58.

——. "Notes pour moi: *L'Âme du bronze.*" *Le Film* 28 (Jan. 28, 1918). Reprinted in Delluc, *Cinéma et cie: Écrits cinématographiques II*: 56–58.

——. "Photographie" (1920). Reprinted in Delluc, *Écrits cinématographiques I: Le cinéma et les cinéastes*, 33.

Depriel, Jean. "À la Gloire du cinéma." *Ciné-Journal* (Oct. 25, 1913): 59–61.

Desnos, Robert. *Fantômas, Les Vampires, Les Mystères de New York*" (1927). Reprinted in Abel, ed., *French Film Theory* 1:398–400.

——. "Picture Palaces" (1927). Reprinted in Hammond, ed., *The Shadow and Its Shadow*, 78–79.

Dévigné, Roger. "De la Mission des Ardennes (1912) à la Mission Alpes-Provence (1939)." *Atlas sonore de la France, l'équipement et les travaux des missions phonographiques du musée de la parole.* Extrait des Annales de l'Université de Paris, 1941.

——. *Musée de la parole et du geste, Institut de phonotèque, Les collections, Le laboratoire, La phonotèque.* Paris: Musée de la parole, 1935.

Doumic, René. "Drama Review: The Cinema Age." *Revue des deux mondes* 133 (Aug. 15, 1913): 919–30. Reprinted in Abel, ed., *French Film Theory* 1:86–89.

Dulac, Germaine. "Cinema at the Service of History: The Role of Newsreels" (1936). Trans. Siân Reynolds. "Germaine Dulac and Newsreel: 3 articles and Introduction." *Screening the Past* 12 (Mar. 2001). See www.latrobe.edu.au/www/screeningthepast/classics/cl0301/srcl12a.htm.

——. *Écrits sur le cinéma (1919–1937).* Ed. Prosper Hillairet. Paris: Paris expérimental, 1994.

——. "L'Essence du cinéma: L'Idée visuelle." *Les Cahiers du mois: Cinéma* 16/17 (1925): 57–66. Reprinted in Dulac, *Écrits sur le cinéma.* 62–67.

——. "Les Esthétiques, les entraves, la cinégraphie intégrale" (1927). Reprinted in Dulac, *Écrits sur le cinéma,* 98–105.

——. "The Expressive Techniques of the Cinema" (1924). Reprinted in Abel, ed., *French Film Theory* 1:305–314.

——. *Liberté* (May 18, 1932) [BNF-AS: RK 582 (1); press clipping].

——. "La Portée éducative et sociale des actualités." *Revue internationale du cinéma éducateur* (Aug. 1934). Reprinted in Dulac, *Écrits sur le cinéma,* 203–207.

Dureau, G. "Les Archives du cinéma." *Ciné-Journal* (Apr. 26, 1913): 3.

——. "Les Films historiques." *Ciné-Journal* (July 5, 1913): 3–4.

Dyssod, Jacques. "En Marge du cinéma." *Mercure de France* (Aug. 16, 1916): 664–73.

"Echos et informations: Un Musée du cinéma." *Le Journal du Ciné-Club* 38 (Oct. 1, 1920): 2.

"L'École du crime." *Ciné-Journal* (July 22, 1916): 25–26.

Encyclopédie par l'image: Le Cinéma. Paris: Librairie Hachette, 1925.

Enquête de René Brunschwik sur une Bibliothèque du Film. In *Cahiers de la République des lettres* (Fall 1927).

Epstein, Jean. "Amour de Charlot." From *Le Cinématographe vu de l'Etna* (1926). Reprinted in Epstein, *Écrits sur le cinéma* 1:150–51.

——. "Art of Incidence." *Comoedia* (Nov. 18, 1927): 4. Reprinted in Epstein, *Écrits sur le cinéma* 1:181–82; and in Abel, ed., *French Film Theory* 1:412–14.

——. *Le Cinématographe vu de l'Etna.* Reprinted in Epstein, *Écrits sur le cinéma* 1:131–52.

——. *Écrits sur le cinéma: 1921–1953.* Vol. 1: *1921–1947.* Introduction by Pierre Leprohon. Paris: Cinéma club/Seghors, 1974.

——. "For a New Avant-Garde." *Cinéa-Ciné-pour-tous* 29 (Jan. 15, 1925): 8–10. Reprinted in Abel, ed., *French Film Theory* 1:349–53.

——. "Magnification." From *Bonjour Cinéma* (1921). Reprinted in Abel, ed., *French Film Theory* 1:235–40.

——. "Magnification and Other Writings." Trans. Stuart Liebman. *October* 3 (1977): 9–25.

——. "On Certain Characteristics of *Photogénie.*" *Cinéa-Ciné-pour-tous* 19 (Aug. 15, 1924): 6–8. Reprinted in Abel, ed., *French Film Theory* 1:314–20.

——. "La Photogénie de l'impondérable" (1935). Reprinted in Epstein, *Écrits sur le cinéma* 1:249–53.

——. "Le Regard du verre." *Les Cahiers du mois* 16/17 (1925). Reprinted in Epstein, *Écrits sur le cinéma* 1:135–37.

——. "Le Sens, 1b," in *Bonjour Cinéma* (1921). Reprinted in Epstein, *Écrits sur le cinéma* 1:85–92.

——. "The Senses 1 (b)" (1921), in *"Bonjour Cinéma* and Other Writings by Jean Epstein." Trans. Tom Milne. *Afterimage* 10 (Autumn 1981): 9–19. Reprinted in Abel, ed., *French Film Theory* 1:241–46.

——. "Timeless Time." Trans. Stuart Liebman. *October* 3 (Spring 1977): 16–20.

Evans, B. Ifor. "Rapport (fragments)." *Bulletin de la Société Autour du Monde* (1928): 63–68.

Exposition du cinématographe: Section du film documentaire et d'enseignement (Apr. 1922) [BNF-AS: Rk 583; exhibition catalogue].

Faure, Élie. "The Art of Cineplastics" (1922). Reprinted in Abel, ed., *French Film Theory* 1:258–68.

Febvre, Lucien. *A Geographical Introduction to History*. Trans. E. G. Mountford and J. H. Paxton. New York: Knopf, 1932.

Feuillade, Louis. *"Scènes de la vie telle qu'elle est."* *Ciné-Journal* 139 (Apr. 22, 1911): 19. Reprinted in Abel, ed., *French Film Theory* 1:54–55.

Flobert, Paul. "Les Amis de la Bibliothèque de la ville de Paris et le cinématographe." *Ciné-Journal* (Feb. 1, 1913): 72.

Forèze, "Le Cinéma il y a trente ans." [BiFi: FVP 045; press clipping].

François-Poncet, André. *Bulletin de la Société Autour du Monde* (June 14, 1931): xviii–xxi.

Fredy, Morgan. "Les Archives cinématographiques." *Le Courrier cinématographique* 6 (Aug. 18, 1911): 5–6.

Freud, Sigmund. "A Note Upon the 'Mystic Writing Pad'" (1925). Reprinted in *The Standard Edition of the Complete Pyschological Works of Sigmund Freud* 19:227–32 (1923–1925). Ed. and trans. James Strachey. London: Hogarth Press, 1981.

——. *The Psychopathology of Everyday Life* (1901). Trans. James Strachey. New York: Norton, 1965.

Frollo, Jean. "Le Cinématographe et l'histoire." *Petit Parisien*, Aug. 14, 1898. Reprinted in Matuszewski, "La Photographie animée," 73–76.

Fuller, Loïe. *Quinze Ans de ma vie*. Preface by Anatole France. Paris: Librairie Félix Juven, 1908.

Gance, Abel. "A Sixth Art." *Ciné-Journal* 185 (Mar. 9, 1912): 10. Reprinted in Abel, ed., *French Film Theory* 1:66–67.

Georges-Michel, Michel. *En Jardinant avec Bergson*. Paris: Albin Michel, 1926.

——. "Henri Bergson nous parle au cinéma." *Le Journal*, Feb. 20, 1914, 7.

Gimpel, Léon. "Principe de la plaque autochrome." *Bulletin de la Société française de la photographie* 9 (Sept. 1931): 178.

Grierson, John, "The Documentary Idea" (1942). Reprinted in Aitken, ed., *The Documentary Film Movement*, 103–115.

——. "First Principles of Documentary" (1932). Reprinted in Aitken, ed., *The Documentary Film Movement*, 81–92.

——. *Grierson on Documentary*. Ed. Forsyth Hardy. Berkeley: U of California P, 1966.

Grimm, Thomas. "La Cinématographie historique." *Petit Journal*, July 15, 1898. Reprinted in Matuszewski, "La Photographie animée," 76–78.

Haugmard, Louis. "The 'Aesthetic' of the Cinematograph." *Le Correspondant* (May 25, 1913): 762–71. Reprinted in Abel, ed., *French Film Theory* 1:84–85.

Hauser, Fernand. "Le 'Bibliophote' cinématographie livres et manuscripts." *Le Journal*, Jan. 23, 1914, 7.

Hédégat, Pascal [Guillaume Apollinaire]. "Le Cinéma à la Nationale." *L'Instransigeant* (Mar. 1, 1910): 1.

L'Herbier, Marcel. "Hermès and Silence." *Le Film* 110–11 (Apr. 29, 1918): 7–12. Reprinted in Abel, ed., *French Film Theory* 1:147–54.

Horn, E. Dr. "La Philosophie et le film." *Revue internationale du cinéma educateur* 6 (June 1932): 498–500.

Hugon, P. D. "Hints to Newsfilm Cameramen" (1915). Reprinted with introduction by Nicholas Hiley in *The Researchers Guide to British Newsreels*, vol. 3 (London: BUFVC, 1993).

Humbourg, Pierre. "Le Film historique: Il faut constituer pour les siècles à venir des archives historiques cinématographiques." *Cinémonde* (Jan. 5, 1933).

Inauguration des Archives de la Parole. Paris: Imprimerie Albert Manier, 1911.

Je Sais Tout (May 18, 1914).

Joffet, R. Letter (typed) from R. Joffet to V. Perrot (Mar. 30, 1953) [BiFi:FVP 054].

Kahn, Albert. *Des Droits et devoirs des gouvernements*. Paris: Imprimerie Vaugirard, 1918.

Kaufman, Boris. "Jean Vigo's *À Propos de Nice*" (1949). Reprinted in Jacobs, ed., *The Documentary Tradition*, 77–79.

Kracauer, Sigfried. "Boredom" (1924). Reprinted in Kracauer, *The Mass Ornament*, 331–36.

——. *History: The Last Things Before the Last*. Princeton: Markus Wiener, 1969.

——. "The Mass Ornament" (1927). Reprinted in Kracauer, *The Mass Ornament*. 75–88.

——. *The Mass Ornament: Weimar Essays*. Trans. Thomas Y. Levin. Cambridge: Harvard UP, 1995.

——. "Photography" (1927). Reprinted in Kracauer, *The Mass Ornament*, 47–64.

——. *The Salaried Masses: Duty and Distraction in Weimar Germany* (1929). Trans. Quintin Hoare. Introduction by Inka Mülder-Bach. London: Verso, 1998.

——. *Theory of Film: The Redemption of Physical Reality* (1960). Introduction by Miriam Bratu Hansen. Princeton: Princeton UP, 1997.

Laurvik, J. Nilsen. "The New Color Photography." *Century Magazine* 75.3 (1908).

Léger, Fernand. "À Propos du Cinéma." *Plans* (Jan. 1931). Reprinted in Marcel L'Herbier, ed., *Intelligence du cinématographe*, 337–40. Paris: Éditions Correa, 1946.

——. "*Ballet mécanique*" (1924). Reprinted in Léger, *Functions of Painting*, 48–51.

——. *Functions of Painting*. Ed. Edward F. Fry. Trans. Alexandra Anderson. New York: Viking, 1965.

——. "The Machine Aesthetic: The Manufactured Object, the Artisan, and the Artist" (1924). Reprinted in Léger, *Functions of Painting*. 52–61.

——. "Painting and Cinema" (1925). Reprinted in Abel, ed., *French Film Theory* 1:372–73.

Le Saint, Lucien. "Les Grands Reportages de Lucien Le Saint." Accessed 2003 (see http://perso.orange.fr/lucien.lesaint)

——. "*La Roue*: Its Plastic Quality" (1922). Reprinted in Abel, ed., *French Film Theory* 1:271–74.

Marcel, Pierre. "L'Histoire de la Grande Guerre: Des Archives, des documents, des preuves." *Ciné-Journal* 16 (Sept. 15, 1915): 15–16.

Matuszewski, Boleslas. "A New Source of History" (1898). Trans. Laura U. Marks and Diane Koszarski. *Film History* 7 (1995): 322–24.

——. "Une Nouvelle Source de l'histoire" (Mar. 25, 1898). Reprinted in Magdalena Mazaraki, ed., *Boleslas Matuszewski: Écrits cinématographiques*. Paris: AFRHC/La Cinémathèque française, 2006.

——. "Une Nouvelle Source de l'histoire." Paris: Noizette et Cie., Apr. 1898.

——. "La Photographie animée: Ce qu'elle est, ce qu'elle doit être." Paris: Imprimerie Noizette, 1898.

Méliès, Georges. "Cinematographic Views." *Annuaire général et international de la photographie* (Paris: Plon, 1907): 362–92. Reprinted in Abel, ed., *French Film Theory* 1:35–47.

Otlet, Paul. *Mundaneum*. Brussels: Union des Associations Internationales, 1928.

Perrot, Victor. "À la Recherche de l'écriture perdue: À l'ombre des hieroglyphes en fleurs l'écriture retrouvée." *Le Cinéopse* 316 (Jan. 1953): 10.

——. "Cinémathèque" [BiFi: FVP 054], handwritten memo dated Dec. 6, 1934.

——. "Handwritten memo on an index card by Victor Perrot dated 1914" [BiFi: FVP 054].

——. "Pour le Cinématographe." *Appel du Vieux Montmartre aux pouvoirs publics, au Conseil Municipal, à la Commission du Vieux Paris, à toutes les Sociétés savantes, à la presse* (Sept. 8, 1918).

——. "Pour la Conservation des films historiques." *Crapouillot* (July 16, 1920).

——. "Rapport présenté par M. Victor Perrot, au nom de la 3ème Sous Commission, sur l'organisation des archives cinématographiques." *Bulletin municipal officiel de la ville de Paris* (May 26–27, 1922): 12–13 [BiFi: FVP 048].

"Les Philosophes à la rescouss." *Le Courrier cinématographique* (Dec. 1, 1917): 16.

"Pourquoi ne crée-t-on pas les Archives nationales du cinéma?" *Scène* (Sept. 11, 1924) [BNF-AS: Rk 582 (1)].

Proust, Marcel. *Jean Santeuil*. Ed. Pierre Clarac. Paris: Gallimard, 1971.

——. *Remembrance of Things Past* (1907–1919). 3 vols. Trans. C. K. Moncrieff, Terence Kilmartin, and Andreas Mayor. New York: Vintage, 1981.

Randerson, William. *Report to the Trustees: Albert Kahn Travelling Fellowships*. London: Kegan Paul, Trench, Trubner, 1926.

Regnault, Félix-Louis. "Les Musées de films." *Biologica: Revue scientifique du médecine* 16 (1912): xx.

La Révolution surréaliste (1924–1929). Rpt., New York: Arno, 1968.

Ricaud, Denis. "Communication de M. Denis Ricaud, Administrateur-Délégué de la Société Pathé Consortium Cinéma." *Exposition du cinématographe: Section du film documentaire et d'enseignement* (Apr. 1922) 10 [BNF-AS: Rk 583; exhibition catalogue].

Riotor, Léon. "Communication de L. Riotor." *Exposition du cinématographe: Section du film documentaire et d'enseignement* (Apr. 1922) 10 [BNF-AS: Rk 583; exhibition catalogue].

——. "Rapport au nom de la 4ème commission (1), sur un projet de création des archives cinématographiques et phonographiques historiques de la ville de Paris." *Conseil Municipal de Paris* (Jan. 3, 1921): 2.

Roustan, M. "Speech." *Bulletin de la Société Autour du Monde* (June 14, 1931): vi–viii.

Souday, Paul. "Les Derniers prophètes: Bergsonisme et cinéma." Originally published in *Paris-Midi* ; reprinted in *Le Temps* (Oct. 12, 1917) and *Le Film* 84 (Oct. 15, 1917): 9–10.

——. "On the Cinema." *Le Temps* (Sept. 6, 1916): 1. Reprinted in Abel, ed., *French Film Theory* 1:130.

Thein, A. "Un Jardin japonais à Paris." *France-Japon* (Aug. 15, 1938): 382–83.

Thierry, Augustin. "Le Cinématographe et l'histoire." *Le Courrier cinématographique* 19 (Nov. 18, 1911): 6.

Vaillat, Léandre. "À la Commission du Vieux-Paris." (c. 1938) [BiFi: FVP 048; press clipping].

Valentin, Albert. "Introduction to Black-and-White Magic" (1927). Reprinted in Hammond, ed., *The Shadow and Its Shadow*, 95–98.

Vautel, Clément. "Propos d'un parisien." *Le Matin* (Feb. 20, 1913) [BiFi: FVP 048].

Verhylle, Armand. "Les Archives familiales." *Le Film* (May 28, 1917): 7.

Vertov, Dziga. "The Birth of Kino-Eye" (1924). Reprinted in *Kino-Eye*, 40–42.

——. "The Factory of Facts" (1926). Reprinted in *Kino-Eye*, 58–59.

——. "Kino-Eye" (1926). Reprinted in *Kino-Eye*, 60–79.

——. *Kino-Eye: The Writings of Dziga Vertov*, 60–79. Ed. with an introduction by Annette Michelson. Trans. Kevin O'Brien. Berkeley: U of California P, 1984.

——. "Kinoks: A Revolution" (1923). Reprinted in *Kino-Eye*, 11–21.

——. "The Same Thing from Different Angles" (1926). Reprinted in *Kino-Eye*, 57.

Vidal de la Blache, Paul. *Principles of Human Geography*. Trans. Millicent Todd Bingham. London: Constable, 1926.

Vignaud, Jean. "L'Histoire vivante." *Ciné-Miroir* (Oct. 30, 1931).

Vigo, Jean. "Toward a Social Cinema" (1930). Reprinted in Abel, ed., *French Film Theory* 2:60–63.

"Le Vrai peut quelquefois." *Filma* 17 (Jan. 15–31, 1918).

Vuillermoz, Émile. "Before the Screen: *Les Frères corses.*" *Le Temps* (Feb. 7, 1917): 3. Reprinted in Abel, ed., *French Film Theory* 1:132–35.

——. "Before the Screen: Hermès and Silence." *Le Temps* (newspaper), Mar. 9, 1918, 3. Reprinted in Abel, ed., *French Film Theory* 1:155–59.

——. "Cinémathèque." *Courrier cinématographique* (Apr. 14, 1923).

——. "La Cinématographie des microbes." *Le Temps* (Nov. 9, 1922).

——. "Devant l'Écran." *Le Temps* (Oct. 10, 1917).

——. "Devant l'Écran." *Le Temps* (Oct. 28, 1917).

——. "La Musique des images." *L'Art cinématographique*, vol. 3. Paris: Librairie Félix Alcan, 1927.

——. "Quelques Films." *Le Temps* (Nov. 22, 1922).

Yhcam. "Cinematography." *Ciné-Journal* 191 (Apr. 20, 1912): 36–37. Reprinted in Abel, ed., *French Film Theory* 1:67–77.

SECONDARY SOURCES

Abel, Richard. *The Ciné Goes to Town: French Cinema, 1896–1914*. Berkeley: U of California P, 1994.

——. "The Contribution of the French Literary Avant-Garde to Film Theory and Criticism (1907–1924)." *Cinema Journal* 3 (Spring 1975): 18–40.

——. *French Cinema: The First Wave, 1915–1929*. Princeton: Princeton UP, 1984.

——. *French Film Theory and Criticism: A History/Anthology*. Vol. 1: *1907–1929*; Vol. 2: *1929–1939*. Princeton: Princeton UP, 1988.

——. "The Thrills of *Grande Peur*: Crime Series and Serials in the Belle Epoque." *The Velvet Light Trap* 37 (Spring 1996): 3–9.

Adler, Judith. "Origins of Sightseeing." In C. Williams, ed., *Travel Culture*, 3–25.

Adorno, Theodor W. "The Curious Realist: On Siegfried Kracauer" (1964). *New German Critique* 54 (Fall 1991): 159–77.

——. *Minima Moralia: Reflections on a Damaged Life* (1951). Trans. E. F. N. Jephcott. London and New York: Verso, 2005.

——. *Negative Dialectics* (1966). Trans. Dennis Redmond. Suhrkamp: Frankfurt am Main, 1970.

Ageron, Charles-Robert. "L'Exposition coloniale de 1931: Mythe républicain ou mythe imperial?" In Pierre Nora, ed., *Les Lieux de mémoire*, vol. 1: *La République*, 561–91. Paris: Gallimard, 1984.

Aitken, Ian. *European Film Theory and Cinema: A Critical Introduction*. Bloomington: Indiana UP, 2001.

Aitken, Ian, ed. *The Documentary Film Movement: An Anthology*. Edinburgh: Edinburgh UP, 1998.

Albert Kahn: Réalités d'une utopie, 1860–1940 (below: *Albert Kahn: Réalitiés*) Boulogne: Musée Albert-Kahn, 1995.

Albert Kahn et le Japon: Confluences (CD-ROM). Boulogne: Musée Albert-Kahn, 2000.

Albert, Phyllis Cohen. "Vichy and the Jews: A Past That Is Not Past." In Peter Medding, ed., *Coping with Life and Death: Jewish Families in the Twentieth Century*, 235–49. Oxford: Oxford UP, 1998.

Aldrich, Robert. *Greater France: A History of French Overseas Expansion*. New York: Palgrave, 1996.

Alloula, Malek. *The Colonial Harem*. Trans. Myrna Godzich and Wlad Godzich. Minneapolis: U of Minnesota P, 1986.

Alpers, Svetlana. *The Art of Describing: Dutch Art in the Seventeenth Century*. Chicago: U of Chicago P, 1983.

Altman, Rick. "From Lecturer's Prop to Industrial Product: The Early History of Travel Films." In Ruoff, ed., *Virtual Voyages*, 61–78.

——. *Silent Film Sound*. New York: Columbia UP, 2004.

Amad, Paula. "*Les Archives de la Planète* d'Albert Kahn (1908–1931): Archives ou contre-archives de l'histoire?" *Cahiers de la cinémathèque* (Special Issue: *Le Cinéma d'Albert Kahn: Quelle place dans l'histoire?*) 74 (Dec. 2002): 19–33.

——. " 'Between the 'familiar text' and the 'book of the world': Touring the Ambivalent Contexts of Travel Films." In Ruoff, ed., *Virtual Voyages*, 99–116.

——. "Cinema's 'sanctuary': From Pre-documentary to Documentary Film in Albert Kahn's *Archives de la Planète*, 1908–1931." *Film History* 13.2 (2001): 138–59.

——. "'Objects became witnesses': Ève Francis as Witness to the Emergence of French Cine-philia and Film Criticism." *Framework: The Journal of Cinema and Media* 46.1 (Spring 2005): 56–73.

——. "'These spectacles are never forgotten': Memory and Reception in Colette's Film Criti-cism." *Camera Obscura: Feminism, Culture and Media Studies* 59 (2005): 119–64.

Anderson, Benedict. *Imagined Communities: Reflections on the Origin and Spread of Na-tionalism.* London and New York: Verso, 1983.

Anderson, Perry. *A Zone of Engagement.* London: Verso, 1992.

André, Jacques. "De la Preuve à l'histoire: Les Archives en France." *Traverses* 36 (Jan. 1986): 25–33 [Revue du Centre de Création industrielle, Centre George Pompidou, Paris, Spe-cial Issue: L'Archive].

Andrew, Dudley. *André Bazin.* New York: Oxford, 1978.

——. *Mists of Regret: Culture and Sensibility in Classic French Film.* Princeton: Princeton UP, 1995.

Andrew, Dudley and Steve Ungar. *Popular Front Paris and the Poetics of Culture.* Cambridge: Harvard UP, 2005.

Antliff, Mark. *Inventing Bergson: Cultural Politics and the Parisian Avant-garde.* Princeton: Princeton UP, 1993.

Appadurai, Arjun. *Modernity at Large: Cultural Dimensions of Globalization.* Minneapolis: U of Minnesota P, 1996.

Les Archives de la Planète, vol. 1: *La France.* Paris: Joël Cuénot, 1978.

Les Archives de la Planète, vol. 2: *Le Monde.* Paris: Joël Cuénot, 1979.

Aubert, Michelle and Jean-Claude Seguin, eds. *La Production cinématographique des frères Lumière.* Paris: Éditions mémoires de cinéma, 1996.

Auslander, Leora. *Taste and Power: Furnishing Modern France.* Berkeley: U of California P, 1996.

Balard, Martine. *Dahomey 1930: Mission Catholique et culte vodoun, l'oeuvre de Francis Aupiais (1877–1945), missionaire et ethnographe.* Perpignan: Presses Universitaires de Perpignan, 1998.

Barden, Garrett. "Method in Philosophy." In Mullarkey, ed., *The New Bergson,* 32–41.

Barsam, Richard. *Nonfiction Film: A Critical History.* Bloomington: Indiana UP, 1992.

Baud-Berthier, Gilles. "The Financial Relations Between France and Japan During the Meiji and Taisho Periods: One Example, Albert Kahn (1860–1940)." *Asian Cultural Studies* 18 (Feb. 1992): 31–41.

——. "Le Métier de la banque." In *Albert Kahn: Réalités,* 119–31.

Baudry, Jean-Louis. "The Apparatus: Metapsychological Approaches to the Impression of Reality in Cinema" (1975). In Rosen, ed., *Narrative, Apparatus, Ideology,* 299–318.

——. "Ideological Effects of the Basic Cinematographic Apparatus" (1970). In Rosen, ed., *Narrative, Apparatus, Ideology,* 286–98.

Bautier, Robert-Henri. "Les Archives." In Samaran, ed., *L'Histoire et ses méthodes,* 1120–1166.

Bazin, André. "An Aesthetic of Reality: Cinematic Realism and the Italian School of the Lib-eration" (1948). In *What Is Cinema?* 2:16–40.

——. *Bazin at Work: Major Essays from the Forties and Fifties*. Ed. Bert Cardullo. Trans. Alain Piette and Bert Cardullo. New York: Routledge, 1997.

——. "A Bergsonian Film: *The Picasso Mystery*" (1956). Reprinted in Bazin, *Bazin at Work*, 211–19.

——. "Cinema and Exploration" (1953–1956). In *What Is Cinema?* 1:154–63.

——. *Le Cinéma français de la Libération à la Nouvelle Vague (1945-1958)*. Paris: Cahiers du cinéma, 1998.

——. "De Sica: Metteur en Scène" (1951). In *Qu'est-ce que le cinéma?*, 311–30. Paris: Les Éditions du Cerf, 2002.

——. "De Sica: Metteur en Scène" (1951). In *What Is Cinema?* 2:61–78.

——. "The Evolution of the Language of Cinema" (1950–1955). In *What Is Cinema?* 1:23–40.

——. "Le Film scientifique: Beauté du hasard." *L'Écran français* (Oct. 21, 1947). Reprinted in Bazin, *Le Cinéma français de la Libération à la Nouvelle Vague (1945-1958)*, 317–21.

——. "The Myth of Total Cinema" (1946). In *What Is Cinema?* 1:17–22.

——. "Ontologie de l'image photographique" (1945). In *Qu'est-ce que le cinéma?*, 9–17. Paris: Les Éditions du cerf, 2002.

——. "The Ontology of the Photographic Image" (1945). In *What Is Cinema?* 1:9–16.

——. "On *Why We Fight*: History, Documentation, and the Newsreel." *Esprit* (1946). Reprinted in Bazin, *Bazin at Work*, 187–92.

——. "*Paris 1900*: À la Recherche du temps perdu." *L'Écran français* (Sept. 30, 1947). Reprinted in Bazin, *Le Cinéma français de la Libération à la Nouvelle Vague (1945-1958)*, 241–43.

——. "*La Terra Trema*" (1948). In *What Is Cinema?* 2:41–46.

——. "*Umberto D*: A Great Work" (1952). In *What Is Cinema?* 2:79–82.

——. *What Is Cinema?* 2 vols. Ed. and trans. Hugh Gray. Berkeley: U of California P, 1967 and 1971.

Beale, Marjorie A. *The Modernist Enterprise: French Elites and the Threat of Modernity, 1900-1940*. Stanford, Calif.: Stanford UP, 1999.

Beausoleil, Jeanne. "Albert Kahn." In *Les Archives de la Planète*, vol. 1: *La France*, 6–19. Paris: Joël Cuénot, 1978.

——. "Albert Kahn et son oeuvre." In *Les Archives de la Planète* 2:6–20.

——. "Les Années Marmoutier." In *Albert Kahn: Réalitiés*, 33–36.

——. "Au Service d'un Idéal de compréhension internationale: Les opérateurs d'Albert Kahn dans le monde." In *Le Cinéma français muet dans le monde, Influences réciproques*, 61–72. Paris: Symposium de la F.I.A.F., 1988.

——. "Introduction." *Irlande 1913: Clichés en couleur pris pour Monsieur Kahn par Mesdemoiselles Mespoulet et Mignon*. 9–17.

——. "Introduction." *Paris-Prétexte ou l'éloge de l'oubli*, 14–53. Ed. Laurent Reiz. Boulogne: Musée Albert-Kahn, 1994.

——. "Préface." *Tunisie: Aperçus de 1909 et 1931*, 7–9. Exposition réalisée par Le Conseil Général des Hauts-de-Seine et la ville de Boulogne-Billancourt, Collections Albert Kahn. Paris: Les Presses artistiques, 1983.

Belloï, Livio. "Lumière and His View: The Cameraman's Eye in Early Cinema." *Historical Journal of Film, Radio, and Television* 15.4 (1995): 461–74.

Bellows, Andy Masaki and Marina McDougall (with Brigitte Berg), eds. *Science Is Fiction: The Films of Jean Painlevé*. Trans. Jeanine Herman. Cambridge: MIT Press, 2000.

Bentley, Michael. "Past and 'Presence': Revisiting Historical Ontology." *History and Theory* 45 (Oct. 2006): 349–61.

Berg, Maxine. *A Woman in History: Eileen Power, 1889–1940*. Cambridge UP, 1996.

Bernard, Youen. "Le Record du monde cinématographique: *L'Abyssinie au temps de Ménélick (1910)*." *1895*, 18 (Summer 1995): 217–21.

Besse, Jean-Marc. *Voir la Terre*. Paris: Actes Sud, 2000.

Bhabha, Homi K. "DissemiNation: Time, Narrative, and the Margins of the Modern Nation." In *The Location of Culture*, 139–70. New York: Routledge, 1994.

Blanchot, Maurice. "Everyday Speech." *The Infinite Conversation*, 238–45. Trans. Susan Hanson. Minneapolis and London: U of Minnesota P, 1993.

Bloch, Étienne and Alfredo Cruz-Ramirez. *Marc Bloch: An Impossible Biography*. Limoges: Culture and Patrimoine en Limousin, 1997.

Bloch, Marc. *Écrits de guerre (1914–1918)*. Ed. Étienne Bloch. Introd. Stéphane Audoin-Rouzeau. Paris: Arman Colin, 1997.

——. *The Historian's Craft* (1941). Trans. Peter Putnam. Introduction by Joseph R. Strayer. New York: Vintage, 1953.

——. *Memoirs of War, 1914–1918*. Trans. with an introduction by Carole Fink. New York: Cambridge UP, 1988.

Bloom, Peter J. *French Colonial Documentary: Mythologies of Humanitarianism*. Minneapolis: U of Minnesota P, 2008.

Bonhomme, Marie. "Correspondances . . . l'art et la philosophie." In *Albert Kahn: Réalités*, 49–54.

Borde, Raymond. *Les Cinémathèques*. Paris: Éditions l'Âge d'homme, 1983.

Borde, Raymond and Pierre Guibbert. "*Le Cinéma au service de l'histoire* (1935): Un film retrouvé de Germaine Dulac." *Archives: Institut Jean Vigo* 44/45 (Nov.–Dec. 1991): 1–12.

Bordwell, David. *French Impressionist Cinema: Film Culture, Film Theory, and Film Style*. New York, Arno, 1980.

Bordwell, David, Janet Staiger, and Kristin Thompson. *The Classical Hollywood Cinema: Film Style and Mode of Production to 1960*. New York: Columbia UP, 1985.

Borges, Jorge Luis. "Museum: On Exactitude in Science" (1935). *Jorge Luis Borges: Collected Fictions*, 325. Trans. Andrew Hurley. New York: Penguin 1999.

Bottomore, Stephen. "'The collection of rubbish': Animatographs, Archives and Arguments: London, 1896–97." *Film History* 7 (1995): 291–97.

——. "Rediscovering Early Non-fiction Film." *Film History* 13.2 (2001): 160–73.

——. "Shots in the Dark—The Real Origins of Film Editing." In Elsaesser, ed., *Early Cinema: Space*, 104–113.

Boulouch, Nathalie. "The Documentary Use of the Autochrome in France." *History of Photography* (Summer 1994): 143–45.

——. "Le Miracle des couleurs." In De Pastre-Robert and Devos, eds., *Les Couleurs du voyage*, 41–51.

Bourdé, Guy and Hervé Martin. *Les Écoles historiques*. Paris: Édition du Seuil, 1997.

Braibant, Charles. "Les Archives de France: Hier, aujourd'hui, demain." Paris: Imprimerie nationale, 1949.

——. "L'Histoire, fille des archives." Paris: Imprimerie Stipa, 1959.

Braudel, Fernand. "History and the Social Sciences: The *longue durée*" (1958). In *On History*, 25–54. Trans. Sarah Matthews. Chicago: Chicago UP, 1980.

——. "Préface de *La Méditerranée*" (1949). Reprinted in *Les Écrits de Fernand Braudel*, vol. 2: *Les Ambitions de l'histoire*, 269–75. Ed. Roselyne de Ayala and Paule Braudel. Paris: Éditions de Fallois, 1997.

Braun, Marta. *Picturing Time: The Work of Étienne-Jules Marey*. Chicago: U of Chicago P, 1992.

Brown. Lloyd A. *The Story of Maps* (1949). New York: Dover, 1979.

Brown, Richard Harvey and Beth Davis-Brown. "The Making of Memory: The Politics of Archives, Libraries, and Museums in the Construction of National Consciousness." *History of the Human Sciences* 11.4 (Nov. 1998): 17–32.

Brownlow, Kevin. *The War, the West, and the Wilderness*. New York: Knopf, 1979.

Bruno, Giuliana. *Streetwalking on a Ruined Map: Cultural Theory and the City Films of Elvira Notari*. Princeton: Princeton UP, 1993.

Buchloh, Benjamin H. D. "Gerhard Richter's *Atlas*: The Anomic Archive." *October* 88 (Spring 1999): 117–45.

Bullot, Erik. *Jardins-Rébus: Histoires de trois jardins remarquables: Tamaris, jardin Albert-Kahn, la Bambouseraie*. Paris: Actes sud, 1999.

Burch, Noël. *Life to Those Shadows*. Trans. Ben Brewster. Berkeley: U of California P, 1990.

Burke, Peter. *The French Historical Revolution: The Annales School, 1929–89*. Stanford, Calif.: Stanford UP, 1990.

Burwick, Frederick and Paul Douglass, eds. *The Crisis in Modernism: Bergson and the Vitalist Controversy*. Cambridge: Cambridge UP, 1992.

Buttimer, Anne. *Society and Milieu in the French Geographic Tradition*. Chicago: Rand McNally, 1971.

Cadé, Michel. "Le Congrès de Tours (25–30 décembre 1920) vu par les Archives de la Planète," *Les Cahiers de la cinémathèque* 74 (Dec. 2002): 85–98.

Les Cahiers de la cinémathèque 74 (Dec. 2002), Special Issue: Le Cinéma d'Albert Kahn: Quelle place dans l'histoire?

Camerawork, Special Issue: Mass Observation (Sept. 1978).

Carbine, Mary. "'The Finest Outside the Loop': Motion Picture Exhibition in Chicago's Black Metropolis, 1905–1928." *Camera Obscura* 23 (May 1990): 9–41.

Cardinal, Roger. "Pausing Over Peripheral Detail." *Framework* 30–31 (1986): 112–30.

Cariou, Marie. *Lectures Bergsoniennes*. Paris: Presses universitaires de France, 1990.

Callahan, Vicki. *Zones of Anxiety: Movement, Musidora, and the Crime Serials of Louis Feuillade*. Detroit: Wayne State UP, 2005,

Caron, Vicki. *Between France and Germany: The Jews of Alsace-Lorraine, 1871–1918*. Stanford, Calif.: Stanford UP, 1988.

Castro, Teresa. "*Les Archives de la Planète*: A cinematographic atlas." *Jump Cut: A Review of Contemporary Media* 4 (Winter 2006).

Çelik, Zeynep and Leila Kinney. "Ethnography and Exhibitionism at the Expositions Universelles." *Assemblage* 13 (Dec. 1990): 34–59.

Chakrabarty, Dipesh. *Provincializing Europe: Post-Colonial Thought and Historical Difference*. Princeton: Princeton UP, 2000.

Charney, Leo. *Empty Moments: Cinema, Modernity, and Drift*. Durham and London: Duke
UP, 1998.

Charney, Leo and Vanessa R. Schwartz, eds. *Cinema and the Invention of Modern Life*.
Berkeley: U of California P, 1995.

Chevalier, Jacques. *Entretiens avec Bergson*. Paris: Librairie Plon, 1959.

——. *Henri Bergson*. Trans. Lilian A. Clare. New York: Macmillan, 1928.

Christie, Ian. "French Avant-Garde Film in the Twenties: From 'Specificity' to Surrealism."
In *Film as Film: Formal Experiment in Film, 1910–1975*, 36–45. London: Hayward Gal-
lery/Arts Council of Britain, 1979.

Clair, René. *Cinema Yesterday and Today* (1970). Ed. R. C. Dale. Trans. Stanley Appelbaum.
New York: Dover, 1972.

——. *"La Roue"* (1923). Reprinted in Abel, ed., *French Film Theory* 1:279.

Clark, T. J., "In a Pomegranate Chandelier." *London Review of Books* (Sept. 21, 2006): 6–8.

Coeuré, Sophie. "Les Centres de Documentation Sociale, 1920–1940." In *Albert Kahn: Réalités*, 201–209.

Coeuré, Sophie and Frédéric Monier. "De l'Ombre à la lumière: Les Archives françaises de
retour de Moscou (1940–2002)." In Sébastien Laurent, ed., *Archives secrets, secrets d'archives? Historiens et archivistes face aux archives sensibles*, 133–48. Paris: CNRS Éditions, 2003.

Coeuré, Sophie and Frédéric Worms, eds. *Henri Bergson et Albert Kahn: Correspondances*.
Boulogne: Musée Albert-Kahn, 2003.

Cohen, Margaret. "Panoramic Literature and the Invention of Everyday Genres." In Charney
and Schwartz, eds., *Cinema and the Invention of Modern Life*, 227–52.

Comay, Rebecca, ed. *Lost in the Archives*. Toronto: Alphabet City Media, 2002.

Combe, Sonia. "Les Fichiers de juifs." *Archives interdites: L'Histoire confisquée*, 194–232.
Paris: La Découverte and Syros, 2001.

Comolli, Jean-Louis. "Machines of the Visible" (in *The Cinematic Apparatus* [1980]). Reprinted in Mast and Cohen, eds., *Film Theory and Criticism*, 741–60.

Conklin, Alice. *A Mission to Civilize: The Republican Idea of Empire in France and West
Africa, 1895–1930*. Stanford, Calif.: Stanford UP, 1997.

Connarty, Jane and Josephine Lanyon, eds. *Ghosting: The Role of the Archive Within Contemporary Artists' Film and Video*. Bristol: Picture This Moving Image, 2006.

Copjec, Joan. *Reading My Desire: Lacan Against the Historicists*. Cambridge: MIT Press,
1994.

Cosandey, Roland. "Some Thoughts on 'Early Documentary.'" In Hertogs and de Klerk, eds.,
Uncharted Territory, 37–50.

Crafton, Donald. *Émile Cohl, Caricature, and Film*. New Jersey: Princeton UP, 1990.

Crary, Jonathan. *Techniques of the Observer: On Vision and Modernity in the Nineteenth
Century*. Cambridge: MIT Press, 1990.

Cultural Studies 18.2–3 (Mar.–May 2004), Special Issue: Everyday Life.

Danks, Adrian. "The Global Art of Found Footage Cinema." In Linda Badley, R. Barton Palmer, and Steven Jay Schneider, eds., *Traditions in World Cinema*, 241–53. New Brunswick, N.J.: Rutgers UP, 2006.

Daughton, James P. "Sketches of the *Poilu*'s World: Trench Cartoons from the Great War." In Mackaman and Mays, eds., *World War I and the Cultures of Modernity*, 35–67.

De Certeau, Michel (in collaboration with Dominique Julia and Jacques Revel). "The Beauty of the Dead: Nisard." In *Heterologies: Discourse on the Other* (1980), 119–36. Trans. Brian Massumi. Minneapolis: U of Minnesota P, 1986.

——. "L'Espace de l'archive ou la perversion du temps." *Traverses* 36 (Jan. 1986): 4–6 [Revue du Centre de Création industrielle, Centre George Pompidou, Paris, Special Issue: L'Archive].

——. *The Practice of Everyday Life*. Trans. Steven. F. Rendall. Berkeley: U of California P, 1984.

——. *The Writing of History* (1975). Trans. Tom Conley. New York: Columbia UP, 1988.

De Klerk, Nico. "A Few Remaining Hours: News Films and the Interest in Technology in Amsterdam Film Shows, 1896–1910." *Film History* 11.1 (1999): 5–18.

——. "Home Away from Home: Private Films from the Dutch East Indies." In Ishizuka and Zimmermann, eds., *Mining the Home Movie*, 148–62.

De la Bretèque, François. "Les Actualités filmées françaises." *Cahiers de la cinémathèque* 66 (July 1997): 3–5, Special Issue: Les Actualités filmées françaises.

——. "Albert Kahn, d'un certain regard sur le monde et sa place dans l'histoire." *Les Cahiers de la cinémathèque* 74 (Dec. 2002): 137–46.

De Pastre-Robert, Béatrice and Emmanuelle Devos. "La Cinémathèque de la ville de Paris." *1895*, 18 (Summer 1995): 107–121.

De Pastre-Robert, Béatrice and Emmanuelle Devos, eds. *Les Couleurs du voyage: L'Oeuvre photographique de Jules Gervais-Courtellemont*. Paris: Cinémathèque Robert-Lynen de la ville de Paris, 2002.

Defert, Daniel. "The Collection of the World: Accounts of Voyages from the Sixteenth to the Eighteenth Centuries." *Dialectical Anthropology* 7 (1982): 11–20.

Delamarre, Mariel Jean-Brunhes. "Jean Brunhes." In *Les Archives de la Planète*, vol. 1: *La France*, 101–107.

Delamarre, Mariel Jean-Brunhes and Jeanne Beausoleil. "Deux Témoins de leur temps: Albert Kahn et Jean Brunhes." In *Jean Brunhes: Autour du Monde*, 91–107.

Deleuze, Gilles. *Bergsonism* (1966). Trans. Hugh Tomlinson and Barbara Habberjam. New York: Zone Books, 1991.

——. *Cinema 1: The Movement-Image* (1983). Trans. Hugh Tomlinson and Barbara Habberjam. Minneapolis: U of Minnesota P, 1997.

——. *Foucault*. Ed. and Trans. Seán Hand. Minneapolis: U of Minnesota P, 1988.

——. "A New Archivist" (1986). In *Foucault*, 1–22.

Delluc, Gilles. *Louis Delluc, 1890–1924: L'Éveilleur du cinéma français au temps des années folles*. Périgueux: Édition pilote 24, 2002.

Delmeulle, Frédéric. "Le Monde selon l'Encyclopédie Gaumont." *1895*, 20 (July 1996): 25–45.

——. "Le Parent pauvre? La Pratique du documentaire chez Gaumont au début des années dix." *1895*, 30 (Oct. 2000): 43–65.

Derrida, Jacques. *Archive Fever: A Freudian Impression*. Trans. Eric Prenowitz. Chicago and London: U of Chicago P, 1996.

——. "Le Cinéma et ses fantômes." Interview with Antoine de Baecque and Thierry Jousse. *Cahiers du cinéma* (Apr. 2001): 74–85.

Deutelbaum, Marshall. "Structural Patterning in the Lumière Films." In John L. Fell, ed., *Film Before Griffith*, 299–310. Berkeley: U of California P, 1983.

Devos, Emmanuelle. "À Travers le Monde." In De Pastre-Robert and Devos, eds., *Les Couleurs du voyage*, 13–34.

Dibbets, Karel and Bert Hogenkamp. *Film and the First World War*. Amsterdam: Amsterdam UP, 1995.

Dickinson, G. Lowes. *Report to the Trustees, Albert Kahn Travelling Fellowships* (Oct.). London: London UP, 1913.

Doane, Mary Ann. *The Emergence of Cinematic Time: Modernity, Contingency, the Archive*. Cambridge: Harvard UP, 2002.

Douglass, Paul. "Bergson and Cinema: Friends or Foes?." In Mullarkey, ed., *The New Bergson*, 209–228.

——. "Deleuze's Bergson: Bergson Redux." In Burwick and Douglass, eds., *The Crisis in Modernism*, 368–88.

Dréville, Jean. "Documentary: The Soul of Cinema" (1930). Reprinted in Abel, ed., *French Film Theory* 2:42–45.

Dubois, Philippe. "Le Regard vertical ou les transformations du paysage." In Jean Mottet, ed., *Les Paysages du cinéma*, 24–44. Paris: Édition Champ Vallon, 1999.

Dujardin, Philippe et al., eds. *L'Aventure du cinématographe, Actes du Congrès mondial Lumière*. Lyon: ALEASI, 1999.

Duvigneau, Marion and Michel Duvigneau. "Les Archives du Service cinématographique du ministère de l'agriculture." *La Gazette des Archives* 173 (1996): 190–200, Special Issue: Le Cinéma et les archives.

Edwards, Elizabeth. "Ordering Others: Photography, Anthropologies, and Taxonomies." In Iles and Roberts, eds., *InVisible Light*, 54–68.

Eksteins, Modris. "The Cultural Impact of the Great War." In Dibbets and Hogenkamp, eds., *Film and the First World War*, 201–212.

Elsaesser, Thomas. "Après Lumière: Une invention sans avenir, dans l'avenir . . . " In Dujardin et al., eds., *L'Aventure du cinématographe*, 279–90.

Elsaesser, Thomas, ed. *Early Cinema: Space, Frame, and Narrative*. London: BFI, 1990.

Enwezor, Okwui. *Archive Fever: Uses of the Document in Contemporary Art*. New York: International Center of Photography, 2008.

Ewen, Elizabeth and Stuart Ewen. "City Lights: Immigrants and the Rise of the Movies." *Channels of Desire: Mass Images and the Shaping of American Consciousness*, 81–105. New York: McGraw-Hill, 1982.

Ezra, Elizabeth. *The Colonial Unconscious: Race and Culture in Interwar France*. Ithaca and London: Cornell UP, 2000.

Farge, Arlette. *Le Goût de l'archive*. Paris: Éditions du Seuil, 1989.

Favier, Jean. *Les Archives*. Paris: Presses Universitaires de France, 1959.

Febvre, Lucien. *A Geographical Introduction to History*. Trans. E. G. Mountford and J. H. Paxton. New York: Knopf, 1932.

Felski, Rita. "Introduction." *New Literary History* 33 (2002): 607–622, Special Issue: Everyday Life.

——. "The Invention of Everyday Life." *New Formations* 39 (1999–2000): 15–31.

Ferro, Marc. *Cinema and History.* Trans. Naomi Greene. Detroit: Wayne State UP, 1988.

Fink, Carole. *Marc Bloch: A Life in History.* Cambridge: Cambridge UP, 1989.

Fogarty, Richard and Michael A. Osborne. "Constructions and Functions of Race in French Military Medecine, 1830–1920." In Peabody and Stovall, eds., *The Color of Liberty,* 206–236.

Ford, Caroline. "Landscape and Environment in French Historical and Geographical Thought: New Directions." *French Historical Studies* 24.1 (2001): 125–34.

Foucault, Michel. *The Archaeology of Knowledge* (1969). Trans. A. M. Sheridan Smith. London: Tavistock, 1972.

——. *The Birth of the Clinic: An Archaeology of Medical Perception* (1963). Trans. A. M. Sheridan. London and New York: Routledge, 2003.

——. *Discipline and Punish: The Birth of the Prison* (1975). Trans. A. Sheridan. Vintage, 1995.

——. "Nietzsche, Genealogy, History" (1971). In *The Foucault Reader,* 76–100. Ed. Paul Rabinow. London: Penguin 1984.

——. "Of Other Spaces" (1967). Trans. Jay Miskowiec. *Diacritics* 16 (Spring 1986): 22–27.

——. *The Order of Things: An Archaeology of the Human Sciences* (1966). London: Routledge, 1989.

——. "Précisions sur le pouvoir: Réponses a certains critiques" (1979). *Dits et écrits: 1954–1988.* Vol. 3: *1976–1979,* 625–35. Paris: Gallimard, 1994.

Foucault, Michel, ed. *I, Pierre Rivière: A Case of Parricide in the Nineteenth Century* (1973). Trans. Frank Jellinek. Lincoln: U of Nebraska P, 1975.

Freeman, Judi. "Bridging Purism and Surrealism: The Origins and Production of Fernand Léger's *Ballet Mécanique*." In Kuenzli, ed., *Dada and Surrealist Film,* 28–45.

Friedberg, Anne. *Window Shopping: Cinema and the Postmodern.* Berkeley: U of California P, 1993.

Fritzsche, Peter. "The Archive." *History and Memory* 17.1 (2005): 15–44.

Frizot, Michel. "Body of Evidence: The Ethnophotography of Difference." In Frizot, ed., *A New History of Photography,* 259–71.

Frizot, Michel, ed. *A New History of Photography.* Köln: Könneman, 1998.

Furlough, Ellen. "*Une leçon des choses*: Tourism, Empire, and the Nation in Interwar France." *French Historical Studies* 25.3 (2002): 441–73.

Fussell, Paul. *The Great War and Modern Memory.* Oxford: Oxford UP, 1976.

Gaines, Jane. "Everyday Strangeness: Robert Ripley's International Oddities as Documentary Attractions." *New Literary History* 33.4 (Autumn 2002): 781–801.

Gaudreault, André. "Film, Narrative, Narration: The Cinema of the Lumière Brothers." In Elsaesser, ed., *Early Cinema,* 68–75.

——. "Theatricality, Narrativity, and 'Trickality': Reevaluating the Cinema of Georges Méliès." *Journal of Popular Film and TV* 15.3 (1987): 110–19.

——. "Les Traces du montage dans la production Lumière." In Dujardin et al., eds., *L'Aventure du cinématographe,* 299–306.

Gauthier, Christophe. "1927, Year One of the French Film Heritage." *Film History* 17 (2005): 289–306.

——. "La Conservation et la consultation des films dans les années 1920: L'Exemple de la cinémathèque Gaumont." *La Gazette des Archives* 173 (1996): 225–30, Special Issue: Le Cinéma et les archives.

——. *La Passion du cinéma: Cinéphiles, ciné-clubs et salles spécialisées à Paris de 1920 à 1929*. Paris: AFRHC, 1999.

Gaycken, Oliver. "'A Drama Unites Them in a Fight to the Death': Some Remarks on a Flourishing of a Cinema of Scientific Vernacularization in France, 1900–1914." *Historical Journal of Film, Radio, and Television* 22.3 (Aug. 2002): 353–74.

Ghali, Noureddine. *L'Avant-garde cinématographique en France dans les années vingt*. Paris: Éditions Paris experimental, 1995.

Gilbert, Sandra M. "'Unreal City': The Place of the Great War in the History of Modernity." In Mackaman and Mays, eds., *World War I and the Cultures of Modernity*, ix–xvi.

Godlewska, Anne. "Napoleon's Geographers: Imperialists or Soldiers of Modernity." In N. Smith and Godlewska, eds., *Geography and Empire*, 31–53.

Golan, Romy. *Modernity and Nostalgia: Art and Politics in France Between the Wars*. New Haven: Yale UP, 1995.

Gomery, Douglas. *Shared Pleasures: A History of Movie Presentation in the United States*. Madison: U of Wisconsin P, 1992.

Green, Nancy L. "The Comparative Gaze: Travelers in France Before the Era of Mass Tourism." *French Historical Studies* 25.3 (2002): 423–40.

Griffiths, Alison. *Wondrous Difference: Cinema, Anthropology, and Turn-of-the-Century Visual Culture*. New York: Columbia UP, 2002.

Grimshaw, Anna. *The Ethnograher's Eye: Ways of Seeing in Modern Anthropology*. New York: Cambridge UP, 2001.

Grogin, R. C. *The Bergsonian Controversy in France, 1900–1914*. Calgary: U of Calgary P, 1988.

Guiomar, Jean-Yves. "Vidal de la Blache's *Geography of France*." In Nora, ed., *Realms of Memory* 2:187–210.

Gunning, Tom. "An Aesthetic of Astonishment: Early Film and the (In)Credulous Spectator." *Art & Text* 34 (Spring 1989): 31–45.

——. "Before Documentary: Early Nonfiction Films and the 'View' Aesthetic." In Hertogs and de Klerk, eds., *Uncharted Territory*, 9–24.

——. "The Cinema of Attractions: Early Film, Its Spectator, and the Avant-Garde." *Wide Angle* 8.3–4 (1986): 63–70.

——. "Loïe Fuller and the Art of Motion: Body, Light, Electricity and the Origins of Cinema." In Richard Allen and Malcolm Turvey, eds., *Camera Obscura Camera Lucida: Essays in Honor of Annette Michelson*, 75–90. Amsterdam: Amsterdam UP, 2003.

——. "New Thresholds of Vision: Instantaneous Photography and the Early Cinema of Lumière." In Terry Smith, ed., *Impossible Presence: Surface and Screen in the Photogenic Era*, 71–99. Sydney: Power, 2001.

——. "Tracing the Individual Body: Photography, Detectives, and Early Cinema." In Charney and Schwartz, eds., *Cinema and the Invention of Modern Life*, 15–45.

——. "'The Whole World Within Reach': Travel Images Without Borders." Reprinted in Ruoff, ed., *Virtual Voyages*, 25–41.

Halbwachs, Maurice. *On Collective Memory*. Ed. and trans. with an introduction by Lewis A. Coser. Chicago: U of Chicago P, 1992.

Hammerton, Jenny. *For Ladies Only: Eve's Film Review, Pathé Cinemagazine, 1921–33*. East Sussex: The Projection Box, 2001.

Hammond, Paul, ed. "Available Light." In Hammond, ed., *The Shadow and Its Shadow: Surrealist Writings on Cinema*. 1–45. London: BFI, 2000.

Hamon, Philippe. *Expositions: Literature and Architecture in Nineteenth-Century France*. Trans. Katia Sainson-Frank and Lisa Maguire. Berkeley: U of California P, 1992.

Hansen, Miriam. *Babel and Babylon: Spectatorship in American Silent Film*. Cambridge: Harvard UP, 1991.

——. "Benjamin and Cinema: Not a One-Way Street." *Critical Inquiry* 25.2 (Winter 1999): 306–343.

——. "Benjamin, Cinema, and Experience: 'The Blue Flower in the Land of Technology.'" *New German Critique* 40 (Winter 1987): 179–224.

——. "Decentric Perspectives: Kracauer's Early Writings on Film and Mass Culture." *New German Critique* 54 (Fall 1991): 47–76.

——. "Introduction" (1997). In Kracauer, *Theory of Film*, vii–xlv.

——. "The Mass Production of the Senses: Classical Cinema as Vernacular Modernism." *Modernism/Modernity* 6.2 (1999): 59–78.

——. *The Other Frankfurt School: Kracauer, Benjamin, and Adorno on Cinema, Mass Culture, and Modernity*. U of California P (forthcoming).

——. "Room-for-Play: Benjamin's Gamble with Cinema." *October* 109 (2004): 3–45.

——. "Universal Language and Democratic Culture: Myths of Origin in Early American Cinema." In Dieter Meindl and Friedrich W. Horlacher, eds., *Myth and Enlightenment in American Literature*, 321–51. Erlangen: Erlanger Forschungen, 1985.

——. "'With Skin and Hair': Kracauer's *Theory of Film*, Marseille 1940." *Critical Inquiry* 19 (Spring 1993): 437–69.

Harootunian, Harry. *History's Disquiet: Modernity, Cultural Practice, and the Question of Everyday Life*. New York: Columbia UP, 2000.

——. *Overcome by Modernity: History, Culture, and Community in Interwar Japan*. Princeton and Oxford: Princeton UP, 2000.

Harrison, Charles, Francis Frascina, and Gill Perry. *Primitivism, Cubism, Abstraction: The Early Twentieth Century*. New Haven: Yale UP, 1993.

Harvey, David. "Cosmopolitanism and the Banality of Geographical Evils." In Jean Comaroff and John L. Comaroff, eds., *Millennial Capitalism and the Culture of Neoliberalism*, 271–310. Durham and London: Duke UP, 2001.

Heffernan, Michael J. "The Politics of the Map in the Early Twentieth Century." *Cartography and Geographic Information Science* 29.3 (2002): 207–226.

——. "The Science of Empire: The French Geographical Movement and the Forms of French Imperialism, 1870–1920." In N. Smith and Godlewska, eds., *Geography and Empire*, 92–114.

Heidegger, Martin. "The Age of the World Picture." *The Question Concerning Technology and Other Essays*. Trans. William Lovitt. New York: Garland, 1977.

Hertogs, Daan and Niko de Klerk, eds. *Nonfiction from the Teens: The 1994 Amsterdam Workshop*. Amsterdam: Netherlands Filmmusueum, 1994.

——. eds. *Uncharted Territory: Essays on Early Nonfiction Film*. Amsterdam: Netherlands Filmmusueum, 1997.

Hervé, Flore. "Exposition d'une collection." *Les Cahiers de la cinémathèque* 74 (Dec. 2002): 37–42.

Heu, Pascal Manuel. "Émile Vuillermoz et la naissance de la critique de cinéma en France." *1895*, 24 (June 1998): 55–75.

Highmore, Ben, ed. *The Everyday Life Reader*. New York and London: Routledge, 2002.

Hill, Chris. "(Re)performing the Archive: Barbara Lattanzi and Hollis Frampton in Dialogue." *Millennium Film Journal* 39–40 (2003): 67–81.

Hodeir, Catherine. "Decentering the Gaze at French Colonial Exhibitions." In Paul S. Landau and Deborah D. Kaspin, eds., *Images and Empires: Visuality in Colonial and Postcolonial Africa*, 233–52. Berkeley: U of California P, 2002.

Horkheimer, Max. "On Bergson's Metaphysics of Time" (1934). Reprinted in *Radical Philosophy* 131 (May–June 2005).

Houston, Penelope. *Keepers of the Frame: The Film Archives*. London: BFI, 1994.

Hughes, H. Stuart. *Consciousness and Society: The Reorientation of European Social Thought 1890–1930* (1958). New York: Vintage, 1977.

Hunt, Lynn. "French History in the Last Twenty Years: The Rise and Fall of the Annales Paradigm." *Journal of Contemporary History* 21 (1986): 209–224.

——. "Introduction: History, Culture, and Text." In Lynn Hunt, ed., *The New Cultural History*, 1–24. Berkeley: U of California P, 1989.

Hüppauf, Bernd. "Emptying the Gaze: Framing Violence through the Viewfinder." *New German Critique* 72 (1997): 3–44.

Hüppauf, Bernd, ed. *War, Violence, and the Modern Condition*. Berlin and New York: Walter de Gruter, 1997.

Hyman, Paula E. *The Emancipation of the Jews of Alsace: Acculturation and Tradition in the Nineteenth Century*. New Haven: Yale UP, 1991.

Iles, Chrissie and Russell Roberts, eds. *InVisible Light: Photography and Classification in Art, Science and the Everyday*. Oxford: Museum of Modern Art Oxford, 1997.

Irlande 1913: Clichés en couleur pris pour Monsieur Kahn par Mesdemoiselles Mespoulet et Mignon. Paris: Département des Hauts-de-Seine/Collections Albert Kahn, 1988.

Ishizuka, Karen and Patricia R. Zimmermann. *Mining the Home Movie: Excavations in Histories and Memories*. Berkeley: U of California P, 2007.

Jacob, Christian. *The Sovereign Map: Theoretical Approaches in Cartography Throughout History*. Trans. Tom Conley. Chicago: U of Chicago P, 2006.

Jacobs, Lewis, ed. *The Documentary Tradition*. New York: Norton, 1979.

Jameson, Fredric. *The Political Unconscious: Narrative as a Socially Symbolic Act*. Ithaca, N.Y.: Cornell UP, 1981.

——. "The Theoretical Hesitation: Benjamin's Sociological Predecessor." *Critical Inquiry* (Winter 1999): 267–88.

Jay, Martin. *The Dialectical Imagination: A History of the Frankfurt School and the Institute of Social Research, 1923–1950*. Berkeley: U of California P, 1973.

——. *Downcast Eyes: The Denigration of Vision in Twentieth-Century Thought*. Berkeley: U of California P, 1993.

Jean Brunhes: Autour du Monde, regards d'un géographe/regards de la géographie. Boulogne: Musée Albert-Kahn, 1993.

Jeanne, René and Charles Ford. *Le Cinéma et la presse, 1895–1960*. Paris: Armand Colin, 1961.

——. *Histoire illustreé du cinéma*. Vol. 1: *Le cinéma muet, 1895–1930*. Paris: Marabout Université, 1966.

Journal of Film Preservation 63 (Oct. 2001), Special Issue: Colonial Cinema / A Borrowed Heritage.

Kaplan, Alice. "Working in the Archives." *Yale French Studies* 77 (1990): 103–116.

Kaplan, Alice and Kristin Ross, eds. *Yale French Studies* 73 (1987), Special Issue: Everyday Life.

Kaplan, Caren. *Questions of Travel: Postmodern Discourses of Displacement*. Durham and London: Duke UP, 1996.

Katz, Joel. "From Archive to Archiveology." *Cinematograph* 4 (1991): 96–103.

Kember, Sarah. "'The Shadow of the Object': Photography and Realism" (1996). In Wells, ed., *The Photography Reader*, 202–217.

Kirby, Lynne. *Parallel Tracks: The Railroad and Silent Cinema*. Durham: Duke UP, 1997.

Kittler, Friedrich. *Discourse Networks, 1800/1900*. Trans. Michael Mettecr with Chris Cullens. Stanford, Calif.: Stanford UP, 1990.

Koch, Gertrud. "Béla Balázs: The Physiognomy of Things." *New German Critique* 40 (Winter 1987): 167–77.

Koetzle, Hans-Michael. *Photo Icons: The Story Behind the Pictures*, vol. 1. Cologne: Taschen, 2002.

Koszarski, Richard. *An Evening's Entertainment: The Age of the Silent Feature Picture, 1915–1928*. New York: Scribener's, 1990.

Krauss, Rosalind. "Photography's Discursive Spaces" (1982). Reprinted in Richard Bolton, ed., *The Contest of Meaning: Critical Histories of Photography*, 287–302. Cambridge: MIT Press, 1999.

Krohn, Esben. "About the First Danish Film Archive." Trans. Thomas C. Christensen. *The First Film Archive* DVD Pamplet (Danish Film Institute, 2002), 11–15. (*See also* www.dfi.dk/bibliotekogarkiver/Filmarkivet/Film+Archive/dvd/thefirstfilmarchive/about/about.htm.)

Kuenzli, Rudolf E., ed. *Dada and Surrealist Film*. Cambridge: MIT Press, 1996.

Kuhn, Annette. *An Everyday Magic: Cinema and Cultural Memory*. London: Tauris, 2002.

Kula, Sam. "Film Archives at the Centenary of Film." *Archivaria* 40 (Fall 1995): 210–25.

Landecker, Hannah. "Cellular Features: Microcinematography and Film Theory." *Critical Inquiry* 31 (Summer 2005): 903–937.

Langbauer, Laurie. *Novels of Everyday Life: The Series in English Fiction, 1850–1930*. Ithaca and London: Cornell UP, 1999.

Lawlor, Leonard and Valentine Moulard. "Henri Bergson." In Edward N. Zalta, ed., *The Stanford Encyclopedia of Philosophy* (Summer 2004 edn.) (*see* http://plato.stanford.edu/archives/sum2004/entries/bergson) (accessed Aug. 19, 2005).

Le Bris, Frédérique. "De l'Image et de son identification." *Les Cahiers de la cinémathèque* 74 (Dec. 2002): 35–36.

———. "Le Quinzième Bulletin, résultat d'une hypothèse." *Les Cahiers de la cinémathèque* 74 (Dec. 2002): 47–48.

Le Gall, Guillaume. *Atget: Life in Paris.* Trans. Brian Holmes. Paris: Hazan Pocket Archives, 1998.

Lebovics, Herman. *True France: The Wars Over Cultural Identity, 1900–1945.* Ithaca and London: Cornell UP, 1992.

Leclerq, Jocelyne. "Albert Kahn et le cinématographe." In *Albert Kahn: Réalités*, 73–78.

Leclerq-Weiss, Jocelyne. "Introduction au cinéma des opérateurs Kahn." *Les Cahiers de la Cinémathèque* 74 (Dec. 2002): 43–46.

———. "Le Procédé Keller-Dorian." *Les Cahiers de la cinémathèque* 74 (Dec. 2002): 53–54.

Lefebvre, Henri. *Critique of Everyday Life* (1947). Vol. 1. Trans. John Moore. London: Verso, 1991.

———. *Everyday Life in the Modern World* (1967). Trans. Sacha Rabinovitch. New Brunswick, N.J.: Transaction, 1990.

Lefebvre, Thierry. "'Scientia': Le cinéma de vulgarisation scientifique au début des années dix." *Cinémathèque* (Autumn 1993): 84–91.

Lefebvre, Thierry, ed. *Images du réel: La Non-fiction en France (1890–1930).* With the collaboaration of Michel Marie and Laurent Veray. Special Issue of *1895*, 18 (Summer 1995).

Lehan, Richard. "Bergson and the Discourse of the Moderns." In Burwick and Douglass, eds., *The Crisis in Modernism*, 306–329.

Lemaire, Françoise, ed. *Les Films militaires français de la Première Guerre Mondiale: Catalogue des films muets d'actualité.* Ivry: Établissement cinématographique et photographique des armées, 1997.

Levie, Françoise. "Paul Otlet et le multimédia." *Transnational Associations/Associations transnationales* 1–2 (2003): 53–59.

Lévi-Strauss, Claude. *Tristes Tropiques* (1955). Trans. John and Doreen Weightman. New York: Penguin, 1973.

Liebman, Stuart. "French Film Theory, 1910–1921." *Quarterly Review of Film Studies* 8.1 (1983): 1–23.

Lippit, Akira Mizuta. *Atomic Light (Shadow Optics).* Minneapolis: U of Minnesota P, 2005.

Livingstone, David N. *The Geographical Tradition: Episodes in the History of a Contested Enterprise.* Oxford: Blackwell, 1992.

Loussouarn, Alain. "La 'Géographie' des vues Albert Kahn à travers trois documents." *Les Cahiers de la Cinémathèque* 74 (Dec. 2002): 77–84.

Lukács, Georg. *History and Class Consciousness* (1923). Trans. Rodney Livingstone. Cambridge: MIT Press, 1971.

———. "Narrate or Describe?" (1936). In Arthur D. Kahn, ed. and trans., *Writer and Critic and Other Essays*, 110–48. New York: Grosset and Dunlap, 1970.

———. *The Theory of the Novel: A Historico-Philosophical Essay on the Forms of Great Epic Literature* (1914–15). Trans. Anna Bostock. Cambridge: MIT Press, 1971.

———. "The Zola Centenary" (1948). *Studies in European Realism: A Sociological Survey of the Writings of Balzac, Stendhal, Zola, Tolstoy, Gorki*, 85–96. Trans. Edith Bone. London: Hillway, 1950.

Mackaman, Douglas and Michael Mays, eds. *World War I and the Cultures of Modernity.* Jackson: UP of Mississippi, 2000.

Malinowski, Bronislaw. "Proper Conditions for Ethnographic Work" (1922). From *Argonauts of the Western Pacific.* Reprinted in Highmore, ed., *The Everyday Life Reader*, 142–44.

Mannoni, Laurent. *Histoire de la Cinémathèque française.* Paris: Gallimard, 2006.

Margulies, Ivone. *Nothing Happens: Chantal Akermans's Hyperrealist Everyday.* Durham: Duke UP, 1996.

Margulies, Ivone, ed. *Rites of Realism: Essays on Corporeal Cinema.* Durham and London: Duke UP, 2003.

Marks, Dan. "Ethnography and Ethnographic Film: From Flaherty to Asch and After." *American Anthropologist* 97.2: 339–47.

Mast, Gerald and Marshall Cohen, eds., *Film Theory and Criticism: Introductory Readings.* New York and Oxford: Oxford UP, 1985.

Matsuda, Matt K. *The Memory of the Modern.* New York: Oxford UP, 1996.

Mazaraki, Magdalena. "Boleslas Matuszewski: Photographe et opérateur." *1895*, 44 (Dec. 2004): 47–66.

Mayne, Judith. "Immigrants and Spectators." *Wide Angle* 5.2 (1982): 32–41.

Mendibil, Didier. "Deux 'Manières': Jean Brunhes et Paul Vidal de la Blache." In *Jean Brunhes: Autour du Monde*, 152–57.

Meusy, Jean-Jacques. "La Diffusion des films de 'non-fiction' dans les établissements parisiens." *1895*, 18 (Summer 1995): 169–99.

——. *Paris-Palaces ou le temps des cinémas (1894–1918).* Paris: CNRS Éditions, 1995.

Meyer, Mark-Paul. "Moments of Poignancy: The Aesthetics of the Accidental and the Casual in Early Nonfiction Film." In Hertogs and de Klerk, eds., *Uncharted Territory*, 51–60.

Milligan, Jennifer. "'What is an Archive?' in the History of Modern France." In Antoinette Burton, ed., *Archive Stories: Facts, Fictions, and the Writing of History*, 159–83. Durham: Duke UP, 2005.

Modern Language Notes 120 (2005), Special Issue: Henri Bergson.

Moholy-Nagy, Laszló. *Painting, Photography, Film* (1925). Trans. Janet Seligman. Cambridge: M.I.T. Press, 1969.

Molinier, Jean-Christophe. *Jardins de ville privés, 1890–1930.* Paris: Éditions Ramsay/de Cortanze/Association Henri and Achille Duchêne/Musée Albert-Kahn, 1991.

Moore, F. C. T. *Bergson: Thinking Backwards.* Cambridge: Cambridge UP, 1996.

Moore, Rachel. *Savage Theory: Cinema as Modern Magic.* Durham: Duke UP, 2000.

Morton. Patricia A. *Hybrid Modernities: Architecture and Representation at the 1931 Colonial Exposition, Paris.* Cambridge and London: MIT Press, 2000.

Mullarkey, John, ed. *The New Bergson.* Manchester: Manchester UP, 1999.

Musser, Charles. "At the Beginning: Motion Picture Production, Representation, and Ideology at the Edison and Lumière Companies." In Lee Grieveson and Peter Krämer, eds., *The Silent Cinema Reader*, 15–30. London: Routledge, 2004.

Naquet, Emmanuel. "Au Delà d'un Alsacien patriote." In *Albert Kahn: Réalitiés*, 37–40.

Nesbit, Molly. *Atget's Seven Albums.* New Haven: Yale UP, 1992.

New Literary History 33.4 (Autumn 2002), Special Issue: Everyday Life.

Nichols, Bill. "Documentary Film and the Modernist Avant-Garde." *Critical Inquiry* 27 (Summer 2001): 580–610.

——. *Introduction to Documentary*. Bloomington: Indiana UP, 2001.

——. *Representing Reality: Issues and Concepts in Documentary*. Bloomington: Indiana UP, 1991.

Nicolas, Marc. "Les Ombres du temps." *Traverses* 36 (Jan. 1986): 86–90 [Revue du Centre de Création industrielle, Centre George Pompidou, Paris, Special Issue: L'Archive].

Nochlin, Linda. *Realism*. London: Penguin, 1971.

Nora, Pierre. "Between Memory and History." In Nora, ed., *Realms of Memory: Rethinking the French Past*, vol. 1: *Conflicts and Divisions*, 1–20. Trans. Arthur Goldhammer. New York: Columbia UP, 1996.

Nora, Pierre, ed. *Realms of Memory*, vol. 2: *The Construction of the French Past*. Trans. Arthur Goldhammer. New York: Columbia UP, 1997.

Nord, Philip. *The Republican Moment: Struggles for Democracy in Nineteenth-Century France*. Cambridge: Harvard UP, 1995.

Norindr, Panivong. *Phantasmatic Indochina: French Colonial Ideology in Architecture, Film, and Literature*. Durham and London: Duke UP, 1996.

O'Brien, Charles. "The 'Cinéma colonial' of 1930s France: Film Narrations as Spatial Practice." In Matthew Bernstein and Gaylyn Studlar, eds., *Vision of the East: Orientalism in Film*, 207–231. New Brunswick, N.J.: Rutgers UP, 1997.

O'Brien, Patricia. "Michel Foucault's History of Culture." In Hunt, ed., *The New Cultural History*, 25–46.

O'Gomes, Isabelle do. "Le Cinema scientifique: L'Oeuvre de Doyen, Thévenard et Comandon." *La Gazette des archives* 173 (1996): 183–89, Special Issue: Le Cinéma et les archives.

O'Shaughnessy, Martin. "Poor Propaganda: French Colonial Films of the 1930s." In Martin Evans, ed., *Empire and Culture: The French Experience, 1830–1940*, 27–40. London: Palgrave Macmillan, 2004.

Ory, Pascal. "Albert Kahn dans l'histoire." In *Albert Kahn: Réalités*, 391–94.

Pagé, Suzanne. *Voilà: Le Monde dans la tête* (exhibition catalog). Paris: Musée d'art moderne de la ville de Paris, 2000.

Painlevé, Jean. "Scientific Film." *La Technique cinématographique* (1955). Reprinted in Bellows and McDougall, eds., *Science Is Fiction*, 160–169.

Panorama des collections Albert Kahn. Boulogne: Musée Albert-Kahn, 1989.

Paris 1910–1931: Au travers des autochromes et des films de la phototèque-cinémathèque Albert Kahn. Paris: Musée Carnavalet, 1982.

Paris, Michael, ed. *The First World War and Popular Cinema*. New Brunswick, N.J.: Rutgers UP, 2000.

Peabody, Sue and Tyler Stovall, eds. *The Color of Liberty: Histories of Race in France*. Durham: Duke UP, 2003.

Pearson, Keith Ansell. "Bergson and Creative Evolution/Involution: Exposing the Transcendental Illusion of Organismic Life." In Mullarkey, ed., *The New Bergson*, 146–67.

Pearson, Keith Ansell and John Mullarkey, eds. *Henri Bergson: Key Writings*. With introduction by Pearson and Mullarkey. New York: Continuum, 2002

Pellerin, Denis. *La Photographie stéréoscopique sous le Second Empire*. Paris: Bibliothèque nationale de France, 1995.

——. "Les Lucarnes de l'infini." *Études photographiques* 4 (May 1998): 27–41.

Peterson, Jennifer. *Education in the School of Dreams: Travelogues and Silent Nonfiction Film*. Duke UP (forthcoming).

Petit, Alain. "Le Premier Élève de Bergson: Un Précurseur alsacien de l'Unesco." *Hommes et Monde* 40 (Nov. 1949): 413–35.

Philo, Chris and Ola Söderström. "Social Geography: Looking for Society in Its Spaces." In Georges Benko and Ulf Strohmayer, eds., *Human Geography: A History for the 21st Century*, 105–138. London: Arnold, 2004.

Piault, Marc Henri. *Anthropologie et cinéma*. Paris: Éditions Nathan, 2000.

Pinney, Christopher and Nicolas Peterson. *Photography's Other Histories*. Durham and London: Duke UP, 2003.

Pomian, Krzysztof. "Les Archives: Du Trésor des Chartes au Caran." In Pierre Nora, ed., *Les Lieux de mémoire* 3.2:162–233. Paris: Éditions Gallimard, 1992.

Ponte, Alessandra. "Archiving the Planet: Architecture and Human Geography." *Daidalos: Architecture, Art, Culture* 66 (Dec. 1997): 120–25.

Poovey, Mary. *A History of the Modern Fact: Problems of Knowledge in the Sciences of Wealth and Society*. Chicago and London: U of Chicago P, 1998.

Posner, Bruce. *Unseen Cinema: Early American Avant-Garde Film, 1893–1941*. New York: Black Thistle Press/Anthology Film Archives, 2001.

Power, Eileen. *Report to the Trustees September 1920–September 1921, Albert Kahn Travelling Fellowship*. London: London UP, 1921.

Rabinovitz, Lauren. *For the Love of Pleasure: Women, Movies, and Culture in Turn-of-the-Century Chicago*. New Brunswick, N.J.: Rutgers UP, 1998.

Rajchman, John. "Foucault's Art of Seeing." *October* 44 (Spring 1988): 88–117.

Ramirez, Francis and Christian Rolot. "Guillaume Apollinaire et le désir de cinéma." *Cinémathèque* (Spring 1995): 50–60.

Ray, Robert B. *How a Film Theory Got Lost and Other Mysteries in Cultural Studies*. Bloomington: Indiana UP, 2001.

Rebérioux, Madeleine. "Preface" (1992) to Charles-Victor Langlois and Charles Seignobos, *Introduction aux études historiques* (1898). Paris: Éditions Kimé, 1992.

Reiz, Laurent. *Paris-Prétexte, ou l'éloge de l'oubli*. Boulogne: Musée Albert-Kahn 1994.

Renov, Michael, ed. "Toward a Poetics of Documentary." *Theorizing Documentary*, 12–36. New York and London: Routledge, 1993.

Reynolds, Siân. "Germaine Dulac and Newsreel: 3 articles and Introduction." *Screening the Past* 12 (Mar. 2001). See www.latrobe.edu.au/www/screeningthepast/classics/cl0301/sr-cl12a.htm.

Rice, Shelley. *Parisian Views*. Cambridge: MIT Press, 1997.

Richard, Pierre-Marc. "Life in Three Dimensions: The Charms of Stereoscopy." In Frizot, ed., *A New History of Photography*, 174–83.

Richards, Thomas. *The Imperial Archive: Knowledge and the Fantasy of Empire*. London and New York: Verso, 1993.

Ricoeur, Paul. *Memory, History, Forgetting*. Trans. Kathleen Blamey and David Pellauer. Chicago: U of Chicago P, 2004.

Ries, Nancy. "Anthropology and the Everyday, from Comfort to Terror." *New Literary History* (Autumn 2002): 725–42.

Rifkin, Adrian. *Street Noises: Parisian Pleasure, 1900–40*. Manchester and New York: Manchester UP, 1993.

Risse, Marielle. "White Knee Socks Versus Photojournalist Vests: Distinguishing Between Travelers and Tourists." In C. Williams, ed., *Travel Culture*, 41–50.

Roberts, John. *The Art of Interruption: Realism, Photography, and the Everyday*. Manchester and New York: Manchester UP, 1998.

Roberts, Russell. "Taxonomy: Some Notes Towards Histories of Photography and Classification." In Iles and Roberts, eds., *InVisible Light*, 9–53.

Robic, Marie-Claire. "Jean Brunhes, un 'géo-photo-graphe' expert aux Archives de la Planète." In *Jean Brunhes: Autour du Monde*, 109–137.

Rohdie, Sam. *Promised Lands: Cinema, Geography, Modernism*. London: BFI, 2001.

Rony, Fatimah Tobing. "The Quick and the Dead: Surrealism and the Found Ethnographic Footage Films of *Bontoc Eulogy* and *Mother Dao: The Turtlelike*." *Camera Obscura* 52 (2003): 129–55.

——. *The Third Eye: Race, Cinema, and Ethnographic Spectacle*. Durham: Duke UP, 1996.

Rosen, Jeff. "Atget's Populism." *History of Photography* (Spring 1994): 50–63.

Rosen, Philip. *Change Mummified: Cinema, Historicity, Theory*. Minneapolis and London: U of Minnesota P, 2001.

Rosen, Philip, ed. *Narrative, Apparatus, Ideology: A Film Theory Reader*. New York: Columbia UP, 1986.

Ross, Kristin. *Fast Cars, Clean Bodies: Decolonization and the Reordering of French Culture*. Cambridge: MIT Press, 1995.

Rotha, Paul. *Documentary Film*. New York: Hastings House, 1970.

Rouch, Jean. *Ciné-Ethnography*. Ed. and trans. Steven Feld. Minneapolis: U of Minnesota P, 2003.

Rudova, Larissa. "Bergsonism in Russia: The Case of Bakhtin." *Neophilologus* 80 (1996): 175–88.

Ruoff, Jeffrey, ed. *Virtual Voyages: Cinema and Travel*. Durham: Duke UP, 2006.

Russell, Catherine. *Experimental Ethnography: The Work of Film in the Age of Video*. Durham: Duke UP, 1999.

——. "Parallax Historiography: The Flâneuse as Cyberfeminist." In Jennifer M. Bean and Diane Negra, eds., *A Feminist Reader in Early Cinema*, 552–70. Durham: Duke UP, 2002.

Sadoul, George. "Cinémathèques et photothèques" (1961). In Samaran, ed., *L'Histoire et ses méthodes*, 1167–1178.

——. *Histoire générale du cinéma*. Vol. 1: *L'Invention du cinéma, 1832–1897* (1948). Paris: Denoël, 1973.

——. *Histoire générale du cinema*. Vol. 2: *Les Pionniers du cinema, 1897–1908* (1948). Paris: Denoël, 1973.

——. *Histoire générale du cinéma*. Vol. 4: *Le Cinéma devient un art, 1909–1920* (1948). Paris: Denoël, 1973.

Said, Edward W. *Culture and Imperialism*. London: Vintage, 1994.

——. "Foucault and the Imagination of Power" (1986). In *Reflections on Exile and Other Essays*, 239–45. Cambridge: Harvard UP, 2002.

——. *Orientalism*. New York: Vintage, 1978.

Saint-Amour, Paul K. "Modernist Reconnaissance." *Modernism/Modernity* 10 (Apr. 2003): 349–80.

Samaran, Charles, ed. *L'Histoire et ses méthodes*. Paris: Gallimard, 1961.

Sandberg, Mark B. "Effigy and Narrative: Looking into the Nineteenth-Century Folk Museum." In Charney and Schwartz, eds., *Cinema and the Invention of Modern Life*, 320–61.

Schaffner, Ingrid and Matthias Winzen, eds. *Deep Storage: Collecting, Storing, and Archiving in Art*. New York and Munich: Prestel-Verlag, 1998.

Schilling, Derek. "Everyday Life and the Challenge to History in Postwar France: Braudel, Lefebvre, Certeau." *Diacritics* 33.1 (Spring 2003): 23–40.

Schlüpmann, Heide. "The Documentary Interest in Fiction." In Hertogs and de Klerk, eds., *Uncharted Territory*, 33–36.

Schmidt, Nicolas. "*Le Pathé Journal*: Toujours d'actualité, entretien avec Thierry Rolland." *CinémAction* 97 (2000), Special Issue: Les Archives du cinéma et de la télévision: 40–42.

Schwartz, Sanford. "Bergson and the Politics of Vitalism." In Burwick and Douglass, eds., *The Crisis in Modernism*, 277–305.

Schwartz, Vanessa R. *Spectacular Realities: Early Mass Culture in Fin-de-Siècle Paris*. Berkeley: U of California P, 1998.

Sebbar, Leïla, Christelle Taraud, and Jean-Michel Belorgey, eds. *Femmes d'Afrique du nord: Cartes postales, 1885–1930*. Paris: Bleu autour, 2002.

Sekula, Allan. "The Body and the Archive." *October* 39 (1986): 3–64.

——. "Reading an Archive: Photography Between Labour and Capital" (1986). In Wells, ed., *The Photography Reader*, 443–52.

Sentilhes, Armelle. "L'Audio-visuel au service de l'enseignement: Projections lumineuses et cinéma scolaire, 1880–1940." *La Gazette des archives* 173 (1996): 165–82, Special Issue: Le Cinéma et les archives.

Serceau, Michel. "Les Archives: Musées, mausolées, cinémathèques, bibliothèques, vidéothèques?" In Serceau and Roger, eds., *CinémAction*, 14–17.

Serceau, Michel and Philippe Roger, eds. *CinémAction* 97 (2000), Special Issue: Les Archives du cinéma et de la télévision.

Shapiro, Gary. *Archaeologies of Vision: Foucault and Nietszche on Seeing and Saying*. Chicago: U of Chicago P, 2003.

Sherman, Daniel J. "The Arts and Sciences of Colonialism." *French Historical Studies* 23.4 (2000): 707–729.

——. *The Construction of Memory in Interwar France*. Chicago: U of Chicago P, 1999.

Sherzer, Dina, ed. *Cinema, Colonialism, Postcolonialism: Perspectives from the French and Francophone Worlds*. Austin, TX: U of Texas P, 1996.

Shetty, Sandhya and Elizabeth Jane Bellamy. "Postcolonialism's Archive Fever." *Diacritics* 30.1 (Spring 2000): 25–48.

Shields, Rob. *Lefebvre, Love, and Struggle: Spatial Dialectics*. London and New York: Routledge, 1999.

Silverman, Debora L. *Art Nouveau in Fin-de-Siècle France: Politics, Psychology, and Style*. Berkeley: U of California P, 1989.

Simmel, Georg. "The Metropolis and Mental Life." *The Sociology of Georg Simmel*, 409–24. Ed. and trans. Kurt H. Wolff. London: Collier-Macmillan, 1950.

Skoller, Jeffrey. *Shadows, Specters, Shards: Making History in Avant-Garde Film*. Minneapolis: U of Minnesota P, 2005.

Slavin, David H. *Colonial Cinema and Imperial France, 1919–1939: White Blind Spots, Male Fantasies, Settler Myths*. Baltimore and London: Johns Hopkins UP, 2001.

Smith, Bonnie G. "Gender and the Practices of Scientific History: The Seminar and Archival Research in the Nineteenth Century." *American Historical Review* 100.4 (Oct. 1995): 1150–1176.

Smith, Leonard V., Stéphane Audoin-Rouzeau, and Annette Becker. *France and the Great War, 1914–1918*. Cambridge: Cambridge UP, 2003.

Smith, Neil and Anne Godlewska, eds. *Geography and Empire*. Oxford: Blackwell, 1994.

Sorlin, Pierre. "Cinema and the Memory of the Great War." In Paris, ed., *The First World War and Popular Cinema*, 5–26.

——. *Le Fils de Nadar: Le Siècle de l'image analogique*. Paris: Éditions Nathan, 1997.

——. "France: The Silent Memory." In Paris, ed., *The First World War and Popular Cinema*, 115–37.

——. "The French Newsreels of the First World War." *Historical Journal of Film, Radio, and Television* 24.4 (2004): 507–515.

Soubeyran, Olivier. "Imperialism and Colonialism versus Disciplinarity in French Geography." In N. Smith and Godlewska, eds., *Geography and Empire*, 244–64.

Soulez, Philippe (completed by Frédéric Worms). *Bergson: Biographie*. Paris: Flamarrion, 1997.

Spivak, Gayatri Chakravorty. *A Critique of Postcolonial Reason: Toward a History of the Vanishing Present*. Cambridge: Harvard UP, 1999.

Steedman, Carolyn. *Dust: The Archive and Cultural History*. New Brunswick, N.J.: Rutgers UP, 2002.

Stewart, Jacqueline. *Migrating to the Movies: Cinema and Black Urban Modernity*. U of California P, 2005.

Stewart, Susan. *On Longing: Narratives of the Miniature, the Gigantic, the Souvenir, the Collection*. Durham and London: Duke UP, 1993.

Stoller, Ann Laura. *Race and the Education of Desire: Foucault's History of Sexuality and the Colonial Order of Things*. Durham and London: Duke UP, 1995.

——. "Tense and Tender Ties: The Politics of Comparison in North American History and (Post)Colonial Studies." *Journal of American History* 88.3 (Dec. 2002): 829–65.

Stovall, Tyler. "Love, Labor, and Race: Colonial Men and White Women in France During the Great War." In Tyler Stovall and Georges Van Den Abbeele, eds., *French Civilization and Its Discontents*, 297–322. Lanham, Md.: Lexington Books, 2003.

——. "National Identity and Shifting Imperial Frontiers: Whiteness and the Exclusion of Colonial Labor after World War I." *Representations* (Nov. 2003): 52–72.

Strain, Ellen. *Public Places, Private Journeys: Ethnography, Entertainment, and the Touristic Gaze*. New Brunswick, N.J.: Rutgers UP, 2003.

Strayer, Joseph R. "Introduction." In Marc Bloch, *The Historian's Craft*, vii–xii.

Streible, Dan. "The Role of Orphan Films in the 21st Century Archive." *Cinema Journal* 46.3 (Spring 2007): 124–28.

SubStance 114 (2007), Special Issue: Henri Bergson.

Sutcliffe, Anthony. *The Autumn of Central Paris: The Defeat of Town Planning, 1850–1970.* London: Edward Arnold, 1970.

Sweeney, Regina. "*La Pudique Anastasie*: Wartime Censorship and French Bourgeois Morality." In Mackaman and Mays, eds., *World War I and the Cultures of Modernity*, 3–19.

Tagg, John. *The Burden of Representation: Essays on Photographies and Histories.* Amherst: U of Massachusetts P, 1988.

Tartakovsky, Danielle. "Les Manifestations de rues dans les actualités cinématographiques Éclair et Gaumont, 1918–1968." *Cahiers de la cinémathèque* 66 (July 1997): 25–32, Special Issue: Les Actualités filmées françaises.

Terdiman, Richard. *Present Past: Modernity and the Memory Crisis.* Ithaca and London: Cornell UP, 1993.

Thévenard, P. and G. Tassel. *Le Cinéma scientifique français.* Introd. Jean Painlevé. Paris: La Jeune Parque, 1948.

Thomas, Martin. *The French Empire Between the Wars: Imperialism, Politics, and Society.* Manchester: Manchester UP, 2005.

Thompson, Elizabeth. *Colonial Citizens: Republican Rights, Paternal Privilege, and Gender in French Syria and Lebanon.* New York: Columbia UP, 2000.

Thompson, Kristin. *Exporting Entertainment: America in the World Film Market, 1907–1934.* London: BFI, 1985.

Tollebeek, Jo. "'Turn'd to dust and tears': Revisiting the Archive." *History and Theory* 43 (May 2004): 237–48.

Toulet, Emmanuelle. "Avant-Propos." *Le Cinéma au rendez-vous des arts, France, années 20 et 30*, 6–9. Paris: Bibliothèque Nationale Française, 1995.

Toulmin, Vanessa. "'Local films for local people': Travelling Showmen and the Commissioning of Local Films in Great Britain, 1900–1902." *Film History* 13.2 (2001): 118–37.

Toulmin, Vanessa and Martin Loiperdinger. "Is It You? Recognition, Representation, and Response in Relation to the Local Film." *Film History* (2005): 7–18.

Toulmin, Vanessa, Simon Popple, and Patrick Russell, eds. *The Lost World of Mitchell and Kenyon: Edwardian Britain on Film.* London: BFI, 2004.

Traverses 36 (Jan. 1986) [Revue du Centre de Création industrielle, Centre George Pompidou, Paris, Special Issue: L'Archive].

Trebitsch, Michel. "Le Robinson juif: Un Film et un texte sur l'université hébraïque de Jérusalem en 1925." *Les Cahiers de la cinémathèque* 74 (Dec. 2002): 99–107.

Trope, Alison. "*Le cinéma pour le cinéma*: Making a Museum of the Modern Image." *The Moving Image: Journal of the Association of Moving Image Archivists* (Spring 2002): 29–68.

Tsivian, Yuri. "Media Fantasies and Penetrating Vision: Some Links between X Rays, the Microscope, and Film." In John E. Bowlt and Olga Matich, eds., *Laboratory of Dreams: The Russian Avant-Garde and Cultural Experiment*, 81–99. Stanford, Calif.: Stanford UP, 1996.

Uricchio, William. "The *Kulturfilm*: A Brief History of an Early Discursive Practice." In Paolo Cherchi Usai and Lorenzo Codelli, eds., *Before Caligari: German Cinema, 1895–1920*, 356–72. Pordenone, Italy: Edizioni Biblioteca dell'Immagine, 1990.

Uricchio, William and Ester Rutten. "Le Film de non-fiction français et le marché néerlandais." *1895*, 18 (Summer 1995): 223–33.

Urry, Scott. *The Tourist Gaze: Leisure and Travel in Contemporary Society*. London: Sage, 1990.

Usai, Paolo Cherchi. *Burning Passions: An Introduction to the Study of Silent Cinema*. Trans. Emma Sansone Rittle. London: BFI, 1994.

——. *The Death of Cinema: History, Cultural Memory, and the Digital Dark Age*. London: BFI, 2001.

Van Dooren, Ine and Peter Krämer. "The Politics of Direct Address." In Dibbets and Hogenkamp, eds., *Film and the First World War*, 97–107.

Vaughn, Dai. "Let there be Lumière." In Elsaesser, ed., *Early Cinema*, 63–67.

——. *"The Man with the Movie Camera"* (1960). Reprinted in Jacobs, ed., *The Documentary Tradition*, 53–59.

Velody, Irving. "The Archive and the Human Sciences: Notes Towards a Theory of the Archive." *History of the Human Sciences* 11.4 (Nov. 1998): 1–16.

Veray, Laurent. "Fiction et 'non-fiction' dans les films sur la Grande Guerre de 1914 à 1928: La Bataille des images." *1895*, 18 (Summer 1995): 235–56.

——. *Les Films d'actualité français de la Grande Guerre*. Paris: Éditions de l'AFRHC, 1996.

——. "Lendemains de Victoire, la fête, le prestige et la mort: Réflexion sur quelques vues d'actualités." *Cahiers de la cinémathèque* 66 (July 1997): 9–15, Special Issue: Les Actualités filmées françaises.

——. "Montrer la Guerre: La Photographie et le cinématographie." In J-J. Becker et al., eds., *Guerre et cultures: 1914–1918*, 229–39. Paris: Armand Colin, 1994.

——. "La Représentation de la guerre dans les actualités françaises de 1914 à 1918." *1895*, 17 (Dec. 1994): 3–52.

Vignaux, Valérie, ed., *1895*, 41 (Oct. 2003). Special Issue: Archives.

Villages et villageois au Tonkin: Autochromes réalisées par Léon Busy pour les "Archives de la Planète." Paris: Département des Hauts-de-Seine/Collections Albert Kahn, 1986.

Virilio, Paul. *War and Cinema: The Logistics of Perception* (1984). Trans. Patrick Camiller. London: Verso, 1989.

Virmaux, Alain and Odette Virmaux, eds. *Les Surréalistes et le cinéma*. Paris: Seghers, 1976.

Waller, Gregory, ed. *Moviegoing in America: A Sourcebook in the History of Film Exhibition*. Madden, Mass.: Blackwell, 2002.

Walz, Robin. *Pulp Surrealism: Insolent Popular Culture in Early Twentieth-Century Paris*. Berkeley: U of California P, 2000.

Wasson, Haidee. *Museum Movies: The Museum of Modern Art and the Birth of Art Cinema*. Berkeley: U of California P, 2005.

Wells, Liz, ed. *The Photography Reader*. London: Routledge, 2003.

Wilder, Gary. "Framing Greater France Between the Wars." *Journal of Historical Sociology* 14.2 (June 2001): 198–225.

Williams, Alan. *Republic of Images: A History of French Filmmaking*. Cambridge: Harvard UP, 1992.

Williams, Carol Traynor, ed. *Travel Culture: Essays on What Makes Us Go.* Westport, Conn., and London: Praeger, 1998.

Williams, Linda. "Film Body: An Implantation of Perversions." In Rosen, ed., *Narrative, Apparatus, Ideology*, 507–534.

Williams, Tami. "Germaine Dulac: Du figurative à l'abstraction." In Nicole Brenez and Christian Lebrat, eds., *Jeune, dure et pure! Une Histoire du cinéma d'avant-garde et expérimental en France*, 78–82. Paris: Cinémathèque française, 2001.

Wing, Paul. *Stereoscopes: The First One Hundred Years.* Nashua, N.H.: Transition, 1996.

Winston, Brian. *Claiming the Real: The Documentary Film Revisited.* London: BFI, 1995.

Winter, Jay. "The Great War and the Persistence of Tradition: Languages of Grief, Bereavement, and Mourning." In Hüppauf, ed., *War, Violence, and the Modern Condition*, 33–45.

——. *Dreams of Peace and Freedom: Utopian Moments in the Twentieth Century.* New Haven: Yale UP, 2006.

——. *Sites of Memory, Sites of Mourning: The Great War in European Cultural History.* Cambridge: Cambridge UP, 1995.

Wood, John. *The Art of the Autochrome: The Birth of Color Photography.* Ames: U of Iowa P, 1993.

Worms, Frédéric. "Agir en Homme de pensée, penser en homme d'action"? In Coeuré and Worms, eds., *Henri Bergson et Albert Kahn: Correspondances*, 111–26.

——. "Portraits du philosophe en professeur et ami." In Coeuré and Worms, eds., *Henri Bergson et Albert Kahn: Correspondances*, 17–38.

Zimmerman, Patricia R. "Morphing History into Histories: From Amateur Film to the Archive of the Future." *The Moving Image* 1.1 (Spring 2001): 109–130.

Zola, Émile. "The Experimental Novel" (1880). Reprinted in George J. Becker, ed., *Documents of Modern Literary Realism*, 162–96. Princeton: Princeton UP, 1963.

——. "Preface to the Second Edition." *Thérèse Raquin* (1867; 2d ed., 1868). Oxford: Oxford UP, 1992, 1–6.

INDEX